Daily Life through World History in Primary Documents

Daily Life through World History in Primary Documents
Lawrence Morris, General Editor

Volume 1: *The Ancient World*
David Matz

Volume 2: *The Middle Ages and Renaissance*
Lawrence Morris

Volume 3: *The Modern World*
David M. Borgmeyer and Rebecca Ayako Bennette

2 THE MIDDLE AGES AND RENAISSANCE

Daily Life through World History in Primary Documents

Lawrence Morris
GENERAL EDITOR AND VOLUME EDITOR

GREENWOOD PRESS
Westport, Connecticut • London

Library of Congress Cataloging-in-Publication Data

Daily life through world history in primary documents / Lawrence Morris, general editor.
        p. cm.
   Includes bibliographical references and index.
   ISBN: 978–0–313–33898–4 (set : alk. paper)
   ISBN: 978–0–313–33899–1 (v. 1 : alk. paper)
   ISBN: 978–0–313–33900–4 (v. 2 : alk. paper)
   ISBN: 978–0–313–33901–1 (v. 3 : alk. paper)
   1. Civilization—History—Sources.   2. Manners and customs—History—Sources.   3. Social history—Sources.   I. Morris, Lawrence, 1972–
   CB69.D35   2009
   909—dc22   2008008925

British Library Cataloguing in Publication Data is available.

Library of Congress Catalog Card Number: 2008008925
ISBN: 978–0–313–33898–4 (set)
        978–0–313–33899–1 (vol. 1)
        978–0–313–33900–4 (vol. 2)
        978–0–313–33901–1 (vol. 3)

First published in 2009

Greenwood Press, 88 Post Road West, Westport, CT 06881
An imprint of Greenwood Publishing Group, Inc.
www.greenwood.com

Printed in the United States of America

The paper used in this book complies with the Permanent Paper Standard issued by the National Information Standards Organization (Z39.48–1984).

10 9 8 7 6 5 4 3 2 1

For those who lived before

CONTENTS

Contents

Contents

PART VII   RECREATIONAL LIFE

PART VIII   RELIGIOUS LIFE

Contents

SET INTRODUCTION

What time we leave work; the food we eat for dinner; how we spend our free time—these small, almost mundane details can shape our lives as powerfully as who is the president or what battles are being fought in a far-distant country. In fact, we often judge major events—wars, legislation, trade deals—by how those events affect our everyday lives. If trade negotiations mean that we can purchase more goods for less money, we may very well support the negotiations: we will be able to eat out more, see more movies, buy more books. If the negotiations mean that we lose our jobs—resulting in skipped meals, bankruptcy, and ulcers caused by stress—we are likely to be much more critical. How an event impacts our daily life frequently determines how we view that event. Daily life, in other words, is very important and always has been.

The study of daily life therefore enables us to examine the cultural norms, concerns, and priorities of societies across time. We learn the vital importance of maritime trade for the citizens of medieval Barcelona, for example, when we examine the detailed law codes by which they carefully regulated the rights and responsibilities of ships' captains and merchants. We understand more deeply the pervasive role of religious ritual in medieval Japan when we read about the exorcisms practiced to combat ailments that we would now consider physical, not spiritual. When we learn about the day-to-day politics of the ancient Roman Republic, we appreciate how radically different life was under the Roman Empire. When we read a letter home from a U.S. soldier fighting in Vietnam, we feel more intimately the pain of separation. By studying daily life, we get a firmer understanding of what it was like to live in a certain era and a certain place. Learning that Constantine I was emperor of Rome in A.D. 313 gives us important information, but learning about the foods prepared by a Roman peasant or how a Roman merchant traveled about on business gives us a better idea of what it was really like to live in Italy during the same time period.

Primary sources, moreover, offer a uniquely valuable way of learning about the past. Primary sources, of course, are documents or artifacts produced by the people under investigation. These sources enable us to listen directly to the voices of the past. A primary source enables us to view the past from the inside, from the point of view of a person alive at the time. Our tour guide to the culture of ancient Egypt is an ancient Egyptian. Primary sources are the ultimate historical authority—there can be no greater expert on ancient Rome than an ancient Roman or on medieval France than a medieval Frenchman or woman or on twentieth-century Africa than a modern African.

Daily Life through World History in Primary Documents, therefore, offers the reader a feast of knowledge. Packed within the covers of this important three-volume set are over 500 documents, each of which offers readers the opportunity to listen to a voice from the past (and sometimes the present) explaining that person's own culture and time. The volumes are organized chronologically as follows:

- Volume 1: *The Ancient World* contains documents from various ancient cultures, including those of Sumeria, Egypt, Israel, China, India, Greece, and Rome, with its primary focus being upon the daily life of Greece and Rome up to roughly the sack of Rome in the fifth century A.D.
- Volume 2: *The Middle Ages and Renaissance* contains documents from various European (e.g., Anglo-Saxon England, Renaissance Italy), Asian (e.g., Tang China, medieval Japan, Mogul India), Middle Eastern (e.g., medieval Persia, early Islamic Arabia), and Latin American (e.g., Aztec Mexico, Inca Peru, Mayan Central America) cultures spanning the period from the fifth to the seventeenth centuries.
- Volume 3: *The Modern World,* covering the birth of modern democracy in the eighteenth century up through the present day, contains documents from various world cultures, including Turkey, West Africa, India, the United States, and Russia.

At the edges of these basic divides, there is some overlap between volumes, demonstrating how each era carries on from the preceding one.

Within each volume, the myriad aspects of daily life are grouped under seven overarching categories: Domestic Life, Economic Life; Intellectual Life, Material Life, Political Life, Recreational Life, and Religious Life. These categories, which were also employed by the award-winning *Greenwood Encyclopedia of Daily Life,* allow for quick reference between all three volumes. Browsing Religious Life in all three volumes, for example, will offer a scintillating introduction to and overview of the major spiritual traditions across time. Under these shared categories, each volume then further subgroups the texts in the way most useful for the time period under discussion. Common subcategories include Women, Marriage, Children, Literature, Transportation, Medicine, Housing, Clothing, Law, Reform, Sports, and Rituals. Under Economic Life in Volume 2, for example, the subcategories employed highlight the important roles played by urban and rural populations, as well as the well-established practice of slavery and the increasingly important role of international trade and commerce.

The scope of *Daily Life through World History in Primary Documents* is truly global. Within these pages, we see documents from countries with such diverse histories and cultures as Japan, Italy, India, West Africa, Persia, the United States, and Central America. Browsing almost any of the subcategories will offer the reader fascinating voices from non-Western cultures. Each section, however, also includes a solid central focus on the major cultures that have shaped the Western world, including Europe and the Americas. None of these cultures exists in a vacuum, however, nor are they entirely dissimilar. Western and non-Western cultures contextualize each other and comment on the common concerns of human beings around the world. Brief analytical essays at the start of each subcategory outline the documents that follow and draw out important themes that weave throughout the documents, charting a cultural conversation that crosses time and place.

To benefit the most from the primary sources, each individual document also is preceded by an analytical introduction that explains and highlights the main features of that particular document. An author of a primary document, just like authors today, may have a bias, a limited perspective, or missing information that results in a slightly inaccurate portrayal of life in a given culture. The non-specialist reader, moreover, may not be familiar with the items and ideas discussed in a document written a thousand years ago, or in a completely different more contemporary culture. The concise analytical introductions preceding each document mitigate these difficulties by providing an expert evaluation and contextualization of the following document. The combination of primary sources and modern historical analyses of those sources offers the reader a balanced perspective and a solid grounding in the modern study of daily life.

Part I in each volume offers a detailed historical overview of the period covered. Each volume also contains a chronology of important world events for the period covered, an appendix of brief biographies of document authors or creators, a glossary defining and describing unfamiliar names and terms encountered in the section and document introductions, and a bibliography of sources used. Glossary terms in the text appear in italics. Many documents are also illustrated, and information can be further accessed through a detailed subject index for the set.

These volumes will be used in many different ways by many different readers, including high school students, college and university undergrads, and interested general readers. Some readers will delve into one volume and browse extensively, gaining an overview of how generations in one era lived their lives. Other readers may be more interested in exploring how one realm of life—political life—for example, has changed from ancient Rome through the present day; those readers will devour the appropriate categories and subcategories from each of the three volumes. Other readers will use the sources to research and support their own written analyses, for assigned essays or for their own independent research. However the reader uses these volumes, I am confident that he or she will enjoy the experience. We have collected an amazing array of intriguing sources that cannot help but capture the interest and the imagination. Enjoy!

SET
ACKNOWLEDGMENTS

Many people have made working on *Daily Life through World History in Primary Documents* rewarding. First of all, the volume editors David Matz, David Borgmeyer, and Rebecca Ayako Bennette, have created interesting and illuminating conversations between the plethora of texts included in their volumes—daily life comes alive in their pages. Dr. William McCarthy also helped to get the project rolling in its early stages. All the editors at Greenwood, and most especially Mariah Gumpert and John Wagner, have supported and encouraged us from day one. I thank Joyce Salisbury in particular for first awakening my interest in the study of daily life. Agus, ar ndóigh, gabhaim buíochas ar leith le mo bhean chéile, Amy, agus le mo chlann, a bhí foighneach agus tuisceanach nuair a bhuailinn an doras amach go dtí an oifig arís eile i ndiaidh an dinnéir chun beagáinín tuilleadh a scríobh. Tá cuid díobh féin istigh san obair seo; go gcúití Dia leo é.

CHRONOLOGY

CHRONOLOGY OF SELECTED EVENTS: THE MIDDLE AGES AND RENAISSANCE

A.D. 410   Rome sacked by Visigoths

527   Justinian becomes Byzantine emperor

c. 550   End of the Gupta Dynasty of northern India

610   Muhammad has visions of the angel Gabriel, leading to the founding of Islam

618   Kao-tsu begins the Tang dynasty in China

622   The Hijrah: Muhammad flees from Mecca to Medina

632   Death of Muhammad

656   Uhtman assassinated, provoking feuding between Shi'a and Sunni Muslims

661   Mu'awiya ibn Abi Sufyan establishes the Muslim Umayyad Caliphate

732   Battle of Tours: Frankish forces under Charles Martel repulse a Muslim invasion of France

750   Abu al-Abbas as-Saffah overthrows the Umayyad Caliphate and creates the Abbasid Caliphate

762   Founding of Baghdad as capital of Abbasid Caliphate

781   Alcuin appointed head of Palace School at Aachen

793   Sack of Lindisfarne: first major Viking raid

800   Charlemagne crowned Emperor of the Romans

836   Abbasid capital moved from Baghdad to Samarra

843   Treaty of Verdun divides Charlemagne's kingdom among his grandsons

846   Po Chu-i (aka Bai Juyi), an influential Chinese poet, dies

863   Cyril and Methodius begin to convert the Slavic peoples to Christianity

c. 878   Treaty of Alfred and Guthrum recognizes Viking control of northern England

c. 900   Classical Maya civilization begins to disintegrate

907   Tang dynasty breaks up into independent kingdoms

909   Al-Mahdi announces the Fatimid Caliphate in northern Africa

960	Sung dynasty founded by Chao K'uang-yin
1016	King Cnut converts to Christianity, encouraging the further spread of Christianity throughout Scandinavia
1054	The Bishop of Rome and the Patriarch of Constantinople excommunicate each other, splitting Christendom into a western Catholic Church and an eastern Orthodox Church
1055	Seljuqs take control of the Abbasid Caliphate
1066	Battle of Hastings: William the Conqueror, Duke of Normandy, conquers England
1076	Kumbi, the capital of Wagadu (Ghana), sacked by Arab forces
1081	Alexius I Comnenus, a famous Byzantine Emperor, ascends to the throne
1095	Council of Clermont: Urban II proclaims the First Crusade
1099	Jerusalem falls to crusader forces
1187	Jerusalem falls to Muslim forces under Saladin
1200	Death of Chu Hsi (Zhu Xi), influential scholar of Confucianism
1204	Constantinople, capital of the Byzantine Empire, sacked by western crusaders
1215	Magna Carta: King John of England is forced to limit royal authority
1227	Genghis Khan dies, having created the Mongol Empire
1240	King Sundiata absorbs the Ghana empire into his Mande empire
1250	Mamluks (slave armies) seize control of Egypt and Syria
1258	Fall of Baghdad: Abbasid Caliphate falls to Mongol armies
1271	Marco Polo departs for Asia
1279	Mongol conquest of China, beginning Yuan dynasty
1281	Osman I begins to build the Ottoman Empire; it will last to 1924
1291	Fall of Acre: Mamluks conquer last remaining crusader outpost in the Middle East
1294	Kublai Khan dies, having ruled over the Mongol Empire at its greatest extent
1304	Birth of Petrarch, major Renaissance thinker
1325	Tenochtitlan (future Aztec capital) is founded
1337	Invasion of Flanders: Start of Hundred Years' War between England and France
1347	Black Death: Bubonic plague spreads through Europe, killing roughly one-third of the population
1368	Ming dynasty in China founded by rebels led by Zhu Yuanzhang
1374	Petrarch, a leading Renaissance intellectual, dies
1417	The Council of Constance ends the papal schism, and the pope returns to Rome from Avignon, France
1431	Joan of Arc, a French military leader, is executed by the English
1435	*Della pittura* by Leon Battista Alberti lays down the foundations of linear perspective in painting
1453	French forces capture Aquitaine, ending the Hundred Years' War with England; Byzantium (Constantinople) falls to Ottoman forces under Mehmed II
1468	Sonni Ali, king of Songhai, captures Timbuktu for his rising empire

1471	Topa Inca becomes king and captures much of Chile, Bolivia, and Argentina
1480	Spanish Inquisition is established
1485	Battle of Bosworth Field: Henry Tudor defeats and kills Richard III, founding the Tudor dynasty in England
1492	Christopher Columbus departs for Asia, finding the Americas by mistake; Isabella and Ferdinand of Spain capture the Muslim Kingdom of Granada
1502	Isma'il I creates the Safavid Dynasty in Iran
1509	Henry VIII ascends to the English throne
1513	Michelangelo finishes painting the Sistine Chapel in Rome
1517	Martin Luther promulgates the *Ninety-Five Theses*, which bring him to the forefront of the Protestant Reformation
1519	Hernán Cortés arrives in Mexico
1520	Suleyman I "The Magnificent" succeeds to the Sultanate of the Ottoman Empire
1521	Fall of Tenochtitlan: Aztec empire falls to Spanish and Native American forces led by Hernán Cortés
1526	Babur founds the Mughal dynasty in northern India
1531	The Virgin of Guadalupe appears to Juan Diego, a Mexican Indian
1533	Cuzco, capital of the Inca empire, falls to Spanish forces under Francisco Pizarro
1534	Henry VIII's Act of Supremacy declares the king, not the pope, to be the head of the Church in England
1536	John Calvin publishes *Institutes of Christian Religion*, a systematic guide to his influential Protestant beliefs
1545	The Council of Trent begins the Catholic Counter-Reformation
1549	Forced labor of Native Americans banned by the Spanish Crown
1570	Pope Pius V excommunicates Elizabeth I
1571	Battle of Lepanto: European allies defeat Ottoman fleet and halt Turkish expansionism; Portugal establishes a colony in Angola, Africa; Tupac Amaru, last independent Inca king, is executed in Cuzco
1582	Pope Gregory XIII introduces the modern calendar, which is quickly adopted by most of Catholic Europe
1588	Spanish Armada: England defeats Spanish invasion
1601	French establish trading post at Tadoussac, North America
1603	Death of Queen Elizabeth I of England
1607	English establish a colony in Jamestown, Virginia
1620	Pilgrims establish colony at Plymouth, Massachusetts
1644	Northern Manchus overthrow the Han-controlled Ming dynasty
1649	English parliamentary forces, having killed King Charles I, establish the Commonwealth
1660	Charles II restored to the English throne
1697	Martin de Ursua conquers Tayasal, the last independent Maya state

Part I
HISTORICAL OVERVIEW

There can be no doubt that the Middle Ages and *Renaissance* witnessed some of the most dramatic changes in the history of *homo sapiens*. This majestic sweep of time, stretching from the fifth century to the seventeenth (though starting and end points are always somewhat arbitrary) witnessed the birth of Islam, the spread of Christianity around the globe, great Chinese imperial dynasties, the discovery of new continents (the Americas from the European perspective, and the rest of the world from the Native American perspective), and numerous cultural flourishings and declines. At the start of the period, Europe, most especially northern Europe, was an economic and largely cultural backwater, whereas the Middle East, North Africa, and Asia maintained great cities and prized learning. By the end of the era, Europe had begun a vast colonial expansion that would result in the English, Spanish, and other European empires of the eighteenth and nineteenth centuries.

The Early Middle Ages (410–1066)

By the time Alaric's Visigothic army stormed Rome in A.D. 410, the Roman empire had been waning for some time. The real center of imperial power had already switched to Byzantium, modern-day Istanbul in Turkey, yet the invasion of these Germanic invaders drove home the point that Imperial Rome, built on the foundations of the Roman Republic, was very much a thing of the past. The Roman Empire would live on without Rome; the *Byzantine Empire* survived into the fifteenth century—Byzantium fell at last only in 1453 to Muslim armies. The Western empire, even after Germanic overlords crowned themselves emperor and attempted to maintain the trappings of imperial rule and order, was a shadow of its former self.

Rome's empire was not the only one to dissolve in the early Middle Ages; so too did the Gupta empire of northern India perish (in the mid-sixth century). Other empires, however, arose. In Europe, the Carolingian dynasty, the most famous monarch of which is *Charlemagne*, "Charles the Great," produced the first large-scale cultural rebirth in northern Europe. After leading the Frankish kingdom in northern France for several years, Charlemagne advanced his kingdom and his power such that he was declared emperor by Pope Leo III in A.D. 800. In addition to enhancing his own power, Charlemagne took an active interest in advancing education. His Palace School at Aachen, run by the famous

Anglo-Saxon scholar Alcuin from 782 onward, became a major center for literary, scientific, and theological studies and one of the most important centers of learning throughout Christian Europe. Charlemagne's united kingdom survived his own death but was broken up among heirs upon the death of Charlemagne's son, Louis the Pious, in A.D. 840.

Charlemagne's kingdom, counted from his imperial crowning to the division of the realm, lasted only 40 years. Contemporary empires in sub-Saharan Africa and China lasted much longer. An empire in western Africa called Wagadu, or the Ghana empire, flourished from at least the 800s, when Arabic accounts mention the empire, up to 1076, when expansionary and missionary Arabs sacked the capital city of Kumbi, though the Ghana empire continued in less vigorous form for two more centuries until succumbing to the Mande leader Sundiata in 1240. Wagadu owed its prosperity to the prime rule of real estate: location, location, location. Straddling the land between the gold mines of southern Africa and the gold customers of northern Africa, Wagadu fostered international trade up and down the western African continent, while also levying a tax on the goods traded. Wagadu's rise to power thus resulted from the shrewd economic exploitation of the empire's lucky location.

In China, the *Tang dynasty* (618–907) produced some of the most important poets and painters of premodern China. Po Chu-i (772–846), perhaps China's greatest poet, lived during this time. The Tang dynasty, founded by Kao-Tsu, built on the cultural reforms of the preceding Sui dynasty. Examinations, for example, were established to ensure that those most deserving of high appointment received the post, rather than those most in favor with the emperor. Of course, favoritism at court did not cease altogether, but the rigor of examination, combined with land redistribution and a commitment to small government, helped the Tang dynasty to thrive in its early years and strengthened it sufficiently to survive the intrigues of characters such as Wu-hou, a powerful queen who established her court in the western provinces and essentially ruled during the illness of her husband Kao-Tsung (649–683). Political stability encouraged economic progress, and the Tang dynasty became a major destination for Persian and later Muslim traders. These merchants introduced non-Chinese customs, and the Tang dynasty embraced them heartily, integrating them into their own traditional culture. In the realm of music, for example, the main genres were court music, common music, and foreign music. By A.D. 907, however, the dynasty had descended into a congregation of squabbling minor kingdoms.

The Americas also witnessed the growth of large, economically complex empires. By A.D. 250, the Maya, who had been living in Central America since at least 1500 B.C., had developed an urban civilization with monumental architecture, including royal palaces, pyramid temples, and ball courts. At its height, Mayan civilization comprised over 40 major cities, with a combined population in the neighborhood of two million. In the tenth century, however, the society broke up quickly, perhaps because of internecine warfare. Major cities were abandoned, though certain Yucatán cities, such as Mayapan, remained inhabited into the 1400s. By the time of the Spanish conquistadors' arrival, however, even these cities had been largely abandoned. Rather than an urbane civilization, the Spanish found a rural, agricultural people living near ruins, such as the large "pyramids" in Palenque and elsewhere, indicative of a far-different past. Although the Spanish eventually seized control of this whole region, the Mayan language continues to be widely spoken throughout the area.

The empires mentioned here developed from political and economic strength. One empire of the period—the Abbasid Caliphate—developed primarily in response to a religious movement that swept the Middle East. During the month of *Ramadan* in the year 610, *Muhammad* (A.D. 570–632) had a vision in which the angel Gabriel came to him and revealed the beginning of the *Koran*. This vision set Muhammad on a long career of missionary zeal. By the time of his death in A.D. 632, Muhammad had witnessed the conversion of almost the entire Arabian Peninsula from paganism, Christianity, or Judaism to Islam, the religion of which Muhammad was the chief prophet. This conversion had resulted from a combination of religious persuasion, political intrigue, and military success. Muhammad's success in welding together a united Arabian kingdom of new monotheists was inherited by his near relations and close associates, resulting in, respectively, the Umayyad (661–750) and Abbasid (750–1258) dynasties, which witnessed a united, although regional, Muslim empire stretching from Persia in the east along northern Africa to Spain in the west.

Another major world religion, although born several centuries before this time period, achieved prominence during the early Middle Ages. Ever since the Edict of Milan in A.D. 313, Christianity had been legal in the Roman Empire, and the new religion grew even more rapidly once believers faced no legal obstacles. By the early fifth century, Christianity had largely displaced the other religions in southern and central Europe and in northern Africa. By 1100, almost all of northern and Eastern Europe had entered "Christendom"; Christianity had become the dominant religion from Iceland in the far northwest, on the edge of the world known to the Europeans, to Constantinople (modern-day Istanbul) in the east.

Christianity, moreover, was not "just" a religion; instead, the organized Church provided a center of intellectual and cultural vigor. Throughout the early Middle Ages, monastic schools offered the main system of formal education. As a result, almost all educated individuals in Europe were involved directly with the Church. Influential intellectuals such as Gregory the Great (c. 540–604), Bede (c. 672–735), and Alcuin (c. 732–804) all saw their primary vocation to be religious; they all were priests and monks.

In addition to promoting education and religion, however, the Church also gathered an increasing amount of political and economic power. Rulers and aristocrats frequently gave significant donations of land and money to monasteries as a form of charity; over time, church institutions became major landowners with significant agricultural incomes. Although individual monks were pledged to personal poverty—they owned no personal possessions—the institutions to which they belonged were frequently very wealthy. This wealth sometimes made Church establishments a target. The Vikings, for example, frequently looted churches in England, Ireland, and France from the ninth to the eleventh centuries. With gold chalices and other precious items, the churches made soft targets for these organized attackers.

The Later Middle Ages (c. 1066–1492)

The year A.D. 1066 by no means marks a major break with the early Middle Ages, but the year usefully marks a major change for the English-speaking world. In 1066 *William the Conqueror*, duke of Normandy, seized the English crown for himself and imported a French-speaking aristocracy. As a result, the English language retained its Germanic substrate but adopted a plethora of French words to the extent that a modern English speaker can often more easily learn French than the historically more closely related language of German.

Politically, however, A.D. 1066 marks the continued development of regional powers that already had formed in the early Middle Ages. Islam and Islamic empires continued to spread throughout middle Africa and into southern Asia, for example, and China remained a major political and economic force.

The Mongol peoples, moreover, perfected the art of empire building during this time period. Genghis Khan (1162–1227) forged the loose confederation of Mongol peoples resident in and around modern-day Mongolia into an effective fighting force of horse archers that made rapid military conquests that were solidified with the administrative help of the conquered peoples themselves. When Khan died, the Mongol Empire stretched from modern-day Russia to the China Sea and from Siberia down to central China. Under Genghis Khan's grandson Kublai (1215–1294), the empire expanded even further, bringing all of China under its aegis and forming the largest geographic empire that has ever existed in human history. Only in the fourteenth century did the empire begin to disintegrate in the face of local and nativist opposition. The Chinese empire fell in 1367 to the rebelling native Ming population, and Russian forces defeated the "Golden Horde," as the western Mongol forces were known, in 1380. The Mongol forces gradually retired back to the traditional homeland of Mongolia.

The Americas also saw the rise of a powerful new empire: the *Aztecs*. The Aztecs moved into central Mexico after the fall of the Toltec kingdom in the early fourteenth century. The Aztecs, also known as the Mexica, settled on the islands in Lake Texcoco and developed an innovative and robust agricultural economy that relied on the rich, fertile mud that lined the bottom of Lake Texcoco. The lush, apparently floating gardens of the Mexica startled the first Europeans to witness their beauty and productivity. Under the fifteenth-century ruler Itzcóatl, the Aztecs began to expand their territorial control through alliance-making and military conquest. By the end of the century, the Aztecs held sway over almost 80,000 square miles, and their capital city of Tenochtitlan had perhaps 140,000 inhabitants. The strong-handed ruling tactics of the Mexica, however, backfired when a new power entered Central American politics: the Spanish. Hernán *Cortés* capitalized on Native American resentment of the Mexica and successfully built allied relationships that empowered the Spaniards' eventual capture of Tenochtitlan in 1521, a year after the famous Aztec leader *Moctezuma*, often called Montezuma, had died in Spanish custody.

As the end of the Aztec empire suggests, the European civilizations themselves would eventually expand into global empires. During the later Middle Ages, Europe's soon-to-come global dominance could not have been realistically predicted, but starting in the eleventh century, European societies launched serious collaborative efforts to expand their areas of political control. In 1095, Pope Urban II urged an audience at the Council of Clermont to give up internecine warfare in Europe and to focus instead on militarily retaking the Holy Lands of Palestine. Ever since Muhammad's early military and conversion campaigns, Christianity had been under threat throughout the Middle East and North Africa. By the eighth century, Muslim forces had succeeded even in wresting Spain from the political control of Christians; the Crusades, in a sense, were the beginning of a large delayed military counterattack against the frequently hostile empires that surrounded European Christendom.

The First Crusade, launched by Urban II, was wildly successful in obtaining its objective; Jerusalem fell to the crusaders on July 15, 1099. Early expansion created a series of Crusader mini-kingdoms along the Palestinian coast and into Syria, despite frequent squabbles among the European rulers. Military setbacks, however, resulted in the loss of much of the northern territory in 1144 and then in the fall of Jerusalem to Saladin's forces in 1187. By 1189, Crusader-held territory was essentially limited to the cities of Antioch and Tripoli. Successive Crusader campaigns recaptured Jerusalem for brief periods (1229–1239 and 1240–1244), before Muslim factions succeeded in maintaining control over the city until 1917, when British troops forced the withdrawal of the Ottomans.

The success of Muslim forces against the west European crusaders paralleled their long-term success against the military forces of eastern Europe. The Byzantine Empire, which was the surviving remnant of the Roman Empire, had bordered Muslim-held lands along its southern and eastern borders ever since Muhammad's initial successes. Throughout the later Middle Ages, the empire increasingly crumbled under the pressure of the Christian kingdoms of western Europe and the Muslim kingdoms to the east and south. In A.D. 1025, the Byzantine Empire stretched from southern Italy, across all of modern-day Serbia, Croatia, and Greece, to the far-eastern sections of modern-day Turkey. By 1265, because of the aggression of western Crusaders and hostile Muslims, the Byzantine Empire had shrunk to include only western Turkey and the central Balkan peninsula. By 1355, the empire had lost Turkey east of the isthmus of Constantinople. Finally, on May 29, 1453, the Ottoman Turks under Mehmed II breached the walls of Byzantium, defeated the remaining Byzantine forces and their Venetian and Genoese allies, and subsumed this last major surviving piece of the ancient Roman Empire into the Ottoman Empire. The Byzantine emperor Constantine was last seen fighting desperately on foot at one of the city's gates. Isolated pockets of resistance, such as Trebizond, were crushed by 1461. The Roman Empire was no more.

The political tensions of this time period frequently mirrored religious differences. The Crusades, for example, clearly targeted the lands held by non-Christians, whereas the expansion of the predominantly Muslim Ottoman Empire precipitated the political collapse of Orthodox Christianity outside of Russia. These wars between members of different religions, however, do not indicate that religious differences were the major instigators of war throughout this time period. Western Europe, for example, engaged in frequent internecine squabbles in which Christian kingdoms battled other Christian kingdoms. To give but one example, France and England fought the intermittent Hundred Years' War (1337–1453) despite professing identical religious beliefs. Similarly, feuding between Shi'a Muslims and Sunni Muslims commenced shortly after the assassination of the leader Uhtman in 656, possibly by the followers of Ali, the cousin of Muhammad himself. These essentially political divides gradually became reinforced by religious divides. As this last episode suggests, religious differences frequently came to mirror political differences.

Several new religious traditions did develop during this time period, at least in part as a result of political events. Christianity, for example, split into two main forms: western

Christianity, centered on the Bishop of Rome as the leader of the global Christian church, and eastern Christianity, centered on the patriarch of Byzantium. These two branches of organized Christianity had become increasingly less interconnected because of political and linguistic differences. The Byzantine Church was centered in the surviving part of the ancient Roman Empire, whereas the western Church viewed Rome as the spiritual center but held sway throughout the multiple kingdoms of western Europe. The Byzantine church, moreover, used Greek in its liturgy and scholarship, and the Roman church used Latin. These political and linguistic differences encouraged separate developments in these two realms of Christianity, and significant theological and practical differences eventually developed. In particular, the west's inclusion of the *filioque* clause in the creed (which asserted that the Holy Spirit proceeded from God the Father and—the change—God the Son) and the growing western consensus that the clergy should be celibate and not marry alienated the sympathies of the Greek-speaking church, to the point that mutual excommunications were issued by the Bishop of Rome and the Byzantine patriarch in 1054. Throughout the later Middle Ages then, Christianity lived with deep schism.

Religious pressures likewise affected Asian and American religious traditions. During the eleventh and twelfth centuries, China's small but prosperous Sung Dynasty produced intellectuals such as Chou Tun-I (1017–1073) and Chu Hsi (1130–1200). Chu Hsi's restructuring and edition of Confucian writings into the Four Books created a system for Confucian study that has dominated Chinese, Japanese, and Korean *Confucianism* ever since. From the fourteenth century onward, the Four Books became the basis of the state examinations that determined careers in the civil service. As a result, the leaders of the Chinese state were, at least theoretically, masters of Confucian philosophy. Chu Hsi encouraged his disciples to explore the nature of the universe with both a sense of reverence and persistent investigation. His pedagogy encouraged not just reading and contemplation but also calligraphy and physical exercise, producing well-rounded individuals.

In Mesoamerica, the spread of Aztec religion corresponded with the military spread of the Aztec kingdom itself. In fact, the pictographic depiction of an enemy city's defeat was a pictogram picturing the burning of that city's temple. Religion and politics were inextricably interwoven. Nonetheless, Aztec religion appears to have been similar to the religions of the Aztecs' neighbors. The Mexica had a specialized priestly class who oversaw the public worship of the many Aztec gods. The priestly vocation was prestigious, though difficult; priests were celibate and made frequent offerings of their own blood. Priests performed these blood offerings by drawing string through lacerations in their tongues and earlobes. The priests would also occasionally sacrifice captured prisoners of war to ensure the continued survival and benevolence of Xipe Totec, the god of fertility.

Although the later Middle Ages, like most eras, witnessed frequent conflict and war, humankind benefited from an increasing codependence and specialization in production. International trade became a major means of creating wealth and increasing productivity. The wars and empire building of this period ironically increased global cooperation. Muslim merchants, following missionaries, created trade routes that stretched from the western Mediterranean into far-east Asia. The Mongol empire created a political unit that stretched from Russia through China and similarly fostered a pan-Eurasian economy. The Crusades, moreover, brought European aristocrats and commoners in direct contact with many of these rich trade routes and arguably increased European interest in luxury goods such as spices and silks. The Aztec empire, moreover, created a vast, prosperous economy, rich in skilled tradesmen and other professionals, that covered much of Mesoamerica. In all of these situations, military expansion efforts, even when they failed as in the case of the Crusades, frequently resulted in long-term economic benefits.

The Renaissance and Early Modern Eras (1492–1660)

The trade routes that developed in the later Middle Ages ultimately spurred the final era of globalization. Columbus set off in 1492 to discover a more direct route to the trade centers of India and Asia, thereby also cutting out the Arab middlemen. By sailing due west across the Atlantic, he hoped to circumnavigate the globe and demonstrate that India could be reached by sailing directly west. What Columbus did not know, however, was that the Americas were in the way. On October 12, 1492, Columbus touched down in the Caribbean. On October 28, he landed in Cuba and became convinced that he had actually landed in Japan. Lack of a translator prevented Columbus from realizing his mistake, but by 1498 it had become clear that the lands at which Columbus had arrived were in fact a previously unknown region of the world and that Asia lay still further to the west. Columbus never did, of course, discover a route to Asia, but his famous voyages launched a wave of colonization, expansion, and profiteering by European powers in the so-called New World.

The wealth of natural resources commandeered by the European powers, especially Spain, Portugal, England, and France, strengthened the European economy and promised fresh starts for those discontented with life at home in Europe, though this European intervention proved disastrous for the native Americans. A deadly combination of military attack, political oppression, and disease unconsciously (and sometimes consciously) imported from Europe resulted in a decline of perhaps 80 percent in the Native American population within a short period of time. By the year 1600, all the major Native American empires in Meso- and South America had been conquered by Spanish conquistador forces. Tenochtitlan, the Aztec capital, fell to Hernán Cortés in 1521, and Cuzco, the center of the Inca Empire in the Andes Mountains of South America, fell to the Spanish conquistador Francisco Pizarro in 1533. Scattered Amerindian tribes survived independently for longer, especially in North America because of the less aggressive policies of the French explorers who held much of the North American continent. U.S. expansionism, however, had destroyed most Native Americans' traditional lifestyles and appropriated their land by 1900.

Africa also possessed vast resources that would gradually attract European investors. During the fifteenth and sixteenth centuries, however, native peoples controlled most of the trade. In North Africa, Muslim Arabs and Berbers who were linked into the vast network of Muslim states controlled the political and economic spheres. Further south, black African nations controlled the trade. The Songhai Empire, for example, controlled the trade along the Niger River and attempted to balance the varying lifestyles of its Muslim urbanites, influenced by the prevailing religion among the wealthy classes throughout north and increasingly central Africa and the polytheistic pastoralists in the countryside.

Sonni Ali, who took power around 1464, led the Songhai kingdom to political unity and dominance within the local region, recapturing Timbuktu (the second largest area in the Songhai region) from the Tuareg. Muhammad I Askia, who ruled 1493–1528, consolidated Sonni Ali's gains. Frequent dynastic squabbles and internal tensions weakened the state, however, and invading Moroccans, equipped with the latest military technology, including firearms, ended Songhai independence in 1591. Guerilla activity in rural Songhai ultimately failed to disrupt the Moroccan grip on the area.

Northern Africa and the coastal Middle East, however, were dominated by the Ottoman Empire. Osman I (1258–1324), the founder of the Ottoman Empire, carved out of the declining Byzantine Empire a small kingdom for himself. His successors expanded their territory, despite setbacks, until, by 1550 during the golden reign of Suleyman I, the Ottomans controlled the Mediterranean sea coasts from modern-day Serbia around the eastern Mediterranean and west to Algiers in Africa. Internal and external pressures led to continued territorial loss from the late seventeenth century onward, until the defeat and dissolution of the remaining empire during World War I.

The Muslim world also saw other, smaller empires during this time period. The Safavid Dynasty controlled modern-day Iran and parts of Iraq from 1502 to 1736 and notably employed an Englishman, Sir Robert Sherley, to modernize the army in 1599, with consequent success in skirmishes against the Ottoman Turks to the west. Further east, in northern India, the *Mughal Dynasty* ruled from its foundation by Babur in 1526, achieving particular strength under Akbar (r. 1566–1605). Poor government and oppression of the large Hindu population undermined Mughal authority and the kingdom during the late seventeenth century. In 1748 the Hindu Maratha caste, comprising strong farmers and soldiers, succeeded in securing most of northern India.

In far-east Asia, the Ming Dynasty of China dominated the early modern era. The Ming Dynasty emerged in the early fourteenth century when the majority Han ethnic group revolted against the Mongol rulers in far-east Asia during a period of severe economic distress. Zhu Yuanzhang joined the rebels and eventually became the main leader. In 1368 the rebels under Zhu Yuanzhang controlled most of modern China, and Zhu Yuanzhang declared himself emperor, thereby starting the Ming Dynasty. Zhu Yuanzhang adopted the name Hongwu as his imperial name. Although Hongwu ruled autocratically and forcefully, he nevertheless succeeded in repairing the agricultural underpinnings of the Chinese economy.

By the early fifteenth century, the Ming Dynasty seemed poised to extend its kingdom overseas. Starting in the year 1405, the naval commander Zheng He completed a series of sea expeditions to the Middle East and the east coast of Africa, bringing back not only trade goods but also emissaries from the countries that he visited. Zheng He and the Ming Dynasty, however, never used these exploratory trips as a means of establishing trading posts or even colonies in the rich lands of the Middle East or in eastern Africa. Instead, the Ming Dynasty concentrated on expanding the territory around central China itself. The Ming Dynasty reached from Mongolia and Turkistan to Korea, Vietnam, and Myanmar, and Chinese merchants traded heavily throughout Southeast Asia and set up communities of expatriates. By the seventeenth century, China and Spain carried on a brisk trade, facilitated by the Spanish base in the Philippines. A gradual weakening of the imperial government, however, enabled the northern Manchus to overthrow the

Hans in 1644. The majority Han population, however, would look back to the Ming Dynasty as a rallying idea against Manchu rule. The Ming Dynasty, despite its autocratic and frequently despotic tendencies, became viewed as a golden era of self-rule.

During the same period that the nations of the world were weaving themselves more tightly into a global economy and—increasingly—a global society, European domestic society also underwent major cultural restructuring. The Renaissance, beginning in the fourteenth century but with roots going far deeper, and the Reformation, beginning in the fifteenth century (but once again with more ancient roots), dramatically changed the religious, intellectual, and political landscape. The Renaissance, which means literally "rebirth," self-consciously attempted to resurrect the glories of ancient Rome and Greece. Authors such as Petrarch (1304–1374) modeled their Latin prose on the works of Cicero, Virgil, and other authors from the first century B.C. In choosing these authors as their paragons, Renaissance authors intentionally slighted the Latin prose of the Middle Ages. Although the intention was to return Latin to the grammatical integrity of a perceived golden age, in reality, choosing a form of the Latin language that no one spoke and that could be acquired only through very diligent study resulted ultimately in a decline of the day-to-day use of the Latin language. Latin had retained pride of place throughout Europe in almost all major spheres of influence (including government, religion, education, and literature) during the Middle Ages. But this everyday Latin had grown very distant from the Latin spoken by Cicero and resembled closely the vernacular Romance languages of the continent. By enforcing an archaic Latin, the Renaissance thinkers unwittingly dealt a deathblow to the language. Increasingly, the vernacular languages (i.e., the languages spoken by the common people) replaced Latin as a form of communication, until, by the late seventeenth century, Latin was used, for the most part, only in the Catholic Church and in intergovernmental correspondence; in sum, Latin still served as a *lingua franca* between learned individuals of different nations, but the vernacular languages had replaced Latin in almost every other situation. This shifting linguistic situation produced some of the most enduring works of literary art, including Shakespeare's plays and Dante's poetic treatment of heaven, hell, and purgatory.

Even though the Renaissance viewed itself as a rebirth, many of its ideas were brand new. In the arts, for example, the Renaissance witnessed the birth of accurate visual perspective. The Italian master *Giotto* (died 1337) conducted early experiments in perspective, and Filippo Brunelleschi (1377–1466) laid out the mathematical foundations of the vanishing point, and other fifteenth-century painters, such as Masaccio and the Dutchman Jan van Eyck, perfected the technique.

Religion changed even more radically during the Renaissance. These religious changes, moreover, reflected deeper cultural shifts. The invention of the printing press in the early fifteenth century, for example, dramatically reduced the cost of books. Previously, scribes needed to laboriously copy out a book by hand; with the printing press, and the growing use of paper instead of velum and other animal skins, thousands of books could be produced during the time that only one book could be copied out by hand. This technological revolution increased supply and decreased the price of books. As a result, the middle class, and even to some degree the lower classes, had ready access to written information. Literacy rates increased steadily, and with literacy came increased education and self-confidence.

A steady belief in the ability of the individual to understand complex texts appears in the philosophies of the major Protestant reformers. The followers of both Martin Luther (1483–1546) and John Calvin (1509–1564), for example, believed that individual believers had the ability to interpret the Bible accurately and correctly. As a result, the Church hierarchy and its head, the pope, did not have the authority to enforce a particular theological interpretation. Instead, the individual Christian had a direct and personal connection with God; a priest was not strictly necessary to bring the believers to God. This interpretation of Christianity, which had deep roots within the mainstream Catholic Church also, became divisive as groups of Christians actively withdrew themselves from communion with their neighbors or with neighboring countries. The religious unity of western Europe, which had produced tremendous accomplishments in education, literature, and military power, dissolved as different regions sided either with reformers or with bishops in union with the pope.

Although the Reformation was, in a sense, a war of ideas, religious questions were often settled by political expediency. *Henry VIII* of England (r. 1509–1547) offers an excellent example. When Henry could not persuade the pope to grant Henry an annulment from his wife, Catherine of Aragon, who had not produced a male heir, Henry declared in 1534 that the king, not the pope, was the head of the Church in England. In this Act of Supremacy, Henry did not set forth a radically different theology. In fact, Henry's orthodoxy had been rewarded by Pope Leo X several years earlier, in 1521, as a reward for Henry's published tome that defended the validity of the seven sacraments against Lutheran theologians. Henry's Act of Supremacy, then, did not seek to establish a new theology, merely a new head of the Church. With the separation from the Catholic Church, however, the new Anglican Church quickly fell under the influence of Reformist theologians. The desire for control over both church and state similarly induced many German princes to separate their national churches from the Church of Rome. By the seventeenth century, England, Scandinavia, and most of northern Germany had separated from communion with the Church of Rome.

The crisis in religion, precipitated by politics to some degree, soon came to destabilize the politicians themselves. The theory of equality—that all human beings possess essentially the same abilities and rights—challenged not just religious hierarchies but also political aristocracies. Monarchy was built on the fundamental assumption that some people—royalty—were more fit to rule than others. The word *aristocracy* means, in fact, "rule by the best"; during the Middle Ages, the "best" became largely synonymous with the noble families. The rethinking of social relationships during the Reformation, however, encouraged the fundamental belief that hierarchies, be they secular or religious, had no special authority or right to rule. The English Civil War (1642–1651) shows the logical continuation of these intellectual ideas. In this war, parliamentary forces, supported by radical Protestants, defeated the king and his forces, who were Catholic sympathizers. After they had captured and beheaded the king, *Charles I,* in 1649, Parliament established a Commonwealth, the first large-scale democracy in Europe since the time of ancient Greece. This democracy did not resemble modern democracy—the poor and women were not allowed to vote, for example—but the Commonwealth represented a dramatic break with the past. The coinage drove home the difference: gone was the king's head, gone was the Latin. In their place stood the shield of England, an abstract symbol clearly representing everyone, and English words that everyone could understand.

The Commonwealth did not last long. The leader of the parliamentary forces, Oliver Cromwell, eventually assumed both the powers and the trappings of kingship, though he eschewed the title and the crown itself. In 1660, less than two years after Cromwell's death in 1658, *Charles II*, the son of the decapitated Charles I, was invited to return to England as king. Britain's experiment with social equality had failed, in no small part because of the corruption and power-grabbing of politicians. The seeds of democracy, however, would take more lasting root in the American and French revolutions during the eighteenth century. These new political undertakings started a genuinely new era in the history of the West, and, ultimately, in the history of the world.

Part II

DOMESTIC LIFE

Domestic life describes the activities, roles, and rhythms that adorn family life. Women and children, both of whom were frequently expected to remain out of the public spotlight during the Middle Ages and Renaissance, have a special connection with domestic life. Throughout much of the past, the home was considered to be the proper place for women and children. These general tendencies, however, were not rules, and we would go far wrong to say that women were excluded from powerful roles. After all, Queen Elizabeth I of England (r. 1558–1603) was perhaps the most powerful monarch in European history. The section on Women's Roles seeks to paint a nuanced picture of the complex roles that women played in the past.

Children, as the following section demonstrates, had similarly complex and conflicting roles. They were supposed to be subservient to their parents and show it in such ritual behavior as standing up and uncovering their heads when their parents entered the room. But children entered the workforce much earlier as well. While children from wealthy families might have many years of education, most children started to work full time as soon as they were able. The luckiest of these children would learn a trade through a formal apprenticeship, though the documents show that many children were desperately homesick. The touching way in which parents frequently talk about their children shows that the parents also missed their children.

The phrase "life cycles" refers to the ritual events that mark important life stages, such as baptisms, weddings, and funerals. Cultures across the world mark such stages, and there appears to be a common human desire to come together, celebrate, and mark important changes in the life of an individual. These ceremonies can also become controversial. Several of the documents in the Life Cycles section describe attempts to restrain lavish celebrations or to deny the celebrations of certain minority groups, such as Quakers. In these situations, life cycles and domestic life clearly played a role in public life.

Life Cycles

Regardless of race or nationality, all human beings go through significant, universal life changes. At the very least, all human beings are born, and all human beings die. Many humans, however, will also take important steps such as marrying. Many of these key stages in life are celebrated through rituals that mark out and sanctify the person making an important transition. Although the particulars of each culture are different, the wide spread of ceremonial life transitions serves to unite cultures around the world.

Baptism (or similar birth rituals) and marriage are excellent examples of ceremonies found in the vast majority of human cultures. The detailed description of European wedding customs provided by Louis de Gaya below (Document 5) demonstrates that all the cultures are alike in celebrating the union of husband and wife, even if most of the interest in de Gaya's account comes from the vivid differences in the ceremonies that celebrate that union. Although German brides carry an onion to cry more effusively, and Polish brides circle a fire three times in a ritual that may predate the arrival of Christianity, both brides nevertheless are specifically and ritually demarcating the transition from being a single woman to being a married woman and—frequently—a mother. The heavy and detailed symbolism investing such rituals is explored in Document 1, regarding the meaning of ritual baptism.

The ritual transitions of the life cycle frequently also became occasions for conspicuous consumption. Perhaps this evolution developed out of the simple fact that a large audience was frequently present to witness an individual's celebration of a life stage. The individual took the opportunity to make a good impression. The seventeenth-century proscription against lavish weddings (Document 3) suggests that such spectacular consumption could even be viewed as harmful to society. A particularly interesting display of wealth surrounds burial, considering that the individual being buried does not get to enjoy the display, even if the deceased provided an elaborate funereal monument, as in the case of Achabar-Sha, described by Thomas Roe (Document 6). Instead, such death monuments seem to benefit the living. Certainly, the Muslims visiting the shrines of the saints receive inspiration and encouragement, but the saints themselves have long since entered paradise according to Muslim tradition.

Certain life stages, then as now, were distinctly unglamorous. Old age in the Middle Ages and the *Renaissance* could be just as troubling as it is today. The gifted Chinese poet Po Chu-i records a quiet life of contentment in the autobiographical poems dealing with his old age (Document 2). They feature a definite sense of peace, but at the same time, the excitement of life has departed. Similarly, although weddings were normally an occasion for ostentatious parties, religious minorities such as the *Quakers* held small weddings, in part because of government and societal opposition (Document 4). While the Scots were celebrating marriage so lavishly that the London government sought to curtail the festivities, the Quaker weddings were not even considered to be valid weddings. Life cycles and their celebrations do unite people and cultures because of their universal practice; perhaps the differences, however, are just as important.

1. The Meaning of Ritual Baptism

Baptisms, or similar infant rituals, welcome young Christians into the world. Baptism, a term that derives from a Greek word meaning "to dip" or "to bathe," involves sprinkling or briefly submersing a new Christian in water. In the traditional Christianity of the Middle

Ages and Europe, baptism generally took place soon after an infant's birth. Baptism conferred church membership and, according to Christian theology, a unity with Christ and his salvation. As a result, if an infant died, he or she would nevertheless enjoy the rewards of heaven by merit of the baptism. Unbaptized children, however, would go to limbo, a place of perfect peace and comfort but devoid of the divine rewards of heaven.

The anonymous author of the sixteenth-century document reproduced here is careful to clarify the symbolism of the baptismal ritual. For example, the author suggests that salt, which is given to the baptized, symbolizes wisdom, and the flame of the candle symbolizes the extinguishing of sin. The author also carefully points out that baptism is only the start of a long journey. The baptized individual must be careful to avoid sins throughout his or her life.

Although the Catholic Church and more conservative churches baptized children, some radical Protestant churches believed that only adults should receive baptism because children were not yet able to make an informed choice on their own behalf. These Protestant congregations nevertheless believed that children should lead Christian lives, even if they were not yet fully professed members of the church.

Only a few words from this document will cause great difficulty to the modern reader: orisons are prayers, gossips are godparents, and Pater Noster, Ave, and Credo are particular prayers.

When a christian man's child is born into this world, it is brought to church and three witnesses cometh with him, that is, Godfather and Godmother and when they be agreed what name shall be to the child, then the priest maketh a sign of the cross in the forehead of the child and sayeth thus: "A token of the holy cross of our Lord Jesu Christ I set in thy forehead and so at the breast in like manner." And then the priest sayeth many orisons over the child commanding the devil to knowledge his sentence and give worship to the living God and true and to Jesu Christ and to the Holy Ghost and depart from this servant of God, and then he putteth salt into the mouth of the child and sayeth thus: "Salt of wisdom, the God be mercifull to thee into everlasting life, Amen." By this salt of wisdom understand God's word, which should be lerned in the mouth of the child when it beginneth to speak as the Apostle sayeth, "Be our word savored with salt evermore in grace." Then the priest wetteth his thomb in spotil and toucheth the child's ear and sayeth, "Be thou opened." That is, understand in all thy five wits, to hear and to seak the word of God with love and dread and holy devotion. For the Judgment of God shall touch in which we should yield account of every idle word. Also the priest toucheth the nostrils of the child for it should smell the odour of wetness of heavenly things, more than every earthly thing. Soon after this the priest biddeth all the people that there be to say a Pater Noster and an Ave and a Credo, beseeking God that the child may rightfully take his Christendom, and well keep it to the ending of his life. And then the priest taketh the child by the right hand and calleth his name and sayeth, "Come thou into the temple of God that thou may have everlasting life and live into world of worlds, Amen." Then the child is brought to the font and the priest calleth it by name and sayeth *Abranuncio Satane et omnibus operibus eius et omnibus pompis eius*, that is, "I forsake Satan, that is the devil, and all his works and all his pomps or prides." And the gossips sayeth, *Abranuncio*, that is "I forsake." Therefore where he is not a false christian man that keepeth not the covenant of these words but afterward wrappeth him in the fiend's pride in heart and in clothing and in wicked working; for if this covenant should be truly kept, all the tokens of pride in man must be done away, saying each token of pride is a pomp of the fiend. After sayeth the priest to the child, "Believest thou in God the Father, Almighty Maker of heaven and earth." The child is dumb and may not speak but and it were of age and might speak, it should answer for itself therefore the gossips, answering, *Credo,* that is, "I believe." After asketh the priest, "And believest thou in Jesu Christ, His only son, our lord, born and suffered," and they say, "I believe." The third time asketh the priest, "And believest thou in the Holy Ghost, in holy church, faith in communion of saints, forgiveness of sins, the rising of flesh, and after the ever-lasting life." And they say, "I believe." Then sayeth the priest *Quid petis,* "What askest thou." They say "Baptism." "Would thou be baptized?" sayeth the priest, and they say *Volo,* "I will." Then the priest taketh the child and sayeth, "I baptize thee in the name of the Father and of the Son and of the Holy Ghost, Amen." And so he plungeth it in the water and commandeth the gossips to lay hand on the child's head, for they been witnesses of his Baptism, and receive the charge to teach it and the truth of his believe that is the commandments and the dooms of God, and to flee the pomps and prides of the fiend, for the common people and all men should know and keep the commandments of God, and priests his holy counsels, and Lords his just dooms, and if they do not this, they be wrongfully called Christian men. And thus blind priests bear false witnesses of young children christened, that afterward serve the devil whom they forsook saying, *Abranuncio.* After these things the priest anointeth the child with oil and lapped in his chrism and taketh it a candel burning in his hand, and sayeth, *Accipe lampadem ardentem irriprehensibilem; custodi baptisinum tuum; serva mandata ut convenit Dominus ad nuptias possis occurrere ei una cum sanctis in aula celestis ut habeas vitam eternam et vivas in secula seculorum, Amen.* That is to say, "Have thou a burning lamp unreprovable; keep thou thy baptism and keep thou the commandments that when the Lord cometh to the weddings, thou mayest be against him as one with the saints in the heavenly hall, that thou have ever lasting life and live into the world of worlds, Amen."

But all christian folk should busily learn to know the greatness of charge which they receive in their baptism. For with four things we be charged in our baptism, although blind priests know it not, when they give to us four Elements in tokening of them. That is salt, and water, and oil, and fire. The first charge is that we take salt of wisdom of God's word and rule our life thereafter and salt our souls that they stink not in sin. For and this heavenly salt fail from men, they should be cast out as Christ teacheth in the gospel. The second charge is, that our ears be opened ever more ready to hear Christs gospel and understand it. For Christ sayeth, "He that hath ears of hearing, Let him hear, and he that readeth, let him understand." The third charge is this, that we keep our Baptism that is the covenant of our baptism, and true belief in the Father and the Son, and the Holy Ghost as the priest apposeth us when we say *Credo.* The fourth charge is this, that we keep the commandements of God, as the priest commandeth us at the font, putting a candle burning in our hand, for as a candle burning is wasted by fire, so sins in our soul should be wasted and destroyed with keeping of the commandments of God, having devout love to him and to our even Christian. And this is the second baptism, that saint John teacheth when he sayeth, "I baptize in water, but another shall come after me stronger than I and he shall baptize you in the Holy Ghost and fire." And without this second baptism may no man be saved, as Christ said to Nichodemus, "Truly, I say to thee, but a man be born again of water and of the Holy ghost, he may not enter into the kingdom of God." Also, Paul teacheth that the first baptism in water only, maketh us not safe, but the asking of a good conscience in God and faith not feigned, the belief that worketh by charity. For Christ sayeth, "He that believeth in me, floods of quick water should flow from his womb," that is the Holy Ghost that Christ calleth the comforter, which floweth ever into the hearts of meek men that make them ready to die; for that man that shall dwell before the blessed face of God in heaven, shall receive the ernest of the Holy Ghost in earth. And this is the second baptism that fleshly priests and swinish people knoweth not, for their hearts be stopped with fleshly lust, that the floods of the Holy ghost may not enter into them, and therefore priests be in peril that teach not the second Baptism. For it sufficeth not to salvation of man to wash his body in water of Baptism and suffer his soul to stink in sin through breaking of the commandments of God. For thus priests read in the holy Psalm, *Increpasti superbos maledicti qui declinant a mandatis tuis,* that is to say, "Thou blamest the proud, they be accursed that bow away from thine behests." And thus God shall blame proud priests for they pursue poor men for the learning of the commandments the which they charge them to keep in the hour of their baptism, and all that bear the name of christian men should cry against this error. For what error is more vile in the sight of God than to bind men to a law and afterward pursue them for the same law, and thus for dread of evil priests, men dare not keep Christ's behests and the ghostly birth of our mother holy church is despised of proud men that know not the bond of their baptism. Amen.

Source: *A Declaracion of the Seremonies Anexid to the Sacrament of Baptyme: What They Sygnyffie and How We Owght to Understande Them.* N.p., 1537, pp. 1–11.

2. Old and Middle Age in Tang China

Po Chu-i (772–846) rose to prominence as a poet during the Chinese Tang dynasty. His descriptive powers and gentle but serious tone make his poems memorable. In the two following poems, he discusses both the changes that come throughout life and his comfortable, though limited, life in advanced old age. According Po Chu-i, the years between 50 and 60 years old are the best. Before this time, the physical passions—the Five Lusts, as Po Chu-i terms them—distract people from the deeper and more important aspects of love. After this time period, disease and weakness prevent people from pursuing their chosen activities.

The second poem, Po Chu-i's last, records his lifestyle in the last days of his life. The poet receives diligent care from servants and grandchildren, and the needs of daily life are placed in his convenient reach. Nevertheless, the poet associates the activities of life as "trifling affairs" and soon goes to sleep basking in the southern sun. The symbolic connection between sleep and death permeates the poem—Po Chu-i is ready to die.

On Being Sixty

Between thirty and forty, one is distracted by the Five Lusts;
Between seventy and eighty, one is a prey to a hundred diseases.
But from fifty to sixty one is free from all ills;

Calm and still—the heart enjoys rest.
I have put behind me Love and Greed; I have done with Profit
   and Fame;
I am still short of illness and decay and far from decrepit age.
Strength of limb I still possess to seek the rivers and hills;
Still my heart has spirit enough to listen to flutes and
   strings.
At leisure I open new wine and taste several cups;
Drunken I recall old poems and sing a whole volume.
Meng-te has asked for a poem and herewith I exhort him
Not to complain of three-score, "the time of obedient ears."

Last Poem

They have put my bed beside the unpainted screen;
They have shifted my stove in front of the blue curtain.
I listen to my grandchildren, reading me a book;
I watch the servants, heating up my soup.
With rapid pencil I answer the poems of friends;
I feel in my pockets and pull out medicine-money.
When this superintendence of trifling affairs is done,
I lie back on my pillows and sleep with my face to the
   South.

Source: *A Hundred and Seventy Chinese Poems*. Translated by Arthur Waley. London: Constable, 1918, pp. 161, 168.

Pottery attendant with three color glaze, Tang dynasty, early eighth century A.D., from tomb at Chungpu near Xian, Shaanxi province, China, 29.7cm. The Art Archive/Genius of China Exhibition.

3. Lavish Weddings Prohibited in England

Baptisms, weddings, and burials were not simply religious and family events—frequently they were also lavish parties. The festivities surrounding these events became so lavish that King James II of England (r. 1685–1688) thought it necessary to issue a proclamation implementing legislation—enacted under Charles II—to restrain the festivities. James's royal proclamation is reproduced here. Although the proclamation puts forth only vague justifications for the imposed restrictions, the restrictions themselves were severe. At weddings, for example, each side was able to bring only four friends, plus their servants, in addition to their family members and teachers. Moreover, they were permitted to change their clothes only twice during the festivities (changing clothes frequently was a way of showing off wealth). Violating these provisions resulted in a fine of 25 percent of the year's personal income—a very substantial sum, although maximums did limit the potential damage done depending on social class.

Indeed, the importance of social class appears clearly in this document. Not only did different social classes suffer different penalties, but they also enjoyed different privileges. The funerals of noblemen were allowed 100 noble guests (servants are not counted), barons were permitted 60 noble guests, and landed gentry 30, whereas lowly Citizens of the Burgh were permitted only 12 noble mourners at their funerals.

A PROCLAMATION AGAINST PENNY-WEDDINGS

James, by the grace of God, King of Great Britain, France and Ireland, Defender of the Faith, To Macers of Our Privy Council, or Messengers at Arms, Our Sheriffs in that part, conjunctly and severally, specially constitute, of Our dearest Royal Brother of ever glorious Memory, Entitled, *Act Restraining the exorbitant Expence of Marriages*, etc. upon the considerations therein-mentioned, the keeping of Penny-Weddings is Prohibited and Discharged, under and with the Certifications and Qualifications thereby expressly provided. And whereas, notwithstanding of the said Act and Prohibtion, divers persons, Vintners and others, have, and still continue to contravene so necessary and useful a Law, to the great contempt of Our Authority, expense, and abuse of Our Leidges, contrary to the design and intent thereof. Therefore, We with Advice of Our Privy Council, Do hereby Ordain the said Act of Parliament to be put in full and vigorous execution against the Contraveners, conform to the tenor thereof in all points. And to the end that all persons may be of new printed, and subjoined hereto, and published in manner underwritten. And therefore, Our Will is, and We Charge you strictly, and Command that incontinent these Our Letter seen, we pass to the Mercatcross of *Edinburgh*, and all the other Mercat-Crosses of the Head-Burghs of the Shires of this Kingdom, and there in Our Royal Name and Authority, by open Proclamation make publication of Our Pleasure in the Premisses, and also read the foresaid Act of Parliament hereunto subjoined, that none may pretend Ignorance, under the Pains and Certifications therein-mentioned.

Given under our Signet at Edinburgh, *the sixth day of December, One thousand six hundred eighty seven. And of our Reign the third year.* God save the King. *Per actum Dominorum Secreti Concilii.* Will. Paterson.

FOLLOWS THE TENOR OF THE ABOVE-MENTIONED ACT OF PARLIAMENT

Act Restraining the exorbitant expence of Marriages, Baptisms, and Burials. September 13, 1681.

Our Sovereign Lord, Considering the great hurt and prejudice, arising to this Kingdom, by the superfluous expence bestowed at Marriages, Baptisms, and Burials. For repressing of which abuse in time coming, His Majesty, with Advice and Consent of His Estates of Parliament, Does Statute and Ordain, That Marriages, Baptisms, and Burials, shall be solemnized, and gone about, in sober, and decent manner. And that at Marriages, besides the married persons, their Parents, Children, Brothers, and Sisters, and the Family wherein they live, There shall not be present at any Contract of Marriage, or in-fare, or meet upon occasion thereof, above four Friends on either side, with their ordinary domestic Servants, and that neither Bride-groom, nor Bride, nor their Parents, or Relations, Tutors, or Curators for them, and to their use, shall make above two changes of Raiment at that time, or upon that occasion. Certifying such persons as shall contravene, if they be Landed persons, They shall be liable in the fourth part of their yearly valued Rent, and those who are not Landed Persons, in the fourth part of their Moveables, Burgesses according to their Condition and Means, not exceeding five hundred Merks Scots, and mean Craftsmen and

Servants, not exceeding one hundred Merks: And if there shall be any greater number of persons that aforesaid, in any House, or Inn, within Burgh, or Suburbs thereof, or within two Miles of the same, where Penny-Weddings are made, that the Master of the House shall be Fined in the Sum of five hundred Merks Scots. And it is statute and Ordained, That at Baptisms, upon that occasion, besides the Parents, Children, Brothers, and Sisters, and those of the Family, there shall not be present above four Witnesses. And Further, His Majesty, with Consent foresaid, Statutes and Ordains, That there shall not be invited to Burials, any greater number of persons than those following, *viz*. To the Burial of Noblemen, and Bishops, and their Wives, not above one hundred Noblemen and Gentlemen: To the Burial of a Baron of Quality, not above Sixty, and other Landed Gentlemen, not above Thirty. And that the Mourners at the Burials of Noblemen, and Bishops, and their Ladies, do not exceed Thirty, and at the Burials of Privy Counsellors, Lords of Session, Barons, Provosts of Burghs, and their Wives, the number of Mourners do not exceed Twenty four, And at the Burials of all other Landed Gentlemen, and Citizens within Burgh, they do not exceed the number of Twelve. And Prohibits, and Discharges the using, or carrying of any Pencils, Banners, and other Honours, at Burials, except only the eight Branches to be upon the Pale, or upon the Coffin, where there is no Pale, under the foresaids penalties respective, in case they contravene. And it is Statute and Ordained, That there be no Mourning Cloaks used at Burials, nor at any other time, under the pain of One Hundred pounds Scots.

Source: James II. *A Proclamation against Penny-Weddings*. Edinburgh: Andrew Anderson, 1687.

4. Quaker Marriages

Originating in seventeenth-century England, the Quakers, like other minority religious groups in Europe, frequently suffered official and unofficial persecution. In the document reproduced here, the Quakers object to the English government's refusal to recognize Quaker marriages as valid—the only licit marriages at the time were those performed within the official Church of England. By offering an example of a marriage certificate to Parliament, the Quakers hoped to prove to the politicians that their marriages also deserved to be recognized as valid by the government.

The marriage certificate clearly meets the major criteria of marriage as understood at that time: the contract is between the man and the woman; neither the man nor the woman is currently married; the proposed marriage has been announced several weeks ahead of time (called reading the banns*) so that anyone might protest; the marriage itself is performed publicly, in front of witnesses; and the man and the woman exchange Christian vows and set their hands ceremonially together. Thus, throughout the document, the Quakers call attention to how similar Quaker marriage is to Anglican (Church of England) marriage. Despite such petitions, the Quakers continued to face official and unofficial obstacles to the practice of their faith, and large numbers therefore immigrated to Penn's Woods, modern-day Pennsylvania, in America, where freedom of religion was a central principle.*

A Quaker Meeting. Unlike most other Christian denominations prior to the twentieth century, any lay person, including women, were allowed to speak during Quaker services. Courtesy of the Library of Congress.

A COPY OF A MARRIAGE-CERTIFICATE OF THE PEOPLE CALLED QUAKERS: IMPORTING THE METHOD USED AMONG THEM

Humbly presented to the Members of Parliament, to manifest the said Peoples' Christian Care, and Righteous Proceedings, not admitting Clandestine or Unwarrantable Marriages amongst them. And therefore they Humbly Request that their Marriages may not be rendered Clandestine or Illegal, nor they or their children exposed to Suffering on that Account.

A.B. Glass-Grinder in Southwark, Son of C.D. of Gilford in *Surrey* Scrivener deceased, and *E.F.* of Little Britain, Daughter of *G.H.* in the *Minories* Shoemaker deceased: Having declared their Intentions of taking each other in Marriage before several public Meetings of the People of God called Quakers in *London,* according to the good Order used amongst them: whose Proceeding therein, after a deliberate consideration thereof, were approved by the said Meetings, they appearing clear of all others, and having Consent of parties and Relations concerned. Now these are to Certifie all whom it may concern, that for the full accomplishing of their said Intentions, this 17th day of *September* in the Year, according to the English Account, One thousand Six Hundred and Eighty Five, They the said *A.B.* and *E.F.* appeared in a public Assembly of the aforesaid People, and others, met together for that end and purpose in their public Meeting-place at the *Bull* and *Mouth London,* and (according to the Example of the Holy Men of God recorded in the Scriptures of Truth) in a solemn manner, he the said *A.B.* taking the said *E.F.* by the Hand, did openly declare as followeth: *Friends, in the fear of the Lord, and in the presence of you his People, I take this my Friend E.F. to be my Wife, promising by the assistance of God, to be to her a faithful and loving Husband, till it please the Lord to separate us by death, [or to the same effect.].*

And then and there in the said Assembly, the said *E.F.* did in like manner declare as followeth: *Friends, in the fear of the Lord, and in the presence of you his Peole, I take this my Friend A.B. to be my Husband, promising to be to him a faithful, obedient and loving Wife, till death separate us, [or to the same effect.]*

And the said *A.B.* and *E.F.* as a further Confirmation thereof, did then and there to these Presents set their Hands; And we whose Names are hereunto subscribed, being present, amongst others, at the solemnizing of their said Marriage and Subscription, in manner aforesaid, as Witnesses thereunto, have also to these Presents subscribed our Names, the Day and Year above-written.

[A list of 37 witnesses follows.]

Source: *A Copy of a Marriage-Certificate of the People Called Quakers.* N.p., 1687.

5. Traditional European Marriage Customs

The colorful account provided in the following document demonstrates the late-medieval and Renaissance interest in ethnography—the study of different cultures. Within the extract, Louis de Gaya surveys the marriage customs of a large number of different European countries. He begins by outlining the marital customs established by the Catholic Church (called frequently the "Romish" Church in the extract) but then proceeds to survey how cultures further removed from Rome tend to have more unusual ceremonies.

According to the author, the Sicilians, for example, tended to consummate their marriages (i.e., have sexual relations) immediately after their engagement, even if they did not plan on marrying for several more years. Germany, meanwhile, had several customs not seen elsewhere: brides carried an onion during the ceremony so that they would be sure to cry (thereby "proving" their virginity), and the bridegroom gave his wife a gift of expensive jewels after they had spent the night together (the custom was called Morgengal).

The Polish, however, are credited with the most unusual customs, which the author believes descend from pagan times. The bride, for example, walked around a fire three times, kicked with her right foot each door in the house before the ceremony, and had her mouth anointed with honey. Once the couple was married, the woman was thrown in bed with the man, and the attendants brought the couple ram's stones (i.e., ram's testicles) to eat to promote the couple's fertility.

These accounts of foreign weddings likely fascinated seventeenth-century Englishmen, at whom the book was aimed, as much as they fascinate modern audiences.

Polygamy, or the use of many Women together, is very usual amongst the Infidels, but it is generally forbidden amongst Christians, who are forbidden, upon pain of death, marrying more than one Woman together; and further she must be married in the Church before the Parson of the Parish. All other Marriages contracted otherwise are declared void and clandestine, the Children born in such are reputed Bastards, and consequently incapable of Succession, and of challenging their Parents' inheritance.

The Ceremonies of Marriages amongst Roman Catholics are prescribed by the Councils. The Council of Trent, for to prevent all abuses in Marriages, declareth and pronounceth all Marriages invalid and void, which have not been celebrated before the Parson of the Parish of the one or the other contracting parties. Wherefore according to the decrees of the Romish Church, as soon as the contracting Parties are agreed, the Parsons of their respective Parishes are bound to proclaim three Banns on three Sundays, or three Holy days consecutively, to the end that if any of the Parishoners know any lawful cause why they may not be joined together, they may reveal it to the Parson of the parish. And in case no body can allege any lawful impediment, then both the parties are conducted by their parents into the Parochial Church of the Woman, where they are betrothed by the Parson of the said parish, who examines them whether they be well contented to be betrothed one to the other, and whether they be not already engaged by promise of Marriage to any other person or persons. This is the Ceremonie, which is called Espousals or betrothing, and is nothing properly but a Nuptial preparation or an engagement, to a future marriage, of which engagement neither of the contracted parties can be released but by the Court of the ordinary, which condemneth him or her that violateth promise, to all damages and expenses whatever, together with a Fine.

There be some Bishoprics where they use to betroth people as soon as they are agreed together, and before the publication of the banns.

The day of marriage being prefixed, the betrothed parties, after they have been at the auricular Confession of their sins, go to receive the Communion the day before their marriage. The next day they are conducted by their friends to Church, where the parson of the parish, having asked them their names and surnames, asks them, one after another, whether they are content to take one another; He asketh them besides if they be not already engaged by any solemn vow, or any promise of Marriage; and whether they will engage to love and keep fidelity one to another. When to all these questions they answer affirmatively, he then blesses a ring, and thirteen pieces of money, which he gives to the Bridegroom.

The Bridegroom sets the Ring upon the fourth finger of the Bride's Right Hand, in saying to her, with the Parson, *with this Ring I thee wed;* then giving her some pieces of money, he goes on saying, *and with this money I thee endow.* The Bride answereth with a compliment set down in the Romish Ceremonial. Then presently the Parson takes the right hands of them both, saying: "Et ego conjungo vos in Nomine Patris, Filii, et Spiritus Sancti." He sprinkleth them, and all the Assembly, with Holy Water.

After the Nuptial Blessing, both the new married Folks are bound to hear Mass with a lighted Taper in their hands, with which they go to kiss the Offertory, and to present the Parson with Bread and Wine.

Then, if the new married Folks were never married before, two of their nearest Relations hold a Sheet over their heads, whilst the Priest readeth some prayers over them.

The Mass being ended, the Parson presenteth the Church Register to the new married couple and to their Relations, to the end that they may sign and seal the Act of Marriage; after that then every one goes away, in the same order as they came.

On that Evening before the new married folks betake themselves to their bed, the Parson, or some other Priest deputed by him, cometh to bless the Nuptial Bed, wherein the Marriage ought to be consumated.

In the most part of *Italy*, they do not use to betroth people in the Church; but the contract of Marriage is made in the presence of the Parson, then the Proclamation of the Banns followeth, they proceed to the Solemnization of the Marriage, which is celebrated wither at Noon, with all Pomp imaginable, or else before the Sun-rising without any noise at all, the Woman being conducted to Church by her Father if living, and if he be dead, by the nearest of her Relations.

At *Venice* when any Gentleman is to marry, as soon as the contract is made, all other Gentlemen resort to the house of the future Bride, whom they call *Novizza;* the Bridegroom also, with his nearest Relations comes thither: He stands at the entry of the House, receiving, with all demonstration of Honour, all his Guests, giving them his right hand as a mark of his entire Affection; The Bride doth do the like to the Women. After the Celebration of Marriage, the Bride enters into a splendid Barge finely decked, her Hair hanging about her shoulders, being set in the most eminent place, that is called, in their Language, *Andar in Trasto*. This they do to the end that every body may take notice that she is a new married Bride, and the Wife of such a Gentleman. But nowadays they have left off something of the ancient Custome, for the *Novizza*'s appear in their Barges many days, with their Hair plaited very high, much like *English* Women's high Towers.

The *Sicilians* did formerly betroth the Man and the Woman at home, and very often were not married till the Hour of Death, or at the extremity of the one, or of the other Parties: But this was forbidden by the order of the Council of *Trent*. The espoused woman did also use to ride through the City with a great Company and Pomp, on horseback; But that is now quite left off, since the Invention of Coaches. But notwithstanding the Prohibition of the foresaid Council even to this day, as soon as the Articles of the Contract are signed, the man enjoys his Spouse with all liberty, and reaps the sweet Fruits of Marriage many years sometimes before the celebration of it.

At the Weddings of their Country people, there is very much dancing, and there is always a great number of Guests, as well of the Relations and others, who bring Presents, after that the Bridegroom hath regaled them three times. Their Feasts usually consist of Meats baked in the Oven, and of Kettles full of Rice boiled in Milk. . . .

Formerly the *Germans* never married Women of any other Nation, but their own; that they might avoid all confusion in their Blood. And they never bestowed their Daughters in Marriage too Young; Bachelors also did not go awooing but very late; So that by that means, the Children which did proceed from two Persons of mature Age, of full Proportion, and of Vigorous strength, were also tall, strong, and vigorous. They, even to this day, will never marry their Sons but to their Maids, which are of a strong constitution of body, tall, and most likely to bear strong and lusty Children. Their Nuptial Ceremonies are in much the same as of the other People in *Europe;* they differ only in this, that the Bride-Maids wear every one a Crown of Gold, or of Flowers, at the Weddings of their fellow Maids, which is not lawful for others to do. All the Guests present the Bride with Jewels or Pieces of Gold and Silver, which they cast into a Basin, which is placed before the Bride, as she sitteth at table in the middle of Women of her near Relations, and they accompany their Presents with civil Acclamations, and good wishes, of Prosperity and Happiness, to the new married Couple.

There are amongst them some free Weddings, in which Men of Honour defray all the charges; and there be some also, in which every one pays his Scot. Their Feasts last at least three days, during which the new married Folks are accompanied with a great number of People, insomuch that a common Handicrafts-man will have oftentimes above sixty Persons at his Wedding: For the more People they have about them, the more are they regarded and esteemed.

As for the Gentlemen and Persons of considerable note, they present their new married Wives with a Chain of Gold, or some Precious Jewel, on the next day morning, after the consummation of Marriage, and this Present they call, in their Language, *Morgengal,* that is to say, the Gift of the morning, because they bestow it upon the Bride, as soon as they are up, as it were to make her some recompence for her Maiden-head, which they have taken away.

If any Maid amongst them hath been so liquorish, as to have tasted of the Horse-Radish before the time; if she, by good fortune, doth not go away with the bag, but is so happy as to marry him, that hath already plaid upon her Fiddle, then the said couple will go to Church very early in the morning, without any Instruments of Music; and, in some places, but especially in Country-Towns, all the Neighbours, crowned with Garlands made of straw, accompany them to Church.

In many places they compel the Daughters at the Marriages to renounce, and disclaim, all their Rights, as well as Paternal as Maternal, and this they do, in casting some straw into their Fathers Houses. Moreover if the Bride doth not shed some Tears, when she goes before the Priest to be joined in marriage, then her Virginity becomes very much suspected, and for that purpose many of them Brides carry Onions, wrapt up in their Handkerchiefs, that they may force some tears out of their Eyes. . . .

In *Poland,* but chiefly in the Country, Of *Prussia* and *Lithuania,* Maids seldom marry under four and twenty Years of Age; and not so neither till they have first wrought, with their own hands, as much stuff, as is sufficient to cloth every one, who must accompany their Bridegroom to Church. Amongst them when any Father seeks a Wife for his Son, he neither regards her Beauty nor Wealth, but only her good Morality, ripeness of Age, and strong constitution of Body. The Women are never married till two of their future Bridegrooms near Relations have had a deep finger in their Pies, and then they use to crave their Father's good consent; those People do still retain many Dregs of the old Superstition of the Heathens: For when the Solemnity of Matrimony is celebrated, the Bride is led three times about a Fire, then they make her sit down, they wash her feet, and with that same water they besprinkle the Nuptial Bed, and all the Utensils of the House. This done, they anoint her Mouth with Honey, they bind her Eyes with a Veil: Then she is conducted towards all the Doors of the House, which she must kick with her right Foot; they afterwards strew every Door with Wheat, Rye, Oats, Barley, Beans and Poppy, declaring that her Bridegroom shall ever enjoy a great abundance of all those good things, if she devoutly retain her Religion, and if she be carefull and industrious in ordering her Family. The evening being come when she must bed with her Bridegroom, they use to cut her hair, then the married Woman takes a Posie, which they fasten on her Head: after that they put on her Head a white Hood, which new married Women wear until they have brought forth a Son, for until that time, they are reputed Maids. The Bride is at last conducted into her Bed-Chamber, whereafter they have shoved and beaten her, they at length cast her into the Bed, into her Bridegroom's arms. And then instead of Sweet Meats or Sack Possets, they bring them a dish of Rams or of Bears stones to eat; For they think that after they have eaten of that meat, they become very prolific and fruitful, and for this reason they never use to kill any gelded creature for their use at their Nuptial Feasts.

Source: Louis de Gaya. *Matrimonial Customs, or, The Various Ceremonies and Divers Ways of Celebrating Weddings Practiced amongst All the Nations in the Whole World Done Out of French.* London: A.S., 1687, pp. 14–28.

6. Muslim Burial

In the following extract, the well-traveled seventeenth-century English ambassador Thomas Roe recounts the Muslim burial customs that he witnessed in his travels in the Middle East and India. Roe clearly recognized the connection between Islam and Judeo-Christianity, given that he repeatedly notes that certain Muslim customs, such as washing the body before burial, burying the dead outside of the city or town limits, and greatly mourning the deceased, parallel customs mentioned in the Bible or practiced by modern-day Jews. Other customs, such as visiting the graves of the saints, clearly parallel Catholic customs, although Roe merely implies this parallel and does not state it directly.

According to Roe, this great reverence for the dead inspired the most impressive architecture in the Muslim world. Beautiful monuments, complete with rich fabrics and ornate gardens, commemorated the Muslim saints and rulers. The richest monument, indeed, commemorated the Mogul Achabar-sha. This monument was constructed so cleverly that it looked like a pyramid made of unbroken marble.

Although Thomas Roe did not share the Islamic faith, he clearly had respect for many aspects of Muslim life. Note that what Roe calls "Misquits" and "Ramjan" are in modern English "mosques" and "Ramadan."

SECTION XVIII. Of their Burials, of the mourning for their Dead, and of their stately Sepulchres and Monuments.

For the Mahometans, it is their manner to wash the Bodies of their Dead before they interr them. An ancient custom as it should seem among the Jews; for it is said of Dorcas, that after she was dead, they washed her Body, as a preparative to her Burial. They lay up none of the Bodies of their Dead in their Misquits, or Churches, (as before) but in some open place in a Grave, which they dig very deep and wide, a Jewish custom, likewise to carry the Bodies of their Dead to bury them out of their Cities and Towns.

Their mourning over their Dead is most immoderate: for, besides that day of general lamentation at the end of their Ramjan, or Lent, (before-mentioned) they howl and cry many whole days for their friends departed, immediately after they have left the world; and after that time is passed over many foolish women, so long as they survive, very often in the year, observe set days to renew their mourning for their deceased friends; and as a people without hope, bedew the graves of their husbands, as of other near relations, with abundance of (seemingly) affectionate tears; as if they were like those mourning women mentioned in Jer. 9.17 who seemed to have tears at command; and therefore were hired to mourn and weep in their solemn lamentations.

And when they thus lament over their dead, they will often put this question to their deaf and dead Carkasses, "Why they would die?" They having such loving wives, such loving friends, and many other comforts: as if it had been in their power to have rescued themselves from that most impartial wounding hand of death. Which carriage of theirs deserves nothing but censure and pity; though, if it be not theatrical, we may much wonder at it, and say of it, as it was said of the mourning in the floor of Atad, Gen. 50.11, That it is a grievous mourning; or, as the mourning of Hadadrimmon in the valley of Megiddon, Zech. 12.11, if we take those lamentations only in a literal sense.

But now further concerning their places of Burial, many Mahometans of the greatest quality in their life-time provide fair Sepulchers for themselves and nearest friends, compassing with a firm wall a good circuit of ground near some Tank, (before spoken of) about which they delight to bury their dead; or else they close in a place for this use, near springs of water, that may make pleasant fountains, near which they erect little Mosquits, or Churches, and near them Tombs built round, or four-square, or in six, or eight squares, with round Vaults, or Canopies of stone over-head, all which are excellently well wrought, and erected upon Pillars, or else made close to be entered by doors every way, under which the bodies of their dead lye interred. The rest of that ground thus circled in, they plant with Fruit-trees; and further set therein all their choicest flowers, as if they would make Elysian fields (such as the Poets dreamed of) wherein their souls might take repose.

There are many goodly Monuments which are richly adorned, built (as before was observed) to the memory of such as they have esteemed Paeres, or Saints (of whom they have a large Calendar) in which are Lamps continually burning; attended by votaries, unto whom they allow Pensions for the maintaining of those lights, and many (transported there with wild devotion) daily resort to those Monuments, there to contemplate the happiness those Paeres (as they imagine) now enjoy. And certainly of all the places that Empire affords, there are none that minister more delight, than some of their Burying places do; neither do they bestow so much cost, nor shew so much skill in Architecture in any other Structures as in these.

Now amongst many very fair Piles there dedicated to the remembrance of their dead, the most famous one is at Secandra, a Village three miles from Agra; it was begun by Achabar-sha the late Mogols Father, who there lies buried; and finished by his Son, who since was laid up beside him. The materials of that most stately Sepulchre are Marble of divers colours, the stones so closely cemented together, that it appears to be but one continued stone, built high like a Pyramid with many curiosities about it, and a fair Mosquit by it; the Garden wherein it stands very large planted (as before) and compassed about with a wall of Marble: this most sumptuous Pile of all the Structures that vast Monarchy affords, is most admired by strangers. Tom Coryat had a most exact view thereof, and so have many other English-men had, all which have spoken very great things of it.

Source: Roe, Thomas. A Voyage to East India. In Pietro della Valle, The Travels of Sig. Pietro della Valle, a Noble Roman, into East-India and Arabia Deserta in Which, the Several Countries, Together with the Customs, Manners, Traffique, and Rites Both Religious and Civil, of Those Oriental Princes and Nations, Are Faithfully Described. London: J. Macock, 1665, pp. 431–33.

Women's Roles

Women make up over 50 percent of the population, yet in many societies they are often not seen in the public eye. Throughout history, in both the West and the East, women have tended to be associated with the home rather than with the world of politics and business. Indeed, when going out in public, women were frequently expected to act in a restrained and conservative manner, as Document 12 indicates. These general patterns, however, do not mean that all opportunities were denied to women in the Middle Ages and *Renaissance*—such a conclusion would be absurd during a period that witnessed the reign of Queen *Elizabeth I* of England (1558–1603), one of the most powerful monarchs ever. Even less privileged women could engage with the world of literature and philosophy, as did Margaret Cavendish (Document 9). Gaelic legend, moreover, preserved stories of warrior women whose prowess and courage in the field matched, or surpassed, their male counterparts (Document 7). Document 8, however, describes the insecure position of women in China in the sixth century.

Despite such examples of prominent women, and despite some authors who considered the possibility that women were superior to men (Document 13), most male thinkers viewed women as inferior to men, although the women nevertheless retained significant rights. The *Koran* (Document 10), for example, although it stated that men were superior, nevertheless guaranteed that women could own property in their own right and that that they were able to inherit money. *Anglo-Saxon* women, meanwhile, had different rights depending on their social class (Document 11); in some ways, lower-class women had more rights but less legal protection.

7. Scottish Warrior Women

In the following sixteenth-century account of ancient Scotland, the author seeks to portray a society of rugged, straightforward individuals. Although ruthless and uncivilized, they are honest and courageous. This picture of early medieval Scotland is mostly imaginative and untrue. Nonetheless, Celtic women did occasionally assume the role of warrior—for example, Queen Boudicca, in what would become southern England, led a revolt against the Romans that resulted in her death in A.D. 60. Medieval Irish legend also preserves the names and exploits of several warrior women said to have lived around A.D. 1: Queen Medb of Connaught and the warlords Aoife and Scáthach in Scotland. These images of warrior women probably reflect a strain of Celtic paganism in which a goddess controlled sovereignty and political power. These legends most likely lie behind the following description of women marching off to war with their husbands.

In these days also the women of our country were of no less courage than the men, for all stout maidens and wives (if they were not with child) marched as well in the field as did the men, and so soon as the army did set forward, they slew the first living creature that they found, in whose blood they not only bathed their swords, but also tasted thereof with their mouths, with no less religion and assurance conceived, than if they had already been sure of some notable and fortunate victory. When they saw their own blood run from them in the fight, they waxed never a whit astonished with the matter, but rather doubling their courages, with more eagerness they assailed their enemies. This also is to be noted of them, that they never sought any victory by treason, falsehood, or sleight, as thinking it a great reproach to win the field any otherwise than by meer manhood, prowess, and plain dealing.

When they went forth unto the wars, each one went with the king at his own cost (except the hired soldier) which custom is yet in use. If any were troubled with the falling evil, or leprosy, or falling frantic, or otherwise was out of his wits, they were diligently sought out, and lest those diseases should pass further by infectious generation unto their issue and posterity, they gelded the men. But the women were secluded to some odd place far off from the company of men, where if she afterward happened to be gotten with child, both she and the infant were run through with the lance. Gluttons and raveners, drunkards, and egregious devourers of victuals were punished also by death, first being permitted to devour so much as they listed, and then drowned in one fresh river or other.

Source: Boetius, Hector. *The Description of Scotland*. In *Chronicles of England, Scotland, and Ireland*, trans. Raphael Holinshed. Vol. 5. London: Johnson, 1808 (originally published 1580), pp. 22–26.

8. Rejected Wife in China

The following poem by Yuan-ti (508–554) expresses emotions of loss and sorrow that feel as real today as they did in the sixth century. The poem, moreover, demonstrates the insecure position of women in many societies, including China. The woman in the poem enters her home only to discover that she has been replaced by a new wife—she has been kicked out of her home in one instant, regardless of her own feelings.

The compassion seen in this poem is surprising, given the hard-nosed background of the author. Yuan-ti had climbed his way to the imperial throne through violent bloodshed. It is said that when eventually forced to abdicate, he heaped together and burned 200,000 books and pictures, proclaiming that the culture of the Liang dynasty would die with him. Such egomania contrasts strikingly with his careful handling of personal emotion in this poem.

Entering the hall, she meets the new wife:
Leaving the gate, she runs into her former husband.
Words stick: she does not manage to say anything:
She presses her hands together and hesitates.
Agitates moon-like fan—sheds pearl-like tears—
Realizes she loves him just as much as ever:
That her present pain will never come to an end.

Source: *A Hundred and Seventy Chinese Poems*. Translated by Arthur Waley. London: Constable, 1918, pp. 15, 90.

9. The Personality of Margaret Cavendish

An English aristocrat, Margaret Cavendish, Duchess of Newcastle (1623–1673), was one of the renowned women of her generation. She was a prolific writer and a serious thinker about the world and human nature. The royalist background of her family, the Lucases, and her marriage to a royalist cavalier meant that she spent much of her adult life in exile, while parliamentary forces controlled England after the execution of King Charles I in 1649. Her determination to express herself enabled her to produce 22 books, despite frequent criticism. Her science fiction novel The Blazing World *is still widely read today.*

In the following autobiographical extract, Margaret Cavendish attempts to describe her personality. Throughout the description, she reveals a woman full of self-confidence, yet restrained and affectionate. Thus, for example, she creates her own fashions, refusing to follow others' tastes and hating for others to follow her. At the same time, she rejoices in the success of others and avoids all envy. She also explicitly defends many of her characteristics, arguing, for example, that self-love is permissible because loving human beings in general is clearly correct. Margaret Cavendish brought a challenging breath of fresh air into an English literary scene that was largely dominated by males.

I think it fit I should speak something of my humour, particularly practice and disposition; as for my humour, I was from my childhood given to contemplation, being more taken or delighted with thoughts than in conversation with a society, insomuch as I would walk two or three hours, and never rest, in a musing, considering, contemplating manner, reasoning with myself of every thing my senses did present; but when I was in the company of my natural friends, I was very attentive of what they said or did; but for strangers I regarded not much what they said, but many times I did observe their actions, whereupon my reason as judge, and my thoughts as accusers, or excusers, or approvers and commenders, did plead, or appeal to accuse, or complain thereto; also I never took delight in closets, or cabinets of toys, but in the variety of fine clothes, and such toys as only were to adorn my person: likewise I had a natural stupidity towards the learning of any other language than my native tongue, for I could sooner and with more facility understand the sense than remember the words, and for want of such memory makes me so unlearned in foreign languages as I am: as for my practice, I was never very active, by reason I was given so much to contemplation; besides my brothers and sisters were for the most part serious, and staid in their actions, not given to sport not play, nor dance about, whose company I keeping, made me so too: but I observed, that although their actions were staid, yet they would be very merry amongst themselves, delighting in each others' company: also they would in their discourse express the general actions of the world, judging, condemning, approving, commending, as they thought good, and with those that were innocently harmless, they would make themselves merry therewith; as for my study of books it was little, yet I chose rather to read, than to employ my time in any other work, or practice, and when I read what I understood not, I would ask my brother, the Lord Lucas, he being learned, the sense or meaning thereof; but my serious study could not be much, by reason I took great delight in attiring, fine dressing, and fashions, especially such fashions as I did invent myself, not taking that pleasure in such fashions as was invented by others: also I did dislike any should follow my fashions,

Margaret Cavendish (1623?–1673), by Peter Ludwig van Schuppen, pub. 1668 (after Abraham van Diepenbeck, c.1655–58). Cavendish's confident and flamboyant pose in this portrait suits her controversial writings. Courtesy of the Library of Congress.

for I always took delight in a singularity, even in accoutrements of habits; but whatsoever I was addicted to, either in fashion of clothes, contemplation of thoughts, actions of life, they were lawful, honest, honourable, and modest, of which I can avouch to the world with a great confidence, because it is a pure truth.

As for my disposition, it is more inclining to be melancholy than merry, but not crabbed or peevishly melancholy, but soft, melting, solitary, and contemplating melancholy; and I am apt to weep rather than laugh, not that I do often either of them; also I am tender-natured, for it troubles my conscience to kill a fly, and the groans of a dying beast strike my soul: also where I place a particular affection, I love extraordinarily and constantly, yet not fondly, but soberly and observingly; not to hang about them as a trouble, but to wait upon them as a servant; but this affection will take no root, but where I think or find merit, and have leave both from Divine and Moral Laws; yet I find this passion so troublesome, as it is the only torment of my life, for fear any evil misfortune, or accident, or sickness, or death, should come unto them, insomuch as I am never freely at rest. Likewise I am grateful, for I never received a curtesy but I am impatient, and troubled until I can return it; also I am chaste, both by nature and education, insomuch as I do abhor an unchaste thought: likewise I am seldom angry, as my servants may witness for me, for I rather chose to suffer some inconveniences than disturb my thoughts, which makes me wink many times at their faults; but when I am angry, I am very angry, but yet it is soon over, and I am easily pacified, if it be not such an injury as may create a hate; neither am I apt to be exceptious or jealous; but if I have the least symptom of this passion, I declare it to those it concerns, for I never let it lie smothering in my breast to breed a malignant disease in the mind, which might break out into extravagant passions, or railing speeches, or indiscreet actions; but I examine moderately, reason soberly, and plead gently in my own behalf, through a desire to keep those affections I had, or at least thought to have; and truly I am so vain, as to be self-conceited, or so naturally partial, to think my friends have as much reason to love me as another, since none can love more sincerely than I, and it were an injustice to prefer a fainter affection, or to esteem the body more than the mind; likewise I am neither spiteful, envious, nor malicious; I repine not at the gifts that Nature, or Fortune bestows upon others, yet I am a great emulator; for though I wish none worse than they are, yet it is lawful for me to wish myself the best, and to do my honest endeavour thereunto; for I think it no crime to wish myself the exactest of Nature's works, my thread of life the longest, my chain of destiny the strongest, my mind the peaceablest, my life the pleasantest, my death the easiest, and the greatest Saint in heaven; also to do my endeavour, so far as honour and honesty doth allow of, to be the highest on Fortune's wheel, and to hold the wheel from turning, if I can, and if it be commendable to wish another's good, it were a sin not to wish my own; for as envy is a vice, so emulation is a virtue; but emulation is in the way of ambition, or indeed it is a noble ambition; but I fear my ambition inclines to vainglory, for I am very ambitious; yet 'tis neither for beauty, wit, titles, wealth, or power, but as they are steps to raise me to Fancy's Tower, which is to live by remembrance in after-ages: likewise I am, that the vulgar calls, proud, nor of a self-conceit, or to slight or condemn any, but scorning to do a base or mean act, and disdaining rude or unworthy persons; insomuch, that I should find any that were rude, or too bold, I should be apt to be so passionate, as to affront them, if I can, unless discretion should get betwixt my passion and their boldness, which sometimes perchance it might, if discretion should crowd hard for place; for though I am naturally bashful, yet in such a cause my spirits would be all on fire; otherwise I am so well bred, as to be civil to all persons, of all degrees or qualities: likewise I am so proud, or rather just to my lord, as to abate nothing of quality of his wife, for if honour be the mark of merit, and his master's royal favour, who will favour none but those that have merit to deserve, it were a baseness for me to neglect the ceremony thereof: also in some cases I am naturally a coward, and in other cases very valiant; so for example, if any of my nearest friends were in danger, I should never consider my life in striving to help them, though I were sure to do them no good, and would willingly, nay cheerfully, resign my life for their sakes: likewise I should not spare my life, if honour bids me die; but in a danger where my friends, or my honour is not concerned or engaged, but only my life to be unprofitably lost, I am the veriest coward in nature, as upon the sea, or any dangerous places or of thieves, or fire, or the like; nay the shooting of a gun, although but a pop-gun, will make me start, and stop my hearing, much less have I courage to discharge one; or if a sword should be held against me, although but in jest, I am afraid: also I am not covetous, so I am not prodigal, but of the two I am inclining to be prodigal, yet I cannot say to a vain prodigality, because I imagine it is to a profitable end; for perceiving the world is given, or apt to honour the outside more than the inside, worshipping show more than substance; and I am so vain, if it be a vanity, as to endeavour to be worshiped, rather than not to be regarded; yet I shall never be so prodigal as to impoverish my friends, or go beyond the limits or facility of our estate, and though I desire to appear to the best advantage, whilst I live in the view of the public worlds, yet I could most willingly exclude myself, so as never to see the face of any creature, but my lord, as long as I live, enclosing myself like an anchoret, wearing a frize gown, tied with a cord about my waste: but I hope my readers will not think me vain for writing my life, since there have been many that have done the like, as Caesar, Ovid, and many more, both men and women; and I know no reason I may not do it as well as they.

Source: Cavendish, Margaret, Duchess of Newcastle. A *True Relation of the Birth, Breeding, and Life of Margaret Cavendish Duchess of Newcastle*. Edited by Sir Egerton Brydges. Kent: Johnson and Warwick, 1814, pp. 29–35.

10. Muslim Women

According to the Western stereotype, Muslim women are oppressed. Images of fully veiled, entirely indistinct women frequently occupy our television screens. Although the Koran does explicitly state that men are superior to women, the rights of women are afforded some specific protection in the Koran, as the following extract demonstrates. In fact, Muslim women enjoyed certain privileges unheard of in most of Europe in the seventh century, most especially the right to inherit property. This right to inheritance demonstrates that women could, at least in theory, become significantly wealthy and therefore command the economic, political, and social power that comes with wealth. Although a man was entitled to inherit twice as much as a woman, females in most European countries of the time were much more thoroughly under the guidance and control of their families. The social position of Muslim women was further advanced by the Koran's commands to respect women, especially one's own mother.

Although the Koran thus respects women, it nonetheless reinforces the notions of gender inequality. This inequality carries over even into punishments. In the following extract, for example, the Koran commands that a prostitute be punished by being walled in without food until she dies of starvation. A man, however, if he repents, escapes punishment. As is to be expected, female slaves had the least rights of all. Thus, although the Koran forbade men to take married women, it explicitly excepted slaves from this protection—a Muslim man was allowed to force a female slave, even if she was already married to someone else. Muslim women lived under a double standard, but they also enjoyed theoretical rights and privileges that were unusual for the time.

SURA IV—WOMEN

In the Name of God, the Compassionate, the Merciful.

O men! fear your Lord, who hath created you of one man, and of him created his wife, and from these twain hath spread abroad so many men and women. And fear ye God, in whose name ye ask mutual favours—and reverence the wombs that bare you. Verily is God watching you!

And give to the orphans their property, and substitute not worthless things of your own for their valuable ones, and enjoy not their property in addition to your own; verily this is a great crime.

And if ye are apprehensive that ye shall not deal fairly with orphans, then, of other women who seem good in your eyes, marry but two, or three, or four; and if ye still fear that ye shall not act equitably, then one only; or the slaves whom ye have acquired: this will make justice on your part easier. And give women their dowry as a free gift; but if of their own free will they kindly give up aught thereof to you, then enjoy it as convenient, and profitable:

And entrust not to the incapable the substance which God hath placed with you as a means of support; but maintain them therewith, and clothe them, and speak to them with kindly speech.

And make trial of orphans until they reach the age of marriage; and if ye perceive in them a sound judgment, then hand over their substance to them; but consume ye it not profusely and hastily only because they have attained their majority. And let the rich guardian not even touch it; and let him who is poor then use it for his support with discretion.

And when ye make over their substance to them, then take witnesses in their presence: God also taketh a sufficient account.

Men ought to have a part of what their parents and kindred leave, and women a part of what their parents and kindred leave: whether it be little or much, let them have a stated portion:

And when they who are of kin are present at the division, and the orphans and the poor, bestow somewhat upon them therefrom; and speak to them with kindly speech:

And let those be afraid to wrong orphans, who, should they leave behind them weakly offspring, would be solicitous on their account. Let them then fear God, and let them propose what is convenient.

Verily they who swallow the substance of the orphan wrongfully, swallow down only fire into their bellies, and shall burn at the flame!

With regard to your children God commandeth you to give the male the portion of two females; and if they be females more than two, then they shall have two-thirds of that which their father hath left: but if she be an only daughter she shall have the half; and the father and mother of the deceased shall each of them have a sixth part of what he hath left, if he have a child; but if he have no child and his parents be his heirs, then his mother shall have the third: and if he have brethren, his mother shall have the sixth, after paying the bequests he shall have bequeathed, and his debts. As to your fathers, or your children, ye know not which of them is the most advantageous to you. This is the ordinance of God. Verily, God is Knowing, Wise!

Half of what your wives leave shall be yours, if they have no issue; but if they have issue, then a fourth of what they leave shall be yours, after paying the bequests they shall bequeath, and debts.

And your wives shall have a fourth part of what ye leave, if ye have no issue; but if ye have issue, then they shall have an eighth part of what ye leave, after paying the bequests ye shall bequeath and debts.

If a man or a woman make a distant relation their heir, and he or she have a brother or a sister, each of these two shall have a sixth; but if there are more than this, then shall they be sharers in a third, after payment of the bequests he shall have bequeathed, and debts, without loss to any one. This is the ordinance of God, and God is Knowing, Gracious!

These are the precepts of God; and whoso obeyeth God and his Prophet, him shall God bring into gardens beneath whose shades the rivers flow, therein to abide for ever: and this, the great blessedness!

And whoso shall rebel against God and his Apostle, and transgress his ordinances, him shall God cause to enter unto Hell-fire, to abide therein for ever; and this, a shameful torment!

If any of your women be guilty of whoredom, then bring four witnesses against them from among yourselves; and if they bear witness to the fact, shut them up within their houses till death release them, or God make some way for them.

And if two men among you commit the crime, then punish them both; but if they repent and amend, then let them be: Verily God is He who relenteth, Merciful!

Only is there relenting on the part of God to those, who have done evil ignorantly, and then turn speedily unto Him. These! God will turn unto them: and God is Knowing, Wise!

But no relenting shall there be on God's part towards those who do evil, until, when death is close to one of them, he sayeth, "Now verily am I turned to God;" nor to those who die unbelievers. These! We have made ready for them a grievous torment!

O believers! it is not allowed you to be heirs of your wives against their will; nor to hinder them from marrying in order to take from them part of the dowry you had given them, unless they have been guilty of undoubted lewdness; but deal kindly with them: for if ye are estranged from them, haply ye are estranged from that in which God hath placed abundant good.

And if ye be desirous to exchange one wife for another, and have given one of them a talent, make no deduction from it. Would ye take it by slandering her, and with manifest wrong?

How, moreover, could ye take it, when one of you hath gone in unto the other, and they have received from you a strict bond of union?

And marry not women whom your fathers have married: for this is a shame and harmful, and an evil way: though what is past may be allowed.

Forbidden to you are your mothers, and your daughters, and your sisters, and your aunts, both on the father and mother's sides, and your nieces on the brother and sister's side, and your foster-mothers, and your foster-sisters, and the mothers of your wives, and your step-daughters who are your wards, born of your wives to whom ye have gone in: (but if ye have not gone unto them, it shall be no sin in you to marry them); and the wives of your sons who proceed out of your loins; and ye may not have two sisters; except where it is already done. Verily, God is Indulgent, Merciful!

Forbidden to you also are married women, except those who are in your hands as slaves: This is the law of God for you. And he hath allowed you, beside this, to seek out wives by means of your wealth, with modest conduct, and without fornication. And give those with whom ye have cohabited their dowry. This is the law. But it shall be no crime in you to make agreements over and above the law. Verily, God is Knowing, Wise!

And whoever of you is not rich enough to marry free and believing women, then let him marry such of your believing maidens as have fallen into your hands as slaves; God well knoweth your faith. Ye are sprung the one from the other. Marry them then, with the leave of their masters, and give them a fair dower: but let them be chaste and free from fornication, and not entertainers of lovers.

If after marriage they commit adultery then inflict upon them half the penalty enacted for free married women. This law is for him among you who is afraid of doing wrong: but if ye abstain, it will be better for you. And God is Lenient, Merciful.

God desireth to make this known to you, and to guide you into the ways of those who have been before you, and He turneth to you with relenting. And God is Knowing, Wise!

And God desireth thus to turn Himself unto you: but they who follow their own lusts, desire that with great swerving should ye swerve from the right way! God desireth to make your burden light to you: for man hath been created weak.

O believers! devour not each other's substance in mutual frivolities; unless there be a trafficking among you by your own consent: and commit not suicide: Of a truth God is merciful to you—

And whoever shall do this maliciously and wrongfully,

We will in the end burn him at hell-fire; for this is easy with God.

If ye avoid the great sins which ye are forbidden, We will blot out your faults and cause you to enter Paradise with honourable entry.

And covet not the gifts by which God hath raised some of you above others. The men shall have a portion according to their deserts, and the women a portion according to their deserts. Of God, therefore, ask his gifts. Verily, God hath knowledge of all things.

To every one have We appointed kindred, as heirs of what parents and relatives, and those with whom ye have joined right hands in contract, leave. Give, therefore to each their portion. Verily, God witnesseth all things.

Men are superior to women on account of the qualities with which God hath gifted the one above the other, and on account of the outlay they make from their substance for them. Virtuous women are obedient, careful during the husband's absence, because God hath of them been careful. But chide those for whose refractoriness ye have cause to fear; remove them into sleeping-chambers apart, and scourge them: but if they are obedient to you, then seek no occasion against them: verily, God is High, Great!

And if ye fear a breach between man and wife, then send a judge chosen from his family and a judge chosen from her family; if they are desirous of agreement, God will effect a reconciliation between them; verily, God is knowing, apprised of all!

And Worship God, and join not aught with Him in worship. Be good to parents, and to kindred, and to orphans, and to the poor, and to a neighbour, a kinsman or near neighbour, and to a familiar friend and to the wayfarer, and to the slaves whom your right hands hold: verily, God loveth not the proud, the vain boaster,

Who are niggardly themselves, and bid others be niggards, and hide away what God of his bounty hath given them. We have made ready a shameful chastisement for the unbelievers.

Source: *El-Koran, or, The Koran.* 2nd ed. Translated by J. M. Rodwell. London: Bernard Quaritch, 1876, pp. 451–57 (verses 1–41).

11. Anglo-Saxon Women

In contrast to the Koranic guidelines given in Document 10 (see Koran in the glossary), early Anglo-Saxon law codes focused relatively little on the rights and privileges of women. In the Laws of Alfred (c. A.D. 890), codified under King Alfred the Great, women are viewed as acted upon, rather than as agents in their own rights. Moreover, the series of laws presented in the following extract stress the importance of female chastity in Anglo-Saxon culture. According to the laws, sleeping with a woman who is not your wife was a serious crime, and the perpetrator was fined a substantial sum. In most cases, however, the fine was paid to a man rather than to the woman herself. Thus, if a villain carried a nun off from a nunnery, he paid compensation to the bishop and to the lord of the church, but not to the woman herself. In fact, the kidnapped nun specifically did not receive any of the villain's assets, even if she bore his child. Similarly, the husband received the money if his wife was seduced.

Paradoxically, commoner women, as opposed to aristocratic women, had somewhat more rights under this system. Thus, a man who sexually harassed a commoner woman

paid the woman herself at least 5 shillings in penalty. The women thus received the money themselves, whereas for wealthier women, the money from the penalty was generally paid to a male. Nevertheless, the fine for abusing wealthier women was much higher, so they were more safely protected by the legal system regardless of whether or not they were entitled to monetary compensation.

8. If anyone takes a nun from a nunnery without the permission of the king or bishop, he shall pay 120 shillings, half to the king, and half to the bishop and the lord of the church, under whose charge the nun is.

    i. If she lives longer than he who abducted her, she shall inherit nothing of his property.

    ii. If she bears a child, it shall inherit no more of the property than its mother.

    iii. If her child is slain, the share of the wergeld due to the mother's kindred shall be paid to the king, but the father's kindred shall be paid the share due to them.

9. If anyone slays a woman with child, while the child is in her womb, he shall pay the full wergeld for the woman, and half the wergeld for the child, [which shall be] in accordance with the wergeld of the father's kindred.

    i. Until the value amounts to 30 shillings, the fine shall be 60 shillings in every case, when the [said] value amounts to this sum, the fine shall be 120 shillings.

    ii. Formerly the fines to be paid by those who stole gold and horses and bees, and many other fines, were greater than the rest. Now all fines, with the exception of that for stealing men, are alike—120 shillings.

10. If anyone lies with the wife of a man whose wergeld is 1200 shillings, he shall pay 120 shillings compensation to the husband; to a husband whose wergeld is 600 shillings, he shall pay 100 shillings compensation; to a commoner he shall pay 40 shillings compensation [for a similar offence].

11. If anyone seizes by the breast a young woman belonging to the commons, he shall pay her 5 shillings compensation.

    i. If he throws her down but does not lie with her, he shall pay 10 shillings compensation.

    ii. If he lies with her, he shall pay 60 shillings compensation.

    iii. If another man has previously lain with her, then the compensation shall be half this amount.

    iv. If she is accused of having previously lain with a man, she shall clear herself by an oath of 60 hides, or lose half the compensation due to her.

    v. If this outrage is done to a woman of higher birth, the compensation to be paid shall increase according to the wergeld.

18. If anyone lustfully seizes a nun, either by her clothes or by her breast, without her permission, he shall pay as compensation twice the sum we have fixed in the case of a woman belonging to the laity.

    i. If a young woman who is betrothed commits fornication, she shall pay compensation to the amount of 60 shillings to the surety of the marriage, if she is a commoner. This sum shall be paid in livestock, cattle being the property tendered, and no slave shall be given in such a payment.

    ii. If her wergeld is 600 shillings, she shall pay 100 shillings to the surety [of the marriage].

    iii. If her wergeld is 1200 shillings, she shall pay 120 shillings to the surety [of the marriage].

25. If anyone rapes the slave of a commoner, he shall pay 5 shillings to the commoner, and a fine of 60 shillings.

    i. If a slave rapes a slave, castration shall be required as compensation.

Source: Attenborough, F. L., ed. and trans. *The Laws of the Earliest English Kings.* Cambridge: Cambridge University Press, 1922, pp. 69–75. With slight modifications.

12. Proper Behavior in Company

The emphasis on female chastity seen in the Anglo-Saxon laws carried on throughout the Middle Ages and the Renaissance, as seen in the following extract from Richard Brathwaite's The English Gentlewoman *(1631). Brathwaite, however, was concerned not only with sexual mores but with a woman's whole behavior.*

Central to Brathwaite's idea of female nobility is a desire for company—women by all means should be out in public and should spend time with their friends. However, what they should do in public is severely curtailed; as he states in an aphorism that has since been transferred to children, women "should be seen, and not heard." A proper woman, in Brathwaite's opinion, should wear her veil constantly in public, should not speak frequently or lightly, and definitely should not exchange any trinkets as signs of affection or love with a man. This restricted code of behavior, however, is correlated with higher status throughout Brathwaite's rhetoric. "Modesty and mildness," for example, are associated with a noblewoman, whereas "simpering-made faces" are indicative of a "Chambermaid." Likewise, suppressing amorous desire will result in making the women "Empresses of that which hath sometimes tyrannized over Emperors." Ultimately, proper behavior is a guarantor of status, wealth, and power. A woman's path to power thus paradoxically requires her careful restraint in public. Brathwaite clearly thought that women desired status and power because he uses these as his motivating forces, instead of religion or abstract morality. Goodness is not its own reward; it brings with it social class and high rank.

We are now to descend to the next branch, which shall show how a *Gentlewoman* of rank and quality (for to such only is my discourse directed) is to *behave herself in Company.*

Society is the solace of the living, for to live without it, were a kind of dying. Companions and friendly Associates are the *Thieves* of time. No hour can be so tedious, which two loving Consorts cannot pass over with delight, and spend without distaste. Be the night never so dark, the place never so mean, the cheerful beams of conceiving consorts will enlighten the one, and their affections mutually planted, enliven the other. What a Desert then were the world without friends? And how poseless those friends without conceiving minds? And how weak those minds, unless united in equal bonds? So then, love is the Cement of our life: life a load without love. Now, *Gentlewomen*, you are to put on your veils, and go into *Company*. Which (I am persuaded) you cannot enter without a maiden-blush, a modest tincture. Herein you are to be most cautious, seeing no place can be more mortally dangerous. Beware therefore with whom you consort, as you tender your repute: for report will brute what you are, by the Company which you bear. *Augustus* being at a combat, discerned the inclinations of his two daughters, *Iulia* and *Livia*, by the Company which frequented them; for grave Senators talked with *Livia*, but riotous persons with *Iulia*. Would you preserve those precious odors of your good names? Consort with such whose names were never branded, converse with such, whose tongues for immodesty were never taxed. As by good words evil manners are corrected, so by evil words are good ones corrupted. Make no reside there, where the least occasion of lightness is ministered; avert your Ear when you hear it, but your heart especially, lest you harbour it. To enter into much discourse or familiarity with strangers, argues lightness or indiscretion: what is spoken of Maids, may be properly applied by an useful consequence to all women: *They should be seen, and not heard.* A Traveler sets himself best out by discourse, whereas their best setting out is silence. You shall have many trifling questions asked, as much to purpose as if they said nothing, but a frivolous question deserves to be resolved by silence. For your *Carriage*, it should neither be too precise, nor too loose. These simpering-made faces partake more of *Chambermaid* than *Gentlewoman*. Modesty and mildness hold sweetest correspondence. You may possibly be wooed to interchange favours: Rings or Ribbons are but trifles; yet trust me, they are no trifles that are aimed at in those exchanges. Let nothing pass from you, that may any way impeach you, or give others advantage over you. Your innocent credulity (I am resolved) is as free from conceit of ill, as theirs, perhaps, from intendment of good: but these intercourses of Courtesies are not to be admitted, lest by this familiarity, an Entry to affection be opened, which before was closed. It is dangerous to enter parley with a beleaguering enemy: it implies want or weakness in the besieged. Chastity is an *enclosed Garden*, it should not be so much as assaulted, lest the report of her spotless beauty become soiled. Such Forts hold out best, which hold themselves least secure, when they are securest. *Nasica*, when the *Roman* Commonwealth was supposed to be in most secure estate, because freed of their enemies, and strongly fenced by their friends, affirmed that though the *Achaians* and *Carthaginians* were both brought under the yoke of bondage, yet they were most in danger, because none were left, whom they might either fear for danger, or who should keep them in awe.

How subject poor *Women* be to lapses, and recidivations, being left their own Guardians, daily experience can sufficiently discover. Of which number, those always proved weakest, who were confidentest of their own strength. Presumption is a daring sin, and ever brings out some untimely birth, which viper-like deprives her unhappy parent of life. I have known diverse so resolute in their undertakings, so presuming of their womanish strength, so constantly devoted to a single life, as in public consorts they held it their choicest merriment to give love the affront, to discourse of affection with an imperious contempt, gear their amorous suitors out of Countenance, and make a very *Whirligig* of love. But mark the conclusion of these insulting spirits: they sport so long with love, till they fall to love in earnest. A moment makes them of Sovereigns' Captives, by slaving them to that deservedly, which at first they entertained so disdainfully. The way then to prevent this malady, is to wean you from consorting with folly. What an excellent impregnable fortress were *Woman*, did not her *Windows* betray her to her enemy? But principally, when she leaves her Chamber to walk on the public Theatre; when she throws off her veil, and gives attention to a merry tale; when she consorts with youthful blood, and either enters parley, or admits of an interview with love. It is most true what the sententious moral sometimes observed: We may be in *security*, so long as we are sequestered from *society*. Then, and never till then, begins the *infection* to be dispersed, when the sound and sick begin to be promiscuously mixed. Tempt not Chastity; hazard not your Christian liberty. You shall encounter with many forward youths, who will most punctually tender their uselesse service to your shadows at the very first sight: do not admit them, lest you prostitute your selves to their prostrate service. *Apelles* found fault with *Protogenes*, in that he could not hold his hands from his Table. Whereas our *Damsels* may more justly find fault with their youthful *Amorists*, for that they cannot hold their hands from under the Table. It is impossible to come off fair with these light-fingered fools. Your only way is to rampire your chaste intentions with Divine and Moral instructions, to stop the source, divert the occasion, subject *affection* to *reason*; so may you become Emperesses of that which hath sometimes tyrannized over Emperors: By this means shall every place where you *publicly* resort, minister to you some object of inward comfort: By this means shall *Company* furnish you with precepts of chastity, enable you in the serious practice of piety, and sweetly conduct you to the port of glory.

Source: Brathwaite, Richard. *The English Gentlewoman, Drawn Out to the Full Body: Expressing What Habiliments Doe Best Attire Her, What Ornaments Doe Best Adorne Her, What Complements Doe Best Accomplish Her.* London: B. Alsop and T. Fawcet, 1631, pp. 40–44.

13. A Man and a Woman Argue over Gender Superiority

Although women generally had fewer social and political roles available to them throughout the Middle Ages and Renaissance, their superiority to men was sometimes debated. Christine de Pisan (1364–c. 1430), for example, defended women by pointing out the many capable women in history and legend and how those women were often betrayed by men. The following fifteenth-century debate follows a similar line of argument. A man and woman debate whether men or women are best. The woman puts forth positive examples, most especially Mary the mother of Christ, whereas the man advances examples of evildoing women, such as Eve. Interestingly, the man does not adduce positive male examples, so perhaps the woman wins the contest?

The author himself, Guillaume Alexis, left the winner of the debate unclear—when he approaches the debating couple, they flee. The reader, as a result, must draw his or her own conclusion. Regardless of these theoretical debates, exceptional women did often control not only their own destinies but also entire countries. The most striking example, of course, is Queen Elizabeth I (1533–1603) of England, who remains one of Britain's most powerful monarchs of all time.

As after ye shall hear, a strife began
which long did endure, with great argument
betwixt the woman and also the man,
which of them could prove to be most excellent.

The Man. The first which I heard was the man, that said:
"Adam our forefather, by woman's shrewd counsel
to eat of an apple, was piteously betrayed.
Well happy is he that with you doth not mell."

The Woman. Jesu of a maiden and virgin, his mother,
was incarnated to redeem that man had lost;
set thou this one now against the other
and woman is more excellent in every cost.

The Man. No women into angels never was transformed,
but women into devils full oft hath been figurate;
for they pride in hell cruelly to be burned.
Unhappy is he that hath one to his make.

The Woman. Many angels to women have been transported
more than to men, for their chastity.
First, our dear lady the angel exorted,
saying the son of God in her conceived should be.

The Man. Joseph by woman was put in prison
and nigh was slain by treason cruel;
David an adulterer with woman was become.
Well happy is he that with them doth not mell.

The Woman. Mankind to deliver out of this worldly pain
and bring him to the joy of the celestial place
god in his mother took nature human.
Who dispraiseth women, God send him no grace.

The Man. For woman was slain the worthy prince Amon;
the love of them causeth much displeasure.
By women was deceived the sage Salomon,
which by the mean of them false idols did adore.

The Woman. That woman is most replete with grace
by good reason, I shall prove plain,
for God in woman first took his place
when into this world he came certain.

The Man. Virgil, the sage clerk of great intelligence,
betrayed was by woman, as written ye may find,
trusting in her grace, in every man's presence
was tied at a window til men did him unbind.

The Woman. God to us by woman paradise hath restored
that before was lost by our great negligence
and above all saints highly hath honored
Mary his mother, woman of most excellence.

The Man. Towns have been destroyed, and cities many one,
diverse men for women be damned deep in hell.
More joyful unto man than woman hath been none.
Well happy is he that with them doth not mell.

The Woman. By the mean of Hester, the judgment was respited
of Assuerus her husband, for the Jews all
which should have died had not he delited
in her high beauty and words petitional.

The Man. Priam, Paris, and Deiphebus,
first by the occasion of women was slain.
Also Troilus, Hector, and Helenus,
and all Troy hath been confounded plain.

The Woman. Judith, 900 men and mo'
made for to fly and yield in confusion
after that Holefernus' head she had cut in two,
which would have destroyed all the region.

The Man. Women their face and forehead doth paint
for to deceive both young and old.
The strong Sampson Dalyda (*sic*) did attaint,
And him betrayed his head when she had poled.

The Woman. Woman is honored in every place
for queen of earth and of heaven high,
which is petitioner for man's trespass
to good on their souls to have mercy.

The Man. Some women can flatter and most can lie
to obtain man's love, they can feign well.
They will never leave it until they die.
Well happy is he that with them doth not mell.

The Woman. Woman is called treasure of grace;
in heaven our lady it is full sure,
for she for man's soul doth so purchase
that thousands she saved by her prayer.

The Man. Some that hath been taken for very sage
by woman's love did so him endeavor
that for it he sold all his heritage
and after hath he died a miserable beggar.

The Woman. Many hath offices and good wages
by women to live right prosperately
benefices and advantages
to maintain men accordingly.

The Man. When a young pigeon a woman hath gotten
she will make him at length as strong as a crane,
for surely she will never forsake him
til that his cropper bone wax very lame.

The Woman. Then look a cawdell you do gyt,
and soon ye look you a better norce,
For I heard say, God gave man wit
to know the better from the worse.

The Man. Women will speak and contrary say,
They will not shame a lie to tell,
To scold and brawl is all their play.
Well happy is he that with them doth not mell.

The Woman. The coming of our lord Jesu,
Many devout woman did prophecye
Sibylls they were that it best knew
For to dispraise women ye do now unwisely.

The Man. One must them give that they desire
To beat or correct them they waxen worse.
They never will stint for to require
As long as a penny is in one's purse.

The Woman. When all the apostles from our lord flied
Women til his death still did him ensue
Never woman our lord denied
As Peter did by ever was true.

The Man. When ye of any man know the intention
Which could be secret ye publish it by and by
Unto your gossips, ye make thereof mention
As soon as ye together beeth, chatting like a pye.

The Woman. Christ after his death for our consolation
First showed unto woman personally
To Mary Magdaleyn after his resurrection
Which for his death bewailed grievously.

The Man. A wife of her husband will have the audience
As chief masters, her tale to tell;
She will cry and weep, except she have the pre-eminence
Well happy is he that with them doth not mell.

The Woman. That a man should a woman for his wife believe
By Abraham is signified plain
For god unto Sara first knowledge did give
That a child should be procreate betwixt the twain.

Source: Alexis, Guillaume. *Here Begynneth an Interlocucyon, with an Argument, betwixt Man and Woman and Which of Them Could Prove to Be Most Excellent.* London: Wynkyn de Worde, 1525, pp. 2–6 (no page numbers in text).

Children

Like those of women (see the previous section), the roles of children are often obscured in the public sector: small children do not run governments, do not usually write high literature, and do not build bridges on their own. That said, children in some ways were much more involved in public life than their modern Western counterparts. Whereas 12-year-old children in the United States and Europe spend their days in classrooms, their medieval and *Renaissance* counterparts were generally already earning a living as assistants or apprentices or even as fully qualified craftsmen. The following documents examine some of the features of children's life that are not covered in other sections of this volume, such as education or games and sports.

The link of affection between parents and children is particularly clear in many documents of the period. This affection, however, did not always take the same forms as it does in the modern day. Document 17, for example, outlines the signs of affection that children showed to their parents; these signs included standing when the parents entered the room, staying quiet when the parents were speaking, and uncovering their heads whenever the parents were present. Although such rituals seem formal by current standards, they were conventional means of demonstrating respect and affection during the Middle Ages and Renaissance. The love that parents showed their children resonates throughout the poems about Golden Bells (Document 14), by the influential Chinese poet Po Chu-i. Although the poet strives to show how children interfere with a busy life and weighty philosophy, the severe sorrow he experiences upon the girl's early demise echoes throughout the poems.

No one can choose his or her own parents. Our upbringing depends entirely on factors outside of our own control. Two radically different upbringings occur in two of the documents featured in this section. Englishwoman Margaret Cavendish (Document 15) was born into a life of aristocratic luxury, until the changing political climate forced her into exile in France. She describes her childhood as paradisiacal—although her father died young, her mother ensured that her children received a sound education, absorbed a strong moral code, and never went without the luxuries of life. Zál, in the legendary *Sháh Námeh* (Document 16), suffered through a dramatically different childhood. Ostracized by the people because of his unusual white hair, the child was left to die on a mountainside before being rescued by the gods. Although unrealistic, the story of Zál nevertheless discusses the damaging effects of peer pressure and the evil of complying with such unreasonable demands. Finally, the theme of premature death, in the cases of Golden Bells and Zál, reminds us that childhood was a dangerous time before the advent of vaccinations, improved nutrition, and modern antibiotics. Most parents expected to lose at least one of their children. The pain of loss, however, was no less.

14. The Early Death of Golden Bells

Children are associated with both joy and exasperation in societies around the world. In these two touching poems by Po Chu-i (772–846), the great Tang dynasty poet, the author explores his feelings about the birth of a new daughter when the author was approaching 40 years old. Although the poet claims to wish he had "a sage's heart" and was therefore able to contemplate great philosophical matters, he finds instead that he is pulled into a simple love for the girl, even though the only real reward he will obtain from the relationship is the pleasure he is getting now from her company.

Tragically, the girl dies before she is three years old, bringing the poet great sorrow. He speaks of himself in the opening line as "ruined and ill." The sorrowing poet, however, uses this sorrow as a moment of meditative contemplation: he reflects that personal relationships inevitably lead to grief and sorrow. As a result, avoiding them is best. Despite such stoical statements, the lament for the deceased daughter makes clear the poet's continuing emotional attachment. Boys are preferred to girls generally in Chinese culture, as the second poem itself makes clear, yet girls were still clearly capable of capturing their parents' love.

Golden Bells

When I was almost forty
I had a daughter whose name was Golden Bells.

Now it is just a year since she was born;
She is learning to sit and cannot yet talk.
Ashamed, to find that I have not a sage's heart,
I cannot resist commonplace thoughts and feelings.
Henceforward I am tied to things outside myself.
My only reward, the pleasure I am getting now.
If I am spared the grief of her dying young,
Then I shall have the trouble of getting her married.
My plan for retiring and going back to the hills must now be postponed for fifteen years!

Remembering Golden Bells

Ruined and ill, a man of two score;
Pretty and guileless, a girl of three.
Not a boy, but still better than nothing:
To soothe one's feeling, from time to time a kiss!
There came a day, they suddenly took her from me;
Her soul's shadow wandered I know not where.
And when I remember how just at the time she died
She lisped strange sounds, beginning to learn to talk,
Then I know that the ties of flesh and blood
Only bind us to a load of grief and sorrow.
At last, by thinking of the time before she was born,
By thought and reason I drove the pain away.
Since my heart forgot her, many days have passed
And three times winter has changed to spring.
This morning, for a little, the old grief came back,
Because, in the road, I met her foster-nurse.

Source: *A Hundred and Seventy Chinese Poems.* Translated by Arthur Waley. London: Constable, 1920, pp. 119–20.

15. A Noblewoman's Childhood

Margaret Cavendish, Duchess of Newcastle (1623–1673), was one of the leading women authors of her time, although her political commitment to the monarchy during the English civil war of the seventeenth century caused her serious trouble throughout her life, including exile and a critical lack of financial resources. In the following extract from her autobiography, Margaret Cavendish relates her aristocratic upbringing as a member of the influential Lucas family. According to Cavendish, the children were trained to seek out a happy medium between pleasure and work. Nonetheless, she points out that their mother, though left a widow and thus subject to financial uncertainty, never spared any money on their education or dress because her mother believed that the child's early years were formative and thus very important. Her mother's educational philosophy can be seen also in her rejection of corporal punishment—rational discussion rather than beating was used to show the children the benefits of righteousness and the wrongs of evil-doing.

The following extract also demonstrates that the Lucas family was very conscious of social class. Although Cavendish notes that even nobles might sometimes be forced to become servants out of pecuniary need, she concurs with the wisdom of her mother's policy that the servants should not be in charge of the children. Rather, the servants were ordered to show the same respect to the children as they did to the mother. Moreover, male servants were not allowed to talk with female servants in the presence of the children for fear that the male servants would behave indiscreetly while attempting to attract the females. In effect, the Lucases believed that the lower classes had lower moral standards than aristocrats; the children, therefore, needed to be protected from them.

As for my breeding, it was according to my birth, and the nature of my sex; for my birth was not lost in my breeding; for as my sisters was, or had been bred, so was I in plenty, or rather with superfluity; likewise we were bred virtuously, modestly, civilly, honourably, and on honest principles: as for plenty, we had not only for necessity, conveniency, and decency, but for delight and pleasure to superfluity; 'tis true we did not riot, but we lived orderly; for riot, even in kings' courts and princes' palaces, brings ruin without content or pleasure, when order in less fortunes shall live more plentifully and deliciously than princes, that live in a hurly-burly, as I may term it, in which they are seldom well served, for disorder obstructs; besides, it doth disgust life, distract the appetites, and yield no true relish to the senses; for pleasure, delight, peace and felicity, live in method and temperance.

As for our garments, my mother did not only delight to see us neat and cleanly, fine and gay, but rich and costly; maintaining us to the height of her estate, but not beyond it; for we were so far from being in debt, before these wars, as we were rather before-hand with the world; buying all with ready money, not on the score; for although after my father's death the estate was divided between my mother and her sons, paying such a sum of money for portions to her daughters, either at the day of their marriage, or when they should come of age; yet by reason she and her children agreed with a mutual consent, all their affairs were managed so well, as she lived not in a much lower condition than when my father lived; 'tis true, my mother might have increased her daughters portions by thrifty sparing, yet she chose to bestow it on our breeding, honest pleasures, harmless delights, out of an opinion, that if she bred us with needy necessity, it might chance to create in us sharking qualities, mean thoughts, and base actions, which she knew my father, as well as herself, did abhor: likewise we were bred tenderly, for my mother naturally did strive to please and delight her children, not to cross and torment them, terrifying them with threats, or lashing them with slavish whips; but instead of threats, reason was used to persuade us, and instead of lashes, the deformities of vice was discovered, and the Graces and Virtues were presented unto us; also we were bred with respectful attendance, every one being severally waited upon; and all her servants in general used the same respect to her children, (even those that were young) as they did to herself; for she suffered not her servants either to be rude before us, or to domineer over us, which all vulgar servants are apt, and ofttimes which some have leave to do; likewise she never suffered the vulgar serving-men to be in the nursery among the nurse-maids, lest their rude love-making might do unseemly actions, or speak unhandsome words in the presence of her children, knowing that youth is apt to take infection by ill examples, having not the reason of distinguishing good from bad; neither were we suffered to have

Pieter de Hooch, Woman with a Child in a Pantry, c. 1660. The mother has tucked up her outer skirt in order to keep it from getting dirty while she goes about her housework. © 2008 Jupiterimages Corporation.

any familiarity with the vulgar servants, or conversation: yet caused us to demean ourselves with an humble civility towards them, as they with a dutiful respect to us; not because they were servants were we so reserved; for many noble persons are forced to serve through necessity; but by reason the vulgar sort of servants are as ill bred as meanly born, giving children ill examples and worse counsel.

As for tutors, although we had for all sorts of virtues, as singing, dancing, playing on music, reading, writing, working, and the like, yet we were not kept strictly thereto; they were rather for formality than benefit; for my mother cared not so much for our dancing and fiddling, singing and prating of several languages, as that we should be bred virtuously, modestly, civilly, honourably, and on honest principles.

Source: Cavendish, Margaret, Duchess of Newcastle. *A True Relation of the Birth, Breeding, and Life of Margaret Cavendish, Duchess of Newcastle.* Edited by Sir Egerton Brydges. Kent: Johnson and Warwick, 1814, pp. 3–6.

16. An Albino Child Abandoned

The national epic of Persian speakers is the Sháh Námeh (Book of Kings) by the eleventh-century poet Firdawsi. Although the Sháh Námeh records mostly legendary history, it nevertheless discusses important social and cultural issues. The following extract, for example, examines the societal mistreatment of those whose physical appearance differs from the norm. When Sám's son turns out to have white hair as an infant, the people suggest that the boy, named Zál, must be a demon and that his father himself was probably also a demon. To stop these rumors, which are undermining Sám's position as leader, the father leaves his son on a mountain, expecting the child to be killed and eaten by a griffin. Rumors and people's prejudice are leading to the death of a child.

The deities, however, have other plans for the child. The griffin actually saves the child and carries the child to his home on the top of the mountain, where he hears a divine voice commanding him to take good care of the child because the child will have an heir of everlasting fame. Although the people sought to destroy the child, the gods worked to save him. Prejudice about physical appearance is thus contrary to the will of the gods.

ZÁL, THE SON OF SÁM

According to the traditional histories from which Firdusi has derived his legends, the warrior Sám had a son born to him whose hair was perfectly white. On his birth the nurse went to Sám and told him that God had blessed him with a wonderful child, without a single blemish, excepting that his hair was white; but when Sám saw him he was grieved:

> His hair was white as goose's wing,
> His cheek was like the rose of spring
> His form was straight as cypress tree—
> But when the sire was brought to see
> That child with hair so silvery white,
> His heart revolted at the sight.

His mother gave him the name of Zál and the people said to Sám, "This is an ominous event, and will be to thee productive of nothing but calamity; it would be better if thou couldst remove him out of sight.

> No human being of this earth
> Could give to such a monster birth;
> He must be of the Demon race,
> Though human still in form and face.
> If not a Demon, he, at least,
> Appears a party-coloured beast."

When Sám was made acquainted with these reproaches and sneers of the people, he determined, though with a sorrowful heart, to take him up to the mountain Alberz, and abandon him there to be destroyed by beasts of prey. Alberz was the abode of the Símurgh or Griffin, and, whilst flying about in quest of food for his hungry young ones, that surprising animal discovered the child lying alone upon the hard rock, crying and sucking its fingers. The Símurgh, however, felt no inclination to devour him, but compassionately took him up in the air, and conveyed him to his own habitation.

> He who is blest with Heaven's grace
> Will never want a dwelling-place
> And he who bears the curse of Fate
> Can never change his wretched state.
> A voice, not earthly, thus addressed
> The Símurgh in his mountain nest—
> "To thee this mortal I resign,
> Protected by the power divine;
> Let him thy fostering kindness share,
> Nourish him with paternal care;
> For from his loins, in time, will spring
> The champion of the world, and bring
> Honour on earth, and to thy name;
> The heir of everlasting fame."

The young ones were also kind and affectionate to the infant, which was thus nourished and protected by the Símurgh for several years.

Source: Firdawsi. *Sháh Námeh*. In *Persian Literature, Comprising the Sháh Námeh, the Rubáiyát, the Divan and the Gulistan*, trans. James Atkinson. Rev. ed., vol. 1. World's Great Classics series. New York: Colonial, 1900, pp. 50–51.

17. Honoring Parents

In Christianity, the Fourth Commandment commands children to honor their parents. The following document explains how one seventeenth-century commentator understood that command. The author, W.C., uses references to the Bible to describe not only how children should behave toward their parents but also what emotions the children should have concerning their parents. For example, the author states, "Children are to be delighted greatly in their Parents presence," although it is unclear how exactly a child who did not have fun with his or her parents should cultivate this emotion.

Although emotions are difficult to control, behavior is perhaps more straightforward. W.C. gives a long list of ways in which children should outwardly show respect for their parents: the children must stand when their parents enter the room, they must uncover their heads as a sign of respect in the presence of their parents, they must bow to their parents when they come to them, they must be completely silent when their parents are speaking, and they must call their parents by respectful titles, such as "Lord." These rituals give a general impression of a very formal relationship between parents and children. This formality can imply to modern readers that the parent–child relationship was not loving, but this assumption is certainly not true. In fact, these formal rituals were ways of demonstrating affection and love, rather than methods of maintaining distance.

Question. How should children honor their Parents with inward honor?
Answer. Children should honor their Parents with inward honor these three ways:

1. First, highly respecting and prizing of them, to have a good opinion, and reverent esteem of them, in regard to that authority that God hath stamped upon them over their children. The contrary to this is a sin,

   1. Forbidden, Prov. 23, 22
   2. Taxed, Ezek. 22:7, Him. 7:6
   3. Cursed, Deut. 27:16.

2. Secondly cordially loving them. What is required of Christians towards their pastor, 1 Thes. 5:12–13. The same should be performed by children to their Parents, there being an analogy and proportion between spiritual and natural Parents; for as spiritual Parents are over them in the Lord, labor among them, and admonish them, and their children should esteem them very highly in love. This love in children to Parents is thus to be expressed:

   1. Children are to be delighted greatly in their Parents presence, to be much affected with the very sight of a Father or Mother, Gen. 45:10, 46:29–31.
   2. Children are to be backward, and loath to part with their Parents, Ruth 1:14–17, 1 Kings 19:20, Deut. 21:13.
   3. Children should express their love by being affected with Parents favors or frowns, Prov. 4:3, Gen. 37:30, 2 Sam. 14:32, Numb. 12:14.
   4. They are to prize very much Parents good counsels, and instructions, yea, their very rebukes, and carefully remembering and recording their most useful sayings, Prov. 4:5–7, 8:21, 3:1, 2:1, 6:21, 7:1–3.
   5. They are cordially to sympathize with their Parents, in their joys or sorrows, Gen. 44:34, 37:35.

6. Yea, this love to their Parents should be expressed by prizing and cleaving to their good Parents special friends, Prov. 27:10. But especially they are to cleave to brethren and sisters of the same Parents, 1 Pet. 3:8, 1 John 5:1, Acts 7:26. . . .

3. By standing in awe of them, by an aweful, reverent, or filial fear of them, Levit. 19:3. This inward filial fear and reverence in children towards their Parents taketh in these particulars:

   1. They are inwardly to awe the very persons, relation, and authority of their Parents, Lev. 19:3.
   2. They are inwardly to awe the commands, reproofs, threats, and corrections of Parents, Jer. 35:6.
   3. They are to fear to lose Parents favour, or to incur their just displeasure, by giving them any just offence, Gen. 27:12.
   4. They are to fear to cross any weighty intents, purposes, or desires of Parents, Judg. 11:36.
   5. They are to fear that trouble, or heart-grief should be occasioned to Parents, if they can prevent it, 1 Sam. 9:5, Gen. 44:34.
   6. They are to fear to fall short of their blessing and benefit of Parents' prayers, and of their godly counsels. This was in good Joseph, Gen. 48:1ff., and profane Esau, Gen. 27:34.

Question. How should children honor their Parents with outward honour?
Answer. Children should honour their Parents outwardly fourteen several ways:

1. First, by an humble and reverent deportment and carriage of the body, either in gesture, speech or action, which may be expressed in these following particulars:

   1. To rise up when our Parents come into our presence, 1 King. 2:19, Levit. 19:32, Judg. 1:14–15, Gen. 31:35.
   2. To uncover the head in token of our reverencing them, Lev. 19:32.
   3. To bow unto them, and do reverence, when they come into their Parents presence, Gen. 41:43, and 48:12, Exod. 18:7, 2 Sam. 14:33, 1 King. 2:19.
   4. To stand before their Parents when any business is imparting by the one to the other, Judg. 1:14–15, Exod. 18:13, 2 King. 5:25.
   5. To be silent whilst our Parents are speaking in our presence, and give ear unto them, Gen. 49:1–2, Job 29:9–10.
   6. When we are by necessary occasions to speak, to use words of submission, and speak reverently, both to, and of our Parents: as Sarah called her husband "Lord," 1 Pet. 3:6, and Rachel said to Laban her father, "Let it not displease my Lord, that I cannot rise up before thee," Gen 31:35, and as Prov. 31:28.
   7. They are to attend reverently to their counsels or instructions, Pro. 4.1.20.
   8. They must meekly and humbly subject themselves to their seasonable corrections, Heb. 12:9, Prov. 13:24, 19:18, 22:15, 23:13–4, 29:15–17, Deut. 21:18–22.
   9. They are to make humble confession to Parents, and to express filial shame and blushing upon occasion of faults and sins against them, especially when Parents deal with children for the same, Heb. 12:9, Luk. 15:21.

2. Secondly, this outward honor that children are to give unto their Parents, may be expressed by covering their failings to prevent dishonor and shame, which otherwise might befall them, Gen. 9:21–2, 23 Prov. 10–12, 1 Pet. 4:8.
3. Thirdly, another duty of outward honor is comprehended under the name of service, or waiting upon; it comprehends all such duties as are used by servants to their Masters, Luk. 15:19–29, 17:8, Phil. 2:22, Mal. 3:17, Gen. 37:12–14, 42:1–3, Ruth 2:2ff. Math. 21:28–30.
4. Fourthly, children should honor their Parents by acquainting them with their secrets of weight, Jud. 14:16, Numb. 10:29–33. Craving their advice, approbation, and leave, in their particular undertakings, Exod. 12:26, 13:14, Josh. 4:6, Exod. 18:8–27, Gen. 34:4, 2 Sam. 13:26, 15:7, Ruth 1:16, 2:2. And their prayer to God for direction therein, and a blessing upon themselves and their concernments, Gen. 27:19–38, 48, 9:13–21.
5. Fifthly, children should honor their Parents by obedience and subjection, Eph. 6:1:

    1. To wholesome counsels and lawful commands.
    2. To reproofs and fitting correction.

First, children being under tuition must be obedient to their Parents' counsels and commands, and be contented therein to be crossed in their own will, Gen. 22:6–10, 37:14, 42:1–3, 48:17–19.

1. In matters of Religion and the fear of the Lord, Gen. 18:19, Deut. 4:9, Josh. 24:15, 1 King. 2:2–3, 1 Chron. 22:11, 2 tim. 3:14–15, compared with 1:5.
2. In civil matters; and that under these two considerations:

1. Considered in their childhood, and so they are to be subject to their Parents for their diet, their apparel, their work, even in the meanest employment, Mal. 3:17, Math. 21:28–30, Luk. 15:19, Gen. 24, 29.
2. Considered in their up-grown years, and so they are to be subject to their Parents for their disposal and that especially in these two particulars:

1. For their disposing into services, Exod. 21:7–12.
2. For their disposing in Marriage, Gen. 24 throughout, Gen. 28:1–8, Gen. 29:18–20, Deut. 7:3–4.

Secondly, children must be subject to their Parents' reproofs and fitting corrections, Prov. 13:24, 19:18, 22, 15, 23:13–14, 29:15–17, Heb. 12:9.

Reasons to persuade children to be obedient unto their Parents

1. The very placing of the commandment may move us much, in that God hath put it before our goods, yea, before our life; to show that obedience ought to be dearer to use than our goods, yea, than our lives.
2. The name of Father and Mother, which are names of nature, full of love, and the more apt to move obedience.
3. Many blessings do attend it; it hath the promise of long life, a thing very amiable, for death is repugnant to nature, Eph. 6:1–2, Prov. 4:10–22.

4. It is a good thing, it is to God acceptable; yea, it is that which God is delighted with, Col. 3:20.
5. It is not only good, but it is right, Eph. 61. We cannot forbear it without injury; it is their own, it is due unto them: and therefore if you keep it back, you do them wrong and injustice.
6. It concerns children to yield obedience unto their Parents, because they watch over their souls, Heb. 13:17. This holds in proportion with natural Parents.
7. The exercise of this duty exceedingly furthereth the exercise of other particular Acts of piety towards God, and righteousness towards others; it will be a means to usher in all other Acts of obedience unto all the commandments, Levit. 19:2–4, Gen. 18:19.
8. It will be a good means to bring other children (though rebellious) into filial obedience: as Jacob's obedience wrought upon Esau, Gen 28:6–9.

Sixthly, children especially of godly Parents, should be observing, minding, prizing, and treasuring up such Parents' good speeches (as one hath expressed) as so many oracles of god, which will evidence to all that their children honor them, Job 15:18, Psalms 44:1–2, Psalms 78:2–3, Prov. 4:3–4, Deut. 6:20 to the end, Exod. 13:14, Josh. 4:6–7, 21, 23.

Seventhly another duty that children should perform is this: cordially and constantly to pray and give thanks to God for their Parents, 1 Tim. 2:1–2, Heb. 13:18, Rom. 10:1. As Subjects should pray and give thanks for their Magistrates, and people for their Minister, and as Paul prayed for Israel, so should children pray and give thanks for their Parents.

Source: W. C. *A Schoole of Nurture for Children, or The Duty of Children in Honouring Their Parents, Unfolded, Proved, and Applied.* London: Simon Miller, 1656, pp. 4–16.

Part III

ECONOMIC LIFE

To supply food and clothes for themselves and their families, people need to work. Economic life, therefore, is an indispensable part of daily life. Some occupations are connected with these basic needs. Prosperous farming families in the Middle Ages, might build their own cabin, grow their own fruits and vegetables, milk their own cows, and make their own clothes from wool shorn from their own sheep. Other occupations are further removed from directly supplying the basics of life—pinners (people who make nails, tacks, and other fasteners) cannot live by eating nails. Instead, they must sell enough product to be able to buy the things that they and their families need. Self-sufficiency, therefore, is one marker of how urban and rural life differed from each other in the Middle Ages and Renaissance.

The following section on urban life examines the complex economies and mutual dependencies that developed during this time period across the world. Major cities, such as London, Madrid, Tenochtitlan (Mexico City), Mecca, and Beijing, continued to grow in size, influence, and power throughout the Middle Ages and Renaissance. Cities offered an economy scale not generally found in the countryside. Craft specialists developed in cities; some people did nothing but make nails; others only butchered animals; others simply exchanged foreign currency for local money. Such specialization enabled more efficient production and frequently superior products than what could be found in rural districts. The growing urban populations and large customer base also attracted competition; in an effort to create a monopoly, craftsmen often banded together in guilds to allow only licensed individuals to sell certain merchandise and services. Royal legislation, furthermore, often gave cities favorable tax breaks—a recognition of the cities' power. Cities were not merely economic and political centers; they could also be spiritual centers, as Mecca—the center of Islamic prayer life—makes clear.

Rural villages may not have been as powerful as cities, but rural life as a whole still dominated the Middle Ages and Renaissance. Throughout the period, most people lived and worked in the countryside. As the sources from the Rural Life section show, rural life was difficult. The vast majority of rural inhabitants lived in meager circumstances, farming lands and estates that belonged to a small group of wealthy landowners, including monasteries. During the earlier Middle Ages, many agricultural laborers were actually slaves—they didn't even own themselves. Other documents indicate a profound distrust between the wealthy landowners and their agricultural laborers; Walter of Henley, for example, accuses the peasants of laziness.

Some occupations, of course, were based neither in the city nor in the countryside, but in both. Merchants traveled vast distances as they brought goods to the most profitable markets, unwittingly helping to match supply and demand. The documents in the section on trade and monetary systems explores how these merchants essentially made the world a smaller place during the course of the Middle Ages and Renaissance. By 1500, Europe, Asia, and the Americas had been interwoven into a web of trade and economic interest.

One of the products sold by merchants was slaves. Modern readers may associate slavery with the southern United States, but slavery was a worldwide phenomenon during the Middle Ages and Renaissance. China, Europe, South America—peoples in these areas and others depended on slaves to provide agricultural labor, entertainment, and sacrificial victims. Despite the prevalence of slavery, many of the documents in the Slavery section demonstrate that intellectuals were uncomfortable with the abuse of fellow human beings. Despite these attempts to restrain the horrors of slavery, the practice continued into the modern era. Economic life was harder for some than for others.

Urban Life

As economies during the Middle Ages moved away from agrarian products toward crafts, trade, and incipient industry, cities grew and became increasingly more important. In the year A.D. 600, political power and economic clout rested primarily in the hands of landed gentry in the countryside; by 1600, cities such as London, Paris, Madrid, Venice, Tenochtitlan, Cuzco, Mecca, Constantinople, and Beijing were clear centers of political control and economic clout. Many of these cities had ancient roots—Beijing had important settlements by the sixth century B.C.—but the Middle Ages witnessed urban life's dramatic rise toward cultural dominance. Document 6 offers an eyewitness tour of the marvels of Tenochtitlan (now Mexico City) during the heyday of the Aztec Empire.

Cities became powerful in part because they made money. The large numbers of potential buyers and willing workers enabled an economy of scale that in turn enabled the efficient manufacture and easy distribution of goods and services. The urban economy, particularly in Europe, was dominated in large part by trade guilds, organizations that determined who could and could not practice a particular craft in a particular city. For example, in the northern English city of the York, the pinners, who made nails and other fasteners, controlled who was able to sell fasteners in the city of York—only members of the pinners' guild. This monopoly control of specific industries undercut competition and helped ensure healthy profits for guild members. The lure of high profits encouraged upwardly mobile families to apprentice their children into these crafts, although sufficient evidence shows that the children themselves were often less pleased with these financial arrangements. Documents 3 and 4 give helpful insights into the guild economy.

Cities were frequently able to leverage their economic clout to gain special privileges. As the city charters in Document 8 show, these privileges came in both financial and political forms. On the one hand, royal authority often canceled the taxes that city merchants would ordinarily need to pay. The equivalent happens today when cities lower business taxes. The increased incentive for economic activity frequently results ultimately in more revenue for everyone. On the other hand, the king also granted the cities a limited form of self-rule. London, for example, elected its own mayor to manage its affairs independently of the crown, but that mayor had to swear loyalty to the king himself.

Although urban life offered literally rich rewards, the spiritual life was not neglected, despite what some critics suggested (Document 1). Certain cities, such as Mecca in the Arabian Peninsula, were themselves considered sacred and were governed by special laws to protect that sanctity, as Document 7 describes. In other cities, such as Tenochtitlan, capital of the Aztec empire in Mexico, the central marketplace (symbolizing economic prosperity) was surpassed only by the temple district (symbolizing spiritual life). The *Aztecs* valued religion over money, and their city layout reflected these priorities. Spiritual life likewise encouraged a concern for the plight of the poor. Monasteries and church institutions, such as the abbey near Stapel mentioned in Document 5, founded and maintained hospitals to care for the sick and dying of the poorer classes, who had flocked to the cities in search of a better life.

The necessity of such hospitals for the poor reminds us that not everyone came out ahead in urban life. Some simply did not succeed economically. Others, such as Jews, were consistently discriminated against by their city-dwelling neighbors. Even when the learned elite recognized the valuable contribution that Jews made to city life (Document 2), the Jews were kept apart from the mainstream and therefore formed a separate community. Many of these separate communities were forcibly evicted during the later Middle Ages. Cities held great promise, but not all of their promises were fulfilled.

1. The Philosophy of Chinese Businessmen

Ch'en Tzu-ang (A.D. 656–698), the author of the following poem, was a controversial poet who delighted in surprising his audience. According to one story, he bought an extremely expensive guitar and announced loudly that he would play it publicly the next day. Once a large crowd had gathered on the following day, Ch'en Tzu-ang picked up the guitar and then smashed it violently against the ground, breaking it into smithereens. He then proceeded to deliver his poems instead.

In the following poem, Ch'en Tzu-ang chides businessmen whose thoughts are predominantly upon the things of this world. As a result, they remain ignorant of the world to come. The poet uses paradoxes, such as seeing the whole world in one cup and entering the Gate of Immutability through Mutation, to represent the difficulty and mystery involved in contemplation of ultimately eternal truths.

Business men boast of their skill and cunning
But in philosophy they are like little children.
Bragging to each other of their successful depredations,
They neglect to consider the ultimate fate of the body
What should they know of the Master of Dark Truth
Who saw the wide world in a jade cup,

By illumined conception got clear of Heaven and Earth,
On the chariot of Mutation entered the Gate of Immutability?

Source: *A Hundred and Seventy Chinese Poems*. Translated by Arthur Waley. London: Constable, 1918, p. 95.

2. A Jewish Ghetto

The Jewish people have a history of extraordinary adversity. The Holocaust of World War II highlights the injustices done to Jews, but the Jewish people were persecuted long before that. Within the first 150 years A.D., Jewish rebellions were repeatedly put down by Roman authorities in Palestine, often with considerable brutality and slaughter. The temple at Jerusalem, for example, was destroyed in A.D. 70, and hundreds of thousands of Jews were massacred in the aftermath of the Bar Kokhba revolt of A.D. 132–135. As a result, the Jewish communities outside of Palestine (called the Diaspora) became as important to Jewish life as the communities remaining in Palestine. Unfortunately, the Jewish Diaspora lived continuously as strangers in foreign lands. The following document, in which Bishop Rudiger Huozmann grants land to a Jewish community at Speyer in Germany in the eleventh century, shows the realities of Jewish life in Christian lands during the High Middle Ages.

The Jews were valued and despised at the same time. As the document notes, Bishop Rudiger attempted to protect the Jews from persecution ("the insolence of the citizens"), but he also invited the Jews to Speyer specifically to "increase the honor" of the city. These contrasting attitudes, despising and valuing the Jews, reflect the ambiguous position of Jews in Christian medieval society. On the one hand, the Jews were not trusted because they were not Christian—they were viewed as enemies of Christ and as potential enemies of the state. On the other hand, Jews had developed great skills in trade and in money-changing; the document specifically grants the Jewish community the right to trade in the harbor and the right to change gold and silver currency. This economic activity boosted not only the Jews' standard of living but also the community of the whole city. Speyer would become wealthier and more prosperous as a result of the Jews' economic and entrepreneurial activities. Speyer wanted to be prosperous, and it needed Jews to be so, however much the citizens distrusted them.

To attract Jewish settlers, the bishop was willing to grant them extensive legal rights and privileges. Not only were they granted trading rights, but they were also granted freedom from thelony, a form of customs tax levied on trade. They were also granted, in return for a fixed rent, a large walled neighborhood, separate from the main town, so that they could live as they wished. Also provided was a cemetery so that Jewish burial customs could be practiced. One of the most interesting concessions was the granting of their own separate law court. The chief rabbi was empowered by the bishop to hear not only cases between Jews but also cases brought against the Jews; the bishop, however, remained as head of the court of appeal.

This document, in sum, demonstrates how highly the learned establishment (e.g., the bishop) valued the Jews, even if the less educated people

THE JEWS' PASSOVER.
Fac-simile of a miniature from a missal of fifteenth century ornamented with paintings
of the School of Van Eyck.
Bibl. de l'Arsenal, Th. lat., n° 199.

A fifteenth-century depiction of a Jewish passover. In accordance with the Hebrew Scriptures, the diners at this seder are eating standing up and with their staffs in hand so as to be ready to flee. © 2008 Jupiterimages Corporation.

55

Christian and Jewish scholars debate theology. The two groups of scholars can be distinguished by their clothing. The Christians are clean-shaven with floppy caps, while the Jewish scholars wear beards and pointed hats in this depiction. Courtesy of Library of Congress.

("the citizens" in this document) esteemed them less. Unfortunately, anti-Jewish sentiment grew as the Middle Ages wore on. During the twelfth century, reports of Jews' massacring innocent Christian children became widespread; these stories were urban legends without factual basis, but they greatly influenced later medieval society. King Edward I expelled the Jews from England in 1290, King Philip IV expelled them from France in 1306, and many other rulers drove the Jews from their territories during the fifteenth and sixteenth centuries.

In the name of the Holy and Indivisible Trinity, I, Rudiger, surnamed Huozmann, Bishop of Speyer, when I made the villa of Speyer into a town, thought I would increase the honor I was bestowing on the place if I brought in the Jews. Therefore I placed them outside the town and some way off from the houses of the rest of the citizens, and, lest they should be too easily disturbed by the insolence of the citizens, I surrounded them with a wall. Now the place of their habitation which I acquired justly (for in the first place I obtained the hill partly with money and partly by exchange, while I received the valley by way of gift from some heirs) that place, I say, I transferred to them on condition that they pay annually three and a half pounds of the money of Speyer for the use of the brethren.

I have granted also to them within the district where they dwell, and from that district outside the town as far as the harbor, and within the harbor itself, full power to change gold and silver, and to buy and sell what they please. And I have also given them license to do this throughout the state. Besides this, I have given them land of the church for a cemetery with rights of inheritance. This also I have added that if any Jew should at any time stay with them, he shall pay no thelony.

Then also just as the judge of the city hears cases between citizens, so the chief rabbi shall hear cases which arise between the Jews or against them. But if by chance he is unable to decide any of them, they shall go to the bishop or his chamberlain. They shall maintain watches, guards, and fortifications about their district, the guards in common with our vassals. They may lawfully employ nurses and servants from among our people. Slaughtered meat which they may not eat according to their law, they may lawfully sell to Christians, and Christians may lawfully buy it. Finally, to round out these concessions, I have granted that they may enjoy the same privileges as the Jews in any other city of Germany.

Lest any of my successors diminish this gift and concession, or constrain them to pay greater taxes, alleging that they have usurped these privileges, and have no episcopal warrant for them, I have left this charter as a suitable testimony of the said grant. And that this may never be forgotten, I have signed it, and confirmed it with my seal as may be seen below. Given on Sept. 15th, 1084, etc.

Source: Altmann, Wilhelm, and Ernst Bernheim, eds. *Ausgewählte Urkunden zur Erläuterung der Verfassungsgeschichte Deutschlands im Mittelalter.* Berlin: Weidmannsche Buchhandlung, 1904.

3. Butchers' Guilds

Guilds were central to the European economy. Essentially, a guild is a licensed monopoly. Only members of a guild were allowed to practice the business of that guild in a particular location. For example, as noted earlier, only members of the pinners' guild in the northern English city of York—pinners are makers of nails and other fasteners—could make and sell nails in York. In return for having this monopoly of trade, the guilds paid the local authorities a fixed sum of money.

The first document given here, written in Paris in 1182, outlines the basics of a trade guild. The guild members did not need to pay any sales tax, but they did need to pay a fixed fee three times a year—roughly the equivalent of $400 dollars each time. As the document suggests, the king farmed out the right to collect these fees to other individuals. In return, the king would receive less money from the individual to whom he granted the right to collect the fees, but the king would also not have the hassle of overseeing the collection of the fees.

In return for paying these flat fees, the butchers' guild was able to control a monopoly of meat products in the city of Paris. No one could open a butcher's shop unless the butchers' guild gave that person permission. The freedom from sales tax likewise was a significant economic advantage.

Although the guild system benefited the guilds and the authorities who received money from the guilds, the monopoly, by its nature, undercut the free market economy. The absence of a free market tends both to reduce the quality of goods offered and to increase the price at which those goods are offered. To counteract this tendency, regulations, as the second document given here demonstrates, were passed to ensure the quality of the product that guilds provided. In the five provisions of the second document, from Tuln in Germany and dated 1237, two provisions attempt to control the quality of the meat: the butchers were held monetarily responsible for bad meat, and they were banned from selling freshly killed animals (most meat was aged in the Middle Ages to enhance its flavor and tenderness). Servants likewise were barred from selling meat; as a result, only professional butchers could sell meat to the public. The third regulation prevents butchers from acting as middlemen, that is, buying meat in country markets (where prices were lower because of less demand) and selling that same meat in city markets (where prices were higher).

Although modern economists recognize that such product mobility is actually good for the economy, the Middle Ages generally viewed such activity as immoral because the middlemen were thought to be profiting off of other people's labor. Finally, the regulations also show increasing anti-Semitism because Jews were forced to pay higher prices for meats, although the higher price also may have reflected the Jewish community's need for meat killed and butchered according to kosher methods. The guild monopolies of the Middle Ages offered economic advantages to certain individuals and economic disadvantages to many others.

PARIS BUTCHER'S GUILD

In the name of the Holy and Indivisible Trinity, Amen. Philip, by the grace of God, King of the Franks. Be it known to all present and future generations that the butchers of Paris came to our presence asking that we could grant and permit them to hold in peace their ancient customs, just as our father and grandfather, Louis of good memory, and other predecessors of ours—the Kings of France—had granted them. On the advice of those who attended us we heard their petition, but, since those customs granted by our father were not in a written charter, we have ordered them to be put into writing, and to be confirmed with our seal.

These are the customs:

1. The butchers of Paris can buy living and dead cattle, and whatever pertains to their trade, freely without tax and without giving any *pedagium* within the area of Paris, from wherever they come, or wherever they are taken, if by chance it should happen that they are being taken anywhere. Fish of the sea, and fish from fresh water, they may likewise buy and sell.
2. No one can be a Paris butcher, nor shall other butchers have their rights, namely, food and drink, unless they wish to concede them of their own will.
3. On the Octave of Christmas, every butcher will give us annually twelve denarii; on the Octaves of Easter and of St. Denis, thirteen denarii to him who holds it in fief from us.
4. Every butcher shall owe an oble for stallage to our reeve for every Sunday on which he cuts pork or beef, and every butcher owes every year to us, at the vintage, one *hautban* of wine.

And in order that all these things may remain secure for ever, we have strengthened this charter by the addition of our seal and signature.

Done at Paris in the year of the Incarnation of the Lord, 1182, in the fourth year of our reign. Witnesses, etc. . . .

GERMAN MEAT REGULATIONS

1. The first is that none of the servants of the butchers shall presume to buy or sell cattle in the city or in the country.
2. The second is that no butcher presume to sell meat on the day on which the animal is killed.
3. The third is that none of them shall dare to attempt the purchase of meat from rural butchers on a market day.
4. The fourth is that if any butcher buys an ox for a talent, a Jew will pay twenty-four denarii for the killing of it, without causing delay for the denarii. Also for cattle which are bought for six solidi, a Jew will pay sixteen denarii for killing. Also for cattle which are bought for half a talent, a Jew will pay twelve denarii. Also for small cattle which are called *chlovieh*, a Jew will pay two denarii; for a lamb a Jew will pay one denarius.
5. Also it has been decreed that if any butcher traffics in bad meat, the master craftsmen will seize that meat until he makes amends in the presence of the mayors.

"Large Kitchen." From *Il Cuoco Segreto Di Papa Pio V* (The Private Chef of Pope Pius V), by Bartolomeo Scappi, Venice, 1570.

Sources: Fagniez, Gustave. *Documents Relatifs à l'Histoire de l'Industrie et du Commerce en France*. Vol. 1. Paris: Picard, 1898, p. 91; Keutgen, F. *Urkunden zur Städtischen Verfassungsgeschichte*. Berlin: Felber, 1901, p. 360. Adjusted by the Lawrence Morris.

4. Apprenticeship

As Document 3 indicates, being a member of a guild could be lucrative. To enter into a guild, a youth generally had to complete an apprenticeship under a member of that guild. Apprenticeship was a complex legal contract in which a craftsman agreed to take on a young man, to feed him and clothe him, and to teach him the craft, in return for certain economic privileges. The major privilege that the craftsman received was the unpaid labor (not counting the housing, clothing, and feeding) of the young assistant. These contractual terms could vary, however. According to the immediately following contract, for example, the young apprentice Michael will receive lodging but no food ("without board").

Although both parties to the contract should benefit, numerous provisions demonstrate that the apprentice relationship was often fraught with difficulty. Both contract extracts presented in this section, for example, force the parents to return their child to the craftsman if the child should run away. Clearly, homesickness or harsh living conditions could cause a young apprentice to flee his new business relationship. The first contract given here wisely provides a get-out clause by which the mother, probably a widow because the father would have made the contract if he were alive, is able to buy out the child's remaining two years of service. Moreover, both contracts make the parents financially responsible for any damage that their children may cause.

Both contracts also clearly demonstrate the great value to be had from a child's induction into a craft. The parents are willing to accept significant financial responsibilities, but the responsibilities of the craftsmen are much less fully sketched out. This disparity in financial obligation shows just how far parents were willing to go to get their children apprenticed. Learning a craft was a ticket to financial security, and it was worth all the homesickness and financial liabilities imposed upon the young apprentice and his family.

AN APPRENTICESHIP IN WEAVING

Be it known to present and future aldermen that Ouede Ferconne apprentices Michael, her son, to Matthew Haimart on security of her house, her person, and her chattels, and the share that Michael ought to have in them, so that Matthew Haimart will teach him to weave in four years, and that he (Michael) will have shelter, and learn his trade there without board. And if there should be reason within two years for Michael to default, she will return him, and Oude Ferconne, his mother, guarantees this on the security of her person and goods. And if she should wish to purchase his freedom for the last two years she may do so for thirty-three solidi, and will pledge for that all that has been stated. And if he should not free himself of the last two years let him return, and Ouede Ferconne, his mother, pledges this with her person and her goods. And the said Ouede pledges that if Matthew Haimart suffers either loss or damage through Michael, her son, she will restore the loss and damage on the security of herself and all her goods, should Michael do wrong. . . .

AN APPRENTICESHIP FOR STEPHEN BORRE

April the ninth. I, Peter Borre, in good faith and without guile, place with you, Peter Feissac, weaver, my son Stephen, for the purpose of learning the trade or craft of weaving, to live at your house, and to do work for you from the feast of Easter next for four continuous years, promising you by this agreement to take care that my son does the said work, and that he will be faithful and trustworthy in all that he does, and that he will neither steal nor take anything away from you, nor flee nor depart from you for any reason, until he has completed his apprenticeship. And I promise you by this agreement that I will reimburse you for all damages or losses that you incur or sustain on my behalf, pledging all my goods, etc., renouncing the benefit of all laws, etc. And I, the said Peter Feissac, promise you, Peter Borre, that I will teach your son faithfully and will provide food and clothing for him.

Done at Marseilles, near the tables of the money-changers. Witnesses, etc.

Source: Blancard, L. *Documents Inédits sur le Commerce de Marseille au Moyen Age*. Vol. 2. Marseilles: Barlatier-Feissat, 1884, p. 33. In Roy Cave and Herbert Coulson, *A Source Book for Medieval Economic History*. New York: Biblo and Tannen, 1965, pp. 256–57.

5. Founding a Hospital

In modern times, hospitals are places were the seriously ill go to become better. In the Middle Ages, hospitals instead were places where only those who were both poor and seriously ill went; death was frequently the outcome. The wealthy classes were treated in their own homes by private doctors and private priests; the poor, on the other hand, relied on hospitals once they became too ill, or too poor, to be cared for by their relatives and friends. Hospitals, thus, were a form of charity and were often sponsored by ecclesiastical institutions.

In the following document, an abbey of monks transfers a hospital from its own lands to the city center of Stapel in the year 1200. To provide for the hospital financially, the abbey pledges to set aside the income from certain pieces of land that it owns. With these proceeds, the abbey hopes to support at least 40 poor people. In addition to providing material benefits to the poor, the abbey also outlines a plan to supply spiritual benefits. They will staff the hospital church, and the priests will provide extreme unction (a ritual confirming forgiveness on the seriously ill) and Christian burial for the hospital inhabitants. The emphasis on death rituals indicates that the monks took a realistic view of how well the hospital would succeed in treating its diseased inhabitants. The hope of the poor would need to be in a better life after death.

Thomas, by divine consent Abbot, and the whole community of the abbey of Saint Trond, to all seeing these presents, greeting in the Lord forever. Taking into consideration the inconvenience arising from the hospital for the sick being on our domain, and seeing the usefulness of the hospital situated in the main street of Stapel, on the advice of honest men, and with the permission of the Lord Bishop James of Palestrina, legate of the apostolic see, we have made the following change, namely, we have assigned to the hospice situated in Stapel, six *bonniers* of land, of which four lie next to our cultivated land near Schuerhoven, and two in another part lying opposite. From this there is paid annually to us five pence as tax from each *bonnier*. Moreover, we grant whatever interest we have in the mill of Stayen to the same house, with this condition, that it be expected to pay annually to us five Liège solidi for the upkeep of the poor to the number of forty. We grant also to the brethren the right to build a chapel in that place, where divine offices may be celebrated, and they may elect a priest from among themselves. He who is elected shall be presented to the abbot; if he be suitable the abbot will approve of him. This priest shall administer to the brethren, and to the sick in that place, all the sacraments of the church and extreme unction. The priest of Holy Sepulcher church shall bury those who die. We desire that these things shall not be to the prejudice of the church of Holy Sepulcher and that all things be granted forever. Whatever the said house is known to have from Lord Wirch of the village of Planken in taxes or rents or other payments shall be paid to our monastery in recompense perpetually. We shall remain as true patron of the said hospice, just as we have been, and it will be always under our protection. Witnesses, etc.

Source: de Smet, J. J. *Monuments pour server a l'Histoire des Provinces de Namur, de Hainaut et de Luxembourg.* Vol. 2. Brussels: M. Hayez, 1870, p. 562. In Roy Cave and Herbert Coulson, *A Source Book for Medieval Economic History.* New York: Biblo and Tannen, 1965, pp. 321–22.

6. A Tour of Mexico City with Moctezuma

Tenochtitlan, as Mexico City was called during the height of the Aztec empire, clearly impressed the Spanish conquistadors, as the following document demonstrates. Throughout the eyewitness account of Bernal Díaz del Castillo, an extract of which is given below, the Aztec city is compared favorably with the great cities of Europe: "Those who had been at Rome and at Constantinople said, that for convenience, regularity, and population, they had never seen the like." The inhabitants likewise are given high praise: Díaz states that their artists equaled such European geniuses as Michelangelo. Although the next generation of Spanish colonialists, especially the profiteering businessmen, would frequently look down upon the Native Americans, many of the original sixteenth-century conquistadors were simply impressed.

The marketplace explored by Hernán Cortés and his men testifies to the thriving economy of the Aztecs. The marketplace dominated one of Tenochtitlan's central squares and was full of an amazing variety of merchandise, from gold to slaves chained to pillars to basic foodstuffs. Very like a modern department store, the marketplace was clearly organized by product. All the gold merchants were in one area, all the armorers in another, all the food merchants in yet another, and so forth. The market was packed, producing a continuous hubbub that could be heard from far away. In addition, legal officials continually policed the area to ensure fair trading practices.

The other center point of Tenochtitlan was the temple. The document makes clear that the temple was even more important than the central market. Although the Aztec king Moctezuma (the more accurate form of the Nahuatl name frequently rendered "Montezuma") allowed the Spaniards to go to the marketplace on their own, he insisted on accompanying them to the temple. Indeed, Moctezuma offered an incense sacrifice before the Spaniards were allowed up into the temple itself. The importance of temples to the Mexica (as the Aztecs are also called) was apparent by the prominence of the buildings themselves. The temple was so tall that the Spaniards were able to survey all of Tenochtitlan from the top of the temple and also were able to see much of the surrounding countryside. The main buildings visible in other towns were likewise temples. The centrality of temples to Mesoamerican culture can also be seen in the Aztec pictographs—the conquering of a people was recorded by a pictorial representation of the destruction of their temple.

But whereas the Aztecs revered the temple, the Spaniards hated it. Although Díaz is complimentary in general to the Mexica civilization, he refers to the Aztec idols as "accursed," and he focuses on the altar stained with the blood of human sacrifices. Once open hostilities broke out between the Spanish, their Native American allies, and the Aztecs, the temple precincts were the sites of some of the fiercest fighting, as the Spanish attempted to destroy the temples and the Aztecs to protect them.

Although the Mexica ultimately lost control of Tenochtitlan to the Spanish, the city survived to become modern-day Mexico City. The very location of the city, originally built up from the bottom of Lake Texcoco so that the city resembled Venice in its need for bridges and boats to get anywhere, is a testimony to the achievements of Mexica civilization.

The place where the artists principally resided was named Escapuzalco, and was at the distance of about a league from the city. Here were the shops and manufactories of all their gold and silver smiths, whose works in these metals, and in jewelry, when they were brought to Spain, surprised our ablest artists. Their painters we may also judge of

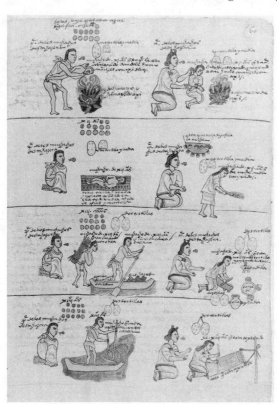

Aztec childhood. This image from the Codex Mendoza shows the upbringing of an Aztec boy (left-hand column) and girl (right-hand column). The boy learns to fish, while the girl learns to bake and weave. Both are punished in the same way, however: they are held over a fire that is burning chiles. © 2008 Jupiterimages Corporation.

by what we now see, for there are three Indians in Mexico, who are named Marcos de Aquino, Juan de la Cruz, and Crespillo, who, if they had lived with Apelles in ancient times, or were compared with Michaelangelo or Berruguete in modern times, would not be held inferior to them. Their fine manufactures of cotton and feathers, were principally brought from the province of Costitlan. The women of the family of the great Montezuma also, of all ranks, were extremely ingenious in these works, and constantly employed; as was a certain description of females who lived together in the manner of nuns.

One part of the city was entirely occupied by Montezuma's dancers, of different kinds, some of whom bore a stick on their feet, others flew in the air, and some danced like those in Italy called by us Matachines. He had also a number of carpenters and handicraft men constantly in his employ. His gardens, which were of great extent, were irrigated by canals of running water, and shaded with every variety of trees. In them were baths of cut stone, pavilions for feasting or retirement, and theatres for shows, and for the dancers and singers; all which were kept in the most exact order, by a number of labourers constantly employed.

When we had been four days in Mexico, Cortes wished to take a view of the city, and in consequence sent to request the permission of his Majesty. Accordingly, Aquilar, Donna Marina, and a little page of our general's called Orteguilla, who already understood something of the language, went to the palace for that purpose. Montezuma was pleased immediately to accede, but being apprehensive that we might offer some insult to his temple, he determined to go thither in person, which he accordingly did, in the same form, and with the same retinue, as when he first came out to meet us, but that he was on this occasion preceded by two lords bearing scepters in their hands, which they carried on high, as a signal of the king's approach. Montezuma, in his litter, with a small rod in his hand, one half of which was gold, and the other half wood, and which he bore elevated like a rod of justice, for such it was, approached the temple, and there quitted his litter and mounted the steps, attended by a number of priests, and offering incense with many ceremonies to his war gods.

Cortes at the head of his cavalry, and the principal part of our soldiers under arms, marched to the grand square, attended by many noblemen of the court. When we arrived there, we were astonished at the crowds of people, and the regularity which prevailed, as well as at the vast quantities of merchandise, which those who attended us were assiduous in pointing out. Each kind had its particular place, which was distinguished by a sign. The articles consisted of gold, silver, jewels, feathers, mantles, chocolate, skins dressed and undressed, sandals, and other manufactures of the roots and fibres of nequen, and great numbers of male and female slaves, some of whom were fastened by the neck, in collars, to long poles. The meat market was stocked with fowls, game, and dogs. Vegetables, fruits, articles of food ready dressed, salt, bread, honey, and sweet pastry made in various ways were also sold here. Other places in the square were appointed to the sale of earthen ware, wooden household furniture such as tables and benches, firewood, paper, sweet canes filled with tobacco mixed with liquid amber, copper axes and working tools, and wooden vessels highly painted. Numbers of women sold fish, and little loaves made of a certain mud which they find in the lake, and which resembles cheese. The makers of stone blades were busily employed shaping them out of the rough material, and the merchants who dealt in gold, had the metal in grains as it came from the mines, in transparent tubes, so that they could be reckoned, and the gold was valued at so many mantles, or so many xiquipils of cocoa, according to the size of the quills. The entire square was enclosed in piazzas, under which great quantities of grain were stored, and where were also shops for various kinds of goods. I must apologize for adding, that boat loads of human ordure were on the borders of the adjoining canals, for the purpose of tanning leather, which they said could not be done without it. Some may laugh at this but I assert the fact is as I have stated it, and moreover, upon all the public roads, places for passengers to resort to, were built of canes, and thatch with straw or grass, in order to collect this material. The courts of justice, where three judges sat, occupied a part of the square, their under-officers going in the market, inspecting the merchandise.

From the square we proceeded to the great temple, but before we entered it we made a circuit through a number of large courts, the smallest of which appeared to me to contain more ground than the great square in Salamanca, with double enclosures built of lime and stone, and the courts paved with large white cut stone, very clean; or where not paved, they were plastered and polished. When we approached the gate of the great temple, to the flat summit of which the ascent was by a hundred and fourteen steps, and before we had mounted one of them, Montezuma sent down to us six priests, and two of his noblemen, to carry Cortes up, as they had done their sovereign, which he politely declined. When we had ascended to the summit of the temple, we observed on the platform as we passed, the large stones whereon were placed the victims who were to be sacrificed. Here was a great figure which resembled a dragon, and much blood fresh spilt. Montezuma came out from an adoratory in which his accursed idols were placed, attended by two priests, and addressing himself to Cortes, expressed his apprehension that he was fatigued; to which Cortes replied, that fatigue was unkown to us.

Montezuma then took him by the hand, and pointed out to him the different parts of the city, and its vicinity, all of which were commanded from that place. Here we had a clear prospect of the three causeways by which Mexico communicated with the land, and of the aqueduct of Chapultepeque, which supplied the city with the finest water. We were struck with the numbers of canoes, passing to and from the main land, loaded with provisions and merchandise, and we could now perceive, that in this great city, and all the others of that neighbourhood which were built in the water, the houses stood separate from each other, communicating only by small drawbridges, and by boats, and that they were built with terraced tops.

We observed also the temples and adoratories of the adjacent cities, built in the form of towers and fortresses, and others on the causeway, all whitewashed, and wonderfully brilliant. The noise and bustle of the market-place below us could be heard almost a league off, and those who had been at Rome and at Constantinople said, that for convenience, regularity, and population, they had never seen the like.

Source: Díaz del Castillo, Bernal. *The True History of the Conquest of Mexico.* London: Harrap, 1927, pp. 175–78. Translation adjusted by Lawrence Morris.

7. Special Laws Governing Mecca

Makkah, or Mecca as it is often spelled in the West, is the holiest city in Islamic tradition. Makkah derives its importance from being the birthplace of Muhammad, the founder of Islam, and from holding al-Haram, the temple district that surrounds the Kaaba shrine, which was used in the local polytheistic religion before the rise of Islam. According to Islamic tradition, the Kaaba was set up by the patriarch Abraham. The central importance of the Kaaba, Haram, and Makkah is marked by Muslim prayer rituals in which the participant must face toward Makkah. The Muslim believer, moreover, must make a pilgrimage (called hajj*) to Makkah at least once in his or her life.*

This sacred nature of Makkah is also reflected in the special laws that governed the city. For example, as the ninth-century Muslim historian al-Baladhuri recorded in the following excerpt from his history Kitab Futuh al-Buldan, *the houses of Makkah could be neither sold nor rented. This prohibition reflects the competing interests in Makkah. On the one hand, Muhammad had declared that Makkah belonged only to the inhabitants of the city—thus, no outsider could buy property there. On the other hand, the necessity of hajj meant that large numbers of pilgrims needed accommodation in the city. To avoid extortionate prices, the pilgrims were instead entitled to free lodging in the city. In effect, Makkah's houses belonged to its inhabitants, but anyone was allowed to stay in them free of charge!*

Although this arrangement is very interesting in theory, the practicalities were tricky. People are naturally reluctant to open their houses to total strangers, of whatever faith. This reluctance can be seen in the pronouncements of various Muslim leaders, called imams, *which allowed houses to be rented or sold. Al-Baladhuri's account is particularly useful as a source because he records these multiple, disagreeing judgments instead of falling into the historian's temptation of supplying only those facts and opinions with which the historian himself or herself agrees.*

Similarly conflicting opinions governed the plants growing in the Haram. Some imams held that plants cultivated by humans could be used but that plants growing uncultivated should not be cut or used by humans. Other religious leaders were much more liberal and allowed greater use of the Haram vegetation. Although the religious leaders disagreed among themselves, they all proclaimed the centrality and holiness of Makkah.

'Amr an-Nâkid from Mujâhid: "Makkah is inviolable," said the Prophet, "It is not legal either to sell its dwellings or to rent its houses."

THE DWELLING PLACES OF MAKKAH NOT TO BE RENTED

Muhammad ibn-Hâtim al-Marwazi from 'Â'ishah who said, "Once I said to the Prophet, 'Build for thee, Prophet of Allah, a house in Makkah that will protect thee against the sun,' to which he replied, 'Makkah is the dwelling place only of those who are already in it.'"

Khalaf ibn-Hishâm al-Bazzâr from ibh-Juraij who said, "I have read a letter written by 'Umar ibn-'Abd-al-'Azîz in which the renting of houses in Makkah is prohibited."

Abu-'Ubaid from ibn-'Umar; the latter said: "The whole of al-Haram is a place of worship."

'Amr an-Nâkid from 'Abd-al-Malik ibn-abi-Sulaimân: A message written by 'Umar ibn-'Abd-al-'Azîz to the chief of Makkah reads: "Let not the inhabitants of Makkah receive rent for their houses because it is not legal for them."

The following tradition regarding the text, "Alike for those who abide therein and for the stranger" was communicated to us by 'Uthmân ibn-abi-Shaibah from 'Abd-ar-Rahmân ibn-Sâbit: By the stranger is meant the pilgrims and visitors who go there and who have equal right in the buildings, being entitled to live wherever they want, provided none of the natives of Makkah goes out of his home.

The following tradition regarding the same text was communicated to us by 'Uthmân on the authority of Mujâhid: The inhabitants of Makkah and other people are alike so far as the dwellings are concerned.

'Uthmân and 'Amr from Mujâhid: 'Umar ibn-al-Khattâb once said to the people of Makkah, "Make no doors for your houses that the stranger may live wherever he wants."

'Uthman ibn-abi-Shaibah and Bakr ibn-al-Haitham from abu-Hasîn—The latter said, "I once told Sa'id ibn-Jubair in Makkah that I wanted to 'abide therein' to which he replied, 'Thou art already abiding therein' and he read 'Alike for those who abide therein and for the stranger.'"

The following tradition in explanation of the same text was communicated to us by 'Uthmân on the authority of Sa'id ibn-Jubair: All people in it are alike whether they are the inhabitants of Makkah or of some other place.

Muhammad ibn-Sa'd from al-Wâkidi: Many cases were brought before abu-Bakr ibn-Muhannad ibn-'Amr ibn-Hazm regarding the rent of the houses of Makkah, and abu-Bakr in each case judged against the tenant. This too in the view of Mâlik and ibn-abi-Dh'ib. But according to Rabî-'ah and abu-az-Zinâd, there is no harm in taking money for renting houses or for selling dwellings in Makkah.

Al-Wâkidi said, "I saw ibn-abi-Dhi'b receiving the rent of his house in Makkah between as-Safa and al-Marwah."

It was said by al-Laith ibn-Sa'd, "Whatever has the form of a house, its rent is legal for its proprietor. As for the halls, the roads, the courts, and the abodes that are in a state of ruins, he who comes to them first can have them first without rent."

A tradition to the same effect was transmitted to me by abu-'Abd-ar-Rahmân al-Awdi on the authority of ash-Shâfi.

Said Sufyân ibn-Sa'îd ath-Thauri: "To rent a house in Makkah is illegal"; and he insisted on that.

According to Al-Auzâ'I, ibn-abi-Laila and abu-Hanîfah, if the rent is made during the nights of the Pilgrimage it is void, but if it is in other nights, whether the one who hires is a neighbor or not, it is all right.

According to certain followers of abu-Yûsuf, its rent is absolutely legal. The one "abiding therein" and the "stranger" are alike only as regards making the circuit of the "House."

THE PLANTS OF THE HARAM

Al-Husain ibn-'Ali ibh-al-Aswad from 'Abd-ar-Rahmân ibn-al-Aswad: The latter found no harm in gathering vegetables, cutting, eating or making any other use of anything else planted by man in Makkah be it palm-trees or otherwise. He only disapproved of this being done with trees and plants that grow of their own accord without the agency of man. From this category *al-idhkir* was excluded. According to al-Hasan ibn-Sâlih, 'Abd-ar-Rahmân allowed it in the case of rotten trees that have decayed and fallen to pieces.

According to the view of Mâlik and ibn-abi-Dh'b, as stated by Muhammad ibn-'Umar-al-Wâkidi, regarding the legality or illegality of felling a tree of the Haram, it is wrong at all events; but if the man who does it is ignorant he should be taught and receive no penalty; if he knows but is impious, he should be punished without paying the value of the trees. He who cuts it may have it for his use. According to abu-Sufyân ath-Thauri and abu-Yûsuf, he should pay the value of the tree he cuts and cannot have the wood for his use. The same view is held by abu-Hanîfah.

According to Mâlik ibn-Anas and ibn-abi-Dhi'b, there is no harm in cutting the branches of the *thumâm* plant and the ends of the senna plant from the Haram to be used as medicine or tooth-picks.

According to Sufyân ibn-Sa'îd, abu-Hanîfah, and abu-Yûsuf, whatever in the Haram is grown by man or was grown by him can be cut with impunity; whatever is grown without the agency of man, its cutter should be responsible for its value.

"I once," said al-Wâkidi, "asked ath-Thauri and abu-Yûsuf regarding the case of one who plants in the Haram something that is not ordinarily grown and which he tends until it grows high, would it be right for him to cut it. They answered in the affirmative. Then I asked about the case of a tree that may grow of its own accord in his garden and that does not belong to the category of trees planted by man, and they said, 'He can do with it whatever he likes.'"

Muhammad ibn-Sa'd from al-Wâkidi: The latter said, "It has been reported to us that ibn-'Umar used to eat in Makkah the vegetables grown in the Haram."

"No pilgrim or visitor of the Haram," said abu-Hanîfah, "shall have his camel graze in the Haram, nor shall he cut grass for it." The same view is held by Zufar. But Mâlik, ibn-abi-Dhi'b, Sufyân, abu-Yûsuf and ibn-abi-Sabrah are of the opinion that there is no harm in having the animals graze, but the man should not cut the grass for them. Ibn-abi-Laila, however, holds that there is no harm in having someone cut the grass.

'Affân and al'Abbas ibn-al-Walîd an-Narsi from Laith: 'Atâ' found no harm in using the vegetables of the Haram as well as what is planted therein including the branches and the tooth-picks, but Mujâhid disapproved of it.

Source: al-Baladhuri, Abbas Ahmad ibn-Jabir. *The Origins of the Islamic State.* Translated by Philip Hitti. New York: Columbia University Press, 1916, pp. 69–73.

8. City Charters

By the thirteenth century, the importance of cities was vitally clear. Just as the cities were growing in population size, their economic prosperity, which ultimately benefited the whole country, grew. The central role of cities in the national economy and in national governance forced the king to grant the inhabitants of cities certain concessions, essentially enabling the cities greater financial freedom and greater self-governance.

The financial advantages of urban life can be seen clearly in the first of the following extracts, in which merchants from the city of York are freed from most taxes not only in York itself but throughout the kingdom of England, which, at the start of the thirteenth century, included much of western France. The king also promises in the extract to pursue anyone who should be so bold as to harm the York merchants. The city of York, and its merchants in particular, thus gained economic advantages from tax relief and increased security for their business transactions.

The importance of self-government can be seen in the final two of the following three extracts. In the charter granted to the English city of Cambridge, the citizens, called burghers, are entitled to elect their own reeve (manager) in return for a fixed lump sum payment to the king. The citizens of London are likewise granted the right to elect annually a mayor. However, the possible dangers of granting too much power to the cities are also highlighted by this document. The mayor must present himself to the king or to the king's representative (the justiciar) and must swear loyalty to the crown. London is granted significant self-rule, provided that it remains loyal to the king himself. From the royal perspective, cities are to be encouraged, but they must also be controlled.

CONFIRMATION FOR THE CITIZENS OF YORK, A.D. 1200

John, by the grace of God, etc. Know that we have granted to our citizens from York all the freedoms and laws and customs, including their merchant guild and their trade guilds in England and Normandy, and the landing tax along the sea coast, just as they held them, freely and well, in the time of King Henry, our great grandfather. And we desire and resolutely instruct that they hold and possess the aforementioned freedoms and customs along with all the freedoms pertaining to the aforementioned merchant guild and trade guilds, freely, peacefully, and without annoyance, just as they once held them in the time of the aforementioned King Henry, our great grandfather, as the charter of our father and the charter of our brother Richard clearly indicates. Moreover, know that we have granted and have confirmed with the present charter to all our citizens of York the quittance of all landing tax, wreck fees, bridge tolls, road tolls, trespass, and all customs throughout England, Normandy, Aquitaine, Andegavia, Pictavia, and all ports and sea coasts in England, Normandy, Aquitaine, Andegavia, Pictavia. Wherefore we desire and resolutely instruct that they should be left in peace, and we prohibit anyone to harass them upon pain of a ten pound penalty, as the charter of King Richard, our brother, clearly indicates. T. G. Archibishop of York, Ph. Bishop, Galfrid son of Peter, count of Essex, etc. Written by the hand of S. Wellensis, archdeacon, and John de Gray, at York, 25 March, in the first year of our reign.

CHARTER TO CAMBRIDGE, A.D. 1207

John, King of England by the grace of God, etc. Know that we have granted and confirmed with this charter to our burghers from Cambridge, the town of Cambridge along with all things pertaining to it, to have and to hold in perpetuity, from us and our heirs and their heirs, provided that they pay annually to our Exchequer the traditional payment, namely 40 white pounds plus twenty pounds profit [. . .]. Wherefore, we desire and firmly instruct that the aforementioned burghers and their heirs have and hold the aforementioned town with all things pertaining to it, freely and peacefully, etc., along with all freedoms and free customs. We have granted to them also that they should create for themselves a reeve, whomever they want whenever they want. Witnessed by lords William of London, Peter Wintoniensis, John of Norwich, Joscelin Bishop of Bath, Galfrid son of Peter Count of Essex Count Alberic, William Brewer, Galfrid de nevilla, Reginald de Cornhill. Written by the and of Hugo de Wells, archdeacon of Wells, at Lamham, 8 May, in the eighth year of our reign.

CHARTER TO LONDON, A.D. 1215

John, King of England by the grace of God, etc. Know that we have granted, and have confirmed with this charter, to our barons of the city of London that they should elect a mayor for themselves every year, who shall be loyal to us, wise, and suitable for city management, and that, once he has been elected, he shall be presented to us, or to our justiciar if we are absent, and should swear loyalty to us; and that, if they wish, they can remove him at the end of the year and put another in his place, or they can keep him, provided that he be shown to us, or to our justiciar if we are absent. We have also granted to these barons, and we have confirmed it with this charter, that they should possess, freely, peacefully, fully, and without annoyance, all the liberties which they have hitherto enjoyed, both in the city of London and outside of it, both on land and on sea, and everywhere, except for our Chamberlainship. Wherefore we desire and resolutely instruct that the aforementioned barons of the city of London elect for themselves a mayor every year in the aforementioned way, and that they hold all the aforementioned liberties freely, peacefully, fully, and without annoyance, along with everything pertaining to such liberties, as has been mentioned above. Witnessed by the lords P. Winton, W. Wygorn, W. Bishop of Coventry, William Brewer, Peter son of Herbert, Galfrid de Lucy, and John son of Hugo. Written by the hand of master Richard de Mariscis, our chancellor, at the New Temple in London, 9 May, in the sixteenth year of our reign.

Source: Stubbs, William, ed. *Select Charters and Other Illustrations of English Constitutional History from the Earliest Times to the Reign of Edward the First*. 9th ed. Revised by H.W.C. Davis. Oxford: Clarendon Press, 1913, pp. 309–12. Translated and adapted by Lawrence Morris.

Rural Life

Throughout the Middle Ages and Renaissance, farming underpinned the economy. The overwhelming majority of people lived in rural communities and spent their days working with animals, plants, and other people. Although the Romantics of the nineteenth century frequently idolized rural life, peasant life in Europe was difficult, harsh, and unjust—look at the ploughman's life examined in Document 12. Not only must he spend his days in the fields outside during the heat of summer and the cold of winter, but he was also a slave, without a significant legal voice and with no control of government. Similarly, the ninth-century Chinese charcoal seller depicted by Po Chu-i (Document 10) spends his life on the margins of society, only to be deprived of his hard-earned profits by wealthy government officials. The medieval social system, moreover, encouraged rigid socioeconomic stratification. As Document 11 shows, each socioeconomic bracket was carefully defined and had its own specific name and specific obligations. Although movement was possible within the system, such movement tended to be unusual and was generally limited.

Despite the attempt to impose order, such rigid social stratification did not bring about peace and harmony in the countryside. As Walter of Henley's guide *Husbandry* shows (Document 14), the wealthy suspected that the peasants were lazy and dishonest. The peasants, however, grew weary of doing all the heavy agricultural work and receiving few of the profits. Agrarian discontent grew markedly in the aftermath of the *Black Death* in the mid-fourteenth century. The plague shrunk the labor force dramatically, which caused peasant labor to be in high demand. In an effort to keep down prices, the ruling classes attempted, in measures such as the one presented in Document 9, to override market forces by fixing the price of labor. In England the issue eventually boiled over into the *Peasants' Revolt of 1381*. Economic inequality and the attempt to override market forces ended in bloodshed.

Many of the victims during the English peasants' revolt were high-ranking churchmen. This animosity toward bishops and abbots was not an attempt to overthrow Christianity; instead, it was an attack on some of the wealthiest landowners in Britain. Monasteries throughout the Middle Ages had been granted land by kings, as seen in Document 13. As a result, monasteries and other religious institutions had vested interests in exploiting peasant labor. Many church organizations and orders, such as the Franciscans, were vociferous in their campaigns to improve the life of the poor, but many religious communities were more interested in maximizing revenue. Ultimately, milking cows was not a great way to earn a living in the Middle Ages and *Renaissance*; rural life's main reward was lots of fresh air.

9. The English Statute of Laborers, 1351

The Statute of Laborers, promulgated in 1351, sought to curb the massive inflation that had affected the English economy since the Black Death of 1347–1348. The statute commanded that all peasants and tradesmen accept the same prices that they did in the early 1340s ("in the twentieth year of the reign of the king that now is [Edward III], or five or six years before"), just before the plague hit. Moreover, the statute forbade peasants to move from their current workplaces, in search of better wages.

The legislation demonstrates effectively how medieval law generally attempted to serve the interests of the wealthy instead of the poor or working classes. Higher wages would clearly benefit the peasants and workmen, yet the document expresses indignation at the peasants' demands for two to three times their previous wages because these pay rates contributed "to great damage of the great men;" the term "great men" here refers to the wealthy aristocrats and landowners, not to the morally virtuous or heroic.

The statute also demonstrates how little medieval rulers understood economic principles. When the Black Death killed approximately one-third of the European population, the supply of laborers was drastically reduced. The aristocrats' demand for laborers, however, remained the same. Modern economic theories of supply and demand indicate that a shock to the supply while demand remains constant will almost inevitably result in a rise in price—exactly what happens today when the Middle Eastern oil supply is threatened. Thus, when the fourteenth-century labor supply shrank while demand remained constant, the price of labor naturally rose. Lacking modern economic theory, medieval rulers attempted to combat this inflation in labor costs by sheer edict. Although the policy was indeed sporadically enforced, a black market in labor developed in which wealthy employers competed for the smaller supply of labor by offering higher wages. In England, continued economic unrest would lead eventually to the Peasants' Revolt of 1381.

Whereas late against the malice of servants, which were idle, and not willing to serve after the pestilence, without taking excessive wages, it was ordained by our lord the king, and by the assent of the prelates, nobles, and other of his council, that such manner of servants, as well men as women, should be bound to serve, receiving salary and wages, in the same places where they were serving in the twentieth year of the reign of the king that now is, or five or six years before; and that the same servants refusing to serve in such manner should be punished by imprisonment of their bodies, as in the said statute is more plainly contained. Whereupon commissions were made to diverse people in every county to inquire and punish all them which offend against the same statue; and now forasmuch as it is given the king to understand in this present parliament, by the petition of the commonalty, that the said servants having no regard to the said ordinance, but to their ease and singular covetousness, do withdraw themselves to serve great men and others, unless they have livery and wages to the double or treble of that they were wont to take in the said twentieth year, and before, to the great damage of the great men, and impoverishing of all the said commonalty, whereof the said commonalty asks for remedy. Wherefore in the said parliament, by the assent of the said prelates, earls, barons, and other great men, and of the same commonalty there assembled, to refrain the malice of the said servants, be ordained and established the things underwritten:

First, that carters, ploughmen, drivers of the plough, shepherds, swineherds, dairy maids, and all other servants, shall take the same liveries and wages as were given in the said twentieth year, or four years before; so that in the country where wheat was usually given, they shall take for the bushel ten pence, or wheat at the will of the giver, till it be otherwise ordained. And that they be allowed to serve by a whole year, or by other usual terms, and not by the day; and that none pay in the time of plowing or hay-making but a penny the day; and a mower of meadows for the acre shall get five pence, or by the day five pence; and reapers of corn in the first week of August two pence, and the second three pence, and so till the end of August, and less in the country where less was wont to be given, without meat or drink, or other courtesy to be demanded, given, or taken; and that such workmen bring openly in their hands to the merchant-towns their instruments, and there they shall be hired in a common place and not privy.

Also, that none take for the threshing of a quarter of wheat or rye over 2 d. ob. and for the quarter of barley, beans, pease, and oats, 1 d. ob. if so much were wont to be given; and in the country where it is used to reap by certain sheaves, and to thresh by certain bushels, they shall take no more nor in other manner than was usual in the said twentieth year and before; and that the same servants be sworn two times in the year before lords, stewards, bailiffs, and constables of every town, to hold and do these ordinances; and that none of them go out of the town, where he dwells in the winter, to serve the summer, if he may serve in the same town, taking as before is said. Saving that the people of the counties of Stafford, Lancaster and Derby, and people of Craven, and of the marches of Wales and Scotland, and other places, may come in time of August, and labor in other counties, and safely return, as they were wont to do before this time; and that those, who refuse to take such oath or to perform what they be sworn to, or have taken upon them, shall be put in the stocks by the said lords, stewards, bailiffs, and constables of the towns for three days or more, or sent to the next jail, there to remain, till they will justify themselves. And that stocks be made in every town for such occasion between this day and the feast of Pentecost.

Also, that carpenters, masons, and tilers, and other workmen of houses, shall not take by the day for their work, but in the manner as they were wont, that is to say: a master carpenter 3 d. and another 2 d.; and master free-stone mason 4 d. and other masons 3 d. and their servants 1 d. ob.; tilers 3 d. and their knaves 1 d. ob.; and other coverers of fern and straw 3 d. and their knaves 1 d. ob.; plasterers and other workers of mudwalls, and their knaves, by the same manner, without meat or drink, 1 s. from Easter to Saint Michael; and from that time less, according to the rate and discretion of the justices, which should be thereto assigned; and that they that make carriage by land or by water, shall take no more for such carriage to be made, than they were wont the said twentieth year, and four years before.

Also, that cordwainers and shoemakers shall not sell boots nor shoes, nor any other thing touching their trade, in any other manner than they were wont in the said twentieth year. Also, that goldsmiths, saddlers, horsesmiths, spurriers, tanners, curriers, tawers of leather, tailors, and other workmen, artificers, and laborers, and all other servants here not specified, shall be sworn before the justices, to do and use their crafts and offices in the manner they were wont to do the said twentieth

European country folk harvesting wheat with scythe and sickle, 1600s. Woodcut. Note the gender roles: men cut the grain while women collect and carry it. North Wind Picture Archives.

year, and in time before, without refusing the same because of this ordinance; and if any of the said servants, laborers, workmen, or artificers, after such oath made, come against this ordinance, he shall be punished by fine and ransom, and imprisonment after the discretion of the justices.

Also, that the said stewards, bailiffs, and constables of the said towns, be sworn before the same justices, to inquire diligently by all the good ways they may, of all them that come against this ordinance, and to certify the same justices of their names at all times, when they shall come into the country to make their sessions; so that the same justices on certificate of the same stewards, bailiffs, and constables, of the names of the rebels, shall do them to be attached by their body, to be before the said justices, to answer of such contempts, so that they make fine and ransom to the king, in case they be convicted; and moreover to be commanded to prison, there to remain till they have found surety, to serve, and take, and do their work, and to sell things in the manner aforesaid; and in case any of them come against his oath, and be thereof convicted, he shall have imprisonment of forty days; and if he be another time convicted, he shall have imprisonment of a quarter of a year, so that at every time that he offends and is convicted, he shall have double pain: and that the same justices, at every time that they come, shall inquire of the said stewards, bailiffs, and constables, if they have made a good and lawful certificate, or if any have not, for gift, procurement, or affinity, and they will be punished by fine and ransom, if they be found guilty; and that the same justices have power to inquire and make due punishment of the said ministers, laborers, workmen, and other servants; and also of hostelers, and of those that sell victual by retail, or other things here not specified, as well at the suit of the party, as by presentment, and to hear and determine, and put the things in execution by the exigend after the first capias, if need be, and to deputize others under them, as many and such as they shall see best for the keeping of the same ordinance; and that they which will sue against such servants, workmen, laborers, for excess taken of them and they be thereof attainted at their suit, they shall have again such excess. And in case that none will sue, to have again such excess, then it shall be levied of the said servants, laborers, workmen, and artificers, and delivered to the collectors of the Quintzime tax, in alleviation of the towns where such excesses were taken.

Source: White, Albert Beebe, and Wallace Notestein, eds. *Source Problems in English History*. New York: Harper, 1915. Slightly modified by Lawrence Morris.

10. A Charcoal Seller in China

The difficulty of rural life is clearly seen in the following poem by the Chinese poet Po Chu-i (A.D. 772–846), in which an old charcoal seller struggles to make a living. Up through the nineteenth century, landless peasants made charcoal in rural forests and hauled their products into villages and cities for sale. Charcoal itself is made by heating wood in the absence of oxygen (so that the wood does not burn); the process and the product are famously dirty.

The manufacture and sale of charcoal was not a lucrative industry. The old man in this poem, for example, clearly has no financial resources to fall back on, so he must continue working despite his advanced age. He is so poor, in fact, that he can barely afford clothes; despite lacking a winter coat, he looks forward to the winter because the cold will increase the need for charcoal and consequently raise the price and thereby increase the peasant's meager income.

In this poem, Po Chu-i blames the wealthy governing elite for the continuation of such poverty in ninth-century China. Just as the snow arrives—to which the charcoal seller had been looking forward—government officials confiscate the peasant's entire stock in exchange for a very small payment. Despite this essential robbery, the peasant has no right to complain within the legal system. Po Chu-i's artistry highlights the contrast and conflict between the poor and the wealthy government officials. Whereas the peasant is caked in black soot, the government "boy" wears a white shirt; whereas the peasant cannot afford a coat with a winter lining, the government official sports a yellow coat—yellow and other bright colors were very expensive in the Middle Ages. In sum, in Po Chu-i's poem, the wealthy take advantage of the poor. Like his product, the charcoal seller is burned up and cast aside.

The Charcoal-Seller

An old charcoal-seller
Cutting wood and burning charcoal in the forests of the Southern Mountain.
His face, stained with dust and ashes, has turned to the colour of smoke
The hair on his temples is streaked with gray: his ten fingers are black.
The money he gets by selling charcoal, how far does it go?
It is just enough to clothe his limbs and put food in his mouth.
Although, alas, the coat on his back is a coat without a lining,
He hopes for the coming of cold weather, to send up the price of coal!
Last night, outside the city, a whole foot of snow;
At dawn he drives the charcoal wagon along the frozen ruts.
Oxen, weary; man, hungry; the sun, already high.
Outside the Gate, to the south of the Market, at last they stop in the mud.
Suddenly, a pair of prancing horsemen. Who can it be coming?
A public official in a yellow coat and a boy in a white shirt.
In their hands they hold a written warrant: on their tongues the words of an order;
They turn back the wagon and curse the oxen, leading them off to the north.
A whole wagon of charcoal!
More than a thousand pieces!
If officials choose to take it away, the woodman may not complain.
Half a piece of red silk and a single yard of damask,
The Courtiers have tied to the oxen's collar, as the price of a wagon of coal.

Source: *A Hundred and Seventy Chinese Poems.* Translated by Arthur Waley. London: Constable, 1918, pp. 137–38.

11. Farming Rents and Social Class

The Middle Ages were very conscious of social class. Instead of having relative notions of "wealthy" and "poor," social class was recognized formally with specific terminology, with special economic privileges, and with defined legal rights.

The document reproduced here (Rectitudines Singularum Personarum, written c. A.D. 1000), outlines the economic position of the three major classes of non-noble freeman in Anglo-Saxon England: the geneat, the cotsetla (called a "cotter" here), and the gebur. The geneat held the highest position of the three. Below these classes, there were slaves (theowas), and above them were the lower-ranking noblemen (thegnas). Although in the agrarian economy of early feudal Europe, freemen performed many of the same farming tasks as slaves, the freemen had the fundamental advantage that they could not be bought or sold and had greater legal power. Slaves themselves, however, were able to have their own private sources of income and could buy themselves out of slavery. Among the three classes examined by the Rectitudines, each lower class had less land and did more service for the local lord. The cotsetla, for example, was obliged to do at least one day's work per week for the lord, whereas the gebur must work at least two days per week for the lord; the higher-ranking geneat had no such fixed days-per-week stipulation. In modern times, we might see a similar economic stratification between those paid by the hour and those paid a yearly salary. Having to work less for the lord, moreover, meant that one could work more for one's self—the higher classes made more money.

Although the classes were carefully distinguished from each other both in theory and in practice, the Rectitudines makes it clear that there were many gray areas and that customs differed from place to place. In a time when many peasants would never travel further than the neighboring parish because of the difficulties and expenses of travel, such systemic differences were visible primarily to the upper classes alone. The cotsetla of one area very well may not have known that he had a significantly worse deal than a cotsetla in a different area. When peasants did become aware of other economic opportunities, as they did in the later Middle Ages, the outcome could be revolt (Document 9).

2. *Geneat-right.* Geneat-right is various according to the rule of the estate; in some places he must pay land-rent, and a swine yearly for grass-rent, and ride and carry with his beasts, and haul loads, work and provide food for his lord, reap and mow, cut deer-hedges, bring travelers to the township, pay church-scot, and alms-money, keep watch and guard the horses, and go on errands far and near, wherever he is ordered.

3. *Cotter's right.* The cotter's right is according to the custom of the estate; in some places he must work each Monday in the year for his hord, or two days in each week at harvest-tide. He has not to pay land-rent. He is wont to have five acres; more, if it is the custom of the estate. And if he have less, it is too little; for his service must be frequent.

4. *Gebur-right.* The gebur's duties are various, in some places heavy, in others light. On some estates the rule is that each week in the year he shall do two days of week-work, whatever is enjoined on him; and three days from Candlemass to Easter; if he lends his horse, he shall do no work while his horse is away. At Michaelmas he must pay ten pence for *gafol*; and at Martinmass twenty-four sesters of malt and two hens; at Easter a lamb or two pence.

Source: Stubbs, William, ed. *Select Charters and Other Illustrations of English Constitutional History from the Earliest Times to the Reign of Edward the First.* 9th ed. Revised by H.W.C. Davis. Oxford: Clarendon Press, 1913, pp. 89–90. Slight modifications by Lawrence Morris.

12. *Peasant Occupations*

Ælfric's Colloquy, *an extract of which follows, was an Old English/Latin phrase book from around the year* A.D. *1000 that was designed to introduce Anglo-Saxon pupils to colloquial Latin. Each Latin phrase was translated into Old English, the language spoken by the Anglo-Saxons. Many of the conversations in the* Colloquy *are unrealistic because Ælfric, the influential monk who authored the textbook, was seeking to teach basic vocabulary, not to create a work of art. Nevertheless, the* Colloquy *does give us some sense of the hardships and difficulties of various peasant occupations.*

The ploughman who appears in the following extract has the worst job, according to the Colloquy. *He must go out to work in the fields every day, in the heat of summer or the frost of winter. Moreover, Anglo-Saxon ploughmen were frequently slaves and were therefore denied many legal and economic privileges—see Document 23 for more information. The shepherd has similar outdoor obligations, and he has the added responsibility of making butter and cheese from the sheep's milk.*

The fisherman, by contrast, boasts that he is making a tidy profit because of the high demand for seafood; as he states, "I cannot catch as much as I can sell." As the Colloquy *points out, being a fisherman required both skill and bravery. In an era in which very few people knew how to swim, going out on the sea or a big river in a small boat was a frightening proposition. The fisherman in the story sensibly declines to go after whales, which are much more dangerous than the shellfish and game fish (e.g., salmon, sturgeon) that the fisherman usually takes. Nevertheless, the "Master" (from the safety of his abbey walls) implies that the fisherman is a coward as a result!*

Master.	What do your companions know?
Disciple.	They are ploughmen, shepherds, oxherds, huntsmen, fishermen, falconers, merchants, cobblers, saltmakers, and bakers.
Master.	What do you say, ploughman! How do you do your work?
Ploughman.	O my lord, I work very hard. I go out at dawn, driving the cattle to the field, and I yoke them to the plough. Nor is the weather so bad in winter that I dare to stay at home, for fear of my lord, but when the oxen are yoked, and the ploughshare and coulter attached to the plough, I must plough one whole field a day, or more.
Master.	Have you any assistant?
Ploughman.	I have a boy to drive the oxen with a goad, and he too is hoarse with cold and shouting.
Master.	What more do you do in a day?
Ploughman.	Certainly I do more. I must fill the manger of the oxen with hay, and water them and carry out the dung.
Master.	Indeed, that is a great labor.
Ploughman.	Even so, it is a great labor for I am not free.
Master.	What have you to say, shepherd? Have you heavy work too?
Shepherd.	I have indeed. In the grey dawn I drive my sheep to the pasture and I stand watch over them, in heat and cold, with my dogs, lest the wolves devour them. And I bring them back to the fold and milk them twice a day. And I move their fold; and I make cheese and butter, and I am faithful to my lord.
Master.	Oxherd, what work do you do?
Oxherd.	O my lord, I work hard. When the ploughman unyokes the oxen I lead them to the pasture and I stand all night guarding them against thieves. Then in the morning I hand them over to the ploughmen well fed and watered . . .
Master.	What is your craft?

Fisherman.	I am a fisherman.
Master.	What do you obtain from your work?
Fisherman.	Food and clothing and money.
Master.	How do you take the fish?
Fisherman.	I get into a boat, and place my nets in the water, and I throw out my hook and lines, and whatever they take I keep.
Master.	What if the fish should be unclean?
Fisherman.	I throw out the unclean fish and use the clean as food.
Master.	Where do you sell your fish?
Fisherman.	In the city.
Master.	Who buys them?
Fisherman.	The citizens. I cannot catch as much as I can sell.
Master.	What fish do you take?
Fisherman.	Herring, salmon, porpoises, sturgeon, oysters, crabs, mussels, periwinkles, cockles, plaice, sole, lobsters, and the like.
Master.	Do you wish to capture a whale?
Fisherman.	No.
Master.	Why?
Fisherman.	Because it is a dangerous thing to capture a whale. It is safer for me to go to the river with my boat than to go with many ships hunting whales.
Master.	Why so?
Fisherman.	Because I prefer to take a fish that I can kill rather than one which with a single blow can sink or kill not only me but also my companions.
Master.	Yet many people do capture whales and escape the danger, and they obtain a great price for what they do.
Fisherman.	You speak the truth, but I do not dare because of my cowardice.

Source: *Anglo-Saxon and Old English Vocabularies.* Vol. 1. Translated by Thomas Wright. London: Trubner, 1884, p. 88. In Roy Cave and Herbert Coulson, *A Source Book for Medieval Economic History.* New York: Biblo and Tannen, 1965, pp. 46–48.

13. A Monastic Fish Farm

Although the fisherman in Document 12 seems to be an independent trader, not all fishermen were so free. In the following document, Louis the Pious, a king of the Franks, grants a fishing spot to the abbey at New Corvey in A.D. 832. Included with the abbey are 32 serfs, tied to the land, who will do all the actual work involved in fishing (e.g., maintaining the fish supply, catching the fish, transporting and selling the fish). The abbey, however, will get all the monetary profit from that fishing. King Louis, on the other hand, hopes to profit spiritually from his donation. The writ declares, "We hope to receive the reward of eternal life through this distribution of temporal gifts."

As a result of such donations, monasteries often grew very wealthy. Although abbots' main concern was supposed to be the spiritual advancement of their subordinate monks, abbots frequently were full-time estate managers, overseeing the complex financial arrangements of the abbey. For example, the monastery's property could be scattered over a large area. As in this case, land grants were described in the vernacular Frankish tongue to specify its precise location.

The importance of monasteries meant that important people were frequently put in charge of them. In the case of Corvey, Warin, the king's own cousin, was the abbot.

The king therefore was giving money not only to an abbey but also to a family member. Church and state were intricately interwoven in the Middle Ages.

Although monasteries did become centers of wealth, it would be a mistake to assume that they therefore always abandoned their spiritual vocation. Corvey, for example, would go on to house one of the largest libraries in western Europe, thereby advancing education and learning throughout medieval Europe. The abbey also produced a plethora of missionaries, who left the comforts of home to bring Christianity to others; perhaps the most famous is St. Ansgar, the "Apostle of Scandinavia."

In the name of our Lord and Saviour, Jesus Christ. Louis, by the grace of God, Emperor Augustus. If, of our charity, we have provided churches in places dedicated to divine worship, and in the same place have made refuges for the servants of God, we not only thereby adhere to the honorable custom of royal munificence, but we hope to receive the reward of eternal life through this distribution of temporal gifts.

Wherefore be it known to all, both present and future, that, by these presents, we have granted for the love of God and for the salvation of our soul, to the monastery which is called New Corvey, which we built in Saxony in honor of Saint Stephen, the first martyr, and at the head of which is our faithful cousin Warin, its first abbot, a certain fishery in the River Weser. This fishery is in the village called Wimode, adjoining the villa of Liusci, the earldom of Count Abbo. And because it is constructed in the likeness of stakes which the inhabitants of the district call *Hocas*, it is known by the natives under the local name of *Hocwar*. It is at present within our

Eadwine the Scribe. The tonsure (shaved head) shows clearly that the scribe was a monk. In his right hand, he holds a feather pen; in his left hand he holds a knife to scrape away any mistakes. From the Canterbury Psalter, c. 1150. © 2008 Jupiterimages Corporation.

right, and the same Count Abbo formerly held it as a benefice from us. But seeing that the same fishery without serfs, who were thought of in this provision, could not be very useful to the brethren, we have granted thirty-two serfs to be wholly and entirely in possession of that monastery. And we have also granted to the monastery whatever Abbo had in benefice pertaining to that same fishery for as long as the monks living there continue to pray for divine clemency for us. And in order that this charter may be held in high regard, and accepted by our faithful people in future, we have ordered it to be sealed with our seal below, and we have signed it with our hand.

Source: Schaten, N. *Annales Paderbornenses.* Vol. 1. Neuhaus: 1693, p. 90. In Roy Cave and Herbert Coulson, *A Source Book for Medieval Economic History.* New York: Biblo and Tannen, 1965, pp. 60–61. Translation adjusted by Lawrence Morris.

14. How to Run a Manorial Estate

Walter of Henley, the author of the following document from the thirteenth century, knew what he was talking about; he had been a bailiff (chief manager of a manorial estate) before he became a monk. The job of running a large manor was complex. For starters, the economy was very mixed. As the following excerpt from Walter's account makes clear, an estate could have dove houses, arable land, pasture land, woods for lumber, beehives, and many other sources of income. A skilled estate manager would need to know the ins and outs of all these industries.

Bailiffs had a proverbial distrust of the peasant workers on an estate. According to Walter, "customary servants neglect their work," and dairymaids lie about the amount of milk produced because "they give away and waste and consume the milk." Much of Husbandry, *the customary English title of Walter's guide to running a manor, is concerned with estimating how much money a manor should be producing to make sure that the laborers are working hard enough. Working for the lord, as a bailiff does, Walter was naturally concerned with eliminating labor inefficiencies, but the modern reader may perhaps have more sympathy for the generally poor farm workers who spent their lives making profits for the wealthy landowners.*

Husbandry *gives us a fascinating insight into thirteenth-century English rural life. Even if we are not interested in figuring out the value of a manor, the document gives us fun facts. For example, the peasant received eight weeks of vacation spread throughout the year in holidays (compare the American custom of two weeks' vacation!). The best time to buy cattle was in late spring, between Easter and Pentecost (Whitsuntide), once the plowing had already been done, and the demand for oxen had subsequently decreased. Most importantly, Walter points out that although a three-field rotation system, in which crops were changed to allow the soil to regain its richness, was common, some places still employed the old-fashioned and less efficient two-field system. Despite bailiffs such as Walter, economic inefficiencies remained.*

Survey your lands and tenements by true and sworn men. First survey your courts, gardens, dove-houses, cartilages, what they are worth yearly beyond the valuation; and then how many acres are in the demesne, and how much is in each *cultura*, and what they should be worth yearly; and how many acres of pasture, and what they are worth yearly; and all other several pastures, and what they are worth yearly; and wood, what you can sell without loss and destruction, and what it is worth yearly beyond the return; and free tenants, how much each holds and by what service; and customary tenants, how much each holds and by what services, and let customs be put in money. And of all other definite things, put what they are worth yearly. And by the surveyors inquire with how much of each sort of corn you can sow an acre of land, and how much cattle you can have on each manor. By the extent you should be able to know how much your lands are worth yearly, by which you can order your living, as I have said before. Further, if your bailiffs or provosts say in their account that so many quarters have been sown on so many acres, go to the extent, and perhaps you shall find fewer acres than they have told you and more quarters sown than was necessary. For you have at the end of the extent the quantity of each kind of corn with which one shall sow an acre of land. Further, if it is necessary to put out more money or less for ploughs, you shall be confirmed by the extent. How? I will tell you.

If your lands are divided in three, one part for winter seed, the other part for spring seed, and the third part fallow, then is a ploughland nine score acres. And if your lands are divided in two, as in many places, the one half sown with winter seed and spring seed, the other half fallow, then shall a ploughland be eight score acres. Go to the extent and see how many acres you have in the demesne, and there you should be confirmed. Some men will tell you that a plough cannot work eight score or nine score acres yearly, but I will show you that it can. You know well that a furlong ought to be forty perches long and four wide, and the king's perch is sixteen feet and a half; then an acre is sixty-six feet in width. Now in ploughing go thirty-six times round to make the ridge narrower, and when the acre is ploughed, then you have made seventy-two furlongs, which are six leagues, for be it known that twelve furlongs are a league. And the horse or ox must be very poor that cannot from the morning go easily in pace three leagues in length from his starting-place and return by three o'clock.

And I will show you by another reason that it can do as much. You know that there are in the year fifty-two weeks. Now take away eight weeks for holy days and other hindrances, then there are forty-four working weeks left. And in all that time the plough shall only have to plough for fallow or for spring or winter sowing three roods and a half daily, and for second fallowing an acre. Now see if a plough were properly kept and followed, if it could not do as much daily. And if you have land on which you can have cattle, take pains to stock it as the land requires. And know for truth if you are duly stocked, and your cattle well guarded and managed, it shall yield three times the land by the extent. If free tenants or customary tenants deny services or customs you will see the definite amount in the extent. . . .

At the beginning of the fallowing and second fallowing and of sowing, let the bailiff, and the messer, or the provost, be all the time with the ploughmen, to see that they do their work well and thoroughly, and at the end of the day see how much they have done, and for so much shall they answer each day after unless they can show a sure hindrance. And because customary servants neglect their work it is necessary to guard against their fraud; further, it is necessary that they are overseen often; and besides the bailiff must oversee all, that they all work well, and if they do not well, let them be reproved. . . .

You know surely that an acre sown with wheat takes three ploughings, except lands which are sown yearly; and that, one with the other, each ploughing is worth sixpence, and harrowing a penny, and on the acre it is necessary to sow at least two bushels. Now two bushels at Michaelmas are worth at least twelvepence, and weeding a halfpenny, and reaping fivepence, and carrying in August a penny; the straw will pay for the threshing. At three times your sowing you ought to have six bushels, worth three shillings, and the cost amounts to three shillings and three halfpence, and the ground is yours and not reckoned. . . .

Sort out your cattle once a year between Easter and Whitsuntide—that is to say, oxen, cows, and herds—and let those that are not to be kept be put to fatten; if you lay out money to fatten them with grass you will gain. And know for truth that bad beasts cost more than good. Why? I will tell you. If it be a draught beast he must be more thought of than the other and more spared, and because he is spared the others are burdened for his lack. And if you must buy cattle, buy them between Easter and Whitsuntide, for then beasts are spare and cheap. And change your horses before they are too old and worn out or maimed, for with little money you can rear good and young ones, if you sell and buy in season. It is well to know how one ought to keep cattle, to teach your people, for when they see that you understand it they will take the more pains to do well.

HOW MUCH MILK YOUR COWS SHOULD YIELD

If your cows were sorted out, so that the bad were taken away, and your cows fed in pasture of slat marsh, then ought two cows to yield a wey of cheese, and half a gallon of butter a week. And if they were fed in pasture of wood, or in meadows after mowing, or in stubble, then three cows ought to yield a wey of cheese and half a gallon of butter a week between Easter and Michaelmas. And twenty ewes which are fed in pasture of salt marsh ought to and can yield cheese and butter as the two cows before named. Now there are many servants and provosts and dairymaids who will contradict this thing, and that is because they give away and waste and consume the milk; and know for certainty the milk is not wasted otherwise but in the same thing, for so much they ought to and can yield, for I have proved it. And you will see it with regard to the three cows that ought to make a wey. One of these cows would be poor, from which one could not have in two days a cheese worth a halfpenny; that would be in six days three cheeses, price three halfpence. And the seventh day shall help the tithe and the waste there may be. Now that will be three halfpence in twenty-four weeks which are between Easter and Michaelmas—that is, three shillings. Now put as much for the second cow, and as much for the third, and then you will have nine shillings, and thereby you have a wey of cheese by ordinary sale. Now one of these three cows would be poor, from which one could not have the third of a pottle of butter a week, and if the gallon of butter is worth sixpence then is the third of a pottle worth a penny. . . .

You can well have three acres weeded for a penny, and an acre of meadow mown for fourpence, and an acre of waste meadow for threepence-halfpenny, and an acre of meadow raised for a penny-halfpenny, and an acre of waste for a penny-farthing. And know that five men can well reap and bind two acres a day of each kind of corn, more or less. And where each takes twopence a day then you must give fivepence an acre, and when four take a penny-halfpenny a day and the fifth twopence, because he is binder, then you must give fourpence for the acre. And, because in many places they do not reap by the acre, one can know by the reapers and by the work done what they do, but keep the reapers by the band, that is to say, that five men or women, whichever you will, who are called half men, make a band, and twenty-five men make five bands, and twenty-five men can reap and bind ten acres a day working all day, and in ten days a hundred acres, and in twenty days two hundred acres by five score. And see then how many acres there are to reap throughout, and see if they agree with the days and pay them then, and if they account for more days than is right according to this reckoning, do not let them be paid, for it is their fault that they have not reaped the amount and have not worked so well as they ought. . . .

If you wish to farm out the issue of your stock, you can take four-and-sixpence clear for each cow and acquit the tithe, and save for yourself the cow and calf; and for a sheep sixpence and acquit the tithe, and keep the sheep and lamb; and a sow should bring you six shillings and sixpence a year and acquit the tithe, and save for yourself the sow; and each goose ought to bring you sevenpence-halfpenny clear and acquit the tithe and save the goose; and each hen should bring you ninepence clear and acquit the tithe and save the hen. And ten quarters of apples and pears should yield seven tuns of cider; and a quarter of nuts should yield four gallons of oil. And each hive of bees ought to yield for two hives a year, one with another, for some yield nothing and other three or four a year, and in some places they are given nothing to eat all winter and in some they are fed then, and where they are fed you can feed eight hives all winter with a gallon of honey; and if you only collect the honey every two years, you should have two gallons of honey from each hive.

Source: Walter of Henley. *Husbandry.* Translated by Elizabeth Lamond. London: Longmans, 1890, pp. 7–9, 11, 19, 23–27, 69, 79–81. In Roy Cave and Herbert Coulson, *A Source Book for Medieval Economic History.* New York: Biblo and Tannen, 1965, pp. 50–55. Modified slightly by Lawrence Morris.

Trade and Monetary Systems

Human communities have almost never lived in complete isolation from each other—there have always been "neighbors." During the Middle Ages and *Renaissance*, however, the peoples of the world began, at one and the same time, to realize just how big and just how small the world was. By the year 1500, Europeans and Chinese had met each other face to face, and Native Americans had laid eyes on the first documented travelers to cross the Atlantic Ocean. Like Christopher Columbus's voyage in 1492, much of this exploration was conducted primarily in the interest of trade. Columbus himself was in search of a shortcut to the lucrative East Indies, whose wares had been on sale in northern European markets from the early Middle Ages, as Document 20 shows. Despite the successes of medieval merchants, trade was not an easy business, and numerous complications could ruin a merchant. Document 21 outlines some of the hazards of shipping products by seas: pirates, storms, crooked captains, and discontented sailors.

International trade and travel brought new ideas along with new products. Marco Polo's fourteenth-century accounts of the Far East found an eager readership in Europe. Document 15 gives an example of one of the new ideas brought back from Asia: paper money. Marco Polo describes with amazement how the Great Khan was able to print money from the bark of trees, instead of using metallic coins like those circulating in Europe. Although Polo incorrectly believed that this innovation had enabled the Khan to acquire his vast wealth, Polo did indicate the requirements for a sound and secure money system: the backing of the government and the faith of the people. Sometimes foreign ideas were so valuable that they were intentionally stolen. Document 18 records a case of industrial espionage from the sixth century A.D.

Not all foreigners' ideas were welcomed, however. The Christian *Byzantine Empire* objected to the propaganda that Muslim Egyptians had started placing on the parchment that they sold to Byzantium (Document 17). A trade war erupted that resulted in the destruction of a hitherto mutually lucrative enterprise; Egypt lost an important customer for its papyrus, and the Byzantine Empire lost not only a major supplier of papyrus but also a market for its coins. Before the trade war, Egypt had used the Byzantine currency as its own local money.

Although international trade helped spur the economies of the world during the Middle Ages and Renaissance, not everyone profited equally. The bankruptcy laws given in Document 16 show that economic failure then as now was a realistic possibility. Fortunately, the legal system protected at least high-status victims from the worst effects: hunger and homelessness. The lower classes were often more disadvantaged. The weavers examined in Document 19 were not allowed to sell their products at full price and were denied all access to political control. Most of them would not have been able to purchase the imported luxury goods for sale in Winchester town center.

15. Marco Polo on Paper Money

Paper money circulated much earlier in the Far East than in Europe; China used paper money as early as the ninth century, whereas paper money did not come into wide circulation in Europe until the seventeenth century. As his description makes clear, the concept of paper money amazed the European Marco Polo. Europe, with its system of metal coins, was still using a "commodity" currency, in which the form of currency (precious metals in this case) was useful and therefore valuable; gold coins could be made into gold rings, for example. Paper money is a "credit" currency, in which the value of the currency derives not from its intrinsic usefulness, but rather solely from the fact that the government and people have assigned it an arbitrary value. Paper money is valuable not because you can make it into paper airplanes but because the central government and other people declare it to be valuable. In fact, even commodity currencies are mostly credit currencies, given that what makes a gold coin valuable is not the fact that it can be turned into a ring but rather the value that the government and people declare the coin to have.

Marco Polo's grasp of modern economics was, of course, slim, but his narrative highlights the necessary ingredients for a strong credit currency: strong government control and the acceptance of the populace. A complex system of seals guarded the currency against counterfeiters and demonstrated government support, and the monetary policy of the mint, which exchanged paper money for precious metals and other substances, ensured that there were no competing currencies in circulation. Moreover, if someone failed to accept the money, the guilty party suffered the death penalty.

Marco Polo felt that the ability to create paper money cheaply and easily had made the Khan the wealthiest ruler in the world because he could simply print more money whenever he wanted. This attitude, however, shows how little inflation was understood. When more money is put into an economic system, the prices of goods rise to absorb the "extra" currency. Net wealth, in fact, remains the same.

BOOK 2, CHAPTER XXIV

How the Great Kaan Causeth the Bark of Trees, Made Into Something Like Paper, to Pass for Money Over All his Country

Now that I have told you in detail of the splendor of this city of the Emperor's, I shall proceed to tell you of the mint which he hath in the same city, in the which he hath his money coined and struck, as I shall relate to you. And in doing so I shall make manifest to you how it is that the Great Lord may well be able to accomplish even much more than I have told you, or am going to tell you, in this Book. For, tell it how I might, you never would be satisfied that I was keeping within truth and reason!

The Emperor's mint then is in this same city of Cambaluc, and the way it is wrought is such that you might say he hath the secret of alchemy in perfection, and you would be right! For he makes his money after this fashion.

He makes them take of the bark of a certain tree, in fact of the mulberry tree, the leaves of which are the food of the silkworms—these trees being so numerous that whole districts are full of them. What they take is a certain fine white skin which lies between the wood of the tree and the thick outer bark, and this they make into something resembling sheets of paper, but black. When these sheets have been prepared they are cut up into pieces of different sizes. The smallest of these sizes is worth a half tornesel; the next, a little larger, one tornesel; one, a little larger still, is worth half a silver groat of Venice; another a whole groat; others yet two groats, five groats, and ten groats. There is also a kind worth one bezant of gold, and others of three bezants, and so up to ten. All these pieces of paper are issued with as much solemnity and authority as if they were of pure gold or silver; and on every piece a variety of officials, whose duty it is, have to write their names, and to put their seals. And when all is pre-

Marco Polo delivering the Pope's letters to Kublai Khan. In this image, Kublai Khan looks misleadingly European, although the attendant in the back does exhibit more stereotypical Asian features. © 2008 Jupiterimages Corporation.

pared duly, the chief officer deputed by the Khan smears the seal entrusted to him with vermilion, and impresses it on the paper, so that the form of the seal remains printed upon it in red; the money is then authentic. Anyone forging it would be punished with death. And the Khan causes every year to be made such a vast quantity of this money, which costs him nothing, that it must equal in amount all the treasure in the world.

With these pieces of paper, made as I have described, he causes all payments on his own account to be made; and he makes them to pass current universally over all his kingdoms and provinces and territories, and whithersoever his power and sovereignty extends. And nobody, however important he may think himself, dares to refuse them on pain of death. And indeed everybody takes them readily, for wheresoever a person may go throughout the Great Khan's dominions he shall find these pieces of paper current, and shall be able to transact all sales and purchases of goods by means of them just as well as if they were coins of pure gold. And all the while they are so light that ten bezants' worth does not weigh one golden bezant.

Furthermore all merchants arriving from India or other countries, and bringing with them gold or silver or gems and pearls, are prohibited from selling to any one but the Emperor. He has twelve experts chosen for this business, men of shrewdness and experience in such affairs; these appraise the articles, and the Emperor then pays a liberal price for them in those pieces of paper. The merchants accept his price readily, for in the first place they would not get so good a one from anybody else, and secondly they are paid without any delay. And with this paper-money they can buy what

A portrait of Marco Polo from a German pamphlet. © 2008 Jupiterimages Corporation.

they like anywhere over the Empire, whilst it is also vastly lighter to carry about on their journeys. And it is a truth that the merchants will several times in the year bring wares to the amount of 400,000 bezants, and the Grand Sire pays for all in that paper. So he buys such a quantity of those precious things every year that his treasure is endless, whilst all the time the money he pays away costs him nothing at all. Moreover, several times in the year proclamation is made through the city that any one who may have gold or silver or gems or pearls, by taking them to the mint shall get a handsome price for them. And the owners are glad to do this, because they would find no other purchaser give so large a price. Thus the quantity they bring in is marvellous, though those who do not choose to do so may let it alone. Still, in this way, nearly all the valuables in the country come into the Khan's possession.

When any of those pieces of paper are spoilt—not that they are so very flimsy neither—the owner carries them to the mint, and by paying three per cent on the value, he gets new pieces in exchange. And if any baron, or any one else soever, hath need of gold or silver or gems or pearls, in order to make plate, or girdles, or the like, he goes to the mint and buys as much as he list, paying in this paper-money.

Now you have heard the ways and means whereby the Great Khan may have, and in fact has, more treasure than all the Kings in the World; and you know all about it and the reason why.

Source: Polo, Marco, and Rustichello of Pisa. *The Travels of Marco Polo: The Complete Yule-Cordier Edition.* 2nd ed. Edited by Henry Yule and Henri Cordier. New York: Scribner, 1903, pp. 423–26. Slightly modified by Lawrence Morris.

16. Twelfth-Century Bankruptcy

The financial inability to pay bills arose in the Middle Ages just as it does today, and the result was frequently the same: bankruptcy. In the following dialogue, a master instructs a student on the rules that the Exchequer (the accounting office and central bank of medieval England) has put into place for debt collection. The document undoubtedly served as a guide as much for those on the brink of financial ruin as for those officials charged with recovering debts.

Much of the dialogue, indeed, concerns the protection of the debtor from his creditors. To protect the debtor, creditors were allowed to seize only the "movable" assets of the debtor—that is, those belongings that could be easily moved, such as money, precious jewels, wine, cattle, and sheep. Creditors were forbidden to seize those assets that were not movable, primarily, of course, the debtor's house, home, and lands. No debtor, therefore, could be made homeless by his creditors, according to these rules.

The law protected not only the debtor's home but also his food supply. According to the document, creditors could not seize any food supplies intended for the use of the debtor, his wife and children, or his household (i.e., his servants and other dependents). Nor could creditors seize so many assets that the debtor was unable to purchase such food supplies for himself. This legislation not only prevented the starvation of the debtor and his family but also ensured the well-being of all the household employees. The financial crisis of the debtor was thus in some ways restrained from creating further financial crises among the debtor's employees.

The privileges of rank, in addition to food and housing, were also protected by the bankruptcy legislation. A knight was specifically allowed to keep his horse regardless of how much he owed. The horse, in fact, served as a badge of knighthood; the Latin eques ("knight") meant essentially "one who owns a horse." As a result, depriving a knight of his horse would be equivalent to demoting the knight from nobleman to commoner. Knights, moreover, supplied much of the king's military power; active warriors, indeed, were entitled to keep not only their horses but also their weapons and armor, despite their debts, precisely so that they could be of continued service to the king in wartime. Only when a knight refused to serve in war or refused to pay scutage (a fixed sum of money that a knight paid to the king in lieu of coming in person to serve in the army) could his horse and weapons be removed from him. Refusing to fight could thus demote a knight to commoner, whereas simple financial insolvency could not.

Although debtors thus had certain protections, the creditors were not powerless. In addition to seizing most of the debtor's belongings, they could also seize the belongings of anyone who was "bound" to the debtor—that is, anyone who was in a feudal relationship with the debtor. In these relationships, a lord would grant property and possessions to another man in return for certain rents, services, or other benefits; when a lord went bankrupt, the creditors could seize those possessions, rents, and benefits that were owed by the lord's men to that bankrupt lord. As a result, bound men had a financial interest in ensuring that their lord remained financially healthy.

Master. . . . The chattels which are lawfully sold, then, of debtors who do not of their own will pay what is demanded of them are those goods which are movable and which move themselves: such are gold, silver, and vessels composed of the same; also precious stones, and changes of vestments and the like; also both kinds of horses, the ordinary ones, namely, and the untamed ones; herds also of oxen and flocks of sheep, and other things of this kind. The nature of fruits also and of some victuals is movable, so that, namely, they may be freely sold, deducting only the necessary expenses of the debtor for his victuals—so that, namely, he may provide for his needs, not his extravagance, and likewise may satisfy nature, not gluttony. Nor are these necessaries furnished to the debtor alone, but to his wife and children and to the household, which he was seen to have had while he was living at his own expense.

Student. Why dost Thou Say "of some" Victuals?

Master. Victuals which are prepared by them for daily use, and which without essential change are suitable for eating—such as bread and drink—may by no means be sold. Of victuals, then, only those are lawfully sold which, aside from necessary uses, had been reserved by the masters themselves that they might be for sale, such as meats laid in salt, cheeses, honey, wines, and the like.

And mark that if that debtor who is not solvent have once obtained the belt of knighthood, though the other things are sold, nevertheless a horse, not any one but the one he uses, shall be reserved for him; lest he who, by rank, has become a knight, may be compelled to go on foot. But if he be a knight who "Delights in the glory of arms, finds pleasure in using his weapons" and who, his merits demanding, ought to be reckoned among the brave, all the armature of his body, together with the horses necessary to carry it, shall be left entirely free by the sellers; so that, when it is necessary, equipped with arms and horses, he can be called to the service of king and kingdom. If, however, this man whom the law has partially favored, hearing of the need of the king or kingdom, shall conceal and absent himself, or, being summoned for this purpose, does not come—provided he serve not at his own expense, but at the king's—and have not given a plain excuse for his absence, the sellers shall not refrain from those arms, etc., either; but, content with the one single horse left to him on account of the dignity of knighthood, he shall be subject to the general rule.

The sheriff, moreover, shall take care to warn his seller that, with regard to the things to be sold, they observe this order: the movable goods of anyone shall first be sold, but they shall spare, as much as possible, the plough oxen, by which agriculture is wont to be carried on; lest, that failing him, the debtor be still further reduced to want in the future. But if even thus, indeed, the sum required is not raised, the plough oxen are not to be spared. When, therefore, all the saleable things that belong especially to him have been sold, if the amount is still not made up, they shall approach the estates of his bondsmen and lawfully sell their chattels, observing at the same time the aforesaid order and rule; for these are known to belong to the lord, as has been said above. This being done, whether the required sum is thus made up or not, our law orders the sellers to quit; unless, perhaps, it be scutage which is required from a lord. For if the chief lord who is bound to the king for scutage does not pay, not only his own, but all the chattels of his knights and bondsmen everywhere, are sold, for the matter of scutages regards his knights in great part; for thy are not due to the king except by knights and by reason of military service. I myself, indeed, whose memory is not yet hoary, have seen how, for the personal debts of those who did not render satisfaction, not only their own, but also the chattels of their knights and bondsmen were lawfully sold. But the law of the illustrious king has decreed that this is to be observed only in the matter of scutages, the order being regarded that first their own, then the goods of others are to be sold. But if the knights have paid to the lord the produce of their fiefs, and are willing to prove this by offering a pledge, the law forbids that their chattels be sold for those payments which are required from the lords.

Likewise the sheriff is to be warned that he diligently and carefully investigate, as well as he can, if there is anyone in his county in debt to that debtor for the payment of money lent to him or deposited with him. But if it be found that there is, the sum which is required from his creditor, the man bound to the king, shall be exacted from that debtor, and he shall be prevented by authority of the public law from being answerable for it to that creditor.

Source: Attributed to Richard, son of Bishop Nigel of Ely. "Dialogue Concerning the Exchequer." In *Select Historical Documents of the Middle Ages*. Ed. Ernest Henderson. London: Bell, 1905, pp. 117–19.

17. A Religious Trade War

Although trade frequently flourished between countries professing different religions, religious divides could seriously impact a nation's economy. The following extract narrates one such economic squabble prompted by a religious difference near the start of the eighth century. The

Byzantine Empire, *referred to as "the Greeks" in the extract, was overwhelmingly Christian, but its lands had shrunk dramatically as Muslim peoples assaulted and conquered its holdings in the Middle East and Turkey. Despite this environment of general animosity and mistrust, the empire traded briskly with its Muslim neighbors in a variety of goods.*

One such tradable commodity was papyrus, called karâtis *in this document (although the term can also refer to packing cloths). Papyrus, of course, is an inexpensive writing material, similar to modern-day paper. Indeed, the word* paper *comes ultimately from the word* papyrus. *Papyrus grows only in certain climates, however; the climate of much of North Africa is ideal for papyrus, but Europe in general cannot sustain a substantial papyrus crop. As a result, by the High Middle Ages, Muslim countries had developed a monopoly on the papyrus trade.*

In return for papyrus, the Greek Empire gave the Egyptian Muslims, the main producers of papyrus, dînârs, *a form of currency. The* dînârs *were not valuable in and of themselves—they were not made from particularly precious metal; instead, the* dînârs *were useful because they served precisely as the form of money used in Egypt. Essentially, the Egyptians were using Byzantine coinage. This situation is not unlike some third-world countries in which U.S. dollars or EU euros are preferred to the local currency. In the case of Egypt, however, there was no local currency; the Byzantine money was the local money.*

This valuable trade route fell apart, however, when the Egyptian leader 'Abd-al-Malik insisted that all sheets of papyrus be shipped with a message in praise of Allah written across the very top. The Christian Byzantine emperor and presumably his people were very unhappy with this religious propaganda, considered heresy by them, emblazoned on their writing supplies. In an attempt to force Egypt to remove the religious propaganda, the Byzantine Empire threatened to cut off the supply of dînârs.

Unfortunately for Byzantium, Egypt was able to call its bluff. Rather than cave into Byzantine demands, the Egyptians began producing their own currency, thereby destroying the need to rely on Byzantine coinage. Although the author of the following document viewed this action as a triumph, the economic reality must have been somewhat different. Because the Byzantine market for papyrus had been essentially destroyed, demand for Egyptian papyrus must have shrunk considerably. The result was undoubtedly a fall in the price of papyrus, which consequently would have reduced the incomes of all workers in the papyrus industry. A religious victory entailed an economic defeat.

The Muslims were not the only ones to suffer. Western Europe in general, cut off from abundant papyrus supplies, turned to parchment, that is, writing materials made from the skins of animals. Parchment was extremely expensive, and the cost made books hard to afford and made literacy itself a luxury. Religious turmoil caused economic distress and a decline in education.

In the following document, the Copts who are mentioned are a still-existing Egyptian Christian group. Although most Egyptians today speak Arabic, the Coptic language (used mostly in church services) derives from the ancient language of Egyptians—the language of the hieroglyphs.

The Greeks used to get the *karâtîs* from Egypt, and the Arabs used to get the *dînars* from the Greeks. 'Abd-al-Malik ibn-Marwân was the first to inscribe on the upper part of these fabrics such phrases as "Declare: Allah is one!" and others with the name of Allah. One day, he received from the Byzantine king a message saying, "You have recently introduced upon your *karâtîs* some inscription that we hate. If you leave that out, well and good; otherwise, you shall see on the *dînârs* the name of your Prophet associated with things you hate." This was too much for 'Abd-al-Malik, who hated to abolish a worthy law that he had established. He thereupon sent for Khâlid ibn-Yâzid ibn-Mu'âwiyah and said to him, "O abu-Hâshim! It is a calamity!" Khâlid replied, "Be free from your fright, Commander of the Believers; declare the use of their *dînârs* illegal; strike new coinage in place of them, and let not these infidels be free from what they hate to see on the fabrics." "Thou hast eased my mind," said 'Abd-al-Malik, "may Allah give thee ease!" He then struck the *dînârs*.

According to 'Awânah ibn-al-Hakam, the Copts used to inscribe the word "Christ" at the top part of the *karâtis*, and to ascribe divinity to him (may Allah be highly exalted above that!), and they used to put the sign of the cross in place of "In the name of Allah, the compassionate, the merciful." That is why the Byzantine king was disgusted, and his anger was aroused with the change that 'Abd-al-Malik introduced.

According to al-Madâ'ini, it was stated by Maslamah ibn-Muhârib that Khâlid ibn-Yazîd advised 'Abd-al-Malik to declare the use of the Greek *dînârs* illegal, to prohibit their circulation and to stop the sending of the *karâtis* to the Byzantine empire. Accordingly, no *karâtis* were carried there for some time.

Source: al-Baladhuri. *Kitab Futuh al-buldan*. In *The Origins of the Islamic State*. Ed. Philip Hitti. New York: Columbia, 1916, 383–84.

18. Industrial Espionage

Reliance on international trade could greatly complicate the political situation. Economic warfare, as Document 17 also demonstrates, could be an effective tool in political conflict. As a result, reducing dependence on foreign trade could increase a nation's or region's political security.

In the following document, the remnant of the Roman Empire in the sixth century A.D. plans to break the Middle East's and India's control of the silk trade through industrial espionage. Indian monks go to Emperor Justinian, describe how silk is made, and offer to procure the silkworm eggs necessary to begin a domestic silk industry. In return for promises of generous financial reward (which is probably what the monks were after), the informants travel back to India and return with the silkworm eggs. According to Procopius, the author of this document, the Roman silk industry, based in Byzantium (Constantinople), took off. Industrial espionage benefited the economy of the Roman Empire and limited dependence on potentially hostile foreign nations.

About the same time there came from India certain monks, and when they had satisfied Justinian Augustus that the Romans no longer should buy silk from the Persians, they promised the emperor in an interview that they should provide the materials for making silk so that never should the Romans seek business of this kind from their enemy the Persians, or from any other people whatsoever. They said that they were formerly in Serinda, which they call the region frequented by the people of the Indies, and there they learned perfectly the art of making silk. Moreover, to the emperor who plied them with many questions as to whether he might have the secret, the monks replied that certain worms were manufacturers of silk, nature itself forcing them to keep always at work; the worms could certainly not be brought here alive, but they could be grown easily and without difficulty; the eggs of single hatchings are innumerable; as soon as they are laid men cover them with dung and keep them warm for as long as it is necessary so that they produce insects. When they had announced these tidings, led on by liberal promises of the emperor to prove the fact, they returned to India. When they had brought the eggs to Byzantium, the method having been learned, as I have said, they changed them by metamorphosis into worms which fed on the leaves of mulberry. Thus began the art of making silk from that time on in the Roman Empire.

Source: Procopius. *Procopii Caesariensis Historiarum Temporis Sui Tetras Altera, De Bello Gótico*. Translated by Claudius Maltretus. Venice: n.p., 1729, bk. 4, ch. 17, p. 212. In Roy Cave and Herbert Coulson, *A Source Book for Medieval Economic History*. New York: Biblo and Tannen, 1965, p. 244.

19. Price Fixing

The scientific study of economics did not begin in earnest until the nineteenth century; medieval authorities, as a result, had to do without its benefits. Although most modern economists advocate the free market, medieval authorities frequently attempted to destroy the free market. The economy was undoubtedly hurt as a result, and individuals suffered.

As the following document shows, the weavers and fullers (preparers of cloth) of the English town of Winchester were disadvantaged politically and economically by the city authorities' attempts to control the price of cloth. City regulations from 1209 prohibited cloth manufacturers from selling their goods to anyone not from Winchester. This prohibition limited the demand for cloth and kept the prices down as a result. In an open market, the weaver would have been able to sell his goods to the highest bidder regardless of where that bidder was from. By limiting competition, however, the city authorities kept down the price of cloth and the profits of the weavers and fullers themselves.

Not only did the weavers and fullers suffer economic discrimination, but they also experienced political disenfranchisement. These cloth manufacturers were not considered "free," and as a result they could not participate actively in the governance of the city, nor could they bring lawsuits against free members of the city. Indeed, to become free, a weaver not only had to become wealthy but also had to renounce his trade. As a result, no weavers or fullers would ever become the political leaders of the city; they would never be the ones passing the laws. Indeed, only by preventing weavers from having any political power could such discriminatory laws as the one seen here be enacted.

THIS IS THE LAW OF THE FULLERS AND WEAVERS OF WINCHESTER

Be it known that no weaver or fuller may dry or dye cloth nor go outside the city to sell it. They may sell their cloth to no foreigner, but only to merchants of the city. And if it happens that, in order to enrich himself, one of the weavers or fullers wishes to go outside the city to sell his merchandise, he may be very sure that the honest men of the city will take all his cloth and bring it back to the city, and that he will forfeit it in the presence of the aldermen and honest men of the city. And if any weaver or fuller sell his cloth to a foreigner, the foreigner shall lose his cloth, and the other shall remain at the mercy of the city for as much as he has. Neither the weaver nor the fuller may buy anything except for his trade but by making agreement with the mayor. No free man can be accused by a weaver or a fuller, nor can a weaver or a fuller bear testimony against a free man. If any of them become rich, and wish to give up his trade, he may forswear it and turn his tools out of the house, and then do as such for the city as he is able in his freedom.

They have this law of the liberty and customs of London, just as they say.

Source: Leach, A. F., ed. *Beverley Town Documents*. London: Selden Society, 1900, pp. 134–35, Appendix II. In Roy Cave and Herbert Coulson, *A Source Book for Medieval Economic History*. New York: Biblo and Tannen, 1965, pp. 242–43.

20. International Trade

No one is able to produce independently everything that he or she needs or wants; as a result, trade with others is necessary. Communities are no different—they must trade with other communities to gain what they themselves cannot produce. This chain of trade can reach extraordinary lengths; Native American products from the Atlantic Coast could reach Native American communities on the Pacific Coast through a series of community exchanges.

Professional merchants could greatly ease this intercommunity and international trade. Merchants provided the smooth and quick delivery of goods to the communities in which those goods were in high demand. The distances that these merchants traveled, and the variety of goods in which they traded, can amaze the modern reader as much as the medieval one. In the following document, city names from across Europe, the Middle East, India, and China piled on top of each other give an idea of the thousands of miles traveled by medieval merchants in the course of earning their living. These merchants brought furs and swords from Europe to the East and brought back spices and perfumes otherwise unobtainable in Europe.

Although the following document, dating from A.D. 847, envisages the same merchants making the whole trip from Europe to China, in reality different merchants generally specialized in different legs of the journey. Some merchants would make the trip across the Arabian Peninsula, and others would carry goods from Middle East ports to the major ports of the European Mediterranean. The document does note, however, the increasing connection between Jews and trade. Deprived of their own homeland, Jews had set up communities throughout Eurasia and as a result were uniquely positioned for international trade. Unlike the Franks, who were largely confined to modern-day France, the Jews lived everywhere. Despite the Jews' economic advantages, however, this lack of a "home" often resulted in discrimination, as Document 19 demonstrates.

These merchants speak Arabic, Persian, Roman (Greek), the language of the Franks, Andalusians, and Slavs. They journey from west to east, from east to west, partly on land, partly by sea. They transport from the west eunuchs, female and male slaves, silk, castor, marten, and other furs, and swords. They take ship in the land of the Franks, on the Western Sea, and steer for Farama (Pelusium). There they load their goods on the backs of camels, and go by land to Kolzum (Suez) in five days' journey over a distance of twenty-five parasangs. They embark in the East Sea (Red Sea) and sail from Kolzum to El-Jar (port of Medina) and Jeddah (port of Mecca); then they go to Sind, India, and China. On their return they carry back musk, aloes, camphor, cinnamon, and other products of the Eastern countries to Kolzum, and bring them to Farama, where they again embark on the Western Sea. Some make sail for Constantinople to sell their goods to the Romans; others go to the palace of the king of the Franks to place their goods.

Sometimes these Jewish merchants prefer to carry their goods from the land of the Franks in the Western Sea, making for Antioch (at the mouth of the Orontes); thence they go by land to Al-Jabia, where they arrive after three days' march. There they embark on the Euphrates for Bagdad, and then sail down the Tigris to Al-Obolla. From Al-Obolla they sail for Oman, Sind, Hind (Hindustan), and China. All this is connected one with another.

These different journeys can also be made by land. The merchants who start from Spain or France go to Sous al-Akza (Morocco), and then to Tangiers, whence they march to Kairuwan (Tunisia), and the capital of Egypt. Thence they go to Al-Kamla, visit Damascus, Al-Kufa, Bagdad, and Basrah, cross Ahwaz, Fars, Kirman, Sind, Hind, and arrive at China. Sometimes they likewise take the route behind Rome, and passing through the country of the Slavs, arrive at Khamlij, the capital of the Khazars. They embark on the Jorjan Sea, arrive at Balkh, betake themselves from there across the Oxus and continue their journey toward Yourts of the Toghosghor, and from there to China.

Source: Jacobs, Joseph. *Jewish Contributions to Civilization*. Philadelphia: Jewish Publication Society, 1919, pp. 194–96. In Roy Cave and Herbert Coulson, *A Source Book for Medieval Economic History*. New York: Biblo and Tannen, 1965, pp. 151–52. Slightly modified by Lawrence Morris.

21. Sailing Laws

The complexity of international trade is amply demonstrated in the following laws from Barcelona in 1258. Not only could merchant ships be attacked by pirates, but in addition, sailors could get sick, ship captains and their merchant clients could have serious disagreements, and elected proctors could assume active command of the ship. As this sampling of laws shows, authorities attempted to foresee and forestall as many problems as possible, but maritime commerce remained a risky, if profitable, way to make a living.

Much of the legislation attempted to clarify the business relationship of the ship's captain and the merchant whose goods he was transporting. To render this relationship more transparent, each ship was commanded by provision 2 to have a clerk who would carefully record the agreements made between the parties. Other legislation, such as requiring the ship to go to sea in the event of a severe storm (provision 1), was designed to keep the ship and its precious cargo safe. Another protective measure required that each mariner carry weapons to defend the ship (and themselves) and that the ship itself carry ballistae, a kind of catapult (provisions 5–7).

The merchants were not the only ones legally protected, however; the sailors themselves were granted rights in law. In particular, the heirs of sailors who died were entitled to full wages, and sick sailors were entitled to at least partial wages depending on the circumstances (provision 20). Finally, provision 21 of these Barcelona statutes ensured that two proctors would be elected by the men of each ship. These proctors, under the advice of two men of their own choosing, had the power to veto decisions by the captain and merchant themselves in the best interest of the community of the entire ship. Such power was rarely used.

Be it known to all that we, James, by the grace of God, King of Aragon, of Majorca, and of Valencia, Count of Barcelona and Urgell, and Lord of Montpellier, hearing the ordinances written below, which you, James Gruny, our faithful servant, have made at our wish and command and with our consent, and which you have drawn up with the advice of the honest water-men of Barcelona and based upon the ordinance of the same, having heard, seen, and understood that the said ordinances were to be made in our honor, and for the use and welfare of the water-men of Barcelona and the citizens of Barcelona, having confirmed the document by the authentic application of our seal, we grant, approve, and confirm all and each of the undermentioned ordinances, made by you and the said honest men on our authority. Wishing that the said ordinances may endure and be observed as long as it shall please us and the said honest water-men of Barcelona, by commanding our mayors, and bailiffs, both present future, that they observe each and all of the undermentioned regulations, firmly and strictly, if they hope confidently for our grace and affection, and that they see that they are observed inviolably, so that they do not allow them to be disturbed by any one.

1. In the first place: we ordain, wish, and command, that the captain of a ship or vessel of any kind and the sailors and mariners shall not leave or depart from the ship or vessel in which they arrived, until all the merchandise, which is on the ship or vessel, be discharged on land, and until that same ship or vessel be emptied of ballast and moored. But the captain of that ship or vessel will be able to go on land with his clerk when he begins to discharge the cargo, if the sea be calm; and if perhaps the weather be such that he cannot discharge the cargo the said captain, if he be on land, shall immediately repair to the said ship or vessel, and if he cannot so repair by reason of the weather, his crew shall have full power and permission to depart with the ship or vessel from the place at which it arrived, and to go to the harbor or put out to sea. Nevertheless, if the said captain be unwilling to go to his ship, his merchants shall be able to order and command him firmly, on behalf of the Lord King and the said James Gruny, to repair to the said ship or vessel and to place upon him such penalty as the said James Gruny is empowered to place upon him. Moreover, the said captain of the ship shall not dare to stay on land until all merchandise which came in the ship or vessel be discharged. And if the merchants wish to disembark from the ship or vessel and a storm should arise after their disembarkation, the captain of the ship or vessel, if he be there, or his crew, shall have permission to withdraw from the place in which he was with that ship or vessel and with the merchandise contained therein, and of going to sea or putting into harbor. But if the mariners should not have done this, let each one incur a penalty of ten solidi of the money of Barcelona, and the captain of a ship fifty solidi, and the captain of a vessel thirty solidi; and over and above the said penalty the captains of ships and vessels shall be condemned to repair all the damage which the said merchants suffered through their fault. But of the penalties, both foregoing and those written below, the King will receive half, and the other half will go to the Order of Water-men of Barcelona. Moreover, these penalties and all those written below shall be paid as long as it be the will of the honest water-men of Barcelona.

2. Also: we order that every ship and vessel shall have a sworn clerk on every voyage, which clerk shall not write anything in the contract book of that ship or vessel unless both parties are present, namely the captain and the merchants, or the captain and his mariners; and the said clerk shall be a good and lawful man, and shall make out the expenses truly and lawfully, and all the mariners shall be expected to swear to the captains of the ships and vessels that to the best of their ability they will save, protect, and defend the captain and all his goods, and his ship or vessel, and its rigging and equipment, and all the merchants going with it, and all their goods and merchandise, by sea and land, in good faith and without fraud. Moreover, the said clerk shall be at least of the age of twenty years, and if the captains of the said ships or vessels do not wish to have the said clerk, they shall not leave Barcelona or any other place in which they may be, until they have another clerk, if they can find one.

3. Also: we command that on every ship which loads at sea, so that it is loaded with merchandise worth 2000 solidi (Barcelona money), the mariners must remain one night with their weapons on the ship; and after any vessel has loaded at sea with merchandise worth 1000 solidi (Barcelona money), half the mariners of that vessel with one officer shall be obliged to stay on their vessel for one night with their arms. Also we command that the captain of a ship or vessel shall have food in his ship or vessel sufficient for fifteen days; namely, bread, wine, salt meat, vegetables, oil, water, and two packets of candles. And if the said captain of ship or vessel be unwilling to do this, let him incur a penalty of twenty solidi, and each of the mariners and crew incur a penalty of five solidi. . . .

5. Also: we command that no boat shall load for a voyage nor send away any living merchandise and if it loads with heavy goods, it shall not dare to load except as far as the middle of the deck, and the captain of the boat shall take his boat, manned and with its rigging, just as is understood between the captain and the merchants whose merchandise it is; and if the said merchants fear they will be held as hostages in any place, the captain of the boat shall not enter with his boat nor go into the place suspected of holding them without the consent of the merchants. Moreover every boat shall be expected to carry two *ballistae* with their equipment, and a hundred spears and two shields; and every sailor is expected to bear a lance and a sword or bill. And if the captains of the boats should not observe this rule, they shall incur a penalty of ten solidi.

6. Also: we command that if any ship or vessel or boat be taken with its company to Barbary or other parts, it shall not take a guard except it be understood between the captain of the vessel and the partners of the said company.

7. Also: we command that every ship's mariner who is expected to do the work of a *ballistarius*, shall carry two *ballistae* of two feet, and one scaling ladder, and three hundred spears, and a helmet, and a breast-plate or corselet, and a straight and a curved sword. Likewise, the *ballistarii* of the other vessels shall be expected to carry the same weapons; but the other mariners on ships shall be expected to bear a breast-plate, and an iron helmet, or *cofa maresa*, and a shield, and two lances, and a straight or a curved sword. And if the said mariners do not have the said arms, the captains of the ships or vessels shall not take them; and if they do take them they shall pay as a penalty fifty solidi for each mariner. . . .

20. Also: we command that if any mariner should die in the service of any ship or vessel, from the time when that ship or vessel moved from the quay or river bank, or from any port, the said mariner shall have all his wages, just as was written in the contract book of that ship or vessel. And if any mariner be sick or be injured in his legs from the time when the ship or vessel put to sea, the captain of the ship or vessel shall give to the said mariner his needs in food for the whole voyage, if the mariner make the voyage, and the mariner shall have all his wages. But if the mariner be unwilling to go on the voyage, he shall not have any wages. But if the mariner has accepted such free victuals for doing work on the said ship or vessel, so that he cannot go on the said voyage to the knowledge of two honest men of the society, he shall have only half his wages; and if the captain of the said ship or vessel shall have paid all the wages of the mariner, he shall not be expected to put another mariner in the place of the one who remained ashore. And if the said captain shall have paid half the wages to the mariner who remained, the captain shall be expected to put another mariner in his place, and to give him the remaining half of the wages which he did not pay. And the merchants will be expected to give the other half of the wages to the mariner placed in the position of the other who did not go.

21. Also: we command that on every ship or vessel departing from the quay of Barcelona there shall be appointed and elected by the men in that ship or vessel two proctors distinguished by their knowledge and lawfulness whose commands they will obey, both the captain of the ship or vessel, and the mariners, and the merchants going in the ship, and all shall be expected to stand by and obey the orders of the two proctors. These two proctors shall elect other men of the ship with the advice of whom they will make and order all things which are to be done on that ship; and whatever is ordered by the seven men shall be strictly obeyed by all going in that ship. But in a vessel the two proctors shall elect another two by the advice of whom they shall ordain all things which are to be obeyed on that vessel. And the election of the two proctors shall be made within four days or eight before the departure of the said ship or vessel from the shores of Barcelona, and as many men of Barcelona as they find in other parts, Arab or Christian, shall be expected to stand by and obey the command and advice of the seven or four. And whatever the elected men do or ordain they shall do and ordain in the name of the Lord King and saving his jurisdiction, and in the name of the Council of the honest watermen of Barcelona. But if the two elected men should depart in ships from the place at which they arrived with the said ship, on their departure let them elect another two with the advice of the said five counselors who shall stand in their places, and those two elected on vessels shall elect another two with the advice of the said two counselors; and if the two elected by these two shall depart, let them elect another two, and thus in order; and whatever shall be done or ordered by those elected shall be strictly observed by all others, and this we command in the name of the Lord King and by virtue of an oath. Given at Barcelona on the twenty-sixth of August, in the year 1258.

Seal of James, by the grace of God, King of Aragon, etc.

Source: de Capmany, A. *Memorias Sobre la Marina, Comercio, y Artes de la Antigua Ciudad de Barcelona.* Vol. 2. Madrid: n.p., 1779–1792, pp. 23–30. In Roy Cave and Herbert Coulson, *A Source Book for Medieval Economic History.* New York: Biblo and Tannen, 1965, pp. 160–68.

Slavery

Before industrialization, rural economies demanded lots of human laborers: plowers, planters, threshers, herdsmen, and so on. Across the world, this high demand for human workers frequently has been met with slave labor in many different forms. The *Aztec* empire of Mexico made prisoners of war into slaves, and in China, certain populations were targeted for enslavement. Early medieval Europe had both slaves, who were either born or sold into slavery, and serfs, who had more legal rights even if they were not "free" in the modern sense of the word.

Although slavery was common, it was rarely pretty. Kind and fair masters existed, but the hardships of slavery come out clearly in the historical sources. Document 25 makes note of slaves' frequent attempts to escape, and Document 24 reports a horrid practice in which female slaves were raped and sold, pregnant, to foreign markets. One particularly evil master, Rauching, even buried two slaves alive when they dared to marry without his permission (Document 26).

The many writings that outline the hardships of slavery demonstrate that intellectuals frequently opposed the damaging effects of this economic system. Po Chu-i, in Document 22, presents a moving story in which the enlightened governor Yang Ch'eng informed the emperor of China that there were no slaves in his province—only people. Po Chu-i was particularly shocked about the damaging effects of slavery on families; he depicts children being taken away from their mothers. As Document 23 shows, having children or a spouse in slavery could effectively ensure that a slave would never seek freedom. Even though local leaders might seek to ameliorate the worst aspects of slavery, most societal institutions were fully integrated into the slavery/serf economy. In Document 27, for example, a religious abbey is given a present of slaves by the king.

22. Philosophical Resistance to Slavery in China

The following poem by the great Tang dynasty poet Po Chu-i (A.D. 772–846) captures the destructive effects of slavery on family life; family members are torn apart from each other in tears, never to meet again. In this particular example, the victims are the dwarfish peoples of a particular Chinese region, but the cruelties of slavery were to be found across the globe in the Middle Ages and well into modern times.

Fortunately for the inhabitants of Tao-Chou, an enlightened governor by the name of Yang Ch'eng ended the practice because of philosophical principles. When the emperor finally demanded to know why the dwarf slaves had not arrived, Yang Ch'eng replied that Tao-Chou had no dwarf slaves, only dwarfish people. Yang Ch'eng was implying that nature produced only people; slaves were produced by cruel tyrants. The emperor was so moved by this philosophical argument that he abolished the custom of enslaving the dwarfs of Tao-Chou. Most slaves around the world had to wait much longer than the ninth century to obtain their freedom.

The People of Tao-Chou

In the land of Tao-chou
Many of the people are dwarfs;

The tallest of them never grow to more than three feet.
They were sold in the market as dwarf slaves and yearly sent to Court;
Described as "an offering of natural products from the land of Tao-chou."
A strange "offering of natural products"; I never heard of one yet
That parted men from those they loved, never to meet again!
Old men—weeping for their grandsons; mothers for their children!
One day—Yang Ch'eng came to govern the land;
He refused to send up dwarf slaves in spite of incessant mandates.
He replied to the Emperor "Your servant finds in the Six Canonical Books
'In offering products, one must offer what is there, and not what isn't there'
On the waters and lands of Tao-chou, among all the things that live
I only find dwarfish people; no dwarfish slaves."
The Emperor's heart was deeply moved and he sealed and sent a scroll
"The yearly tribute of dwarfish slaves is henceforth annulled."
The people of Tao-chou,
Old ones and young ones, how great their joy!
Father with son and brother with brother henceforward kept together;
From that day for ever more they lived as free men.
The people of Tao-chou
Still enjoy this gift.
And even now when they speak of the Governor
Tears start to their eyes.
And lest their children and their children's children should forget the Governor's name,
When boys are born the syllable "Yang" is often used in their forename.

Source: *A Hundred and Seventy Chinese Poems.* Translated by Arthur Waley. London: Constable, 1918, pp. 123–25.

23. Anglo-Saxon Slaves

Like other early medieval peoples, the Anglo-Saxons of England accepted slavery as a natural part of economic enterprise. Selling oneself or one's family into slavery could bring a person enough money to escape high debts or, for that matter, to secure sufficient food. The following extracts from the Laws of King Alfred (c. 871) give a sample of the legal issues surrounding slaves.

Alfred the Great's system distinguishes between the rights of a Christian slave and those of a non-Christian slave. A non-Christian slave in this context would be a Dane or Norseman, pagan Vikings who had seized control of most of northern and eastern England. According to Alfred's law code, a Christian (i.e., an Anglo-Saxon in practice) had the right to go free after seven years of service. Presumably, a Dane did not have the same opportunity.

Even given the opportunity, a slave might be coerced into remaining a slave, as the document points out. A slave owner had no obligation to free a slave's wife if she had been a previous slave of the master. Freedom in this case, therefore, would mean that the slave would have to abandon his wife and child; few people were willing to do that. The possibility of freedom, although theoretically present, was, in practice, limited.

Slaves, moreover, were open to abuse. Alfred's law code makes specific provisions for what should happen if the slave owner's son slept with a female slave. Such rapes were probably common; otherwise, legislation against them would not be necessary. According to the law code, the slave must either be set free or be married to the son. Although the woman having to marry the man who violated her does not seem like a positive outcome to many modern readers, such legislation was actively attempting to secure and safeguard the interests of the slave victim—surely a step in the right direction. The word theow in this document is the Old English word for slave.

11. These are the laws which you shall set for them. If any one buy a Christian *theow*, let him serve six years; the seventh he shall be free without purchase. With such clothing as he went in, with such goes he out. If he has a wife of his own, she will go out with him. If, however, the lord has given him a wife, she and her child will be the lord's. But if the *theow* should say: "I will not depart from my lord, nor from my wife, nor from my child, nor from my goods," let his lord then bring him to the door of the Temple, and bore his ear through with an awl, in token that he ever after shall be a *theow*.

12. If any one sell his daughter to servitude, let her not be altogether such a *theow* as other female slaves are. He ought not to sell her away among a strange folk. But if he who bought her care not for her, let her go free among a strange folk. If, however, he allows his son to cohabit with her, let him marry her; and let him see that she has clothing, and that which is the worth of her maidenhood, that is, the dowry; let him give her that. If he does unto her none of these things, then let her be free. . . .

43. To all freemen let these days be given, but not to *theow*-men and *esne*-workmen: twelve days at Yule, and the day on which Christ overcame the devil, and the commemoration day of St. Gregory, and seven days before Easter and seven days after, and one day at St. Peter's tide and St. Paul's, and in harvest the whole week before St. Marymass, and one day at the celebration of All-Hallows and the four Wednesdays in the four Ember weeks. To all *theow*-men be given, to those to whom it may be most desirable to give, whatever any man shall give them in God's name, or they at any of their moments may deserve.

Source: Thorpe, Benjamin. *Ancient Laws and Institutes of England*. London: Eyre, 1840, pp. 5–9. In Roy Cave and Herbert Coulson, *A Source Book for Medieval Economic History*. New York: Biblo and Tannen, 1965, pp. 275–76.

24. A Slave Market

The following document paints one of the bleakest pictures of slavery: females purchased in their homeland, raped repeatedly to make them pregnant, and then sent as slaves to a foreign land. The document, from c. 1066, may perhaps exaggerate the nefarious activities of the Bristol traders (Bristol was a western English port), but it also highlights the truly frightening prospects and injustices that could befall slaves. Denied any realistic legal protection, slaves depended primarily on the goodwill of their masters. All too often, that goodwill was lacking.

There is a maritime town, called Bristol, which is on the direct route to Ireland, and so suitable for trade with that barbarian land. The inhabitants of this place with other Englishmen often sail to Ireland for the sake of trade. Wulfstan banished from among them a very old custom which had so hardened their hearts that neither the love of God nor the love of King William could efface it. For men whom they had purchased from all over England they carried off to Ireland; but first they got the women with child and sent them pregnant to market. You would have seen queues of the wretches of both sexes shackled together and you would have pitied them; those who were beautiful and those who were in the flower of youth were daily prostituted and sold amidst much wailing to the barbarians. Oh, execrable crime, wretched dishonor, men who remind us of beasts, to sell into slavery their nearest relative because of their necessities.

Source: Cunningham, W. *The Growth of English Industry and Commerce during the Early and Middle Ages.* Cambridge: Cambridge University Press, 1890, p. 82. In Roy Cave and Herbert Coulson, *A Source Book for Medieval Economic History.* New York: Biblo and Tannen, 1965, pp. 298–99.

25. Runaway Slaves

The poor living conditions of slaves naturally encouraged them to run away. This perceived economic problem of runaways became so severe that special legislation controlling the return of runaway slaves was deemed necessary. In the following document, promulgated by Henry, King of the Romans (the son of Holy Roman Emperor Frederick II) in 1224, a legal procedure for securing the return of runaway slaves is outlined. Slave owners were allowed to enter the cities of Alsace in search of their runaway slaves. If they located a slave whom they claimed to own, the slave owners needed to prove their case through the use of witnesses. The preferred witnesses were family members, but witnesses from the actual district also sufficed. The family members needed not necessarily know the slave—medieval law often favored the oaths of high-ranking nobility over the evidence of eyewitnesses.

Henry, by the grace of God, King of the Romans and ever Augustus. We make known to all, both present and future, that (since the question has been debated between our cities of Alsace, and the nobles and ministerials of the same province, about those men of theirs who had fled to those cities and who might so flee in the future) this same question may be settled forever; and, that each side may enjoy its proper rights, the following decision has been made by us: That if any person pertaining to any noble or ministerial betake himself to our cities with the idea of staying there, and his lord wish to reclaim him, the lord ought to be allowed to take him, if he has seven relatives on the mother's side, who are commonly called *nagilmage*, who will swear that he belongs to the lord by right of ownership. But if for any reason the lord be unable to obtain the relatives or friends, let him obtain two suitable witnesses from the neighborhood from which the fugitive came, and let him prove that he had that man in his undisturbed possession by right of ownership before he betook himself to our cities, and with his witnesses let him take oath on the relics of the saints, and so let his man be restored to him. We also decree and firmly ordain that all nobles and ministerials, as has been said, being desirous of obtaining their men, may enter our cities in peace and security and depart without hurt or injury. At their request a safe-conduct will be furnished them by the bailiffs and council of our cities. And in order that there might be enduring evidence of this, we have ordered this present charter to be written, and have confirmed it with our seal. Given at Basle, December sixteenth, 1224.

Source: Weiland, L., ed. *Legum*, M.G.H. Hanover: n.p., 1896, Vol. 2, sec. 4, p. 403. In Roy Cave and Herbert Coulson, *A Source Book for Medieval Economic History*. New York: Biblo and Tannen, 1965, pp. 278–79.

26. Egregious Cruelty

The lack of viable legal standing exposed slaves to the capricious whims of their masters. Although some slave owners treated their slaves fairly, others were cruel and violent. In the following extract, the sixth-century author Gregory of Tours recounts the horrific cruelty of one especially diabolical slave owner. Rauching, as the evil lord is named, delights in torturing his servants for any perceived misdeeds. He burns the legs of slaves if they hold a candle in front of him by accident, and he buries alive two lovers who presume to fall in love without his official permission. This outrageous cruelty was fortunately uncommon during Gregory's time; the story is interesting to us, as it was to Gregory's audience, precisely because the story is so unusual.

Although church organizations themselves often owned slaves, they also attempted to alleviate some of the suffering of these most oppressed human beings. In this extract, the slaves flee to a church. By doing so, they are seeking sanctuary—the protection of the church against their enemies. The priest of the church, in conformity with the law codes, refuses to release the slaves to their master until the master agrees to treat the slaves well. In this case, the priest requires Rauching to testify that he will not separate the two and will allow them to remain husband and wife.

Unfortunately, the good intentions of the parish priest are unable to halt the evil cunning of Rauching, who does keep the lovers together—buried alive in a coffin. Although Gregory of Tours clearly disapproves of such actions, the account makes it clear that secular lords often did have more power than their local church leaders.

The widow of Godwin married Rauching, a man of great vanity, swollen with pride, shameless in his arrogance, who acted towards those subject to him as though he were without any spark of human kindness, raging against them beyond the bounds of malice and stupidity and doing unspeakable injuries to them. For if, as was customary, a slave held a burning candle before him at dinner, he caused his shins to be bared, and placed the candle between them until the flame died; and he caused the same thing to be done with a second candle until the shins of the torchbearer were burned. But if the slave tried to cry out, or to move from one place to another, a naked sword threatened him; and he found great enjoyment in the man's tears.

They say that at that time two of his slaves, a man and a girl, fell in love—a thing which often happens—and that when their affection for each other had lasted for a period of two years, they fled together to a church. When Rauching found this out, he went to the priest of that place and asked him to return the two slaves immediately, saying that he had forgiven them. Then the priest said to him, "You know what veneration is due to the churches of God. You cannot take them unless you take an oath to allow them to remain together permanently, and you must also promise that they will be free from corporal punishment." But he, being in doubt and remaining silent for some time, at length turned to the priest and put his hands upon the altar, saying, "They will never be separated by me, but rather I shall cause them to remain in wedlock; for though I was annoyed that they did such things without my advice, I am perfectly happy to observe that the man did not take the maid of another in wedlock, nor did she take the slave of another."

The simple priest believed him and returned the two slaves who had been ostensibly pardoned. He took them, gave thanks, and returned to his house, and straightway ordered a tree to be cut down. Then he ordered the trunk to be ground to the depth of three or four feet, and the trunk to be placed therein. Then placing the girl as if she were dead, he ordered the slave to be thrown on top of her. And when the cover had been placed upon the trunk he filled the grave and buried them both alive, saying, "I have not broken my oath and I have not separated them."

Source: Migne, J. P. *Patrologiae Cursus Completus*. Vol. 71. Paris: n.p., 1849, p. 318. In Roy Cave and Herbert Coulson, *A Source Book for Medieval Economic History*. New York: Biblo and Tannen, 1965, pp. 289–90. Translation modified slightly by Lawrence Morris.

27. A Present of Serfs

Although the Church sought to alleviate some of the suffering experienced by slaves and serfs (see Document 26), it also benefited from the slave system. In the following document, from c. 938, Richelinde gives the monastery of Saint Tronde a present of serfs; in return, Richelinde hopes to receive eternal life.

The present itself is certainly not selfless. In addition to gaining eternal life through the present, Richelinde is enriching his son, who is the abbot of the monastery. Richelinde is essentially increasing his son's economic prestige while hoping to gain heaven to boot. Although the serfs are explicitly allowed in the grant to have their own possessions and to work for themselves, Richelinde still compels them to pay a yearly tax. He will continue to receive economic benefits from his gift.

It is unclear whether the serfs themselves will have a better life under monastic control. On the positive side, the families do seem to have remained intact; Richelinde grants the monastery whole families: husbands, wives, and children. Even their new lord is really an "old" lord—they probably knew Richelinde's son Reyner when he was growing up.

Be it known to all the faithful of the Holy Church of God that if we have surrendered something of our fortune to the shrines of the saints, we are confident that we shall undoubtedly receive from God, who rewards all deeds, unfailing reward at the end of this life. Wherefore I, Richelinde, in the name of God, wish as a charitable person to make a perpetual gift to the monastery of Saint-Trond, which is built in the place called Sarcigny, near the river Melterbekk, in the county of Hasbany, where the precious confessor of Christ now rests, and where my son, Reyner, is abbot over a multitude of monks who live under the regular rule of the Order of Sempringham. And this is what I give: for the good of my soul, that after the course of this earthly life I might be worthy of receiving the gifts of eternal life—I give serfs of these names: Eve-rard and his wife Ricimar, with their children, Wiburch, Betswint, Hanezin with her daughter, Ratsmunt with her daughter, Imma, Wigira with her daughter, Meniza, Iseka with her children, Rikera with her daughter, Hererat, Hildekin, Berenger, Amiza; albeit on the condition that, after my death, each year on the feast of Saint Trond, they take care to pay in taxes, God willing, two denarii, and that they owe service to no one as long as they shall live. Let this hold good for them and for their children. But if they should have anything or be able to acquire anything they shall have those things conceded to them. And those things are in their power for their lifetime to dispose of how they wish. Except that while they live, anything of theirs that is useful to the aforesaid monastery they should give freely and charitably, and they should do this of their own free will. They shall live in dependence upon and under the protection of that same monastery. And if it should happen, which God forbid, that they should be killed, an estimate of their goods shall be given to the monastery.

Source: Piot, C., ed. *Cartulaire de l'Abbaye de Saint-Tond.* Brussels: Académie Royale de Belgique, 1870, p. 7. In Roy Cave and Herbert Coulson, *A Source Book for Medieval Economic History.* New York: Biblo and Tannen, 1965, pp. 295–96.

Part IV

INTELLECTUAL LIFE

The Middle Ages and Renaissance witnessed a radical transformation in intellectual life that has left indelible marks on modern society. At the start of the Middle Ages, intellectual life focused on spiritual matters and favored the preservation of traditional knowledge. By the end of the Renaissance, intellectual life focused on materialistic concerns and innovative experimentation. Scholarship had shifted perceptibly from a focus on the heavens to a focus on the earth, and from accepting inherited opinions to subjecting all knowledge to empirical observation. Each of the three following sections, Education, Science and Medicine, and Language and Literature, bears witness to this monumental paradigm shift.

The Middle Ages witnessed the development of large, multifaceted centers of learning: the university. In late antiquity, formal education was provided by loose associations of teachers and students. In the early Middle Ages, monasteries became the centers of serious intellectual work. By the twelfth century, however, large, frequently state sponsored, universities were developing in cities such as Bologna, Paris, and Oxford. These centers for learning differed strikingly from monasteries. While monasteries focused particularly, but not exclusively, on theology, the new universities attracted students much more interested in secular pursuits. Indeed, as the documents in the Education section demonstrate, students seem to have pursued partying as much as they pursued sacred knowledge. Critics of the universities, moreover, criticized the tendency to learn for the sake of curiosity, instead of learning for the sake of serving God and fellow human beings.

The Science and Medicine section reveals that these fields followed the general trends of education. Whereas the universities seemed to abandon a focus on spirituality and theology, scientists in particular turned away from theology to empirical and experimental methodologies. A prime example is Galileo Galilei, whose observations of the planets and the sun led him finally to reject the tenet that the sun moved around the earth; instead he advocated the Copernican theory that the earth moved around the sun. In doing so, he rejected most contemporaneous scientific theory and the literal interpretation of biblical passages that implied that the sun moved around the earth. For Galileo, as for other followers of empiricism or experimental methodologies, what he could see and reason for himself held more weight than what he read in books. This quest for experimental proof led to many advances; William Harvey, for example, discovered through experiments on live animals how the heart circulates blood. The section examines these thinkers and others as well as traditional approaches to health care and to knowledge.

The Language and Literature section explores some of the most enduring achievements in language. The switch from learned languages to vernacular languages parallels the general shift from traditional thinking to experimental approaches. Throughout the Middle Ages, Latin (the language of ancient Rome) remained the language of education, learning, and government even though the languages of the common people had changed significantly. Italian was very similar to Latin—its parent language—but it was not the same thing. In other countries, such as England, Latin was even further from the vernacular language. In the Renaissance, however, vernacular languages, such as Italian, English, and Arabic began to displace Latin as the medium of learned conversation. As a result, learning became more available to those without the wealth to purchase lessons in Latin. At the same time, the invention of the printing press in the fifteenth century made reading material less expensive and more readily available. While these developments were occurring in Europe, Arab countries rejected Greek—the old language of government in the eastern Mediterranean—in favor of Arabic.

Education

The Middle Ages witnessed the birth of many aspects of the modern educational system. Whereas the classical world relied on private tutors and loose associations of scholars, the Middle Ages saw the rise of formalized institutions of higher learning and the wide spread of collective education for younger ages. The first universities, in the modern sense of the word, developed in the twelfth century, in cities such as Bologna, Paris, and Oxford. Unlike earlier learning communities, such as monastery schools, these institutions were dedicated in practice to the pure search for knowledge, both secular and religious (although the dividing line between these fields was not distinct).

This quest for knowledge for knowledge's sake originally disturbed conservative thinkers. Previously, under monastery schools, knowledge, at least theoretically, served God and the Church; an entirely different perspective reigned in universities by the thirteenth century. According to reactionaries such as Jacques de Vitry (Document 1), the quest for knowledge, when divorced from God's service, led to the sins of curiosity, vanity, simony, and a general disinterest in the salvation of souls.

Songs composed by university students (Document 3) certainly seem to confirm Vitry's skepticism about the moral fiber of the educational system. These songs revel in the physical passions; they glorify drinking and womanizing and generally endorse the unbridled seeking of physical pleasure. The only curb on these vices, according to the songs, was the total poverty that students endured. Poverty, rather than personal restraint, kept students from fully indulging their passions. Fierce hatreds and national divisions also arose among the scholars; according to Vitry, each nationality was stereotyped in derisive ways, and a general sense of animosity filled the classrooms.

Although the picture painted by Vitry and the student songs themselves imply that the students were irresponsible, hateful vagabonds, the students were in reality among the most privileged and influential social groups. As Document 2 demonstrates, public legislation economically advantaged students by exempting them from a wide range of taxes, curbing their lodging expenses at the expense of other citizens, and granting them substantial legal protections. The recipients of these benefits, moreover, came from the wealthiest families in the kingdom. There was no free, public education in the Middle Ages and *Renaissance*, so only those students with parents wealthy enough to send them to private schools were able to acquire the education necessary to enter a university. In essence, only children from the upper middle classes and aristocracy commonly entered universities. These same students, upon graduation, would assume some of the most important positions in the government of church and state. When Vitry criticizes university students, he is criticizing the future leaders of the nation and the most influential members of society.

Aspects of education changed significantly during the Renaissance, beginning in the fourteenth century. This change is most clear in the realm of language. Whereas the Middle Ages used Latin as a living language in the realms of law, church, government, and international commerce, the Renaissance rejected medieval Latin in favor of the Latin written by the Romans of the first century B.C. As a result, educators such as Roger Ascham (Document 4) advocated that the student not learn to speak Latin until he (formal education was aimed almost exclusively at males) had learned to read and write in the style of Cicero. Although Ascham did intend the students to gain a spoken command of the language eventually, the failure to teach Latin as a spoken language gradually resulted in the decline of the language—at the same time, however, the local spoken vernaculars (e.g., English, French, Italian) gained importance (see the Language and Literature section).

Ascham also radically changed pedagogical approaches (Document 5). Instead of harsh punishments, including beating, Ascham urged the creation of a trusting, peaceful relationship between teacher and student. According to Ascham—and modern educational theory—students learn more when they want to learn, as opposed to when they are afraid not to learn. Education in English (rather than in Latin), the banning of corporal punishment, and a trusting, professional relationship between teacher and student are all modern movements that have their roots in Renaissance ideals.

1. University Life and National Stereotypes

Jacques de Vitry, a thirteenth-century French intellectual most famous for writing a history of the Middle East, severely criticized the lifestyle of students at the University of Paris. According to Vitry, few students were interested in personal edification, which was the aim of Christian education. Instead, they sought knowledge merely for material gain, for a reputation as a learned man, or for simple curiosity, instead of for the salvation of their souls.

Worse still, ethnic strife created deep divides in the student body. According to the stereotypes, the English drank excessively, the Germans angered easily, the Burgundians (people from central France) lacked intelligence, the Sicilians exhibited cruelty, and so on. Vitry's list in the second of the following paragraphs effectively gives a succinct list of medieval ethnic stereotypes.

Almost all the students at Paris, foreigners and natives, did absolutely nothing except learn or hear something new. Some studied merely to acquire knowledge, which is curiosity; others to acquire fame, which is vanity; others still for the sake of gain, which is cupidity and the vice of simony. Very few studied for their own edification, or that of others. They wrangled and disputed not merely about the various sects or about some discussions; but the differences between the countries also caused dissensions, hatreds and virulent animosities among them and they impudently uttered all kinds of affronts and insults against one another.

They affirmed that the English were drunkards and had tails; the sons of France proud, effeminate and carefully adorned like women. They said that the Germans were furious and obscene at their feasts; the Normans, vain and boastful; the Poitevins, traitors and always adventurers. The Burgundians they considered vulgar and stupid. The Bretons were reputed to be fickle and changeable, and were often reproached for the death of Arthur. The Lombards were called avaricious, vicious and cowardly; the Romans, seditious, turbulent and slanderous; the Sicilians, tyrannical and cruel; the inhabitants of Brabant, men of blood, incendiaries, brigands and ravishers; the Flemish, fickle, prodigal, gluttonous, yielding as butter, and slothful. After such insults from words they often came to blows.

I will not speak of those logicians before whose eyes flitted constantly "the lice of Egypt," that is to say, all the sophistical subtleties, so that no one could comprehend their eloquent discourses in which, as says Isaiah, "there is no wisdom." As to the doctors of theology, "seated, in Moses' seat," they were swollen with learning, but their charity was not edifying. Teaching and not practicing, they have "become as sounding brass or a tinkling cymbal," or like a canal of stone, always dry, which ought to carry water to "the bed of spices." They not only hated one another, but by their flatteries they enticed away the students of others; each one seeking his own glory, but caring not a whit about the welfare of souls.

Having listened intently to these words of the Apostle, "If a man desire the office of a bishop, he desireth a good work," they kept multiplying the prebends, and seeking after the offices; and yet they sought the work decidedly less than the preeminence, and they desired above all to have "the uppermost rooms at feasts and the chief seats in the synagogue, and greetings in the market." Although the Apostle James said, "My brethren, be not many masters," they on the contrary were in such haste to become masters that most of them were not able to have any students except by entreaties and payments. Now it is safer to listen than to teach, and a humble listener is better than an ignorant and presumptuous doctor. In short, the Lord had reserved for Himself among them all only a few honorable and timorous men who had not stood "in the way of sinners," nor had sat down with the others in the envenomed seat.

Teaching law at University of Bologna, Italy, from a fifteenth-century Italian manuscript. Students sit on either side taking notes while the teacher lectures from the podium. The Art Archive/Museo Civico Bologna/Gianni Dagli Orti.

Source: de Vitriaco, Jacobus. *Hist. occid.* Bk. 2, ch. 7. Translated from the Latin in the University of Pennsylvania, Department of History, *Translations and Reprints from the Original Sources of European History.* Vol. 3. Philadelphia: University of Pennsylvania Press, 1907, pp. 19–20.

2. Student Privileges at the University of Heidelberg

Being a university student carried significant prestige during the Middle Ages and Renaissance. By and large, university students (called clerks) came from wealthy families, and their university education marked them out for potentially important roles in the governance of both church and state. Along with this prestige and importance came a variety of legal and economic privileges, as the following Charter of Privileges issued by Rupert I, Count Palatine of the Rhine, to the University of Heidelberg (founded 1386), indicates.

First and foremost, the scholars were not subject to the normal workings of law and order. Instead of the students being answerable to the city magistrates or the representatives of the king, Rupert entrusted the bishop with the responsibility of policing the student community and enforcing the rule of law. In particular, students were free from the immediate payment of fines and were generally entrusted to their schoolmaster instead of being forced to dwell in prison while they awaited trial. Students, however, were not to leave town until the date of their trial. In effect, the clerks benefited from a separate legal system geared just for themselves, whereas the average citizen faced a much more robust and severe judiciary.

The students enjoyed economic benefits as well. To prevent the "extortionate prices of lodgings" charged by the local citizens, one university delegate and one delegate from the city would inspect each rental unit and would determine the price of that unit for one year's rental. In effect, this form of price-fixing undercut the workings of the free market. The large demand for student housing had the power to drive up prices; through price-fixing, the students were protected from considerable expenses, but the townspeople were denied potentially much larger profits. Such favoritism carried over into taxes. The students were exempted from most forms of sales and import taxes, whereas the ordinary citizen had to pay them. Essentially, students, who were generally from the wealthiest families, paid the fewest taxes. As a result of this double standard, one can see why the students may have needed protection from being "oppressed by the citizens!"

Lest in the new community of the city of Heidelberg, their misdeeds being unpunished, there be an incentive to the scholars of doing wrong, we ordain, with provident counsel, by these presents, that the bishop of Worms, as judge ordinary of the clerks of our institution, shall have and possess, now and hereafter while our institution shall last, prisons, and an office in our town of Heidelberg for the detention of criminal clerks. These things we have seen fit to grant to him and his successors, adding these conditions: that he shall permit no clerk to be arrested unless for a misdemeanor; that he shall restore any one detained for such fault, or for any light offense, to his master, or to the rector if the latter asks for him, a promise having been given that the culprit will appear in court and that the rector or master will answer for him if the injured parties should go to law about the matter. Furthermore, that, on being requested, he will restore a clerk arrested for a crime on slight evidence, upon receiving a sufficient pledge—sponsors if the prisoner can obtain them, otherwise an oath if he cannot obtain sponsors—to the effect that he will answer in court the charges against him; and in all these things there shall be no pecuniary exactions, except that the clerk shall give satisfaction, reasonably and according to the rule of the aforementioned town, for the expenses which he incurred while in prison. And we desire that he will detain honestly and without serious injury a criminal clerk thus arrested for a crime where the suspicion is grave and strong, until the truth can be found out concerning the deed of which he is suspected. And he shall not for any cause, moreover, take away any clerk from our aforesaid town, or permit him to be taken away, unless the proper observances have been followed, and he has been condemned by judicial sentence to perpetual imprisonment for a crime.

We command our advocate and bailiff and their servants in our aforesaid town, under pain of losing their offices and our favor, not to lay a detaining hand on any master or scholar of our said institution, nor to arrest him or allow him to be arrested, unless the deed be such that that master or scholar ought rightly to be detained. He shall be restored to his rector or master if he is held for a slight cause, provided he will swear and promise to appear in court concerning the matter; and we decree that a slight fault is one for which a layman, if he had committed it, ought to have been condemned to a light pecuniary fine. Likewise, if the master or scholar detained be found gravely or strongly suspected of the crime, we command that he be handed over by our officials to the bishop or to his representative in our said town, to be kept in custody.

By the tenor of these presents we grant to each and all the masters and scholars that, when they come to the said institution, while they remain there, and also when they return from it to their homes, they may freely carry with them both coming and going, throughout all the lands subject to us, all things which they need while pursuing their studies, and all the goods necessary for their support, without any duty, levy, imposts, tolls, excises, or other exactions whatever. And we wish them and each one of them, to be free from the aforesaid imposts when purchasing corn, wines, meat, fish, clothes and all things necessary for their living and for their rank. And we decree that the scholars from their stock in hand of provisions, if there remain over one or two wagonloads of wine without their having practiced deception, may, after the feast of Easter of that year, sell it at wholesale without paying tax. We grant to them, moreover, that each day the scholars, of themselves or through their servants, may be allowed to buy in the town of Heidelberg, at the accustomed hour, freely and without impediment or hurtful delay, any eatables or other necessaries of life.

Lest the masters and scholars of our institution of Heidelberg may be oppressed by the citizens, moved by avarice, through extortionate prices of lodgings, we have seen fit to decree that thenceforth each year, after Christmas, one expert from the university on the part of the scholars, and one prudent, pious, and circumspect citizen on the part of the citizens, shall be authorized to determine the price of the students' lodgings. Moreover, we will and decree that the various masters and scholars shall, though our bailiff, our judge and the officials subject to us, be defended and maintained in the quiet possession of the lodgings given to them free or of those for which they pay rent. Moreover, by the tenor of these presents, we grant to the rector and the university, or to those designated by them, entire jurisdiction concerning the payment of rents for the lodgings occupied by the students, concerning the making and buying of books, and the borrowing of money for other purposes by the scholars of our institution; also concerning the payment of assessments, together with everything that arises from, depends upon, and is connected with these.

Source: Ogg, Frederic Austin. *A Source Book of Mediaeval History.* New York: American, 1908, pp. 348–50. With slight modifications from *Select Historical Documents of the Middle Ages,* ed. and trans. Ernest F. Henderson. London, 1896, pp. 262–66.

3. The Scholar's Poverty and Drunkenness

The stereotype of the poor but fun-loving student, still found throughout Western culture, has its origins in the Middle Ages. University students in the twelfth and thirteenth centuries crafted many songs celebrating their love of wine and women and lamenting their lack of financial solvency. This goliardic poetry, as the satirical songs are known, should not be confused with the actualities of student life, just as similar genres today (e.g., National Lampoon's Animal House) depict a faux ideal rather than the reality of college life. Although some medieval students were poor, and some were drunkards, most students in fact came from wealthy families, studied sufficiently hard to receive degrees, and found lucrative employment.

The first of the following songs was intended to ask for alms, that is, gifts of money. The poet emphasizes his poverty by pointing out his poor clothing and argues that this poverty is distracting him from the learning that he loves. As a result, he encourages the inhabitants of X-town (the performer would fill in that name with the town in which he happened to be— e.g., Paris) to follow the example of St. Martin, who famously gave a share of his clothing to a beggar. In return for this charity, the poor scholar prays for the soul of his benefactors.

Whereas the first poem offers up a genuine prayer, the second poem twists religious language ("blest") into a praise of wine. In fact, the poem mimics a hymn to the Blessed Virgin Mary but changes the object of praise from the mother of God to wine. Many found such reinterpretations blasphemous, and church councils throughout the thirteenth century passed provisions aimed at curbing the outrages of the goliards. These approaches had little effect, and the stereotype of the fun-loving college student survives to this day.

The Wandering Scholar

I, a wandering scholar lad,
Born for toil and sadness,
Oftentimes am driven by
Poverty to madness.
Literature and knowledge I
Fain would still be earning,
Were it not that want of pelf
Makes me cease from learning.
These torn clothes that cover me
Are too thin and rotten;
Oft I have to suffer cold,
By the warmth forgotten.
Scarce I can attend at church,
Sing God's praises duly;
Mass and vespers both I miss,

Though I love them truly.
Oh, you pride of X-town,
By thy worth I pray thee,
Give the suppiant help in need,
Heaven will sure repay thee.
Take a mind unto thee now
Like unto St. Martin;
Clothe the pilgrim's nakedness,
Wish him well at parting.
So may God translate your soul
Into peace eternal,
And the bliss of saints be yours
In his realm eternal.

A Sequence in Praise of Wine

Wine the good and bland, though blessing
of the good, the bad's distressing,
Sweet of taste by all confessing,
Hail, thou world's felicity!
Hail thy hue, life's gloom dispelling;
Hail thy taste, all tastes excelling;
By thy power, in this thy dwelling,
Deign to make us drunk with thee!
Oh, how blest for bounteous uses
Is the birth of pure vine-juices!
Safe's the table which produces
Wine in goodly quality.
Oh, in colour how auspicious!
Oh, in odour how delicious!
In the mouth how sweet, propitious
To the tongue enthralled by thee!
Blest the man who first thee planted,
Called thee by the name enchanted!
He whose cups have ne'er been scanted
Dreads no danger that may be.
Blest the belly where thou bidest!
Blest the tongue where thou residest!
Blest the mouth through which thou glidest,
And the lips thrice blest by thee!
Therefore let wine's praise be sounded,
Healths to topers all propounded;
We shall never be counfounded,
Toping for eternity!
Pray we: here be thou still flowing,
Plenty on our board bestowing,
While with jocund voice we're showing
How we serve thee—Jubilee!

Sources: Symonds, John Addington. *Wine, Women, and Song: Mediaeval Latin Student's Songs*. London: n.p., 1884, pp. 136–37. In Frederic Austin Ogg. *A Source Book of Mediaeval History*. New York: American, 1908, pp. 354–55. Translation modified slightly by Lawrence Morris.

4. A Renaissance Education

Since the fourteenth century, a cultural movement called the Renaissance had been spreading. The Renaissance, meaning "rebirth," viewed itself as the rebirth of ancient Greek and Latin learning; as such, it rejected the cultural and literary norms of the Middle Ages. By the 1570s, the Renaissance had gained a firm hold in England, as this excerpt from Roger Ascham's Scholemaster *indicates. Ascham rejected the standard educational practices of his day—all of them current during the Middle Ages—that involved learning Latin as a living language. Latin was spoken at all times in school, and the student quickly became familiar with the basics of commercial, ecclesiastical, and governmental Latin. This work-a-day Latin, however, was not acceptable to Ascham. Ascham rejected this living language approach and instead encouraged students to model themselves on "Tully," as the first-century* B.C. *Roman orator and author Cicero was known throughout the Middle Ages and Renaissance. Needless to say, the spoken Latin of the late Middle Ages differed considerably from the polished written Latin of the Roman Republic in the first century* B.C. *In effect, Ascham was rejecting the current Latin entirely, in favor of a long dead language. The result, of course, was ultimately the death of Latin.*

The death of Latin was not Ascham's aim, however. He states explicitly that his goal is to have his students speaking Latin—only a very particular and classical variety of Latin. To achieve this goal, Ascham had the students translate Cicero's letters repeatedly from Latin into written English and then from English into written Latin again, until they were able to reproduce Cicero's Latin style flawlessly. Only after they had mastered such technical difficulties did Ascham allow them to move on to expressing themselves orally. Although some scholars following these methods, such as John Milton, did achieve great proficiency in Latin, the higher standards inevitably led to the decay of the language as an everyday medium of communication.

If Ascham's system of education had unintended detrimental side effects, his understanding of the role of child psychology in education is outstanding. In conformity with many modern pedagogical theories, Ascham noted that praise of good work and gentle criticism of a few flaws resulted in much greater student progress than the repeated lambasting of many faults. The higher student morale effectively encouraged the student to try harder. Ascham likewise pointed out the necessity of building trust in the student–teacher relationship; a lack of trust, Ascham contended, would lead the child to cheat on his (in this time period, female students of Latin were rare) homework to hide his lack of knowledge. In a trusting relationship, however, the student would ask questions instead. Trust clearly led to greater student learning.

After the child hath learned perfectly the eight parts of speech, let him then learn the right joining together of substantives with adjectives, the noun with the verb, the relative with the antecedent. And in learning farther his syntax, by mine advice, he shall not use the common order in common schools, for making of Latins: whereby, the child commonly learneth, first, an evil choice of words (and right choice of words, sayeth Caesar, is the foundation of eloquence), then a wrong placing of words, and lastly, an ill framing of the sentence, with a perverse judgement, both of words and sentences. These faults, taking once root in youth, be never, or hardly, plucked away in age. Moreover, there is no one thing that hath more, either dulled the wits, or taken away the will of children from learning, then the care they have to satisfy their masters in making of Latins.

For the scholar is commonly beat for the making, when the Master were more worthy to be beat for the mending, or rather marring of the same; the master many times, being as ignorant as the child, what to say properly, and fitly to the matter.

Two schoolmasters have set forth in print, either of them a book, of such kind of Latins, Horman and Whittington.

A child shall learn of the better of them, that which another day if he be wise, and come to judgement, he must be fain to unlearn again.

There is a way touched in the first book of Cicero, *De Oratore*, which wisely brought into Schools, truly taught and constantly used, would not only take wholly away this butcherly fear in making of Latins, but would also, with ease and pleasure, and in short time as I know by good experience, work a true choice and placing of words, a right ordering of sentences, an easy understanding of the tongue, a readiness to speak, a facility to wright, a true judgment both of his own and other men's doings, what tongue soever he doth use.

The way is this: after the three concordances learned, as I touched before, let the Master read unto him the Epistles of Cicero, gathered together, and chosen out by Sturmius, for the capacity of children.

First, let him teach the child, cheerfully and plainly, the cause, and matter of the letter. Then, let him construe it into English, so oft, as the child may easily carry away the understanding of it. Lastly parse it over perfectly. This done thus, let the child, by and by, both construe and parse it over again, so, that it may appear, that the child doubteth in nothing, that his master taught him before. After this, the child must take a paper book, and sitting in some place, where no man shall prompt him, by himself, let him translate into English his former lesson. Then, showing it to his master, let the master take from him his Latin book, and pausing an hour, at the least, then let the child translate his own English into Latin again, in another paper book. When the child bringeth it, turned into Latin, the Master must compare it with Tullies book, and lay them both together, and where the child doth well, either in chosing, or true placing of Tully's book, let the master praise him, and say, here you do well. For I assure you, there is no such whetstone to sharpen a good wit and encourage a will to learning, as is praise.

But if the child miss, either in forgetting a word, or in changing a good with a worse, or misordering the sentence, I would not have the master either frown or chide with him, if the child have done his diligence, and used no truantship therein. For I know by good experience, that a child that take more profit of two faults gently warned of, then of four things rightly hit. For then the master shall have good occasion to say unto him: "A, Tullie would have used such a word, not this; Tullie would have placed this word here, not there; would have used this case, this number, this person, this degree, this gender; he would have used this mood, this tense, this simple, rather than this compound; this adverb here not there; he would have ended the sentence with this verb, not with that noun or participle, etc."

In these few lines, I have wrapped up, the most tedious part of Grammar and also the ground of almost all the Rules, that are so busily taught by the Master, and so hardly learned by the Scholar, in all common Schools, which after this sort, the master shall teach without all error, and the scholar shall learn without great pain, the master being led by so sure a guide and the scholar being brought into so plain and easy a way. And therefore, we do not contemn the Rules, but we gladly teach Rules, more plainly, sensibly, and orderly, than they be commonly taught in common schools. For, when the master shall compare Tullie's book with the scholar's translation, let the master first lead and teach his scholar, to join the Rules of his Grammar book, with the examples of his present lesson, until the Scholar, by himself, be able to fetch out of his Grammar, every rule for every example. So, as the Grammar book be ever in the Scholar's hand, and also used of him, as a Dictionary, for every present use. This is a lively and perfect way of teaching of Rules: where the common way, used in common Schools, to read the Grammar alone by itself, is tedious for the master, hard for the Scholar, cold and uncomfortable for them both.

Let your Scholar be never afraid to ask you any doubt, but use discretely the best allurements ye can to encourage him to the same, lest, his overmuch fearing of you, drive him to seek some misorderly shift, as to seek to be helped by some other book, or to be prompted by some other Scholar, and to go about to beguile you much, and himself more.

With this way of good understanding the matter, plain construing, diligent parsing, daily translating, cheerfull admonishing, and heedfull amending of faults, never leaving behind just praise for well doing, I would have the scholar brought up withal, till he had read and translated over the first book of Epistles chosen out by Sturmius, with a good piece of a Comedy of Terence also.

All this while, by mine advice, the child shall use to speak no Latin. For, as Cicero sayeth in like matter, with like words, "Loquendo, male loqui discunt." And that excellent learned man, G. Budaeus, in his Greek Commentaries, sore complaineth that when he began to learn the Latin tongue, use of speaking Latin at the table, and elsewhere, unadvisedly, did bring him to such an evil choice of words, to such a crooked framing of sentences, that no one thing did hurt or hinder him more, all the days of his life afterward, both for readiness in speaking, and also good judgement in writing.

In very deed, if children were brought up in such an house or such a school, where the Latin tongue were properly and perfectly spoken, as Tib. and Ca. Gracci were brought up, in their mother Cornelia's house, surely, then the daily use of speaking were the best and readiest way to learn the Latin tongue. But now, commonly, in the best Schools in England, for words, right choice is smally regarded, true property wholly neglected, confusion is brought in, barbariousness is bred up so in young wits, as afterward they be not only marred for speaking, but also corrupted in judgment: as with much a do, or never at all, they be brought to right frame again.

Yet all men covet to have their children speak Latin, and so do I very earnestly too. We both, have one purpose: we agree in desire, we wish one end, but we differ somewhat in order and way, that leadeth rightly to that end. Other would have them speak at all adventures: and, so they be speaking, to speak, the Master careth not, the Scholar knoweth not, what. This is, to seem, and not to be; except it be, to be bold without shame, rash without skill, full of words without wit. I wish to have them speak so, as it may well appear, that the brain doth govern the tongue, and that reason leadeth forth the talk. Socrates' doctrine is true in Plato, and well marked, and truly better uttered by Horace in *Arte poetica*, that, wheresoever knowledge doth accompany the wit, there best utterance doth always await upon the tongue; For, good understanding must first be bred in the child, which being nourished with skill, and use of writing (as I will teach more largely hereafter) is the only way to bring him to judgement and readiness in speaking, and that in far shorter time (if he follow constantly the trade of this little lesson) than he shall do, by common teaching of the common schools of England.

Source: Ascham, Roger. *The Scholemaster or Plaine and Perfite Way of Teaching Children to Understand, Write, and Speake the Latin Tong but Specially Purposed for the Private Bringing Up of Youth in Ientlemen and Noble Mens Houses, and Commodious Also for All Such as Have Forgot the Latin Tonge.* Aldersgate: John Day, 1573, pp. 1–3. Slightly adapted by Lawrence Morris.

5. Corporal Punishment, Quick Wits, and Too Much Math

As the sixteenth-century English scholar Roger Ascham noted in the previous extract (Document 4), he practiced a pedagogical method very different from that of his contemporaries. In particular, Ascham criticized harshly the practice of corporal punishment. As Ascham argues in the next extract, corporal punishment often had little to do with the student's behavior. Rather, beating was often the result of a schoolmaster's simply having a bad day. As Ascham claims, "For when the schoolmaster is angry with some other matter, then will he soonest fall to beat his scholar." Moreover, failing students were frequently beaten even though they were genuinely trying to understand the material. As a result, the schoolmaster was not punishing bad behavior, but rather simply punishing someone for their "nature," or "genes" as we might say today.

Ascham's defense of slow students, moreover, extends to stating that they are often the best individuals later on. According to Ascham, students change over time, so that students who are smart early on become slower as they grow, whereas slow pupils likewise become more intelligent. Finally, Ascham is wary of those who are too quick in mathematics and the sciences then associated with math, such as music. Ascham claims that mathematicians and musicians are "solitary" and "unfit to live with others." As his reference to his previously mentioned book on "shooting" makes clear, Ascham believed strongly in the value of a well-rounded life. In the extract below, "fond" in Renaissance English means "stupid," not "loving."

If your scholar do miss sometimes, in marking rightly these foresaid six things, chide not hastily, for that shall both dull his wit and discourage his diligence, but admonish him gently, which shall make him both willing to amend and glad to go forward in love and hope of learning.

I have now wished, twice or thrice, this gentle nature to be in a Schoolmaster. And that I have done so, neither by chance nor without some reason, I will now declare at large, why in mine opinion, love is fitter than fear, gentleness better than beating, to bring up a child rightly in learning.

With the common use of teaching and beating in common schools of England, I will not greatly contend; which, if I did, it were but a small grammatical controversy, neither belonging to heresy nor treason, nor greatly touching God nor the Prince;

although in very deed, in the end, the good or ill bringing up of children doth as much serve to the good or ill service of God, our Prince, and our whole country, as any one thing doth beside.

I do gladly agree with all good Schoolmasters in these points: to have children brought to good perfectness in learning; to all honesty in manners; to have all faults rightly amended; to have every vice severely corrected; but for the order and way, that leadeth rightly to these points, we somewhat differ. For commonly, many Schoolmasters, some, as I have seen, more, as I have heard tell, be of so crooked a nature, as, when they meet with a hard witted scholar, they rather break him, they bow him, rather mar him, than mend him. For when the schoolmaster is angry with some other matter, then will he soonest fall to beat his scholar, and though he himself should be punished for his folly, yet must he beat some scholar for his pleasure, though there be no cause for him to do so, nor yet fault in the scholar to deserve so. These ye will say, be fond schoolmasters, and few they be, that be found to be such. They be fond in deed, but surely over many such be found everywhere. But this will I say, that even the wisest of your great beaters, do as oft punish nature, as they do correct faults. Yea, many times, the better nature, is sorer punished. For, if one by quickness of wit, take his lesson readily, another by hardness of wit taketh it not so speedily, the first is always commended, the other is commonly punished, when a wise schoolmaster should rather discretely consider the right disposition of both their natures, and not so much weigh what either of them is able to do now, as what either of them is likely to do hereafter. For this I know, not only by reading of books in my study, but also by experience of life, abroad in the world, that those, which be commonly the wisest, the best learned, and best men also, when they be old, were never commonly the quickest of wit, when they were young. The causes why, amongst other, which be many, that move me thus to think, be these few which I will reckon. Quick wits commonly be apt to take, unapt to keep, soon hot and desirous of this and that, as cold, and soon weary of the same again; more quick to enter speedily, than able to persever; even like our sharp tools, whose edges be very soon turned. Such wits delight themselves in easy and pleasant studies, and never pass far forward in high and hard sciences. And therefore the quickest wits commonly may prove the best poets, but not the wisest Orators, ready of tongue to speak boldly, not deep of judgment, either for good counsel or wise writing. Also, for manners and life, quick wits commonly be in desire newfangled, in purpose unconstant, light to promise any thing, ready to forget every thing, both benefit and injury, and thereby neither fast to friend nor fearful to foe; inquisitive of every trifle, not secret in greatest affairs; bold with any person, busy in every matter; soothing such as be present, nipping any that is absent; of nature also, always flattering their betters, envying their equals, despising their inferiours, and by quickness of wit, very quick and ready to like none so well as themselves. . . .

Some wits, moderate enough by nature, be many times marred by overmuch study and use of some sciences, namely Music, Arithmetic, and Geometry. These sciences, as they sharpen men's wits overmuch, so they change men's manners over sore, if they be not moderately mingled, and wisely applied to some good use of life. Mark all Mathematical heads, which be only and wholly bent to those sciences, how solitary they be themselves, how unfit to live with others, and how unapt to serve in the world. This is not only known now by common experience, but uttered long before by wise men's judgment and sentence. Galen sayeth: Much Music marreth mens' manners, and Plato hath a notable place of the same thing in his books *de Rep.* well marked also, and excellently translated by Tullie himself. Of this matter I wrote once more at large twenty year ago, in my book of shooting; now I thought but to touch it, to prove that overmuch quickness of wit, either given by nature, or sharpened by study, doth not commonly bring forth either greatest learning, best manners, or happiest life in the end.

Source: Ascham, Roger. *The Scholemaster or Plaine and Perfite Way of Teaching Children to Understand, Write, and Speake the Latin Tong but Specially Purposed for the Private Bringing Up of Youth in Ientlemen and Noble Mens Houses, and Commodious Also for All Such as Have Forgot the Latin Tonge.* Aldersgate: John Day, 1573, pp. 4–6. Spelling modified by Lawrence Morris.

Science and Medicine

Some of the most dramatic changes between the *Renaissance* and the modern world have taken place in the realm of science and medicine. The documents in this section give witness to these changes. In *Genji Monogatari* (Document 6), for example, a gravely ill, wealthy woman's health care consists of monks chanting hymns and burning incense at her bedside, whereas a modern Japanese woman would seek care in a hospital. By and large, spiritual causes of disease have yielded almost completely to physical explanations of the disease process.

This change in the theory and management of disease resulted from the scientific empirical method. In the empirical method, conclusions are drawn only from observable phenomena, not from tradition or previous authors. William Harvey, for example, as Document 7 shows, refused to accept the unsubstantiated theories that he found in books about the circulation of blood; instead, he himself performed operations on animals so that he could witness firsthand the operations of the heart.

Such innovation caused controversy. Harvey had fierce critics who refused to believe his conclusions. Galileo Galilei (Document 8), whose direct observation of the stars caused him to reject the standard theories that the earth did not move, suffered more than simple criticism. As a result of poor political judgment and his own self-belief, Galileo ran afoul of Pope Urban VIII, a former friend, and lived the remainder of his life in house arrest, although he was still able to research and publish on less controversial subjects. Then as now, science raised ethical and religious issues.

Although doctors of the Middle Ages and Renaissance did not understand the role of microorganisms in disease, they nevertheless devised many pharmaceutical remedies (Documents 9, 10, and 12). Although many of these medicines did not attack the underlying causes of disease, some of them, such as camphor and traditional Chinese medicine, are still widely used as supplements to antibiotics and other modern Western treatments, whereas other treatments, such as the burning of herbs against plague, encouraged the development of more sanitary conditions overall.

The scientific area that has changed least is perhaps mathematics. As Document 11 shows, the learned Indian thinker Brahmagupta had already formalized many key mathematical principles, still in use today, before the year A.D. 650.

6. Death by Possession

Genji Monogatari, or Tale of Genji, *written shortly after 1000, allegedly by the Lady Murasaki Shikibu, is sometimes considered the world's first novel. The novel explores Japanese imperial politics through the lives of fictional characters. Although the work is entirely fictional, it gives insight into the stereotypes or fantasies of Japanese court life and is widely considered one of the most important works of Japanese literature.*

In the following extract, Genji (the illegitimate but prestigious son of the Japanese emperor) is reconciled with his wife, Aoi, who is giving birth while very ill. The passage gives insight into the contemporary medical treatment of such difficult deliveries. In this case, the medical treatment is entirely spiritual, not physical. The healers, monks from the monastery of Tendai, treat Aoi by chanting and performing healing rituals. When a male child is born alive, these monks take credit for having achieved the successful outcome. Although Genji is skeptical about the spiritual world, he is converted when Lady Rokujo, a jealous mistress, speaks through the mouth of his own wife. As the passage makes clear, though, Lady Rokujo is not even consciously aware that her spirit is possessing and destroying Aoi; Rokujo is confused as to why her own clothes smell of incense (we are to understand that she smells of the incense being used to cure Aoi). In the end, Lady Aoi dies from spiritual possession. The doctors—that is, the monks—are able to help her, but they cannot cure her completely.

At last the priests arrived to fetch the girl away. They took a grave view of the mother's condition and gave her the benefit of their presence by offering up many prayers and incantations. But week after week she remained in the same condition, showing no symptom which seemed actually dangerous, yet all the time (in some vague and indefinite way) obviously very ill. Genji sent constantly to enquire after her, but she saw clearly that his attention was occupied by quite other matters. Aoi's delivery was not yet due and no preparations for it had been made, when suddenly there were signs that it was close at hand. She was in great distress, but though the healers recited prayer upon prayer their utmost efforts could not shift by one jot the spiteful power which possessed her. All the greatest miracle-workers of the land were there; the utter failure of their ministrations irritated and perplexed them. At last, daunted by the potency of their incantations, the spirit that possessed her found voice and, weeping bitterly, she was heard to say: "Give me a little respite; there is a matter of which Prince Genji and I must speak." The healers nodded at one another as though to say, "Now we shall learn something worth knowing," for they were convinced that the "possession" was speaking through the mouth of the possessed, and they hurried Genji to her bedside. Her parents thinking that, her end being near, she desired to give some last secret injunction to Genji, retired to the back of the room. The priests too ceased their incantations and began to recite the *Hokkeyo* in low impressive tones. He raised the bed-curtain. She looked lovely as ever as she lay there, very big with child, and any man who saw her even now would have found himself strangely troubled by her beauty. How much the more then Prince Genji, whose heart was already overflowing with tenderness and remorse! The plaited tresses of her long hair stood out in sharp contrast to her white jacket. Even to this loose, sick-room garb her natural grace imparted the air of a fashionable gown! He took her hand. "It is terrible," he began, "to see you looking so unhappy!" He could say no more. Still she gazed at him, but through his tears he saw that there was no longer in her eyes the wounded scorn that he had come to know so well, but a look of forbearance and tender concern; and while she watched him weep her own eyes brimmed with tears. It would not do for him to go on crying like this. Her father and mother would be alarmed; besides, it was upsetting Aoi herself, and meaning to cheer her he said: "Come, things are not so bad as that! You will soon be much better. But even if anything should happen, it is certain that we shall meet again in worlds to come. Your father and mother too, and many others, love you so dearly that between your fate and theirs must be some sure bond that will bring you back to them in many, many lives that are to be." Suddenly she interrupted him: "No, no. That is not it. But stop these prayers awhile. They do me great harm," and drawing nearer to him she went on, "I did not think that you would come. I have waited for you till all my soul is burnt with longing." She spoke wistfully, tenderly; and still in the same tone recited the verse "Bind thou, as the seam of a skirt is braided, this shred, that from my soul despair and loneliness have sundered." The voice in which these words were said was not Aoi's, nor was the manner hers. He knew someone whose voice was very like that. Who was it? Why, yes; surely only she—the Lady Rokujo. Once or twice he had heard people suggest that something of this kind might be happening; but he had always rejected the ideas as hideous and unthinkable, believing it to be the malicious invention of some unprincipled scandalmonger, and had even denied that such "possession" ever took place. Now he had seen one with his own eyes. Ghastly, unbelievable as they were, such things did happen in real life. Controlling himself at last he said in a low voice: "I am not sure who is speaking to me. Do not leave me in doubt." Her answer proved only too conclusively that he had guessed aright. To his horror her parents now came back to the bed, but she had ceased to speak, and seeing her now lying quietly her mother thought the attack was over, and was coming towards the bed carrying a basin of hot water when Aoi suddenly started up and bore a child. For the moment all was gladness and rejoicing; but it seemed only too likely that the spirit which possessed her had but been temporarily dislodged; for a fierce fit of terror was soon upon her, as though the thing (whatever it was) were angry at having been put to the trouble of shifting, so that there was still grave anxiety about the future. The Abbot of Tendai and the other great ecclesiastics who were gathered together in the room attributed her easy delivery to the persistency of their own incantations and prayers, and as they hastily withdrew to seek refreshment and repose they wiped the sweat from their brows with an expression of considerable self-satisfaction. Her friends who had for days been plunged in the deepest gloom now began to take heart a little, believing that although there was no apparent improvement yet now that the child was safely born she could not fail to mend. The prayers and incantations began once more, but throughout the house there was a new feeling of confidence; for the amusement of looking after the baby at least gave them some relief from the strain under which they had been living for so many days. Handsome presents were sent by the ex-Emperor, the Royal Princes and all the Court, forming an array which grew more dazzling each night. The fact that the child was a boy made the celebrations connected with his birth all the more sumptuous and elaborate.

The news of this event took Lady Rokujo somewhat aback. The last report she had heard from the Great Hall was that the confinement was bound to be very dangerous.

And now they said that there had not been the slightest difficulty. She thought this very peculiar. She had herself for a long while been suffering form the most disconcerting sensations. Often she felt as though her whole personality had in some way suddenly altered. It was as though she were a stranger to herself. Recently she had noticed that a smell of mustard-seed incense for which she was at a loss to account was pervading her clothes and hair. She took a hot bath and put on other clothes; but still the same odour of incense pursued her. It was bad enough even in private to have this sensation of being as it were estranged from oneself. But now her body was playing tricks upon her which her attendants must have noticed and were no doubt discussing behind her back. Yet there was not one person among those about her with whom she could bring herself to discuss such things and all this pent-up misery seemed only to increase the strange process of dissolution which had begun to attack her mind.

Now that Genji was somewhat less anxious about Aoi's condition, the recollection of his extraordinary conversation with her at the crisis of her attack kept on recurring in his mind, and it made so painful an impression upon him that though it was now a long time since he had communicated with Rokujo and he knew that she must be deeply offended, he felt that no kind of intimacy with her would ever again be possible. Yet in the end pity prevailed and he sent her a letter. It seemed indeed that it would at present be heartless to absent himself at all from one who had just passed through days of such terrible suffering and from her friends who were still in a state of the gravest anxiety, and all his secret excursions were abandoned. Aoi still remained in a condition so serious that he was not allowed to see her. The child was as handsome an infant as you could wish to see. The great interest which Genji took in it and the zest with which he entered into all the arrangements which were made for its welfare delighted Aoi's father, inasmuch as they seemed signs of a better understanding between his daughter and Genji; and though her slow recovery caused him great anxiety, he realized that an illness such as that through which she had just passed must inevitably leave considerable traces behind it and he persuaded himself that her condition was less dangerous than one might have supposed. The child reminded Genji of the Heir Apparent and made him long to see Fujitsubo's little son again. The desire took such strong hold upon him that at last he sent Aoi a message in which he said: "It is a very long time since I have been to the Palace or indeed have paid any visits at all. I am beginning to feel the need of a little distraction, so today I am going out for a short while and should like to see you before I go. I do not want to feel that we are completely cut off from one another." So he pleaded, and he was supported by her ladies who told her that Prince Genji was her own dear Lord and that she ought not to be so proud and stiff with him. She feared that her illness had told upon her looks and was for speaking to him with a curtain between, but this too her gentlewomen would not allow. He brought a stool close to where she was lying and began speaking to her of one thing or another. Occasionally she put in a word or two, but it was evident that she was still very weak. Nevertheless it was difficult to believe that she had so recently seemed almost at the point of death. They were talking quietly together about those worst days of her illness and how they now seemed like an evil dream when suddenly he recollected the extraordinary conversation he had had with her when she was lying apparently at her last gasp and filled with a sudden bitterness, he said to her: "There are many other things that I must one day talk to you about.

But you seem very tired and perhaps I had better leave you." So saying he arranged her pillows, brought her warm water to wash in and in fact played the sick-nurse so well that those about her wondered where he had acquired the art. Still peerlessly beautiful but weak and listless she seemed as she lay motionless on the bed at times almost to fade out of existence. He gazed at her with fond concern. Her hair, every ringlet still in its right place, was spread out over the pillow. Never before had her marvelous beauty so strangely impressed him. Was it conceivable that year after year he should have allowed such a woman to continue in estrangement from him? Still he stood gazing at her. "I must start for the Palace," he said at last; "but I shall not be away long. Now that you are better you must try to make you mother feel less anxious about you when she comes presently; for though she tries hard not to show it, she is still terribly distressed about you. You must begin now to make an effort and sit up for a little while each day. I think it is partly because she spoils you so much that you are taking so long to get well." As he left the room, robed in all the magnificence of his court attire she followed him with her eyes more fixedly than ever in her life before. The attendance of the officers who took part in the autumn session was required, and Aoi's father accompanied Genji to the Palace, as did also her brother who needed the Minister's assistance in making their arrangements for the coming political year. Many of their servants went too and the Great Hall wore a deserted and melancholy aspect. Suddenly Aoi was seized with the same choking-fit as before and was soon in a desperate condition. This news was brought to Genji in the Palace and breaking off his Audience he at once made for home. The rest followed in hot haste and though it was Appointment Evening they gave up all thought of attending the proceedings, knowing that the tragic turn of affairs at the Great Hall would be considered a sufficient excuse. It was too late to get hold of the abbot from Mount Tendai or any of the dignitaries who had given their assistance before. It was appalling that just when she seemed to have taken a turn for the better she should so suddenly again be at the point of death, and the people at the Great Hall felt utterly helpless and bewildered. Soon the house was full of lackeys who were arriving from every side with messages of sympathy and enquiry; but from the inhabitants of that stricken house they could obtain no information, for they seemed to do nothing but rush about from one room to another in a state of frenzy which it was terrifying to behold.

Remembering that several times already her "possession" had reduced her to a trance-like state, they did not for some time attempt to lay out the body or even touch her pillows, but left her lying just as she was. After two or three days however it became clear that life was extinct.

Source: *Tale of Genji*. Translated by Arthur Waley. Boston: Houghton, 1926.

7. William Harvey on the Circulation of Blood

The seventeenth-century Englishman William Harvey is credited with discovering the circulation of blood. Although Harvey was, of course, building on the work of other scientists, his Exercitatio Anatomica de Motu Cordis et Sanguinis in Animalibus *(1628) established the basic principles of the heart's role in moving blood through the circulatory system.*

What enabled this discovery, and similar discoveries, was the empirical method, by which scientific conclusions are based on observable phenomena. Although the empirical method is the major method of learning and scholarship in the present era, it was still a relative newcomer in the seventeenth century. Medieval and Renaissance medicine generally followed the precepts of classical authorities and their interpreters. The writings of the second-century A.D. physician Galen of Pergamum, for example, remained the essential textbook throughout this time period. Only by rejecting this tradition, however, could scientists hope to advance knowledge. As Harvey puts it in his first chapter, which follows, he "sought to discover these from actual inspection, and not from the writings of others."

The particular method Harvey employed is controversial even today: vivisection. To examine the workings of the heart, Harvey restrained animals of many different species and then cut into their chest cavities, pulled away the bone and muscle, and looked at the beating heart. No pain medicine was administered. The pain suffered by the vertebrates must have been intense, and the operation was, as a rule, fatal. In fact, as Harvey notes in the second chapter, the motions of the dying heart were particularly informative. Without these experiments, however, the medical understanding of the heart—which has ultimately led to important and common operations such as heart bypass surgery—would have remained primitive. Although controversial today, Harvey's methodology did not cause significant moral dilemmas at the time. Harvey notes that he had critics, but these critics did not object to his methods; rather, they simply did not believe his results. Animal experimentation was accepted throughout this time period, though dissection of human corpses was frowned upon and often forbidden by law. The ethics of scientific research was as controversial then as it is now, though the areas of concern have changed.

CHAPTER 1. THE AUTHOR'S MOTIVES FOR WRITING

When I first gave my mind to vivisections, as a means of discovering the motions and uses of the heart, and sought to discover these from actual inspection, and not from the writings of others, I found the task so truly arduous, so full of difficulties, that I was almost tempted to think with Fracastorius, that the motion of the heart was only to be comprehended by God. For I could neither rightly perceive at first when the systole and when the diastole took place, nor when and where dilatation and contraction occurred, by reason of the rapidity of the motion, which in many animals is accomplished in the twinkling of an eye, coming and going like a flash of lightning; so that the systole presented itself to me now from this point, now from that; the diastole the same; and then everything was reversed, the motions occurring, as it seemed, variously and confusedly together. My mind was therefore greatly unsettled, nor did I know what I should myself conclude, nor what believe from others; I was not surprised that Andreas Laurentius should have said that the motion of the heart was as perplexing as the flux and reflux of Euripus had appeared to Aristotle.

At length, and by using greater and daily diligence, having frequent recourse to vivisections, employing a variety of animals for the purpose, and collating numerous observations, I thought that I had discovered what I so much desired, both the motion and the use of the heart and arteries; since which time I have not hesitated to expose my views upon these subjects, not only in private to my friends, but also in public, in my anatomical lectures, after the manner of the Academy of old. These views, as usual, please some more, others less; some chid and calumniated me, and laid it to me as a crime that I had dared to depart from the precepts and opinion of all anatomists; others desired further explanations of the novelties, which they said were both worthy of consideration, and might perchance be found of signal use. At length, yielding to the requests of my friends, that all might be made participators in my labours, and partly moved by the envy of others, who, receiving my views with uncandid minds and understanding them indifferently, have essayed to traduce me publicly, I have been moved to commit these things to the press, in order that all may be enabled to form an opinion both of me and my labours. This step I take all the more willingly, seeing that Hieronymus Fabricius of Aquapendente, although he has accurately and learnedly delineated almost every one of the several parts of animals in a special work, has left the heart alone untouched. Finally, if any use or benefit to this department of the republic of letters should accrue from my labours, it will, perhaps, be allowed that I have not lived idly, and, as the old man in the comedy says:

> For never yet hath any one attained
> To such perfection, but that time, and place,
> And use, have brought addition to his knowledge;
> Or made correction, or admonished him,
> That he was ignorant of much which he
> Had thought he knew; or led him to reject
> What he had once esteemed of higher price.

So will it, perchance, be found with reference to the heart at this time; or others, at least, starting from hence, the way pointed out to them, advancing under the guidance of a happier genius, may make occasion to proceed more fortunately, and to inquire more accurately.

CHAPTER 2. OF THE MOTIONS OF THE HEART, AS SEEN IN THE DISSECTION OF LIVING ANIMALS

In the first place, then, when the chest of a living animal is laid open and the capsule that immediately surrounds the heart is slit up or removed, the organ is seen now to move, now to be at rest; there is a time when it moves, and a time when it is motionless.

These things are more obvious in the colder animals, such as toads, frogs, serpents, small fishes, crabs, shrimps, snails, and shell-fish. They also become more distinct in warm-blooded animals, such as the dog and the hog, if they be attentively noted when the heart begins to flag, to move more slowly, and, as it were, to die: the movements then become slower and rarer, the pauses longer, by which it is made much more easy to perceive and unravel what the motions really are, and how they are performed. In the pause, as in death, the heart is soft, flaccid, exhausted, lying as it were at rest.

In the motion, and interval in which this is accomplished, three principal circumstances are to be noted:

1. That the heart is erected, and rises upwards to a point, so that at this time it strikes against the breast and the pulse is felt externally.

William Harvey. The open book showing a diagram of the heart makes reference to Harvey's most important discovery: the circulation of blood. © 2008 Jupiterimages Corporation.

2. That it is everywhere contracted, but more especially towards the sides, so that it looks narrower, relatively longer, more drawn together. The heart of an eel taken out of the body of the animal and placed upon the table or the hand, shows these particulars; but the same things are manifest in the heart of small fishes and of those colder animals where the organ is more conical or elongated.

3. The heart being grasped in the hand, it is felt to become harder during its action. Now this hardness proceeds from tension, precisely as when the forearm is grasped, its tendons are perceived to become tense and resilient when the fingers are moved.

4. It may further be observed in fishes, and the colder blooded animals, such as frogs, serpents, etc., that the heart, when it moves, becomes of a paler colour, when quiescent of a deeper blood-red color.

From these particulars it appeared evident to me that the motion of the heart consists in a certain universal tension—both contraction in the line of its fibres, and constriction in every sense. It becomes erect, hard, and of diminished size during its action; the motion is plainly of the same nature as that of the muscles when they contract in the line of their sinews and fibres; for the muscles, when in action, acquire vigour and tenseness, and from soft become hard, prominent and thickened: in the same manner the heart.

We are therefore authorized to conclude that the heart, at the moment of its action, is at once constricted on all sides, rendered thicker in its parietes and smaller in its ventricles, and so made apt to project or expel its charge of blood. This, indeed, is made sufficiently manifest by the fourth observation preceding, in which we have seen that the heart, by squeezing out the blood it contains becomes paler, and then when it sinks into repose and the ventricle is filled anew with blood, that the deeper crimson colour returns. But no one need remain in doubt of the fact, for if the ventricle be pierced the blood will be seen to be forcibly projected outwards upon each motion or pulsation when the heart is tense.

These things, therefore, happen together or at the same instant: the tension of the heart, the pulse of its apex, which is felt externally by the striking against the chest, the thickening of the parietes, and the forcible expulsion of the blood it contains by the constriction of its ventricles.

Hence the very opposite of the opinions commonly received appears to be true: inasmuch as it is generally believed that when the heart strikes the breast and the pulse is felt without, the heart is dilated in its ventricles and is filled with blood; but the contrary of this is the fact, and the heart, when it contracts, is emptied. Whence the motion which is generally regarded as the diastole of the heart, is in truth its systole. And in like manner the intrinsic motion of the heart is not the diastole but the systole; neither is it in the diastole that the heart grows firm and tense, but in the systole, for then only, when tense is it moved and made vigorous.

Neither is it by any means to be allowed that the heart only moves in the line of its straight fibres, although the great Vesalius, giving this notion countenance, quotes a bundle of osiers bound into a pyramidal heap in illustration; meaning, that as the apex is approached to the base, so are the sides made to bulge out in the fashion of arches, the cavities to dilate, the ventricles to acquire the form of a cupping glass and so to suck in the blood. But the true effect of every one of its fibres is to constinge the heart at the same time that they render it tense; and this rather with the effect of thickening and amplifying the walls and substance of the organ than enlarging its ventricles. And, again, as the fibres run from the apex to the base, and draw the apex towards the base, they do not tend to make the walls of the heart bulge out in circles, but rather the contrary; inasmuch as every fibre that is circularly disposed, tends to become straight when it contracts; and is distended laterally and thickened, as in the case of muscular fibres in general, when they contract, that is, when they are shortened longitudinally, as we see them in the bellies of the muscles of the body at large. To all this let it be added that not only are the ventricles contracted in virtue of the direction and condensation of their walls, but further, that those fibres, or bands, styled *nerves* by Aristotle, which are so conspicuous in the ventricles of the larger animals, and contain all the straight fibres (the parietes of the heart containing only circular ones), when they contract simultaneously, by an admirable adjustment all the internal surfaces are drawn together, as if with cords, and so is the charge of blood expelled with force.

Neither is it true, as vulgarly believed, that the heart by any dilatation or motion of its own, has the power of drawing the blood into the ventricles; for when it acts and becomes tense, the blood is expelled; when it relaxes and sinks together it receives the blood in the manner and wise which will by and by be explained.

Source: Harvey, William. *On the Motion of the Heart and Blood in Animals.* Translated by Robert Willis. New York: Collier, 1909–1914. In *Great Books of the Western World.* Vol. 26. Chicago: Encyclopaedia Britannica, 1990, 273–75.

8. Galileo Galilei on the Earth and Sun

Galileo Galilei (1564–1642) was one of the most brilliant mathematicians and physicists of his day. Although Galileo made significant discoveries in numerous areas, including navigation and gravity, his espousal of Nicolaus Copernicus's theory of heliocentrism and his resulting disputes with the Roman Inquisition have made him famous.

Galileo, like many scientists of his generation (see Document 7), determined that the observable world, rather than the received opinions found in books, was the ultimate authority in scientific matters. As a result, he was willing to argue, based on his observations with telescopes that he developed, that the sun (and not Earth) was indeed the center of the universe, even though several Biblical passages in passing implied that the sun moved around Earth. Holding these opinions caused controversy—many physicists of the time disagreed with Galileo for academic reasons. Some theologians also were worried about this apparent disregard for the Bible. Cardinal Bellarmine ordered Galileo not to hold or defend publicly the Copernican theory in 1615; when Galileo's friend Maffeo Cardinal Barberini was elected Pope Urban VIII, however, Galileo received permission to publish his ideas. Pope Urban, however, asked Galileo to discuss heliocentrism from a hypothetical perspective and to include other methods of explaining the observable phenomena.

The book Galileo published, however, angered the pope. The following extract makes the reasons for this anger apparent. Rather than viewing heliocentrism as a hypothesis, Galileo suggested that the Copernican theory was the only legitimate view. In fact, he named the opponent of heliocentrism "Simplicius," which basically means "very uneducated one" in Latin. Rather than producing an impartial textbook of theories of the universe, Galileo published an outright and inflammatory attack on the pope's own personal opinions.

Galileo did not perhaps anticipate the swift and angry reaction. Brought before the Roman Inquisition in 1633, Galileo was punished by house arrest and was forbidden to publish more on the subject. Although Galileo's university career was officially over, he continued to research and to publish until the time of his death. In the following extract, a careful reader with some experience in astronomy will be able to prove the heliocentrism of the solar system by following the instructions of the character Salviatus.

SIMPLICIUS. I do not as yet very well apprehend this structure, but it may be that with a drawing one may better and more easily discourse concerning the same.

SALVIATUS. Good; and, indeed, for your greater satisfaction and astonishment, I want you to draw it yourself and to see that, although you think you do not apprehend it, yet you understand it very perfectly; and only by answering to my interrogations you shall design it exactly. Take therefore a sheet of paper and compasses. Let this white paper be the immense expanse of the Universe, in which you are to distribute and dispose its parts in order, according as reason shall direct you. And, first, since without my instruction you verily believe that the Earth is placed in this Universe, therefore note a point at pleasure, about which you intend it to be placed, and mark it with some characters.

SIMP. Let this mark A be the place of the terrestrial globe.

SALV. Very well. I know, secondly, that you understand perfectly that the Earth is not within the body of the Sun, nor so much as contiguous to it, but distant some space from the same; therefore, assign to the Sun what other place you like, as remote from the Earth as you please, and mark this in like manner.

SIMP. Here it is; let the place of the solar body be O.

SALV. These two being constituted, we should think of placing Venus in such manner that its site and motion may agree with what the experience of the senses shows us and therefore recall to mind that which, either by the past discourses or your own observations, you have learnt to befall that star and afterwards assign to it that state which you think agrees with the same.

SIMP. Supposing those appearances expressed by you, and which I have likewise read in the little treatise of Conclusions, to be true, namely, that that star never recedes from the Sun beyond a certain interval of 40 degrees or thereabouts, so that it never comes either to opposition with the Sun, or so much as to quadrature, or yet to the sextile aspect; and, more than that, supposing that it appears at one time almost forty times greater than at another, namely, very great, when being retrograde it goes to the verspertine conjunction of the Sun, and very small when, with a motion straight forwards, it goes to the matutine conjunction; and moreover, it being true that, when it appears big, it shows with a corniculate or horned figure, and, when it appears little, it seems perfectly round—these appearances, I say, being true, I do not see how one can choose but affirm the said star to revolve in a circle about the Sun, for that the said circle cannot in any wise be said to encompass or to contain the Earth within it, nor to be inferior to the Sun, that is, between it and the Earth, nor yet superior to the Sun. That circle cannot encompass the Earth, because Venus would then sometimes come to opposition with the Sun; it cannot be inferior, for then Venus in both its conjunctions with the Sun would seem horned; nor can it be superior, for then it would always appear round and never cornicular; and therefore I will draw for Venus the circle *CH* about the Sun, without encompassing the Earth.

SALV. Having placed Venus, it is requisite that you think of Mercury, which, as you know, always keeping about the Sun, does recede less distance from it than Venus; therefore, consider with yourself what place is most convenient to assign it.

SIMP. It is not to be questioned but that, this planet imitating Venus, the most proper place for it will be a lesser circle within this of Venus, in like manner about the Sun; we may therefore upon these considerations draw its circle, marking it with the characers *BG*.

SALV. But Mars, where shall we place it?

SIMP. Mars, because it comes to an opposition with the Sun, its circle must of necessity encompass the Earth; but I see that it must necessarily encompass the Sun also, for coming to conjunction with the Sun, if it did not move over it but were below it, it would appear horned, as Venus and the Moon; but it shews always round, and therefore it is necessary that it should no less include the Sun within its circle than the Earth. And because I remember that you did say that when it is in opposition with the Sun it seems sixty times bigger than when it is in the conjunction, I think that a circle about the centre of the Sun that takes in the Earth will very well agree with these phenomena; which I note and mark *DI*, where Mars in the point *D* is near to the Earth and opposite to the Sun; but, when it is in the point *I*, it is at conjunction with the Sun but very far from the Earth. And because the same appearances are observed in Jupiter and Saturn, although with much lesser difference in Jupiter than in Mars, and with yet less in Saturn than in Jupiter, I understand that we should very aptly save all the phenomena of these two planets, with two circles in like manner drawn about the Sun, and this first for Jupiter, marking it *EL*, and another above that for *Saturn* marked *FM*.

SALV. You have behaved yourself bravely hitherto. And because (as you see) the measure of the approach and recession of the three superior planets is given by double the distance between the Earth and the Sun, this makes greater difference in Mars than in Jupiter, the circle *DI* of Mars being lesser than the circle *EL* of Jupiter; and likewise because this *EL* is less than this circle *FM* of Saturn, the said difference is also yet lesser in Saturn than in Jupiter, and that exactly answers the phenomena. It remains now that you assign a place to the Moon.

Girl with an armillary. The armillary mapped the constellations in relation to the earth, and symbolized understanding and education, c. 1520. © 2008 Jupiterimages Corporation.

SIMP. Following the same method (which seems to me very conclusive), since we see that the Moon comes to conjunction and opposition with the Sun, it is necessary to say that its circle encompasses the Earth, but yet it does not follow that it must environ the Sun, for then at the time of its conjunction it would not seem it could ever eclipse the Sun, as it often does; it is necessary therefore to assign it a circle about the Earth, which should be this NP, so that, being placed in P, it will appear from the Earth A to be in conjunction with the Sun, and, placed in N, it appears opposite to the Sun, and in that position it may fall under the Earth's shadow and be obscured.

SALV. Now, Simplicius, what shall we do with the fixed stars? Shall we suppose them scattered through the immense abuses of the Universe, at different distances from one determinate point; or else placed in a surface spherically distended about a centre of its own, so that each of them may be equidistant from the said centre?

SIMP. I would rather take a middle way and would assign them a circle described about a determinate centre and comprised with two spherical surfaces, to wit, one very high and concave, and the other lower, and convex, betwixt which I would constitute the innumerable multitude of stars, but yet at diverse altitudes, and this might be called the sphere of the Universe, containing within it the circles of the planets already by us described.

SALV. But now we have all this while, Simplicius, disposed the mundane bodies exactly according to the order of Copernicus, and we have done it with your hand; and moreover to each of them you have assigned peculiar motions of their own, except to the Sun, the Earth, and starry sphere; and to Mercury with Venus you have ascribed the circular motion about the Sun, without encompassing the Earth; about the same Sun you make the three superior planets, Mars, Jupiter, and Saturn, to move, comprehending the Earth within their circles. The Moon in the next place can move in no other manner than about the Earth, without taking in the Sun, and in all these emotions you agree also with Copernicus. There remain now three things to be decided between the Sun, the Earth, and fixed starts, namely *rest*, which seems to belong to the Earth; the *annual motion* under the zodiac, which appears to pertain to the Sun; and the *diurnal motion*, which seems to belong to the starry sphere and to be imparted by it to all the rest of the Universe, the Earth excepted. And it being true that all the circles of the planets, I mean Mercury, Venus, Mars, Jupiter, and Saturn, do move about the Sun as their centre, rest seems with so much more reason to belong to the said Sun than to the Earth, inasmuch as in a movable sphere it is more reasonable that the centre stand still than any other place remote from the centre; to the Earth, therefore, which is constituted in the midst of movable parts of the Universe, I mean between Venus and Mars, one of which makes its revolution in nine months and the other in two years, the motion of a year may very aptly be assigned, leaving rest to the Sun. And, if that be so, it follows of necessary consequence that, likewise, the diurnal motion belongs to the Earth; for if, the Sun standing still, the Earth should not revolve about itself but have only the annual motion about the Sun, our year would be no other than one day and one night, that is, six months of day and six months of night, as has already been said. You may consider withal how aptly the precipitate motion of twenty-four hours is taken away from the Universe, and the fixed stars, that are so many Suns, are made in conformity to our Sun to enjoy a perpetual rest. You see, moreover, what facility one meets with in this rough drawing to render the reason of so great appearances in the celestial bodies.

SAGREDUS. I very well perceive that facility, but, as you collect, from this simplicity, great probabilities for the truth of that system, others haply could make thence contrary deductions: wondering, not without reason, why being the ancient system of the Pythagoreans, and so well corresponding to the phenomena, it has in the succession of so many thousand years had so few followers and has been refuted even by Aristotle himself, and why later Copernicus himself has had no better fortune.

SALV. My dear Sagredus, if it has ever been your fate, as it has been mine, many and many a time, to hear what kind of idiocies are enough to make the vulgar contumacious and refractory, I will not say to agreeing but even to listening to these new ideas, I believe that your wonder at the paucity of those who are followers of that opinion would be much diminished. But small regard, in my judgment, ought to be had of such thick souls as think it a most convincing proof to confirm and steadfastly settle them in the belief of the Earth's immobility to see that in the same day they cannot dine at Constantinople and sup in Japan, and that the Earth, as being a most grave body, cannot clamber above the Sun and then slide headlong down again. Of such as these, whose number is infinite, we need not make any reckoning, nor need we record their fooleries or strive to gain to our side, as partakers in subtle and difficult opinions, individuals in whose definition the kind only is concerned and the difference

F. Villamœna Fecit

Galileo Galilei: This quiet portrait depicts one of the most controversial thinkers of his time. © 2008 Jupiterimages Corporation.

is wanting. Moreover, what ground do you think you could be able to gain, with all the demonstrations of the world, upon brains so stupid as are not able of themselves to know their utter follies? But my wondering, Sagredus, is very different from yours. You wonder that so few are followers of the Pythagorean opinion; and I am amazed how there could be any yet left till now that do embrace and follow it. Nor can I sufficiently admire the eminence of those men's intelligence who have received and held it to be true, and with the sprightliness of their judgments offered such violence to their own senses that they have been able to prefer that which their reason dictated to them to what sensible appearances represented most manifestly on the contrary. That the reasons against the diurnal vertiginous revolution of the earth, by you already examined, do carry great probability with them, we have already seen; as, also, that the Ptolemaics and Aristotelians with all their spectators did receive them for true is indeed a very great argument of their efficacy; but those experiences which overtly contradict the annual motion have yet so much more of an appearance of convincingness that (I say it again) I cannot find any bounds for my admiration how reason was able in Aristarchus and Copernicus to commit such a rape upon their senses as, in despite thereof, to make herself mistress of their belief.

Source: Galileo Galilei. *Salusbury, The Systeme of the World: In Four Dialogues, Wherein the Two Grand Systemes of Ptolomy and Copernicus Are Largely Discoursed Of.* Translated by Thomas Salusbury. 1661; Galileo Galilei. *Dialogue on the Great World Systems in the Salusbury Translation.* Revised, annotated, and introduced by Giorgio de Santillana. Chicago: University of Chicago Press, 1953, pp. 336–41.

9. A Muslim Doctor

Usamah ibn-Munqidh, who died in 1188, was an influential Syrian writer from a powerful family. One particular physician, ibn-Butlan, in the service of his great grandfather, made a lasting impression on the author. In the following extract, Usamah ibn-Munqidh describes how ibn-Butlan cured a particularly bad head cold: the doctor piled camphor onto the woman's head. Camphor does have antimicrobial properties and is used today, with menthol, in topical cold-alleviation products, such as Vicks VapoRub. By curing the lady's cold, the doctor not only alleviated her symptoms but also enabled her to return to mainstream society; the woman had been wrapping her head in many scarves in an attempt to keep her head warm, but once cured, she was able to return to wearing a single veil. Ultimately, this account from ibn-Munqidh's Kitab al-i'tibar is probably meant to be humorous.

There lived in Aleppo a woman, one of the notable women of the city, named Barrah. She was afflicted with a bad cold in the head. She would wrap her head up with old cotton, a hood, a piece of velvet and some napkins until she looked as though she wore a huge turban on her head, and she would still appeal for relief against the cold. She called ibn-Butlan and complained to him about her malady. He said to her, "Procure for me early tomorrow fifty *mithqals* of camphor with a strong smell, which thou canst either borrow or rent from some perfumer with the understanding that it will be returned intact." She procured the camphor for him. In the morning, the physician removed all that she had on her head and stuffed her hair with the camphor. Then he put back the wraps she had on her head. All that while she was appealing for relief against the cold. After sleeping for a short time, she woke up complaining of the heat and the tiresome weight on her head. The physician began to remove one piece at a time from her head until nothing was left but one veil. Then he shook off the camphor from her hair and all her cold disappeared. After that, she was contented with one veil for her head.

Source: Usamah ibn-Munqidh. *An Arab-Syrian Gentleman and Warrior in the Period of the Crusades: Memoirs of Usamah ibn-Munqidh.* Translated by Philip Hitti. New York: Columbia University Press, 1929, pp. 216–17.

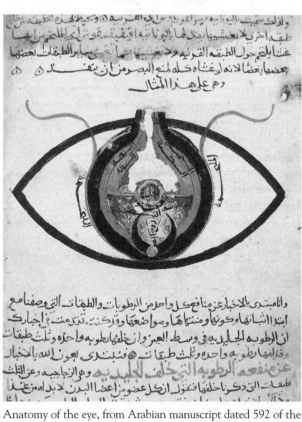

Anatomy of the eye, from Arabian manuscript dated 592 of the Hegira (A.D. 1214) by Al-Mutadibih. The Arab countries excelled in science and mathematics during the Middle Ages. The Art Archive / Egyptian Museum Cairo / Gianni Dagli Orti.

10. Chinese Medical Recipes

The Ben Cao Gang Mu, from which the following extract derives, is even today the major textbook of traditional Chinese medicine, even though its main author, Li Shizhen (Li Shi-chen) wrote in the late sixteenth century. Although many of these cures seem unlikely to Westerners (for example, the dropping of turtle urine in the ears to cure deafness), traditional Chinese medicine remains popular in the Orient and has gathered an increasingly large following in Europe and North America.

199 e TERRAPIN URINE

According to *Sun Kuang-hsien's Pei Men So Yen* the tortoise is a licentious animal and copulates with snakes. So take a tortoise put it in an earthenware basin and hold up a mirror. When the animal sees its reflection it will have desire and urinate, a utensil should be quickly held out to receive it. A slower method is to hold a lighted paper under the sacrum. In *Li Shi-chen's* day people obtained quicker results by pricking the nose of the animal with a pine needle or a pig's bristle.

Uses. *Ch'en Ts'ang-ch'i.* Dropped in the ear for deafness. *Li Shi-chen.* Placed under the tongue for slurred speech in the adult after a seizure. For children dumb from fright. Applied to the back and chest for hunchback and pidgeon breast. A hair dye used with leeches.

208 c TURTLE FAT

Uses. On the last day of the year pull out any white hairs and run turtle fat into the holes and they will not grow again. If it is desirable to grow the hair again and it does not do so, apply the milk from a white bitch.

225 b CLAM SHELL POWDER

Li Shih-chen says that this is a mixture of all kinds of sea shells from clams and oysters as distinct from fresh water products and powdered mussel shells. There is a kind of drug of threadlike appearance which disintegrates in water called *hai fen*, which on account of its name is bought by mistake. Being collected from the sea beaches it is good for removing phlegm and is demulcent.

PROPERTIES. SALINE, COOLING AND NONPOISONOUS

Directions. According to *Chu chen-hung*, because clam shells have been calcined they cannot be put into decoctions. *Wu Ch'in* said that only purple edged shells should be used. Others mistook powdered pumice for this article, the names being confused with *hai shi*.

Uses. To remove all types of phlegm, for hernia, gonorrhoea, leucorrheoa. Taken with cypress and ginger juice for pain in the stomach, *Chu Chen-heng, Pen-t'sao Pu-yi.* For water retention, to dissolve phlegm, for asthmatic cough, nausea, edema. A diuretic. For spermatorrhoea, painful indigestion, constipation. A carminative expelling gas, for swollen neck glands, and all toxic swellings, and all women's blood diseases. Mixed with oil it is applied to burns, *Li Shi-chen.*

The powder mixed with oil and wax to form a pill the size of a soap bean (nearly an inch), tied in a pig's kidney and steamed, is given once daily for night blindness, *Chang Tze-ho's Ju Men Shih-ch'in* (Yuan).

Source: *Chinese Materia Medica: Turtle and Shellfish Drugs.* Translated by Bernard E. Read. Beijing: Peking Natural History Bulletin, 1937, pp. 11–12, 27, 57–58.

11. Brahmagupta on Algebra

Brahmagupta, who flourished in the early seventh century in India, was a profound mathematician and astronomer whose discoveries influenced scientists not only in India but also in Arabia and, through the Muslim world, in Europe. His most famous work, Brahmesphuta-siddhanta (A.D. 628), from which the following extract comes, outlines the basic principles of mathematics and astronomy.

1. He, who distinctly and severally knows addition and the rest of the twenty logistics, and the eight determinations including measurement by shadow, is a mathematician.

2. Quantities, as well numerators as denominators, being multiplied by the opposite denominator, are reduced to a common denomination. In addition, the numerators are to be united. In subtraction, their difference is to be taken.

3. Integers are multiplied by the denominators and have the numerators added. The product of the numerators, divided by the product of the denominators, is multiplication of two or of many terms.

4. Both terms being rendered homogenous, the denominator and numerator of the divisor are transposed: and then the denominator of the dividend is multiplied by the [new] denominator; and its numerator, by the [new] numerator. Thus division [is performed].

5. The quantity being made homogenous, the square of the numerator, divided by the square of the denominator, is the square. The root of the homogenous numerator, divided by the root of the denominator, is the square-root.

6. The cube of the last term is to be set down; and, at the first remove from it, thrice the square of the last multiplied by the preceding; then thrice the square of this preceding term taken into that last one; and finally the cube of the preceding term. The sum is the cube.

7. The divisor for the second non-cubic [digit] is thrice the square of the cubic-root. The square of the quotient, multiplied by three and by the preceding, must be subtracted from the next [non-cubic]; and the cube from the cubic [digit]: the root [is found].

Source: *Algebra, with Arithmetic and Mensuration, from the Sanscrit of Brahmegupta and Bhascara.* Translated by Henry Thomas Colebrooke. London: John Murray, 1817, pp. 277–80.

12. Treating the Plague

The plague, be it the bubonic plague or another more localized endemic, posed serious health risks throughout the Middle Ages and Renaissance. Before the discovery of microorganisms, medical theory believed that bad odors spread disease. Because of this theory, the prevention of plague centered on creating a sweet-smelling environment through burning herbs, such as rosemary. Although scientifically inaccurate, these prescriptions may have done some good, given that offensive-smelling rubbish was removed from the dwelling, thereby increasing public sanitation.

The following extract is a good example of Renaissance medicine. Designed as a self-help book for those too poor to afford a university-trained physician but wealthy enough to read, the book gives medicinal recipes for the prevention and curing of plague. Just like other cookbooks of the period, the quantity of each ingredient to be used is very vague. The writer backs up his recommendations with the testimony of a man from Andover, who apparently has succeeded in containing the disease.

PLAGUE AND PESTILENCE

Herein are contained diverse and sundry good rules and easy Medicines, which are made with little charge, for the poorer sort of people, as well for the preservation of all people from the Plague before infection, as for the curing and ordering of them after such time as they shall be infected.

A PRESERVATIVE BY CORRECTING THE AIR IN ALL HOUSES

Take *Rosemary* dryed, *Juniper, Bay-leaves,* or *Frankincense,* and cast the same upon the coals in a chafing-dish, and receive the fume or smoke thereof into your head. If you will, put a little *Lavender* or *Sage* that is dryed, into the fire with the rest; it will do much good.

Also to make your fires in earthen pans (rather to remove about your Chambers, then in Chimneys) shall be better to correct the airs in your houses, then otherwise.

A PRESERVATIVE AGAINST THE PLAGUE

Take a handfull of *Herb-grace,* otherwise called *Rue,* a handful of *Elder-leaves,* a handful of red *Sage,* and a handful of red *Bramble-leaves,* and stamp them well together, and strain them through a fine linen cloth, with a quart of white *Wine,* then take a quantity of *Case Ginger,* and mingle it with them, and drink a good draught thereof both morning and evening for the space of nine days together, and by God's grace it will preserve you.

AN EXCELLENT GOOD DRINK TO BE TAKEN EVERY MORNING FOR A PRESERVATIVE AGAINST THE PLAGUE, AND FOR TO AVOID INFECTION

Take a handful of *Winter-Savery,* and boil the same in a quart of good *wine-Vinegar,* with a spoonful of *Grains* being very fine beaten, and put into the same, then put into it a quantity of fine *Sugar,* and so drink a good draught thereof every morning fasting.

When you must of necessity come into any place where any infectious persons are, it is good for you to smell to the root of *Angelica, Gentian,* or *Valerian,* and to chew any of these in your mouth.

A SPECIALL PRESERVATIVE AGAINST THE PLAGUE

Take five spoonfuls of *wine-Vinegar,* three spoonfuls of fair *running-Water,* half a spoonful of *Treacle of Jene,* and of *Bole armeniac* as much as a small nut, being beaten to powder, and drink this every morning and every evening. *Proved by M. Knight of Andover.*

Escaping the Black Death. These fourteenth-century flagellants seek to escape the plague by repentance, self-mortification, and faith in God. © 2008 Jupiterimages Corporation.

Take vi leaves of *Sorrel*, and wash them with *Water* and *Vinegar*, and let them lie to steep in the said *Water* and *Vinegar* a good while, then eat them fasting and keep in your mouth and chew now or then either *Stewall*, or the root of *Angelica*, or a little *Cinnamon*, for any of these is marvellous good.

MEDICINES TO BE USED AFTER INFECTION TAKEN

Forasmuch as the greatest cause of the Plague doth stand rather in poison, than in any putrefaction of humors, as other Agues do, the chiefest way is to move much sweating, and to defend the hart by some cordial thing.

Source: A. T. *A Rich Storehouse or Treasury for the Diseased*. London: Thomas Purfoot and Ralph Blower, 1596.

Language and Literature

As the linguist Noam Chomsky has argued, human beings develop language instinctively. All human societies across the globe have a well-developed verbal language, and these verbal languages often have surprising grammatical similarities. Although language is essential to the smooth operation of every realm of daily life—complicated work simply cannot be done efficiently without language—language comes to artistic perfection in the realm of literature. Whereas language is a means or a tool in other branches of life, the beauty of language is frequently the end and goal of literature.

Because literature is so thoroughly tied up with language, only fluent speakers of that language can fully relish a work of high literature. The beauty of the images in the poetry of Li Po (Document 15) will strike any reader in translation, but only a speaker of Chinese can appreciate the beauty of the words themselves. Likewise, Dante's *Divine Comedy* in English translation can strike readers as a treatise, but the original Italian *Divina Commedia* remains completely and utterly poetry. Dante himself outlines his love for his native tongue and discusses why others are less keen in Document 14.

The close ties between a language and the people who speak that language can also be used to create political statements. When the Islamic kingdoms switched from Greek (a foreign language in central Arabia) to Arabic, they were asserting a nationalistic self-confidence in themselves (Document 16). The Arab kingdoms were ready to throw off the trappings of the *Byzantine Empire* and to assert their own Arab identity—non-Arabs may have been much less pleased with these developments. Likewise, when Petrarch advocated a return to the Latin of Cicero (see Document 13), he was not making a merely linguistic point; instead, he was in reality urging a return to a whole series of cultural values that Petrarch associated with ancient Rome, including rational discussion, rule of law, and a vigorous Italian empire. Language politics mirror personal and national political positions.

Politics can pervade more than just language, of course; literature often contains direct and obvious political statements. Document 17, by the renowned Persian epic author Firdawsi, contains a clear political and moral lesson: tyrannical kings should be overthrown by the divinely inspired people. The villain in the episode is a magic-wielding king, and the hero is an honest and family-loving blacksmith. Right overcomes injustice.

Although literature allows us insight into the life and times of the past, we must remember that the window offered by literature is narrow—most authors were from the upper, educated classes and were male. The illiterate poor, by definition, had little access to written forms of communication, and women were often viewed in the Middle Ages and Renaissance as not fit for serious writing. As a result, the Japanese *Genji Monogatari* (Document 18) by Murasaki Shikibu, along with European works by authors such as Margery *Kempe* and *Christine de Pisan*, is a refreshing change of perspective. Murasaki Shikibu herself was intimately familiar with Japanese court life, and her classic novel is sensitive to the emotions, insights, and position of women in upper-class Japanese society.

13. Petrarch to Cicero

Petrarch (1304–1374), or Francesco Petrarca as he is known in Italian, is often viewed as the father of the European Renaissance and certainly was the most influential scholar of his day. Through his essays and scholarship, Petrarch urged Europe to rediscover fully the thought and ideals of ancient Rome and, to a lesser extent, ancient Greece. As the following document shows, Petrarch idolized in particular the Latin writings of Marcus Tullius Cicero (106–43 B.C.), the Roman philosopher, orator, and politician. Although Latin remained the linguistic medium of all serious communication in the Middle Ages, the Latin used had developed considerably from Cicero's day. The Latin of the medieval courts, governments, schools, and traders would have been virtually unintelligible to the Latin-speakers of first-century B.C. Rome. Petrarch urged a return to the cultural standards of classical antiquity in language, culture, and thought.

Although Europe widely embraced this return to the classical aesthetics of Greece and Rome, Cicero represented more than just a great thinker and writer to Petrarch—he was also an Italian patriot. Toward the close of the letter that Petrarch wrote to his dead predecessor, Cicero, Petrarch laments that the Roman Empire has collapsed. Not only does Rome not control as far as the Danube (i.e., modern-day Germany and Hungary) and Ganges (India), but furthermore, she does not even control the whole of the Italian peninsula. The peninsula, in fact, had broken up into small city-states that squabbled interminably among themselves. Petrarch's longing for Ciceronian language and thought, therefore, cannot be separated from his longing for an Italian empire.

In English-speaking countries, Petrarch has suffered the fate that he laments in Cicero: although he is widely spoken of, he is little read. The following selection helps remedy that problem slightly.

If my earlier letter gave you offence,—for, as you often have remarked, the saying of your contemporary in the *Andria* is a faithful one, that compliance begets friends, truth only hatred,—you shall listen now to words that will soothe your wounded feelings and prove that the truth need not always be hateful. For, if censure that is true angers us, true praise, on the other hand, gives us delight.

You lived then, Cicero, if I may be permitted to say it, like a mere man, but spoke like an orator, wrote like a philosopher. It was your life that I criticised; not your mind, nor your tongue; for the one fills me with admiration, the other with amazement. And even in your life I feel the lack of nothing but stability, and the love of quiet that should go with your philosophic professions, and abstention from civil war, when liberty had been extinguished and the republic buried and its dirge sung.

See how different my treatment of you is from yours of Epicurus, in your works at large, and especially in the *De Finibus*. You are continually praising his life, but his talents you ridicule. I ridicule in you nothing at all. Your life does awaken my pity, as I have said; but your talents and your eloquence call for nothing but congratulation. O great father of Roman eloquence! not I alone but all who deck themselves with the flowers of Latin speech render thanks unto you. It is from your well-springs that we draw the streams that water our meads. You, we freely acknowledge, are the leader who marshals us; yours are the words of encouragement that sustain us; yours is the light that illumines the path before us. In a word, it is under your auspices that we have attained to such little skill in this art of writing as we may possess. . . .

You have heard what I think of your life and your genius. Are you hoping to hear of your books also; what fate has befallen them, how they are esteemed by the masses and among scholars? They still are in existence, glorious volumes, but we of today are too feeble a folk to read them, or even to be acquainted with their mere titles. Your fame extends far and wide; your name is mighty, and fills the ears of men; and yet those who really know you are very few, be it because the times are unfavourable, or because men's minds are slow and dull, or, as I am the more inclined to believe, because the love of money forces our thoughts in other directions. Consequently right in our own day, unless I am much mistaken, some of your books have disappeared, I fear beyond recovery.

It is a great grief to me, a great disgrace to this generation, a great wrong done to posterity. The shame of failing to cultivate our own talents, thereby depriving the future of the fruits that they might have yielded, is not enough for us; we must waste and spoil, through our cruel and insufferable neglect, the fruits of your labours too, and of those of your fellows as well, for the fate that I lament in the case of your own books has befallen the works of many another illustrious man.

It is of yours alone, though, that I would speak now. Here are the names of those among them whose loss is most to be deplored: the *Republic*, the *Praise of Philosophy*, the treatises on the *Care of Property*, on the *Art of War*, on *Consolation*, on *Glory*,—although in the case of this last my feeling is rather one of hopeful uncertainty than of certain despair. And then there are huge gaps in the volumes that have survived. It is as if indolence and oblivion had been worsted, in a great battle, but we had to mourn noble leaders slain, and others lost or maimed. This last indignity very many of your books have suffered, but more particularly the *Orator*, the *Academics*, and the *Laws*. They have come forth from the fray so mutilated and disfigured that it would have been better if they had perished outright.

Now, in conclusion, you will wish me to tell you something about the condition of Rome and the Roman republic: the present appearance of the city and whole country, the degree of harmony that prevails, what classes of citizens possess political power, by whose hands and with what wisdom the reins of empire are swayed, and whether the Danube, the Ganges, the Ebro, the Nile, the Don, are our boundaries now, or in very truth the man has arisen who "bounds our empire by the ocean-stream, our fame by the stars of heaven," or "extends our rule beyond Garama and Ind," as your friend the Mantuan has said. Of these and other matters of like nature I doubt not you would very gladly hear. Your filial piety tells me so, your well-known love of country, which you cherished even to your own destruction. But indeed it were better that I refrained. Trust me, Cicero, if you were to hear of our condition to-day you would be moved to tears, in whatever circle of heaven above, or Erebus below, you may be dwelling. Farewell, forever.

Written in the world of the living; on the left bank of the Rhone, in Transalpine Gaul; in the same year, but in the month of December, the 19th day.

Source: Petrarch. *Petrarch: The First Modern Scholar and Man of Letters*. Edited and translated by James Harvey Robinson. New York: G.P. Putnam, 1898, pp. 249–52.

14. Dante on the Italian Language

Dante Alighieri (1265–1321) is the Italian writer whose work has had the greatest influence on later Italian and world literature. His most famous work is La Divina Commedia *(The Divine Comedy), in which the narrator journeys through hell, purgatory, and heaven. An extract from this famous work can be found in Document 17 in Part VIII: Religious Life.*

Although Dante's poetry has become famous, his decision to write in the Italian language was controversial. Throughout the Middle Ages, Latin (the language of the ancient Romans) was the prestige language—all serious literature and business were conducted in Latin. The vernacular (i.e., the language of the common people), however, had already carved out a niche in entertainment literature, especially love poetry. Beyond providing simple entertainment, however, such poetry could also explore philosophical positions. Petrarch, for example, explored the triviality of mortal life in comparison with the heavenly reward in his Canzoniere. Dante's Divina Commedia, however, has an even more serious tone. His choice of the Italian vernacular for his work rather than the "serious" Latin therefore remains a courageous choice.

Not only did Italian literature face the challenge of Latin literature, but it also faced the challenge of Provençal literature. Provençal was the language spoken in southern France (i.e., Provence) and northeastern Spain. It had developed an active literary and poetical tradition by the eleventh century and became celebrated across western Europe. Because of its influence, many Italian (and Spanish) writers, such as Alberto Malaspina, wrote in Provençal instead of their own native language. In choosing Italian, Dante was staking a claim to the intrinsic capacity of the Italian language to convey meaning as precisely and as meaningfully as Latin and Provençal.

Because of the contested position of Italian, Dante felt the need to defend its merits in several places. His treatise De vulgari eloquentia (On the Eloquence of the Vernacular) deals explicitly with the value of Italian. The following extract, from Il Convivio, likewise outlines why some authors have chosen to ignore Italian and why Dante holds the language so dear.

To the perpetual infamy and suppression of the evil men of Italy who prize the vernacular of another and disprize their own, I declare that their impulse arises from five detestable causes. The first, blindness in discernment; the second, disingenuous excusing; the third, desire of vainglory; the fourth, the prompting of envy; the fifth and last, abjectness of mind or pusillanimity. And each one of these guilty tendencies has so great a following that there be few exempt from them.

Of the first one may thus discourse: like as the sensitive part of the mind hath its eyes whereby it apprehendeth the difference of things in so far as they are coloured externally, even so hath the rational part its eye whereby it apprehendeth the difference of things in so far as they be ordained to some certain end; and this same eye is discernment. And like as he who is blind with the eyes of sense must ever judge of evil or good according to others, so he who is blind of the light of discernment must ever follow in his judgment after mere report, true or false. And so, whensoever the leader is blind, he himself, and also the one, blind likewise, who leaneth upon him, must needs come to an evil end. Wherefore it is written, that the blind shall lead the blind and so shall they both fall into the ditch. Now this same report hath long been counter to our vernacular, for reasons which will be discoursed below. Following the which, the blind ones spoken of above, who are almost without number, with their hands upon the shoulders of these liars, have fallen into the ditch of the false opinion from which they know not how to escape. To the habit of this light of discernment the populace are specially blinded, because they are occupied from the beginning of their lives with some trade, and so direct their minds to it, by force of necessity, that they give heed to nought else. And because the habit of a virtue, whether moral or intellectual, may not be had of a sudden, but must needs be acquired by practice, and they devote their practice to some art, and are not careful to discern other things, it is impossible for them to have discernment. Wherefore it comes to pass that they often cry long live their death and death to their life, if only someone raise the cry. And this is the most perilous defect involved in their blindness. Wherefore

Boethius considers popular glory an empty thing, because he sees that it has no discernment. Such are to be regarded as sheep and not men; for if one sheep were to fling itself over a precipice of a thousand paces all the others would go after it; and if one sheep leap for any reason as it passes a street all the others leap, although they see nothing to leap over. And ere now I myself have seen one after another leap into a well because one leapt into it (thinking, I suppose, that it was leaping over a wall), although the shepherd, wailing and shouting, set himself with arms and breast before them.

The second sect who oppose our vernacular is made up by disingenuous excusings. There are many who love to be thought masters rather than to be such; and to avoid the opposite (to wit, not being thought such) they ever find fault with the material of their art that is furnished them, or else the instrument; for example, a bad smith finds fault with the iron furnished him, and a bad harper finds fault with the harp, thinking to throw the blame of the bad knife or the bad music upon the iron and upon the harp, and to remove it from himself. And in like manner there be some, and they are not few, who would have men think them poets; and to excuse themselves for not poetizing, or for poetizing badly, they accuse and blame the material, to wit their own vernacular, and praise that of others, which they are not required to forge. And if anyone would see how far this iron is really to be blamed, let him look upon the works which the good artificers make from it, and he will recognize the disingenuousness of those who by blaming it think to excuse themselves. Against such as these Tully cries out in the beginning of a book of his, which is called the book *Concerning the Goal of Good;* because in his time

Dante Alighieri. Although Dante lived much of his life in exile, he nevertheless became Italy's most treasured poet. Dover Pictorial Archives

they found fault with the Latin of the Romans and commended the Grammar of the Greeks, for the like reasons for which these others now make the Italian speech cheap and that of Provence precious.

The third sect against our vernacular is made up by desire of vainglory. There are many who by handling things composed in some tongue not their own, and by commending the said tongue, look to be more admired than by handling things in their own tongue; but it is blameworthy to commend it beyond the truth, in order to vaunt oneself for such acquirement.

The fourth is made up the prompting of envy. As was said above, there is envy wherever there is similarity. Amongst men of one tongue there is similarity in vernacular; and because one cannot handle it as another can, envy springs up. So the envious man goes subtly to work and doth not find with him who poetises the fault of not knowing how to write, but finds fault with that which is the material of his work, so that by slighting the work on that side he may deprive the poet of honour and fame; as one should find fault with the steel of a sword for the sake of discrediting not the steel, but the whole work of the master.

The fifth and last sect is impelled by abjectness of mind. The large-souled man ever exalts himself in his heart, and so counterwise the small-souled man ever holds himself less than he really is. And because magnifying and minifying always have regard to something in comparison to which the large-souled man makes himself great and the small-souled man makes himself little, it comes to pass that the large-souled man always makes others of less account than they are, and the small-souled man of more. And because with the same measure wherewith a man measures himself he measures the things that are his, which are as it were a part of himself, it comes to pass that the large-souled man's things always seem to him better than they are, and the things of others worse; and the small-souled man always thinks his things of little worth, and the things of others of much. Wherefore many, by reason of his abjectness, depreciate their own vernacular and praise that of others.

And all these together make up the detestable wretches of Italy who hold cheap that costly vernacular, if which be vile in ought it is only in so far as it sounds upon the prostitute lips of these adulterers, by whose guidance the blind men go of whom I made mention under the head of the first cause. . . .

And all these causes have been at work begetting and strengthening the love which I bear to my vernacular, as I will briefly show. A thing is near in proportion as of all the things of its kind it is most closely united to a man; wherefore a son is nearest to his father; and of all arts medicine is nearest to the doctor, and music to the musician, because they are more closely united to them than are the rest; of all lands that is nearest to a man wherein he maintains himself, because it is more closely united to him. And thus a man's proper vernacular is nearest to him, inasmuch as it is most closely united to him; for it is singly and alone in his mind before any other; and not only is it united to him essentially, in itself, but also incidentally, inasmuch as it is conjoined with the persons closest to him, as his relatives, his fellow-citizens, and his own people. Such, then, is a man's own vernacular, which we will not call near, but most nearest to him. Wherefore, if nearness be the seed of friendship, as was said above, it is clear that it is amongst the causes of the love which I bear to my tongue, which is most near to me above the others. It was the abovesaid cause, namely that that is most closely untied which at first has sole possession of the mind, that gave rise to the custom which makes first-born sons succeed alone, as the closer, and because closer, more loved.

Again its excellence makes me its friend. And here you are to know that every excellence proper to a thing is to be loved in that thing; as in masculinity to be well bearded, and in femininity to be well smooth of beard over all the face. As in a setter, good scent, and in a boarhound, good speed. And the more proper is the excellence the better is it to be loved; wherefore, though every virtue is to be loved in man, that is most to be loved in him which is most human; and that is justice, which abides only in the rational or intellectual part, to wit in the will. This is so much to be loved that, as the Philosopher says in the fifth of the *Ethics*, they who are its foes, as are robbers and plunderers, love it; and therefore we see that its contrary, to wit injustice, is most hated; as treachery, ingratitude, forgery, theft, rapine, cheating, and their likes. Which be such inhuman sins that, to shield himself from the infamy thereof, long usage alloweth that man may speak of himself, as was said above, and that he have leave to declare himself faithful and loyal. Of this virtue I shall hereafter speak more at length in the fourteenth treatise, and here leaving it I return to the matter at hand. That has been shown, then, to be the most proper excellence of a thing which is most loved and praised in it; and we must see in each case what that excellence is. Now we see that in all matters of speech rightly to manifest the conception is the most loved and commended. This, then, is its prime excellence. And inasmuch as this excellence abideth in our vernacular, as hath been shown above, in another chapter, it is clear that it is of the causes of the love which I bear to the said vernacular; because, as already said, excellence is a cause that generates love.

Source: Dante Alighieri. *The Convivio of Dante Alighieri*. Translated by Philip Wicksteed. London: Dent, 1924, pp. 48–56.

15. The Poetry of Li Po

Li Po (A.D. 701–62) is the most famous poet of the Tang dynasty and is considered one of the best Chinese poets of all time. He led a life of dissolution, addicted in particular to drinking, but he became a favorite of the emperor and the emperor's household. He allegedly crafted some of his best poetry while under the influence of alcohol, though we may doubt the accuracy of this tradition: Li Po undoubtedly attempted to become a "character" by highlighting his inebriation when considerable sober forethought probably went into most of his poems. According to legend, his alcoholism led directly to his death; in a drunken stupor he attempted to embrace the reflection of the moon in a river while he drifted alone in a boat. The legend encapsulates two of the major themes in Li Po's poetry, the beauty of nature and lonesome solitude, as the proceeding selections will demonstrate.

A Tortoise

A tortoise I see
on a lotus-flower resting:
A bird amid the reeds

and the rushes is nesting;
A light skiff propelled
by some boatman's fair daughter,
Whose song dies away
over the fast-flowing water.

In the Mountains on a Summer Day

Gently I stir a white feather fan,
With open shirt sitting in a green wood.
I take off my cap and hang it on a jutting stone;
A wind from the pine-tree trickles on my bare head.

Clearing at Dawn

The fields are chill; the sparse rain has stopped;
The colours of Spring teem on every side.
With leaping fish the blue pond is full;
With singing thrushes the green boughs droop.
The flowers of the field have dabbled their powdered cheeks;
The mountain grasses are bent level at the waist.
By the bamboo stream the last fragment of cloud
Blown by the wind slowly scatters away.

To Tan Ch'iu

My friend is lodging high in the Eastern Range,
Dearly loving the beauty of valleys and hills.
At green Spring he lies in the empty woods,
And is still asleep when the sun shines on high.
A pine-tree wind dusts his sleeves and coat;
A pebbly stream cleans his heart and ears.
I envy you, who far from strife and talk
Are high-propped on a pillow of blue cloud.

Self-Abandonment

I sat drinking and did not notice the dusk,
Till falling petals filled the folds of my dress.
Drunken I rose and walked to the moonlit stream;
The birds were gone, and men also few.

Drinking Alone by Moonlight: Three Poems

1

   A cup of wine under the flowering trees;
I drink alone, for no friend is near.
Raising my cup I beckon the bright moon,
For he, with my shadow, will make three men.
The moon, alas! is no drinker of wine;

Listless, my shadow creeps about at my side.
Yet with the moon as friend and the shadow as slave
I must make merry before the Spring is spent.
To the songs I sing the moon flickers her beams;
In the dance I weave my shadow tangles and breaks.
While we were sober, three shared the fun;
Now we are drunk, each goes his way.
May we long share our odd, inanimate feast,
And meet at last on the Cloudy River of the Sky.

2

Is thick-spread with a carpet of fallen flowers.
Who in Spring can bear to grieve alone?
Who, sober, look on sights like these?
Riches and Poverty, long or short life,
By the Maker of Things are portioned and disposed;
But a cup of wine levels life and death
And a thousand things obstinately hard to prove.
When I am drunk, I lose Heaven and Earth.
Motionless—I cleave to my lonely bed.
At last I forget that I exist at all,
And at that moment my joy is great indeed.

3

If High Heaven had no love for wine,
There would not be a Wine Star in the sky.
If Earth herself had no love for wine,
There would not be a city called Wine Springs.
Since Heaven and Earth both love wine,
I can love wine, without shame before God.
Clear wine was once called a Saint
Thick wine was once called a Sage.
Of Saint and Sage I have long quaffed deep,
What need for me to study spirits and *hsien?*
At the third cup I penetrate the Great Way;
A full gallon—Nature and I are one.
But the things I feel when wine possesses my soul
I will never tell to those who are not drunk.

Sources: First poem: Giles, Herbert. *A History of Chinese Literature*. New York: Appleton, 1901, p. 156. Others: *More Translations from the Chinese*. Translated by Arthur Waley. London: George Allen, 1919, pp. 20–23.

16. Arabic Replaces Greek in the Islamic World

Al-Baladhuri was an influential ninth-century Muslim intellectual who spent most of his life in Baghdad and in Syria. He is most known for his history of the rise of the Arab kingdoms in the Middle East, an extract of which is printed here. As the Arab, and specifically Islamic, kingdoms grew in power and confidence, they became more independent and nationalistic, devising at various points, for example, their own currency and dating system (based on the date of Muhammad's flight to Medina). In the following document, for example, the year 81 equals A.D. 703.

Part of Arabic independence can be seen in the switch from Greek to Arabic as the language of official record keeping. The Islamic world had inherited the well-run bureaucratic system of the Byzantine Empire, which was predominantly Greek speaking. To aid in the transition, the new Arab kingdoms largely kept the Greek system for their own record keeping. The changeover in language, thus, reflects a new level of nationalistic self-confidence in the Arab world's ability to manage complex domestic and international issues. The document, however, presents a colorful story describing the cause of the linguistic shift: a Greek scribe urinated in an inkwell. Whether or not such an incident ever occurred, the clear growth of nationalistic pride remains evident.

AL-BALADHURI'S *KITÂB FUTÛH AL-BULDÂN*

Greek remained the language of the state registers until the reign of 'Abd-al-Malik ibn-Marwân, who in the year 81 ordered it changed. The reason was that a Greek clerk desiring to write something and finding no ink urinated in the inkstand. Hearing this, 'Abd-al-Malik punished the man and gave orders to Sulaimân ibn Sa'd to change the language of the registers. Sulaimân requested 'Abd-al-Malik to give him as subsidy the *kharâj* of the Jordan province for one year. 'Abd-al-Malik granted his request and assigned him to the governorship of the Jordan. No sooner had the year ended, than the change of the language was finished and Sulaimân brought the registers to 'Abd-al-Malik. The latter called Sarjûn and presented to him the new plan. Sarjûn was greatly chagrined and left 'Abd-al-Mallik sorrowful. Meeting certain Greek clerks, he said to them, "Seek your livelihood in any other profession than this, for God has cut it off from you."

The total tax of the Jordan which was thus assigned as subsidy was 180,000 *dînârs*, that of Palestine was 350,000; that of Damascus 400,000; that of Hims with Kinnasrîn and the regions called today al-'Awâsim, 800,000, and according to others 700,000.

Source: al-Baladhuri, Abbas Ahmad ibn-Jabir. *The Origins of the Islamic State.* Translated by Philip Kuri Hitti. Vol. 1. New York: Columbia University Press, 1916, p. 301.

17. Firdawsi, "Poet of Paradise"

Firdawsi, whose name means "poet of paradise," produced the most famous epic in the Persian language. His work, Sháh Námeh (Book of Kings), completed in 1010, chronicles the legendary careers of Persia's ancient rulers. The Persian language has changed so little that modern Persian speakers are still able to understand the work when it is read aloud. Although sometimes considered tedious by Western audiences, the Sháh Námeh holds the same place in Iran as Homer's Odyssey and Iliad do in Greece, Europe, and North America.

The next extract describes the defeat of the tyrant-king Zohák by a young boy, Feridún, and his blacksmith ally, Kavah. Zohák is a magical tyrant who demands the sacrifice of young children every year, until Kavah refuses to send his own children and joins forces with Feridún. Kavah's leather apron becomes the flag for the rebellion and an object of worship for later generations. As in Homer's works, which feature capricious divine intervention, magic plays a large role in the fighting depicted in Sháh Námeh. *Zohák commands the allegiance of demons and peris (fallen angels who try to do good), and Feridún is able to slay such foes with his mace.*

Although Sháh Námeh *functions as entertainment and was treated in former times as a kind of history, it also functioned as a didactic manual of good kingship and responsible citizenship. Zohák, though a king, loses the respect of his people by unnecessarily wasting their lives; faced with such circumstances, the people, just like Kavah, have the right and the responsibility to overthrow the government. It is perhaps no surprise that Firdawsi himself, according to legend, was forced to flee from King Mahmud, who controlled Iran during much of Firdawsi's lifetime and who was unfriendly to the Shi'ite Muslim majority in Iran.*

KAVAH, THE BLACKSMITH

Zohák having one day summoned together all the nobles and philosophers of the kingdom, he said to them: "I find that a young enemy has risen up against me; but notwithstanding his tender years, there is no safety even with an apparently insignificant foe. I hear, too, that though young, he is distinguished for his prowess and wisdom; yet I fear not him, but the change of fortune. I wish therefore to assemble a large army, consisting of Men, Demons, and Peris, that this enemy may be surrounded, and conquered. And, further, since a great enterprise is on the eve of being undertaken, it will be proper in future to keep a register or muster-roll of all the people of every age in my dominions, and have it revised annually." The register, including both old and young, was accordingly prepared.

At that period there lived a man named Kavah, a black-smith, remarkably strong and brave, and who had a large family. Upon the day on which it fell to the lot of two of his children to be killed to feed the serpents, he rose up with indignation in presence of the king, and said:

> "Thou art the king, but wherefore on my head
> Cast fire and ashes? If thou has the form
> Of hissing dragon, why to me be cruel?
> Why give the brains of my beloved children
> As serpent-food, and talk of doing justice?"
> At this bold speech the monarch was dismayed,
> And scarcely knowing what he did, released
> The blacksmith's sons. How leapt the father's heart,
> How warmly he embraced his darling boys!
> But now Zohák directs that Kavah's name
> Shall be inscribed upon the register.
> Soon as the blacksmith sees it written there,
> Wrathful he turns towards the chiefs assembled,
> Exclaiming loud: "Are ye then men, or what,
> Leagued with a Demon!" All astonished heard,
> And saw him tear the hated register,
> And cast it under foot with rage and scorn.

Kavah having thus reviled the king bitterly, and destroyed the register of blood, departed from the court, and took his children along with him. After he had gone away, the nobles said to the king:

"Why should reproaches, sovereign of the world,
Be thus permitted? Why the royal scroll
Torn in thy presence, with a look and voice
Of proud defiance, by the rebel blacksmith?
So fierce his bearing, that he seems to be a bold confederate of this Feridún."
Zohák replied: "I know not what o'ercame me,
But when I saw him with such vehemence
Of grief and wild distraction, strike his forehead,
Lamenting o'er his children, doomed to death,
Amazement seized my heart, and chained my will.
What may become of this, Heaven only knows,
For none can pierce the veil of destiny."
Kavah, meanwhile, with warning voice set forth
What wrongs the nation suffered, and there came
Multitudes round him, who called out aloud
For justice! justice! On his javelin's point
He fixed his leathern apron for a banner,
And lifting it on high, he went abroad
To call the people to a task of vengeance.
Wherever it was seen crowds followed fast,
Tired of the cruel tyranny they suffered.
"Let us unite with Feridún," he cried,
And from Zohák's oppression we are free!"
And still he called aloud, and all obeyed
Who heard him, high and low. Anxious he sought
For Feridún, not knowing his retreat:
But still he hoped success would crown his search.
The hour arrived, and when he saw the youth,
Instinctively he knew him, and thanked Heaven
For that good fortune. Then the leathern banner
Was splendidly adorned with gold and jewels,
And called the flag of Kavah. From that time
It was a sacred symbol; every king
In future, on succeeding to the throne,
Did honor to that banner, the true sign
Of royalty, in veneration held.

Feridún, aided by the directions and advice of the blacksmith now proceeded against Zohák. His mother wept to see him depart, and continually implored the blessing of God upon him. He had two elder brothers, whom he took along with him.

Desirous of having a mace formed like the head of a cow, he requested Kavah to make one of iron, and it was accordingly made in the shape he described. In his progress, he visited a shrine or place of pilgrimage frequented by the worshippers of God, where he besought inspiration and aid, and where he was taught by a radiant personage the mysteries of the magic art, receiving form him a key to every secret.

Bright beamed his eye, with firmer step he strode,
His smiling cheek with warmer crimson glowed.

When his two brothers saw his altered mien, the pomp and splendor of his appearance, they grew envious of his good fortune, and privately meditated his fall. One day they found him asleep at the foot of a mountain, and they immediately went to the top and rolled down a heavy fragment of rock upon him with the intention of crushing him to death; but the clattering noise of the stone awoke him, and, instantly employing the knowledge of sorcery which had been communicated to him, the stone was suddenly arrested by him in its course. The brothers beheld this with astonishment, and hastening down the mountain, cried aloud: "We know not how the stone was loosened from its place: God forbid that it should have done any injury to Feridún." Feridún, however, was well aware of this being the evil work of his brothers, but he took no notice of the conspiracy, and instead of punishing them, raised them to higher dignity and consequence.

They saw that Kavah directed the route of Feridún over the mountainous tracts and plains which lie contiguous to the banks of the Dijleh, or Tigris, close to the city of Bagdád. Upon reaching that river, they called for boats, but got no answer from the ferryman; at which Feridún was enraged, and immediately plunged, on horseback, into the foaming stream. All his army followed without delay, and with the blessing of God arrived on the other side in safety. He then turned toward the Bait-el-Mukaddus, built by Zohák. In the Pahlavi language it was called Kunuk-duz-mokt. The tower of this edifice was so lofty that it might be seen at the distance of many leagues, and within that tower Zohák had formed a talisman of miraculous virtues. Feridún soon overthrew this talisman, and destroyed or vanquished successively with his mace all the enchanted monsters and hideous shapes which appeared before him. He captured the whole building, and released all the black-eyed damsels who were secluded there, and among them Shahrnáz and Arnawáz, the two sisters of Jemshíd before alluded to. He then ascended the empty throne of Zohák, which had been guarded by the talisman, and the Demons under his command; and when he heard that the tyrant had gone with an immense army toward Ind, in quest of his new enemy, and had left his treasury with only a small force at the seat of his government, he rejoiced, and appropriated the throne and the treasure to himself.

From their dark solitudes the Youth brought forth
The black-haired damsels, lovely as the sun,
And Jemshíd's sisters, long imprisoned there;
And gladly did the inmates of that harem
Pour over their gratitude on being freed
From that terrific monster; thanks to Heaven
Devoutly they expressed, and ardent joy.

Feridún inquired of Arnawáz why Zohák had chosen the route towards Ind; and she replied, "For two reasons: the first is, he expects to encounter thee in that quarter; and if he fails, he will subdue the whole country, which is the seat of sorcery, and thus obtain possession of a renowned magician who can charm thee into his power.

He wishes to secure within his grasp
That region of enchantment, Hindústan,
And then obtain relief from what he feels;
For night and day the terror of thy name
Oppresses him, his heart is all on fire,
And life is torture to him."

Source: Firdawsi. *Sháh Námeh.* In *Persian Literature, Comprising the Sháh Námeh, the Rubáiyát, the Divan and the Gulistan,* trans. James Atkinson. Rev. ed., vol. 1. World's Great Classics series. New York: Colonial, 1900, pp. 31–34.

18. Genji Monogatari, *a Masterpiece of Japanese Literature*

The Genji Monogatari, *or* Tale of Genji, *is considered one of the great masterpieces of Japanese literature. Written by the female courtier Murasaki Shikibu (c. 978–c. 1014), the novel documents the refinement of tenth-century court life by examining the life and relationships of Prince Genji. The following extract follows the early career of a courtly woman who becomes one of the emperor's lovers. Her success in attracting the emperor earns her the envy and distrust of other courtesans, who attempt to lock her out and abuse her serving women. Nevertheless, she bears a son to the emperor and is moved to an apartment close to the emperor's own quarters, thus preserving her from the worst of the ill treatment. The young boy born to this woman and the emperor becomes the main character of the story.*

Japanese court culture featured a very formal and technical etiquette and language. This translation keeps many of the Japanese titles. Niogo and kioyi, for example, are titles for ladies of the court, a Dainagon is a court official, and Hakamagi is a ceremony in which boys wear trousers for the first time (they wear looser garments in their first years of life). Yokihi, mentioned in the story, was a beautiful woman who so distracted the Emperor Hsuan Tsung in the eighth century that a rebellion broke out.

CHAPTER 1: THE CHAMBER OF KIRI

In the reign of a certain Emperor, whose name is unknown to us, there was, among the Niogo and Kôyi of the Imperial Court, one who, though she was not of high birth, enjoyed the full tide of Royal favor. Hence her superiors, each one of whom had always been thinking—"I shall be the one," gazed upon her disdainfully with malignant eyes, and her equals and inferiors were more indignant still.

Such being the state of affairs, the anxiety which she had to endure was great and constant, and this was probably the reason why her health was at last so much affected, that she was often compelled to absent herself from Court, and to retire to the residence of her mother.

Her father, who was a Dainagon, was dead; but her mother, being a woman of good sense, gave her every possible guidance in the due performance of Court ceremony, so that in this respect she seemed but little different from those whose fathers and mothers were still alive to bring them before public notice, yet, nevertheless, her friendliness made her oftentimes feel very diffident from the want of any patron of influence.

These circumstances, however, only tended to make the favor shown to her by the Emperor wax warmer and warmer, and it was even shown to such an extent as to become a warning to after-generations. There had been instances in China in which favoritism such as this had caused national disturbance and disaster; and thus the matter became a subject of public animadversion, and it seemed not improbable that people would begin to allude even to the example of Yó-ki-hi.

In due course, and in consequence, we may suppose, of the Divine blessing on the sincerity of their affection, a jewel of a little prince was born to her. The first prince who had been born to the Emperor was the child of Koki-den-Niogo, the daughter of the Udaijin (a great officer of State). Not only was he first in point of age, but his influence on his mother's side was so great that public opinion had almost unanimously fixed upon him as heir-apparent. Of this the Emperor was fully conscious, and he only regarded the new-born child with that affection which one lavishes on a domestic favorite. Nevertheless, the mother of the first prince had, not unnaturally, a foreboding that unless matters were managed adroitly her child might be superseded by the younger one. She, we may observe, had been established at Court before any other lady, and had more children than one. The Emperor, therefore, was obliged to treat her with due respect, and reproaches from her always affected him more keenly than those of any others.

To return to her rival. Her constitution was extremely delicate, as we have seen already, and she was surrounded by those who would fain lay bare, so to say, her hidden scars. Her apartments in the palace were Kiri-Tsubo (the chamber of Kiri); so called from the trees that were planted around. In visiting her there the Emperor had to pass before several other chambers, whose occupants universally chafed when they saw it. And again, when it was her turn to attend upon the Emperor, it often happened that they played off mischievous pranks upon her, at different points in the corridor, which leads to the Imperial quarters. Sometimes they would soil the skirts of her attendants, sometimes they would shut against her the door of the covered portico, where no other passage existed; and thus, in every possible way, they one and all combined to annoy her.

The Emperor at length became aware of this, and gave her, for her special chamber, another apartment, which was in the Kôrô-Den, and which was quite close to those in which he himself resided. It had been originally occupied by another lady who was now removed, and thus fresh resentment was aroused.

When the young Prince was three years old the Hakamagi took place. It was celebrated with pomp scarcely inferior to that which adorned the investiture of the first Prince. In fact, all available treasures were exhausted on the occasion. And again the public manifested its disapprobation. In the summer of the same year the Kiri-Tsubo-Kôyi became ill, and wished to retire from the palace. The Emperor, however, who was accustomed to see her indisposed, strove to induce her to remain. But her illness increased day by day; and she had drooped and pined away until she was now but a shadow of her former self. She made scarcely any response to the affectionate words and expressions of tenderness which her Royal lover caressingly bestowed upon her. Her eyes were half-closed: she lay like a fading flower in the last stage of exhaustion, and she became so much enfeebled that her mother appeared before the Emperor and entreated with tears that she might be allowed to leave. Distracted by his vain endeavors to devise means to aid her, the Emperor at length ordered a Te-gruma to be in readiness to convey her to her own home, but even then he went to her apartment and cried despairingly: "Did not we vow that we would neither of us be either before or after the other even in traveling the last long journey of life? And can you find it in your heart to leave me now?" Sadly and tenderly looking up, she thus replied, with almost failing breath:

> "Since my departure for this dark journey,
> Makes you so sad and lonely,
> Fain would I stay though weak and weary,
> And live for your sake only!"
> "Had I but known this before—"

She appeared to have much more to say, but was too weak to continue. Overpowered with grief, the Emperor at one moment would fain accompany her himself, and at another moment would have her remain to the end where she then was.

At the last, her departure was hurried, because the exorcism for the sick had been appointed to take place that evening at her home, and she went. The child Prince, however, had been left in the Palace, as his mother wished, even at that time, to make her withdrawal as privately as possible, so as to avoid any invidious observations on the part of her rivals. To the Emperor the night now became black with gloom. He sent messenger after messenger to make inquiries, and could not await heir return with patience. Midnight came, and with it the sound of lamentation. The messenger, who could do nothing else, hurried back with the sad tidings of the truth. From that moment the mind of the Emperor was darkened, and he confined himself to his private apartments.

Source: Murasaki Shikibu. *Genji Monogatari*. In *Japanese Literature*, trans. Suyematz Kenchio. Rev. ed. World's Great Classics series. New York: Colonial, 1900, pp. 11–14.

Part V
MATERIAL LIFE

Material Life theoretically covers all the physical objects that we encounter in day-to-day life. This volume focuses on three key aspects of our material existence in the Food and Drink, Housing and Furniture, and Clothing and Personal Appearance sections. These categories cover some of humankind's most basic needs.

Although food, shelter, and clothing are necessary for human existence, they also play an important symbolic role in society. Indeed, the symbolic meanings of material goods are often as important as the needs that those material objects fill. The Clothing and Personal Appearance section, for example, offers many examples of how clothing reveals socioeconomic status or internal virtues. The guidelines on women's clothing in the Koran, for example, aim to encourage modesty. In a similar vein, the English author Brathwaite argues that luxurious clothing makes people soft and decadent.

Food also carries symbolic meanings, as the Food and Drink section demonstrates. The ambassador Thomas Roe, for example, praises the Muslims for their simple diet; in Roe's opinion, this simple diet consisting of meat stews and hearty breads demonstrates an honesty that is missing from the fancy European cuisine then in favor in England. Boetius similarly links Scotland's change in diet with a decline in manliness! Like clothing, food and eating rituals could also demark status. The Aztec emperor Moctezuma, for example, ate before anyone else in his court. The order of eating in society reinforces the sociopolitical hierarchy. Authors in the Middle Ages and Renaissance also understood that diet had an important role in maintaining good health, although modern nutritionists might not agree with Stanihurst's praise of Irish whiskey as a powerful curative medicine.

Just like a culture's culinary traditions, housing can reveal a lot about a society. Large, expensive houses with lavish furnishings obviously display wealth and economic power. Houses can also reflect the physical environment, however. Many of the houses discussed in the Housing and Furniture section were clearly adapted to their environments; thus, houses in warm countries frequently featured terraces and large double-doors in an effort to entice a breeze indoors. The objects of material life are necessary for survival, but they are also necessary to express ourselves and our role in the world.

Food and Drink

Fortunately, most people today eat several times a day. Famine, of course, still wreaks tragedy across the globe, but the provision of a stable food supply to a large percentage of the earth's population remains one of the major achievements of the twentieth century and has confounded the pessimistic predictions of people such as Thomas *Malthus,* who suggested that the earth's population would outstrip its food supply by the mid-eighteenth century. The opposite, in fact, has occurred, though grave problems in distributing the global harvest remain.

The common threat of famine in the Middle Ages and *Renaissance,* however, placed an importance on food that a supermarket shopper will find hard to appreciate. In almost all the passages in this section, however, food plays a symbolic role that far exceeds its more literal role of sustaining human physical existence. In Document 1, for example, Boetius uses a description of the ancient Scottish to suggest that contemporaneous Scottish society has become "soft" and is too dependent on unnecessary luxuries. In fact, many discussions of food stress the benefits of temperance and self-restraint. The English ambassador Thomas Roe (Document 6), for example, praises the Muslim population of India for their simple diet of meat stews and inexpensive breads, and Yoshida Kenko (Document 4) argues against the excessive consumption by the Japanese of the alcoholic drink sake. Perhaps the greatest champion of simplicity was Po Chu-i. This *Tang dynasty* poet succeeds in painting a beautiful and enticing picture of an inexpensive food: bamboo shoots (Document 3). Unlike Thomas Roe, not only does Po Chu-i not only praise simple foods—he makes us want to eat them.

According to these authors, temperance encouraged good health. Boetius suggested that overindulgence in spices, for example, could result in death. Other foods, however, were credited with healthful properties. In the sixteenth century, Richard Stanihurst (Document 2) claimed that Irish whiskey cured a variety of illnesses, including excessive gas and even skin diseases. Although modern nutritionists may not agree with Stanihurst's conclusions, the link between food and good health, seen in these medieval and Renaissance sources, certainly continues to this day.

Food, especially formal dining, also helped to reinforce societal structures. By eating by himself, separated from his retainers by a movable screen, the *Aztec* ruler *Moctezuma* emphasized that he was different, indeed, that he was better than the others present during the meal (Document 5). Likewise, the variety of dishes served by Moctezuma, as by the Muslim leaders discussed by Roe, emphasized the wealth and luxury of the hosts. Food, then, indicated not only the political standing but also the economic power of the host. When authors such as Bernal Díaz del Castillo described a meal, therefore, they gave insight not only into the foods and diet of a nation but also into the societal structures that organized the population. Frequently, the authors then used these observations about foreign cultures to criticize and correct aspects of the authors' own societies. Writing about food was writing about life.

1. The Scottish Diet: Past and Present

Like many history writers, Hector Boetius, the author of the passage reproduced here, reveals more about the customs of his own time period—the sixteenth century—than about the remote past. In Boetius's eyes, contemporary Scotland had become a much worse place. Using the metaphor of food, Boetius contrasts the straightforward, temperate diners of the past with the gluttonous population of his own time. Boetius uses the image of ancient Scotland to criticize both the frequency and the preciosity of the modern Scottish diet. According to Boetius, his contemporary Scots ate three meals a day, whereas their ancestors were happy with two meals a day. In fact, Boetius even claims that some eat so much that they are forced to vomit ("depart") the surplus. The second character defect that Boetius outlines is a delight in gourmet foods. In the ancient past, the Scots were satisfied with simple food—they made simple breads and ate fish, beef, and game. His own generation, however, has become obsessed with obtaining foreign spices and "drugs" with which to make their food tastier. Boetius even goes so far as to suggest that such foreign products are actually "poison" and pictures their devourers as dying from sudden convulsions. The author took a strong position in favor of foods "made in Scotland." Increased global trade, however, ensured that a strong supply of spice reached all of the British Isles despite the objections of xenophobic, moralizing historians.

In sleep they were competent, in meat and drink sober, and contented with such food as was ready at hand and prepared with little cost. Their bread consisted of such stuff as grew most readily on the ground, without all manner of sifting and boldting, whereby to please the palate; but baked up as it came from the mill without any curiosity, which is a great abasing of the force thereof unto our daily nourishment. The flesh whereon they chiefly fed, was either such as they got by hunting, wherein they took great delight, and which increased not a little their strength and nimbleness, or else cattle as they bred at home, whereof beef was accounted the principal, as it is yet in our days, though after another manner and far discrepant from the use and custom of other countries. The "stirkes" or young beefets ungelded, we either kill young for veal, or geld, to the end that they may serve afterward for tillage in earing of the ground, but the cow calves and heifers are never killed till they be with calf, for then are they fattest and most delicious to the mouth. The common meat of our elders was fish, howbeit not only or so much for the plentie thereof, as for that our lands lay often waste and untilled, because of the great warres which they commonly had in hand. They brake also their fast early in the morning with some slander repast, and so continued without any other diet until suppertime, in which they had but one dish, whereby it came to pass, that their stomachs were never overcharged, nor their bones desirous of rest through the fullness of their bellies. At such time as they determined of set purpose to be merry, they used a kind of Aquavite void of spices and only consisting of such herbs & roots as grew in their own gardens, otherwise the common drink was ale; but in time of war, when they were forced to lie in camp, they contented themselves with water as readiest for their turns. Each soldier also had so much meal as might serve him for a day which he made up in cakes, and baked on the coals, as the Romans sometimes used to do, and the emperor Caracalla himself (as Herodian hath remembered). Seldom did they eat any flesh in their tents, except they got it from their adversaries; such as they had likewise was eaten half raw, because they supposed the juice thereof so used to nourish very abundantly. But fish was much more plentiful amongst them, especially when they wanted their usual preys, or could not attain unto them.

They brought furthermore from their houses to the field with them, a vessel of butter, cheese, meal, milk, and vinegar tempered together as a shoot-anchor against extreme hunger, which they would feed and suck out the moisture, when other provision could not be gotten. . . .

But how far we in these present days are swerved from the virtues and temperance of our elders, I believe there is no man so eloquent, nor indued with such utterance, as that he is able sufficiently to express. For whereas they gave their minds to doughtiness, we apply our selues to drunkenness; they had plenty with sufficiency, we have inordinate excess with superfluity; they were temperate, we effeminate; and so is the case now altered with us, that he which can devour and drink most, is the noblest man and most honest companion, and thereto hath no peer if he can once find the vein, though with his great travel to purvey himself of the plentifullest number of new fine and delicate dishes, and best provoke his stomach to receive the greatest quantity of them, though he never make due digestion of it.

Being thus drowned in our delicate gluttony, it is a world to see how we stuff ourselves both day and night, never ceasing to engorge and pour in, till our bellies be so full that we must needs depart. Certes it is not supposed meet that we should now content ourselves with breakfast and supper only, as our elders have done before, nor enough that we have added our dinners unto their aforesaid meals, but we must have thereto our beverages and rare suppers, so that small time is spared wherein to occupy ourselves in any godly exercise, sith almost the whole day and night do scarcely suffice for the filling of our paunches. We have also our merchants, whose charge is not to look out and bring home such things as necessarily pertain to the maintenance of our lives, but unto the furniture of our kitchen, and these search all the secret corners of our forests for venison, of the air for fowls, and of the sea for fish, for wine also they travel not only into France, whose wines do now grow into contempt, but also into Spain, Italy and Greece; nay Africa is not void of our factors, no, nor Asia, and only for fine and delicate wines if they might be had for money.

In like sort they gad over all the world for sweet and pleasant spices, and drugs (provokers unto all lust and licentiousness of behaviour) as men that adventure their own lives to bring home poison and destruction unto their countrymen, as if the mind were not already sufficiently bereft of her image of the divinity, but must yet more be clogged and overladen with such a franked case, therewithall to be extinguished outright, which already dwelleth or is buried rather in such an ugly sepulchre. The body likewise being oppressed with such a heap of superfluous food, although otherwise it be indued with an excellent nature, cannot be able to execute his office, nor keep himself upright, but must needs yield as overcome, and to be torn in pieces and rent with sundry maladies.

Hereof also it commeth to pass, that our countrymen travelling into the colder regions are nowadays, contrary to their former usage, taken sometime with fevers, whereby their inward parts do burn and parch as it were with continual fire, the only cause whereof we may ascribe unto those hot spices and drugs which are brought unto us from the hot countries. Others of them are so swollen and grown full of humors that they are often taken suddenly, and die of vehement apoplexies, and although here and there one or two recover for a little while, yet are they but dead people, reviving again, leading the rest of their lives like shadows, and walking about as if they were buried already.

Source: Boetius, Hector. *The Description of Scotland.* In *Chronicles of England, Scotland, and Ireland,* trans. Raphael Holinshed. Vol. 5. London: Johnson, 1808, pp. 22–26.

2. Irish Whiskey

English sources have frequently used whiskey as a symbol of Ireland. Whiskey did appear to be a unique drink to the English, who preferred beer and imported wine throughout most of the Middle Ages and Renaissance; whiskey remained the preserve of Ireland and Scotland and symbolized the difference between England and its Gaelic neighbors. As a symbol of difference, however, whiskey, being an alcoholic drink, frequently served as a negative stereotype suggesting that the Irish and Scots were alcoholics incapable of leading sober and rational lives. This negative association, for example, dominated the cartoons of "apelike" Irishmen that appeared in the popular British periodical Punch *in the nineteenth century. In the sixteenth century, however, whiskey could still be presented as an actually healthful drink. In the following description of Ireland provided by the Anglo-Irish writer Richard Stanihurst (1547–1618), whiskey is presented as the true fulfillment of its Latin name: aqua vitae, "water of life."*

Stanihurst paints whiskey ultimately as a healthy dietary supplement rather than as an intoxicating beverage. According to Stanihurst, whiskey could cure a wide range of diseases, including colds, gas pains, stomach ills, and skin diseases (if applied topically). Stanihurst suggests that the water of life can even help cardiovascular disease. The alcoholic content of the product that Stanihurst recommends was clearly high—the best whiskey could be set afire. This high alcoholic content would indeed have some antimicrobial effects, just as rubbing alcohol has, but whiskey surely is not, and never was, a cure-all and is certainly not considered a medicine in the modern era.

The soil is low and waterish, including diverse little Islands, environed with lakes and marsh. Highest hills have standing pools on their tops. Inhabitants especially new come, are subject to distillations, rheums, and fluxes. For remedie whereof, they use an ordinary drink of *Aqua vitae*, being so qualified in the making, that it drieth more, and also inflameth less than other hot confections do. One Theoricus wrote a proper treatise of *Aqua vitae*, wherein he praiseth it unto the ninth degree. He distinguisheth three sorts thereof, *Simplex*, *Composita*, and *Perfectissima*. He declareth the simples and ingredients thereto belonging. He wisheth it to be taken as well before meat as after. It drieth up the breaking out of hands, and killeth the flesh worms, if you wash your hands therewith. It scoureth all scurf and scalds from the head, being therewith daily washed before meals. Being moderately taken (sayeth he) it sloweth age, in strengtheneth youth, it helpeth digestion, it cutteth phlegm, it abandoneth melancholie, it relisheth the heart, it lighteneth the mind, it quickeneth the spirits, it cureth the hydropsie, it healeth the strangurie, it pounceth the stone, it expelleth gravel, it puffeth away ventositie, it keepeth and preserveth the head from whirling, the eyes from dazzling, the tongue from lisping, the mouth from maffling, the teeth from chattering, and the throat from rattling; it keepeth the weasan from stifling, the stomach from wambling, and the heart from swelling, the belly from wirtching, the guts from rumbling, the hands from shivering, and the sinews from shrinking, the veins from crumpling, the bones from aching, and the marrow from soaking. Ulstadius also ascribeth thereto a singular praise, and would have it to burn being kindled, which he taketh to be a token to know the goodness thereof. And truly it is a sovereign liquor, if it be orderly taken.

Source: Stanihurst, Richard. *A Treatise Conteining a Plaine and Perfect Description of Ireland, in Raphael Holinshed, Chronicles of England, Scotland, and Ireland.* Vol. 6. London: Johnson, 1808, p. 8.

3. Bamboo Shoots: A Chinese Delicacy

Po Chu-i (772–846), the famous Tang dynasty poet, who served for several years as a governor in remote provinces, focused on noticing and expressing the beauty of everyday life. In the following poem, Po Chu-i relates how a posting in a rural province has enabled him to indulge his love of boiled bamboo shoots. In the poem, Po Chu-i recognizes one of the central facts of economics—supply and demand determine price. When Po Chu-i was stationed at Lo-yang, the eastern capital of the Tang dynasty, he could barely find bamboo shoots. Now stationed in the mountains, he is able to buy the delicacies for a pittance.

The cheapness of bamboo shoots, however, does not decrease Po Chu-i's delight in eating them. Instead, he celebrates the bamboo by describing the process of cooking them in beautiful detail. His celebration of the common things in life is not, however, a simple culinary poem. Instead, his valuation of the simple, of the everyday, continues a political commitment, expressed by Po Chu-i in other poems, to support the poor and downtrodden population in his contemporary society. Within the context of Po Chu-i's corpus, the praise of bamboo becomes a praise of the workingman and woman.

Eating Bamboo-Shoots

My new province is a land of bamboo-groves:
Their shoots in spring fill the valleys and hills.
The mountain woodman cuts an armful of them
And brings them down to sell at the early market.
Things are cheap in proportion as they are common;
For two farthings, I buy a whole bundle.
I put the shoots in a great earthen pot
And heat them up along with boiling rice.
The purple nodules broken, like an old brocade;
The white skin opened, like new pearls.
Now every day I eat them recklessly;
For a long time I have not touched meat.
All the time I was living at Lo-yang
They could not give me enough to suit my taste,
Now I can have as many shoots as I please;
For each breath of the south-wind makes a new bamboo!

Source: *A Hundred and Seventy Chinese Poems.* Translated by Arthur Waley. London: Constable, 1918, p. 149.

4. Japanese Sake

The Tsurezuregusa, *written by Yoshida Kenko (c. 1282–c. 1350), in the* zuihitsu, *or "stream-of-consciousness," style has become a classic in Japan. The* Tsurezuregusa *(Essays in Idleness) discusses contemporary Japanese customs and generally laments the disappearance of the older ways. At the same time, Yoshida Kenko associates beauty with impermanence; true beauty cannot last forever.*

In the following extract, the author laments a widespread overindulgence in sake, an alcoholic beverage made from fermented rice. In elaborate depth, Yoshida describes the stupidities that those drunk on sake perform. In every case, the drunkard violates both good taste and reason. Nevertheless, Yoshida does list some situations in which he believes the imbibing of sake is justified. In most instances, Yoshida pictures the drinker having a small amount of liquor in a quiet, intimate, or natural setting, such as in a flowery field or with a small group of close friends. These distinctions indicate that sake is not, in fact, disliked by Yoshida—rather, he merely detests shameless and outrageous displays of public drunkenness. Drinking should be done in moderation and in private.

There are many things in this world that I do not understand. For example, you give other people sake to drink, and you think this is enjoyable. I can't understand why. The drinker grimaces, he frowns, he watches for an opportunity to throw away the sake or to escape, but the host traps him, holds him back, and forces him to drink. Next, intelligent men become all at once fools and do stupid things. Healthy people fall ill under our very eyes, and lie down, dead to the world. What an absurd way to celebrate a festival! The next day they have a headache, they can't eat anything, they let out long sighs, they can no longer remember the things of the night and say that they were in another life. They neglect both private and public business, no matter how important, and become ill. To make people go through this is neither hospitable nor decent. How can one who has seen such harsh things not view them with distaste and irritation? If we heard that a similar custom existed in some foreign country, we would undoubtedly find it bizarre and outrageous.

Seeing these things happen shocks the heart. Some thoughtful people, who are important, foolishly hold themselves proudly and start gabbing. They tilt their hat, they unknot their belts, they roll up their sleeves; they have such a stunned look that they become almost unrecognizable. Women push back their hair, shamelessly showing their forehead. They throw back their heads and seize the hand of the man to whom they are offering the drink. Some rude fellow, taking a bit of fish, raises it to someone else's lips and then eats the rest himself—a disgusting sight! Everyone sings at the top of their lungs and dances. An old monk, urged to dance, uncovers a dark black shoulder and performs a strange unwatchable dance. The people who look at this in enjoyment repulse and detest me. Next, the drunkard boasts greatly of his skills and qualities (which the others find hideously tiresome), and he cries out in his drunkenness. Commoners quarrel and argue, generating fear and anxiety. The intoxicated crowd behaves like ruffians; they grab things that you do not want to give them. They fall off the veranda, or from a horse, or out of the carriage, and end up injured. Those who can't use a vehicle teeter in the street, they lean against the walls or against the gates, and perform all sorts of stupidities. An old monk, wearing the priestly sash, stops a young boy and tells him about some foolishness—what a pitiful sight. Would that, either in this life or in the life to come, sake offered something actually interesting!

In this world, sake brings with it a host of wrongs—the victim loses his money and his health. Although one calls the man of a hundred cures, ten thousand diseases come to him. Although it's said that sake makes you forget sadness, in fact drunk people remember past miseries and bemoan them. With regard to the future life, sake destroys the wisdom of men, it burns like fire the roots of goodness, increases one's faults, encourages one to violate all the commandments and to fall into hell. "He who gives other people drink will be born without hands for five hundred lives." That is what Buddha said about the matter.

Although sake is indeed detestable, there are some occasions when one cannot justly refuse it. Sake increases pleasure if offered on a bright moonlit night, on a snowy morning, or amongst the flowers when you are at peace. If, on a tedious day, a friend suddenly arrives, then it is enjoyable to receive him with a bit of sake. If in the palace, one sees a bit of sake pleasantly offered, along with some cakes and other things, it is very agreeable. In a small room, during the winter, cooking something—then it is pleasant to drink some sake with a few close friends. In a temporary hut on a voyage, or in some remote place, it is pleasant to drink a bit of the herb. Occasionally, someone who doesn't like to drink should have a bit anyway, especially if a superior urges it. Likewise, it is fine for someone to have sake when someone with whom they want to network loves sake, and, while drinking, they strike up a friendship. In every case, we are always strangely indulgent of the faults of a drinking partner.

Source: *Anthologie de la literature japonaise des origins au xxe siècle.* Ed. Michel Revon. Paris: Delagrave, 1919, pp. 297–99. Translated from the French by Lawrence Morris.

5. Moctezuma's Feasts

The author of the following extract, Bernal Díaz del Castillo, traveled with Hernán Cortés to Mexico in 1519 in the ultimately successful Spanish attempt to subjugate the much-hated Aztec empire. As an eyewitness to much of the Spanish campaign, Castillo provides valuable insight into how the Spanish viewed and understood the Native American cultures of early sixteenth-century America.

In the following extract elaborating the dining customs of the Aztec ruler Moctezuma (called "Montezuma" in this translation), Bernal Díaz del Castillo highlights those customs that emphasize the royalty and difference of Moctezuma. For example, Díaz claims that, according to rumor, Moctezuma ate the flesh of young children. Although the Aztecs did occasionally practice ritual cannibalism, the flesh of young children never played a staple role in the Native American diet. By deciding to report the rumor, however, Díaz paints Moctezuma as very different from the Spanish leaders, indeed as vaguely monstrous. Díaz's claim that Moctezuma stopped this practice as a result of Cortés's intervention likewise suggests that the Spanish conquistadors were "civilizing" influences on the native population.

At the same time, Díaz mentions details of the Aztec ruler's feast that would not be out of place in any European royal court during the high Middle Ages. Moctezuma, like any king, eats a wide variety of foods—the variety proving the wealth and luxury of the court. Similarly, the king watches entertainment provided by jesters while he eats, and just like a European monarch, he gives morsels of particularly delicious food to favored guests and counselors.

Unlike most European potentates, however, Moctezuma generally eats by himself. Although he has counselors present and female servants, Moctezuma eats first. The servants even place a screen in front of Moctezuma to shield him from the view of others. Only after Moctezuma has finished his meal does his vast retinue of administrators, guards, and servants eat. Such rituals ultimately serve to reinforce the social and political hierarchies. Meals do not just satisfy hunger—they also remind everyone who is in charge.

Montezuma's cooks had upwards of thirty different ways of dressing meats, and they had earthen vessels so contrived as to keep them always hot. For the table of Montezuma himself, above three hundred dishes were dressed, and for his guards, above a thousand. Before dinner, Montezuma would sometimes go out and inspect their preparations, and his officers would point out to him which were the best, and explained of what birds and flesh they were composed; and of those he would eat. But this was more for amusement than any thing else. It is said that at times the flesh of young children was dressed for him; but the ordinary meats were domestic fowls, pheasants, geese, partridges, quails, venizon, Indian hogs, pigeons, hares, and rabbits, with many other animals and birds peculiar to the country. This is certain; that after Cortes had spoken to him relative to the dressing of human flesh, it was not practiced in the palace. At his meals, in the cold weather, a number of torches of bark of a wood which makes no smoke and has an aromatic smell, were lighted, and that they should not throw too much heat, screens, ornamented with gold, and painted with figures of idols, were placed before them. Montezuma was seated on a low throne, or chair, at a table proportioned to the height of his seat. The table was covered with white cloths and napkins, and four beautiful women presented him with water for his hands, in vessels which they called Xicales, with other vessels under them like plates, to catch the water; they also presented him with towels. Then, two other women brought small cakes of bread, and when the king began to eat, a large screen of wood, gilt, was placed before him, so that people should not during that time see him. The women having retired to a little distance, four ancient lords stood by the throne, to whom Montezuma from time to time spoke or addressed questions, and as a mark of particular favor, gave to each of them a plate of that which he was eating. I was told that these old lords, who were his near relations, were also counselors and judges. The plates which Montezuma presented to them, they received with high respect, eating what was in them without taking their eyes off the ground. He was served on earthenware of Cholua, red and black. While the king was at table, no one of his guards, or in the vicinity of his apartment, dared for their lives make any noise. Fruit of all the kinds that the country produced was laid before him; he ate very little, but from time to time, a drink prepared from cocoa, and of a stimulative, or corroborative quality, as we were told, was presented to him in golden cups. We could not at that time see if he drank it or not, but I observed a number of jars, above fifty, brought in, filled with foaming chocolate, of which he took some, which the women presented to him. At different intervals during the time of the dinner, there entered certain Indians, hump-backed, very deformed, and ugly, who played tricks of buffoonery, and others who they said

Moctezuma. Facsimile of the copper plate in the Venice edition of Solis' *Conquista* (1715), based on earlier images. Although this portrait is somewhat fanciful, it does depict some genuine Aztec clothing and equipment, such as their elaborate feather shield. Chaibis.

were jesters. There was also a company of singers and dancers, who afforded Montezuma much entertainment. To these he ordered the vases of chocolate to be distributed. The four female attendants then took away the cloths, and again with much respect presented him with water to wash his hands, during which time Montezuma conversed with the four old noblemen formerly mentioned, after which they took their leave with many ceremonies. One thing I forgot, and no wonder, to mention in its place, and that is, that during the time Montezuma was at dinner, two very beautiful women were busily employed making small cakes with eggs and other things mixed therein. These were delicately white, and when made they presented them to him on plates covered with napkins. Also another kind of bread was brought to him in long loaves, and plates of cakes resembling wafers. After he had dined, they presented to him three little canes highly ornamented, containing liquid amber, mixed with an herb they call tobacco; and when he had sufficiently viewed and heard the singers, dancers, and buffoons, he took a little of the smoke of one of these canes, and then laid himself down to sleep; and thus his principal meal concluded. After this was over, all his guards and domestics sat down to dinner, and as near as I could judge, above a thousand plates of those eatables that I have mentioned were laid before them, with vessels of foaming chocolate, and fruit in an immense quantity. For his women and various inferior servants, his establishment was of a prodigious expense; and we were astonished, amidst such a profusion, at the vast regularity that prevailed.

Source: Díaz, Bernal del Castillo. *The True History of the Conquest of Mexico*. Translated by Maurice Keatinge. London: Harrap, 1927, pp. 171–73. Translation slightly modified by Lawrence Morris.

6. Muslim Indian Cuisine

The Englishman Sir Thomas Roe was an influential political agent, served as an ambassador to the Mughal dynasty emperor and to Constantinople during the early seventeenth century, and wrote copiously about his experiences. Unlike some of his contemporaries, Roe frequently praised the customs of the foreign peoples among whom he traveled. In the following extract, Roe describes the diet of Muslims (called "Mahometans" in the extract) in what is today northern India. According to Roe, their diet consisted chiefly of a spicy meat stew, and those too poor to afford this dish survived on a simple flat bread served with a small amount of butter. Roe's description of the delicious dishes served during a formal dinner in a perfumed tent shows how willingly Roe noted the good points of the cultures he visited. The great variety of dishes served at the dinner—upwards of 50—resembles the royal dinners of the Aztec ruler Moctezuma described in Document 5. Roe also notes that almonds formed the basis of many sweet dishes. Most of all, Roe approved of the Muslims' refusal to overindulge in food—they scrupulously avoided gluttony. According to Roe, their abstemiousness was rewarded with long lives and freedom from disease.

SECTION X. OF THEIR DIET, THEIR COOKERY IN DRESSING IT, &C.

And though this Country affords very much variety of excellent good Provisions, yet the Mahometans feed not freely on any flesh, but on that which is strange, and forbidden (of the Hindoos Diet I shall speak afterwards): but for the Mahometans they are a people, as I conceive, not much given to their Palate; but are very careful of, and temperate in their Diet, as having learn'd by experience, that full bellies do more oppress, than strengthen the body, that too much of the Creature doth not comfort but destroy Nature; It being a tried truth, that Gluttony reacheth, and kills those whom swords cannot touch. All Diseases of the body for the most part being contracted to it by Surfeits, in one kind or other; and therefore they keep themselves to a thin Diet, and eat not to pamper and please their Appetite, but to satisfie and support nature, which is contented with a little every where, but with less in hot Countries, where men's digestion of food is not so quick and good; this being further a tried truth, that those bodies are most strong, active, and healthy, which are most temperate.

Therefore though they have abundance of flesh and fowl, and have fish too, yet are they temperate in all of them. For Swine's flesh, it is an abomination unto the Mahometans; and therefore they touch it not. And for other kind of flesh, they eat very little of them alone, to make their full meals of them, for they dress no kind of flesh in great pieces, or whole joynts, nor scarce any of their fowls whole.

For boiling of flesh in water, or baking or roasting any flesh, are pieces of Cookery (if I observed well) they know not; but they stew all their flesh as their Kid and other Venison, &c. out into sippets, or slices, or little parts, to which they put Onions, and Herbs, and Roots, and Ginger, (which they take there green out of the earth) and other Spices, with some butter, which ingredients when as they are well proportioned, make a Food that is exceedingly pleasing to all Palates, at their first tasting thereof most savoury Meat, haply that very dish which Jacob made for his Father Isaac, when he got the blessing, Gen. 27.

With their flesh and herbs, etc., they sometimes stew Hens and other Foul cut in pieces, which is like that the Spaniards call an Oleo, but more toothsome.

But their great common standing dish there is Rice, which they boil with more Art than we: for they boil the grain so as that it is full, and plump, and tender, but not broken in boyling; they put to it a little green Ginger, and Pepper, and Butter, and this is the ordinary way of their dressing it, and so 'tis very good.

Sometimes they boil pieces of flesh, or Hens, and other Fowl cut in pieces in their Rice, which dish they call Pillau; as they order it, they make it a very excellent, and a very well-tasted Food.

Once my Lord Ambassadour had an Entertainment there by Asaph Chan, who invited him to dinner (and this was the only respect in that kind he ever had, while he was in East India). That Asaph Chan was a Man made by his great Alliances, the greatest Subject and Favourite in all that Empire; for his Sister was the Mogol's most beloved Wife, and his Daughter was married unto Sultan Caroon the Prince, and very much beloved by him, but of all these, more afterward. This Asaph Chan entertained my Lord Ambassador in a very spacious and a very beautiful Tent, where none of his followers besides my self, saw, or tasted of that Entertainment.

That Tent was kept full of a very pleasant Perfume; in which tents the King and Grandees there take very much delight. The floor of the Tent was first covered all over with very rich and large Carpets, which were covered again in the places where our dinner stood, with other good Carpets, made of stitched Leather, to preserve them which were richer; and these were covered again with pure white and fine Callico Clothes, and all these covered with very many dishes of Silver, but for the greater part of those Silver dishes they were not larger than our largest trencher-plates, the brims of all of them gilt.

We sat in that large Room as it were in a Triangle; The Ambassadour on Asaph Chan's right hand a good distance from him, and my self below; all of us on the ground, as they there all do when as they eat, with our Faces looking each to the other, and every one of us had his several mess. The Ambassadour had more dishes by ten, and I less by ten, than our entertainer had, yet for my part I had fifty dishes. They were all set before us at once, and little paths left betwixt them, that our entertainer's servants (for only they waited) might come and reach them to us one after another, and so they did. So that I tasted of all set before me, and of most did but taste, though all of them tasted very well.

Now of the provision itself, for our larger dishes, they were filled with Rice, dressed (as before described.) And this Rice was presented to us, some of it white, in its own proper colour, some of it made yellow with Saffron, and some of it was made green, and some of it put into a purple colour, but by what Ingredient I know not, but this I am sure, that it all tasted very well; And with Rice thus ordered, several of our dishes were furnished, and very many more of them with flesh of several kinds, and with Hens, and with other sort of Fowl cut in pieces, as before I observed in their Indian Cookery.

To these we had many Jellies, and Culices; Rice ground to flower, and then boyled, and after sweetned with Sugar-Candy and Rose-Water to be eaten cold. The flower of Rice mingled with sweet Almonds, made as small as they could, and with some of the most fleshy parts of Hens stewed with it, and after the flesh so beaten into pieces, that it could not be discerned, all made sweet with Rose-Water and Sugar-Candy, and scented with Amber-Grease; this was another of our dishes, and a most luscious one, which the Portugals call Mangee Real, Food for a King. Many other dishes we had, made up in Cakes of several forms, of the finest of the wheat-flower, mingled with Almonds and Sugar-Candy, whereof some were scented, and some not. To these Potatoes excellently well dressed, and to them divers Sallads, and the curious fruits of that Country, some preserved in Sugar, and others raw, and to these many Roots candied, Almonds blanched, Raisons of the Sun, Prunellas, and I know not what, of all enough to make up that number of dishes before named; and with these quelque chose, was that entertainment made up.

And it was better a great deal, than if it had consisted of full and heaped up dishes, such as are sometimes amongst us provided, for great and profuse entertainments. Our Bread was of very good and excellent Wheat, made up very white and light, in round Cakes; and for our Drink, some of it was brewed for ought I know, ever since Noah his Flood, that good innocent water, being all the Drink there commonly used (as before) and in those hot Climates (it being better digested there than in any other parts) it is very sweet, and allays thirst better than any other Liquor can, and therefore better pleaseth, and agreeth better with every Man that comes and lives there, than any other Drink.

At this entertainment we sat long, and much longer than we could with ease cross-legged, but all considered, our Feast in that place was better than Apicius, that famous

Epicure of Rome, with all his witty Gluttony (for so Paterculus calls it, ingeniosa Gula,) could have made with all provisions had from the Earth, and Air, and Sea.

My Lord Ambassadour observed not that uneasy way of sitting at his meat, but as in his own House had Tables and Chairs, etc. Served he was altogether in Plate, and had an English, and Indian Cook to dress his diet, which was very plentiful, and cheap likewise; so that by reason of the great variety of provisions there, his weekly account for his House-keeping came but to little.

The meaner sort of people there eat Rice boiled with their green-Ginger and a little Pepper, after which they put Butter into it, which is their principal dish, and but seldom eaten by them: But their ordinary Food is made (not of the flour of Wheat) but of a coarse well tasted Grain, made up in round broad and thick Cakes, which they bake upon their thin iron plates (before spoken of) which they carry with them, when as they travel from place to place; when they have baked those Cakes, they put a little Butter on them: And doubtless the poor people find this a very hearty Food, for they who live most upon it, are as strong as they could be, if they had their diet out of the King's Kitchin. I shall here say no more of this, but proceed to speak.

Source: Roe, Thomas. *A Voyage into the East Indies*. In Pietro della Valle, *The Travels of Sig. Pietro della Valle, a Noble Roman, into East-India and Arabia Deserta in Which, the Several Countries, Together with the Customs, Manners, Traffique, and Rites Both Religious and Civil, of Those Oriental Princes and Nations, Are Faithfully Described*. London: Macock, 1665, pp. 406–09.

Housing and Furniture

Food and shelter are the basic necessities of life. Being necessary, however, is not the same as being simple. Indeed, the necessities of life also offer some of the greatest scope for conspicuous consumption. In the extract from *Gawain and the Green Knight* (Document 9), the anonymous author highlights how expensive and luxurious every aspect of Bertilak's castle is. Every detail—towers, high walls, silk carpets, and ermine-lined robes—creates the impression of immense wealth and privilege. In this case, the wealth highlights the nobility and generosity of the host and serves as an ideal to be strived for, but never attained, by the audience.

The reality of medieval estates could be very different from the ideal. The accounting of one of *Charlemagne*'s royal estates (Document 7) shows that rural estates were valued primarily for their agricultural wealth, not for the luxuriousness of the buildings themselves. According to the document, this royal estate, for example, had 1,800 measures of barley, but only one set of bed sheets. The luxurious silk tapestries and carpets that Gawain encounters in the deep woods of medieval England would rarely appear in such a location in reality. People generally brought their own supplies.

Forms of shelter are by no means universal across the globe. Local climactic and cultural conditions affect what form and construction of buildings best serve the inhabitants. In Thomas Roe's account of the buildings he saw in the empire of the *Mughal dynasty* of northern India in the seventeenth century (Document 8), the hot climate and nomadic lifestyle of the inhabitants had a clear impact on the kind of buildings they constructed and how they used those buildings. In the cities, for example, the Indians built large terraces and large double doors to pull the cooling breeze inside. The houses, moreover, were largely unornamented because the inhabitants would frequently follow their traditional nomadic lifestyle for part of the year and therefore did not waste money on fixed furnishings and also because the noblemen held their houses only at the king's pleasure and could lose those houses at any time. The temporary nature of these houses thus inhibited any large expense on complex ornamentation or bulky furnishings. Instead, the Indians relied on carpets and blankets for their beds and decorations.

The Indian rainy season lay behind yet another aspect of Indian architecture that Roe found fascinating: the large wells and water tanks, some of which were over one mile wide. These cleverly constructed tanks collected water during the rainy season and then kept that water for communal use throughout the long dry season. Necessity bred ingenuity.

7. One of Charlemagne's Estates

The accounting that follows offers a clear picture of a royal estate in the countryside belonging to the Frankish king Charlemagne (c. 742–814). As the description indicates, although the estate belonged to the king, it was by no means outrageously luxurious. The main house had 3 main rooms and 11 smaller chambers for female inhabitants, plus one cellar. Moreover, there were bedclothes for just one bed, plus one tablecloth and one towel. One hopes that 11 people did not show up at the same time on a whim! Of course, servants would equip the house fully before any scheduled royal visits, which were undoubtedly infrequent. Many of the functions we associate with a house, moreover, were performed in separate buildings. Thus, outside but still within the central courtyard was the kitchen, plus various work buildings such as a mill, granary, and barn.

The most important aspect of the estate, however, was not the house, but rather the agricultural business that took place on the estate. Most of the account describes in precise detail the quantities of agricultural goods that the rich farmlands had produced. In an era before the ready transportation of goods, the agricultural products were suitably diverse, including both livestock and wheat, barley, peas, and so on. The combined nature of the report—a description of the house and the agricultural business together—indicates that such rural houses served primarily as organizational centers rather than as residences for the king. The number of barley measures was ultimately much more important than the number of bedsheets.

We found in the imperial estate of Asnapium a royal house built of stone in the very best manner, having 3 rooms. The entire house was surrounded with balconies and it had 11 apartments for women. Underneath was 1 cellar. There were 2 porticoes. There were 17 other houses built of wood within the courtyard, with a similar number of rooms and fixtures, all well constructed. There was 1 stable, 1 kitchen, 1 mill, 1 granary, and 3 barns.

The yard was enclosed with a hedge and a stone gateway, and above was a balcony from which distributions can be made. There was also an inner yard, surrounded by a hedge, well arranged, and planted with various kinds of trees.

Of vestments: coverings for 1 bed, 1 table-cloth, and 1 towel.

Of utensils: 2 brass kettles, 2 drinking cups, 2 brass cauldrons, 1 iron cauldron, 1 frying pan, 1 grammalin, 1 pair of andirons, 1 lamp, 2 hatchets, 1 chisel, 2 augers, 1 axe,

1 knife, 1 large plane, 1 small plane, 2 scythes, 2 sickles, 2 spades edged with iron, and a sufficient supply of utensils of wood.

Of farm produce: old spelt from last year, 90 baskets which can be made into 450 weight of flour, and 100 measures of barley. From the present year, 110 baskets of spelt, of which 60 baskets had been planted, but the rest we found, 100 measures of wheat, 60 sown, the rest we found, 98 measures of rye all sown, 1,800 measures of barley, 1,100 sown, the rest we found; 430 measures of oats; 1 measure of beans; 12 measures of peas. At 5 mills were found 800 measures of small size. At 4 breweries, 650 measures of small size, 240 given to clergymen, the rest we found. At 2 bridges, 60 measures of salt and 2 shillings. At 4 gardens, 11 shillings. Also honey, 3 measures; about 1 measure of butter; lard, from last year 10 sides; new sides, 200, with fragments and fats; cheese from the present year, 43 weights.

Of cattle: 51 head of larger cattle; 5 three-year-olds; 7 two-year-olds; 7 yearlings; 10 two-year old colts; 8 yearlings; 3 stallions; 16 cows; 2 asses; 50 cows with calves; 20 young bulls; 38 yearling calves; 3 bulls; 260 hogs; 100 pigs; 5 boars; 150 sheep with lambs; 200 yearling lambs; 120 rams; 30 goats with kids; 30 yearling kids; 3 male goats; 30 geese; 80 chickens; 22 peacocks.

The Coronation of Charlemagne by Pope Leo II (A.D. 800). © 2008 Jupiterimages Corporation.

Also concerning the manors which belong to the above mansion: in the villa of Grisio we found domain buildings where there are 3 barns and a yard enclosed by a hedge. There were, besides, 1 garden with trees, 10 geese, 8 ducks, 30 chickens.

In another villa we found domain buildings and a yard surrounded by a hedge, and within 3 barns; 1 arpent of vines; 1 garden with trees; 15 geese; 20 chickens.

In a third villa, domain buildings, with 2 barns; 1 granary; 1 garden and 1 yard well enclosed by a hedge.

We found all the dry and liquid measures just as in the palace. We did not find any goldsmiths, silversmiths, blacksmiths, huntsmen, or persons engaged in other services.

The garden herbs which we found were lily, putchuck, mint, parsley, rue, celery, libesticum, sage, savory, juniper, leeks, garlic, tansy, wild mint, coriander, scullions, onions, cabbage, kohlrabi, betony. Trees: pears, apples, medlars, peaches, filberts, walnuts, mulberries, quinces.

Source: Oggs, Frederic Austin. *A Source Book of Mediaeval History.* New York: American, 1908, pp. 127–29.

8. Indian Houses, Furnishings, and Wells

Sir Thomas Roe, the great seventeenth-century English diplomat, traveled extensively in the Middle East and India. In the extract reproduced here, he records the details of the buildings and houses that he saw during his stay in the realm of the Mughal dynasty of northern India. Throughout his description, Roe notes how the hot climate of India, with its seasonal rains, and the Indians' way of life affected the architecture. For example, he notes that even the wealthiest inhabitants rarely built deluxe and luxurious abodes because they spent part of the year leading the traditional nomadic lifestyle of their ancestors. Given that a large part of their year was spent living in tents, the aristocrats decided not to waste money decorating only part-time homes. Moreover, according to Roe, all the houses were granted to the wealthy by the Mughal ruler himself, so the inhabitants could not count on living in the same house forever. The temporary nature of their abode made permanent investment in the houses unwise.

The hot climate, moreover, encouraged an architecture that sought to alleviate the heat. The houses featured large terraces, for example, so that the inhabitants could spend much of the time in the cooling breeze, and the upper stories also featured double doors that could be opened wide to encourage the breeze inside. The houses did not feature chimneys because fires for heat were unnecessary, and fires for cooking were generally located as far from the living quarters as possible to avoid the excess heat.

Houses in the city were built of sturdy stone and timber, but the poor villages in the countryside featured less expensive materials. According to Roe, the village huts were built immediately next to each other, sharing the same walls, and were constructed out of mud and sticks—a kind of wattle and daub construction, undoubtedly. The timing of construction was important; the houses were built immediately after the rainy season so that the walls would have cured hard by the time the rains came again.

Neither city houses nor rural houses featured furniture to any great degree. The inhabitants of northern India, according to Roe, would lie down on soft blankets and carpets, or at most in a cot or hammock, when they went to bed. Similarly, they would sit on the floor. The ease with which carpets, as opposed to chairs, can be moved obviously suited the nomadic lifestyle. Roe believed that this simple life could have significant health benefits. He attributes the good posture and absence of physical deformities to the Indian habit of sleeping on the back without pillows.

The climatic conditions likewise encouraged a great ingenuity in the construction of vast wells and water tanks. These stone and earth structures would be cleaned just before the rainy season to maintain the purity of the water and would then collect water during the entire rainy season. This water would then last throughout the dry season until the next rainy season came. Special access points and stairs were provided so that anyone from the neighboring cities could descend into the well on foot to collect water.

The natural landscape also clearly impressed Roe. His account frequently mentions the lions that would enter the Englishmen's camps at night and devour domestic animals, including a pet dog in one case. The roaring of lions around his camp seemed to still reverberate in Roe's ears, given the vividness of the description.

Roe's depiction of India shows how very different the habitations of the Mughal dynasty were from the elaborately furnished homes of Europe. India, however, does not appear inferior as a result. Rather, the roaring of lions outside nomadic tents seems fundamentally romantic, swashbuckling, and exciting.

SECTION IX. OF THEIR BUILDINGS IN VILLAGES, TOWNS, AND CITIES; HOW THEIR HOUSES ARE FURNISHED; OF THEIR SARRA'S OR HOUSES FOR THE ENTERTAINMENT OF PASSENGERS; OF THEIR TENTS, WELLS, AND OF THEIR PLACES OF PLEASURE, &C.

I Observed before the richness of their Soil, and how those Provinces are watered by many goodly Rivers, fed with abundance of Springs; and how their Fields are clothed with very much plenty of Corn of divers kind, sold there at such low rates that every one may there eat bread without scarceness.

Now I come to take notice of their Buildings; and here I must tell my Reader, that this People are not much taken or infected with that plague of Building (as the Italians call it) wishing the love of it as a Curse to possess the thoughts of them they most hate; and therefore, as the stones in India are not all precious, so the Houses there are not at all Palaces; the poor there cannot erect for their dwellings fair Piles, and the Grandees do not cover their heads under such curious Roofs, as many of the Europeans do. The reason, first, because all the great men there live a great part of the year, (in which their Months are more temperate, as from the middle of September, to the midst of April) in Tents, Pavilions, or moveable habitations, which, according to their fancies, changing they remove from place to place, changing their air as often as they please. And secondly, because all the great men there have their Pensions and whole subsistence from the King, which they hold upon very fickle and uncertain terms; for as they are settled upon, and continued unto them by the King's favour, so are they forfeited and lost by his frown. Of which more afterward.

Yet though they make not much use of them, they have in plenty excellent good materials for building, as Timber, Bricks, stone and marble of divers kinds and colours, of which I have seen some very good Vaults and Arches well wrought, as in their Mosquits or Churches, so in some of their high-erected Tombs, (of which more afterward) and so in some other places likewise.

For their buildings in Cities and Towns, there are some of them handsome, others fair, such as are inhabited by Merchants, and none of them very despicable. They build their houses low, not above two stories, and many of their tops flat and thick, which keep off the violence of the heat; and those flat tops, supported with strong Timber, and coated over with a plaster (like that we call plaster of Paris) keep them dry in the time of the Rains.

Those broad Terraces, or flat Roofs, some of them lofty, are places where many people may stand (and so they often do) early in the morning, and in the evening late, like Chameleons, to draw, and drink in fresh air; and they are made after this fashion, for prospect, as well as pleasure. Those houses of two stories have many of them very large upper rooms, which have many double doors in the sides of them, like those in our Balconies, to open and let in fresh air, which is likewise conveyed in unto them, by many lesser lights made in the walls of those rooms, which are always free and open; The use of glass windows, or any other shuttings, being not known there, nor in any other very hot Countries. Neither have they any Chimneys in their buildings, because they never make any use of fire but to dress their food, which fire they make against firm wall, or without their Tents against some bank of Earth, as remote as may be from the places where they use to keep, that they may receive no annoyance from the heat thereof.

It is their manner in many places, to plant about, and amongst their buildings, trees which grow high and broad, the shadow whereof keeps their houses by far more cool; this I observ'd in a special manner when we were ready to enter Amadavar; for it appeared to us, as if we had been entring a Wood, rather than a City. That Amadavar is a very large and populous City, entered by many fair Gates girt about with an high and thick Wall of Brick, which mounts above the tops of their houses, without which wall there are no suburbs.

Most of the houses within the City are of Brick, and very many of them ridged and covered with Tiles. But for their houses in their Aldeas or Villages, which stand very thick in that Country, they are generally very poor and base. All those Country-dwellings are set up close together; for I never observed any house there to stand single, and alone. Some of their houses in those villages are made with earthen walls, mingled with straw, set up immediately after their Rains, and having a long season after to dry them thoroughly, stand firm, and so continue; they are built low, and many of them flat: but for the generality of those Country-Villages, the Cottages in them are miserably poor, little, and base; so that as they are built with a very little charge, set up with sticks rather than Timber, if they chance to fire (as many times they do) for a very little they may be re-edified.

Those who inhabit the Country-Villages, are called Coolees. These till the ground, and breed up Cattle, and other things for provision, as Hens, etc. They who plant the Sugar, the Cotton-wool, and Indigo, etc., for their Trades and Manufactures, they are kept in Cities and Towns, about which are their choicest fruits planted. In their Cities and Towns, without their dwellings, but fix't to them, are pend-houses where they shew and sell their provisions, as bread, and flower-cakes made up with Sugar, and fruits, and other things; and there they show their manufactures, and other Commodities, some of which they carry twice every day to sell in the Bazar or Market.

I saw two houses of the Mogol's, one at Mandoa, the other at Amadaver, which appeared large & stately, built of excellent stone well squared and put together, each of them taking up a large compass of ground; but we could never see how they were contrived within, because there are none admitted, strangers or others, to have a sight of those houses, while the King's wives and women are there, which must not be seen by any but by himself, and his servants the Eunuchs.

The Mogol's Palace Royal is at Agra his Metropolis (of which more afterward) but for the present I shall take a little notice of a very curious Grot I saw belonging to his house at Mandoa, which stood a small distance from it, for the building of which there was a way made into a firm Rock, which showed it self on the side of an Hill, Canopied over with part of that Rock. It was a place that had much beauty in it by reason of the curious workmanship bestowed on it; and much pleasure by reason of its coolness.

That City Mandoa I speak of, is situated upon a very high mountain, the top whereof is flat, and plain, and spacious. From all parts that lie about it but one; the ascent is very high, and steep; and the way to us seemed exceeding long, for we were two whole days climbing up the Hill, with our Carriages, which we got up with very much difficulty; not far from the bottom of which Hill, we lodged at a great town called Achabar-pore, where we ferried over a broad River (as we did in other places) for I observed no bridges made there over any of their Rivers where their high-ways lie. That Hill on which Mandoa stands, is stuck round (as it were) with fair trees, that keep their distance so one from and below the other that there is much delight in beholding them either from the bottom or top of that Hill.

In those vast and far extended Woods, there are Lions, Tigers, and other beasts of Prey, and many wild Elephants. We lay one night in that wood with our Carriages, and those Lions came about us discovering themselves by their Roaring; but we keeping a very good fire all night, they came not near enough to hurt either our selves, or cattle. Those cruel Beasts are night-walkers for in the day they appear not.

After when (through God's most gracious assistance) we had overcome those difficulties and dangers, we came into a plain and even Country; in which travelling a few days more, we first met with my Lord Ambassador marching towards Mandoa with that great King, with whom I then settled, and continued with him, till he was returned home.

We were in our journey to the Court from the beginning of January, till the end of March, we resting a while at Brampore, which is a very spacious and populous City, where we had a Factory. And after that, we were violently detained in our journey by Sultan Caroon the Prince, whom we met in his march towards Brampore, & a very marvelous great retinue with him. The reason why he interrupted us in our course was, that he might see the Presents we had for his Father the King; but we having command from the Ambassador to tell him, that we durst not open them, till we came to the King, we most humbly craved his pardon to spare us in that; so presenting him with a pair of Rich Gloves (though they be things they wear not in those hot Countries) and a rich embroidered bag for perfume (which amongst many other things of the like kind were brought from England to be given away for Presents) after that he had carried us back three days journey, he let us go, taking further order for our safe convoy.

And now Reader, thou mayest suppose us almost settled in Mandoa, the place then of the Mogol's residence, not much inhabited before we came thither, having more ruins by far about it, than standing houses. But amongst the Piles of building that had held up their heads above Ruin, there were not a few unfrequented Mosquits, or Mahometan Churches; yet I observed, that though the people who attended the King there, were marvellously straightened for room, wherein they might dispose of very great numbers of most excellent horses, which were now at that place, they would not make stables of any of those Churches, though before that time, they had been forsaken, and out of use.

One of those deserted Mosquits, with some large Tomb near it, both vaulted over head (which shall be after described) were the best places there to be gotten for my Lord Ambassadour and his Company to lodge and be in, we carrying our bedding, and all things appertaining thereto, all necessaries belonging to our Kitchen, and every thing beside for bodily use, from place to place, as we occasionally removed. Here we stayed with the Mogol from the middle of April, till the twentieth of September following, and then began our progress with him, towards the City Amadavar.

Our abiding place at Mandoa, was very near one of the sides of that vast Wilderness, out of which, some of those wild beasts oft-times in the night came about our habitation, and seldom returned back without a Sheep, or a Goat, or a Kid, some of which we always kept about us for our provision. And it was a wonderful great mercy, those furious, and ravening, and hunger-bit Creatures, did not make their prey sometimes in the dark and silent nights, while we were sleeping, on some of our bodies, the fore-part of our dwelling standing upon pillars; and there was nothing in those open distances, that had any strength in it to keep them from us.

One night, early in the Evening, there was a great Lion which we saw, came into our Yard, (though our Yard was compassed about with a stone-wall, that was not low). And my Lord Ambassadour having a little white neat Shock, that ran out barking at him, the Lion presently snapt him up, leapt again over the wall, and away he went.

But for a ravening and roaring Lion, as I believe that he cannot be made tame when he is old; yet certainly he may be bred tame, being kept full, and high fed. For the

Mogol, at my being there, had a very great Lion (I often saw) which went up and down, amongst the people that frequented his Court, gently as a dog, and never did hurt; only he had some Keepers which did continually wait upon him.

For those wild and cruel Beasts, one of our English-men watching in a tree by night, (that stood not far from our dwelling) with a fire-lock charged with some small bullets, shot a Tiger, and killed him stone-dead, as he was coming towards us. It was a large beast, higher than an Irish-Greyhound, with grizzled hair, a long head, & sharp and short picked ears, having a mouth filled with cruel teeth; after which (we usually keeping a little fire without our house every night) were not so much troubled with those night-walkers.

Now to return to that from which I am occasionally digressed, I told you before what their buildings are. And now for the furniture that the greatest men have in them, it is Curta supellex, very little; they being not beautified with hangings, nor with any thing besides to line their walls; but where they are best adorned, they are kept very white, and set off with a little neat painting and nothing else; for they have no Chairs, no stools, nor Couches, nor Tables, nor Beds, enclosed with Canopies, or Curtains, in any of their Rooms. And the truth is, that if they had them, the extreme heat there would forbid the use of many of them; all their bravery is upon their Floors, all which are made even with fine Earth or Plaster, on which they spread their most excellent Carpets in their Tents, as well as in their dwelling houses, laying some coarse thing under to preserve them; on which they sit (as Tailors on their shop-boards) when they meet together, putting off their shoes (which they usually wear as slippers and their feet bare in them) when they come to tread upon those soft Pavements, and keeping them off till they remove thence, this helps to keep cool their feet, and is very pleasant in those hot Countries. On those Carpets they sleep in the night time, or else upon an hard Quilt, or lying upon a flight and low Bed-stead they call a Cot, bottomed with broad Girt-web made of Cotton-wool. But wherever they lie, they stretch themselves out at their full length when they go to sleep, usually upon their backs, without any Pillow, or Bolster, to raise up their heads. Very many of the meaner sort of people (as I have often observed) lie thus stretched out to take their rest upon the ground, in the dry season of the year, with a white Callico-cloth spread all over them, which makes them to appear like so many dead corpses laid forth for burial. This lying so even, and at length with their bodies thus extended, may be one reason why the people there are all so straight limbed, having none crooked amongst them; and another, because they never girt, nor lace in their bodies (as before was observed). Some of those slight Bedsteads, they call Cots, in their standing houses hang by ropes, a little above ground, which are fastened to the four corners thereof; moved gently up and down, by their servants, to lull them asleep.

They have no Inns in those parts for the entertainment of strangers; but in some great Towns large Houses they call Sarras very substantially built, with brick, or stone, where any Passengers may find house-room and use it without any recompence; but there is nothing to be had beside room, all other things they must provide and bring with them, as when they lodge in Tents.

Amongst their Buildings I must take special notice of their Wells and Tanks, upon both which in very many places they bestow exceeding much cost in stone-work; for their Wells which are fed with Springs, they make them round, but very wide and large.

They are wrought up with firm stones laid in fine Plaster; they usually cover those Wells with a building over-head, and with Oxen draw water out of them, which riseth up in many small Buckets, whereof some are always going down, others continually coming up, and emptying themselves, in troughs, or little rills, made to receive, and convey the water whither they please.

Their Tanks are made in low places, and many of them very deep and large (one mile, and some of them much more in compass) made round or four-square, or in more squares, about which there is a low stone-wall, that hath many doors in it, and within that wall steps, made one below the other round about it, that go down to the bottom thereof, (which is paved likewise); those steps are made of well squared lasting stone, laid firm, and even in very good order, for people that have not plenty of water otherwise, to go down and take it. These great receptacles of water, are made near places that are very populous; filled when that long season of rain (before spoken of) comes, immediately before which time, they cleanse them, that the water may be more clear, and wholesome. They hold water all the dry season of the year.

Source: Roe, Thomas. *A Voyage into the East Indies.* In Pietro della Valle, *The Travels of Sig. Pietro della Valle, a Noble Roman, into East-India and Arabia Deserta in Which, the Several Countries, Together with the Customs, Manners, Traffique, and Rites Both Religious and Civil, of Those Oriental Princes and Nations, Are Faithfully Described.* London: Macock, 1665, pp. 398–404. Spelling has been altered slightly.

9. The Welcome at an English Manor House

The best way to explore medieval and Renaissance housing is, of course, to take a tour of the many such houses that remain. Fictional descriptions of contemporary housing, however, can offer a unique understanding not only of an edifice but also of the use and symbolic importance of that edifice. The magnificent late fourteenth-century Middle English masterpiece Gawain and the Green Knight, *for example, highlights how a wealthy home built prestige by offering a warm welcome to noble guests. In the extract reproduced here, the anonymous author recounts how Gawain, an Arthurian knight, comes upon an unexpected castle in a deep wood in the middle of winter as an answer to his prayer for refuge and a place to hear Mass over the Christmas holiday. This English manor house appears literally in answer to his prayers.*

In no way does Gawain *paint an accurate description of a typical medieval welcome— silk carpets, for example, would be out of the question for almost all rural estates. The passage does, however, depict an ideal to which the audience could aspire. A nobleman would offer a prominent guest silk carpets if he could. Other aspects of Gawain's welcome are more possible, however. Fourteenth-century hosts eager to please a prestigious guest would undoubtedly welcome them heartily, remove their armor, bring them to a warm room, bring them rich attire (no need to pack a suitcase!), and have an elaborate meal prepared. The more important the guest, the more luxurious and elaborate would be the clothes, food, and welcome offered. In this way, the status of both the guest and the host can be measured. In the following passage from* Gawain and the Green Knight, *therefore, the incredibly rich clothes and bedroom decorations reveal both the host's wealth and the host's generosity, but also the honor that the host feels is due to Gawain. Honor, ultimately, is measured materialistically.*

Of course, the elaborate exterior of the manor house—it features a multitude of chimneys, towers, windows, and walls—foreshadows the elaborate welcome within. The architectural details of this home reflect the most recent fashions of the late Middle Ages. In the early Middle Ages, even the wealthiest of buildings featured more simple, solid designs in the Romanesque style. The Gothic style of open spaces, elaborate towers, fancy decorations, and large windows began to sweep Europe in the twelfth century. The most elaborate workmanship was usually to be found in cathedrals, which could draw on a large economic base, so the elaborate craftsmanship of the private castle in Gawain and the Green Knight *is even more impressive.*

Gawain and the Green Knight *is written in alliterative verse in a northwest dialect of Middle English. In the following translation, the editor has attempted to present the material simply and clearly and has abandoned the goal of capturing the detailed intricacies of the verse for the sake of more colloquial clarity.*

When he had just finished making the sign of the cross three times, he noticed a dwelling place with a moat in the midst of the wood. On a knoll above a glade, underneath the boughs of many giant trees, in the middle of the moat, stood the most handsome castle that a knight ever owned. It was built in a meadow with a park all around it. The palace was thoroughly enclosed with pickets, and surrounded for two miles by trees. The nobleman contemplated the side of that stronghold as it shimmered and glowed through the fair oaks. Then he removed his helmet deftly and offered thanks to Jesus and St. Gilian, those noblemen who had shown him this sight and listened to his cry. "Good lodging," he said, "I ask of you yet." Then he spurred Gringolet with his golden spurs, and he sped to the main gate and the knight came quickly to the drawbridge. The bridge was stoutly pulled up, and the gates were securely closed. The walls were skillfully constructed: they feared no wind's blast.

The warrior waited with his horse on the bank by the deep moat that enclosed the habitation. The wall stood very deep in the water and rose up to a huge height. It featured well carved stone up to the cornices, with horizontal projections in the best style below the battlements. There were pretty turrets strewed along the top, and many lovely windows looked out cleverly. That knight had never seen a better barbican. Further in, he espied the lofty and wide hall set with towers and many ornamental pinnacles, carved with wondrous skill. He examined the many chalk-white chimneys scattered along the castle's roof: they gleamed brightly. So many painted pinnacles projected everywhere in the castle that it seemed almost as if cut out of paper. The knight expected a pleasant time, if he could manage to get inside, to lodge in that dwelling for the holidays. He called out, and a polite, polished porter came at once. He did his job and greeted the knight errant.

"Good sir," said Gawain, "will you go as a messenger to the high lord of this house to ask lodging for me?" "Yes, by Peter," said the porter, "and I am positive that you will be welcome to stay as long as you like." Then the man went swiftly and returned as quickly, accompanied by a group to welcome the knight. They let down the huge drawbridge and went out in a group and kneeled down on their knees upon the cold earth to welcome this man who seemed most worthy. They invited him to come through the opened-wide gates. He quickly made them rise and rode over the bridge. Several men held his saddle while he alighted and then strong men led the steed to a stable. Knights and squires came then to lead this nobleman joyfully into the hall. When he took off his helmet, they hastened to take it from his hand and to serve him. They took his sword and his shield, and then each of the knights embraced him heartily, and many proud men strove to give that prince honor. They brought him in his armor into the hall where the blazing fire burned upon the floor. Then the lord of the people came out from his private room to greet honorably the guest; He said, "You are welcome to make use of everything here. Everything is yours, to use and enjoy at your pleasure." "Many thanks," said Gawain, "May Christ reward you." The happy men embraced each other.

Gawain gazed on the man who proffered him such a warm greeting. The man that owned the castle was bold, huge, and in the prime of life. His beard was large and intensely reddish-brown. He stood firmly on two massive legs, and had a face like fire, and was courteous in his speech. He appeared truly to Gawain to be a good leader of knights. The lord brought him into the room and commanded that a servant be brought immediately. Many men appeared at once. They brought him to a beautiful bedroom with luxurious bedclothes and silk curtains with golden hems and embroidered blankets lined with ermine. There were drapes hanging from gold rings, and rich, red tapestries of silk hung on the walls, and carpeted the floors as well. There the knight's armor was removed while they chatted pleasantly. The men quickly brought him a selection of rich robes to put on. As soon as he put one on and wrapped it around himself, the man's limbs shone brightly and resembled spring itself. They were of the opinion that Christ had never made a more handsome knight. It seemed that he had to be the best prince anywhere in the world where fierce men battle in the field.

A chair draped with cloths and padded with beautifully quilted cushions was placed for Sir Gawain in front of the chimney and a charcoal fire. Then a jolly mantle of rich, embroidered cloth, lined with fur—ermine in fact—with a hood of the same quality was placed upon him. He sat in that chair nobly arrayed, and warmed up quickly, and his spirits revived. A table was soon set up, decorated with a clean, bright table cloth, and laid with a salt cellar and silver spoons. The man washed and went to eat. Servants waited on him well, and brought him delicious stews in vast quantities, along with many kinds of fish. Some fish were baked in bread, and others were grilled over hot coals; some were poached, and some were stewed with spices. All the sauces were skillfully prepared and the man enjoyed them. The nobleman frequently proclaimed it a true feast, while the men beseeched him at the same time: "Accept this penitential fare graciously for now, and later we'll do better." The man grew very merry as the wine went to his head.

Source: *Sir Gawain and the Green Knight.* 2nd ed. Ed. J.R.R. Tolkien and E. V. Gordon. Oxford: Clarendon Press, 1967, lines 763–900. Translated for this volume by Lawrence Morris.

Clothing and Personal Appearance

According to an old adage, "Clothing makes the man." Or woman, for that matter. The documents presented in this section certainly seem to agree. Of course, documents that expressly examine clothing are likely to highlight the important role of clothing in self-presentation in daily life, yet the use of clothing across time and cultures to delineate and reveal socioeconomic class as well as personal taste indicates that clothing does play a central role in structuring societal and personal interactions.

Sumptuary laws, in which certain social classes are ordered to wear certain kinds of clothing, were prevalent across the globe, from medieval Europe to seventeenth-century South America. Clothing under such legislation serves as a readily apparent marker of political and economic power. The poor are marked as poor, and the wealthy are marked as wealthy. Of course, even without such legislation (as in the case of the modern-day United States), the differences between the wealthy and the poor can frequently be seen in clothing, but these differences are not enshrined in law. Document 13 gives a good overview of the practicalities of one system of clothing regulations: the fashions of the Incas of Peru and their subject peoples. At the pinnacle of the system stood the founder of the Inca people, *Manco Capac*. All the other tribes were permitted to imitate the Inca leader and his family in some respects but were never allowed to adopt exactly the same fashions. The ruling class determined what fashions were good, and the lower social classes could imitate, but never obtain, those same fashions. This structure naturally made Inca culture the center and pinnacle of achievement while debasing the previous tribal traditions of the conquered peoples.

The tribal or national traditions of dress were often greatly valued, as seen in Richard Brathwaite's remarks on Englishwomen's clothing of the seventeenth century (Documents 11 and 12). Brathwaite, however, was even more concerned with the morality of clothing. According to Brathwaite, an excessive interest in fancy clothing and foreign fashions corrupts the soul. Arguing from the biblical book of Genesis, where God dressed Adam and Eve in the skins of animals, Brathwaite claims that the modern desire for soft, luxurious, full clothing represents an indulgent debasement. Ultimately, instead of having wardrobes full of fine clothing, the wealthy should spend this money on clothing the poor. Only fools, moreover, value a people based on their appearance—much better to attract someone using internal qualities rather than external appearance. In sum, Brathwaite radically rejects the idea, seen in the Inca culture as well as in Brathwaite's contemporary Britain, that wealthy fashions are the best fashions.

Islamic law also saw fashion as a location of morality. However, unlike Brathwaite in the seventeenth century, who saw wealthy fashion as the main enemy, the seventh-century principles contained in the *Koran* saw immodest fashion as the most dangerous temptation. The passage extracted in Document 10 provides the rational for Muslim women covering themselves in veils, either with simple headscarves or in full-length *hijab*. According to the Koran, such veiling will protect a woman's beauty from the gaze of men; the women should appear unveiled only in front of those who will not notice the beauty (children, relations, other women) or who are permitted to enjoy that beauty (husbands). Modest clothing therefore serves to control male lust.

The connections and connotations of clothing that these documents describe show that clothing and personal appearance are not, in fact, strictly personal. Clothing is fundamentally a way of communicating with others. Even when we do not speak or interact with someone, our appearance suggests to that person what we are like and what background we have. Clothing is not personal; it is a cultural construct as expressive and meaningful as language.

10. Women's Dress in the Koran

The passage from the Koran reprinted here provides the major textual backing for the practice of Muslim women wearing veils. The vagueness of the passage has allowed for multiple interpretations. Thus, in some regions, women wear full covering from head to foot (called hijab), whereas in other regions women wear a simple headscarf.

Regardless of interpretation, the purpose of the veils remains the same: the women reserve their "ornaments" (i.e., their physical beauty) primarily for their husbands, although the formality of veiling is not needed when dealing with close relations or with those unlikely to be aroused by the woman's appearance, such as small children. Veiling, therefore, serves primarily as a means of combating male desire and unwanted male attention.

And speak to the believing women that they refrain their looks, and observe continence; and that they display not their ornaments, except those which are external; and that they draw their veils over their bosoms, and display not their ornaments, except to their husbands or their fathers, or their husbands' fathers, or their sons, or their husbands' sons, or their brothers, or their brothers' sons, or their sisters' sons, or their women, or their slaves, or male domestics who have no natural force, or to children who note not women's nakedness. And let them not strike their feet together, so as to discover their hidden ornaments. And be ye wholly turned to God, O ye believers! Haply it shall be well with you.

Forced baptism of Muslim women, wearing hijab, in Granada after the Reconquista by the Catholic Kings in 1492. Painted wood relief, c. 1500. Bildarchiv Preussischer Kulturbesitz/Art Resource, NY.

Source: *El-Koran, or, The Koran.* 2nd ed. Translated by J. M. Rodwell. London: Bernard Quaritch, 1876, p. 492 (sura 24, verse 31).

11. Sinful Dress

A person's clothing can make a powerful impression and imply what kind of a person he or she is. Even today, this supposed connection between clothing and internal qualities remains strong—we get a different impression from someone in jeans and a T-shirt than from someone in a business suit. The Middle Ages and Renaissance were no different; in fact, people from those eras believed even more strongly in a connection between external appearance and internal character. In the extract that follows, the author, an Englishman named Richard Brathwaite, discusses what clothing is inappropriate, indeed, sinful, for a human being to wear.

Brathwaite classifies the abuse of clothing into four categories: inappropriate degree, excessive softness, foreign fashions, and simply too much. "Degree" refers to social class; throughout the Middle Ages and Renaissance, people were expected to dress in a manner that indicated what their social class was. In fact, sumptuary laws frequently attempted to legislate exactly what kinds of clothes any particular social class could wear. Such laws rarely succeeded in their ambitions—people of all classes consistently strove to wear the best clothing they could afford.

Brathwaite adds a further twist, however, by suggesting that all current styles of human clothing are excessive by noting that God gave Adam and Eve the skins of animals to wear in Genesis, but today humans have chosen instead to wear worm excrement, by which he means silk.

"Softness of apparel" refers to luxurious clothes with smooth textures. Once again referring to the clothing of the ancestors referenced in the Bible, consisting of rough skins and animal hair, Brathwaite suggests that human beings are becoming like their clothes: soft and effeminate. Better, according to Brathwaite, would be to adopt the animal skins of John the Baptist, if we want to be close to God.

Outlandish is the word Brathwaite chooses to describe foreign clothes. The word actually meant "foreign" (out + land) during Brathwaite's time but was already coming to contain the sense of strange and over-the-top that the word has today. Brathwaite's biblical citation is misleading here—although Brathwaite considers non-English clothing to be outlandish, the biblical personages of course were referring to Jewish clothing. English clothing, in fact, was very outlandish from a Jewish perspective.

Finally, Brathwaite discusses "superfluity of apparel," by which he refers to two practices: (1) having too many changes of clothing and (2) having clothes made with too much cloth. The second criticism is perhaps the hardest to understand from a modern perspective because of changes in fashion. Today, clothing tends to contain more or less only the amount of cloth needed to cover the body; in the Middle Ages and Renaissance, however, clothes often had large amounts of extra cloth in the design. A prime example, which Brathwaite criticizes, is the long, billowing sleeves that often reached all the way to the ground. The purpose of such extra cloth was to show off wealth. Cloth was expensive, and more of it indicated that the wearer had the financial means to spend large amounts of money on clothing. Brathwaite, perhaps sensibly, suggests that the extra cloth should simply be given to the poor and naked, who cannot afford to buy anything new. Brathwaite successfully turns the question "What shall I wear tonight?" into a moral dilemma.

REPROOF TOUCHING APPAREL MAY BE OCCASIONED FROM FOUR RESPECTS

First, when any one weareth *Apparel* above their degree, exceeding their estate in precious attire. Whence it is that *Gregory* sayeth, "There be some who are of opinion, that the wearing of precious or sumptuous *Apparel* is no sin, which, if it were no fault, the divine Word would never have so punctually expressed, nor historically related, how the *Rich man*, who was tormented in hell, was clothed with Purple and Silk. Whence we may note, that touching the matter or subject of attire, human curiosity availeth highly. The first stuff or substance of our garments, was very mean, to wit, Skin with Wool. Whence it is we read, that God made *Adam* and his wife *Coats of Skins*, that is, of the Skins of dead beasts. Afterwards (see the gradation of this vanity derived from human singularity) they came to *Pure Wool*, because it was lighter than Skins. After that to *rinds of trees*, to wit, *Flax*. After that to the *dung and ordure of Worms*, to wit, *Silk*. Lastly, to *Gold and Silver, and precious Stones*. Which preciousness of attire highly displeaseth God. For instance whereof (which the very Pagans themselves observed) we read that the very first among the *Romans*, whoever wore *Purple*, was struck with a Thunder-bolt, and so dyed suddenly, for a terror and mirror to all succeeding times, that none should attempt to lift himself proudly against God in precious attire.

The second point reprehensible is, *Softness* or *Delicacy* of *Apparel*: Soft Clothes introduce soft minds. Delicacy in the *habit*, begets an *effeminacy* in the *heart*. *John the Baptist,* who was sanctified in his mother's womb, wore sharp and rough garments. Whence we are taught, that the true servant of God is not to wear garments for beauty or delight, but to cover his nakedness; not for State or Curiosity, but necessity and convenience. Christ sayeth in his Gospel, "They that are clad in soft raiments are in Kings' houses." Whence appeareth a main difference betwixt the servants of Christ and of this world. The servants of this world seek delight, honour, and pleasure in their attire; whereas the servants of Christ so highly value the garment of innocence, as they loath to stain it with outward vanities. It is their honour to *put on* Christ Jesus; other robes you may rob them of, and give them occasion to joy in your purchase.

The third thing reproveable is, *foreign Fashions:* When we desire nothing more than to bring in some Outlandish habit different from our own, in which respect (so Apishly-antic is man) it becomes more affected than our own. Against such the Lord threatneth, "I will visit the Princes and the Kings' children, and all such as are clothed with strange Apparel." Which "strange Apparell" is after diverse fashions and inventions, wholly unknown to our Ancestors. Which may appear sufficiently to such, who within this 30, or 40, or 60 years never saw such cutting, carving, nor indenting as they now see.

The fourth thing reproveable is, *Superfluity of Apparell*, expressed in these three particulars: first, in those who have diverse changes and suits of Clothes; who had rather have their garments eaten by moths, than they should cover the poor members of Christ. The naked cry, the needy cry, and shriekingly complain unto us, how they miserably labour and languish of hunger and cold. What avails it them that we have such changes of raiments neatly plaited and folded; rather than we will supply them, they must be starved? How do such rich Moth-worms observe the Doctrine of Christ, when he sayeth in his Gospel, *"He that hath two Coats let him give one to him that hath none?"*

Secondly, we are to consider the *Superfluity* of such who will have long garments, purposely to seem greater: yet, which of these can add one cubit to his stature? This puts me in remembrance of a conceited story which I have sometimes heard, of a diminutive Gentleman, who demanding of his Tailor, what yards of Satin would make him a Suit, being answered far short in number of what he expected: with great indignation replied,

"Such an one of the *Guard* to my knowledge had thrice as much for a Suite, and I will second him." Which his Tailor with small importunacy condescended to, making a *Gargantuan's Suite* for this *Ounce of man's flesh*, reserving to himself a large portion of shreds, purposely to form a fitter proportion for his *Ganymede* shape.

The third *Superfluity* ariseth from their vanity, who take delight in wearing great sleeves, misshapen Elephantine bodies, trains sweeping the earth, with huge pokes to shroud their fantastic heads, as if they had committed some egregious fact which deserved that censure; for in the Eastern Countries it hath been usually observed, that such light Women as had distained their honour, or laid a public imputation on their name, by consenting to any libidinous act, were to have their heads sewed up in a poke, to proclaim their shame, and publish to the world the quality of their sin.

Source: Brathwaite, Richard. *The English Gentlewoman, Drawn Out to the Full Body: Expressing What Habiliments Doe Best Attire Her, What Ornaments Doe Best Adorne Her, What Complements Doe Best Accomplish Her.* London: B. Alsop and T. Fawcet, 1631, pp. 13–16.

12. National Dress, Modesty, and Mates

In the extract reproduced here, the seventeenth-century Englishman Richard Brathwaite discusses the temptations of fancy and fanciful dress. According to Brathwaite, many women dress richly to attract a mate. Indeed, Brathwaite even acknowledges that he knows some men who are in fact struck by beautiful clothing. However, Brathwaite avers that these men are largely fools, possessing little intelligence (called "wit" in the language of the day), and are therefore largely not worth attracting because they are attracted to appearances rather than realities. Using the metaphor of musical instruments, he implies that it is much better to appreciate a violin because of its beautiful sound than to appreciate it because of its beautiful case. Therefore, according to Brathwaite, women do better in improving their internal character—especially their humility, modesty, and chastity—than they do in improving their external appearance.

Brathwaite is particularly critical of England's propensity to borrow the fashions of other cultures. He argues that whereas the Italians, French, and others are content with their own national costume—which frequently also delineates the sex, state, and family of the wearer—Englishwomen alone seek out other nations' costume, thereby both abandoning the traditions of their ancestors and proving their insufferable delight in new fashions. Although twenty-first-century fashions do not much resemble the fashions of the seventeenth century, curiously, stereotypes about women's love of clothing and shopping continue today.

As that is ever held most *generous* which is least *affected*, most *genuine* which is least *forced*; so there is nothing which confers more true glory on us, than in displaying our own Country's garb by that we wear upon us. The Crow in the fable was sharply taxed for her borrowed feathers; the *fable*, though it spoke of a *Crow*, the *Moral* pointed at a *man*. *Habit* (we say) is a *Custom*; why should it be our *custom* to change our *Habit?* With what constancy some other Nations observe their native attire, Histories both ancient and modern will sufficiently inform us. Nothing is held more contemptible with them, than apishly to imitate foreign fashions. Prescription is their Tailor, antiquity their Tutor. Amongst the ancient Heathen, even their very habit distinguished Widows from Matrons, Matrons from Virgins. So as not only sexes, states, conditions, years, but even lineages, races, and families were remarkably discovered.

We usually observe such a fashion to be *French*, such an one *Spanish*, another *Italian*, this *Dutch*, that *Poland*. Meantime where is the *English?* Surely, some precious Elixir extracted out of all these. She will neither rely on her own invention, nor compose herself to the fashion of any one particular Nation, but make herself an Epitomized confection of all. Thus becomes she not only a stranger to others, but to herself. It were to be wished, that as our Country is jealous of her own invention in contriving, so she were no less cautious in her choice of wearing. *Gregory* the Great thought that *Angles* did nearly symphonize with *Angels*, not so much in letter, as in favour and feature: Were it not pity that these should darken their beauty with veils of deformity?

Truth is, there is nothing which confers more native beauty on the *wearer*, than to be least affective in whatsoever she shall wear. She asperseth a great blemish on her better part, who ties herself to that formality, as she dare not put off the least trifle that she wears, nor put on ought more than she wears, lest she should lose the opinion of Compleat. There is a native modesty even in attire as well as gesture, which better becomes, and would more fully accomplish her, if *fashion* were not such a *pearl* in her eye, as it keeps her from the sight of her own vanity. I confess, light heads will be easily taken with such toys: yea, I have sometimes observed a fantastic dressing strike an amorous inconsiderate Gosling sooner into a passionate *ah me,* with a careless lovesick wreathing of his enfolded arms, than some other more attractive object could ever do. But what is the purchase of one of these *Green-wits* worth? What benefit can a young *Gentlewoman* reap in enjoying him, who scarcely ever enjoyed himself? Means he may have, but so meanly are they seconded by inward abilities, as his state seems fitter to manage him, than he to marshal it. A long Locke he has got, and the art to frizzle it; a Ring in a string, and the trick to handle it: for his discourse, to give him his true Character, his silence approves him better; for his wit, he may laugh at a conceit, and his conceit never the wiser; for his other parts, disclaiming his substance, I appeal to his picture. Now, *Gentlewoman,* tell me, do you trim yourself up for this *Popinjay?* Would you have the *fool* to wear you, after so many *follies* have outworn you? Let modesty suit you, that a discreeter mate may choose you.

Be it your prime honour to make civility your director. This will incomparably more grace you, than any fantastic attire, which, though it beget admiration, it closeth always with derision. You cannot possibly detract more from the renown of your Country, where you received birth and education, than by too hot a quest or pursuit after Outlandish fashions. Play not the *Dotterell,* in this too apish and servile *Imitation;* let other Countries admire your Constancy and Civility: while they reflect both on what you wear and what you are. Be it your glory to improve your Country's fame. Many eyes are fixed on you, and many hearts will be taken with you, if they behold those two Ornaments, *Modesty,* and *Humility,* ever attending you; Discretion will be more taken and enamoured with these, than toys and feathers. There is nothing so rough but may be polished; nor ought so outwardly faire but may be disfigured. Whereas the beauty of these two cannot by adulterate Art be more graced, by the aged furrows of time become defaced, or by any outward Occurrence impaired.

There are many beauteous and sumptuous *Cases,* whose *Instruments* are out of tune. These may please the *eye,* but they neither lend nor leave a sweet accent in the *Ear.* May-buds of fading beauty; Fruits which commonly *fall* before they be *ripe,* and tender small sweetness to them that *reap.* These Baths of voluptuous delights, chaste feet disdaine to approach. Virtue must either be suited with Consorts like herself, or they must give her leave solely to enjoy herself. Be you *Maids of honour* to this maiden Princess. Consecrate your day to virtuous actions, your night to usefull recollections. Think how this *World* is your *Stage,* your *Life* an Act. The *Tiring-house,* where you bestowed such care, cost and curiosity, must be shut up, when your *Night* approacheth. Prepare Oil for your virgin Lamps; marriage robes for your chaste souls; that advancing the honour of your Country here on Earth, in your translation from hence, you may find a Country in heaven.

Source: Brathwaite, Richard. *The English Gentlewoman, Drawn Out to the Full Body: Expressing What Habilliments Doe Best Attire Her, What Ornaments Doe Best Adorne Her, What Complements Doe Best Accomplish Her.* London: B. Alsop and T. Fawcet, 1631, pp. 22–25.

13. Inca Fashions

Garcilaso de la Vega, called "El Inca," had a special insight into the cultures of Peru: his mother was an Inca princess, and his father was a Spanish conquistador. Thus, he had access to the worlds of both Native American and European elites. His firsthand accounts of the Incas provide accurate insights into the traditions of the Native American peoples of the Andes.

According to Garcilaso, the fashions of the Native Americans were strictly regimented to indicate both to what tribe a person belonged and with what favor that tribe was held. The center of fashion was the original Inca, Manco Capac, who proclaimed himself the child of the Sun and therefore a god. His own fashion, which he passed down to the Incas, the elite ruling class of Andean society during the time of the Conquistadors, was striking: a shaved head except for a finger-wide strip of hair, a thin colored headband called a llautu, and ears pierced with studs as wide as a red-wine-glass's mouth. The less important tribes were commanded gradually to adopt similar fashions; the closer their own allotted fashion to the fashion of the Inca himself, the more respected that tribe was. The vassal tribes, for example, wore a llautu, but theirs was black rather than multicolored; they had their ears pierced, but their studs were much smaller and made of materials such as wool or reeds. In this way, Inca fashion replicated the power structure of the society. At the top was the divine Inca emperor and his family; every other tribe attempted to imitate the Incas but was never allowed to succeed.

THE HONOURABLE BADGES WHICH THE INCA GAVE TO HIS FOLLOWERS

In the above affairs, and in other similar occupations, the Inca Manco Ccapac was occupied during many years, conferring benefits on his people; and, having experienced their fidelity and love, and the respect and adoration with which they treated him, he desired to favour them still farther by ennobling them with titles, and badges such as he wore on his own head, and this was after he had persuaded them that he was a child of the Sun. The Inca Manco Ccapac, and afterwards his descendants, in imitation of him, were shorn, and only wore a tress of hair one finger in width. They were shaven with stone razors, scraping the hair off, and only leaving the above-mentioned tress. They used knives of stone, because they had not invented scissors, shaving themselves with great trouble, as any one may imagine. When they afterwards experienced the facility and ease afforded by the use of scissors, one of the Yncas said to an old schoolfellow of mine: "If the Spaniards, your fathers, had done nothing more than bring us scissors, looking-glasses, and combs, we would have given all the gold and silver there is in our land, for them." Besides having their heads shaved, they bored their ears, just as women are usually bored for ear-rings; except that they increased the size of the hole artificially (as I shall more fully relate in the proper place) to a wonderful greatness, such as would be incredible to those who have not seen it, for it would seem impossible that so small a quantity of flesh as there is under the ear, could be so stretched as to be able to surround a hole of the size and shape of the mouth of a pitcher. The ornaments they put in the holes were like stoppers, and if the lobes were broken the flesh would hang down a quarter of a *vara* in length, and half a finger in thickness. The Spaniards called the Indians *Orejones* (large-eared men) because they had this custom.

The Incas wore, as a head-dress, a fringe which they called *llautu*. It was of many colours, about a finger in width, and a little less in thickness. They twisted this fringe three or four times round the head, and let it hang after the manner of a garland.

These three fashions, the *llautu*, the *shaving*, and the *boring of the ears*, were the principal ones that were introduced by the Inca Manco Ccapac. There were others which we shall describe presently, and which were peculiar to the sovereign, no one else being permitted to use them. The first privilege that the Inca granted to his vassals was to order them to imitate him in wearing a fringe; only it was not to be of many colours like the one worn by the Inca, but of one colour only, and that colour was black.

After some time another fashion was granted to the people, and they were ordered to go shaven, but in a fashion differing one from another, and all from the Inca, that there might be no confusion in the distinctions between nations and provinces, and that they might not have too near a resemblance to the Inca. Thus one tribe was ordered to wear the tail plait like a cap for the ears; that is, with the forehead and temples bare, and the plaits reaching down so as to cover the ears on either side. Others were ordered to cut the tail plait so as only to reach halfway down the ears, and others still shorter. But none were allowed to wear the hair so short as that of the Inca. It is also to be observed that all these Indians, and especially the Incas, took care not to let the hair grow, but always kept it at a certain length, that it might not appear after one fashion, but each nation kept to its own, which was decreed and ordained by the hand of the Inca.

After several months and years had elapsed, the Inca granted his people another privilege, more important than those already mentioned, which was that of boring their ears. This privilege, however, was limited with reference to the size of the hole, which was not to be so much as half that of the Inca, and each tribe and province wore a different stopper in the ear hole. To some he granted the privilege of wearing a wisp of straw in their ears, the size of a little finger, and these were of the nations called Mayu and Cancu. Others were to have a tuft of white wool, which was to come out on each side as far as the length of the first joint of a man's thumb, and these were of the nation called Pòques. The nations called Muyna and Huarac Cillqui were ordered to wear ear ornaments made of common reeds, called by the Indians *tutura*. The nation of Rimac-tampu and its neighbours wore their ear ornament made of the pole which is called *maguey* in the Windward Islands, and *chuchau* in the general language of Peru. When the bark is removed, the pith is very soft and light. The three tribes called Urcos, Yucay, and Tampu, all living in the valley of the river Yucay, were ordered as a particular favour and honour, to wear a larger hole in their ears than any of the other nations. But, that it might not reach to half the size of the Inca's hole, he gave them a measure of the size of his hole, as he had done to all the other tribes. He also ordered their stoppers to be made of the reed *tutura*, that they might more resemble those of the Ynca. They called the ornaments ear stoppers, and not ear drops, because they

Inca holding a quipu. The quipu, a rope with knotted strings, was used to keep administrative records and accounts throughout the Inca Empire. The Art Archive/ John Meek.

did not hang from the ears, but were closed by the sides of the hole, like a stopper in the mouth of a jar.

Besides the signs which were intended to prevent confusion between one tribe and another, the Inca ordered other differences in the fashion of his vassals, which they said were intended to show the degree of favour and trust in which they were held, according as they resembled the badges of the Inca. But he did not like one vassal more than another from any caprice, but in conformity with reason and justice. Those who most readily followed his precepts, and who had worked most in the subjugation of the other Indians were allowed to imitate the Inca most closely in their badges, and received more favours than the others. He gave them to understand that all he did with regard to them was by an order and revelation of his father the Sun. And the Indians, believing this, were well satisfied with every thing that was ordered by the Inca, and with any manner in which he might treat them; for, besides believing that his orders were revelations of the Sun, they saw, by experience, the benefits that were derived from obedience to them.

Source: El Inca Garcilaso de la Vega. *First Part of the Royal Commentaries of the Yncas.* Translated by Clements R. Markham. Vol. 1. London: Hakluyt Society, 1869, pp. 84–87.

Part VI
POLITICAL LIFE

Political Life describes the ways in which people group together to advance their mutual self-interests. The development of legal systems is a prime example: individuals agree to give up certain freedoms in return for greater protection. Of course, people do not always have a choice in government; monarchies, in which a king theoretically rules the entire nation, dominated the Middle Ages and Renaissance. Nor did a strong government always establish peace. Some of the most powerful nations were also the most belligerent—they gained power at the cost of other peoples and other governments.

The Government and Hierarchy section examines how societies were governed. Social hierarchy is inextricably bound up with government during the Middle Ages and Renaissance. The prevailing model of government—kingship—rested on a theoretical framework of class distinction in which the king stood uppermost, followed by aristocrats, then freemen, and then serfs and slaves. Each member of society had a clearly defined role within the social hierarchy, and this role corresponded more or less directly with that individual's political power. Kings, in fact, were thought to be chosen by God for their roles of leadership. Nevertheless, centralizing power in the hands of a king and his confidantes did cause civil unrest. In 1215 the barons (an influential group of aristocrats) gathered and forced King John to sign the Magna Carta, a declaration that radically limited the rights and prerogatives of the king. The Magna Carta did not establish a democracy, as we understand that word today. First of all, King John almost immediately broke the terms of the agreement. More important, although the Magna Carta did envision a kind of small parliament, political power was still limited to the wealthy aristocracy. Barons would be the ones to control the king under Magna Carta. Another strong check on royal power was the Church. Throughout this time period, Church and state vied for ultimate control; this contest resulted frequently in an unintended and limited system of checks and balances.

The Legal Systems section discusses the ways in which societies sought to maintain justice and equity within their realms. Three main legal traditions dominated Europe during this time period: Roman law, Germanic law, and Church law. The great emperor Justinian in the sixth century sponsored a codification of Roman law—both individual statutes and general principles—that has remained highly influential until the present day. Germanic law tended to be more straightforward and reflected the agricultural concerns of the people—fines are laid out with careful attention, for example, to how many pigs were stolen. Operating in parallel to civil law was Church law. Throughout the Middle Ages and Renaissance, Church law oversaw the clergy and adjudicated issues of morality and theology. A suspected heretic, for example, would be tried in Church courts, though any punishments would be enforced by civil courts. Church law, called canon law, survives today, though its influence on society has been greatly diminished. Most early medieval law focused on torts, that is, the payment of fines. For crimes such as murder for which a perpetrator would go to jail today, a perpetrator in Anglo-Saxon England would be required to pay a fine. In the absence of jails, in fact, most penalties were financial. If the guilty person could not pay the fine, he or she faced possible execution. Not only were there no public jails, but there was also no well-organized police force. Victims and their families were the ones who would track down the guilty. As a result much of the early legislation sought to regulate what victims could and could not do once they found the guilty party.

The military campaigns of England, the Aztecs, China, and others, demonstrates that medieval and Renaissance nations understood the role of warfare in pursuing international politics. The Warfare section explores the tactics, technology, and philosophy behind the practice of war. While European nations relied upon heavy armor and siege weaponry, the Mongols—who created the largest empire of the period—carved out their kingdom through the use of versatile and highly skilled horse-archers. The document on Japanese Samurai, shows the high respect that culture paid to those who fell in battle. Regardless of differences in the philosophy and conduct of war, one thing united all warfare: violence. People always died in war. As the Tang dynasty poet Ts'ao Sung stated, "For a single general's reputation / Is made out of ten thousand corpses."

Government and Hierarchy

Governmental systems and social hierarchies were so closely interwoven throughout the Middle Ages and *Renaissance* that they must be treated in the same section. The major form of government during this period—kingship—is after all predicated on the concept of social hierarchy: there is one person at the top, a group of aristocrats just below him, and then everyone else. These social systems at times developed out of warlord societies, as seen in the social class and government of early *Anglo-Saxon* England (Document 3), in which aristocrats, called *thegnas*, were originally the top warriors in the king's troop. Kings, moreover, were often viewed either as divine or as ruling with divine approval. The Anglo-Saxon kings of the eighth century frequently traced their ancestry back to the Germanic god Woden, and Thomas Cranmer, a sixteenth-century archbishop of Canterbury in England viewed the king as appointed by God (Document 8).

Despite the rhetoric of divine kingship, in practice real restrictions were placed on the king's power. The Magna Carta of 1215 (Document 5) famously sought to erect a group of barons who could restrict and constrain King *John* of England. Parliament (an advisory body drawn from the body of citizens) gained increasing power throughout this time period—indeed, elected individuals have replaced kings in most countries of the modern world. As Document 6 demonstrates, however, medieval and Renaissance parliamentary bodies were not necessarily fully democratic. Members of Parliament were generally drawn from the wealthiest sectors of society—indeed, the poor, who made up the majority of the population, were not allowed to vote at all.

The other force operating to restrict royal power was the Church. For example, *Unam sanctam* (Document 7), a bull (or papal charter) issued by Pope Boniface VIII in 1302, explicitly contended that the Pope and Church were superior in rank and authority to the king. Kings as a result did not have the right to tax the Church or interfere in other ways with the clergy. Such competition for power extends as far back as the time of Christ himself—the gospels argue that Jesus was executed because of the fear that his power challenged the power of the Roman emperor in Jerusalem. "The Donation of Constantine" (Document 9 under "Priests and Rituals" in Part VIII: Religious Life) was another sally in the competition between church and state.

The king was not the only one to wield power—all aristocrats and wealthy individuals commanded respect and power. In China, as discussed by Tsung Ch'en in Document 4, a system of clientship operated. In this system, an individual would give expensive gifts to the powerful in hopes of increased career prospects and influential recommendations. In western Europe, the system was even more formalized. Feudal relationships formalized personal contracts between individuals in which the less wealthy served the more wealthy in return for material benefits (Documents 1 and 2).

1. A Vassal's Contract

The social and economic structure of early medieval life depended on personal relationships between noblemen and their clients. The following contract, from seventh-century France, provides a good example of this economic relationship; an indigent individual agrees to serve and honor a wealthier man in return for food, clothing, and other material benefits. To some degree, modern employment is no different from these contracts: an employee receives money, with which to buy food, clothing, shelter, and luxuries, in return for doing work for a wealthier individual or corporation.

Unlike modern employment, however, early medieval contracts could be for life. In this contract, the oath-taker renounces the right ever to withdraw from the "control or guardianship" of the lord. Although either party to the contract can purchase his way out of the relationship for a specified amount, the wealthier party would obviously find it easier to pay the sum than the less wealthy party. Taking an oath of allegiance could not be undertaken lightly. The following document has blanks that could be filled in with the individual names and figures to suit individual relationships.

To that magnificent lord _____, I, _____. Since it is well known to all how little I have wherewith to feed and clothe myself, I have therefore petitioned your piety, and your goodwill has decreed to me, that I should hand myself over, or commend myself, to your guardianship, which I have thereupon done; that is to say, in this way, that you should aid and succor me, as well with food as with clothing, according as I shall be able to serve you and deserve it.

And so long as I shall live I ought to provide service and honor to you, compatible with my free condition; and I shall not, during the time of my life, have the right to withdraw from your control or guardianship; but must remain during the days of my life under your power or defense. Wherefore it is proper that if either of us shall wish to withdraw himself from these agreements, he shall pay _____ shillings to the other party, and this agreement shall remain unbroken.

Source: *University of Pennsylvania Translations and Reprints*, trans. Edward P. Cheyney. Vol. 4, no. 3, pp. 3–4. In *A Source Book of Mediaeval History*, Ed. Frederic Austin Ogg. New York: American, 1908, pp. 205–06.

2. Enfeoffment

Document 1 describes a relatively poor man, in need of food and clothing, entering into a business relationship, but noblemen also entered into lifelong social and economic contracts. The next document describes the ceremony through which William, Count of Flanders, having in 1127 inherited his position from his father, reestablished the feudal relationships that his father had established. The ceremony consists of six steps. First, the client kneels down before the count, places his hand between the two hands of the count, and receives a kiss from the count. Next, the client swears homage to the count. Then the client swears his loyalty upon the relics—the bones and clothing—of the saints; failing to fulfill such an oath would be sacrilege, and the violator would fear punishment in hell. Finally, after the oaths, the count uses a rod to symbolically confirm the rights and privileges that the clients had acquired from William's father, Count Charles. By the end of the ceremony, clients and count have established a formal working relationship and have been bound to each other through sacred rights.

Through the whole remaining part of the day those who had been previously enfeoffed by the most pious count Charles, did homage to the count, taking up now again their fiefs and offices and whatever they had before rightfully and legitimately obtained. On Thursday, the seventh of April, homages were again made to the count, being completed in the following order of faith and security:

First they did their homage thus. The count asked if he was willing to become completely his man, and the other replied, "I am willing," and with clasped hands, surrounded by the hands of the count, they were bound together by a kiss. Secondly, he who had done homage gave his fealty to the representative of the count in these words, "I promise on my faith that I will in future be faithful to Count William, and will observe my homage to him completely, against all persons, in good faith and without deceit." Thirdly, he took his oath to this upon the relics of the saints. Afterwards, with a little rod which the count held in his hand, he gave investitures to all who by this agreement had given their security and homage and accompanying oath.

Source: Galbert de Bruges. *De multro, traditione, et occisione gloriosi Karoli comitis Flandirarum.* In *University of Pennsylvania Translations and Reprints*, trans. Edward P. Cheyney. Vol. 4, no. 3, p. 18. In Frederic Austin Ogg, *A Source Book of Mediaeval History*. New York: American, 1908, pp. 218–19.

3. Rank and Wealth

Like most medieval and Renaissance societies, Anglo-Saxon England possessed a fixed class system based primarily on wealth. At the head of the system was the theoden *(pronounced "thay-oh-den"), the king in modern language. By the time the following document was written in the second quarter of the eleventh century, England had a centralized monarchy, the head of which was called "cing." In earlier times, however,* theoden *could refer to a local warlord who held independent control of a certain tract of land.*

Below the theoden *in rank stood the* eorl, *which has become in modern English "earl." A more common rank, however, was the* thegn *(pronounced "thane"). In origin, a* thegn *was an aristocratic warrior in the service of a local king or* theoden. *By the eleventh century, however,* thegn *referred to a powerful nobleman, who might or might not also be an effective warrior. A* thegn *had a similar amount of power as a duke on the continent. Below the* thegn *stood the* ceorl *(pronounced "cherl"), the lowest widely recognized rank of a successful freeman. The* ceorl *would generally own enough land to produce self-sufficiency. Slaves (*theowas*) completed the social hierarchy; see Document 23 under "Slavery" in Part III: Economic Life for more information about their lives.*

Although wealth and service to the king are the main methods of advancement according to this document, other paths were possible. Priest scholars, for example, were ranked as thegns *provided that they did not break the rules of their orders. Even merchants, outside of the traditional landed economy around which traditional social hierarchy was built, could achieve* thegn *status if they made three trips overseas. Although conservative, social class systems evolved and adapted to the changing socioeconomic conditions.*

Of People's Ranks and Law

1. It was once, in the laws of the English, that people and law went by ranks, and then were the counselors of the nation of worship worthy, each according to his condition: *eorl* and *ceorl*, *thegn* and *theoden*.
2. And if a *ceorl* thrived, so that he had fully five hides of his own land, church and kitchen, bell-house and *burh*-gate seat, and special duty in the king's hall, then was he thenceforth of *thegn*-right worthy.
3. And if a *thegn* thrived, so that he served the king, and on his summons rode among his household; if he then had a *thegn* who him followed, who had five hides to the king's *ut-ware*, and in the King's hall served his lord, and thrice with his errand went to the king; he might thenceforth represent his lord with his fore-oath at various needs, and conduct his plaint lawfully, wheresoever he ought.
4. And he who so prosperous a viceregent had not, swore for himself according to his right, or if forfeited.
5. And if a *thegn* thrived, so that he became an *eorl*, then he was thenceforth worthy of *eorl*-right.
6. And if a merchant thrived, sot that he fared thrice over the wide sea by his own means, then was he thenceforth of *thegn*-right worthy.
7. And if there were a scholar, who thrived through learning, so that he had holy orders, and served Christ; then was he thenceforth of rank and power so much worthy, that he rightfully belonged to those orders, if he conducted himself as he should; unless he should misdo, so that he might not perform those orders' ministry.

Source: Thorpe, Benjamin. *Ancient Laws and Institutes of England.* London: Eye and Spottiswoode, 1840, p. 191. In Roy Cave and Herbert Coulson, *A Source Book for Medieval Economic History.* New York: Biblo and Tannen, 1965, p. 316. Translation modified by Lawrence Morris.

4. Flunkeyism in China

The author of this document, Tsung Ch'en, was a sixteenth-century Chinese official and national hero; he successfully defended Fuzhou against the Japanese around 1560. His stratagem involved opening the gate, as if to let in the invaders, and then slaughtering them in an ambush.

In the passage presented here, however, Tsung Ch'en criticizes the informal sociopolitical system that controlled the upper echelons of Chinese society. In this client system, wealthy and powerful individuals would accept gifts from inferiors in return for speaking well of them and recommending them for good jobs. These inferiors, moreover, had to undergo great humiliation to secure this preferment. According to Tsung Ch'en, the supplicant would first need to bribe the porter two days in a row to be allowed in to see the master. Once allowed access to the master, the supplicant would need to prostrate himself on the floor several times and repeatedly beg the master to accept a costly gift. Once the master had accepted the gift, however, the supplicant would return to his home and brag to his friends that he had high contacts—the supplicant would expect better career prospects from then out.

Similar client systems existed in ancient Rome, and the fundamental relationship between wealthy and less wealthy is similar to the feudal relationships of medieval Europe. Nonetheless, Tsung Ch'en considered the system completely corrupt and humiliating—commitment to duty alone should determine advancement in Tsung Ch'en's eyes.

I was very glad at this distance to receive your letter which quite set my mind at rest, together with the present you were so kind as to add. I thank you very much for your good wishes, and especially for your thoughtful allusion to my father.

As to what you are pleased to say in reference to official popularity and fitness for office, I am much obliged by your remarks. Of my unfitness for office I am only too well aware; while as to popularity with my superiors, I am utterly unqualified to secure that boon.

How indeed does an official find favour in the present day with his chief? Morning and evening he must whip up his horse and go dance attendance at the great man's door. If the porter refuses to admit him, then honied words, a coaxing air, and money drawn from the sleeve may prevail. The porter takes in his card; but the great man does not come out. So he waits in the stable among grooms, until his clothes are charged with the smell; in spite of hunger, in spite of cold, in spite of a blazing heat. At nightfall, the porter who had pocketed his money comes forth and says his master is tired and begs to be excused, and will he call again next day. So he is forced to come once more as requested. He sits all night in his clothes. At cock-crow he jumps up, performs his toilette, and gallops off and knocks at the entrance gate. "Who's there?" shouts the porter angrily; and when he explains, the porter gets still more angry and begins to abuse him, saying, "You are in a fine hurry, you are! Do you think my master sees people at this hour?" Then is the visitor shamed, but has to swallow his wrath and try to persuade the porter to let him in. And the porter, another fee to the good, gets up and lets him in; and then he waits again in the stable as before, until perhaps the great man comes out and summons him to an audience.

Now, with many an obeisance, he cringes timidly towards the foot of the dais step: and when the great man says "Come!" he prostrates himself twice and remains long without rising. At length he goes up to offer his present, which the great man refuses. He entreats acceptance; but in vain. He implores, with many instances; whereupon the great man refuses. He entreats acceptance, but in vain. He implores, with many instances; whereupon the great man bids a servant take it. Then two more prostrations, long drawn out; after which he arises, and with five or six salutations he takes his leave.

On going forth, he bows to the porter, saying, "It's all right with your master. Next time I come you need make no delay." The porter returns the bow, well pleased with his share in the business. Meanwhile, our friend springs on his horse, and when he meets an acquaintance flourishes his whip and cries out, "I have just been with His Excellency. He treated me very kindly, very kindly indeed."

And then he goes into detail, upon which his friends begin to be more respectful to him as a *protegé* of His Excellency. The great man himself says, "So-and-so is a good fellow, a very good fellow indeed;" upon which the bystanders of course declare that they think so too.

Such is the popularity with one's superiors in the present day. Do you think that I could be as one of these? No! Beyond sending a complimentary card at the summer and winter festivals, I do not go near the great from one year's end to another. Even when I pass their doors I stuff my ears and cover my eyes and gallop quickly past as if some one was after me. In consequence of this want of breadth, I am of course no favourite with the authorities; but what care I? There is a destiny that shapes our ends and it has shaped minc towards thc path of duty alonc. For which, no doubt, you think me an ass.

Source: *Gems of Chinese Literature: Prose.* 2nd ed. Ed. Herbert A. Giles. London: Bernard Quaritch, 1923, pp. 223–25.

5. Magna Carta (June 15, 1215)

The Great Charter, or Magna Carta as it is known in Latin, set the first major limits on medieval kingship. The document arose out of a conflict between King John of England and rebellious aristocrats dissatisfied with the king. This dissatisfaction resulted in large part from the king's attempt to increase the level of taxation dramatically through income taxes and through special laws pertaining to forests. Other sources of dissatisfaction included the loss of most of England's possessions in France during John's reign and the argument between the king and the Pope Innocent III over who had the right to appoint archbishops, which resulted in all church services in England being temporarily suspended. The aristocrats, called barons, gathered together in 1215 and forced King John to concede certain rights and protections, which were then recorded and promulgated in the Magna Carta.

The Magna Carta covers a large number of very specific legal questions, such as the financial position of widows, but the most important concessions are found in clauses 12, 14, and 61. Clauses 12 and 14 force the king to gain the permission of a council of aristocrats before raising taxes (called "aid" and "scutage"). Clause 61, moreover, empowers a group of 25 barons to take direct action against the monarch if he fails to fulfill the clauses of the Great Charter. In particular, the barons are permitted to seize all the king's possessions, and the public is to swear allegiance to the barons. In effect, clause 61 makes the 25 barons the effective rulers of England, not the king. Because of this dramatic shift in power, the Magna Carta is often viewed as a step away from kingship and toward parliamentary democracy.

Once King John had freed himself from the barons' control, however, he rescinded the Great Charter, thereby provoking the First Barons' War. King John died of dysentery in the middle of the war in 1216, and his son, King Henry III, reissued the Magna Carta, albeit in modified form without the controversial clause 61. Although the Magna Carta as originally signed therefore never carried full legal force, it remained a powerful symbol of the limitation of a king's rights. Kings would not hold absolute power, at least in England.

John, by the grace of God, king of England, lord of Ireland, duke of Normandy and Aquitaine, and count of Anjou, to the archbishops, bishops, abbots, earls, barons, justiciars, foresters, sheriffs, stewards, servants, and to all his bailiffs and liege subjects, greeting. Know that, having regard to God and for the salvation of our soul, and those of all our ancestors and heirs, and unto the honor of God and the advancement of holy church, and

King Edward I, 1239–1307, of England, confirming Magna Carta, from manuscript "Statutes of England," in Latin and French, fourteenth century. (Douce 35 folio 25r). The Art Archive/Bodleian Library Oxford.

for the reform of our realm, by advice of our venerable fathers, Stephen archbishop of Canterbury, primate of all England and cardinal of the holy Roman Church, Henry archbishop of Dublin, William of London, Peter of Winchester, Jocelyn of Bath and Glastonbury, Hugh of Lincoln, Walter of Worcester, William of Coventry, Benedict of Rochester, bishops, of master Pandulf, subdeacon and member of the household of our lord the Pope, of brother Aymeric (master of the Knights of the Temple in England), and of the illustrious men William Marshall earl of Pembroke, William earl of Salisbury, William earl of Warenne, William earl of Arundel, Alan of Galloway (constable of Scotland), Waren Fitz Gerald, Peter Fits Herbert, Hubert de Burgh (seneschal of Poitou), Hugh de Neville, Matthew Fitz Herbert, Thomas Basset, Alan Basset, Philip d'Aubigny, Robert of Roppesley, John Marshall, John Fitz Hugh, and others, our liegemen.

1. In the first place we have granted to God, and by this our present charter confirmed for us and our heirs for ever that the English church shall be free, and shall have her rights entire, and her liberties inviolate; and we will that it be thus observed; which is apparent from this that the freedom of elections, which is reckoned most important and very essential to the English church, we, of our pure and unconstrained will, did grant, and did by our charter confirm and did obtain the ratification of the same from our lord, Pope Innocent III, before the quarrel arose between us and our barons: and this we will observe, and our will is that it be observed in good faith by our heirs for ever. We have also granted to all freemen of our kingdom, for us and our heirs for ever, all the underwritten liberties, to be had and held by them and their heirs, of us and our heirs for ever.

2. If any of our earls or barons, or others holding of us in chief by military service shall have died, and at the time of his death his heir shall be of full age and owe "relief," he shall have his inheritance on payment of the ancient relief, namely the heir or heirs of an earl, 100 pounds for a whole earl's barony; the heir or heirs of a baron, 100 pounds for a whole barony; the heir or heirs of a knight, 100 shillings at most for a whole knight's fee; and whoever owes less let him give less, according to the ancient custom of fiefs.

3. If, however, the heir of any of the aforesaid has been under age and in wardship, let him have his inheritance without relief and without fine when he comes of age.

4. The guardian of the land of an heir who is thus under age, shall take from the land of the heir nothing but reasonable produce, reasonable customs, and reasonable services, and that without destruction or waste of men or goods; and if we have committed the wardship of the lands of any such minor to the sheriff, or to any other who is responsible to us for its issues, and he has made destruction or waste of what he holds in wardship, we will take of him amends, and the land shall be committed to two lawful and discreet men of that fee, who shall be responsible for the issues to us or to him to whom we shall assign them; and if we have given or sold the wardship of any such land to anyone and he has therein made destruction or waste, he shall lose that wardship, and it shall be transferred to two lawful and discreet men of that fief, who shall be responsible to us in like manner as aforesaid.

5. The guardian, moreover, so long as he has the wardship of the land, shall keep up the houses, parks, fishponds, stanks, mills, and other things pertaining to the land, out of the issues of the same land; and he shall restore to the heir, when he has come to full age, all his land, stocked with ploughs and "waynage," according as the season of husbandry shall require, and the issues of the land can reasonably bear.

6. Heirs shall be married without disparagement, yet so that before the marriage takes place the nearest in blood to that heir shall have notice.

7. A widow, after the death of her husband, shall forthwith and without difficulty have her marriage portion and inheritance; nor shall she give anything for her dower, or for her marriage portion, or for the inheritance which her husband and she held on the day of the death of that husband; and she may remain in the house of her husband for forty days after his death, within which time her dower shall be assigned to her.

8. No widow shall be compelled to marry, so long as she prefers to live without a husband; provided always that she gives security not to marry without our consent, if she holds of us, or without the consent of the lord of whom she holds, if she holds of another.

9. Neither we nor our bailiffs shall seize any land or rent for any debt, so long as the chattels of the debtor are sufficient to repay the debt; nor shall the sureties of the debtor be distrained so long as the principal debtor is able to satisfy the debt; and if the principal debtor shall fail to pay the debt, having nothing wherewith to pay it, then the sureties shall answer for the debt; and let them have the lands and rents of the debtor, if they desire them, until they are indemnified for the debt which they have paid for him, unless the principal debtor can show proof that he is discharged thereof as against the said sureties.

10. If one who has borrowed from the Jews any sum, great or small, die before that loan can be repaid, the debt shall not bear interest while the heir is under age, of whomsoever he may hold; and if the debt fall into our hands, we will not take anything except the principal sum contained in the bond.

11. And if any one die indebted to the Jews, his wife shall have her dower and pay nothing of that debt; and if any children of the deceased are left underage, necessaries shall be provided for them in keeping with the holding of the deceased; and out of the residue the debt shall be paid, reserving, however, service due to feudal lords; in like manner let it be done touching debts due to others than Jews.

12. No scutage nor aid shall be imposed on our kingdom, unless by common counsel of our kingdom, except for ransoming our person, for making our eldest son a knight, and for once marrying our eldest daughter; and for these there shall not be levied more than a reasonable aid. In like manner it shall be done concerning aids from the city of London.

13. And the city of London shall have all its ancient liberties and free customs, as well by land as by water; furthermore, we decree and grant that all other cities, boroughs, towns, and ports shall have all their liberties and free customs.

14. And for obtaining the common counsel of the kingdom against the assessing of an aid (except in the three cases aforesaid) or of a scutage, we will cause to be summoned the archbishops, bishops, abbots, earls, and greater barons, severally by our letters; and we will moreover cause to be summoned generally, through our sheriffs and bailiffs, all others who hold of us in chief, for a fixed date, namely, after the expiry of at least forty days, and at a fixed place; and in all letters of such summons we will specify the reason of the summons. And when the summons has thus been made, the business shall proceed on the day appointed, according to the counsel of such as are present, although not all who were summoned have come.

15. We will not for the future grant to anyone license to take an aid from his own free tenants, except to ransom his body, to make his eldest son a knight, and once to marry his eldest daughter; and on each of these occasions there shall be levied only a reasonable aid.

16. No one shall be distrained for performance of greater service for a knight's fee, or for any other free tenement, than is due therefrom.

17. Common pleas shall not follow our court, but shall be held in some fixed place.

18. Inquests of *novel disseisin*, of *mort d'ancester*, and of *darrein presentment*, shall not be held elsewhere than in their own county courts and that in manner following,—We, or, if we should be out of the realm, our chief justiciar, will send two justiciars through every county four times a year, who shall, along with four knights of the county chosen by the county, hold the said assize in the county court, on the day and in the place of meeting of that court.

19. And if any of the said assizes cannot be taken on the day of the county court, let there remain of the knights and freeholders, who were present at the county court on that day, as many as may be required for the efficient making of judgments, according as the business be more or less.

20. A freeman shall not be amerced for a slight offense, except in accordance with the degree of the offense; and for a grave offense he shall be amerced in accordance

with the gravity of the offense, yet saving always his "contenement;" and a merchant in the same way, saving his "merchandise;" and a villein shall be amerced in the same way, saving his "wainage"—if they have fallen into our mercy: and none of the aforesaid amercements shall be imposed except by the oath of honest men of the neighborhood.

21. Earls and barons shall not be amerced except through their peers, and only in accordance with the degree of the offence.

22. A clerk shall not be amerced in respect of his lay holding except after the manner of the others aforesaid; further, he shall not be amerced in accordance with the extent of his ecclesiastical benefice.

23. No village or individual shall be compelled to make bridges at river-banks, except those who from of old were legally bound to do so.

24. No sheriff, constable, coroners, or others of our bailiffs, shall hold pleas of our Crown.

25. All counties, hundreds, wapentakes, and trithings (except our *demesnemanors*) shall remain at old rents, and without any additional payment.

26. If any one holding of us a lay fief shall die, and our sheriff or bailiff shall exhibit our letters patent of summons for a debt which the deceased owed to us, it shall be lawful for our sheriff or bailiff to attach and catalogue chattels of the deceased, found upon the lay fief, to the value of that debt, at the sight of law-worthy men, provided always that nothing whatever be thence removed until the debt which is evident shall be fully paid to us; and the residue shall be left to the executors to fulfil the will of the deceased; and if there be nothing due from him to us, all the chattels shall go to the deceased, saving to his wife and children their reasonable shares.

27. If any freeman shall die intestate, his chattels shall be distributed by the hands of his nearest kinsfolk and friends, under supervision of the church, saving to every one the debts which the deceased owed to him.

28. No constable or other bailiff of ours shall take corn or other provisions from any one without immediately tendering money therefore, unless he can have postponement thereof by permission of the seller.

29. No constable shall compel any knight to give money in lieu of castle-guard, when he is willing to perform it in his own person, or (if he cannot do it from any reasonable cause) then by another responsible man. Further, if we have led or sent him upon military service, he shall be relieved from guard in proportion to the time during which he has been on service because of us.

30. No sheriff or bailiff of ours, or other person, shall take the horses or carts of any freeman for transport duty, against the will of the said freeman.

31. Neither we nor our bailiffs shall take, for our castles or for any other work of ours, wood which is not ours, against the will of the owner of that wood.

32. We will not retain beyond one year and one day, the lands of those who have been convicted of felony, and the lands shall thereafter be handed over to the lords of the fiefs.

33. All kiddles for the future shall be removed altogether from Thames and Medway, and throughout all England, except upon the seashore.

34. The writ which is called *praecipe* shall not for the future be issued to any one, regarding any tenement whereby a freeman may lose his court.

35. Let there be one measure of wine throughout our whole realm; and one measure of ale; and one measure of corn, to wit, "the London quarter;" and one width of cloth (whether dyed, or russet, or "halberget"), to wit, two ells within the selvages; of weights also let it be as of measures.

36. Nothing in future shall be given or taken for a writ of inquisition of life or limbs, but freely it shall be granted, and never denied.

37. If any one holds of us by fee-farm, by socage, or by burgage, and holds also land of another lord by knight's service, we will not (by reason of that fee-farm, socage, or burgage) have the wardship of the heir, or of such land of his as is of the fief of that other; nor shall we have wardship of that fee-farm, socage, or burgage, unless such fee-farm owes knight's service. We will not by reason of any small serjeanty which any one may hold of us by the service of rendering to us knives, arrows, or the like, have wardship of his heir or of the land which he holds of another lord by knight's service.

38. No bailiff for the future shall, upon his own unsupported complaint, put any one to his "law," without credible witnesses brought for this purpose.

39. No freeman shall be taken or imprisoned or *disseised* or exiled or in anyway destroyed, nor will we go upon him nor send upon him, except by the lawful judgment of his peers or by the law of the land.

40. To no one will we sell, to no one will we refuse or delay, right or justice.

41. All merchants shall have safe and secure exit from England, and entry to England, with the right to tarry there and to move about as well by land as by water, for buying and selling by the ancient and right customs, quit from all evil tolls, except (in time of war) such merchants as are of the land at war with us. And if such are found in our land at the beginning of the war, they shall be detained, without injury to their bodies or goods, until information be received by us, or by our chief justiciar, how the merchants of our land found in the land at war with us are treated; and if our men are safe there, the others shall be safe in our land.

42. It shall be lawful in future for any one (excepting always those imprisoned or outlawed in accordance with the law of the kingdom, and natives of any country at war with us, and merchants, who shall be treated as is above provided) to leave our kingdom and to return, safe and secure by land and water, except for a short period in time of war, on grounds of public policy—reserving always the allegiance due to us.

43. If any one holding of some escheat (such as the honor of Wallingford, Nottingham, Boulogne, Lancaster, or of other escheats which are in our hands and are baronies) shall die, his heir shall give no other relief, and perform no other service to us than he would have done to the baron, if that barony had been in the baron's hand; and we shall hold it in the same manner in which the baron held it.

44. Men who dwell without the forest need not henceforth come before our justiciars of the forest upon a general summons, except those who are impleaded, or who have become sureties for any person or persons attached for forest offenses.

45. We will appoint as justices, constables, sheriffs, or bailiffs only such as know the law of the realm and mean to observe it well.

46. All barons who have founded abbeys, concerning which they hold charters from the kings of England, or of which they have long-continued possession, shall have the wardship of them, when vacant, as they ought to have.

47. All forests that have been made such in our time shall forthwith be disafforested; and a similar course shall be followed with regard to river-banks that have been placed "in defense" by us in our time.

48. All evil customs connected with forests and warrens, foresters and warreners, sheriffs and their officers, river-banks and their wardens, shall immediately be inquired into in each county by twelve sworn knights of the same county chosen by the honest men of the same county, and shall, within forty days of the said inquest, be utterly abolished, so as never to be restored, provided always that we previously have intimation thereof, or our justiciar, if we should not be in England.

49. We will immediately restore all hostages and charters delivered to us by Englishmen, as sureties of the peace or of faithful service.

50. We will entirely remove from their bailiwicks, the relations of Gerard Athee (so that in future they shall have no bailiwick in England); namely, Engelard of Cigogne, Peter, Guy, and Andrew of Chanceaux, Guy of Cigogne, Geoffrey of Martigny with his brothers, Philip Mark with his brothers and his nephew Geoffrey, and the whole brood of the same.

51. As soon as peace is restored, we will banish from the kingdom all foreign-born knights, cross-bowmen, serjeants, and mercenary soldiers, who have come with horses and arms to the kingdom's hurt.

52. If any one has been dispossessed or removed by us, without the legal judgment of his peers, from his lands, castles, franchises, or from his right, we will immediately restore them to him; and if a dispute arise over this, then let it be decided by the five-and-twenty barons of whom mention is made below in the clause for securing the peace. Moreover, for all those possessions, from which any one has, without the lawful judgment of his peers, been disseised or removed, by our father, King Henry, or by our brother, King Richard, and which we retain in our hand (or which are possessed by others, to whom we are bound to warrant them) we shall have respite until the usual term of crusaders; excepting those things about which a plea has been raised, or an inquest made by our order, before our taking of the cross; but as soon as we return from our expedition (or if perchance we desist from the expedition) we will immediately grant full justice therein.

53. We shall have, moreover, the same respite and in the same manner in rendering justice concerning the disafforestation or retention of those forests which Henry our father and Richard our brother afforested, and concerning wardship of lands which are of the fief of another (namely, such wardships as we have hitherto had by reason of a fief which any one held of us by knight's service), and concerning abbeys founded on other fiefs than our own, in which the lord of the fief claims to have right; and when we have returned, or if we desist from our expedition, we will immediately grant full justice to all who complain of such things.

54. No one shall be arrested or imprisoned upon the appeal of a woman, for the death of any other than her husband.

55. All fines made with us unjustly and against the law of the land, and all amercements imposed unjustly and against the law of the land, shall be entirely remitted, or else it shall be done concerning them according to the decision of the five-and-twenty barons of whom mention is made below in the clause for securing the peace, or

according to the judgment of the majority of the same, along with the aforesaid Stephen, archbishop of Canterbury, if he can be present, and such others as he may wish to bring with him for this purpose, and if he cannot be present the business shall nevertheless proceed without him, provided always that if any one or more of the aforesaid five-and-twenty barons are in a similar suit, they shall be removed as far as concerns this particular judgment, others being substituted in their places after having been selected by the rest of the same five-and-twenty for this purpose only, and after having been sworn.

56. If we have disseised or removed Welshmen from lands or liberties, or other things, without the legal judgment of their peers in England or in Wales, they shall be immediately restored to them; and if a dispute arise over this, then let it be decided in the marches by the judgment of their peers; for tenements in England according to the law of England, for tenements in Wales according to the law of Wales, and for tenements in the marches according to the law of the marches. Welshmen shall do the same to us and ours.

57. Further, for all those possessions from which any Welshman has, without the lawful judgment of his peers, been disseised or removed by King Henry our father or King Richard our brother, and which we retain in our hand (or which are possessed by others, to whom we are bound to warrant them) we shall have respite until the usual term of crusaders; excepting those things about which a plea has been raised or an inquest made by our order before we took the cross; but as soon as we return (or if perchance we desist from our expedition), we will immediately grant full justice in accordance with the laws of the Welsh and in relation to the foresaid regions.

58. We will immediately give up the son of Llywelyn and all the hostages of Wales, and the charters delivered to us as security for the peace.

59. We will do toward Alexander, King of Scots, concerning the return of his sisters and his hostages, and concerning his franchises, and his right, in the same manner as we shall do toward our other barons of England, unless it ought to be otherwise according to the charters which we hold from William his father, formerly King of Scots; and this shall be according to the judgment of his peers in our court.

60. Moreover, all these aforesaid customs and liberties, the observance of which we have granted in our kingdom as far as pertains to us toward our men, shall be observed by all of our kingdom, as well clergy as laymen, as far as pertains to them toward their men.

61. Since, moreover, for God and the amendment of our kingdom and for the better allaying of the quarrel that has arisen between us and our barons, we have granted all these concessions, desirous that they should enjoy them incomplete and firm endurance for ever, we give and grant to them the underwritten security, namely, that the barons choose five-and-twenty barons of the kingdom, whomsoever they will, who shall be bound with all their might, to observe and hold, and cause to be observed, the peace and liberties we have granted and confirmed to them by this our present Charter, so that if we, or our justiciar, or our bailiffs or any one of our officers, shall in anything bear fault toward any one, or shall have broken any one of the articles of the peace or of this security, and the offense be notified to four barons of the foresaid five-and-twenty, the said four barons shall repair to us (or our

justiciar, if we are out of the realm) and, laying the transgression before us, petition to have that transgression redressed without delay. And if we shall not have corrected the transgression (or, in the event of our being out of the realm, if our justiciar shall not have corrected it) within forty days, reckoning from the time it has been intimated to us (or to our justiciar, if we should be out of the realm), the four barons aforesaid shall refer that matter to the rest of the five-and-twenty barons, and those five-and-twenty barons shall, together with the community of the whole land, distrain and distress us in all possible ways, namely, by seizing our castles, lands, possessions, and in any other way they can, until redress has been obtained as they deem fit, saving harmless our own person, and the persons of our queen and children; and when redress has been obtained, they shall resume their old relations toward us. And let whoever in the country desires it, swear to obey the orders of the said five-and-twenty barons for the execution of all the aforesaid matters, and along with them, to molest us to the utmost of his power; and we publicly and freely grant leave to every one who wishes to swear, and we shall never forbid anyone to swear. All those, moreover, in the land who of themselves and of their own accord are unwilling to swear to the twenty-five to help them in constraining and molesting us, we shall by our command compel the same to swear to the effect aforesaid. And if any one of the five-and-twenty barons shall have died or departed from the land, or be incapacitated in any other manner which would prevent the foresaid provisions being carried out, those of the said twenty-five barons who are left shall choose another in his place according to their own judgment, and he shall be sworn in the same way as the others. Further, in all matters, the execution of which is entrusted to these twenty-five barons, if perchance these twenty-five are present, that which the majority of those present ordain or command shall be held as fixed and established, exactly as if the whole twenty-five had concurred in this; and the said twenty-five shall swear that they will faithfully observe all that is aforesaid, and cause it to be observed with all their might. And we shall procure nothing from any one, directly or indirectly, whereby any part of these concessions and liberties might be revoked or diminished; and if any such thing has been procured, let it be void and null, and we shall never use it personally or by another.

62. And all the ill-will, hatreds, and bitterness that have arisen between us and our men, clergy and lay, from the date of the quarrel, we have completely remitted and pardoned every one. Moreover, all trespasses occasioned by the said quarrel, from Easter in the sixteenth year of our reign till the restoration of peace, we have fully remitted to all, both clergy and laymen, and completely forgiven, as far as pertains to us. And, on this head, we have caused to be made for them letters testimonial patent of the lord Stephen, archbishop of Canterbury, of the lord Henry, archbishop of Dublin, of the bishops aforesaid, and of Master Pandulf as touching this security and the concessions aforesaid.

63. Wherefore it is our will, and we firmly enjoin, that the English Church be free, and that the men in our kingdom have and hold all the aforesaid liberties, rights, and concessions, well and peaceably, freely and quietly, fully and wholly, for themselves and their heirs, of us and our heirs, in all respects and in all places for ever, as is aforesaid. An oath, moreover, has been taken, as well on our part as on the part

of the barons, that all these conditions aforesaid shall be kept in good faith and without evil intent. Given under our hand—the above-named and many others being witnesses—in the meadow which is called Runnymede, between Windsor and Staines, on the fifteenth day of June, in the seventeenth year of our reign.

Source: *Source Problems in English History.* Albert Beebe White and Wallace Notestein, eds. and trans. New York: Harper and Brothers, 1915. Translation modified by Lawrence Morris.

6. The Manner of Holding Parliament in England

On a day-to-day basis, the English Parliament, like parliaments in Spain and elsewhere, attempted to curtail the power of the king and to supervise the monarch's activities. The following document, from the fourteenth century, describes the workings of Parliament as practiced under King Edward the Confessor (died 1066). Although the document purports to describe ancient practices, it ultimately sets forth the theoretical workings of an ideal parliament—what the author would like parliament to be in the fourteenth century. By giving the contemporary parliament ancient roots, the document lends Parliament authority and credibility.

The importance of social class is clear in this extract. The members of Parliament are divided strictly by their hierarchical social class. At the most basic level, there are three grades of "peer" (voting member): the clergy, the knights, and the citizens (i.e., wealthy inhabitants of the cities). This basic three-fold division can be further subdivided to create six grades: king; bishops and other important religious figures; clergy; earls, barons, and other magnates; knights of the shires; and citizens. During parliamentary disputes, each of these grades formulates its own written response to a parliamentary question. If the total Parliament cannot decide, then a subset of Parliament is elected, and that committee attempts to resolve the issue. If that committee cannot agree, then a still smaller committee is chosen out of their number. Eventually, if disagreements continue, all decision making is vested in just one member of Parliament, although the king must still ratify those decisions.

Throughout, the document stresses the important role of the lower social grades. For example, whereas only two bishops are appointed to a committee, five citizens are appointed. The lower-level peers thus have a greater voice and greater decision-making power within the kingdom, at least on the theoretical level. As the document states, "the commonalty of parliament" must make decisions, not the great magnates alone. This refusal to cater to the interests of the super-rich and powerful can be seen likewise in the rules governing the order in which questions are addressed. According to the document, "he who first made a proposition shall act first" with "no respect being had for the persons of any one." The idea of "first come, first served," rather than wealth and power, determined the order of business on the agenda.

Finally, the document outlines the kinds of "aid"—that is, financial assistance in the form of taxes—that Parliament could give the king. Most importantly for the kingdom, aid could be sought to fight a war. Yet more personal reasons for requesting tax money could also be advanced; the king could request money to knight one of his sons or to marry one of his daughters. In these scenarios, much of the money would be spent on parties and revelries for the king, his family, and their friends. Although such occasions may seem like frivolous uses of tax monies, such events could be important ways of securing international alliances—they were the business lunches and golf-outings of the Middle Ages.

CONCERNING DIFFICULT CASES AND JUDGMENTS

When a dispute, a doubt, or a difficult case, whether of peace or war, comes up in the kingdom or out of it, that case shall be drawn up in writing and read in full parliament; and, if it be necessary, it shall be enjoined—through the king, or on the part of the king if he be not present—on each of the grades of peers, that each grade shall go apart by itself; and that that case shall be delivered to their clerk in writing; and that they, in a fixed place, shall cause that case to be read before them, so that they may ordain and consider among themselves how, in that case, they shall best and most justly proceed; according as they themselves are willing to answer before God for the person of the king, and for their own persons, and also for the persons of those whose persons they represent. And they shall draw up in writing their replies and views; so that when all their responses, plans and views, on this side and on that, have been heard, it may be proceeded according to the better and more healthful plan, and according as, at length, the majority of the parliament shall agree. And if, through discord between them and the king and some magnates—or, perhaps, between the magnates themselves—the peace of the kingdom is endangered, or the people or the country troubled; so that it seems to the king and his council to be expedient that that matter shall be treated of and emended through the attention of all the peers of his kingdom; or if, through war, the king or the kingdom are in trouble; or if a difficult case come up before the chancellor of England; or a difficult judgment be about to be rendered before the justices, and so on: and if perchance, in such deliberations, all, or at least the majority, can not come to an agreement; then the earl seneschal, the earl constable, the earl marshall, or two of them, shall elect twenty five persons from all the peers of the realm—two bishops, namely, and three representatives for the whole clergy; two counts, and three barons; five knights of the shires; five citizens, and five burgesses; which make twenty five. And those twenty five can elect from themselves twelve and resolve themselves into that number; and those twelve, six, and resolve themselves into that number; and those who were hitherto six, three, and resolve themselves into that number. And those three can not resolve themselves into fewer, unless by obtaining permission from our lord the king. And, if the king consent, those three can resolve into two; and of those two, one into the other; and so at length that man's decision shall stand above the whole parliament. And thus, by resolving from twenty five persons into one single person, if a greater number cannot be concordant and make a decision, at last one person alone, as has been said, who cannot disagree with himself, shall decide for all; it being allowed to our master the king, and to his council, to examine and amend such decisions after they have been written out—if they can and will do this. In such manner that this same shall then be done in full parliament, and with the consent of parliament, and not behind parliament.

CONCERNING THE BUSINESS OF PARLIAMENT

The matters for which parliament has been summoned ought to be deliberated upon according to the calendar of parliament, and according to the order of the petitions delivered and filed; no respect being had for the persons of any one; but he who first made a proposition shall act first. In the calendar of parliament all the business of parliament should be called up in this order: first what concerns war, if there is war, and what concerns other matters relating to the persons of the king, the queen and their children; secondly, what concerns the common affairs of the kingdom, such as the making of laws against defects of original laws, judicial and executive, after the judgments have been rendered—which things, most of all, are common affairs; thirdly, there should be called the separate matters, and this according to the order of the petitions filed, as has been said.

CONCERNING THE DAYS AND HOURS OF PARLIAMENT

Parliament ought not to be held on Sundays, but it can be held on all other days; that day always being excepted, and three others, namely: All Saints', and Souls', and the nativity of John the Baptist. And it ought to begin each day in the middle of the first hour; at which hour the king is bound to be present in parliament, together with all the peers of the kingdom. And parliament ought to be held in a public place, and not in a private nor in a secret place. On feast days parliament ought to begin at the first hour, on account of the Divine Service.

CONCERNING THE GRADES OF PEERS

The king is the head, beginning and end of parliament; and thus he has no peer in his grade, and the first grade consists of the king alone. The second grade consists of the archbishops, bishops, abbots, priors, who hold by barony. The third grade consists of the representatives of the clergy. The fourth, of earls, barons, and other magnates and chiefs, whose holding is of the value of a county and barony—as has been explained in the clause concerning laymen. The fifth is of knights of the shires. The sixth, of citizens and burgesses. And thus parliament consists of six grades. But it must be known that even though any one of the said grades except the king be absent—provided, however, that all have been forewarned by reasonable summonses of parliament—nevertheless, it shall be considered as a full parliament. . . .

CONCERNING THE STANDING OF THOSE WHO SPEAK

All the peers of parliament shall sit, and no one shall stand except when he speaks; and he shall so speak that every one in parliament may hear him. No one shall enter the parliament, or go out from parliament, unless through the one door; and whenever anyone says something that is to be deliberated upon by the parliament, he shall always stand when he speaks; the reason is that he may be heard by his peers, for all his peers are judges and justices.

CONCERNING AID TO THE KING

The king does not usually ask aid from his kingdom unless for imminent war, or for knighting his sons, or for marrying his daughters; and then such aids ought to be sought in full parliament; and to be delivered in writing to each grade of the peers of parliament; and to be replied to in writing. And be it known that if such aids are to be granted, all the peers of parliament ought to consent. And be it known that the two knights who come to parliament for the shire, have a greater voice in parliament, in granting and refusing, than a greater earl of England; and likewise, if the representatives of the clergy are all of one mind, than the bishop himself. And this is the case in all matters which ought to be granted, refused or done through the parliament. And this is evident, that the king can hold parliament with the commonalty of his kingdom, without the bishops, earls and barons, provided they have been summoned to parliament, even though no bishop, earl or baron, answer to his summons. For, formerly, kings held their parliaments when no bishop, earl or baron was present. But it is another matter, on the contrary, if the commonalty—the clergy and the laity—have been summoned to parliament, as they have a right to be, and are not willing to come for certain causes; as if they were to maintain that the lord king did not rule them as he ought to, and were to signify in what especial respect he did not do so; then it would not be a parliament at all, even though the archbishops, bishops, counts and barons and all their peers, were present with the king. And so it is necessary that all things which are to be affirmed or cancelled, granted or denied, or done by the parliament, should be granted by the commonalty of the parliament, which consists of the three grades or divisions of parliament: viz. of the representatives of the clergy, the knights of the shires, the citizens and burgesses, who represent the whole commonality of England; and not by the magnates. For each of them is in parliament for his own person alone, and not for any one else.

Source: *Select Charters and Other Illustrations of English Constitutional History from the Earliest Times to the Reign of Edward the First*, ed. William Stubbs. 9th ed. Revised by H.W.C. Davis. Oxford: Clarendon Press, 1913, p. 502. In *Select Historical Documents of the Middle Ages*. Ed. and trans. by Henderson, Ernest F. London: Bell, 1921, pp. 151–65. Translation slightly modified by Lawrence Morris.

7. Church and State: The Papal Bull Unam Sanctam

Issued in November 1302, the famous papal bull Unam sanctam *attempted to finalize the theoretical relationship between church and state. In no uncertain terms, the bull's promulgator, Pope Boniface VIII, stated that the Church had ultimate authority and power of judgment over the state. In other words, the pope was greater than the king because the spiritual life was ultimately greater than the secular life. Moreover, using the image of a two-headed monster, the pope argued that the world needed ultimately just one head—not two heads. Thus, the Church and state were not equals; rather, the Church was superior to the state.*

Although Unam sanctam *set forth a theoretical, philosophical, and theological position, its motivation was ultimately political. Pope Boniface's release of* Unam sanctam *was a response to the growing infringement of secular princes on Church properties. To finance their intermittent war against each other, both Edward I of England and Philip IV of France turned to taxing the clergy. Although the kings levied this taxation as a matter of political expediency—to gain more money for their wars—the actions did have theological consequences; in effect, taxing the clergy suggested that kings had the right to force the Church to pay money. In other words, the state had ultimate control over the Church. Seen in this light, Boniface's actions in* Unam sanctam *appear to defend the Church from outside interference.*

Boniface was not shy about playing politics and developed a reputation for such during his lifetime. Elected pope upon the abdication of Celestine V, Boniface imprisoned his predecessor in a castle. When Celestine died soon thereafter, contemporaries suspected foul play and cast suspicion on Boniface. The great Italian poet Dante Alighieri so disliked Boniface's political position that the poet pictures Boniface in hell in the Divine Comedy.

We are compelled, our faith urging us, to believe and to hold—and we do firmly believe and simply confess—that there is one holy catholic and apostolic church, outside of which there is neither salvation nor remission of sins; her Spouse proclaiming it in the canticles: "My dove, my undefiled, is but one, she is the choice one of her that bore her;" which represents one mystic body, of which body the head is Christ; but of Christ, God. In this church there is one Lord, one faith and one baptism. There was one ark of Noah, indeed, at the time of the flood, symbolizing one church; and this being finished in one cubit had, namely, one Noah as helsman and commander. And, with the exception of this ark, all things existing upon the earth were, as we read, destroyed. This church, moreover, we venerate as the only one, the Lord saying through His prophet: "Deliver my soul from the sword, my darling from the power of the dog." He prayed at the same time for His soul—that is, for Himself the Head—and for His body, which body, namely, he called the one and only church on account of the unity of the faith promised, of the sacraments, and of the love of the church. She is that seamless garment of the Lord which was not cut but which fell by lot. Therefore of this one and only church there is one body and one head—not two heads as if it were a monster: Christ, namely, and the vicar of Christ, St. Peter, and the successor of Peter. For the Lord Himself said to Peter, "Feed my sheep." My sheep, He said, using a general term, and not designating these or those particular sheep; from which it is plain that He committed to Him all His sheep. If, then, the Greeks or others say that they were not committed to the care of Peter and his successors, they necessarily confess that they are not the sheep of Christ; for the Lord says, in John, that there is one fold, one shepherd, and one only. We are told by the word of the gospel that in this His fold there are two swords: a spiritual, namely, and a temporal. For when the apostles said "Behold here are two swords"—when the apostles were speaking of the church—the Lord did not reply that this was too much, but enough. Surely he who denies that the temporal sword is in the power of Peter wrongly interprets the word of the Lord when He says: "Put up thy sword in its scabbard." Both swords, the spiritual and the material, therefore, are in the power of the church; the one, indeed, to be wielded for the church, the other by the church; the one by the hand of the priest, the other by the hand of kings and knights, but at the will and sufferance of the priest. One sword, moreover, ought to be under the other, and the temporal authority to be subjected to the spiritual. For when the apostle says "there is no power but of God, and the powers that are of God are ordained," they would not be ordained unless sword were under sword and the lesser one, as it were, were led by the other to great deeds. For according to St. Dionysius the law of divinity is to lead the lowest through the intermediate to the highest things. Not therefore, according to the law of the universe, are all things reduced to order equally and immediately; but the lowest through the intermediate, the intermediate through the higher. But that the spiritual exceeds any earthly power in dignity and nobility we ought the more openly to confess the more spiritual things excel temporal ones. This also is made plain to our eyes from the giving of tithes, and the benediction and the sanctification; from the acceptation of this same power, from the control over those same things. For the truth bearing witness, the spiritual power has to establish the earthly power, and to judge it if it be not good. Thus concerning the church and the ecclesiastical power is verified the prophecy of Jeremiah: "See, I have this day set thee over the nations and over the kingdoms," and the other things which follow. Therefore if the earthly power err, it shall be judged by the spiritual power; but if the lesser spiritual power err, by the greater. But if the greatest, it can be judged by God alone, not by man, the apostle bearing witness. A spiritual man judges all things, but he himself is judged by no one. This authority, moreover, even though it is given to man and exercised through man, is not human but rather divine, being given by divine lips to Peter and founded on a rock for him and his successors through Christ himself whom he has confessed; the Lord himself saying to Peter: "Whatsoever thou shalt bind," etc. Whoever, therefore, resists this power thus ordained by God, resists the ordination of God, unless he makes believe, like the Manichean, that there are two beginnings. This we consider false and heretical, since by the testimony of Moses, not "in the beginnings," but "in the beginning" God created the Heavens and the earth. Indeed we declare, announce, and define, that it is altogether necessary to salvation for every human creature to be subject to the Roman pontiff.

Source: *Select Historical Documents of the Middle Ages.* Ed. and trans. by Ernest F. Henderson. London: Bell, 1921, pp.435–37.

PHILIP IV.

King Philip of France (1790). © 2008 Jupiterimages Corporation.

8. Divine Right of Kings

The issue of the dividing line between church and state remained a vexed question throughout the Middle Ages and Renaissance. While popes such as Boniface VIII (c. 1235–1303) laid claim to ultimate authority (see Document 7), kings attempted to carve out their own sphere of influence. The monarchical backlash to papal authority can be seen clearly in the English Reformation of the sixteenth century. Thomas Cranmer (1489–1556), who was archbishop of Canterbury under both King Henry VIII (1491–1547) and his son King Edward VI (1537–1553), worked to create not only a Protestant church in England but also a king-dominated society.

In the following sermon, Cranmer defends the notion of kingship and argues that the king has ultimate authority. According to Cranmer, the social class system is a form of natural order imposed by God; any destabilizing of that order not only is forbidden by God but also will lead to a lack of safety. Cranmer argues that a society without a king and his government officials (such as judges) would quickly sink into anarchy, and the people therefore would have to fear for the safety of their property and for their lives. More importantly, kings are God's ministers and are divinely appointed. In fact, Cranmer goes to great lengths to convince the audience that rebellion from even an unrighteous and evil tyrant is contradictory to God's law. The intertwining of politics and religion here is obvious, and it is perhaps no surprise that the king ordered priests to read this collection of Cranmer's sermons throughout England. The English Church had become an effective vehicle for royalist propaganda.

The spelling of this sixteenth-century document has been left mostly as it appears in the earliest printed version; if you get stuck on a word, try pronouncing it out loud. Although

*spelled differently from modern English, Renaissance English was pronounced almost ex-
actly the same.*

An exhortacion, concernyng good ordre and obedience, to rulers and magistrates.

Almightie God hath created and appointed all thinges, in heaven, the earth, and waters, in a moste excellent and perfect ordre. In heaven, he hath appoynted distinct orders
and states of Archangelles and Angels. In the earth he hath assigned kynges, princes, with
other governors under them, all in good and necessary ordre. The water above is kept and
raineth doune in due time and season. The sunne, mone, sterres, rainbow, thunder, lightning, cloudes, and al birdes of the aire, do kepe their ordre. The earth, trees, seedes,
plantes, herbes, corne, grasse, and all maner of beastes, kepe them in their ordre. All the
partes of the whole yeare, as winter, somer, monethes, nightes and dayes, continue in their
ordre. All kyndes of fishes in the sea, rivers and waters, with all fountaynes, sprynges, yea,
the seas themselves, kepe their comely course and ordre. And man hymself also, hath al
his partes, both within and without: as soule, harte, mynd, memory, understandyng, reason, speache, withall and singuler corporall membres of his body, in a profitable, necessary
and pleasaunt ordre. Every degre of people, in their vocation, callyng, and office, hath
appoynted to them, their duetie and ordre. Some are in high degree, some in lowe, some
kynges and princes, some inferiors and subjectes, priestes, and laymen, masters and servauntes, fathers and children, husbandes and wifes, riche and poore, and every one have
nede of other: so that in all thinges, is to be lauded and praysed the goodly ordre of God,
without the whiche, no house, no citie, no common wealth, can continue and endure.

For where there is no right ordre, there reigneth all abuse, carnall libertie, enormitie,
syn, and babilonicall confusion. Take awaye kynges, princes, rulers, magistrates, judges,
and such states of Gods ordre, no man shall ride or go by the high way unrobbed, no man
shall slepe in his owne house or bed unkilled, no man shall kepe his wife, children, and
possessions in quietness; all thynges shal be common, and there must nedes folow all
mischief and utter destruction, both of soules, bodies, goodes and common wealthes. But
blessed be God, that we in this realme of England fele not the horrible calamities, miseries and wretchedness, which al they undoubtedly fele and suffre, that lacke this godly
ordre. And praised be God, that we knowe the great excellent benefite of God, shewed
towards us in this behalfe. God hath sente us his high gifte, our most dere sovereigne lord
king Edward the sixth, with godly wise, and honorable counsail, with other superiors and
inferiors in a beautifull ordre. Wherefore, let us subjectes do our bounden duties, giving
hartie thankes to God, and praiyng for the preservacion of this Godly ordre.

Let us all obey even from the botome of our hartes, al their Godly procedynges,
lawes, statutes, proclamacions, and injunctions, with all other Godly orders. Let us
considre the scriptures of the holy ghost, whiche perswade and conmaunde us all obediently to be subject: First and chiefly, to the kynges majestie, supreme head over all, and
next, to his honorable counsail, and to all other noble men, magistrates and officers,
which by Gods goodness be placed and ordered: for almightie God, is the onely author
and provider of thys forenamed state and ordre, as it is written of God, in the boke of
the proverbes: through me, kynges do reigne; through me counsailors make just lawes,
through me, doo princes beare rule, and all judges of the earth execute judgement: I am
lovyng to them, that love me.

Here let us marke wel, and remembre, that the high power and aucthoritie of kynges, with theyr makyng of lawes, judgementes, and officers, are the ordinaunces, not of man, but of God: and therfore is this word (through me) so many tymes repeted. Here is also well to be considered and remembred, that this good ordre is appoynted of Gods wisedom, favor, and love, specially for them that love god, and therfore he saith: I love them, that love me. Also, in the boke of wisedom we may evidently learne, that a kynges power, aucthoritie, and strength, is a greate benefite of God, geven of his great mercy, to the comfort of our greate misery. For thus wee rede there spoken to kynges. Heare o ye kynges and understand: learne ye that be judges of the endes of the earth: give eare ye, that rule the multitudes: for the power is geven you of the lord, and the strength from the highest.

Let us learne also here by the infallible word of God, that kinges and other supreme and higher officers, are ordeined of god who is most highest, and therfore they are here diligentely taught, to apply themselfes, to knowledge and wisedom, necessary for the orderynge of Gods people, to their governaunce committed. And they be here also taught by almighty God, that thei should reknowledge themselfes, to have all their power and strength, not from Rome, but immediatly of God most highest. We rede in the boke of Deuteronomy, that al punishement perteineth to God, by this sentence: vengeaunce is mine, and I will reward. But this sentence we must understand, to pertein also unto the magistrates, which do exercise Gods roume in judgement and punishing, by good and godly lawes, here in the earth. And the places of scripture whiche seme to remove from among al christian men, judgement, punishment, or kyllyng, ought to be understand, that no man (of his owne private aucthoritie) may be judge over other, may punish, or may kill. But we must refer al judgement to god, to kynges and rulers, and judges under them, which be Gods officers, to execute justice, and by plain wordes of scripture, have their aucthoritie and use of the swoord, graunted from God, as we are taught by S. Paule the dere and elect Apostle of our sauior Christ, whom we ought diligently to obeye, even as we would obey our savior Christ, if he were present. Thus S. Paule writeth to the Romans, "Let every soule submit hymself, unto the aucthoritie of the higher powers, for there is no power, but of God, the powers that be, be ordeined of God, whosoever therfore resisteth the power, resisteth the ordinaunce of God, but they that resist, shall receive to themselfes dampnacion: for rulers are not fearful to them that do good, but to them that do evill. Wilt thou be without feare of the power? Do well then, and so shalt thou be praysed of the same: for he is the minister of God, for thy wealthe. But and if thou do that, whiche is evill, then feare, for he beareth not the swourde for naught, for he is the minister of God, to make vengeaunce on hym, that doth evill." Wherfore ye must nedes obey, not onely for feare of vengeaunce, but also, because of conscience, and even for this cause pay the tribute, for they are Gods ministers, servyng for the same purpose.

Here let us al learne of S. Paule, the elect vessel of God, that all persones having soules, (he excepteth none, nor exempteth none, neither priest, apostle, nor prophet, saieth. s. Chriso.) do owe of bounden duetie, and even in conscience, obedience, submission and subjection, to the hygh powers, which be constituted in aucthoritie by God, forasmuch as thei be Gods liuetenauntes, Gods presidentes, Gods officers, Gods commissioners, Gods judges, ordeyned of God hymself, of whom onely thei have al their power, and all their aucthoritie. And the same s. Paule threateneth no lesse pain, then everlasting dampnacion to al disobedient persons, to al resisters, against this generall and conmon aucthoritie, forasmuch as they resist not man, but God, not mannes devise and invencion, but Gods wisedon, Gods ordre, power, and aucthoritie.

And here (good people) let us all marke diligently, that it is not lawfull for inferiors and subjectes, in any case to resist the superior powers: for s. Paules wordes be playn, that whosoever resisteth, shall get to themselfes dampnacion: for whosoever resisteth, resisteth the ordinaunce of God. Our savior Christe him self and his apostles, received many and diverse injuries of the unfaithfull and wicked men in aucthoritie: yet we never rede, that thei, or any of then, caused any sedicion or rebellion agaynst aucthoritie. We rede oft, that they paciently suffered al troubles, vexacions, slaunders, pangues, and paines, and death it self obediently, without tumulte or resistence. They committed their cause to him, that judgeth righteously, and prayed for their enemyes hartely and earnestly. They knew that the aucthoritie of the powers, was Gods ordinaunce, and therfore bothe in their wordes and dedes, they taught ever obedience to it, and never taught, nor did the contrary. The wicked judge Pilat sayd to Christe: knowest thou not that I have power to crucifye thee, and have power also to lose thee? Jesus aunswered: "Thou couldest have no power at all against me, except it were geven the from above." Wherby Christe taught us plainly, that even the wicked rulers have their power and aucthoritie from God. And therfore it is not lawfull for their subjectes, by force to resyst then, although they abuse their power; muche lesse then it is lawfull for subjectes to resiste their godly and christian princes, whiche do not abuse their aucthoritie, but use the same to Gods glory, and to the profyte and commoditie of Gods people. The holy apostle S. Peter commaundeth servauntes to be obedient to their masters, not onely, if they be good and gentle, but also, if they be evil and froward: affirmyng, that the vocation and callyng of Gods people, is to bee pacient, and of the sufferyng syde. And there he bringeth in, the pacience of our savior Christ to perswade obedience to governors, yea, although they be wycked and wrong dooers. But let us now heare S. Peter himself speake, for his own wordes certifye best our conscience. Thus he uttereth them in his firste Epistle: Servauntes obeye your Masters with feare, not onely, if they be good and gentle, but also, if they bee froward: For it is thanke worthy, if a man for conscience towarde God, suffereth grief, and suffreth wronge undeserved: for what praise is it, when ye be beaten for your faultes, if ye take it paciently, but when ye do wel, if you then suffre wrong, and take it paciently, then is there cause to have thanke of God: for hereunto verily were ye called. For so did Christ suffre for us, leavyng us an example, that we should follow his steppes. All these be the very wordes of Saint Peter.

Saint David also teacheth us a good lesson in this behalfe, who was many tymes most cruelly and wrongfully persecuted of kyng Saule, and many tymes also put in jeoperdy and daunger of his life, by kyng Saule and his people: yet he never resysted, neither used any force or violence against

Investiture of knight by King, from fourteenth-century manuscript. The kneeling knight shows the close relationship between religious and secular symbolism during the Middle Ages. The Art Archive/Biblioteca Nazionale Marciana Venice/Alfredo Dagli Orti.

kyng Saule, his mortall enemy, but did ever to his liege Lorde and master kyng Saule, moste true, most diligent, and most faithfull service. In so muche, that when the lord God had given kyng Saule into Davides handes in his own cave, he would not hurt him, when he myght without all bodily perill, easly have slain hym: no, he would not suffre any of his servauntes, once to lay their handes upon kyng Saule, but praied to god in this wise: lord, kepe me from doyng that thyng unto my master, the lordes anoynted: kepe me that I laye not my hande upon him, seyng, he is the anoynted of the lorde: for as truly as the lorde liveth, (except the lorde smyte him, or except his day come, or that he go doune to warre, and in battaill perishe) the Lorde be mercifull unto me, that I lay not my hand upon the lordes anoynted. And that Dauid mighte have killed his enemye kyng Saule, it is evidently proved, in the first boke of the kynges, both by the cuttyng of the lap of Saules garment, and also by the playn confession of kyng Saule. Also another time (as it is mentioned in the same boke) when the most unmercifull, and most unkynd kyng Saule did persecute poore Dauid, God did agayn give kyng Saule into Davides handes, by castyng of kyng Saul and his whole army, into a dead slepe: so that David and one Abisai with him, came in the night into Saules hoste, wher Saule lay slepyng, and his speare stacke in the ground at his hed. Then said Abisai unto David: God hath delivered thyne enemy into thy handes, at this tyme, now therfore let me smyte him once with my spear to the earth, and I will not smyte him agayn the seconde tyme: meanyng thereby to have kylled hym with one stroke, and to have made him sure for ever. And David answered, and sayd to Abisai, destroy him not: for who can lay his handes on the lordes anoynted and be guiltless? And David said furthermore: as sure as the lord liveth, the lord shall smite him, or his day shall come to dye, or he shall descend into battaill, and there perish. The lord kepe me fron laiyng my handes vpon the lordes anoynted. But take thou now the speare that is at his head, and the cruse of water, and let us go: and so he did.

Source: Cranmer, Thomas. *Certayne Sermons, or Homelies Appoynted by the Kynges Maiestie, to Be Declared and Redde, by All Persones, Vicars, or Curates, Euery Sondaye in Their Churches, Where They Have Cure.* 1547. Spelling modified slightly by Lawrence Morris.

Legal Systems

Human societies have turned to formal legal systems to provide clear guidelines for peaceful coexistence and the profitable exchange of goods. However, the complexity and concepts of any legal system may differ from those of another legal system. The law is certainly not the same everywhere. *Anglo-Saxon* law, for example, allowed individuals to seek their own private vigilante justice, provided that certain procedures designed to promote peaceful outcomes were followed. The rather straightforward proclamations of the ninth-century Anglo-Saxon king *Alfred the Great* (Document 12) contrast with the complex compilation of Roman law codes initiated by the Roman Emperor *Justinian* in the sixth century. The legal advisors under Justinian not only established what the law was but also offered a theory of basic legal concepts, such as possession (Document 14). In all cases, however, the legal codes tend to reflect the legal needs of the particular society. Anglo-Saxon law addresses vendetta, for example, whereas other early Germanic law codes distinguish carefully between different forms of livestock theft (Document 13). Such concern with rural matters reflects the importance of rural life in their society.

Not only do different countries have different laws, but additionally, the same country may have different but contemporaneous law codes. Throughout much of western Europe, two laws existed side by side: secular law and Church law (Documents 9 and 11). Church law covered moral and religious matters, as well as internal Church affairs, whereas secular law tended to cover crime affecting property or persons.

Perhaps the most spectacular aspect of medieval law was the trial by ordeal, in which two opponents would determine who was right by fighting or by undergoing some other physical contest. As Document 10 shows, these ordeals attracted large crowds eager to see who would win and who would be severely injured. Despite the fascination of this form of trial, the vast majority of cases were decided in a way that we would recognize today—by a judge listening to witnesses. It was an unfortunate aspect of the times, however, that the testimony of wealthy high-status individuals inevitably carried more weight than the testimony of the poor. It was nearly impossible for the lower classes to win a case against a wealthy individual.

9. Church Law

As noted previously, throughout the Middle Ages and Renaissance, two major legal systems existed: secular law and Church law. Ecclesiastic and canon law governed the internal workings of the Church but could also serve as the main judge of clergymen. A good example comes from the following extract from the Council of Trent (1545–1563). As part of the efforts of Roman Catholic self-reformation, the council addressed the issue of clerics who, contrary to their vows of celibacy, kept concubines, that is, lovers. Although clerical celibacy did not become the norm until the early Middle Ages—after all, many of the Apostles, such as Peter, were married—by the year 1000 all the clergy in western Europe were expected to be single and celibate. In the following decrees, the Council of Trent sought to ensure celibacy by punishing delinquent priests in their pocketbooks: womanizing prelates would need to pay one-third of their total income as a fine, and repeat offenders would have their entire income confiscated and would face excommunication if they did not reform. Moreover, the council forbade the illegitimate sons of priests to hold office in the same establishment as their father, a formerly rather commonplace, though criticized, custom.

The urgency of reform can be seen in the legal structure established by these decrees. The local bishop, instead of lower-ranking officials or a legal court, was given all the authority to determine guilt and to punish the womanizing priests. Vesting authority in one individual in this manner streamlined justice; there was no need for lawyers and complicated legal procedures. The absence of a right of appeal, however, meant that there were also no checks and balances.

CHAPTER XIV

The Manner of Proceeding Against Clerics who Keep Concubines is Prescribed

How shameful a thing, and how unworthy it is of the name of clerics who have devoted themselves to the service of God, to live in the filth of impurity, and unclean bondage, the thing itself doth testify, in the common scandal of all the faithful, and the extreme disgrace entailed on the clerical order. To the end, therefore, that the ministers of the Church may be recalled to that continency and integrity of life which becomes them; and that the people may hence learn to reverence them the more, that they know them to be more pure of life: the holy Synod forbids all clerics whatsoever to dare to keep concubines, or any other woman of whom any suspicion can exist, either in their own houses, or elsewhere, or to presume to have any intercourse with them: otherwise they shall be punished with the penalties imposed by the sacred canons, or by the statutes of the (several) churches. But if, after being admonished by their superiors, they shall not abstain from these women, they shall be ipso facto deprived of the third part of the fruits, rents, and proceeds of all their benefices whatsoever, and pensions; which third part shall be applied to the fabric of the church, or to some other pious place, at the discretion of the bishop. If, however, persisting in the same crime, with the same or some other woman, they shall not even yet have obeyed upon a second admonition, not only shall they thereupon forfeit all the fruits and proceeds of their benefices and pensions, which shall be applied to the places aforesaid, but they shall also be suspended from the administration of the benefices themselves, for as long a period as shall seem fit to the Ordinary, even as the delegate of the Apostolic See. And if, having been thus suspended, they nevertheless shall not put away those women, or, even if they shall have intercourse with them, then shall they be for ever deprived of their ecclesiastical benefices, portions, offices, and pensions of whatsoever kind, and be rendered thenceforth incapable and unworthy of any manner of honours, dignities, benefices and offices, until, after a manifest amendment of life, it shall seem good to their superiors, for a cause, to grant them a dispensation. But if, after having once put them away, they shall have dared to renew the interrupted connexion, or to take to themselves other scandalous women of this sort, they shall, in addition to the penalties aforesaid, be smitten with the sword of excommunication. Nor shall any appeal, or exemption, hinder or suspend the execution of the aforesaid; and the cognizance of all the matters above-named shall not belong to archdeacons, or deans, or other inferiors, but to the bishops themselves, who may proceed without the noise and the formalities of justice, and by the sole investigation of the truth of the fact.

As regards clerics who have not ecclesiastical benefices or pensions, they shall, according to the quality of their crime and contumacy, and their persistance therein, be punished, by the bishop himself, with imprisonment, suspension from their order, inability to obtain benefices, or in other ways, conformably with the sacred canons.

Bishops also, if, which God forbid, they abstain not from crime of this nature, and, upon being admonished by the provincial Synod, they do not amend, shall be ipso facto suspended; and, if they persist therein, they shall be reported by the said Synod to the most holy Roman Pontiff, who shall punish them according to the nature of their guilt, even with deprivation if need be.

CHAPTER XV

The Illegitimate Sons of Clerics are Excluded from Certain Benefices and Pensions

That the memory of paternal incontinency may be banished as far as possible from places consecrated to God, where purity and holiness are most especially beseeming; it shall not be lawful for the sons of clerics, not born in lawful wedlock, to hold, in those churches wherein their fathers have, or had, an ecclesiastical benefice, any benefice whatsoever, even though a different one; nor to minister in any way in the said churches; nor to have pensions out of the revenues of benefices which their fathers hold, or have aforetime held. And if a father and son shall be found, at this present time, to hold benefices in the same church; the son shall be compelled to resign his benefice, or to exchange it for another out of that church, within the space of three months, otherwise he shall be ipso jure deprived thereof; and any dispensation in regard of the aforesaid shall be accounted surreptitious. Moreover, any reciprocal resignations which shall from this time forth be made by fathers who are clerics in favour of their sons, that one may obtain the benefice of the other, shall be wholly regarded as made in fraudulent evasion of this decree, and of the ordinances of the canons; nor shall the collations that may have followed, by virtue of resignations of this kind, or of any other whatsoever made fraudulently, be of avail to the said sons of clerics.

Source: *The Council of Trent: The Twenty-Fifth Session; The Canons and Decrees of the Sacred and Oecumenical Council of Trent.* Edited and translated by J. Waterworth. London: Dolman, 1848, pp. 270–72.

10. Trial by Ordeal

Ordeals, with their battles to the death or injury, are a famous part of medieval justice but did not, in fact, play a major role in the medieval justice system. The elites in both the Church and state, as seen in Document 9, understood that a rational system of justice, using evidence and sworn witnesses, provided justice more surely than recourse to life-threatening competitions in the name of God. On the popular level, however, ordeals remained alive. Seventeenth-century witch trials, for example, still involved dunking suspected witches in water to see if they would float unnaturally.

The grasping of heated objects was one of the most common ordeals. In the following extract, from Gregory of Tours's sixth-century Books of Miracles (Libri miraculorum), *two men in a dispute over religion decide to pluck a ring from a cauldron of boiling water; the man who is not harmed by the water will prove that his doctrine is correct. Comically, one of the participants loses confidence and attempts to protect his arm by covering it in ointment and urges his adversary to go first, in hopes, no doubt, that his opponent will be badly burned! While the two stand arguing, a third religious man comes along and proves the correctness of orthodox Christianity by plunging his arm into the boiling water and retrieving the ring while remaining unharmed. When the Arian heretic attempts to do the same, the flesh of the heretic's armed is completely burned off.*

The fear and excitement generated by an ordeal is clear from the extract. Neither disputant wants to go first, and one of them has attempted to cheat. Meanwhile, a large crowd gathers around to see the outcome of the ordeal and, gruesomely, to see violent injury done to one or both parties. The interest aroused by the ordeal highlights the extraordinary nature of the event: ordeals were rare and therefore intriguing. At the same time, ordeals could evidently be convincing; Gregory of Tours relates the story precisely because he believes that the readers will be convinced by the outcome of the ordeal.

Arianism, the heresy that Gregory attempts to disprove by recording this story, taught that Jesus and the Holy Spirit were not equal to God the Father, whereas orthodox Christianity, followed by Gregory of Tours and by the characters of Iacinthus and the ointment-wearing deacon in the story, held that Jesus and the Holy Spirit were equal to the Father.

An Arian priest, disputing with a deacon of our religion, made venomous assertions against the Son of God and the Holy Spirit, as is the habit of that sect. But when the deacon had discoursed a long time concerning the reasonableness of our faith, and the heretic, blinded by the fog of unbelief, continued to reject the truth (according as it is written, "Wisdom shall not enter the mind of the wicked") the former said: "Why weary ourselves with long discussions? Let acts demonstrate the truth. Let a kettle be heated over the fire and someone's ring be thrown into the boiling water. Let him who shall take it from the heated liquid be approved as a follower of the truth, and afterwards let the other party be converted to the knowledge of this truth. And understand, O heretic, that this our party will fulfill the conditions with the aid of the Holy Spirit; you shall confess that there is no inequality, no dissimilarity, in the Holy Trinity." The heretic consented to the proposition and they separated, after appointing the next morning for the trial. But the fervor of faith in which the deacon had first made this suggestion began to cool through the instigation of the enemy. Rising with the dawn, he bathed his arm in oil and smeared it with ointment. But nevertheless he made the round of the sacred places and called in prayer on the Lord. What more shall I say? About 9 am they met in the market place. The people came together to see the show. A fire was lighted, the kettle was placed upon it, and when it grew very hot the ring was thrown into the boiling water. The deacon invited the heretic to take it out of the water first. But he promptly refused, saying, "You who did propose this trial should take it out." The deacon, all of a tremble, bared his arm. When the heretic priest saw it besmeared with ointment he cried out: "With magic arts you have thought to protect yourself: you have made use of these salves, but what you have done will not avail." While they were thus quarreling, there came up a deacon from Ravenna named Iacinthus, who inquired what the trouble was about. When he learned the truth, he drew his arm out from under his robe at once and plunged his right hand into the kettle. Now the ring that had been thrown in was a little thing and very light, so that it was tossed about by the water as chaff would be blown about by the wind. And searching for it a long time, he found it after about an hour. Meanwhile the flame beneath the kettle blazed up mightily, so that the greater heat might make it difficult for the ring to be followed by the hand; but the deacon extracted it at length and suffered no harm, protesting rather that at the bottom the kettle was cold while at the top it was just pleasantly warm. When the heretic beheld this, he was greatly confused and audaciously thrust his hand into the kettle saying, "My faith will aid me." As soon as his hand had been thrust in, all the flesh was boiled off the bones clear up to the elbow. And so the dispute ended.

Source: Gregory of Tours, *Libri miraculorum*, ch. 80. Text in Monumenta Germaniae Historica, *Scriptores merovingicarum*, vol. 1, p. 542. Trans. by Arthur Howland in *University of Pennsylvania Translations and Reprints*, vol. 4, no. 4, pp. 10–11. In *A Source Book of Mediaeval History*. Ed. by Frederic Austin Ogg. New York: American, 1908, pp. 198–200. Translation modified slightly by Lawrence Morris.

11. Separation of Church and State

When the Norman duke William the Conqueror won control of England in 1066, he imported continental legal practices to his new kingdom. One of these practices was a strict separation of church and state. In this decree from the early 1070s, William orders that bishops no longer hear cases in the hundred courts (where secular legal cases were heard) but instead hear them in a special episcopal court at a place of the bishop's choosing. Although William thus removed the bishops from the secular courts, he also removed the secular law officers (sheriffs, reeves, and crown ministers) from the episcopal courts by outlawing their interference with episcopal law. Finally, William sought to limit trial by ordeal by confining it solely to church law, and even then the ordeal had to be under the direct supervision of the bishop.

William, King of the English by the grace of God, to R. Bainardo, G. de Magnavilla, P. de Valoines, and to my other faithful followers from Essex, Hartfordshire, and Middlesex, greetings. May you, and all my faithful who remain in England, know that I have ordered that a common council of archbishops, bishops, abbots, and chief men of my kingdom amend the episcopal laws that have been used in England up until my time although they are poor and not in accordance with the precepts of holy canon law. Moreover, I command and instruct by my royal authority that no bishop or archdeacon hear pleas concerning episcopal law in the hundred courts anymore, nor bring any case relating to the guidance of souls to the secular courts. Instead, let anyone called for a case or charge pertaining to episcopal law go to the place which the bishop shall choose and announce for this purpose, and there the called shall respond to the case or charge, and let him do right before God and the bishop, not according to the laws of the hundred courts, but according to the canons and episcopal law. If anyone, carried away by pride, refuses to come to the episcopal court, let him be called three times; if he does not come to make amends, let him be excommunicated, and the strength and the justice of the king or his deputy shall enforce this excommunication as necessary. Whoever refuses to come to the episcopal court when called shall pay reparations for each time he refused to come. I also declare, and proclaim with my authority, that no sheriff or reeve or crown minister, nor any lay man, should interfere with the law belonging to the bishop, and no lay man should bring another to trial by ordeal without the episcopal court. Trial by ordeal shall not be conducted anywhere, except at the episcopal seat or in a place that the bishop has appointed.

Source: *Select Charters and Other Illustrations of English Constitutional History from the Earliest Times to the Reign of Edward the First.* 9th ed. Ed. by William Stubbs. Revised by H.W.C. Davis. Oxford: Clarendon Press, 1913, pp. 99–100. Translated and adapted by Lawrence Morris for this encyclopedia.

12. Vendetta and Tort Law

In many early medieval law codes, such as in Anglo-Saxon England, the legal system was based on tort law, in which an aggressor or a criminal pays a fine to the victim instead of going to prison. Whereas an aggressor who knocked out a victim's eye in the modern day would go to jail for assault and battery, the same culprit, according to the following excerpt from the law code issued by the ninth-century Anglo-Saxon king Alfred the Great, would need to pay a little more than 66 shillings in monetary compensation. Fines, rather than imprisonment, were the main form of punishment.

Another difference from modern legal systems was the reliance on personal vengeance to ensure justice. In an era before police forces, the victim and the victim's family ensured that justice occurred. Alfred's laws, however, already bear witness to attempts to curb the role of personal and violent vengeance in the administration of justice. In the first codes quoted here, for example, the victim must first give the criminal a chance to make monetary restitution. The victim therefore may surround the criminal's house, but he is not permitted to commence open warfare. If the victim is not powerful enough to besiege the criminal's house, then the victim can seek assistance from the local ealdorman, who may, in turn, request assistance from the king, if necessary.

A notable exception to this prohibition of sudden vengeance is made for crimes of passion. According to the law code, a man can fight immediately if he finds his wife in suspicious circumstances with another man or indeed if he finds any female relative with an inappropriate male.

42. Also we enjoin, that a man who knows his adversary to be residing at home, shall not have recourse to violence before demanding justice of him.

    i. If he has power enough to surround his adversary and besiege him in his house, he shall keep him therein seven days, but he shall not fight against him if he will consent to remain inside. And if, after seven days, he will submit and hand over his weapons, he shall keep him unscathed for thirty days, and send formal notice of his position to his kinsmen and friends.

    ii. If, however, he flees to a church, the privileges of the church shall be respected, as we have declared above.

    iii. If, however, he has not power enough to besiege him in his house, he shall ride to the *ealdorman* and ask him for help. If he will not help him, he shall ride to the king before having recourse to violence.

    iv. And further, if anyone chances on his enemy, not having known him to be at home, and if he will give up his weapons, he shall be detained for thirty days, and his friends shall be informed [of his position]. If he is not willing to give up his weapons, then violence may be used against him, he shall pay any sum which he incurs, whether wergeld or compensation for wounds, as well as a fine, and his kinsman shall forfeit his claim to protection as a result of his action.

    v. We further declare that a man may fight on behalf of his lord, if his lord is attacked, without becoming liable to vendetta. Under similar conditions a lord may fight on behalf of his man.

    vi. In the same way a man may fight on behalf of one who is related to him by blood, if he is attacked unjustly, except it be against his lord. This we do not permit.

    vii. A man may fight, without becoming liable to vendetta, if he finds another man with his wedded wife, within closed doors or under the same blanket; or if he finds another man with his legitimate daughter or sister; or with his mother, if she has been given in lawful wedlock to his father.

44. 30 shillings shall be given as compensation for a wound on the head, if both bones are pierced.

    i. If the outer bone only is pierced, 15 shillings shall be given as compensation.

45. If a wound an inch long is inflicted under the hair, one shilling shall be given as compensation.
    i. If a wound an inch long is inflicted in front of the hair, 2 shillings shall be paid as compensation.
46. If either ear is struck off, 30 shillings shall be given as compensation.
    i. If the hearing is stopped, so that he cannot hear, 60 shillings shall be given as compensation.
47. If anyone knocks out a man's eye, he shall give him 66 shillings, 6 pence and the third part of a penny as compensation.
    i. If it remains in the head, but he can see nothing with it, one-third of the compensation shall be withheld.
48. If anyone strikes off another's nose, he shall pay him 60 shillings compensation.
49. If anyone knocks out another's front tooth, he shall pay 8 shillings as compensation for it.
    i. If it is a black tooth, 4 shillings shall be given as compensation.
    ii. A man's canine tooth shall be valued at 15 shillings.
50. If anyone strikes another's jaws so violently that they are fractured, he shall pay 15 shillings compensation.
    i. If a man's chin-bone is broken in two, 12 shillings shall be given as compensation.
51. If a man's throat is pierced, 12 shillings shall be paid as compensation.
52. If, as the result of another's actions, a man's tongue is torn from his mouth, the compensation shall be the same as that for an eye.
53. If a man is wounded in the shoulder, so that the synovia flows out, 30 shillings shall be paid as compensation.
54. If the arm is fractured above the elbow, 15 shillings must be paid as compensation for it.
55. If both bones in the arm are broken, the compensation shall be 30 shillings.
56. If the thumb is struck off, 30 shillings must be paid as compensation for it.
    i. If the nail is struck off, 5 shillings must be paid as compensation for it.
57. If the first finger is struck off, the compensation shall be 15 shillings; for the nail of the same 3 shilling.
58. If the middle finger is struck off, the compensation shall be 15 shillings; for the nail of the same, 2 shillings compensation shall be paid.
59. If the third finger is struck off, 17 shillings must be paid as compensation for it; and for the nail of the same, 4 shillings must be paid as compensation.
60. If the little finger is struck off, 9 shillings must be paid as compensation for it, and one shilling must be paid as compensation for the nail of the same, if it is struck off.
61. If a man is wounded in the belly, 30 shillings shall be given to him as compensation.
    i. If he is pierced right through, 20 shillings shall be paid for each orifice.
62. If a man's thigh is pierced, 30 shillings shall be given to him as compensation.
    i. If it is fractured, 30 shillings shall also be the compensation.
63. If the shin is pierced below the knee, 12 shillings must be paid as compensation for it.
    i. If it is fractured below the knee, 30 shillings shall be given to him as compensation.

64. If the big toe is struck off, 20 shillings shall be given to him as compensation.
    i. If it is the second toe which is struck off, 15 shillings shall be given to him as compensation.
    ii. If the middle toe is struck off, 9 shillings must be paid as compensation for it.
    iii. If it is the fourth toe which is struck off, 6 shillings must be paid as compensation for it.
    iv. If the little toe is struck off, 5 shillings shall be given to him as compensation.
65. If a man is so badly wounded in the testicles that he cannot beget children, 80 shillings shall be paid to him as compensation for it.

Source: *The Laws of the Earliest English Kings*. Ed. and trans. by F. L Attenborough Cambridge: Cambridge University Press, 1922, pp. 83–91.

13. Stealing Livestock

This brief extract from seventh-century German laws reveals the importance of the rural economy. The punishments for the theft of pigs and cows are determined according to precise distinctions between the animals involved. The theft of a suckling pig, for example, carries a penalty of 120 denarii, whereas the theft of a weaned pig carries a penalty one-third as severe: 40 denarii. The theft of a whole herd of 25 or more pigs carries the truly heavy penalty of 2500 denarii; the penalty indicates that theft of a whole herd could leave the owner destitute and at risk of starvation. Livestock was valued so highly by the Germans that even animals that drifted into a neighbor's crops were protected; harming the animal could result in repaying the price of the animal, and attempting to cover up the crime would result in a whopping 600 denarii additional fine. Stealing and harming livestock were clearly serious crimes in the rural societies of the early medieval Germanic world.

II. Concerning thefts of pigs

1. If any one steal a suckling pig and it be proved against him, let him be judged guilty of *chrane calcium*, i.e. 120 denarii, which make 3 solidi.
2. If any one steal a pig that is weaned and it be proved against him, let him be judged guilty of *chrane calcium*, i.e., 40 denarii, which make 1 solidi. . .
14. If any one steal 25 pigs and there be no more in the herd, and it be proved against him, let him be judged guilty of *sonista*, i.e. 2500 denarii, which make 62 solidi.

III. Concerning thefts of cattle

4. If any one steal the unyoked bull which is the leader of the herd, let him be judged guilty of *charohitum*, i.e., 8000 denarii, which make 45 solidi.
5. But if that bull be kept for the cows of three villages in common, let him who stole it be judged guilty of *chammitum*, i.e., three times 45 solidi.
6. If any one steal the king's bull, let him be judged guilty of *anteotho*, i.e., 3600 denarii, which make 90 solidi, besides *capitale* and *delitura*.

IX. Concerning damage done among crops or in any enclosure

1. If any one find cattle or a horse or any flocks among his crops he ought not to harm them in any way.
2. And if he does so and confess it, let him pay *capitale* in place of the damage; but he shall keep the injured beast for himself.
3. But if he does not confess, and it be proved against him, let him be judged guilty of 600 denarii, which make 15 solidi, besides *capitale* and *dilatura*.

Source: Gengler, H. G. *Germanische Rechtsdenkmäler*. Erlangen: F. Enke, 1875, p. 267. In Roy Cave and Herbert Coulson, *A Source Book for Medieval Economic History*. New York: Biblo and Tannen, 1965, pp. 307–08.

14. The Code of Justinian

The Code of Justinian, a law code drawn up by the Roman emperor Justinian (483–565), remained the most influential legal document throughout the Middle Ages and much of the Renaissance. Upon assuming the throne of the Roman Empire, Justinian appointed a team of lawyers to collect and recodify the existing body of Roman law. The result was a series of books that united Roman law and presented that law in an easily accessible manner. The finished work carefully indicated which emperors enacted the laws and how legal thinkers had understood the law. The kingdoms of western Europe would continually look to the Code of Justinian as a source of authoritative legal precedent.

The following extract, from the Digest, discusses the notion of the legal possession of goods and how to acquire it. Legal possession is one of the most important legal concepts. Without the concept of possession, private property could not exist. Anyone would be able to take property away from anyone else. Possession is thus necessary for economic security. Possession also played an important role in family life because Roman parents possessed their children. The same laws that applied to things applied to certain classes of people.

CONCERNING ACQUIRING OR LOSING POSSESSION.

1. Paulus, On the Edict, Book LIV.

Possession, as Labeo says, is derived from the term *sedes*, or position, because it is naturally held by him who has it.

1. Nerva, the son, asserts that the ownership of property originated from natural possession, and that the trace of this still remains in the case of whatever is taken on the earth, on the sea, and in the air, for it immediately belongs to those who first acquire possession of it. Likewise, spoils taken in war, and an island formed in the sea, gems, precious stones, and pearls found upon the shore, become the property of him who first obtains possession of them.
2. We also acquire possession by ourselves.
3. An insane person, or a ward, cannot begin to acquire possession without the authority of his curator or guardian; because, although the former may touch the

property with their bodies, they have not the disposition to hold it, just as where anyone places something in the hands of a man who is asleep. A ward can begin to obtain possession by the authority of his guardian. Ofilius, and Nerva, the son, however, say that a ward cannot begin to obtain possession without the authority of his guardian, for possession is a matter of fact, and not of law. This opinion may be accepted where the ward is of such an age as to be capable of understanding what he is doing.

4. Where a husband gives possession to his wife for the purpose of making her a donation, several authorities hold that she is in actual possession, as a question of fact cannot be annulled by the Civil Law. And, indeed, what use would it be to say that the wife is not in possession, as the husband immediately lost it when he no longer desired to retain it?

5. We also acquire possession by means of a slave or a son who is under our control; and this is the case with property constituting his peculium, even if we are ignorant of the fact, as was held by Sabinus.

Cassius and Julianus: because those whom we have permitted to have peculium are understood to be in possession with our consent. Therefore, an infant and an insane person can obtain possession of property forming peculium, and can acquire it by usucaption; an heir also can do this, where a slave belonging to the estate makes a purchase.

6. We can also acquire possession through anyone whom we possess in good faith as a slave, even though he belongs to another, or is free. If, however, we have possession of him fraudulently, I do not think that we can acquire possession through his agency. He who is in possession of another can neither acquire property for his master nor for himself.

7. When we are joint-owners of a slave, we can individually acquire property through him to the full amount, as if he were one of our own slaves, if he intends to make the acquisition for one of his masters; just as is the case of acquiring ownership.

8. We can obtain possession through a slave in whom we have the usufruct in the same way that he is accustomed to acquire property for us by means of his labor; nor does it make any difference if we do not actually possess him, for the same rule applies to a son.

9. Moreover, he through whom we desire to obtain possession should be such a person as to be able to understand what possession means.

10. Therefore, if you send a slave, who is insane, to take possession, you will by no means be considered to have acquired it.

11. If you send a boy under the age of puberty to take possession, you will begin to do so; just as a ward acquires possession, and especially by the authority of his guardian.

12. There is no doubt that you can obtain possession by means of a female slave.

13. A ward can acquire possession by means of a slave, whether the latter has arrived at the age of puberty, or not, if he directs him to take possession with the authority of his guardian.

14. Nerva, the son, says that we cannot acquire possession by means of one of our slaves who is a fugitive, although it has been held that he remains in our possession as long

as he is not in that of another; and therefore that, in the meantime, property can be acquired by him through usucaption. This opinion, however, is adopted on account of public convenience, so that usucaption may take place as long as no one has obtained possession of the slave. It is the opinion of Cassius and Julianus that possession may be acquired by such a slave, as well as by those whom we have in a province.

15. Julianus says that we cannot acquire possession by means of a slave who has been actually given in pledge, for he is held to be possessed by the debtor in one respect, that is to say, for the purpose of usucaption. Nor can the slave who is pledged acquire property for the creditor, because although the latter may have possession of him, he cannot acquire property through him by means of a stipulation, or in any other way.

16. The ancients thought that we could acquire anything by means of a slave belonging to an estate, because he was part of the said estate. Hence, a discussion arose whether this rule should not be extended farther so that where some slaves were bequeathed, the others could be possessed by the act of one of them. It was also discussed whether this would be the case if they were all purchased or donated together.

The better opinion is that I cannot, under such circumstances, acquire possession by the act of one of them.

17. If a slave is partially bequeathed to an appointed heir, he can acquire possession of the land of the estate for him, in proportion to his share in the said slave, by virtue of the legacy.

18. The same rule will apply if I order a slave owned in common to accept an estate, because I obtain possession of my share of it on account of my interest in him.

19. What we have stated with reference to slaves also applies where they themselves desire to acquire possession for us; for if you order your slave to take possession, and he does so with the intention of acquiring the property not for you, but for Titius, possession is not acquired for you.

20. Possession is acquired by us by means of an agent, a guardian, or a curator. But when they take possession in their own names, and not with the intention of merely rendering their services, they cannot acquire possession for us.

On the other hand, if we say that those who obtain possession in our name do not acquire it for us, the result will be that neither he to whom the property was delivered will obtain possession, because he did not have the intention of doing so, nor will he who delivered the article retain it, as he has relinquished possession of the same.

21. If I order a vendor to deliver the property to my agent, while it is in our presence, Priscus says that it will be held to have been delivered to me.

The same rule will apply if I order my debtor to pay to another the sum which is due to me, for it is not necessary to take possession bodily and actually, but this can be done merely by the eyes and the intention. The proof of this appears in the case of property which, on account of its weight, cannot be moved, as columns, for instance; for they are considered to have been delivered if the parties consent, with the columns before them; and wines are held to have been delivered when the keys of the wine-cellar have been handed to the purchaser.

22. Municipalities cannot possess anything by themselves, because all the citizens cannot consent. They do not possess the forums, and the temples, and other things of this kind, but they make use of them promiscuously. Nerva, the son, says that they can acquire, possess, and obtain by usucaption, the peculium of their slaves; others, however, hold the contrary; as they do not have possession of the slaves themselves.

2. Ulpianus, On the Edict, Book LXX.

The present rule is that municipalities can both hold possession and acquire by usucaption, and that this can be done through a slave, or a person who is free.

3. Paulus, On the Edict, Book LXX.

Moreover, only corporeal property can be possessed.

1. We obtain possession by means of both the body and the mind, and not by these separately. When, however, we say that we obtain possession by the body and the mind, this should not be understood to mean that where anyone desires to take possession of land he must walk around every field, as it will be sufficient for him to enter upon any part of the land, as long as it is his intention to take possession of it all, as far as its boundaries extend.

2. No one can obtain possession of property which is uncertain; as, for instance, if you have the intention and desire to possess everything that Titius has.

3. Neratius and Proculus think that we cannot acquire possession solely by intention, if natural possession does not come first. Therefore, if I know that there is a treasure on my land, I immediately possess it, as soon as I have the intention of doing so; because the intention supplies what is lacking in natural possession.

Again, the opinion of Brutus and Manilius, who hold that anyone who has had possession of land for a long time has also had possession of any treasure to be found there, even though he was ignorant of its existence, is not correct. For he who does not know that there is any treasure there does not possess it, although he may have possession of the land; and, if he was aware of its presence, he cannot acquire it by long possession, because he knows that it is the property of someone else.

Several authorities hold that the opinion of Sabinus is the better one; namely, that he who knows that there is a treasure on his land does not gain possession of it unless it has been removed from its place, because it is not in our custody. I concur in this opinion.

4. We can hold possession of the same thing by several different titles; for example, certain authorities think that he who obtains property by usucaption does so not only as a purchaser, but as the owner. For if I am the heir of him who has possession as a purchaser I possess the same property, but as purchaser and as heir; for while ownership can only be established by a single title, this is not the case with possession.

5. On the other hand, several persons cannot have possession of the same thing without division; for, indeed, it is contrary to nature that while I hold something you should also be considered to hold it. Sabinus, however, says that he who gives property held by a precarious title possesses it himself, as well as he who received it with the risk. Trebatius, also, approves this opinion, for he thinks that one person can have possession justly, and another unjustly, but that both of them cannot possess it either unjustly or justly.

Labeo contradicts him, since, in the case of complete possession, it does not make much difference whether anyone has possession justly or unjustly. This is correct, for the same possession cannot be held by two persons, any more than you can be considered to stand on the very place on which I am standing, or to sit exactly where I am seated.

6. When possession is lost, the intention of the party in possession must be considered. Therefore, although you may be on a tract of land, still, if you do not intend to retain it, you will immediately lose possession. Hence, possession can be lost by the intention alone, although it cannot be acquired in this way.
7. If, however, you have possession solely by intention, even though another may be on the land, you will still have possession of the same.
8. If anyone should give notice that a house is invaded by robbers, and the owner, being overcome with fear, is unwilling to approach it, it is established that he loses possession of the house. But if a slave or a tenant, through whose agency I actually possess property, should either die, or depart, I will retain possession by intention.
9. If I deliver an article to another, I lose possession of the same; for it has been decided that we hold possession until we voluntarily relinquish it, or are deprived of it by force.
10. If a slave, of whom I am in possession, asserts that he is free, as Spartacus did, and is ready to maintain his freedom in court, he will not be considered to be in possession of the master whom he is preparing to oppose. This, however, is only correct when he has remained for a long time at liberty; otherwise, if, from his condition as a slave, he demands his freedom, and petitions for a judicial decision on this point, he, nevertheless, remains under my control, and I hold possession of him by intention, until he has been pronounced to be free.
11. We possess by intention the places to which we resort in summer and in winter, although we leave them at certain times.
12. Moreover, we can have possession by intention, and also corporeally, by means of another, as we have stated in the case of a tenant and a slave. The fact that we possess certain property without being aware of it as is the case where slaves obtain peculium), should not present any difficulty, for we are held to possess it by both the intention and the actual agency of the slaves.
13. Nerva, the son, thinks that we can possess movable property, with the exception of slaves, as long as it remains in our charge; that is to say, as long as we can obtain natural possession of it, if we wished to do so. For if a flock should be lost, or a vase should fall in such a way that it cannot be found, it immediately ceases to be in our possession, although no one else can obtain possession of it; but the

case is different where anything cannot be found which is in my charge, because it still remains in the neighborhood, and diligent search will discover it.

14. Likewise, wild animals which we shut up in enclosures, and fish which we throw into ponds, are in our possession. But fish which are in a lake, or wild animals that wander in woods enclosed by hedges, are not in our possession, as they are left to their natural freedom; for otherwise, if anyone purchased the woods, he would be considered to have possession of all the animals therein, which is false.

15. Moreover, we have possession of birds which we have shut up or tamed, and subjected to our control.

16. Certain authorities very properly hold that pigeons, which fly away from our buildings, as well as bees which leave our hives, and have the habit of returning, are possessed by us.

17. Labeo and Nerva, the son, have given it as their opinion that I cease to possess any place which a river or the sea has overflowed.

18. If you appropriate any property which has been deposited with you, with the intention of stealing it, I cease to have possession of the same. If, however, you do not move it from its place, and have the intention of denying that it was deposited with you, several ancient authorities, and among them Sabinus and Cassius, very properly hold that I still retain possession, for the reason that a theft cannot be committed without handling the article, nor can theft be committed by mere intention.

19. The rule that no one can himself change his title to the possession of property has been established by the ancient authorities.

20. If, however, he who deposited an article with me, or lent it to me, should sell or give me the same thing, I will not be considered to have changed the title by which I hold possession, since I did not have possession.

21. There are as many kinds of possession as there are ways of acquiring property which does not belong to us; as, for example, by purchase, by donation, by legacy, by dowry, as an heir, by surrender as reparation for damage committed, by occupancy, as in the case where we obtain property from the land or the sea, or from the enemy, or which we ourselves create. And, in conclusion, there is but one genus of possession, but the species are infinite in number.

22. Possession may be divided into two kinds, for it is acquired either in good, or in bad faith. The opinion of Quintus Mucius, who included among the different kinds of possession that given by order of a magistrate, for the purpose of preserving the property, or where we obtain possession because security against threatened injury is not furnished, is perfectly ridiculous. For where anyone places a creditor in possession for the purpose of preserving property, or where this is done because security has not been furnished against threatened injury, or in the name of an unborn child, he does not really grant possession, but merely the custody and supervision of the property. Hence, when a neighbor does not give security against threatened injury, and we are placed in charge, and this condition continues for a long time, the Praetor, upon proper cause being shown, will permit us to obtain actual possession of the property.

4. Ulpianus, On the Edict, Book LXVII.

A father immediately possesses whatever his son acquires as a part of his peculium, although he may not be aware that he is under his control. Moreover, the same rule should be adopted even if the son is in possession of another as a slave.

5. Paulus, On the Edict, Book LXIII.

If I owe you Stichus under the terms of a stipulation, and I do not deliver him, and you obtain possession of him in some other way, you are a depredator. Likewise, if I should sell you any property and do not deliver it, and you obtain possession of the same without my consent, you will not do so as a purchaser, but as a depredator.

6. Ulpianus, On the Edict, Book LXX.

We say that he holds anything clandestinely who takes possession of it by stealth, suspecting that the other party, not knowing what he has done, may raise a controversy, and fearing that he will contend his right. He, however, who does not take possession secretly, but conceals himself, is in such a position that he is not considered to have clandestine possession. For not the manner in which he acquired possession, but the beginning of his acquiring it, should be taken into account, nor does anyone begin to acquire possession clandestinely who does so in good faith, with the knowledge or consent of him to whom the property belongs, or for any other good reason. Hence Pomponius says that he obtains clandestine possession who, fearing that some future controversy may arise, and the person of whom he is apprehensive being ignorant of the fact, takes possession by stealth.

1. Labeo says that where a man goes to a market, leaving no one at home, and on his return from the market finds that someone has taken possession of his house, the latter is held to have obtained clandestine possession. Therefore, he who went to the market still retains possession, but if the trespasser should not admit the owner on his return, he will be considered to be in possession rather by force than clandestinely.

7. Paulus, On the Edict, Book LIV.

If the owner is unwilling to return to the land because he fears the exertion of superior force, he will be considered to have lost possession. This was also stated by Neratius.

8. The Same, On the Edict, Book LXV.

As possession cannot be acquired except by intention and a corporeal act, so in like manner, it cannot be lost, except in a case where the opposite of both of these things takes place.

9. Gaius, On the Edict, Book XXV.

Generally speaking, we are considered to have possession when anyone as an agent, a host, or a friend, holds it in our name.

10. Ulpianus, On the Edict, Book LXIX.

Where anyone leases property, and afterwards claims it by a precarious title, he is considered to have abandoned his lease. If he claims it at first by a precarious title, and afterwards leases it, he is considered to hold possession under the lease; for whatever is done last should rather be taken into consideration. Pomponius, also, is of this opinion.

1. Pomponius discusses a very nice question; namely, whether a man who leases land, but claims it by a precarious title, does so, not for the purpose of possessing it, but merely to remain in possession; for there is a great difference, as it is one thing to possess, but quite another to be in possession. Persons placed in possession for the purpose of preserving the property, as legatees or neighbors, on account of threatened injury, do not possess the property but are in possession of the same for the purpose of caring for it. When this is done both of the above ways are merged into one.

2. Where anyone leases land, and asks to be placed in possession by a precarious title, if he leased it for one sesterce there is no doubt that he holds it at will, as a lease for only that sum is void. If, however, he leases it for a fair rent, it must then be ascertained what was done first.

11. Paulus, On the Edict, Book LXV.

He possesses justly who does so by the authority of the Praetor.

12. Ulpianus, On the Edict, Book LXX.

He who has the usufruct of property is held to possess it naturally.

1. Ownership has nothing in common with possession, and therefore an interdict Uti possidetis is not refused to one who has begun proceedings to recover the property, for he who does so is not held to have relinquished possession.

13. The Same, On the Edict, Book LXXII.

Pomponius relates that stones were sunk in the Tiber by a shipwreck and were afterwards recovered; and he asks whether the ownership remained unchanged during the time that they were in the river. I think that the ownership, but not the possession, was retained. This instance is not similar to that of a fugitive slave, for the slave is considered to be possessed by us, in order to prevent him from depriving us of possession; but the case of the stones is different.

1. Where anyone makes use of the agency of another, he should do so with the liabilities and defects attaching to it. Hence, with reference to the time during which the vendor has had possession of the property, we also take into consideration the questions of violence, secrecy, and precarious title.

2. Moreover, where anyone returns a slave to the vendor, the question arises whether the latter can profit by the time that the slave was in possession of the purchaser. Some authorities think that he cannot, for the reason that the return of the slave annuls the sale; others hold that the purchaser can profit by

Church and State. Justinian and his ministers with Maximian, bishop of Ravenna. On the right are representatives of the Church; on the left are representatives of the state. Reproduction of a mosaic at Ravenna. North Wind Picture Archives.

the time of possession by the vendor, and the vendor by that of the purchaser. This opinion, I think, should be adopted.

3. If a freeman, or a slave belonging to another who is serving in good faith, purchases property, and a third party acquires possession of the same, neither the alleged slave, when he becomes free, nor the real owner can profit by the time that the property has been in the hands of a bona fide possessor.

4. Where an heir did not possess in the first place, the question arose whether he can profit by the possession of the testator. And, indeed, possession is interrupted between the parties to the sale, but many authorities do not hold the same opinion with reference to heirs, as the right of succession is much more extensive than that of purchase. It is, however, more in accordance with a liberal interpretation of law that the same rule should be adopted concerning heirs which applies to purchasers.

5. Not only does the possession of the testator, which he had at the time of his death, benefit the heir, but also that which he had at any time whatsoever has this effect.

6. With reference to dowry also, if property has been either given or received as such, the time of possession will profit either the husband or the wife, as the case may be.

7. Where anyone has transferred property by a precarious title, the question arises whether he can profit by the time during which it was in possession of the person to whom it was transferred. I think that he who transfers it by a precarious title cannot profit by the time of possession, as long as the title continues to be precarious; but if he again acquires possession, and the precarious title is extinguished, he can profit by the possession during the time when the property was held by a precarious title.

8. In a certain case, it was asked if a manumitted slave has possession of property forming part of his peculium (his peculium not having been given to him) and his master desires to profit by the time it was held by the freedman, possession of the property having been surrendered, whether he can do so. It was decided that he should not be granted the benefit of the time of possession, because his conduct was clandestine and dishonest.

9. Where property has been restored to me by order of court, it has been decided that I am entitled to the benefit of the time during which it was held by my opponent.

10. It must, however, be remembered that a legatee is entitled to the benefit of the time when the property was in the hands of the testator. But let us see whether he will be benefited by the time that the property was in the possession of the heir. I think that, whether the legacy was bequeathed absolutely or conditionally, it should be held that the legatee can profit by the time that it was in the possession of the heir, before the condition was fulfilled, or the property, delivered. The time that it was in the possession of the testator will always profit the legatee, if the legacy or the trust is genuine.

11. Moreover, he to whom property is donated has a right to profit by the time it was possessed by the person who made the donation.

12. Times of possession are applicable to those who themselves have possession of what is their own; but no one will be entitled to this privilege unless he himself has been in possession.

13. Again, time of occupancy will be of no advantage where the possession is defective; possession, however, which is not defective, causes no injury.

Source: *The Civil Law*. Translated by S. P. Scott. Cincinnati: Central Trust Company, 1932.

Warfare

War serves as a central tool of political life in many cultures. Although certain groups, such as strict Buddhists, *Quakers,* and *Mennonites,* refrain from violence, all modern nations and most political units throughout time have maintained armies for the express purpose of maintaining political independence or acquiring additional political influence and hegemony. Even when other motives seem to generate warfare, the desire for political control frequently lies behind the violence. For example, although the First Crusade, proclaimed by Pope Urban II in 1095 (Document 15), ostensibly sought to establish peace in Europe and to protect the religion of Christianity, the

Crusade ultimately established European political control over Jerusalem and over key parts of the Middle East. The motives of the crusaders were undoubtedly mixed; they went to defend Christianity, but they also wanted to make potential profit. Similarly, although war in Mesoamerica served to capture prisoners for sacrifice (Document 21), a city-state's defeat also led frequently to its political subjugation. War in all these cultures provided a valuable tool of politico-economic policy.

Although the underlying purpose of war has remained remarkably similar across time and space, the practice and techniques of war differ considerably. The Mongols of the thirteenth century (Document 17), for example, developed extremely mobile horse-mounted archers whose speed and flexibility allowed them to strike at both tactical and strategic weak points while escaping counterattacks; European armies, by contrast, consisted largely of heavily armed, relatively slow-moving units, such as armored knights and pikemen. European accounts of battles, moreover, often stress the role of technology in strategic planning and tactical engagement. In the description of the siege of Jerusalem in Document 16, for example, the towers used to attack the city walls receive significant attention, and Díaz del Castillo describes the mobile defensive platforms employed by the Spanish against the *Aztecs* during the first battle for Tenochtitlan, modern-day Mexico City (Document 20). The immediate goals of combat could also be different. Whereas armies in late medieval Europe and Asia generally aimed to kill their opponents, Aztec warriors often sought to wound their opponents to catch them alive for later ritual sacrifice to the sun god. These different practices of war inevitably helped to tip the outcomes of individual engagements. European armies had great difficulty repulsing Mongol attacks, and the Aztecs found the Spanish, with their technological superiority and "shoot-to-kill" mentality, a difficult opponent.

Despite varying purposes and techniques, a universal outcome of war was human suffering. The toll of human casualties in the first Aztec–Spanish battle in Tenochtitlan so shocked both sides that the date has come to be called *la noche triste*, meaning "the sorrowful night." Raymond d'Aguiliers, recalling the slaughter of the Muslims who had fled to the Temple of Solomon, claims that the victorious crusading knights rode in a pool of blood that reached to the riders' knees. Even if we allow room for exaggeration, the slaughter must have been devastating (Document 20).

Conversely, however, this immense suffering also created glory, especially for the conquerors. In China, Ts'ao Sung, a Tang dynasty poet, criticized generals for gaining promotion, honor, and glory by slaughtering thousands and depriving ordinary civilians of material sustenance (Document 18). Raymond d'Aguiliers indicates that the capture of Jerusalem and the slaughter of the Muslims therein redounded to the glory of God. Bernal Díaz del Castillo describes the suffering of Spanish prisoners of wars, who were sacrificed to the Aztec gods, to demonstrate just how courageous, and presumably glorious, he himself was when he entered battle notwithstanding the potentially fearful consequences. The Japanese samurai Sanemori (Document 19) likewise gained glory for himself by entering into a combat situation from which he could not by any reasonable means escape alive. By choosing death in battle, by willfully undergoing a certain kind of suffering, the samurai gained a lasting fame. Suffering, either imposing it or enduring it, preceded glory in war.

15. Pope Urban II Proclaims the First Crusade

In the following important speech, Pope Urban II proclaims the First Crusade at the Council of Clermont in 1095. Several different versions of the speech survive, suggesting that each historian relied largely on memory and oral history rather than on an official document. In this version, given by Fulcher of Chartres, Urban sets forth two goals: (1) to stem the tide of internal violence in Europe and (2) to secure control of the Holy Lands. In his opening comments, Urban criticizes lax priests who do not protect their congregations and then exhorts everyone to keep peace and to refrain from theft and banditry. The pope reserves particular criticism for those who rob bishops, priests, nuns, and religious pilgrims. Because Urban held authority primarily over the Church and not the state, the punishment he recommends for these criminals is also Church-related: anathema, that is, exclusion from the Church.

Whereas the first part of the speech addresses internal violence, the second part examines violence that has come from outside the Christian community. The pope turns to address the continuing Muslim invasion of the Byzantine Empire (which he calls Romania), the eastern edge of medieval Christendom. Ever since the seventh-century A.D., Muslim armies had been forcefully expanding their territories, across Arabia and North Africa and into Spain and the Byzantine Empire. Urban calls on knights, who had been breaking the peace by fighting and plundering each other, to put their skills at the service of their fellow Christians by pushing back the Muslim armies. In effect, Urban seeks to channel the aggression of European knights away from internally destructive paths and toward external expansion and defense of Christian lands.

Like most medieval Christians, the pope had relatively little understanding of Islam as a religion; he states that Muslims worship devils, for example, which is, of course, untrue. Indeed, medieval Christianity and Islam shared many similar tenets. For example, as a reward for those answering his call, the pope offers an everlasting reward: the remission of all sins, and therefore the gaining of heaven, for all those who die while undertaking the crusade. The promise of heaven for those who die fighting mirrors the Muslim idea that those who die on jihad will go to heaven.

"Most beloved brethren, urged by necessity, I, Urban, by the permission of God chief bishop and prelate over the whole world, have come into these parts as an ambassador with a divine admonition to you, the servants of God. I hoped to find you as faithful and as zealous in the service of God as I had supposed you to be. But if there is in you any deformity or crookedness contrary to God's law, with divine help I will do my best to remove it. For God has put you as stewards over his family to minister to it. Happy indeed will you be if he finds you faithful in your stewardship. You are called shepherds; see that you do not act as hirelings. But be true shepherds, with your crooks always in your hands. Do not go to sleep, but guard on all sides the flock committed to you. For if through your carelessness or negligence a wolf carries away one of your sheep, you will surely lose the reward laid up for you with God. And after you have been bitterly scourged with remorse for your faults, you will be fiercely overwhelmed in hell, the abode of death. For according to the gospel you are the salt of the earth. But if you fall short in your duty, how, it may be asked, can it be salted? O how great the need of salting! It is indeed necessary for you to correct with the salt of wisdom this foolish people which is so devoted to the pleasures of this world, lest the Lord, when He may wish to speak to them, find them putrefied by their sins unsalted and stinking. For if He shall find worms, that is, sins, in them, because you have been negligent in your duty, He will command them as worthless to be thrown into the abyss of unclean things. And because you cannot restore to Him His great loss, He will surely condemn you and drive you from His loving presence. But the man who applies this salt should be prudent, provident, modest, learned, peaceable, watchful, pious, just, equitable, and pure. For how can the ignorant teach others? How can the licentious make others modest? And how can the impure make others pure? If anyone hates peace, how can he make others peaceable? Or if anyone has soiled his hands with baseness, how can he cleanse the impurities of another? We read also that if the blind lead the blind, both will fall into the ditch. But first correct yourselves, in order that, free from blame, you may be able to correct those who are subject to you. If you wish to be the friends of God, gladly do the things which you know will please Him. You must especially let all matters that pertain to the church be controlled by the law of the church. And be careful that simony does not take root among you, lest both those who buy and those who sell be beaten with the scourges of the Lord through narrow streets and driven into the place of destruction and confusion. Keep the church and the clergy in all its grades entirely free from the secular power. See that the tithes that belong to God are faithfully paid from all the produce of the land; let them not be sold or withheld. If anyone seizes a bishop let him be treated as an outlaw. If anyone seizes or robs monks, or clergymen, or nuns, or their servants, or pilgrims, or merchants, let him be anathema. Let robbers and incendiaries and all their accomplices be expelled from the church and anathematized. If a man who does not give a part of his goods as alms is punished with the damnation of hell, how should he be punished who robs another of his goods? For thus it happened to the rich man in the gospel; he was not punished because he had stolen the goods of another, but because he had not used well the things which were his.

"You have seen for a long time the great disorder in the world caused by these crimes. It is so bad in some of your provinces, I am told, and you are so weak in the administration of justice, that one can hardly go along the road by day or night without being attacked by robbers; and whether at home or abroad one is in danger of being despoiled either by force or fraud. Therefore it is necessary to re-enact the truce, as it is commonly called, which was proclaimed a long time ago by our holy fathers. I exhort and demand that you each try hard to have the truce kept in your diocese. And if anyone shall be led by his cupidity or arrogance to break this truce, by the authority of God and with the sanction of this council he shall be anathematized."

After these and various other matters had been attended to, all who were present, clergy and people, gave thanks to God and agreed to the pope's proposition. They all faithfully promised to keep the decrees. Then the pope said that in another part of the world Christianity was suffering from a state of affairs that was worse than the one just mentioned. He continued:

"Although, O sons of God, you have promised more firmly than ever to keep the peace among yourselves and to preserve the rights of the church, there remains still an important work for you to do. Freshly quickened by the divine correction, you must apply the strength of your righteousness to another matter which concerns you as well as God. For your brethren who live in the east are in urgent need of your help, and you must hasten to give them the aid which has often been promised to them. For, as most of you have heard, the Turks and Arabs have attacked them and have conquered the territory of Romania as far west as the shore of the Mediterranean and the Hellespont, which is called the Arm of St. George. They have occupied more and more of the lands of those Christians, and have overcome them in seven battles. They have killed and captured many, and have destroyed the churches and devastated the empire. If you permit them to continue thus for awhile with impunity, the faithful of God will be much more widely attacked by them. On this account I, or rather the Lord, beseech you as Christ's heralds to publish this everywhere and to persuade all people of whatever rank, foot-soldiers and knights, poor and rich, to carry aid promptly to those Christians and to destroy that vile race from the lands of our friends. I say this to those who are present, it's meant also for those who are absent. Moreover, Christ commands it.

"All who die by the way, whether by land or by sea, or in battle against the pagans, shall have immediate remission of sins. This I grant them through the power of God with which I am invested. O what a disgrace if such a despised and base race, which worships demons, should conquer a people which has the faith of omnipotent God and is made glorious with the name of Christ! With what reproaches will the Lord overwhelm us if you do not aid those who, with us, profess the Christian religion! Let those who have been accustomed unjustly to wage private warfare against the faithful now go against the infidels and end with victory this war which should have been begun long ago. Let those who for a long time have been robbers, now become knights. Let those who have been fighting against their brothers and relatives now fight in a proper way against the barbarians. Let those who have been serving as mercenaries for small pay now obtain the eternal reward. Let those who have been wearing themselves out in both body and soul now work for a double honor. Behold! On this side will be the sorrowful and poor, on that, the rich; on this side, the enemies of the Lord, on that, his friends. Let those who go not put off the journey, but rent their lands and collect money for their expenses; and as soon as winter is over and spring comes, let hem eagerly set out on the way with God as their guide."

Source: Bongars. *Gesta Dei per Francos*, vol. 1, pp. 382 f. Translated in *A Source Book for Medieval History*, ed. Oliver J. Thatcher and Edgar Holmes McNeal. New York: Scribners, 1905, pp. 513–17.

16. Crusades: The Fall of Jerusalem, 1099

Several crusaders wrote memoirs of their adventures. The following account, written by Raymond d'Aguiliers, gives an eyewitness account of the crowning victory of the First Crusade: the 1099 crusader capture of Jerusalem, a city of major importance for Judaism, Christianity, and Islam.

This document offers valuable insight into both the practical and the psychological dimensions of medieval warfare. With regard to the practical, Raymond highlights the role of technology in determining victory. The Frankish crusaders constructed elaborate siege machines, such as tall towers with bridges that can be swung down, to overcome the walls defending the city. Similarly, the use of specially constructed long-burning flaming arrows played a crucial role in driving back the defenders from the wall. These devices were made even more potent by a clever strategy that involved a surprise nighttime redeployment of the war machines to a section of the walls that was less protected.

Despite apparent technological and strategic superiority, the ultimate outcome of the battle still depended largely on psychology. As Raymond's account makes clear, the crusaders held a strong belief that God was on their side, and this faith gave them confidence and courage. At the crucial juncture of the battle, moreover, just as the crusaders were beginning to be discouraged, a mysterious knight waving them forward from the Mount of Olives renewed their enthusiasm and rallied the troops, driving them onward to victory.

Raymond d'Aguiliers also gives an accurate account of the usual end awaiting the inhabitants of a conquered city: random death and destruction. Although both modern and medieval fiction like to portray knightly combat as genteel and courteous, in reality, medieval warfare was just as brutal as modern warfare. In this account, Raymond notes that women were not spared and that many people suffered torture, decapitation, or dismemberment. As Raymond states, "the city was filled with corpses and blood."

Later, all of our people went to the Sepulchre of our Lord rejoicing and weeping for joy, and they rendered up the offering that they owed. In the morning, some of our men cautiously ascended to the roof of the Temple and attacked the Saracens both men and women, beheading them with naked swords; the remainder sought death by jumping down into the temple. When Tancred heard of this, he was filled with anger.

The Duke and the Counts of Normandy and Flanders placed Gaston of Beert in charge of the workmen who constructed machines. They built mantlets and towers with which to attack the wall. The direction of this work was assigned to Gaston by the princes because he was a most noble lord, respected by all for his skill and reputation. He very cleverly hastened matters by dividing the work. The princes busied themselves with obtaining the material, while Gaston supervised the construction. Likewise, Count Raymond made William Ricau superintendent of the work on Mount Zion and placed the Bishop of Albara in charge of the Saracens and others who brought in the timber. The Count's men had taken many Saracen castles and villages and forced the Saracens to work, as though they were their serfs. Thus for the construction of machines at Jerusalem fifty or sixty men carried on their shoulders a great beam that could not have been dragged by four pair of oxen. What more shall I say? All worked with a singleness of purpose, no one was slothful, and no hands were idle. All worked without wages, except the artisans, who were paid from a collection taken from the people. However, Count Raymond paid his workmen from his own treasury. Surely the hand of the Lord was with us and aided those who were working!

When our efforts were ended and the machines completed, the princes held a council and announced: "Let all prepare themselves for a battle on Thursday; in the meantime, let us pray, fast, and give alms. Hand over your animals and your boys to the artisans and carpenters, so that they may bring in beams, poles, stakes, and branches to make mantlets. Two knights should make one mantlet and one scaling ladder. Do not hesitate to work for the Lord, for your labors will soon be ended." This was willingly done by all. Then it was decided what part of the city each leader should attack and where his machines should be located.

Meanwhile, the Saracens in the city, noting the great number of machines that we had constructed, strengthened the weaker parts of the wall, so that it seemed that they could be taken only by the most desperate efforts. Because the Saracens had made so many and such strong fortifications to oppose our machines, the Duke, the Count of Flanders, and the Count of Normandy spent the night before the day set for the attack moving their machines, mantlets, and platforms to that side of the city which is between the church of St. Stephen and the valley of Josaphat. You who read this must not think that this was a light undertaking, for the machines were carried in parts almost a mile to the place where they were to be set up. When morning came and the Saracens saw that all the machinery and tents had been moved during the night, they were amazed. Not only the Saracens were astonished, but our people as well, for they recognized that the hand of the Lord was with us. The change was made because the new point chosen for attack was more level, and thus suitable for moving the machines up to the walls, which cannot be done unless the ground is level; and also because that part of the city seemed to be weaker having remained unfortified, as it was some distance from our camp. This part of the city is on the north.

Count Raymond and his men worked equally hard on Mount Zion, but they had much assistance from William, and the Genoese sailors, who, although they had lost their ships at Joppa, as we have already related, had been able, nevertheless, to save ropes, mallets, spikes, axes, and hatchets, which were very necessary to us. But why delay the story? The appointed day arrived and the attack began. However, I want to say this first, that, according to our estimate and that of many others, there were sixty thousand fighting men within the city, not counting the women and those unable to bear arms, and there were not many of these. At the most we did not have more than twelve thousand able to bear arms, for there were many poor people and many sick. There were twelve or thirteen hundred knights in our army, as I reckon it, not more. I say this that you may realize that nothing, whether great or small, which is undertaken in the name of the Lord can fail, as the following pages show.

Our men began to undermine the towers and walls. From every side stones were hurled from the *tormenti* and the *petrahae*, and so many arrows that they fell like hail. The servants of God bore this patiently, sustained by the premises of their faith, whether they should be killed or should presently prevail over their enemies. The battle showed no indication of victory, but when the machines were drawn nearer to the walls, they hurled not only stones and arrows, but also burning wood and straw. The wood was dipped in pitch, wax, and sulphur; then straw and tow were fastened on by an iron band, and, when lighted, these firebrands were shot from the machines. They were bound together by an iron band, I say, so that wherever they fell, the whole mass held together and continued to burn. Such missiles, burning as they shot upward, could not be resisted by swords or by high walls; it was not even possible for the defenders to find safety down behind the walls. Thus the fight continued from the rising to the setting sun in such splendid fashion that it is difficult to believe anything more glorious was ever done. Then we called on Almighty God, our Leader and Guide, confident in His mercy. Night brought fear to both sides. The Saracens feared that we would take the city during the night or on the next day for the outer works were broken through and the ditch was filled so that it was possible to make an entrance through the wall very quickly. On our part, we feared only that the Saracens would set fire to the machines that were moved close to the walls, and thus improve their situation. So on both sides it was a night of watchfulness, labor, and sleepless caution: on one side, most certain hope, on the other doubtful fear. We gladly labored to capture the city for the glory of God, they less willingly strove to resist our efforts for the sake of the laws of Mohammed. It is hard to believe how great were the efforts made on both sides during the night.

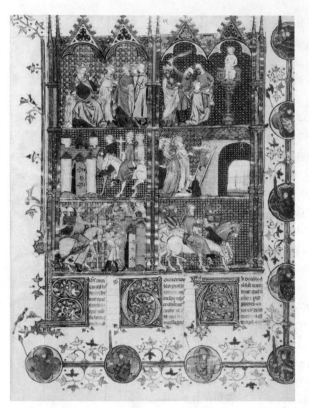

A fourteenth-century depiction of the fall of Jerusalem to the crusaders during the First Crusade, 1096–1099. © 2008 Jupiterimages Corporation.

When the morning came, our men eagerly rushed to the walls and dragged the machines forward, but the Saracens had constructed so many machines that for each one of ours they now had nine or ten. Thus they greatly interfered with our efforts. This was the ninth day, on which the priest had said that we would capture the city. But why do I delay so long? Our machines were now shaken apart by the blows of many stones, and our men lagged because they were very weary. However, there remained the mercy of the Lord which is never overcome nor conquered, but is always a source of support in times of adversity. One incident must not be omitted. Two women tried to bewitch one of the hurling machines, but a stone struck and crushed them, as well as three slaves, so that their lives were extinguished and the evil incantations averted.

By noon our men were greatly discouraged. They were weary and at the end of their resources. There were still many of the enemy opposing each one of our men; the walls were very high and strong, and the great resources and skill that the enemy exhibited in repairing their defences seemed too great for us to overcome. But, while we hesitated, irresolute, and the enemy exulted in our discomfiture, the healing mercy of God inspired us and turned our sorrow into joy, for the Lord did not forsake us. While a council was being held to decide whether or not our machines should be withdrawn, for some were burned and the rest badly shaken to pieces, a knight on the Mount of Olives began to wave his shield to those who were with the Count and others, signalling them to advance. Who this knight was we have been unable to find out. At this signal our men began to take heart, and some began to batter down the wall, while others began to ascend by means of scaling ladders and ropes. Our archers shot burning firebrands, and in this way checked the attack that the Saracens were making upon the wooden towers of the Duke and the two Counts. These firebrands, moreover, were wrapped in cotton. This shower of fire drove the defenders from the walls. Then the Count quickly released the long drawbridge which had protected the side of the wooden tower next to the wall, and it swung down from the top, being fastened to the middle of the tower, making a bridge over which the men began to enter Jerusalem bravely and fearlessly. Among those who entered first were Tancred and the Duke of Lorraine, and the amount of blood that they shed on that day is incredible. All ascended after them, and the Saracens now began to suffer.

Strange to relate, however, at this very time when the city was practically captured by the Franks, the Saracens were still fighting on the other side, where the Count was attacking the wall as though the city should never be captured. But now that our men had possession of the walls and towers, wonderful sights were to be seen. Some of our men (and this was more merciful) cut off the heads of their enemies; others shot them with arrows, so that they fell from the towers; others tortured them longer by casting them into the flames. Piles of heads, hands, and feet were to be seen in the streets of the city. It was necessary to pick one's way over the bodies of men and horses. But these were small matters compared to what happened at the Temple of Solomon, a place where religious services are ordinarily chanted. What happened there? If I tell the truth, it will exceed your powers of belief. So let it suffice to say this much, at least, that in the Temple and porch of Solomon, men rode in blood up to their knees and bridle reins. Indeed, it was a just and splendid judgment of God that this place should be filled with the blood of the unbelievers, since it had suffered so long from their blasphemies. The city was filled with corpses and blood. Some of the enemy took refuge in the Tower of David, and, petitioning Count Raymond for protection, surrendered the Tower into his hands.

Now that the city was taken, it was well worth all our previous labors and hardships to see the devotion of the pilgrims at the Holy Sepulchre. How they rejoiced and exulted and sang a new song to the Lord! For their hearts offered prayers of praise to God, victorious and triumphant, which cannot be told in words. A new day, new joy, new and perpetual gladness, the consummation of our labor and devotion, drew forth from all new words and new songs. This day, I say, will be famous in all future ages, for it turned our labors and sorrows into joy and exultation; this day, I say, marks the justification of all Christianity, the humiliation of paganism, and the renewal of our faith. "This is the day which the Lord hath made, let us rejoice and be glad in it," for on this day the Lord revealed Himself to His people and blessed them.

On this day, the Ides of July, Lord Adhemar, Bishop of Puy, was seen in the city by many people. Many also testified that he was the first to scale the wall, and that he summoned the knights and people to follow him. On this day, moreover, the apostles were cast forth from Jerusalem and scattered over the whole world. On this same day, the children of the apostles regained the city and fatherland for God and the fathers. This day, the Ides of July, shall be celebrated to the praise and glory of the name of God, who, answering the prayers of His Church, gave in trust and benediction to His children the city and fatherland which He had promised to the fathers. On this day we chanted the Office of the Resurrection, since on that day He, who by His virtue arose from the dead, revived us through His grace. So much is to be said of this.

Source: Raymond d'Aguiliers. *Historia Francorum qui Ceperint Iherusalem.* In *The First Crusade: The Accounts of Eyewitnesses and Participants.* Ed. by August C. Krey. Princeton, NJ: Princeton University Press, 1921, pp. 257–62.

17. Marco Polo on Mongol Warriors in the Thirteenth Century

Although other adventurers had reached China before Marco Polo, his literary account of his voyages became the first widely read work about Oriental peoples and cultures. The Mongols, or the Tartars as they are called in the following extract, were famous warriors who possessed a kingdom stretching from eastern Europe to China. According to his account, Marco Polo visited and befriended the Great Khan, the ruler of the Mongol empire. Although Marco Polo embellished many of his accounts with fictional details or myths that he had heard from other travelers, his description of Mongol warriors appears to be accurate because it matches the descriptions found in many other sources.

Like European knights, the Mongol warriors excelled in horsemanship; unlike the Europeans, however, who weighed themselves down with heavy armor, the Mongols prized speed and tactics over heavy armor and weapons. As a result, Mongol armies, armed with bows and light leather armor, frequently outmaneuvered European armies, striking at the weakest defenses and retreating before any counterattack could arrive. Tensions within the Mongol empire, rather than military defeat, kept the Mongols from creating an empire that included all of Europe and Asia.

CHAPTER LIV: CONCERNING THE TARTAR CUSTOMS OF WAR

All their harness of war is excellent and costly. Their arms are bows and arrows, sword and mace; but above all the bow, for they are capital archers, indeed the best that are known. On their backs they wear armor of cuirbouly, prepared from buffalo and other hides, which is very strong. They are excellent soldiers, and passing valiant in battle. They are also more capable of hardships than other nations; for many a time, if need be, they will go for a month without any supply of food, living only on the milk of their mares and on such game as their bows may win them. Their horses also will subsist entirely on the grass of the plains, so that there is no need to carry store of barley or straw or oats; and they are very docile to their riders. These, in case of need, will abide on horseback the livelong night, armed at all points, while the horse will be continually grazing.

Of all troops in the world these are they which endure the greatest hardship and fatigue, and which cost the least; and they are the best of all for making wide conquests of country. And this you will perceive from what you have heard and shall hear in this book; and (as a fact) there can be no manner of doubt that now they are the masters of the biggest half of the world. Their troops are admirably ordered in the manner that I shall now relate.

You see, when a Tartar prince goes forth to war, he takes with him, say, 100,000 horse. Well, he appoints an officer to every ten men, one to every hundred, one to every thousand, and one to every ten thousand, so that his own orders have to be given to ten persons only, and each of these ten persons has to pass the orders only to another ten, and so on; no one having to give orders to more than ten. And every one in turn is responsible only to the officer immediately over him; and the discipline and order that comes of this method is marvellous, for they are a people very obedient to their chiefs. Further, they call the corps of 100,000 men a Tuc; that of 10,000 they call a Toman; the hundred Guz. And when the army is on the march they have always 200 horsemen, very well mounted, who are sent a distance of two marches in advance to reconnoitre, and

Fourteenth-century depiction of the departure of Marco Polo and his fleet from Venice. Note the prominent canal and Piazza San Marco—Venice's most important neighborhood. © 2008 Jupiterimages Corporation.

these always keep ahead. They have a similar party detached in the rear, and on either flank, so that there is a good look-out kept on all sides against a surprise. When they are going on a distant expedition they take no gear with them except two leather bottles for milk; a little earthenware pot to cook their meat in; and a little tent to shelter them from rain. And in case of great urgency they will ride ten days on end without lighting a fire or taking a meal. On such an occasion they will sustain themselves on the blood of their horses, opening a vein and letting the blood jet into their mouths, drinking till they have had enough, and then staunching it.

They also have milk dried into a kind of paste to carry with them; and when they need food they put this in water, and beat it up till it dissolves, and then drink it. It is prepared in this way; they boil the milk, and when the rich part floats on the top they skim it into another vessel, and of that they make butter; for the milk will not become solid till this is removed. Then they put the milk in the sun to dry. And when they go on an expedition, every man takes some ten pounds of this dried milk with him. And of a morning he will take a half pound of it and put it in his leather bottle, with as much water as he pleases. So, as he rides along, the milk-paste and the water in the bottle get well churned together into a kind of pap, and that makes his dinner.

When they come to an engagement with the enemy, they will gain the victory in this fashion. They never let themselves get into a regular medley, but keep perpetually riding round and shooting into the enemy. And as they do not count it any

Cavalry attack of Seljuk army shows arms and armour of the Mongols, from *Compendium of Chronicles, or World History*, by Rashid al-Din, 1247–1318, minister to the Mongol Ilkhanid dynasty, Tabriz, Iran. The Art Archive/Edinburgh University Library.

shame to run away in battle, they will sometimes pretend to do so, and in running away they turn in the saddle and shoot hard and strong at the foe, and in this way make great havoc. Their horses are trained so perfectly that they will double hither and thither, just like a dog, in a way that is quite astonishing. Thus they fight to as good purpose in running away as if they stood and faced the enemy, because of the vast volleys of arrows that they shoot in this way, turning round upon their pursuers, who are fancying that they have won the battle. But when the Tartars see that they have killed and wounded a good many horses and men, they wheel round bodily, and return to the charge in perfect order and with loud cries; and in a very short time the enemy are routed. In truth they are stout and valiant soldiers, and inured to war. And you perceive that it is just when the enemy sees them run, and imagines that he has gained the battle, that he has in reality lost it; for the Tartars wheel round in a moment when they judge the right time has come. And after this fashion they have won many a fight.

All this that I have been telling you is true of the manners and customs of the genuine Tartars. But I must add also that in these days they are greatly degenerated; for those who are settled in China have taken up the practices of the idolaters of the country, and have abandoned their own institutions; whilst those who have settled in the Middle East have adopted the customs of the Saracens.

Source: Polo, Marco, and Rustichello of Pisa. *The Book of Ser Marco Polo the Venetian Concerning the Kingdoms and Marvels of the East.* Edited by Henry Yule. Vol. 1. London: John Murray, 1903, pp. 260–63. Translation slightly modified by Lawrence Morris.

18. Opposition to War in China

This moving poem by the late Tang dynasty poet Ts'ao Sung (fl. A.D. 870–920) poignantly contrasts two, perhaps diametrically opposed, aspects of warfare: glory and suffering. On the one hand, warfare had established the political dominance and economic clout of the Tang dynasty in the seventh and eighth centuries A.D., establishing a kingdom that stretched from modern-day Japan and Korea to central Asia; on the other hand, war, especially internal wars, often destroyed the lives of ordinary civilians. Ts'ao Sung, for example, lived to see the collapse of the Tang dynasty because of pressure from independent military governors, especially Zhu Wen, who overthrew the government and seized the emperorship for himself in 907. However, Zhu Wen was himself overthrown and killed by his own son in 923.

The poem that follows reflects on how the ruthless actions of warlords such as Zhu Wen caused suffering to the ordinary people while gaining power and glory for the warlords. Ts'ao Sung calls attention especially to the serious societal effects of warfare in the first stanza: turning cultivated fields into battlefields destroys the crops, with the resulting privation, suffering, and possible starvation of the local civilians. The second stanza makes the point more bluntly: a general's glory depends on the deaths of thousands.

The hills and rivers of the lowland country
You have made your battle-ground.
How do you suppose the people who live there

Will procure firewood and hay?
Do not let me hear you talking together
About titles and promotions;
For a single general's reputation
Is made out of ten thousand corpses.

Source: *A Hundred and Seventy Chinese Poems.* Trans. by Arthur Waley. New York: Knopf, 1919, p. 150.

19. Samurai Hairstyles

A samurai was a member of the warrior caste of medieval Japanese society. Theoretically, the warriors followed a strict code of honor, called bushido, which governed their conduct, but in reality the ideals of loyalty and personal integrity advocated by bushido frequently went unheeded in favor of personal advantage. Nevertheless, aspects of bushido could and did influence the conduct of individual warriors.

In the narrative reproduced here, taken from a narrative history called Genpei Seisuiki written during the Kamakura era (A.D. 1185–1333), one of the core concepts of bushido—glory, or meiyo—informs the behavior of a samurai advanced in years. The samurai, Sanemori by name, reflects on the fact that his years of glory are over now that he has turned 70. At the same time, he laments that younger warriors criticize older warriors no matter what their seniors do. If the older warrior attacks, he is viewed as foolhardy, but if he retreats, he is viewed as cowardly. Younger warriors might even refuse to fight an older warrior. To avoid such age discrimination, Sanemori dyes his gray hairs dark and advances into a suicidal combat, attacking two warriors by himself. According to Genpei Seisuiki, when Sanemori was inevitably killed and his extraordinary commitment to achieving continual glory in battle revealed, he gained universal respect. Sanemori had completed his mission.

WHY SANEMORI DYED HIS HAIR

A Samurai in the service of the Heike lived in the land of Musashi and was called Nagai no Saito Betto Sanemori. One day, he reflected, "I am over 70 years old; I cannot expect more glory. I cannot escape from death. It doesn't matter where I die—it's all the same." So he put on his clothing of red silk and his armor, and placed on his shoulder 18 feathers from a falcon's tail, and he headed out into combat on his own, facing death. In the army of Kiso, there was a man named Tezuka no Taro Mitsumori, who lived in the land of Sinano. When he saw Sanemori, he drew close to him. Likewise, Sanemori, seeing Tezuka, strode towards him. Tezuka said, "Who are you, that you fight on your own? Are you a general or a regular samurai? You are provoking me. Say your name! Me, I am called Tezuka no Taro Kanazashi no Mitsumori, from the town of Suwa, in the land of Shinano. I am a good opponent. Tell me your name and let's begin!" They urged their horses together. "I have heard of you," said Sanemori. "I will not reveal my name, however, for various reasons, but I have no ill-feeling towards you. Strike off my head and show it to the Ghennji—you will be well rewarded. Do not cast my head into the river; the lord Kiso should recognize me. I am fighting on my own because I have renounced life. It is pleasant to fight any enemy! Come, Tezuka!" Saying this, he threw away his bow and advanced on Tezuka. One of Tezuka's samurai, in order to protect him, threw himself in between them. Sanemori seized him and said, "You are a servant of Tezuka, I cannot show you mercy!" Sanemori took hold of his shoulder-piece, seized the bridle, dragged him from his horse, and threw him down to the ground, so that the feet of this servant were plunged deep into the ground. When Tezuka saw this, in order to save the life of his servant, he seized the shoulder-piece of his enemy, gave a shout, and descended from his horse. Sanemori, grabbing Tezuka's samurai, drew his own sword and chopped off the samurai's head. At the same time, Tezuka, keeping hold of Sanemori's right shoulder-piece, drove his sword through Sanemori all the way to the guard. He then cut off his head.

Tezuka, carrying the head of his enemy, came before the lord Kiso and said, "Mitsu-mori has won the head of a courageous warrior! When I asked him to tell me his name, he replied, 'I have reasons for not doing so. The lord Kiso will recognize me.' And he did not say his name. His embroidered silk, though, indicated that he was a samurai. I wondered if he was a general, but he did not have any soldiers. I wondered if he was a man from the West, but he had the accent of Tokaido. When I wondered if he were young, I saw that the wrinkles in his face suggested that he was more than 70. When I considered that he might be an old man, I realized that his black hair and beard showed him to be in full vigor. Whose head, then, is this?" Kiso exclaimed: "Oh, no! This must be Saito Betto of Musashi. Nevertheless, since I was young when I knew him, he ought to be covered

by white hair by now. How can it be that his hair and beard are still black? Nevertheless, the rest of his face resembles him perfectly. It is very strange. Higutchi is a long-time friend of his; he should be able to recognize him." He then sent for Higutchi. Higutchi took the head and glanced at it, and began to cry out, "Oh, no! What a sad thing! It is Sanemori. But why this black hair and beard? Yes, I remember. Sanemori often said, 'Old men who take the bow and arrows off to combat ought to dye their hair black. If in peacetime the young mock white hair, even more do they do so in time of war. If an old man attacks, they say that he lacks wisdom; if he retreats, they insult him by calling him a coward. One doesn't dare compete with these young people. As regards the enemy, they think the old are just nothings. The white hairs of old age are a true sorrow. The lord Shunzei wrote a poem about it:

Who does not have the young vegetables
That grow in the valley
Gathers years
In vain;
My cuffs are all wet!
Men should leave behind some words so that they may be remembered in the future.' Some, of course, dye their hair black."

A nineteenth-century Ukiyo-e print illustration showing Ronin (a freelance Samurai), sword in hand, moving toward a long-handled sword. Courtesy of the Library of Congress.

Having said this, since they had been close friends for some years, Higutchi Jiro Kanemitsu asked for some water and washed the head, which became clearly the head of an old man covered with white hair. There was no more doubt that it was Sanemori. Kioyu, from China, made himself famous in later times by purifying his ears in a river; Sanemori, from Japan, captured the respect of all by dying his hair black for the field of battle.

Source: *Genpei Seisuiki.* In *Anthologie de la littérateur japonaise des origins au XXe siècle.* Ed. by Michel Revon. Paris: Delagrave, 1919, pp. 211–44. Translated and modified by Lawrence Morris.

20. La Noche Triste: *A Battle in Mexico City*

La Noche Triste, *Spanish for "the sorrowful night," refers to the escape of Hernán Cortés's conquistador army from Tenochtitlan (modern-day Mexico City) on the night of July 1, 1520, during the first battle between Spanish forces and Aztec warriors in the capital of the Aztec empire. The Spaniards and their Native American allies had arrived as honored guests of the Aztec emperor Moctezuma in November 1518, but relations between the Aztecs and their guests quickly soured when Cortés took Moctezuma as an unofficial hostage. Matters became much worse when Pedro de Alvarado slaughtered numerous Aztec nobles in the main temple during Cortés's absence. When Cortés returned to Tenochtitlan, open warfare erupted, resulting in the death of Moctezuma at the hands of either the Spanish or the Aztecs themselves. Cortés's men, heavily outnumbered, attempted to flee the city, taking with them as much gold and booty as they could. Hundreds of Spanish and thousands of Native Americans were killed. Because of the large death toll on both sides, July 1 is commemorated as La Noche Triste in Mexico.*

The following account of the battle comes from the pen of Bernal Díaz del Castillo (c. 1492–1583), a conquistador who served with Cortés and fought during La Noche Triste. Although Díaz del Castillo was an eyewitness of the events, he did not begin to write his history until almost 50 years after the events occurred, so we may question the accuracy of some of the smaller details in the account, although the overall picture is confirmed by other surviving accounts. The account highlights several interesting aspects of the conflict. First, Díaz del Castillo highlights the Spanish reliance on technology and their attempts to gain technological superiority. The Spanish metal sword and the musket, combined with the Spaniards' body armor, gave the Spanish both more destructive force and more protection in comparison with the Native American warriors. As the passage recounts, the Spanish attempted to further these advantages by building moveable bulwarks to provide cover and firing positions for up to 25 men each.

Second, the choice of target—the main temple in Tenochtitlan—demonstrates the role of strategy in the Spanish campaign. In sixteenth-century Mesoamerican culture, temples served as the symbolic heart of a city and its people. Aztec paintings, for example, record a victory over a neighboring people by showing the enemy's temple broken and in flames. The Spanish attack on the temple of Tenochtitlan, the Aztec capital, therefore was an attack on the very heart of the Aztec empire. The symbolic importance of the target demonstrates the understanding the Spanish conquistadors had of Mesoamerican culture and also explains the fierce resistance that the conquistadors met there. Generally outnumbered, the Spanish conquistadors concentrated on strategically important targets, such as Moctezuma or the temple, instead of attempting to control the whole city or territory.

Díaz's account also frequently highlights how the unique geography of Tenochtitlan affected the battle. Much of the city consisted of narrow avenues built up out of the water of

Lake Texcoco and separated by canals. This city plan inhibited the usual European tactics of cavalry charges and burning buildings, and the street system funneled forces into narrow bottlenecks. The failure of the usual tactics led to widespread panic among the fleeing Spanish forces and the complete breakdown of united action. In the situation of each man for himself, Cortés and other leaders of the campaign fled on horseback, leaving behind large bodies of their own troops. Although Díaz records criticism of this apparently cowardly action, he nevertheless defends this abandonment by claiming that nothing could have saved the victims and that the entire army would have been slaughtered if they had attempted to stay together. Finally, Díaz records how the soldiers split their acquired treasure among themselves. This scene reminds us of a central motive for the conquest of Mexico and for European exploration and settlement in the Americas in general: material profit.

On this day we lost ten or twelve soldiers, and all of us who came back were severely wounded. From the period of our return we were occupied in making preparation for a general sally on the next day but one, with four military machines constructed of very strong timber, in the form of towers, and each capable of containing twenty five men under cover, with port holes for the artillery and also for the musquetiers and crossbowmen. This work occupied us for the space of one day, except that we were obliged likewise to repair the breaches made in our walls, and resist those who attempted to scale them in twenty different places at the same time. They continued their reviling language, saying that the voracious animals of their temples had now been kept two days fasting, in order to devour us at the period which was speedily approaching, when they were to sacrifice us to their gods; that our allies were to be put up in cages to fatten; and that they would soon repossess our ill acquired treasure. At other times they plaintively called to us to give them their king, and during the night we were constantly annoyed by showers of arrows, which they accompanied by shouts and whistlings.

At day break on the ensuing morning, after recommending ourselves to God, we sallied out with our turrets, which as well as I recollect were called *burros* or *mantas*, in other places where I have seen them, with some of our musquetry and cross-bows in front, and our cavalry occasionally charging. The enemy this day showed themselves more determined than ever, and we were equally resolved to force our way to the great temple, although it should cost the life of every man of us; we therefore advanced with our turrets in that direction. I will not detail the desperate battle which we had with the enemy in a very strong house, nor how their arrows wounded our horses, notwithstanding their armour, and if at any time the horsemen attempted to pursue the Mexicans, the latter threw themselves into the canals, and others sallied out upon our people and massacred them with large lances.

As to setting fire to the buildings, or tearing them down, it was utterly in vain to attempt; they all stood in the water, and only communicating by draw bridges, it was too dangerous to attempt to reach them by swimming, for they showered stones from their slings, and masses of cut stone taken from the buildings, upon our heads, from the terraces of the houses. Whenever we attempted to set fire to a house, it was an entire day before it took effect, and when it did, the flames could not spread to others, as they were separated from it by the water, and also because the roofs of them were terraced.

We at length arrived at the great temple, and immediately and instantly above four thousand Mexicans rushed up into it, without including in that number other bodies who occupied it before, and defended it against us with lances, stones, and darts. They thus prevented our ascending for some time, neither turrets, nor musquetry, nor cavalry availing, for although the latter body several times attempted to charge, the stone pavement of the courts of the temple was so smooth that the horses could not keep their feet, and fell. From the steps of the great temple they opposed us in front, and we were attacked by such numbers on both sides, that although our guns swept off ten or fifteen of them at each discharge, and that in each attack of our infantry we killed many with our swords, their numbers were such that we could not make any effectual impression, or ascend the steps. We were then forced to abandon our turrets, which the enemy had destroyed, and with great concert, making an effort without them, we forced our way up. Here Cortes shewed himself the man that he really was. What a desperate engagement we then had! Every man of us was covered with blood, and above forty dead upon the spot. It was God's will that we should at length reach the place where we had put up the image of our Lady, but when we came there it was not to be found, and it seems that Montezuma [i.e. Moctezuma], actuated either by fear or by devotion, had caused it to be removed. We set fire to the building, and burned a part of the temple of the gods Huitzilopochtli and Tezcatepuco. Here our Tlascalan allies served us essentially. While thus engaged, some setting the temple on fire, others fighting, above three thousand noble Mexicans with their priests were about us, and attacking us, drove us down six and even ten of the steps, while others who were in the corridors, or within the side the railings and concavities of the great temple, shot such clouds of arrows at us that we could not maintain our ground, when thus attacked from every part. We therefore began our retreat, every man of us being wounded, and forty six left dead upon the spot. We were pursued with a violence and desperation which is not in my power to describe, nor in that of any one to form an idea of who did not see it. During all this time also other bodies of the Mexicans had been continually attacking our quarters, and endeavoring to set fire to them. In this battle, we made prisoners two of the principal priests. I have often seen this engagement represented in the paintings of the natives, both of Mexico and Tlascala, and our ascent into the great temple. In these our party is represented with many dead, and all wounded. The setting fire to the temple when so many warriors were defending it in the corridors, railings, and concavities, and other bodies of them on the plain ground, and filling the courts, and on the sides, and our turrets demolished, is considered by them as a most heroic action.

With great difficulty we reached our quarters, which we found the enemy almost in possession of, as they had beaten down a part of the walls; but they desisted in a great measure from their attacks on our arrival, still throwing in upon us however showers of arrows, darts, and stones. The night was employed by us in repairing the breaches, in dressing our wounds, burying our dead, and consulting upon our future measures. No gleam of hope could be now rationally formed by us, and we were utterly sunk in despair. Those who had come with Narvaez showered maledictions upon Cortes, nor did they forget Velasquez by whom they had been induced to quit their comfortable and peaceable habitations in the island of Cuba. It was determined to try if we could not procure from the enemy a cessation of hostilities, on condition of our quitting the city; but at day break they assembled round our quarters and attacked them with greater fury than ever, nor could our fire arms repel them, although they did considerable execution.

Meso-American warriors. Each people-group and each rank of warrior had a distinctive costume. Feather-shields, as shown here, were prized Aztec artistic works, as well as defensive tools. © 2008 Jupiterimages Corporation.

[Omitted here is a passage detailing the death of Moctezuma when he was sent to try to broker a peace treaty.]

Orders were now given to make a portable bridge of very strong timber, to be thrown over the canals where the enemy had broken down the bridges, and for conveying, guarding, and placing this, were assigned one hundred and fifty of our soldiers and four hundred of the allies. The advanced guard was composed of Sandoval, Azevido el Pulido, F. de Lugo, D. de Ordas, A. de Tapia, and eight more captains of those who came with Narvaez, having under them one hundred picked soldiers, of the youngest and most active. The rear guard was composed of one hundred soldiers, mostly those of Narvaez, and many cavalry, under the command of Alvarado and Velasquez de Leon. The prisoners, with Donna Marina and Donna Luisa, were put under the care of thirty soldiers and three hundred Tlascalans; and Cortes, with A. de Avila, C. de Oli, Bernardino Vasquez de Tapia and other officers, with fifty soldiers, composed a reserve, to act wherever occasion should require.

By the time that all this was arranged night drew on. Cortes then ordered all the gold which was in his apartment to be brought to the great saloon, which being done, he desired the officers of his Majesty, A. de Avila and Gonzalo Mexia, to take his Majesty's due, in their charge, assigning to them for the conveyance of it eight lame or wounded horses, and upwards of eighty Tlascalans. Upon these were loaded as much as they could carry of the gold which had been run into large bars, and much more remained heaped up in the saloon. Cortes then called to his secretary Hernandez and other royal notaries and said, "Bear witness that I can be no longer responsible for this gold; here is to the value of above six hundred thousand crowns, I can secure no more than what is already packed; let every soldier take what he will, better so than that it should remain for those dogs of Mexicans." As soon as he had said this, many soldiers of those of Narvaez, and also some of ours fell to work, and loaded themselves with treasure. I never was avaricious, and now thought more of saving my life which was in much danger; however when the opportunity thus offered, I did not omit seizing out of a casket, four *calchihuis*, those precious stones so highly esteemed amongst the Indians; and although Cortes ordered the casket and its contents to be taken care of by his major domo, I luckily secured these jewels in time, and afterwards found them of infinite advantage as a resource against famine.

A little before midnight the detachment which took charge of the portable bridge set out upon its march, and arriving at the first canal or aperture of water, it was thrown across. The night was dark and misty, and it began to rain. The bridge being fixed, the baggage artillery, and some of the cavalry passed over it, as also the Tlascalans with the gold. Sandoval and those with him passed, also Cortes and his party after the first, and many other soldiers. At this moment the trumpets and shouts of the enemy were heard, and the alarm was given by them, crying out, "Taltelulco, Taltelulco, out with your canoes! The Teules are going, attack them at the bridges!" In an instant the enemy were upon us by land, and the lake and canals were covered with canoes. They immediately flew to the bridges, and fell on us there, so that they entirely intercepted our line of march. As misfortunes do not come single, it also rained so heavily that some of the horses were terrified, and growing restive fell into the water, and the bridge was broken in at the same time. The enemy attacked us here now with redoubled fury, and our soldiers making a stout resistance, the aperture of water was soon filled with the dead and dying men, and horses, and those who were struggling to escape, all heaped together, with artillery, packs, and bales of baggage, and those who carried them. Many were drowned here, and many put into the canoes and carried off for sacrifice. It was dreadful to hear the cries of the unfortunate sufferers, calling for assistance and invoking the Holy Virgin or St. Iago, while others who escaped by swimming, or by clambering upon the chests, bales of baggage, and dead bodies, earnestly begged for help to get up to the causeway. Many who, on their reaching the ground, thought themselves safe were there seized or knocked in the head with clubs.

Away went whatever regularity had been in the march at first; for Cortes and the captains and solders who were mounted clapt spurs to their horses and galloped off, along the causeway; nor can I blame them, for the cavalry could do nothing against the enemy, of any effect; for when they attacked them, the latter threw themselves into the water on each side of the causeway, and others from the houses with arrows, or on the ground with large lances, killed the horses. It is evident we could make no battle with them in the water, and without powder, and in the night, what else could we do than what we did; which was, to join in bodies of thirty or forty soldiers, and when the Indians closed upon us, to drive them off with a few cuts and thrusts of our swords, and then hurry on, to get over the causeway as soon as we could. As to waiting for one another, that would have lost us all; and had it happened in the day time, things would have been even worse with us. The escape of such as were fortunate enough to effect it, was owing to God's mercy, who gave us force to do so; for the very sight of the number of the enemy who surrounded us, and carried off our companions in their canoes to sacrifice, was terrible. About fifty of us, soldiers of Cortes, and some of those of Narvaez, went together in a body, by the causeway; every now and then parties of Indians came up, calling us Luilones, a term of reproach, and attempting to seize us, and we, when they came within our reach, facing about, repelling them with a few thrusts of our swords, and then hurrying on. Thus we proceeded, until we reached the firm ground near Tacuba, where Cortes, Sandoval, De Oli, Salcedo, Dominguez, Lares, and others of the cavalry, with such of the infantry soldiers as had crossed the bridge before it was destroyed, were already arrived. When we came near them, we heard the voices of Sandoval, De Oli, and De Morla, calling to Cortes who was riding at their head, that he should turn about, and assist those who were coming along the causeway, and who complained that he had abandoned them. Cortes replied that those who had escaped owed it to a miracle, and if they returned to the bridges all would lose their lives. Notwithstanding, he, with ten or twelve of the cavalry and some of the infantry who had escaped unhurt, countermarched and proceeded along the causeway; they had gone however but a very short distance when they met P. de Alvarado with his lance in his hand, badly wounded, and on foot, for his chestnut mare had been killed; he had with him three of our soldiers, and four of those of Narvaez, all badly wounded, and eight Tlascalans covered with blood. While Cortes proceeded along the causeway, we reposed in the enclosed courts hard by Tacuba. Messengers had already been sent out from the city of Mexico, to call the people of Tacuba, Ezcapuzalco, and Teneyuca together, in order to intercept us. In consequence they now began to surround and harass us with arrows, and stones, and to attack us with lances headed with the swords which had fallen into their hands on the preceding night. We made some attacks upon them, and defended ourselves as well as we could.

To revert to Cortes and his companions, when they learned from Alvarado that they were not to expect to see any more of our soldiers, the tears ran from their eyes, for Alvarado had with him in the rear guard, Velasquez de Leon, with above twenty more of the cavalry, and upwards of one hundred infantry. On enquiry Cortes was told that they were all dead, to the number of one hundred and fifty more. Alvarado also told them that after the horses had been killed, about eighty assembled in a body and passed the first aperture, upon the dead bodies and heaps of luggage; I do not perfectly recollect if he said that he passed upon the dead bodies, for we were more attentive to what he related to Cortes of the deaths of J. Velasquez and above two hundred more companions, those of Narvaez included, who were with him, and who were killed at that canal. He also said that at the other bridge God's mercy saved them, and that the whole of the causeway was full of the enemy.

Source: Díaz del Castillo, Bernal. *The True History of the Conquest of Mexico.* Translated by Maurice Keatinge. London: Harrap, 1927, pp. 249–52, 256–60.

21. Human Sacrifice in War

One of the deciding factors in the conflict between the Aztec empire and the Spanish conquistadors and their allies, led by Hernán Cortés, involved their different attitudes toward war. As Bernal Díaz del Castillo (c. 1492–1583), a soldier in Cortés's expedition that conquered the Aztec empire, notes in the following extract, the Mesoamericans viewed war as an opportunity to take prisoners, some of whom would be sacrificed, whereas others would be enslaved or potentially ransomed back. Although European warfare in the Middle Ages also frequently involved the taking of prisoners for political and economic profit, by the sixteenth century, the emerging superpowers of Europe, with the increased firepower of the musket that allowed a simple soldier to defeat an aristocratic knight, increasingly shot to kill rather than to capture. The different goals of the Spaniards (killing) and the Aztecs (capturing) increased the technological imbalance between the two combatants: the Spanish wielded muskets, canon, metal swords, and mounted troops, whereas the Aztecs relied on obsidian blades, slings, and bows and arrows. These differences in approach and equipment in part resulted in the difference in kill ratios between the two groups: Spanish casualties frequently measured in the hundreds, whereas Aztec casualties measured in the thousands.

However, the Aztec practice of sacrificing captured prisoners to the Aztec gods did have powerful psychological effects. In this passage, Díaz del Castillo admits that witnessing the sacrifice of 72 captured Spaniards, in which their hearts were surgically ripped, pulsating, from their bodies and offered to the sun god, filled him with fear. According to Díaz, however, this fear did not turn him into a coward; instead, he continued to enter battle and to fight courageously despite the awareness of the fate that awaited him should he be captured and held by the enemy.

Now that I am past these furious combats, through which, praised be God he was pleased to conduct me safe, I have to mention a certain particularity relative to myself, and it is this. When I saw the sacrifice of our seventy-two countrymen, and their hearts taken out and offered to the war god of the Mexicans, I had a sensation of fear. Some may consider this as want of firmness; but if they weigh it duly, they will find that it was in truth the result of too much courage, which caused me to run into extreme and uncommon dangers; for in that day I considered myself a most valiant soldier, and was so esteemed by all; and was used to do that which was attempted by the boldest, and I was always under the eye of my captain. As I have before observed, when I saw my companions sacrificed, their hearts taken out palpitating, and their legs and arms cut off and eaten, I feared it might one day or other be my own lot, for they had me in their hands twice, but it was God's will that I should escape; but I remembered, and thought on what I had seen, and from this time I feared that cruel death; and this I mention, because before I went into battle, I felt a great depression and uneasiness about my heart, and then recommending myself to God and his blessed mother our Lady, the instant I was engaged with the enemy it left me. Still I am surprised that it came upon me when I should have felt more valiant than ever, on account of the many battles in which I had been engaged. But I declare I never

A depiction from the Codex Magliabicciano of Aztec temple sacrifice. Most victims were captured prisoners of war. © 2008 Jupiterimages Corporation.

knew what fear was, until I saw the massacre of the seventy two soldiers. Let those cavaliers who have been in desperate battles and mortal dangers now decide what was the cause of my fears; I say that it was excess of courage; and for this reason; that I knew the greatness of the danger into which I was determined to go, and knowingly, and voluntarily, encountered it. Many engagements are related in my history besides those I was at; but if my body were of iron, I could not have been at all; and I was much oftener wounded than whole.

I must observe, that the Mexicans did not kill our soldiers, but wounded, and carried them off, to sacrifice alive, to their gods.

Source: Díaz del Castillo, Bernal. *The True History of the Conquest of Mexico*. Translated by Maurice Keatinge. London: Harrap, 1927, pp. 359–60.

Part VII
RECREATIONAL LIFE

Recreational life is often viewed today as an escape from the working world. The Middle Ages and Renaissance, however, generally viewed recreation as preparation for the real world. The Games and Sports section presents several documents that discuss the pastime of hunting, which was surely the most popular sport among aristocratic males. As Margaret Cavendish makes clear, hunting served as preparation for war. Many of the same skills did indeed transfer over from hunting to war. Noblemen always hunted on horseback and they also fought on horseback. The deft horse-riding skills learned by chasing deer through woods undoubtedly equipped the gentlemen with the ability to control their horse adeptly when in the midst of battle. Hunting dangerous quarry like boar also helped to build up courage and a sense of confidence in the face of danger. Aristocrats owned all the land during this time period, and so were the only ones able to hunt animals, although the other social classes frequently helped in the hunt, serving as beaters (people who beat bushes to drive the wild animals in a certain direction), for example. The lower social classes turned to storytelling, music, and dancing to amuse themselves, but they had much less leisure time than the aristocrats, who prided themselves on doing no manual labor of any kind. The least wealthy and powerful in the social hierarchy had almost no leisure time; slaves in Anglo-Saxon England had only four days off during a calendar year, and even on those days many slaves went to markets to sell some of their own crafts in the hopes of securing some extra money.

The Performing Arts section examines how music, drama, and other intangible productions adorned daily life. In the absence of television and movies, performing arts were one of the most common pastimes during the Middle Ages and Renaissance. The theatres in the London suburbs, for example, attracted a liberal cross-section of society. Everyone from the lower aristocracy to the tradesmen attended theatres and relished the comedy, pathos, and tragedy that frequently appeared in one and the same performance. The upper aristocrats also loved drama, but they often had private performances. The best of the plays presented to the public discussed important philosophical and political issues, as seen in the extract from Shakespeare's *Merchant of Venice*. Music was perhaps the most widely available performing art. Peasants as well as aristocrats learned to sing, and everyone was expected to perform to help pass a long winter's evening. The Native Americans, just like Europeans, also used song to woo their lovers. Music was the language of passion.

The Visual Arts section shows that those arts also have a strong connection with nonrecreational life. Modern advertising, for example, frequently relies on finding just the right picture. According to Thomas Elyot, an ability to draw enabled the skilled individual to make maps and to design engines of war. Leon Battista Alberti, argued that a painting was an exercise in logic. Collecting the visual arts could also bring social prestige to the collector; Hsu Hsieh therefore warned that we should use ancient art to bring ourselves into contact with the great minds of the past, and instead of using art as a form of ostentatious display designed to show off.

Recreational life did offer an escape from the working world, but it ultimately developed skills, attitudes, and philosophies that helped the participants to do better in every area of their lives.

Games and Sports

Although play often appears to be an escape from the demands of daily life, it frequently serves in fact to prepare for the demands of "serious" life. An excellent example comes from hunting, the most esteemed pastime for aristocrats throughout almost the whole world. Usamah ibn-Munqidh (Document 5) enjoyed hunting partridges in Syria just as much as George Tuberville enjoyed hunting boar in England (Document 6). At least part of the central importance of hunting for aristocratic life derived from the sport's close connection with war, a connection that Margaret Cavendish makes clear in Document 1. Both hunting and war demanded excellent horsemanship, a willingness to kill, and (depending on the prey) courage.

Throughout Europe in the Middle Ages and *Renaissance*, where almost all land was owned by an aristocrat, hunting remained the preserve of the upper classes, that is, the social class that owned the land. Social class played a wider role than simply controlling hunting, however. The possession of leisure time itself was largely the preserve of the wealthy alone—the lower social classes not only needed to work more but also were frequently *ordered* to work more. The laws of the ninth-century *Anglo-Saxon* king *Alfred the Great* (Document 2) spell out how different the allotments of leisure time among the social classes could be. Although the law code lays out a series of holidays and vacation periods, these days off are specifically not granted to slaves. Instead, slaves have only four days off, and even those days could not be spent on true relaxation; as the law code makes clear, enterprising slaves would use these days to hawk their goods in the hopes of eventually being able to buy themselves out of slavery. Although aristocrats could spend hours every day chasing boars through the forest, every day was a workday for slaves.

Even in play, Renaissance audiences were advised not to go overboard. A *Fool's Complaint* (Document 3) criticizes those who, for example, wiggle while bowling or who absent-mindedly hit walls as they walk down the street. Such absent-minded activities destroyed credibility and diminished the performer's social position. Self-control and dignified presence were necessary not just at work, but also in play. Nevertheless, people could still enjoy themselves and could even indulge in very physical pleasures legitimately. The Englishman Thomas Roe recounted with relish the Eastern practice of massage as a means to relax the mind and body (Document 4). Even in massage, though, the themes of class and control remain: the aristocrat orders a subservient individual to give the massage; in return, of course, the masseur-barber receives a fee. Leisure time was not free.

1. Aristocratic Pastimes

Margaret Cavendish, Duchess of Newcastle, was one of the leading aristocratic English-women of the seventeenth century. Despite criticism and her own self-effacement, Cavendish nevertheless published frequently both imaginative fiction and creative philosophical arguments. Although, as an author, Cavendish broke into a realm that in her time was generally reserved for men, in the following extract from her autobiography, she reinforces the division between men and women in their pastimes. Whereas Margaret Cavendish and her sisters enjoyed taking walks and chatting, her brothers devoted their time principally to fencing, shooting, and wrestling. These "games" demonstrate clearly how the male aristoc-racy viewed military preparation as an all-consuming part of life. The price of war, after all, was high; as Margaret Cavendish notes, two of her brothers were killed in combat. Playing war needed to be serious.

Their practice was, when they met together, to exercise themselves with fencing, wrestling, shooting, and such like exercises, for I observed they did seldom hawk or hunt, and very seldom or never dance, or play music, saying it was too effeminate for masculine spirits; neither had they skill, or did use to play, for ought I could hear, at cards or dice, or the like games, nor given to any vice, as I did know, unless to love a mistress were a crime, not that I know any they had, but what report did say, and usually reports are false, at least exceed the truth.

As for the pastimes of my sisters when they are in the country, it was to read, work, walk, and discourse with each other; for though two of my three brothers were married, my brother the Lord Lucas to a virtuous and beautiful lady, daughter to Sir Christopher Nevile, son of the Lord Abergavenny, and my brother Sir Thomas Lucas to a virtuous lady of an ancient family, one Sir John Byron's daughter; likewise, three of my four sisters, one married Sir Peter Killegrew, the other Sir William Walter, the third Sir Edmund Pye, the fourth as yet unmarried, yet most of them lived with my mother, especially when she was at her country-house, living most commonly at London half the year, which is the Metropolitan city of England: but when they were at London, they were dispersed into several houses of their own, yet for the most part they met every day, feasting each other like Job's children. But this unnatural war came like a whirlwind, which felled down their houses, where some in the wars were crushed to death, as my youngest brother Sir Charles Lucas, and my brother Sir Thomas Lucas; and though my brother Sir Thomas Lucas died not immediately of his wounds, yet a wound he received on his head in Ireland shortened his life.

But to rehearse their recreations. Their customs were in winter time to go sometimes to plays, or to ride in their coaches about the streets to see the concourse and recourse of people; and in the spring time to visit the Spring-garden, Hyde-park, and the like places; and sometimes they would have music, and sup in barges upon the water;

these harmless recreations they would pass their time away with; for I observed, they did seldom make visits, nor never went abroad with strangers in their company, but only themselves in a flock together agreeing so well, that there seemed but one mind amongst them: and not only my own brothers and sisters agreed so, but my brothers and sisters in law, and their children, although but young, had the like agreeable natures and affectionable dispositions: for to my best remembrance I do not know that ever they did fall out, or had any angry or unkind disputes. Likewise, I did observe, that my sisters were so far from mingling themselves with any other company, that they had no familiar conversation or intimate acquaintance with the families to which each other were linked to by marriage, the family of the one being as great strangers to the rest of my brothers and sisters, as the family of the other.

But sometime after this war began, I know not how they lived.

Source: Cavendish, Margaret, Duchess of Newcastle. A *True Relation of the Birth, Breeding, and Life of Margaret Cavendish, Duchess of Newcastle*. Edited by Sir Egerton Brydges. Kent: Johnson and Warwick, 1814, pp. 7–10.

2. Legal Holidays

Throughout medieval Europe, most holidays were religious holidays. Although the dates of many holidays demonstrate pre-Christian origins, by the Middle Ages the holidays had been thoroughly converted into Christian celebrations. The date of All Saints, for example, falls on the same day as the Irish samhain, *our Halloween, which celebrated the harvest, the beginning of the Celtic new year, and a time of possibility in which the realms of the dead and the living were intermingled. The feast of All Saints (November 1) picked up on these pre-Christian themes of unity between the living and the dead to celebrate the unity of all Christians, dead or alive, in Christ.*

In the following extract from the laws of the Anglo-Saxon king Alfred the Great, promulgated around A.D. 890, an interesting distinction is made between free men and slaves. The free men, not surprisingly, are granted many more holidays than the slaves. The work of slaves ultimately facilitated the rest of free men. The slaves, however, were granted four particular days in which they could sell wares that they had made or had been given. By selling enough on these, and other days, slaves might eventually be able to buy themselves out of slavery and finally have Christmas off.

43. The following days shall be granted as holidays to all free men, though not to slaves and hired labourers: twelve days at Christmas and the day on which Christ overcame the devil; the anniversary of St Gregory; seven days before Easter and seven days after; one day at the festival of St. Peter and St. Paul; and in autumn, the full week before St. Mary's mass; and one day at the celebration of All Saints. The four Wednesdays in the four Ember weeks shall be granted as holidays to all slaves whose chief desire is to sell anything which has been given to them in God's name, or which they are able to acquire by their labour in any portions of time at their disposal.

Source: Attenborough, F. L., ed. and trans. *The Laws of the Earliest English Kings*. Cambridge: Cambridge University Press, 1922, p. 85.

3. A Fool's Activities

Although the modern reader may associate "Gotham" primarily with the dark city of Batman fame, Renaissance England knew that Gotham was not, in fact, a big, gritty city; rather, Gotham was the home of fools—silly individuals who knew little and understood less. In the following extract from The Fool's Complaint to Gotham College, *the anonymous author describes some activities that, in his own opinion, show that someone is a fool. Most of these activities, such as talking to yourself or playing with gates as you walk down the street, are simply forms of absent-mindedness or informality. Plenty of bowlers today can be seen in the midst of the gyrations that the author of* The Fool's Complaint *castigates so strongly.*

The objections to these innocent diversions reveal some of the cultural assumptions and priorities of seventeenth-century England. The criticism of absent-minded behaviors emphasizes that anyone who wishes to appear sensible must, absolutely must, remain self-possessed, dignified, reserved, and in control at all times. Even when having fun (e.g., bowling), you should not "let your hair down."

I. First of all, wherefore any person or persons that shall talk to themselves as they walk in the streets, or at any time when they are alone, or in a house private, may be censured for fools three months, within which term of time if they abstain therefrom, and reform this their foolery, their punishment then to be taken off; but in case that they shall not amend this fault, that some three terms of the said time, or thereabouts, may be peremptory set down to be inflicted upon them; within which limited time they shall bring a certificate of their reformation and amendment, upon pain of being held for approved attainted and converted fools, and accordingly to command your aforesaid elder brothers and ancients of the Company to find them guilty, and to see them afterwards severely punished, as violators and breakers of the laws.

II. They who shall walk along the streets, casting their cloak under one arm, and stretching out their fingers, playing with the wall, and making indentures with their fingers' ends, let them be admitted Scholars of your house and College, provided always that they have six months of approbation granted unto them, in which you to command them to be reformed; otherwise in default thereof to ordaine that the Warden, Sub-Warden, or Dean of the College, and in their absence the Senior Fellow, put his coat upon him (according to the custom of the house) his cap and his bable, and other ornaments belonging to his degree, and ever afterwards be held a professed fool.

III. Whosoever walking through any place paved with brick, or stone, shall pitch their toes or heels, walking by a direct line, stride or corner of the said brick or pavement, may be condemned to the same punishment as aforesaid.

IV. That whosoever shall play at bowls, seeing the bowl run awry, shall wry their body with it, thinking to make the bowl run the more on that side, and govern itself as they direct it with these mimic gestures, if they should be seen to practice this their error, we must declare them for brothers already professed. And further, that the libe be also understood of those who use the apish action, when they see something fall down from some high place to the ground, shrinking their shoulders, wiping their mouths, or turning out the whites of their eyes, that the like censure may pass.

Source: *The Fooles Complaint to Gotham College.* London: Ridibundus [sic], 1643.

4. Leisure Time in East India

In the following extract from the seventeenth-century account of his travels in Muslim India, English ambassador Thomas Roe describes the pastimes and diversions of the wealthier inhabitants. Some of the recreational pursuits practiced by the Indian aristocracy resemble the pastimes of the European aristocracy of the same period. Like European nobles, Indian aristocrats enjoyed spending time in luxurious gardens, hunting wild game, and playing chess (a game that originated in India). Other Indian customs were impractical in northern Europe. Although India has the weather to render a swimming pool enjoyable, only brave individuals swim in non-heated pools in the British Isles. Thomas Roe was particularly impressed by Indian "jugglers," who were, in fact, magicians. Roe particularly enjoyed their trick of making turkeys disappear in wicker baskets.

Perhaps the most striking pastime described by Thomas Roe is the custom of receiving massages. The custom was sufficiently new to the English ambassador that he did not have a way of expressing the concept quickly. The modern reader might not even recognize that Thomas Roe is describing a massage in his attempt to describe the process: "Thus taking their ease, they call for Barbers, who very gently gripe their arms, and shoulders, and other parts, they can in any measure grasp, and they strike likewise very softly those parts with the sides of their hands; it is very pleasing as they do it, and causeth their blood to stir in their veins; it is therefore very much used in those parts."

Roe's enthusiastic description ("it is very pleasing as they do it") suggests that he missed his masseur once he had returned to England.

For their places of pleasure, they are in their Groves, where their curious Fruit-trees (before described) grow; but especially in their Gardens, wherein they plant little Vineyards that afford marvelous fair and sweet Grapes, which they cut green, for their eating, or make Raisons of them. But for Wine, they make none, because their Mahomet forbids the drinking thereof. In those Gardens likewise, they have many Pomegranate trees, with all other of the choicest fruits and flowers their Country affords; to which Nature daily yields such a supply, as that there is beauty to be seen in those Trees, and Plants, and that continually. In the middle of those Gardens, they have such Wells (as before are described) the tops whereof stand a good deal higher than the planted ground, which lies even, and flat below them, from whence water is conveyed in narrow open passages (they knowing not the use of Leaden-Pipes) to all the parts of them in the dry season of the year. In those Gardens likewise they have little round Tanks to bathe in; whose sides and bottoms are made firm and smooth with that plaster before named; they are filled by aquaducts from those Wells, and they can empty them when they please, as well as fill them. The water that is conveyed into those small Tanks, usually runs down broad stone Tables, that have many hollows made in them, like to scallop-shells, which water in its passage makes such a pretty murmur, as helps to tie their senses with the bonds of sleep, in the hot seasons of the day when they constantly keep their houses, and then they lie down near them on their Carpets, to be lulled asleep. Those bathing places are within, or very near their Garden-houses, which usually are by far more neat, than any other of their dwelling.

In such a Garden-house, with all those accommodations about it, my Lord Ambassadour lay with his company at Surat, the last three months before he left East-India. And further, in those hot seasons of the day; the people of better quality lying or sitting on their Carpets, or Pallats, have servants standing about them, who continually beat the air upon them with Flabellas, or Fans, of stiffened leather, which keeps off the flies from annoying them, and cool them as they lie. Thus taking their ease, they call for Barbers, who very gently gripe their arms, and shoulders, and other parts, they can in any measure grasp, and they strike likewise very softly those parts with the sides of their hands; it is very pleasing as they do it, and causeth their blood to stir in their veins; it is therefore very much used in those parts, to such as do not heat their blood by bodily motion.

For their pastimes within doors, they have Cards, but much different from ours in the figures made in them, and in their greater number of suits. Those Cards I have often seen; and have been more often told, that they have very good skill in that most innocent and ingenious game we call Chess.

They delight themselves sometimes with the Company of Mountebanks, and Jugglers. For their Mountebanks; they keep venomous Snakes in baskets, and will suffer themselves to be bitten or stung by them; which part thus bitten, or stung, presently swells, and immediately after that, they cure themselves again by Oils and Powders, which they apply unto the place, and then offer to sell them unto the people standing by.

Their Jugglers are the cunningest that ever I saw, to do strange things by sleight of hand, as in this trick I shall here name: where I have observed them to lay down scuttles or broad open Wicker-baskets upon the ground, three or four one upon another, all which appeared empty, as they laid them down; but taking them up again one after the other, in the bottom of them there would appear, three or four living Turtle-doves: which they would cover again with the same Scuttles, and tossing and turning them as they took them off, and up the second time, none of those pretty creatures were to be seen any more. But how they first conveyed them thither, and how after thence, we could not possibly discover.

For their Pastimes abroad they have Hawks of diverse kinds, greater and less, and Partridges, and other choice Fowl great store to fly at. They have Hares, and Antilopes, with other wild Beasts to hunt, and these not a few. Their dogs for chase are made somewhat like our Grey-hounds, but much less, who never open in the pursuit of their game. They hunt likewise with Leopards trained up and made fit for their sport, who by leaping seize on that they pursue: but by reason of the heat of the Country, those sports are not there much used. The Mogol when he hunts, carries Hawks and Dogs, and all things beside with him, to make him pastime; that if one sport fail, he may be pleased with another. They say, that they have a curious Device to take wild fowls that use the water; into which a fellow goes, with a fowl of that kind he desires to catch, whose skin is stuffed so artificially, as that with a noise he counterfeits that fowl, it appears to be alive, the man keeps all his body but head under water, on which he fastens that counterfeit fowl to stand fore-right on the top thereof, and thus coming amongst them, he plucks them (as they say) by their legs under water at his pleasure. But this I have only by tradition.

For other pastimes abroad, this I am sure of, that when the weather is more temperate, they shoot much in their Bows, and are very excellent Marks-men, somewhat like those left-handed men spoken of Judg. 20.16. And with their Guns in which they shoot single bullets (for they have not the use of small-shot) they are somewhat long in taking their aim, but they will come very neer the mark.

Others delight themselves very much in managing their excellent Horses; But so shall not I delight my Reader, if I dwell too long in particulars.

Source: Roe, Thomas. *A Voyage into the East Indies.* In Pietro della Valle, *The Travels of Sig. Pietro della Valle, a Noble Roman, into East-India and Arabia Deserta in Which, the Several Countries, Together with the Customs, Manners, Traffique, and Rites Both Religious and Civil, of Those Oriental Princes and Nations, Are Faithfully Described.* London: Macock, 1665, pp. 404–06.

5. An Animal Lover in Arabia

Hunting, in part because of its similarity to war, dominated aristocratic leisure life throughout Eurasia. Not everyone, however, delighted in these blood sports. In the following extract from a twelfth-century memoir, the influential Syrian-born Muslim aristocrat Usamah ibn Munqidh describes the Koranic scholar Abu-Turab, who was a family friend. Abu-Turab would abstain from the hunt and one day even went so far as to lie about the location of a partridge that had taken refuge near him from the hunting falcons. The other hunter, however, did not take kindly to this deception; he found the partridge, broke its legs, and fed it to the falcon. Usamah ibn Munqidh himself, who fought against the European crusaders, took after the hunter, although his account of the animal-loving Abu-Turab reveals a much gentler side of Islamic civilization.

My father (may Allah's mercy rest upon his soul!) related to me the following in his own words:

I used to go out to the hunt accompanied by al-Ra'is abu-Turab Haydarah ibn-Qatramatar (may Allah's mercy rest upon his soul!), who was my father's sheikh and under whom my father memorized the Koran and studied Arabic. When we arrived at the hunting field, Abu-Turab would dismount from his mare, sit on a rock, and read the Koran while we would be hunting around him. With the chase done, he would ride along with us.

Abu-Turab related to me the following: "Sir, as I was sitting once on a rock a small partridge came all of a sudden trotting heavily along, because of exhaustion, towards the rock on which I was sitting. As soon as it took cover underneath the rock, a falcon appeared, coming after it, but was still at some distance from it. The falcon alighted opposite me while Lu'lu was screaming, 'Look out! Look out, O our master!' He then came galloping, while I was praying, 'O Allah, conceal the partridge so that he may not see it,' and said, 'Our master, where is the partridge?' I replied, 'I did not see anything. It did not come here.' He then dismounted from his mare and went around the rock looking underneath it. There he saw the partridge and said, 'I thought the partridge was here, but thou dost insist that it is not.' He took it, sir, broke its legs and threw it to the falcon, as my heart was breaking for it."

Source: Usamah ibn-Munqidh. *An Arab-Syrian Gentleman and Warrior in the Period of the Crusades: Memoirs of Usamah ibn-Munqidh.* Translated by Philip Hitti. New York: Columbia University Press, 1929, p. 224.

6. Hunting Wild Boar

Hunting was the premier sport for aristocrats during the Middle Ages. Hunting demanded intensive training, quality horsemanship, and personal courage. In short, hunting demanded the same skills that warfare demanded. Hunting, therefore, formed the pastime of the aristocracy, the elite warrior class of society.

Many animals took part in the hunt. Hounds and dogs chased the prey, horses carried the main huntsmen, and deer, bears, and boars served as game. Of the prey, the boar particularly captured the medieval imagination. The late fourteenth-century heroic romance Gawain and the Green Knight *depicts a series of hunts. Although the huntsmen chase the deer and the fox, only the boar puts up a genuine fight, and Bertilak ultimately must grapple with the boar hand to hand to vanquish this prey.*

In the following extract from a sixteenth-century handbook on hunting, the author, George Tuberville, similarly recognizes the singular vigor of the boar as game. Tuberville notes, for example, that the boar alone can kill a hound with just one blow. In one episode, Tuberville witnessed a boar slay more than 35 hounds in one hunt. Tuberville therefore notes that boar mastiffs rather than hounds should be used in hunting the boar. Nevertheless, Tuberville recognized that hounds were frequently used for hunting boar, so he gives practical details on how to organize the chase. He recommends, for example, that placing bells around the hounds' necks may frighten the boar into flight, instead of attacking the hounds, and that horses may be further protected by having a cloak placed over them. Even then, however, the horses and riders should remain in constant motion around the boar to avoid the boar's effective attack.

Having described the hunting of an Hart, and all other deer according to my simple skill, I have thought good to set down here a little treatise of the hunting at the wild boar, and of his properties, although he ought not to be counted amongst the beasts of venerie which are chasable with hounds, for he is the proper pray of a mastiff and such-like dogs, for as much as he is a heavy beast, and of great force, trusting and affying himself in his tusks and his strength, and therefore will not lightly flee nor make chase before hounds, so that you cannot (by hunting of the boar) know that goodness or swiftness of them, and therewithal to confess a truth, I think it great pity to hunt (with a good kennel of hounds) at such chases, and that for such reasons and considerations as follow.

First, he is the only beast which can dispatch a hound at one blow, for though other beasts do bite, snatch, tear, or rend your hounds, yet there is hope of remedy if they be well attended; but if a boar do once strike your hound and light between the four quarters of him, you shall hardly see him escape, and therewithal this subtilty he hath, that if he be run with a good kennel of hounds, which he perceiveth hold in round and follow him hard, he will flee into the strongest thicket that he can find, to the end he may kill them at leisure one after another, the which I have seen by experience oftentimes. And amongst others I saw once a boar chased and hunted with fifty good hounds at the least, and when he saw that they were all in full cry, and held in round together, he turned head upon them, and thrust amidst the thickest of them. In such sort that he slew sometimes six or seven (in manner) with twinkling of an eye: and of the fifty hounds there went not twelve sound and alive to their masters' houses. Again if a kennel of hounds be once used to hunt a boar, they will become lither, and will never willingly hunt, fleeing chases again. For as much as they are (by him) accustomed to hunt with more ease, and to find great scent. For a boar is a beast of very hot scent, and that is contrary to light fleeing chases, which are hunted with more pain to the hound, and yet therewith do not leave so great scent. And for these causes, whosoever meaneth to have good hounds for an hart, hare, or roe-deer, let him not use them to hunt the boar; but since men are of sundry opinions, and love to hunt such chases as lie most commodiously about their dwelling places, I will here describe the property of the boar, and how they may hunt him. And the manner of killing him either with the sword or boar-spear, as you shall also see it set you in a portraiture hereafter in his place. . . .

and by such means a huntsman being early in the woods may judge the subtlety or craft of the boar, and according to that which he shall perceive, he may prepare to hunt with hounds which are hot or temperate. For it be a great boar, and one that hath lain long at rest, he shall do well to hunt him with hounds that will stick to him; and the huntsmen on horseback be ever amongst them, charging the board, and forcing him as much as they may to discourage him: for if you hunt such a boar with four or five couple of hounds, he will make small account of them, and when they have a little chased him, he will take courage, and keep them still at bay, running upon any thing that he seeth before him; but if he perceive himself charged and hard laid unto with hounds and huntsmen, then he will become astonished, and lose courage, and then he is enforced to flee and to seek the country abroad. You must set relays also, but that must be of the staunchest and best old hounds of the kennel, for if you should make your relays with young hounds, and such as are swift and rash, then when a boar is any thing before the rest of the hounds in chase, he might easily kill them in their fury, at their first coming in to him. But if he be a boar which is accustomed to flee endways before the hounds, and to take a champayne countrey, then you shall cast off but four or five couple of hounds at the first and set all the rest at Relays, about the entry of the fields where you think likely that he will flee. For such a boar will seldom keep hounds at a bay, unless he be forced: and if he stand at bay, the huntsmen must ride in unto him as secretly as they can without much noise, and when they be near him, let them cast round about the place where he standeth, and run upon him all at once, and it shall be hard if they give him not one scoth with a sword, or some wound with a boar-spear; and let them not strike low, for then they shall commonly hit him on the snout, because he watcheth to take all blows upon his tusks or thereabouts. But let them lift up their hands high, and strike right down, and let them beware that they strike not towards their horses, but that other way, for on that side that a boar feeleth himself hurt, he turneth head straightways whereby he might the sooner hurt or kill their horses, if they stroke towards them. And if they be in the plain, then let cast a cloak about their horses, and they may the better ride about the boar, and strike at him as they pass: but stay not long in a place. It is a certain thing experimented and found true, that if you hang bells upon collars and your hounds necks, a boar will not so soon strike at them, but flee endways before them, and seldom stand at Bay.

Source: Tuberville, George. *Noble Arte of Venerie or Hunting* (1576). In *Tuberville's Book of Hunting*. Oxford: Clarendon Press, 1908, pp. 148–49, 157–59.

Performing Arts

Although the concept of "the performing arts" conveniently groups together diverse art forms such as music, drama, and dance, the continuum between these arts and any other leisure activity was much stronger in the Middle Ages. Although today most people listen to live music in a concert setting, with a strong divide between performer and audience, medieval and *Renaissance* music was frequently performed in settings in which every audience member was also a participant. Every aristocrat, following Thomas Elyot's advice in *The Governour*, for example, (Document 7) would have some skill in music and would be able to play for friends in an informal gathering. A similar situation held true for Peru, as Garcilaso de la Vega demonstrates in Document 8. Music was so integrated into Inca society that tunes were used to convey personal messages.

Although music could be very participatory, drama conformed more closely to modern concepts of a "show." Actors might be professionals or might be drawn from the ranks of the local clergy or the local trade guild, but during the performance, some were audience members, and others were performers. The performances, however, were rarely stuffy affairs. As the humorous Digby play about the tragic slaughter of the innocents (Document 9) demonstrates, European society could find humor in unlikely places. The humor, however, was a tool of moral criticism—not a flippant or disrespectful cheap laugh. The wildly popular plays of William Shakespeare, as seen in Document 10, reinforced and helped create both a dynamic sense of group identity and a sense of the corresponding evils of racial stereotypes. In all these productions, serious issues were discussed in entertaining ways. As these documents demonstrate repeatedly, recreational life informed continually the other dimensions of daily life.

7. *The Necessity of Music*

The Governour, by Thomas Elyot, was one of the most influential manuals of sixteenth-century England. In this work, Elyot laid out a comprehensive system for the education of aristocratic children. In the extract that follows, Elyot describes the proper role of music within that educational system. According to Elyot, music is necessary to give the mind a break from more serious academic pursuits. Music allows the mind to recover the energies spent on more difficult material. Elyot also defends the practice of music by citing the examples of famous people from the Bible and Greek antiquity who enjoyed and played music. Although David, who was widely credited as being the author of the biblical psalms, seems like Elyot's strongest example, the author actually spends much more time describing the Greeks' love of music, focusing on the examples of Achilles and Alexander the Great. This preference for classical antiquity reflects the growing strength of the European-wide Renaissance, which rediscovered the pleasures of classical antiquity.

Elyot's need to defend music, however, reveals that the inclusion of music in the curriculum might cause controversy. There would, of course, be no need to defend music if all his audience clearly prized music. The last part of the following extract gives some insight into this potential resistance to music: public performance of music would shame an aristocrat because, just as if he were seen performing manual labor, the aristocrat would be engaging in the same activities as paid servants. Elyot therefore underlines the importance of never performing publicly—to do so turned a nobleman into a hired hand, albeit a professional musician. Music, then, however worthy, must remain a private hobby for the aristocracy, not a public show. Although Elyot's sixteenth-century language may pose a few difficulties for modern readers, the general argument will be clear.

IN WHAT WISE MUSIC MAY BE TO A NOBLEMAN NECESSARY: AND WHAT MODESTY OUGHT TO BE THEREIN

The discretion of a tutor consisteth in temperaunce; that is to say, that he suffer not the child to be fatigate with continual study or learning, wherewith the delicate and tender wit may be dulled or oppressed, but that there may be therewith interlaced and mixed some pleasant learning and exercise, as playing on instruments of music, which moderately used and without diminution of honor (that is to say, without wanton countenance and dissolute gesture) is not to be contemned. For the noble king and prophet David, king of Israel (whom almighty God said he had chosen as a man according to his heart or desire) during his life, delighted in music. And with the sweet harmony that he made on his harp, he constrained the evil spirit that vexed king Saul to forsake him, continuing the time that he harped.

The most noble and valiant princes of Greece oftentimes, to recreate their spirits and in augmenting their courage, embraced instruments musical.

Thus did the valiant Achilles (Homer sayeth) who after the sharp and vehement contention, between him and Agamemnon, for the taking away of his concubine; whereby he being set in a fury, had slain Agamemnon, emperor of the Greeks' army, had not Pallas the goddess withdrawn his hand. In which rage, he all inflamed, departed with his people to his own ships, that lay at road, intending to have returned to his country; but after he had taken to him his harp (whereon he had learned to pay of Chiron the Centaur, which also taught him feats of arms, with physic and surgery) and playing thereon, had sung the gests and acts martial of the ancient princes of Greece, as Hercules, Perseus, Perithous, Theseus, and his cousin Jason, and of diverse other of semblable value and prowess. He was therewith assuaged of his fury, and reduced into his first state of reason, in such wise that in redoubling his rage, and that thereby should not remain to him any note of reproach, he retaining his fierce and sturdy countenance, so tempered himself in the entertainment and answering the messengers that came to him from the residue of the Greeks, that they reputing all that his fierce demeanor to be (as it were) a divine majesty, never embraided him with any inordinate wrath or fury.

And therefore the great king Alexander, when he had vanquished Ilion, where some time was set the most noble city of Troy, being demanded of one, if he would see the harp of Paris, who ravished Helen, he thereat gently smiling answered: it was not the thing that he much desired, but had rather see the harp of Achilles, whereto he sang, not the illecebrous delectations of Venus, but the valiant acts and noble affairs of excellent princes.

But in this commendation of music, I would not be thought to allure noble men to have so much delectation therein, that in playing and singing only, they should put their whole study and felicity, as did the emperor Nero, which all a long summer's day would sit in the theatre (an open place where all the people of Rome beheld solemn acts and plays) and in the presence of all the noble men and senators, would play on his harp and sing without ceasing. And if any man happened by long sitting to sleep, or by any other countenance, to show himself to be weary, he was suddenly bobbed on the face by the servants of Nero, for that purpose attending. Or if any person were perceived to be absent, or were seen to laugh at the folly of the emperor, he was forthwith accused, as it were of misprision, whereby the emperor found occasion to commit him to prison, or to put him to tortures. O what misery was it, to be subject to such a minstrel, in whose music was no melody but anguish and dolor?

It were therefore better that no music were taught to a noble man, than by the exact knowledge thereof, he should have therein inordinate delight; and by that be elected to wantonness, abandoning gravity and the necessary cure and office in the public weal to him committed.

King Philip, when he heard that his son Alexander did sing sweetly and properly, rebuked him gently, saying, "But Alexander, be ye not ashamed, that ye can sing so well and cunningly?" Whereby he meant that the open profession of that craft was but of a base estimation, and that it sufficed a noble mean, having therein knowledge, either to use it secretly, for the refreshing of his wit, when he hath time of solace, or else only hearing the contention of noble musicians, to give judgment in the excellency of their cunnings. These be the causes, whereunto having regard, music is not only tolerable, but also commendable. For as Aristotle sayeth: "Music in the old time was numbered among sciences, for as much as nature seeketh not only how to be in business well occupied, but also how in quietness to be commendably despoiled." And if the child be of a perfect inclination and towardness of virtue, and very aptly disposed to this science, and ripely doth understand the reason and concordance of tunes, the tutors office shall be to persuade him to have principally in remembrance his estate, which maketh him exempt from the liberty of using this science in every time and place; that is to say, that it only serveth for recreation, after tedious or laborious affairs. And to show him, that a gentleman playing or singing in a common audience appaireth his estimation, the people forgetting reverence when they behold him in similitude of a common servant or minstrel. Yet notwithstanding, he shall commend the perfect understanding of music, declaring how necessary it is for the better attaining the knowledge of a public weal, which, as I before said, is made of an order of estates and degrees, and by reason thereof containeth in it a perfect harmony, which he shall afterward more perfectly understand, when he shall happen to read the books of Plato and Aristotle of public weals, wherein be written diverse examples of music and geometry. In this form may a wise and circumspect tutor, adapt the pleasant science of music to a necessary and laudable purpose.

Source: Elyot, Sir Thomas. *The Boke Named the Governour*. London: Thomas Berthelet, 1537, pp. 21–33. With adaptations by Lawrence Morris.

8. Inca Music

Garcilaso de la Vega, the author of the following extract, had a unique insight into the Peruvian culture of the sixteenth century. The illegitimate but loved son of a Spanish conquistador and an Inca princess, Garcilaso had access to both the Spanish and the Native American cultures, traditions, and perspectives. His testimony therefore carries particular importance.

In his discussion of Inca music, Garcilaso notes one of the instruments still associated with the Andes: panpipes. Throughout his account, Garcilaso's praise for Inca music reveals his admiration for the Native American culture. By noting that the Inca flautists could play any organ tune, for example, Garcilaso shows that the Native Americans are the equals of the European musicians. This equal ability, however, does not mean that the two musical traditions were the same. Garcilaso highlights the uniqueness of each Inca tune. Unlike the European popular musical tradition, in which the same musical notes might carry different words—and thus different meanings—each tune within the Inca repertoire carried only one meaning and interpretation. As a result, playing a tune could be as powerful a form of communication as literature. According to Garcilaso, love-struck youths in particular used the persuasion of traditional Inca tunes to woo their beloved.

In music they had acquired a knowledge of some tunes, which the Indians of the Collas district played on instruments made of hollow reeds, four or five being tied in a row, each one having the point higher than its neighbour, like an organ. These canes were fastened in fours, different one from another. One of them ran in high notes and the others each higher in the scale; so that the four natural voices, treble, tenor, contralto, and counter-bass were represented by the four sets of reeds. When an Indian played on one of these pipes, another answered on a fifth or any other note; then another played on another note, sometimes rising to the high notes, and at others going down, but always in tune. They did not understand accompaniments on different keys, but always played in one compass. The players were Indians instructed for the amusement of the king, and for the lords his vassals, and although their music was so simple, it was not generally practiced, but was learnt and attained to by study. They had *la* flutes with four or five notes, like those of shepherds; but they were not made on a scale, each one being of only one note. Their songs were composed in measured verses, and were for the most part written to celebrate amorous passions expressive now of joy now of sorrow, now of the kindness now of the cruelty of the fair.

Each song had its appropriate tune, and they could not put two different songs to the same tune. Thus the enamoured swain, playing his flute at night, with the tune that belonged to it, apprised the lady and the whole world of the state of his feelings, arising from the smiles or frowns of the object of his love. But if two tunes were used for the same song, it could not be known what sentiment the lover wished to express; for it may be said that he talked with his flute. One night a Spaniard met an Indian girl of his acquaintance, and asked her to go with him to his lodging. The girl said, "Sir! let me go whither I desire; for know you not that that flute is calling me with much love and tenderness, so that it obliges me to go towards it. Leave me, then. I cannot help going, for love drags me to where the flute-player will be my husband, and I his wife."

They did not play the songs composed to celebrate their warlike deeds, because they were not fit to play before ladies, nor to express on their flutes. But they were sung at the principal festivals, in memory of their victories. When I departed from Peru in the year 1560, I left five Indians in Cuzco who played the flute very well, from any music book for the organ that was placed before them. They belonged to Juan Rodriguez de Villalobos, formerly a citizen of that town. At present, being the year 1602, they tell me that there are so many Indians expert in playing on instruments, that they may be met with in all directions. In my time the Indians did not use their voices, because, no doubt, they were not sufficiently good, and because they did not understand singing; but, on the other hand, many mestizos had very good voices.

An Andean woman weaves on a loom. From *History of the Inca Kingdom, Nueva Coronica y buen Gobierno*, c. 1587; manuscript with illustrations by Guaman Poma de Ayala, Peru. The Art Archive/Archaeological Museum Lima/Gianni Dagli Orti.

Source: El Inca Garcilaso de la Vega. *First Part of the Royal Commentaries of the Yncas.* Translated by Clements R. Markham. Vol. 1. London: Hakluyt Society, 1869, pp. 191–93.

9. Mystery Plays

Live drama thrived in medieval Europe. Traveling troupes of actors as well as locally based companies frequently delighted large crowds of spectators in pub courtyards and public squares. Many of the surviving scripts deal with religious themes, both because such themes were popular and because precious writing resources were more likely to be reserved for sacred themes. Although the plays are religious, they are not necessarily humorless. In fact, humor remains one of the most striking aspects of medieval religious drama. The extract from the Digby play, for example, deals with Herod's ordering the death of all infants in Israel, yet despite the tragic theme, the play aims for comic relief by inserting the non-biblical character of Watkin, a cowardly messenger who wants to be a knight. Watkin is eager to kill the children but is deathly afraid of women. The humor of Watkin's false courage, however, is by no means blasphemous. By emphasizing Watkin's cowardice, the play highlights how the proposed act itself—killing innocent and defenseless children—is itself cowardly. As a result, even though the play treats senseless slaughter humorously, the humor makes a serious point.

Watkin

Now a largess, my lord: I am right well apaid,
If I do not well lay my head upon a stock;
I shall go show your knights how ye have said,
And arm myself manly, and go forth on the flock;
And if I find a young child, I shall chop it on a block,
though the mother be angry, the child shall be slain,
But yet I dread no thing more than a woman with a Rock,
For if I see any such, by my faith I return!

Herod

What, shall a woman with a Rock drive thee away?
Fie on thee traitor! Now I tremble for anger.
I have trusted thee long and many a day;
A bold man and an hardy I thought thou haddest been.

Watkin

So am I, my lord, and that shall be seen
That I am a bold man and best dare abide;
And there come an hundred women I will not flee,
But from tomorrow till night with them I dare chide.
And therefore my lord, ye may trust unto me,
for all the children of Israel your knights and I shall kill.
I will not spare one, but dead they shall be
If the father and mother will let me have my will.

An elaborate stage set. In the far right corner is a "hell mouth," a common representation of the entrance to Hell. Bridgeman-Giraudon/Art Resource, NY.

Herod

Thou lord, take heed what I say thee til,
And high thee to my knights as fast as thou can;
Say, I command them everywhichwise that they spill blood
Around in every province, and spare for no man.

Watkin

Nay, Nay, my lord, we will spare for no man
Though there come a thousand in a rought;
For your knights and I will kill them all if we can.
But for the women, that is all my doubt.
And if I see any walking by,
I will take good heed until she be gone,
And as soon as I spy that she is out,
By my faith into the house I will go anon!
And thus I promise you, that I shall never sleep,
but evermore wait to find the children alone,
And if the mother come in, under the bench will I creap
And lie still there until she be gone.
Then manly I shall come out and her children slay,
And when I have done, I shall run fast away.
If she found her child dead, and took me there alone,
By my faith I am sure we should make a fray.

Herod

Nay, harlot, abide still with my knights, I command thee,
Until the children be slain all the whole rout,
And when thou comest home again, I shall advance thee
If thou quite thee like a man, while thou art one.
and if thou play the coward, I put thee out of dought,
Of me thou shalt neither have fee nor advantage.
Therefore I charge you the country be well sought,
And when thou comest home, shalt have thy wage.

Watkin

Yes, sire, by my troth, ye shall well know,
While I am out, how I shall acquit me,
For I purpose to spare neither high nor low,
If there be no man will smite me.
The most I fear: the women will beat me.
Yet shall I take good heart to me and look well about,
And look that your knights be not far from me,
For if I be alone, I may soon get a clout.

Herod

I say, hie thee hence! That thou were gone,
And unto my knights, look ye take the way,

And say, I charge them that my commandment be done
In all haste possible without more delay.
And if there be any that will say you "nay,"
Rid him of his life out of hand anon.
And if thou quite thee well unto my pay,
I shall make thee a knight adventurous when thou comest home.

Watkin

Sir knights, I must go forth with you—
Thus my lord commanded me for to do.
And if I quite me well while I am amoung you,
I shall be made a knight adventurous when I come home.
For one thing I promise you, I will fight anon,
if my heart fail not when I shall begin,
for they fight like devils with rocks when they spin.

First Soldier

Watkin, I love thee, for thou art ever a man.
If thou quit thee well in this great voyage,
I shall speak to my lord for thee that I can,
That thou shalt no more be neither groom nor page.

Second Soldier

I will speak for thee that thou shalt have better wage
If thou quite thee manly among the women,
For they be as fierce as a lion in a cage
When they are broken out, to reave men of their lives.

Source: *The Digby Plays*. Ed. by F. J. Furnivall. London: Early English Text Society, 1896, pp. 7–10. Minor linguistic modifications made by Lawrence Morris.

10. William Shakespeare Explores Race and Nationality

The Merchant of Venice, *a play by England's most famous playwright, William Shakespeare (1564–1616), demonstrates how drama could help create a sense of nation and race. In* The Merchant of Venice, *the Venetian merchant Antonio borrows money from the Jewish moneylender, Shylock, with a pound of flesh as collateral. When Antonio's business enterprise fails unexpectedly, Shylock claims his pound of flesh in court. In the following extract from the court scene, racial terminology defines the characters and their ambitions. Antonio, for example, consistently uses merely the word "Jew" to refer to Shylock, rather than Shylock's own name. As a result, Shylock is robbed of individuality and is made a representative of an entire race. Shylock's negative aspects, comprising vengeance and a lack of mercy, are thus projected onto the entire Jewish race.*

The play, as a result, is frequently interpreted as anti-Semitic, but Shakespeare's work is more complex than that. Although a stereotypical presentation of Jewish people as

*grasping and merciless does indeed pervade the play, the Venetians themselves are not ab-
solved from all faults. In a convincing speech, for example, Shylock points out that the Venetians frequently mistreat their slaves; in fact, the entire Venetian state seems based on creating
and enforcing discrepancies of class and power. The very anti-Semitism of the Venetian
state in the play proves Shylock's point. Nonetheless, all of Renaissance society endorsed such
national, racial, and class distinctions. Regardless of how unfair those distinctions may have
been, Shakespeare's audience accepted them as a matter of course and entirely natural.*

Duke

I am sorry for thee: thou art come to answer
A stony adversary, an inhuman wretch
Uncapable of pity, void and empty
From any dram of mercy.

Antonio

I have heard
Your Grace hath ta'en great pains to qualify
His rigorous course; but since he stands obdurate,
And that no lawful means can carry me
Out of his enemy's reach, I do oppose
My patience to his fury; and am armed
To suffer, with a quietness of spirit,
The very tyranny and rage of his.

Duke

Go one, and call the Jew into the court.

Sailor

He is ready at the door: he comes, my lord.
  Enter Shylock.

Duke

Make room, and let him stand before our face.
Shylock, the world thinks, and I think so too,
That thou but lead'st this fashion of thy malice
To the last hour of act; and then 'tis thought
Thou'llt show thy mercy and remorse more strange
than is thy strange apparent cruelty;
And where thou now exact'st the penalty,
Which is a pound of this poor merchant's flesh,
Thou wilt not only loose the forfeiture,
But, touched with human gentleness and love,
Forgive a moiety of the principal;
Glancing an eye of pity on his losses,
That have of late so huddled on his back,

Enow to press a royal merchant down,
And pluck commiseration of his state
From brassy bosoms and rough hearts of flint,
From stubborn Turks and Tartars, never trained
to offices of tender courtesy.
We all expect a gentle answer, Jew.

Shylock

I have possessed your Grace of what I purpose;
And by our holy Sabbath have I sworn
To have the due and forfeit of my bond:
If you deny it, let the danger light
Upon your charter and your city's freedom.
You'll ask me, why I rather choose to have
A weight of carrion-flesh than to receive
Three thousand ducats: I'll not answer that:
But, say, it is my humour: is it answer'd?
What if my house be troubled with a rat,
And I be pleased to give ten thousand ducats
To have it baned? What, are you answered yet?
Some men there are love not a gaping pig;
Some, that are mad if they behold a cat;
And others, when the bagpipe sings in the nose,
Cannot contain themselves: for affection,
Mistress of passion, sways it to the mood
Of what it likes or loathes. Now, for your answer:
As there is no firm reason to be rendered,
Why he cannot abide a gaping pig;
why he, a harmless necessary cat;
Why he, a woolen bag-pipe; but of force
Must yield to such inevitable shame
As to offend, himself being offended;
So can I give no reason, nor I will not,
More than a lodged hate and a certain loathing
I bear Antonio, that I follow thus
A losing suit against him. Are you answered?

Bassianus

This is no answer, thou unfeeling man,
To excuse the current of thy cruelty.

Shylock

I am not bound to please thee with my answer.

Bassianus

Do all men kill the things they do not love?

Shylock

Hates any man the thing he would not kill?

Bassianus

Every offence is not a hate at first.

Shylock

What, wouldst thou have a serpent sting thee twice?

Antonio

I pray you, think you question with the Jew:
You may as well go stand upon the beach,
And bid the main flood bate his usual height;
You may as well use question with the wolf,
Why he hath made the ewe bleat for the lamb;
You may as well forbid the mountain pines
To wag their high tops, and to make no noise,
When they are fretten with the gusts of heaven;
You may as well do anything most hard,
As seek to soften that—than which what's harder?—
His Jewish heart: therefore, I do beseech you,
Make no more offers, use no farther means,
But with all brief and plain conveniency
Let me have judgment and the Jew his will.

Bassianus

For thy three thousand ducats here is six.

Shylock

If every ducat in six thousand ducats
Were in six parts and every part a ducat,
I would not draw them; I would have my bond.

Duke

How shalt thou hope for mercy, rendering none?

Shylock

What judgment shall I dread, doing no wrong?
You have among you many a purchased slave,
Which, like your asses and your dogs and mules,
You use in abject and in slavish parts,
Because you bought them: shall I say to you,
Let them be free, marry them to your heirs?

William Shakespeare, as depicted in the 1623 *First Folio* (the first collected works of Shakespeare's plays). The conservative dress presents the image of a serious, upstanding citizen, though his plays could cause controversy. © 2008 Jupiterimages Corporation.

Why sweat they under burdens? Let their beds
Be made as soft as yours, and let their palates
Be seasoned with such viands? You will answer
"The slaves are ours," so do I answer you:
The pound of flesh, which I demand of him,
Is dearly bought; 'tis mine and I will have it.
If you deny me, fie upon your law!
There is no force in the decrees of Venice.
I stand for judgment: answer, shall I have it.

Source: Shakespeare, William. *The Merchant of Venice*. Edited by Robert Sharp. Richmond, VA: Johnson, 1903, pp. 101–05. With minor adaptations.

Visual Arts

The power of the visual arts is obvious. Dramatic photographs can capture buyers more easily than a product's name or a newspaper's headline. Photography, of course, is a modern art, but the Middle Ages and *Renaissance* still valued the visual arts highly. Renaissance intellectuals, such as Leon Battista Alberti (Document 13) or any pupil following Thomas Elyot's curriculum (Document 12), frequently counted painting among their list of accomplishments.

Medieval and Renaissance thinkers did not value the visual arts purely because of beauty—rather the arts frequently served as an aid to other skills. Elyot claims, for example, that a skill in drawing will prove invaluable for the construction of maps during military campaigns and in the design of new military weapons. The claim remains somewhat unconvincing, however, considering that few of his readers ever invented new military machines, although the ability to draw a diagram would indeed aid in the construction of such new technology. Alberti, on the other hand, values the visual arts in part because they are a study in logic. In the principles of good art that he lays out in this section (Document 13), Alberti stresses that a painting should be logical: if the centaurs have violently crashed a wedding, there should be no wine glasses left unbroken on the tables. Art similarly serves as a means of closely observing the natural world, especially animals and human beings.

Collecting art provided a pleasant pastime for those who could afford it. As Hsu Hsieh points out, however, many people collected art not for the art's sake, but to show off in front of their friends and acquaintances (Document 11). Expensive art had become a status symbol. Hsu Hsieh views this trend as ultimately debasing. According to Hsu Hsieh, the love of antiques should focus on encountering the great minds of the past, not on demonstrating ostentatious wealth. Hsieh, therefore, refuses to obsess about antiques and prefers instead to read the great writings of the past so that he can emulate the great men of history. By so doing, he aspires to become a great thinker himself, read by others in the future. Art, for Hsu Hsieh, offers a means of bettering oneself.

For all these thinkers, Elyot, Alberti, and Hsu Hsieh, the visual arts meant more than simple beauty or ornamentation. Art had the power to teach about the world, to change the course of history, and to transform the viewer.

11. *Antiques and the Love of the Past in China*

The following extract, from the seventeenth-century Chinese scholar Hsu Hsieh, examines the practice of antique hunting. According to Hsu Hsieh, collecting antiques was a popular pastime during his era, but not because people loved the objects themselves. Rather, people collected expensive antiques primarily to demonstrate that they were wealthier than others. These objects of art were prized not because they were beautiful, but because they were expensive.

Hsu Hsieh contrasts his own love of the past with this more common love of antiques. Hsu Hsieh views himself as a true antiquarian—a true lover of the past. Whereas his contemporaries love relics from the past because of their current price, Hsu Hsieh loves the men of the past—their objects he treats with simple respect, but he devours the ideas of the past. As a result, Hsu Hsieh prefers to read ancient books, where he can encounter the minds of antiquity directly. Instead of treasuring a thousand-year-old inkstand, he continues to view the inkstand primarily as just an inkstand. With that ink, however, Hsu Hsieh hopes to become an "antique" in his implied definition of the word: a thinker whose writings command respect and offer guidance in the future.

For some years I had possessed an old inkstand, left at my house by a friend. It came into ordinary use as such, I being unaware that it was an antique. However, one day a connoisseur told me it was at least a thousand years old, and urged me to preserve it carefully as a valuable relic. This I did, but never took any further trouble to ascertain whether such was actually the case or not. For supposing that this inkstand really dated from the period assigned, its then owner must have regarded it simply as an inkstand. He could not have known that it was destined to survive the wreck of time and come to be cherished as an antique. And while we prize it now, because it has descended to us from a distant past, we forget that then, when antiques were relics of a still earlier period, it could not have been of any value to antiquarians, themselves the moderns of what is antiquity to us!

The surging crowd around us thinks of naught but the acquisition of wealth and material enjoyment, occupied only with the struggle for place and power. Men lift their skirts and hurry through the mire; they suffer indignity and feel no sense of shame. And if from out this mass there arises one spirit purer and simpler than the rest, striving to tread a nobler path than they, and amusing his leisure, for his own gratification, with guitars, and books, and pictures and other relics of olden times—such a man is indeed a genuine lover of the antique. He can never be one of the common herd, though the common herd always affect to admire whatever is admittedly admirable. In the same way, persons who aim at advancement in their career, will spare no endeavour to collect the choicest rarities, in order, by such gifts, to curry favour with their superiors; who, in their turn, will take pleasure in ostentatious display of their collections of antiquities. Such is but a specious hankering after antiques, arising simply from a desire to eclipse one's neighbours. Such men are not genuine lovers of the antique. Their tastes are those of the common herd after all, though they make a great show and filch the reputation of true antiquarians, in the hope of thus distinguishing themselves from their fellows, ignorant as they are that what they secure is the name alone without the reality.

The man whom I call a genuine antiquarian is he who studies the writings of the ancients, and strives to form himself upon their model though unable to greet them in the flesh; who ever and anon, in his wanderings up and down the long avenue of the past, lights upon some choice fragment which brings him in an instant face to face with the immortal dead. Of such enjoyment there is no satiety. Those who truly love antiquity, love not the things, but the men of old; since a relic in the present is much what it was in the past—a mere thing. And so if it is not to things, but rather to men, that devotion is due, then even I may aspire to be some day an antique. Who shall say that centuries hence an antiquarian of the day may not look up at me as I have looked up to my predecessors? Should I then neglect myself, and foolishly devote my energies to trifling with things?

Such is the popular enthusiasm in these matters. It is shadow without substance. But the theme is endless, and I shall therefore content myself with this passing record of my old inkstand.

Source: *Gems of Chinese Literature: Prose.* 2nd ed. Ed. by Giles A. Herbert. London: Bernard Quarittch, 1923, pp. 228–29.

12. Painting for Noblemen

Although the European aristocracy enjoyed collecting the visual arts, including both contemporaneous and classical art, a career in the visual arts was nevertheless viewed as beneath the status of a nobleman. An aristocrat could purchase art, but he was expected not to become an artist himself.

Thomas Elyot, in his manifesto on education, The Governour *(1537), attempts to counter these social class prejudices by highlighting how useful the visual arts are to a gentleman's "proper" role as general and governor. Elyot names a long list of famous kings and princes who painted or carved, and he claims that skill in drawing will help princes to produce more accurate military maps, which will in turn lead to greater military success, resulting ultimately in increased security for the prince's home country. Painting, Elyot claims, will increase homeland security. Elyot likewise suggests that the ability to diagram has aided kings in the past in the invention of new war-machines. The visual arts, in sum, are a tool of war.*

Although the connection between skill in carving and success in war is tenuous at best, Elyot mentions other reasons to value artistic skill that remain convincing even today: visual imagery helps students learn and can move viewers more powerfully than written or spoken words. Elyot's claim that visual representations of historical events can be more memorable concurs with modern understandings of learning styles, in which reading material, auditory lectures, and visual diagrams all play a role. Few readers, moreover, will doubt how visual material—photographs, for example—can cut directly and emotionally to the heart of an issue.

Despite his attempts to demonstrate the utility of the visual arts to the upper classes, Elyot nevertheless relegates artistic skills to second place in his educational curriculum. Elyot states that pupils interested in the arts should receive art lessons only "in vacant times from other more serious learning," that is, outside of regular class times. The arts are meant to supplement regular classes, not to supplant them. Because art will not be the nobleman's focus, he will never be a professional artist; hence, Thomas Elyot, contrary to his critics' claims, will not be turning noblemen into "masons or painters," terms used derisively to describe working-class craftsmen. Rather than non-aristocratic painters, who are "stained or embrewed with sundry colors," Elyot's students will be noblemen who also happen to be able to paint.

If the child be of nature inclined (as many have been) to paint with a pen, or to form images in stone or tree, he should not be therefrom withdrawn, or nature be rebuked, which is to him benevolent, but putting one to him, which is in that craft wherein he deliteth, most excellent, in vacant times from other more serious learning, he should be in the most pure wise instructed in painting or carving. And now perchance some envious reader will hereof take occasion to scorn me, saying that I had well hied me to make a noble man a mason or painter. And yet if either ambition or voluptuous idleness would have suffered that reader to have seen histories, he should have found excellent princes, as well in painting as in carving, equal to noble artificers. Such were Claudius Titus, the son of Vespasian, Hadrian, both Antonines, and diverse other emperors and noble princes, whose works of long time remained in Rome and other cities, in such places where all men might behold them, as monuments of their excellent wits and virtuous occupation, in eschewing of idleness.

And not without necessary cause, princes were in their childhood so instructed: for it served them afterward for devising of engines for the war; or for making them better that be already devised. For as Vitruvius (which writeth of building to the emperor Augustus) sayeth: "Al torments of war, which we call engines, were first invented by kings or governors of hosts, or if they were devised by other, they were by them made much better."

Also by the feat of portraiture or painting a captain may describe the country of his adversary, whereby he shall eschew the dangerous passages with his host or navy; also perceive the places of advantage, the form of embatailing of his enemies, the situation of his camp, for his most surety, the strength or weakness of the town or fortress, which he intendeth to assault. And that, which is most specially to be considered in visiting his own dominions, he shall set them out in figure in such wise that at his eye shall appear to him, where he shall employ his study and treasure, as well for the safeguard of his country as for the commodity and honor thereof, having at all times in his sight the surety and feebleness, advancement and hindrance of the same. And what pleasure and also utility is it to a man, which intendeth to edify himself, to express the figure of the work that he purposeth, according as he hath conceived it in his own fantasy. Wherein by often amending and correcting, he finally shall so perfect the work unto his purpose, that there shall neither ensure any repentance nor in the employment of his money he shall be by other deceived.

Moreover, the feat of portraiture shall be an elective to every other study or exercise. For the wit thereto disposed shall always covet congruent matter, wherein it may be occupied. And when he happeneth to read or hear any fable or history, forthwith he apprehendeth it more desirously and retaineth it better than any other that lacketh the said feat, by reason that he hath found matter apt to his fantasy. Finally, every thing that portraiture may comprehend will be to him delectable to read or hear. And where the lively spirit and that which is called the grace of the thing is perfectly expressed that thing more persuadeth and steereth the beholder, and sooner instructeth him, than the declaration in writing or speaking doth the reader or hearer. Experience we have thereof in learning of geometry, astronomy, and cosmography, called in English the description of the world. In which studies I dare affirm a man shall more profit in one week by figures and charts, well and perfectly made, than he shall by the only reading or hearing the rules of that science, by the space of half a year at the least. Wherefore the late writers deserve no small commendation, which added to the authors of those sciences apt and proper figures.

And he that is perfectly instructed in portraiture and happeneth to read any noble and excellent history whereby his courage is inflamed to the imitation of virtue, he forthwith taketh his pen or pencil, and with a grave and substantial study, gathering to him all the parts of imagination, endeavoureth himself to express lively, and (as I might say) actually, in portraiture, not only the fact or affair, but also the sundry affections of every personage in the history recited, which might in any wise appear or be perceived in their visage, countenance, or gesture; with like diligence as Lysippus made in metal King Alexander, fighting and struggling with a terrible lion of incomparable magnitude and fierceness, whom, after long and difficult battle with wonderfull strength and clean might at the last he overthrew and vanquished. Wherein he so expressed the similitude of Alexander, and of his lords standing about him, that they all seemed to live. Among whom the prowess of Alexander appeared excelling all other, the residue of his lords after the value and estimation of their courage, every man set out in such forwardness, as they than seemed more prompt to the helping of their master, that is to say, one less afeared than another.

Phidias the Athenian, whom all writers do commend, made of ivory the simulacrum or image of Jupiter, honored by the gentiles, on the high hill of Olympus, which was done so excellently, that Pandenus, a cunning painter, thereat admarvelling, required the craftsman to show him where he had the example or pattern of so noble a work. Then Phidias answered that he had taken it out of three verses of Homer the poet: the sentence whereof ensueth as well as my poor wit can express it in English.

> Then Jupiter, the father of them all
> Thereto assented with his brows black,
> Shaking his hair, and therewith did let fall
> A countenance that made all heaven to quake.

Where it is to be noted that Thetis, the mother of Achilles, desired Jupiter to incline his favor to the part of the Trojans.

Now (as I have before said), I intend not by these examples to make of a prince or nobleman's son a common painter or carver, which shall present himself openly, stained or embrewed with sundry colors, or powdered with the dust of stones that he cutteth, or perfumed with tedious savours of the metals by him gotten; but verily mine intent and meaning is only that a noble child, by his own natural disposition and not by coercion, may be induced to receive perfect instruction in these sciences.

Source: Elyot, Sir Thomas. *The Boke Named the Governour.* London: Thomas Berthelet, 1537, pp. 23–26.

13. *Painting with the Renaissance Masters*

Leon Battista Alberti (1404–1472) was a quintessential "Renaissance man," in the sense that he was learned in a wide variety of intellectual and artistic fields. His writings, for example, span the gamut from advice on how to raise a family to the following extract from Della pittura, *his famous treatise on the arts. In addition to being an accomplished writer, Alberti also found fame as a practical artist in the fields of architecture and painting.*

Della pittura, the Italian version of his slightly earlier Latin work De pictura, *remains Alberti's most remembered work because it sets out the basic principles of linear perspective. The art of the Middle Ages was generally "flat," with distance indicated by simply placing figures behind each other. Artists such as Giotto were rapidly moving to perspective, but it was Alberti who laid down the theoretical principles that are contained in the concept of a "vanishing point." Although Alberti, like Giotto, was a pioneer in painting, he nonetheless made frequent allusions to the art of the ancient Greeks, a common practice throughout the self-styled "Renaissance," which means "rebirth" and refers to the alleged rebirth of ancient Greek and Roman culture.*

In this extract, Alberti describes what, in his view, are the most important parts of any painting: circumscription (the outlined drawing of figures) and composition (the placement of figures). He also discusses many subpoints, such as the need for logic in the painted scene (which he calls istoria). His guide offers an excellent insight into how educated Italians evaluated artwork. He also reveals some of the tricks of the trade, such as a translucent veil with a grid marked on it; the painter looks through the grid, notes where the lines of his subject fall on that grid, and then reproduces those lines exactly on this lightly (or mentally) gridded paper.

Therefore, painting is composed of circumscription, composition and reception of light. In the following we shall treat of them most briefly.

First we will treat of circumscription. Circumscription describes the turning of the outline in the painting. It is said that Parrhasius, the painter who talked with Socrates in Xenophon, was most expert in this and had examined these lines carefully. I say that in this circumscription one ought to take great pains to make these lines so fine that they can scarcely be seen. The painter Apelles used to practice this and to compete with Protogenes. Because circumscription is nothing but the drawing of the outline, which when done with too apparent a line does not indicate a margin of the plane but a neat cleavage, I should desire that only the movement of the outline be inscribed. To this, I insist, one must devote a great amount of practice. No composition and no reception of light can be praised where there is not also a good circumscription—that is, a good drawing—which is most pleasant in itself. Here is a good aid for whoever wishes to make use of it. Nothing can be found, so I think, which is more useful than that veil which among my friends I call an intersection. It is a thin veil, finely woven, dyed whatever colour pleases you and with larger threads [marking out] as many parallels as you prefer. This veil I place between the eye and the thing seen, so the visual pyramid penetrates through the thinness of the veil. This veil can be of great use to you. Firstly, it always presents to you the same unchanged plane. Where you have placed certain limits, you quickly find the true cuspid of the pyramid. This would certainly be difficult without the intersection. You know how impossible it is to imitate a thing which does not continue to present the same appearance, for it is easier to copy painting than sculpture. You know that as the distance and the position of the centre are changed, the thing you see seems greatly altered. Therefore the veil will be, as I said, very useful to you, since it is always the same thing in the process of seeing. Secondly, you will easily be able to constitute the limits of the outline and of the planes. Here in this parallel you will see the forehead, in that the nose, in another the cheeks, in this lower one the chin and all outstanding features in their place. On panels or on walls, divided into similar parallels, you will be able to put everything in its place. Finally, the veil will greatly aid you in learning how to paint when you see in it round objects and objects in relief. By these things you will be able to test with experience and judgment how very useful our veil can be to you.

Nor will I hear what some may say, that the painter should not use these things, because even though they are great aids in painting well, they may perhaps be so made that he will soon be able to do nothing without them. I do not believe that infinite pains should be demanded of the painter, but paintings which appear in good relief and a good likeness of the subject should be expected. This I do not believe can ever be done without the use of the veil. Therefore, let us use this intersection, that is the veil, as we have said. Then, when a painter wishes to try his skill without the veil, he should note first the limits of objects within the parallels of the veil. Or he may study them in another manner by imagining a line intersected by its perpendicular wherever these limits are located. But since the outlines of the planes are frequently unknown to the inexpert painter—doubtful and uncertain as in the faces of man where he does not discern the distance between the forehead and the temples—it would be well to teach him how he can come to understand them.

This is clearly demonstrated by nature. We see in flat planes that each one reveals itself by its lines, lights and shades. Again spherical concave planes are divided into many planes as if chequered with spots of light and shade. Therefore each part with its highlights, divided by those which are dark, would thus appear as many planes. However, if one continuous plane, beginning shadowy, becomes little by little lighter, then note the middle of it with a very fine line so that the method of colouring it will be less in doubt.

Circumscription, which pertains not a little to composition, remains to be treated. For this it is well to know what composition is in painting. I say composition is that rule in painting by which the parts fit together in the painted work. The greatest work of the painter is the *istoria*. Bodies are part of the *istoria*, members are parts of the bodies, planes are parts of the members. Circumscription is nothing more than a certain rule for designing the outline of the planes, since some planes are small as in animals, others are large as those of buildings and colossi.

Concerning the small planes the precepts given up to here will be enough—precepts which we demonstrated when we learned how to use the veil. Perhaps we should find new rules for the larger planes. We must remember what has been said above in the instruction on planes, rays, the pyramid, the intersection, and on the parallels of the pavement, the centric point and line. On the pavement, drawn with its lines and parallels, walls and similar planes which we have called jacent are to be built. Here I will describe just briefly what I do. First I begin with the foundation. I place the width and the length of the wall in its parallels. In this laying out I follow nature. I note that, in any squared body which has right angles, only two on joined sides can be seen at one time. I observe this in describing the foundations of the walls. I always commence first of all with the nearest plane, the greatest of those which are equidistant from the cross-section. These I put before the others, describing their width and height in those parallels of the pavement in such a way that for as many *braccia* as I choose they occupy as many parallels. To find the middle of each parallel, I find where the diameters mutually intersect. And thus, as I wish, I draw the foundations. Then the height follows by not at all difficult rules. I know the height of the wall contains in itself this proportion, that as much as it is from the place where it starts on the pavement to the centric line, so much it rises upwards. When you wish this quantity of the pavement up to the centric line to be the height of a man, there will, therefore, be these three *braccia*. Since you wish your wall to be twelve braccia, you go up three times the distance from the centric line to that place on the pavement. With these rules we shall be able to draw all planes which have angles.

The way in which circles are drawn remains to be treated. Circles are drawn from angles. I do it in this manner. In a space I make a quadrangle with right angles, and I divide the sides of this quadrangle in the painting. From each point to its opposite point I draw lines and thus the space is divided into many small quadrangles. Here I draw a circle as large as I want it so the lines of the small quadrangles and the lines of the circle cut each other mutually. I note all the points of this cutting; these places I mark on the parallels of the pavement in my painting. It would be an extreme and almost never-ending labour to divide the circle in many places with new minor parallels and with a great number of points to complete the circle. For this reason, when I have noted eight or more intersections, I continue the circle in the painting with my mind, guiding the lines from point to point. Would it perhaps be briefer to derive it from a shadow? Certainly, if the body which made the shadow were in the middle, located by rule in its place.

We have considered in what way with the aid of the parallels the large angular and round planes are drawn. Since we have finished the circumscription, that is the way of drawing. Composition remains to be treated.

It would be well to repeat what composition is. Composition is that rule of painting by which the parts of the things seen fit together in the painting. The greatest work of the painter is not a colossus, but an *istoria*. *Istoria* gives greater renown to the intellect than any colossus. Bodies are part of the *istoria*, members are parts of the bodies, planes part of the members. The primary parts of painting, therefore, are the planes. That grace in bodies which we call beauty is born from the composition of the planes. A face which has its planes here large and there small, here raised and there depressed—similar to the faces of old women—would be most ugly in appearance. Those faces which have the planes joined in such a way that they take shades and lights agreeable and pleasantly, and have no harshness of the relief angles, these we should certainly say are beautiful and delicate faces.

Therefore, in this composition of planes grace and beauty of things should be intensely sought for. It seems to me that there is no more certain and fitting way for one who wishes to pursue this than to take them from nature, keeping in mind in what way nature, marvelous artificer of things, has composed the planes in beautiful bodies. In imitating these it is well both to take great care and to think deeply about them and to make great use of our above-mentioned veil. When we wish to put into practice what we have learned from nature, we will always first note the limits to which we shall draw our lines.

Up to here we have talked of the composition of planes; members follow. First of all, take care that all the members are suitable. They are suitable when size, function, kind, colour and other similar things correspond to a single beauty. If in a painting the head should be very large and the breasts small, the hand ample and the foot swollen, and the body puffed up, this composition would certainly be ugly to see. Therefore, we ought to have a certain rule for the size of the members. In this measuring it would be useful to isolate each bone of the animal, on this add its muscles, then clothe all of it with its flesh. Here someone will object that I have said above that the painter has only to do with things which are visible. He has a good memory. Before dressing a man we first draw him nude, then we enfold him in draperies. So in painting the nude we place first his bones and muscles which we then cover with flesh so that it is not difficult to understand where each muscle is beneath. Since nature has here carried the measurements to a mean, there is not a little utility in recognizing them. Serious painters will take this task on themselves from nature. They will put as much study and work into remembering what they take from nature as they do in discovering it. A thing to remember: to measure an animate body, take one of its members by which the others can be measured. Vitruvius, the architect, measured the height of man by the feet. It seems a more worthy thing to me for the other members to have reference to the head, because I have noticed as common in all men that the foot is as long as from the chin to the crown of the head. Thus one member is taken which corresponds to all the other members in such a way that none of them is non-proportional to the others in length and width.

Then provide that every member can fulfill its function in what it is doing. A runner is expected to throw his hands and feet, but I prefer a philosopher while he is talking to show much more modesty than skill in fencing. The painter Demon represented hoplites in a contest so that you would say one was sweating while another, putting down his weapons, clearly seemed to be out of breath. Ulysses has been painted so that you could recognize his insanity was only feigned and not real. An *istoria* is praised in Rome in which Meleager, a dead man, weighs down those who carry him. In every one of his members he appears completely dead—everything hangs, hands, fingers and head; everything falls heavily. Anyone who tries to express a dead body—which is certainly most difficult—will be a good painter, if he knows how to make each member of a body flaccid. Thus, in every painting take care that each member performs its function so that none by the slightest articulation remains flaccid. The members of the dead should be dead to the very nails; of live persons every member should be alive in the smallest part. The body is said to live when it has certain voluntary movements. It is said to be dead when the members no longer are able to carry on the functions of life, that is, movement and feeling. Therefore the painter, wishing to express life in things, will make every part in motion—but in motion he will keep loveliness and grace. The most graceful movements and the most lively are those which move upwards into the air.

Again we say that in composition the members ought to have certain things in common. It would be absurd if the hands of Helen or of Ophigenia were old and gnarled, or if Nestor's breast were youthful and his neck smooth; or Ganymede's forehead were wrinkled and his thighs those of a labourer; if Milo, a very strong man, were to have short and slender flanks; if a figure whose face is fresh and full should have muscular arms and fleshless hands. Anyone painting Achemenides, found by Aeneas on the island, with the face which Virgil describes and the other members not following such consumptiveness, would be a painter to laugh at. For this reason, all the members ought to conform to a certain appropriateness. I should also like the members to correspond to one colour, because it would be little becoming for one who has a rosy, white and pleasant face to have the breast and the other members ugly and dirty. Therefore, in the composition of members we ought to follow what I have said about size, function, kind and colour. Then everything has its dignity. It would not be suitable to dress Venus or Minerva in the rough wool cloak of a soldier; it would be the same to dress Mars or Jove in the clothes of a woman. The antique painters took care in painting Castor and Pollux to make them appear brothers, but in the one a pugnacious nature appeared and in the other agility. They also took pains to show under the robe of Vulcan his handicap of hobbling—so great was their diligence in expressing the function, kind and dignity of whatever they painted.

The fame of the painter and of his art is found in the following—the composition of bodies. Certain things said in the composition of members also apply here. Bodies ought to harmonize together in the *istoria* in both size and function. It would be absurd for one who paints the Centaurs fighting after the banquet to leave a vase of wine still standing in such tumult. We would call it a weakness if in the same distance one person should appear larger than another, or if dogs should be equal to horses, or better, as I frequently see, if a man is placed in a building as in a closed casket where there is scarcely room to sit down. For these reasons, all bodies should harmonize in size and in function to what is happening in the *istoria*.

The *istoria* which merits both praise and admiration will be so agreeably and pleasantly attractive that it will capture the eye of whatever learned or unlearned person is looking at it and will move his soul. That which first gives pleasure in the *istoria* comes from copiousness and variety of things. In food and in music novelty and abundance please, as they are different from the old and usual. So the soul is delighted by all copiousness and variety. For this reason, copiousness and variety please in painting. I say that *istoria* is most copious in which in their places are mixed old, young, maidens, women, youths, young boys, fowls, small dogs, birds, horses, sheep, buildings, landscapes and all similar things. I will praise any copiousness which belongs in that *istoria*. Frequently the copiousness of the painter begets much pleasure when the beholder stands staring at all the things there. However, I prefer this copiousness to be embellished with a certain variety, yet moderate and grave with dignity and truth. I blame those painters who, where they wish to appear copious, leave nothing vacant. It is not composition but dissolute confusion which they disseminate. There the *istoria* does not appear to aim to do something worthy but rather to be in tumult.

Source: Alberti, Leon Battista. *On Painting*. Translated by John R. Spencer. New Haven, CT: Yale University Press, © 1956, 67–73. Used by permission of Yale University.

Part VIII
RELIGIOUS LIFE

Religious life has stirred some of humankind's deepest emotions. Men and women have suffered hardship, persecution, and death for the sake of maintaining their religion. Missionaries have left their home countries and traveled great distances to introduce others to the beliefs they hold dear. The Deities and Doctrines section focuses on what some of these religious beliefs were during the Middle Ages and Renaissance. Some religions were born during this time. Muhammad (A.D. 570–632) started the religion of Islam after he had visions of the angel Gabriel. Other religions continued to develop; Shinto produced *Kojiki*, the most important textual description of traditional Japanese religion. The Protestant Reformation in sixteenth-century Europe produced new forms of Christianity during this period. New religious beliefs could spread rapidly; during this time period, Christianity became the religion of Europe. Buddhism dug deeper roots into China and Japan, and Islam swept the Arab world and into Spain, Africa, and western Asia. Religious beliefs often spread peacefully. Other times, new religious beliefs were met with resistance. Sir John Oldcastle was executed for continuing to advocate a Lollard form of Christianity, while Confucianists criticized the growth of Buddhism in China.

Most religions worldwide have specialists who help and guide others in prayer. these specialists are usually called priests, and the ceremonies that priests, and other believers, perform are called rituals. The Priests and Rituals section discusses the roles that these professionals and ceremonies played during the Middle Ages and Renaissance. Worship, in the form of oral prayer or physical actions, dominated religious rituals. The centrality of prayer in Muslim life so impressed the Englishman Thomas Roe that he used their example to rebuke the lax prayer lives of Europeans. Priests were natural leaders in their local and national communities, and, as a result, they could wield huge political, as well as religious, power. The Donation of Constantine, a medieval forgery, attempted to place a significant part of western Europe directly under the political power of the Pope. Kings attempted to resist the usurpation of their own political power by regulating religion and priests within their kingdom. Religious life often intersected directly with political life.

Most, but not all, religions explored the question of what happens after death. Eyewitness accounts of the afterlife appear frequently. What happens in the next life, however, can vary greatly from one tradition to the other. One document from China, for example, describes a soul that is stuffed up a giant's sleeve until the soul calls for help from Buddha. Xibalba, the kingdom of the dead in Maya religion, is a place of torment, featuring a house of knives and a house of bats, among others. Most religions offer a chance to escape from the worst sufferings of the afterlife. Often, as the documents show in the Death and the Afterlife section, living a virtuous and kind life in this world will lead to a good life in the next world. Death, then, was not the end for most peoples, and the afterlife encouraged people to live kindly, generously, virtuously, and courageously. Sir John Oldcastle could go to his death calmly because he fully expected to enter Paradise. Of course, their lack of fear could also make religious enemies even more dangerous.

Religious life could inspire some of the noblest actions, but also could create tremendous conflict.

Deities and Doctrines

By the Middle Ages, many of the world's prominent religions—Judaism, Christianity, Buddhism, and Hinduism—were well established. Even so, all these religions continued to develop, and other major religions (Islam in particular) were born, while other religions developed their first written texts (*Shinto*, for example).

The birth of Islam from *Muhammad*'s (A.D. 570–632) visionary experiences has had global consequences for the medieval and modern world. Islam grew out of the religious melting pot of early medieval Arabia, in which Jewish, Christian, and tribal religions mixed freely, and sometimes violently. Muhammad himself combined a gift for religious preaching with the skill of a military commander. Document 6 outlines some of the key principles of Islam and some of its religious origins.

Christianity underwent particularly dramatic changes during the *Renaissance*, as the Protestant Reformation of the sixteenth century created new Christian churches independent of the hierarchical governing systems headquartered in the Mediterranean. As Document 3 indicates, reformers such as John Calvin stressed that the Bible, rather than the pope or bishops, was the ultimate, or even the sole, authority in doctrinal matters. This reverence for the scriptures, however, frequently went hand in hand with less literal readings of the New Testament. Calvin, for example, held that the Eucharist was deeply symbolic of Christ's body and blood, whereas the Roman Catholic hierarchy had a more philosophically literal understanding of Christ's words: "This is my body." Early Catholic thinkers responded to the thirst for the gospel books by providing biblical paraphrases, some of them quite moving (e.g., Nicholas Love's *Mirror of the Blessed Life of Jesus Christ* was particularly popular; see Document 2), but none of them were able to satisfy the laity's demand for direct access to the New Testament.

Change and innovation in religion have frequently caused strife and conflict. The challenge to medieval Christianity posed by the European reformers often resulted in violent interventions. Document 7, for example, relates the trial of Sir John Oldcastle, who in the early fifteenth century was tried for heresy, found guilty, and eventually punished with death. Such discord was hardly just a European phenomenon; Document 4 demonstrates resistance of *Confucianism* to the growing popularity in China of Buddhism, which had spread from northern India and was considered foreign—and therefore bad—by thinkers such as Han Wen-Kung (A.D. 768–824).

Religion, however, was also frequently a force for compassion. The lynchpin of the mystic thought of Julian of Norwich (Document 1) was compassion. Influenced by the "affective piety" of the late Middle Ages, in which the believer focused on emotionally responding to Christ's life and message, Julian argued that the suffering of Christ taught believers to have compassion for and mercy on their fellow sinners. According to Julian, sin caused the sinner suffering, and this suffering pulled compassion and mercy from Christ just as contemplation of Christ's suffering pulled compassion from the Christian believer.

Indeed, one of the basic tenets of many religions, including Shinto (Document 5) in Japan, is that God (or the gods) created the universe. As a result, the physical world is in some sense divine and is in some sense divinely good. These religions are fundamentally optimistic. The world may be getting worse and worse, but it always has some chance of returning to its original pristine connection with the heavens. Paradise, or Eden, may be lost, but it can still be regained.

1. Julian of Norwich: A Mystic's Vision of Christ

Mystic visions have played a role in Christianity since its earliest days. The biblical book of Revelation, for example, consists of an apocalyptic vision. Christians in the Middle Ages continued to experience visions of God. Some mystics, such as Bridget of Sweden, became famous internationally and were considered saints in their own lifetimes. Others, such as the author of the following extract, the English mystic Julian of Norwich (1342–c. 1416), achieved only a local celebrity; people from eastern England knew of Julian and visited her, but she did not become renowned outside of her local area.

Julian's lack of international fame is partly due to the fact that she was not particularly unique. Several late medieval women experienced visions, and many more lived the same austere lifestyle as Julian of Norwich. These women, called anchorites, walled themselves into a room from which they never emerged for the rest of their lives. Food and other necessities were delivered to them in their room, and waste products were carted away. Although these anchorites never left the one room, they were not necessarily cut off from the outside world. Julian, for example, regularly received visitors seeking her advice about spiritual matters. Although these women were not priests, they were considered religious experts.

Julian used her renown to preach a simple, but meaningful, message focusing on compassion. As a result of a near-death experience that she underwent at the age of 30 (described in part in the extract), Julian came to realize fully that existence is radically dependent on God's love. Julian described later in her work that God has compassion for sinners in the same way that people have compassion for Christ on the cross. Just as Christians cannot look at the cross and not feel sorry for Christ, so Christ cannot look at sinners and not feel compassion for them. As a result, sin does not tear us away from God—it is simply not that powerful. Instead, sin causes God to feel more compassion for, indeed to love, that sinner more. Although Julian's theology is more complex than this summary can suggest, her message was one of peace, forgiveness, and trust in Christ.

As the following extract makes clear, meditating on the sufferings of Christ was key to Julian's visionary experience. Julian's vision begins in earnest when the curate (local priest) holds up a crucifix for the dying Julian to gaze on; seeing the cross triggers Julian's compassion for her dying Lord. This compassion then leads ultimately to further understanding of Christ's compassion for us. Although Julian's longing to feel Christ's pains, his "passion" in the sense of suffering, may strike some modern readers as odd, fascination with the suffering of Christ was common in the later Middle Ages. This form of piety, in which the believer seeks to become emotionally united with the suffering Christ, is called "affective piety."

And when I was thirty years old and a half, God sent me a bodily sickness in which I lay three days and three nights, and on the fourth night I took all the rites of Holy Church and expected not to live to daytime, but after this I languished for two days and two nights. And on the third night, I thought often that I was about to die, as did those who were with me. Since I was still young, I thought it a great pity to die, not because there was something on earth that I wanted to live for, nor because I was afraid of any pain (for I trusted in God's mercy), but rather because I wanted to live so that I might love God better and for a longer time, so that I might have more knowledge and love of God in the bliss of Heaven. For the time that I had lived here seemed so little and so short, as if it were nothing in comparison to the reward of endless bliss. Wherefore I thought, "Good Lord, may my living no longer be to Your worship?" And I understood by my reason and by feeling the pain that I was going to die, and I assented fully to it, that all my will should be in accordance with God's will. Thus I lasted until day, and by then my body was numb from the middle down. Then I was propped up in a sitting position, in order to have more freedom of heart to be at God's will, and to think on God while my life should last.

My curate was sent for to be at my death, and by the time he came my eyes had lost focus and I was unable to speak. He placed the cross before my face and said, "I have brought you the image of thy creator and Savior. Look upon it and take comfort." I thought I was fine already, because my eyes were looking up straight into heaven where I trusted to come by the mercy of God, but I nevertheless consented to look on the face of the Crucifix, if I could; and so I did, because I thought that I might be able to look straight ahead longer than I could upwards. After this my sight began to fail, and it was all dark around me in the chamber, as if it had been night, save on the image of the cross wherein I beheld a common light, and I knew not how. All that was beside the cross was ugly to me, as if it had been overrun with devils. After this, the other part of my body began to die, so that I had barely any feeling left, with shortness of breath; and then I expected to die shortly.

Suddenly all my pain was taken from me, and I was as healthy in all my body as I ever was before. I marveled at this sudden change, for I thought it was the mysterious working of God, and not of nature; but, despite this feeling of ease, I did not expect to live longer. Nor was this feeling of ease true ease for me, because I thought that I would rather be delivered out of this world. Then it suddenly came into my mind that I should desire the second wound of our Lord's gracious gift, that my body might be fulfilled with the thought and feeling of His blessed passion, for I wished that His pains would be my pains, with compassion and consequent longing for God. But in this I never desired the bodily sight or showing of God, but compassion as a kind soul might have with our Lord Jesus that for love would become a mortal man; and therefore I desired to suffer with Him.

Then I suddenly saw the red blood trickle down from under the garland, hot and fresh and right plentifully, as if it were the time of His passion when the garland of thorns was pressed on His blessed head. Right so, both God and man, the same that suffered thus for me, I conceived truly and mightily that it was Himself showed me it without any go-between.

And in the same showing, suddenly the Trinity filled the heart utterly with great joy; and I understood that it would be like this in heaven without end, for everyone that will go there. For the Trinity is God, God is the Trinity. The Trinity is our maker and keeper, the Trinity is our everlasting lover, everlasting joy and bliss, by our Lord Jesus Christ; and this was shown first and foremost, for where Jesus appeareth, the blessed Trinity is understood, as I see it.

And I said, "Blessings, Lord." This I said for reverence in my meaning with a mighty voice, and full greatly was I astonished for wonder and marvel that I had, that He that is so reverend and dreadful would be so comfortable with a sinful creature living in wretched flesh. This I took to be the time of my temptation, for I thought that, by the permission of God, I would be tempted by devils before I died. With this sight of the blessed passion, with the Godhead that I saw in my understanding, I knew well that it was strong enough for me, yes, and to all creatures living, against all the devils of Hell and spiritual temptation.

Then He brought our blessed Lady to my understanding. I saw her spiritually in bodily likeness, a simple and meek maid, young of age and little grown beyond childhood, in the stature that she was when she conceived the child. Also God showed the wisdom and the truth of her soul, wherein I understood the reverent beholding with which she beheld her God and maker, marveling with great reverence that He would be born of her that was a simple creature of His own making. And this wisdom and truth, knowing the greatness of her maker and the littleness of herself, that is made, caused her to say full meekly to Gabriel, "Behold, I am God's handmaid." In this sight I understood truly that she is more than all that God made beneath her in worthiness and grace. For above her is nothing that is made but the blessed manhood of Christ, as I see it.

At this same time, our Lord showed to me a spiritual sight of His friendly loving. I saw that He is to us everything that is good and comfortable for us. He is our clothing, that for love wraps us up, covers us, and all surrounds us in tender love, that He may never leave us, being to us everything that is good, as I understand it. He then showed me also a little thing the size of a hazelnut in the palm of my hand, and it was as round as a ball. I looked thereupon with the eye of my understanding and thought, "What may this be?" And it was generally answered thus: "It is all that is made." I marveled how it might last, for it seemed to me that it might suddenly have fallen and been destroyed, because it was so small. And I was answered in my understanding: "It will always last because God loves it; and so does everything owe existence to the love of God."

Source: Julian of Norwich. *Shewings*. Chapters 3–5. Translated and adapted by Lawrence Morris for this encyclopedia. See also *A Book of Showings to the Anchoress Julian of Norwich*. 2 vols. Ed. by Edmund Colledge and James Walsh. Toronto: Pontifical Institute of Mediaeval Studies, 1978.

2. Nicolas Love on the Benefits of Meditating on Christ's Life

Nicholas Love (d. c. 1424) was one of the leading English churchmen of the early fifteenth century. Love was particularly concerned with the proper religious education of the laity, and his influential The Mirror of the Blessed Life of Jesus Christ *(c. 1410) offered a model of Christian spirituality for the average Christian. In* The Mirror, *as the following excerpt shows, Love advocates meditation on the life of Christ as a means of making spiritual progress and of cultivating a virtuous life. The Mirror leads the reader through the life of Christ, while making useful observations about the spiritual significance of moments in Christ's life. Love also encourages an active use of the imagination; he urges the reader to imagine the scene so vividly that it actually comes to life before one's eyes.*

Works such as The Mirror *also highlight the divide between the clergy and the laity during the later Middle Ages. Bishops, priests, theologians, and the clergy in general were expected to read the Bible in Latin. Most laypeople, however, were unable to read Latin and therefore did not have direct access to biblical texts. Two movements developed to address the laity's hunger for information about Christ. One movement advocated translating the Bible into English, and the other movement created paraphrases of the Bible interspersed with commentary. Nicholas Love belonged to the latter movement; the first movement was viewed as potentially heretical by the early 1400s. Although officially sanctioned Bible translations did circulate, many translations were associated with the English Christian sect known as the Lollards, a group that was considered heretical by the Church hierarchy. For the most part, the clergy believed that laypeople did not have enough education to understand the Bible correctly, and therefore the hierarchy advocated the production of more explanatory texts instead of direct Bible translations. Although this position seems snooty by today's standards, it is true that the vast majority of the laity did not have a significant amount of formal schooling and were much less educated than the higher-ranking ecclesiastical clergy. Just as school officials today do not allow students free access to all chemicals in a science laboratory, Church officials thought it unwise to allow free access to all aspects of the Bible.*

Among other virtuous commandments of the holy virgin Cecile, it is written that she always carried the gospel of Christ hidden in her breast; that is, she chose certain very devout passages out of the blessed life of our lord Jesus Christ written in the gospel, in which she set her meditation and her thought night and day with a clean heart and full attention. And when she had so fully gone over the whole manner of his life, she began again. And so, with a liking and sweet taste, spiritually chewing in that manner the gospel of Christ, she set and carried it always in the privacy of her breast. I counsel you to do the same. For, among all the spiritual exercises, I believe that this is the most necessary and the most profitable, and that it may bring to the highest degree of good living whoever greatly despises the world, with patience in the face of suffering and adversity, for gaining and increasing virtues. For truly, you will never find a better way than the blessed life of our lord Jesus, who was always perfect and without fault, to teach people first of all, to strengthen their hearts against vanities and the deceptive pleasures of the world, and to strengthen them in the midst of tribulations and adversities, and, furthermore to keep them from vices and to gain virtues.

First, as I say, the frequent and habitual meditation upon the blessed life of Jesus strengthens the soul and heart against vanities and the deceptive pleasures of the world. This is openly seen in the above-mentioned Cecile; when she filled her heart so fully with the life of Christ, the vanities of the world were unable to enter into her. Indeed, amongst all the great pomp of weddings, where many vain things are done, such as songs and organ playing, she set her heart firmly in God, saying and praying: "Lord, let my heart and my body be clean and undefiled, so that I shall not be counfounded."

Second, where would martyrs get their strength against the various tortures, except, as Saint Bernard says, that they set all their heart and devotion on the passion and the wounds of Christ. When a martyr's body is torn to pieces, and he is nevertheless joyful and glad despite all his pain, where do you believe that his soul and heart are then? Truly, they are in the wounds of Christ; indeed the wounds are not closed, but rather open and wide so that they can enter in, or else the martyr would feel the hard iron and would not be able to bear the pain and the sorrow, but would soon fail and deny God. And not only martyrs, but also confessors, virgins, and all that live righteously, despising the world, keep patience, and are even joyful and glad in soul as we frequently see, despite tribulations, sicknesses, and penitential deeds. How so? Because their hearts, through devout meditation of Christ's blessed life, are more in Christ's body than in their own bodies.

Thirdly, that it keeps vices away and disposes one to gain virtues can be shown by the fact that the perfection of all virtues is to be found in Christ's life. For where will you find so clear an example and setting forth of noble charity, of perfect poverty, of deep humility, of patience and other virtues, as in the blessed life of Jesus Christ. Wherefore Saint Bernard says that anyone who wishes to gain virtues does so in vain if he looks anywhere but to the lord of virtues, whose life is the mirror of temperance and all other virtues. Behold the great comfort and spiritual profit that is in the devout contemplation of Christ's blessed life.

Wherefore, you who desire to feel truly the fruit of this book, you must with all your thought and effort make present in your soul those things that books record were said or done by our lord Jesus, and that busily, continually, and with pleasure, as if you heard them with your very own ears, or saw them with your eyes, all the while ignoring and leaving behind all other concerns and occupations.

And although the beginning of this book concerns the blessed life of Christ at his incarnation, nevertheless we may first devoutly imagine and contemplate some things done earlier, concerning God and his angels in heaven, and also about the blessed virgin, our Lady, Saint Mary on earth. And, since this book is divided and separated into seven sections, after the seven days of the week, those that wish should contemplate the proper section on that day. Therefore, on Monday, the first workday of the week, does this spiritual work begin, recounting first the devout desire of the holy angels in heaven for man's restoring and for his salvation, so as to stir men to worship them especially on that day, since holy church keeps them especially in mind on that day. And the subjects in this book are pertinent and profitable for meditation on the aforementioned days, but also during special times of the year; for example, during advent, one can read and devoutly contemplate from the beginning the Nativity of our Lord Jesus, and so forth.

Source: Love, Nicholas. *The Mirror of the Blessed Life of Jesus Christ*. Translated and modified by Lawrence Morris for this volume. See also Nicholas Love, *The Mirror of the Blessed Life of Jesus Christ*. Ed. by Michael Sargent. Exeter: University of Exeter Press, 2004.

3. John Calvin on Scripture and Miracles

John Calvin (1509–1564) was a major leader of the Protestant Reformation, the religious movement that swept northern Europe in the sixteenth century. The Reformation sought to return the Christian Church to what the reformers thought were the original beliefs of Christianity, as outlined in the New Testament. According to the reformers, the medieval Church had allowed idolatrous practices to creep into Christian worship, and it was therefore necessary to strip the Church of such accretions. Tradition, therefore, was not a safe guide to valid Christian worship; instead, the sacred scriptures alone provided access to legitimate and divinely appointed Christianity.

Although Reformation rhetoric claimed to value scriptures more than did the official Catholic Church, in reality, both sides believed in the binding authority of scripture—they differed not in a reverence for the New Testament but rather in how to interpret the New Testament. The Roman Catholic hierarchy, for example, interpreted Christ's words at the last supper, "This is my body," in a much more literal way than Calvin, who thought that these words were richly symbolic but that the bread did not in any real way change into the body of Christ.

In the following extract, Calvin outlines and refutes some of the objections that Catholics made to his teachings. Judging from the space that Calvin allotted to each rebuttal, he found the Reformation Church's apparent lack of miracles to be the most troubling point raised by the Catholic hierarchy. Calvin's need to refute this point in depth suggests that his contemporaries found miracles to be convincing evidence of doctrinal orthodoxy.

Calvin's mastery of biblical argument is clear in the extract, but in keeping with the times, Calvin did not limit his argument to academic concerns alone. He also included ad hominem attacks; in this extract, for example, he argues that priests resist the Reformation just because they want to keep their jobs in the Catholic Church so that they can continue to eat gourmet cuisine (a metaphor for excessive interest in earthly goods). Although some priests probably were motivated by financial incentives, the majority of Catholics were clearly sincere in their beliefs, and Calvin's attack seems underhanded by today's standards, especially when we consider that Calvin prefaced his work to King Francis I of France in an effort to secure political, and perhaps even financial, backing for his own Church system. Sixteenth-century standards of argument, however, were more permissive than modern academic standards.

Look not to our adversaries (I mean the priesthood, at whose beck and pleasure others ply their enmity against us), and consider with me for a little by what zeal they are actuated. The true religion which is delivered in the Scriptures, and which all ought to hold, they readily permit both themselves and others to be ignorant of, to neglect and despise; and they deem it of little moment what each man believes concerning God and Christ, or disbelieves, provided he submits to the judgment of the Church with what they call implicit faith; nor are they greatly concerned though they should see the glory of God dishonoured by open blasphemies, provided not a finger is raised against the primacy of the Apostolic See and the authority of holy mother Church. Why, then, do they war for the mass, purgatory, pilgrimage, and similar follies, with such fierceness and acerbity, that though they cannot prove one of them from the word of God, they deny godliness can be safe without faith in these things—faith drawn out, if I may so express it, to its utmost stretch? Why? Just because their belly is their God, and their kitchen their religion; and they believe, that if these were away they would not only not be Christians, but not even men. For although some wallow in luxury, and others feed on slender crusts, still they all live by the same pot, which without that fuel might not only cool, but altogether freeze. He, accordingly, who is most anxious about his stomach, proves the fiercest champion of his faith. In short, the object on which all to a man are bent, is to keep their kingdom safe or their belly filled; not one gives even the smallest sign of sincere zeal.

Nevertheless, they cease not to assail our doctrine, and to accuse and defame it in what terms they may, in order to render it either hated or suspected. They call it new, and of recent birth; they carp at it as doubtful and uncertain; they bid us tell by what miracles it has been confirmed; they ask if it be fair to receive it against the consent of so many holy Fathers and the most ancient custom; they urge us to confess either that it is schismatical in giving battle to the Church, or that the Church must have been without life during the many centuries in which nothing of the kind was heard. Lastly, they say there is little need of argument, for its quality may be known by its fruits, namely, the large number of sects, the many seditious disturbances, and the great licentiousness which it has produced. No doubt, it is a very easy matter for them, in presence of an ignorant and credulous multitude, to insult over an undefended cause; but were an opportunity of mutual discussion afforded, that acrimony which they now pour out upon us in frothy torrents, with as much license as impunity, would assuredly boil dry.

The Geneva Bible. Produced under John Calvin's auspices, this English-language Bible aimed to encourage the Protestant Reformation in England. The title page image of the Jews crossing the Red Sea symbolically represents Protestant believers resisting the Catholic Church.

1. First, in calling it new, they are exceedingly injurious to God, whose sacred word deserved not to be charged with novelty. To them, indeed, I very little doubt it is new, as Christ is new, and the Gospel new; but those who are acquainted with the old saying of Paul, that Christ Jesus "died for our sins, and rose again for our justification" (Rom. iv. 25), will not detect any novelty in us. That it long lay buried and unknown is the guilty consequence of man's impiety; but now when, by the kindness of God, it is restored to us, it ought to resume its antiquity just as the returning citizen resumes his rights.

2. It is owing to the same ignorance that they hold it to be doubtful and uncertain; for this is the very thing of which the Lord complains by his prophet, "The ox knoweth his owner, and the ass his master's crib; but Israel doth not know, my people doth not consider" (Isaiah i. 3). But however they may sport with its uncertainty, had they to seal their own doctrine with their blood, and at the expense of life, it would be seen what value they put upon it. Very different is our confidence—a confidence which is not appalled by the terrors of death, and therefore not even by the judgment-seat of God.

3. In demanding miracles from us, they act dishonestly; for we have not coined some new gospel, but retain the very one the truth of which is confirmed by all the miracles which Christ and the apostles ever wrought. But they have a peculiarity which we have not—they can confirm their faith by constant miracles down to the present

day! Nay rather, they allege miracles which might produce wavering in minds otherwise well disposed; they are so frivolous and ridiculous, so vain and false. But were they even exceedingly wonderful, they could have no effect against the truth of God, whose name ought to be hallowed always, and everywhere, whether by miracles, or by the natural course of events. The deception would perhaps be more specious if Scripture did not admonish us of the legitimate end and use of miracles. Mark tells us (Mark xvi.20) that the signs which followed the preaching of the apostles were wrought in confirmation of it; so Luke also relates that he Lord "gave testimony to the word of his grace, and granted signs and wonders to be done" by the hands of the apostles (Acts xiv.3). Very much to the same effect are those words of the apostle, that salvation by a preached gospel was confirmed, "the Lord bearing witness with signs and wonders, and with divers miracles" (Heb ii. 4). Those things which we are told are seals of the gospels, shall we pervert to the subversion of the gospel? What was destined only to confirm the truth, shall we misapply to the confirmation of lies? The proper course, therefore, is, in the first instance, to ascertain and examine the doctrine which is said by the Evangelist to precede; then after it has been proved, but not till then, it may receive confirmation from miracles. But the mark of sound doctrine given by our Saviour himself is its tendency to promote the glory not of men, but of God (John vii. 18; viii. 50). Our Saviour having declared this to be test of doctrine, we are in error if we regard as miraculous, works which are used for any other purpose than to magnify the name of God. And it becomes us to remember that Satan has his miracles, which, although they are tricks rather than true wonders, are still such as to delude the ignorant and unwary. Magicians and enchanters have always been famous for miracles, and miracles of an astonishing description have given support to idolatry: these, however, do not make us converts to the superstitions either of magicians or idolaters. In old times, too, the Donatists (in Joan. Tract. 23), "The Lord put us on our guard against those wonder-workers, when he foretold that false prophets would arise, who, by lying signs and diverse wonders, would, if it were possible, deceive the very elect" (Matth. xxiv. 24). Paul, too, gave warning that the reign of antichrist would be "withal power, and signs and lying wonders" (2 Thess. ii. 9).

But our opponents tell us that their miracles are brought not by idols, not by sorcerers, not by false prophets, but by saints: as if we did not know it to be one of Satan's wiles to transform himself "into an angel of light" (2 Cor. xi. 14). The Egyptians, in whose neighbourhood Jeremiah was buried, anciently sacrificed and paid other divine honours to him (Hieron. in Praef. Jerem). Did they not make an idolatrous abuse of the holy prophet of God? And yet, in recompense for so venerating his tomb, they thought that they were cured of the bite of serpents. What, then, shall we say but that it has been, and always will be, a most just punishment of God, to send on those who do not receive the truth in the love of it, "strong delusion, that they should believe a lie"? (2 Thess. ii. 11). We, then, have no lack of miracles, sure miracles, that cannot be gainsaid; but those to which our opponents lay claim are mere delusions of Satan, inasmuch as they draw off the people from the true worship of God to vanity.

Source: Calvin, John. *Institutes of Christian Religion*. Translated by Henry Beveridge. Grand Rapids, MI: William B. Eerdmans, 1845, pp. 7–10. Reprinted 1989.

4. A Confucian Tract against Buddhism

Politics and religion have mixed throughout human history. Just as religious leaders such as John Calvin (Document 3) hoped to gain political support for their religious move-ments in sixteenth-century Europe, so too did Confucianists such as Han Wen-Kung (A.D. 768–824) attempt to gain imperial favor in Tang dynasty China. In the follow-ing extract, Han Wen-Kung urges the emperor to reject Buddhism in favor of traditional Confucianism.

Han Wen-Kung based his argument on two main points: (1) the emperors before the rise of Buddhism were longer-lived and enjoyed longer reigns than those emperors who embraced Buddhism, and (2) Buddhism is a fundamentally foreign religion that does not encapsulate traditional Chinese values. Although modern Western audiences associate the Far East strongly with Buddhism today, Han Wen-Kung's second point reflects a time in which Buddhism's origins in India were widely known and recognized. Han Wen-Kung achieved such prominence as a Confucian scholar that many serious Confucianists tradi-tionally wash their hands in rose water before picking up his works.

ON A BONE FROM BUDDHA'S BODY

Your Majesty's servant would submit that Buddhism is but a cult of the barbarians, and that its spread in China dates only from the later Han dynasty, and that the an-cients knew nothing of it.

Of old, Huang Ti sat on the throne one hundred years, dying at the age of one hun-dred and ten. Shao Hao sat on the throne eighty years and died at the age of a hundred. Chuan Hsu sat on the throne seventy-nine years and died at the age of a hundred and fifty. The Emperor Yao sat on the throne ninety-eight years and died a the age of a hun-dred and eighteen; and the Emperors Shun and Yu both attained the age of one hundred years. At that epoch the Empire was tranquil, and the people happy in the attainment of old age; and yet no Buddha had yet reached China. Subsequently, the Emperor T'ang of the Yin dynasty reached the age of a hundred years; his grandson T'ai Mou reigned for seventy-five years; and Wu Ting reigned for fifty-nine years. Their exact ages are not given in the annals, but at the lowest computation these can hardly have been less than a hundred years. Wen Wang of the Chou dynasty reached the age of ninety-seven, Wu Wang reached the age of ninety-three; and Mu Wang reigned for one hundred years; and as at that date likewise the Buddhist religion had not reached China, these examples of longevity cannot be attributed to the worship of the Lord Buddha.

The Buddhist religion was in fact introduced during the reign of Ming Ti of the Han dynasty; and that Emperor sat on the throne but eighteen years. After him came rebel-lion upon rebellion with short-lived monarchs.

During the Sung, Ch'I Liang, Ch'en, Yuan and Wei dynasties, and so on down-wards, the Buddhistic religion gradually spread. The duration of those dynasties was comparatively short, only the Emperor Wu Ti of the Liang dynasty reigning for so long as forty-eight years. Thrice he devoted himself to the service of Buddha; at the sacrifices in his ancestral shrines no living victims were used; he daily took but one single meal, and that composed of fruits and vegetables; yet he was harassed by the rebel Ho Ching and died of hunger at T'ai-ch'eng, soon after which his dynasty came to an end. He sought happiness in the worship but found misfortune instead; from which it must be clear to all that Buddha himself is after all but an incompetent god.

When Kao Tsu obtained the Empire he contemplated the extermination of this religion; but the officials of that day were men of limited capabilities; they did not understand the way of our rulers of old; they did not understand the exigencies of the past and present; they did not understand how to avail themselves of His Majesty's wisdom, and root out this evil. Therefore, the execution of this design was delayed, to your servant's infinite sorrow.

Now your present Majesty, endowed with wisdom and courage such as are without parallel in the annals of the past thousand years, prohibited on your accession to the throne the practice of receiving candidates, whether male or female, for priestly orders, prohibiting likewise the erection of temples and monasteries; which caused your servant to believe that the mantle of Kao Tsu had descended on Your Majesty's shoulders. And even should prohibition be impossible, patronage would still be out of the question. Yet your servant has now heard that instructions have been issued to the priestly community to proceed to Feng-hsiang and receive a bone of Buddha, and that from a high tower in the palace Your Majesty will view its introduction into the Imperial Palace; also that orders have been sent to the various temples, commanding that the relic be received with the proper ceremonies. Now, foolish though your

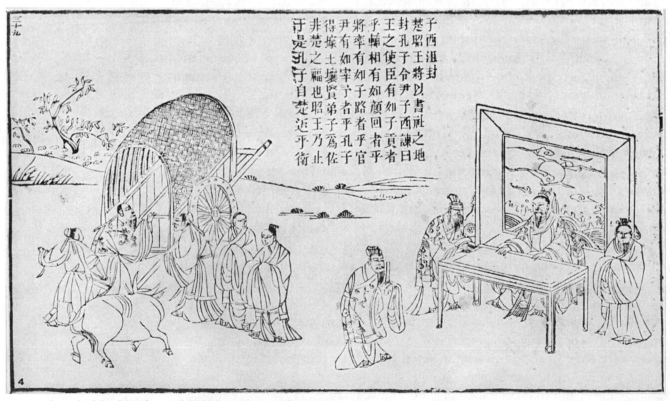

A scene from the life of Confucius. © 2008 Jupiterimages Corporation.

servant may be, he is well aware that your Majesty does not do this in the vain hope of deriving advantages therefrom; but that in the fullness of our present plenty, and in the joy which reigns in the hearts of all, there is a desire to fall in with the wishes of the people in the celebration at the capital of this delusive mummery. For how could the wisdom of Your Majesty stoop in participation in such ridiculous beliefs? Still the people are slow of perception and easily beguiled; and should they behold Your Majesty thus earnestly worshipping at the feet of Buddha they would cry out, "See! the Son of Heaven, the All-Wise, is a fervent believer; who are we, his people, that we should spare our bodies?" Then would ensue a scorching of heads and burning of fingers; crowds would collect together, and tearing off their clothes and scattering their money, would spend their time from morn to eve in imitation of Your Majesty's example. The result would be that by and by young and old, seized with the same enthusiasm, would totally neglect the business of their lives; and should Your Majesty not prohibit it, they would be found flocking to the temples, ready to cut off an arm or slice their bodies as an offering to the God. Thus would our traditions and customs be seriously injured, and ourselves become a laughing-stock on the face of the earth; truly, no small matter! For Buddha was a barbarian. His language was not the language of China; his clothes were of an alien cut. He did not utter the maxims of our ancient rulers, nor conform to the customs which they have handed down. He did not appreciate the bond between prince and minister, the tie between father and son. Supposing, indeed, this Buddha had come to our capital in the flesh, under an appointment from his own State, then your Majesty might have received him with a few words of admonition, bestowing on him a banquet and a suit of clothes, previous to sending him out of the country with an escort of soldiers, and thereby have avoided any dangerous influence on the minds of the people. But what are the facts? The bone of a man long since dead and decomposed, is to be admitted, forsooth, within the precincts of the Imperial Palace! Confucius said, "Pay all respect to spiritual beings, but keep them at a distance." And so, when the princes of old paid visits of condolence to one another, it was customary for them to send on a magician in advance, with a peach wand in his hand, whereby to expel all noxious influences previous to the arrival of his master. Yet now Your Majesty is about to causelessly introduce a disgusting object, personally taking part in the proceedings without the intervention either of the magician or of his peach wand. Of the officials, not one has raised his voice against such an act. Therefore our servant, overwhelmed with shame, implores Your Majesty that this bone may be handed over for destruction by fire or water, whereby the root of this great evil may be exterminated for all time, and the people know how much the wisdom of Your Majesty surpasses that of ordinary men. The glory of such a deed will be beyond all praise. And should the Lord Buddha have power to avenge this insult by the infliction of some misfortune, then let the vials of his wrath be poured out upon the person of your servant who now calls Heaven to witness that he will not repent him of his oath.

In all gratitude and sincerity your Majesty's servant now humbly resents, with fear and trembling, this Memorial for your Majesty's benign consideration.

Source: Giles, Herbert A. *Gems of Chinese Literature: Prose.* 2nd ed. London: Bernard Quaritch, 1923, pp. 124–28.

5. The Cosmic Beginning, as Told in the Japanese Text Kojiki

The Kojiki, written down from oral tradition in the year 712, is the oldest text in a form of the Japanese language and is a central sacred text for the Shinto religion. Shinto, the indigenous religion of Japan, is a loosely organized religion that consists of traditional rituals and folk beliefs—there is no recognized central governing body.

The start of the Kojiki, given here, outlines the creation of the earth. Much of this creation results from the sexual intercourse of two major deities, the Male-Who-Invites and the Female-Who-Invites, though some deities are created by other means. The deity Metal-Mountain-Prince, for example, was born from the vomit of the Female-Who-Invites.

Although this creation story is foreign to Western audiences, the basic principles of the Kojiki story are similar to those contained in the Judeo-Christian tradition: the divine creation of the physical world, the continued connection between heaven and earth, and divine justice. Of course, Shinto differs in so far as it is polytheistic, and it associates individual deities very closely with specific physical features (e.g., the Sea-Deity). In this regard, however, Shinto resembles other polytheistic religions, such as Greek paganism (e.g., Poseidon as sea-god). Similar to other religions, the Kojiki cosmogony also establishes gender roles—the gods produce bad offspring when the woman speaks before the man and good offspring when the man speaks before the woman.

THE BEGINNING OF HEAVEN AND EARTH

The names of the Deities that were born in the Plain of High Heaven when the Heaven and Earth began were the Deity Master-of-the-August-Centre-of-Heaven, next the High-August-Producing-Wondrous Deity, next the Divine-Producing-Wondrous-Deity. These three Deities were all Deities born alone, and hid their persons. The names of the Deities that were born next from a thing that sprouted up like unto a reed-shoot when the earth, young and like unto floating oil, drifted about medusa-like, were the Pleasant-Reed-Shoot-Prince-Elder Deity, next the Heavenly-Eternally-Standing-Deity. These two Deities were likewise born alone, and hid their persons.

The five Deities in the above list are separate Heavenly Deities.

THE SEVEN DIVINE GENERATIONS

The names of the Deities that were born next were the Earthly-Eternally-Standing-Deity, next the Luxuriant-Integrating-Master-Deity. These two Deities were likewise Deities born alone, and hid their persons. The names of the Deities that were born next were the Deity Mud-Earth-Lord next his younger sister the Deity Mud-Earth-Lady; next the Germ-Integrating-Deity, next his younger sister the Life-Integrating-Deity; next the Deity Elder-of-the-Great-Place, next his younger sister the Deity Elder-Lady-of-the-Great-Place; next the Deity Perfect-Exterior, next his younger sister the Deity Oh-Awful-Lady; next the Deity the Male-Who-Invites, next his younger sister the Deity the Female-Who-Invites. From the Earthly-Eternally-Standing Deity down to the Deity the Female-Who-Invites in the previous list are what are termed the Seven Divine Generations.

THE ISLAND OF ONOGORO

Hereupon all the Heavenly Deities commanded the two Deities His Augustness the Male-Who-Invites and Her Augustness the Female-Who-Invites, ordering them to "make, consolidate, and give birth to this drifting land." Granting to them an heavenly jewelled spear, they [thus] deigned to charge them. So the two Deities, standing upon the Floating Bridge of Heaven, pushed down the jewelled spear and stirred with it, whereupon, when they had stiffed the brine till it went curdle-curdle, and drew [the spear] up, the brine that dripped down from the end of the spear was piled up and became an island. This is the Island of Onogoro.

COURTSHIP OF THE DEITIES THE MALE-WHO-INVITES AND THE FEMALE-WHO-INVITES

Having descended from Heaven onto this island, they saw to the erection of an heavenly august pillar, they saw to the erection of an hall of eight fathoms. Then the August Male-Who-Invites asked his younger sister the August Female-Who-Invites, "How is your body made?" She responded, "My body grew by growing, but there is one part that did not grow fully." Then the August Male-Who-Invites said, "My body grew by growing, but there is one part that grew too much. Therefore, would it be good for me to insert this part that grew too much into your part that did not grow fully, so that I will generate regions?" "It would be good." Then the August Male-Who-Invites said, "Since this is so, let us place together our august parts, running around this celestial column." Having made this agreement, the August Male-Who-Invites said, "Run around from the right, and I'll run from the left." When they had run around, the August Female-Who-Invites said, "O pleasant and lovable youth!" and the August Male-Who-Invites said, "O pleasant and lovely maiden!" When they finished, the August Male-Who-Invites said to his sister, "A woman should not speak first." Nevertheless, they began the work of creation in bed, and they produced a son named Hirudo. This child they placed in a boat of reeds, and let it float away. Next they gave birth to the Island of Aha. This likewise is not reckoned among their children.

BIRTH OF THE EIGHT LANDS

Hereupon the two Deities took counsel, saying: "The children to whom we have now given birth are not good. It will be best to announce this in the august place of the Heavenly Deities." They ascended forthwith to Heaven and enquired of Their Augustnesses the Heavenly Deities. Then the Heavenly Deities commanded and found out by grand divination, and ordered them, saying: "They were not good because the woman spoke first. Descend back again and amend your words." So thereupon descending back, they again went round the heavenly august pillar as before. Thereupon his Augustness the Male-Who-Invites spoke first: "Ah! what a fair and lovely maiden! Afterwards his younger sister Her Augustness the Female-Who-Invites spoke: "Ah! what a fair and lovely youth!" When they had finished speaking in this way, they lay together and they produced a child, the Island of Ahaji, Ho-no-sa-wake. Next they gave birth to the Island of Futa-no in Iyo. This island has one body and four faces, and each face has a name. So the Land of Iyo is called Lovely-Princess; the Land of Sanuki is called Prince-Good-Boiled-Rice; the Land of Aha is called the Princess-of-Great-Food; the Land of Tosa is called Brave-Good-Youth. Next they gave birth to the Islands of Mitsu-go near Oki, another name for which [islands] is Heavenly-Great-Heart-Youth. This island likewise has one body and four faces and each face has a name. So the land of Tsukushi is called White-Sun-Youth; the Land of Toyo is called Luxuriant-Sun-Youth; the Land of Hi is called Brave Sun-Confronting-Luxuriant-Wondrous-Lord-Youth; the Land of Kumaso is called Brave-Sun-Youth. Next they gave birth to the Island of Iki, another name for which is Heaven's One-Pillar. Next they gave birth to the Island of Tsu, another name for which is Heavenly-Hand-net-Good-Princess. Next they gave birth to the Island of Sado. Next they gave birth to Great-Yamato-the-Luxuriant-Island-of-the-Dragon-Fly, another name for which is Heavenly-August-Sky-Luxuriant-Dragon-fly-Lord-Youth. The name of "Land-of-the-Eight-Great-Islands" therefore originated in these eight islands having been born first. After that, when they had returned, they gave birth to the Island of Ko[-shima] in Kibi, another name for which [island] is Brave-Sun Direction-Youth. Next they gave birth to the Island of Adzuki, another name for which is Oho-Nu-De-Hime. Next they gave birth to the Island of Oho [-shima], another name for which is Oho-Tamaru-Wake. Next they gave birth to the Island of Hime, another name for which is Heaven's-One-Root. Next they gave birth to the Island of Chika, another name for which is Heavenly-Great-Male. Next they gave birth to the Island[s] of Futa-go, another name for which is Heaven's-Two-Houses, (Six islands in all from the Island of Ko, in Kibi to the Island of Heaven's-Two-Houses).

BIRTH OF THE VARIOUS DEITIES

When they had finished giving birth to countries, they began afresh giving birth to Deities. So the name of the Deity they gave birth to was the Deity Great-Male-of-the-Great-Thing; next they gave birth to the Deity Rock-Earth-Prince; next they gave birth to the Deity Rock-Nest-Princess; next they gave birth to the Deity Great-Door-Sun-Youth; next they gave birth to the Deity Heavenly-Blowing-Male; next they gave birth to the Deity Great-House-Prince; next they gave birth to the Deity Youth-of-the-Wind-Breath-the-Great-Male; next they gave birth to the Sea-Deity, whose name is the Deity Great-Ocean-Possessor; next they gave birth to the Deity of the Water-Gates, whose name is the Deity Prince-of-Swift-Autumn; next they gave birth to his younger sister the Deity Princess-of-Swift-Autumn. (Ten Deities in all from the Deity-Great-Male-of-the-Great-Thing to the Deity Princess-of-Autumn.) The names of the Deities given birth to by these two Deities Prince-of-Swift-Autumn and Princess-of-Swift-Autumn from their separate dominions of river and sea were: the Deity Foam-Calm; next the Deity Foam-Waves; next the Deity Bubble-Calm; next the Deity Bubble-Waves; next the Deity Heavenly-Water-Divider; next the Deity Earthly-Water-Divider; next the Deity Heavenly-Water-Drawing-Gourd-Possessor; next the Deity Earthly-Water-Drawing-Gourd-Possessor. (Eight Deities in all from the Deity Foam-Prince to the Deity Earthly-Water-Drawing-Gourd-Possessor.) Next they gave birth to the Deity of Wind, whose name is the Deity Prince-of-Long-Wind. Next they gave birth to the Deity of Trees, whose name is Deity Stem-Elder, next they gave birth to the Deity of Mountains, whose name is the Deity Great-Mountain-Possessor. Next they gave birth to the Deity of Moors, whose name is the Deity Thatch-Moor-Princess, another name for whom is the Deity Moor-Elder. (Four Deities in all from the Deity Prince-of Long-Wind to Moor-Elder.) The names of the Deities given birth to by these two Deities, the Deity Great-Mountain-Possessor and the Deity Moor-Elder from their separate dominions of mountain and moor were: the Deity Heavenly-Elder-of-the-Passes; next the Deity Earthly-Elder-of-the-Passes; next the Deity Heavenly-Pass-Boundary, next the Deity Earthly-Pass-Boundary; next the Deity Heavenly-Dark-Door; next the Deity Earthly Dark-Door; next the Deity Great-Vale-Prince; next the Deity Great-Vale-Princess. (Eight Deities in all from the Deity Heavenly-Elder-of-the-Passes to the Deity Great-Vale-Princess.) The name of the Deity they next gave birth to was the Deity Bird's-Rock-Camphor-tree-Boat, another name for whom is the Heavenly-Bird-Boat. Next they gave birth to the Deity Princess-of-Great-Food. Next they gave birth to the Fire-Burning-Swift-Male-Deity, another name for whom is the Deity Fire-Shining-Prince, and another name is the Deity Fire-Shining-Elder.

RETIREMENT OF HER AUGUSTNESS
THE PRINCESS-WHO-INVITES

Through giving birth to this child her august private parts were burnt, and she sickened and lay down. The names of the Deities born from her vomit were the Deity Metal-Mountain-Prince and next the Deity Metal-Mountain-Princess. The names of the Deities that were born from her feces were the Deity Clay-Viscid-Prince and next the Deity Clay-Viscid-Princess. The names of the Deities that were next born from her urine were the Deity Mitsuhanome and next the Young-Wondrous-Producing-Deity. The child of this Deity was called the Deity Luxuriant-Food-Princess. So the Deity the Female-Who-Invites, through giving birth to the Deity-of-Fire, at length divinely retired. (Eight Deities in all from the Heavenly-Bird-Boat to the Deity Luxuriant-Food-Princess.) The total number of islands given birth to jointly by the two Deities the Male-Who-Invites and the Female-Who-Invites was fourteen, and of Deities thirty-five. (These are such as were given birth to before the Deity Princess-Who-Invites divinely retired. Only the Island of Onogoro, was not given birth to, and moreover the Leech-Child and the Island of Aha are not reckoned among the children).

So then His Augustness the Male-Who-Invites said: "Oh! Thine Augustness my lovely younger sister! Oh that I should have exchanged thee for this single child!" And as he crept round her august pillow, and as he crept round her august feet and wept, there was born from his august tears the Deity that dwells at Konomoto near Unewo on Mount Kagu, and whose name is the Crying-Weeping-Female-Deity. So he buried the divinely retired Deity the Female-Who-Invites on Mount Hiba at the boundary of the Land of Idzumo and the Land of Hahaki.

THE SLAYING OF THE FIRE-DEITY

Then His Augustness the Male-Who-Invites, drawing the ten-grasp sabre that was augustly girded on him, cut off the head of his child the Deity Shining-Elder. Hereupon the names of the Deities that were born from the blood that stuck to the point of the august sword and bespattered the multitudinous rock-masses were: the Deity Rock-Splitter, next the Deity Root-Splitter, next the Rock-Possessing-Male-Deity. The names of the Deities that were next born from the blood that stuck to the upper part of the august sword and again bespattered the multitudinous rock-masses were: the

Awfully-Swift-Deity, next the Fire-Swift-Deity, next the Brave-Awful-Possessing-Male-Deity, another name for whom is the Brave-Snapping-Deity, and another name is the Luxuriant-Snapping Deity. The names of the Deities that were next born from the blood that collected on the hilt of the august sword and leaked out between his fingers were: the Deity Kura-okami and next the Deity Kura-mitsuha. All the eight Deities in the above list, from the Deity Rock-Splitter to the Deity Kura-mitsuha, are Deities that were born from the august sword. The name of the Deity that was born from the head of the Deity Shining-Elder, who had been slain was the Deity Possessor-of-the-True-Pass-Mountains. The name of the Deity that was next born from his chest was the Deity Possessor-of-Descent-Mountains. The name of the Deity that was next born from his belly was the Deity Possessor-of-the-Innermost-Mountains. The name of the Deity that was next born from his private parts was the Deity Possessor-of-the-Dark-Mountains. The name of the Deity that was next born from his left hand was the Deity Possessor-of-the-Dense[ly-Wooded]-Mountains. The name of the Deity that was next born from his right hand was the Deity Possessor-of-the-Outlying, Mountains. The name of the Deity that was next born from his left foot was the Deity Possessor-of-the-Moorland-Mountains. The name of the Deity that was next born from his right foot was the Deity Possessor-of-the-Outer-Mountains. (Eight Deities in all from the Deity Possessor-of-the-True-Pass-Mountains to the Deity Possessor-of-the-Outer-Mountains). So the name of the sword with which [the Male-Who-Invites] cut off [his son's head] was Heavenly-Point-Blade-Extended, and another name was Majestic Point-Blade-Extended.

Source: Chamberlain, Basil Hall. *Translation of "Ko-ji-ki": or "Records of Ancient Matters."* Kobe: Asiatic Society of Japan, 1919, pp. 15–37. Chamberlain's Latin passages translated by Lawrence Morris.

6. Islamic Tradition

The sacred text of Islam is the Koran, *which contains the teachings of Muhammad (A.D. 570–632). Muslims believe that Muhammad received the text directly from God, although non-Muslim scholars trace the influence of contemporaneous Christian and Jewish traditions on the text. In common with Judeo-Christianity, for example, Islam shares a conception of life after death. In this extract, for example, the righteous will be awarded with delicious fruit, refreshing non-inebriating drink, and beautiful companions. The evil-doers shall be forced to eat the fruit of the tree Ez-zakkoum, which grows from the depths of hell, and will have boiling water for the drink.*

The connection of Islam with Judeo-Christianity, which Islam considers also to be "religions of the book" and therefore having some contact with God, can be seen in the list of prophets named in this extract. The passage cites as warners *(i.e., prophets) many of the chief characters of the Hebrew scriptures: Noah, Abraham, Isaac, Moses, Aaron, Elijah (Elias), and Jonah (Jonas). Within this rhetoric, Muhammad becomes the last and greatest in a line of men sent by God to correct and teach the human race.*

Sura 37—The Ranks

In the name of God, the Compassionate, the Merciful.
By the angels who range themselves in rank for Songs of Praise,

And by those who repel demons,

And by those who recite the Koran for warning,

Truly your God is One,

Lord of the Heavens and of the Earth, and of all that is between them, and Lord of the East.

Verily We have adorned the lower heaven with the adornment of the stars;

They serve also as a guard against every rebellious Satan,

That they overhear not the exalted Chiefs, for they are darted at from every side,

Driven off and consigned to a lasting torment;

While, of one steal a word by stealth, then a glistening flame pursueth him.

Ask the Meccans then, Are they, or the angels whom We have made, the stronger creation?
    Ay, of adhesive clay have We created them.

But thou marvellest and they mock;

And when they are warned, no warning do they take;

And when they see a sign, they fall to mocking,

And say, "Lo, this is no other than clear sorcery;

What! when dead, and become dust and bones, shall we indeed be raised?

Our sires also of olden time?"

Say, Yes; and ye shall be of no account,

For, one shout only, and lo! they gaze around them

And say, "Oh! woe to us! this is the day of reckoning;

This is the day of decision which ye gainsaid as an untruth."

"Gather together those who have acted unjustly, and their consorts, and the gods whom they
    worshipped

Beside God; and guide them to the road for Hell.

Set them forth: verily they shall be questioned."

"How now, that ye help not one another?"

But on this day they shall submit themselves to God,

And shall turn towards one another with mutual questionings;

They say, "In sooth, ye came to us in well-omened sort:"

But they answer, "Nay, it was ye who would not believe; and we had no power over you. Nay,
    ye were people given to transgress;

Just, therefore, is the doom which our Lord hath passed upon us. We shall surely taste it—

And we made you err, for we had erred ourselves."

Partners therefore shall they verily be in punishment on that day.

Lo, thus will We deal with the wicked

Who, when it was said to them, "There is no God but God," were proudful

And exclaimed, "Shall we in sooth abandon our gods for a crazed poet?"

Nay rather, he cometh with the Truth and confirmeth the Sent Ones of old.

Ye shall verily taste the painful punishment,

And ye shall not be rewarded but as ye have wrought,

But the sincere servants of God

Shall have a stated provision

Of fruits; and honoured shall they be

In the gardens of delight,

Upon couches face to face;

A cup shall be borne round among them from a fountain,

Limpid, delicious to those who drink;

It shall not oppress the sense, nor shall they therewith be inebriated,

And they shall address one another with mutual questions.

Saith one of them, "I truly had a bosom friend,

Who said, 'Art thou indeed of those who credit it?

When we are dead, and become dust and bones, shall we indeed be judged?'"

He shall say to those around him, "Will ye look down?"

And he shall look down, and see him in the midst of hell.

He shall say to him, "By God, thou hadst almost brought me to destruction;

And, but for the favour of my Lord, I had surely been of those given over into torment."

"Are we not then liable to die," say the blessed,

"Any other than our first death? and have we escaped the torment?"

Lo, this is indeed the great felicity!

For the like of this should the travailers travail!

Is this the better repast or the tree Ez-zakkoum?

Verily We have made it for a subject of discord to the wicked:

Lo, it is a tree which cometh up from the bottom of hell;

Its fruit is as it were the heads of Satans;

And, lo! the damned shall surely eat of it and fill their bellies with it:

then verily shall they have thereupon a mixture of boiling water;

Then verily shall they return to hell.

Lo, they found their fathers erring,

And they hastened on in their footsteps;

Also before them the greater number of the ancients had erred,

Though We had sent warners among them;

See then what was the end of these warned ones,

Except of God's sincere servants.

Noah called on Us of old, and We returned a gracious answer,

And we saved him and his family out of the great distress,

And We made his offspring the survivors;

And We left for him with posterity,

"Peace be on Noah throughout the worlds!"

Thus verily do We reward the well-doers;

Verily he was one of our believing servants;

Then the rest We drowned.

And truly, of his fellowship was Abraham,

When he brought to his Lord a perfect heart,

When he said to his father and to his people, "What is this ye worship?

Prefer ye with falsehood gods to God?

And what deem ye of the Lord of the worlds?"

So gazing he gazed towards the stars,

And said, "In sooth I am ill:"

And they turned their back on him and departed.

Then he went aside to their gods and said, "Do ye not eat?

What aileth you that ye do not speak?"

Then he turned upon them, with the right hand striking:

Then his tribesmen rushed on him with hurried steps—

He said, "Worship ye what ye carve,

When God hath created you, and the idols ye make?"

They said, "Build up a pyre for him and cast him into the glowing flame,"

And they chose to plot against him, but We brought them very low.

And he said, "Verily, I repair to my Lord who will guide me:

O Lord give me a son, of the righteous,"

So We announced to him a gracious youth.

And when he attained to such an age that he could assist him in work

His father said to him "My son, I have seen in a dream that I should sacrifice thee; consider therefore what thou seest right."

He said, "My father, do what thou art bidden; of the patient, if God please, shalt thou find me."

And when they had surrendered themselves to the will of god, he laid him down upon his
forehead:

Then cried We unto him, "O Abraham!

Now hast thou satisfied the vision." Lo, thus do We recompense the righteous!

This was indeed a clear trial,

And we ransomed his son with a costly victim,

And we left for him among posterity,

"Peace be on Abraham!"

Thus do We reward the well-doers;

Verily he was of our believing servants.

And We announced Isaac to him—a righteous Prophet—

And on him and on Isaac We bestowed our blessing. And among their offspring was a righteous
man and one to his own hurt an undoubled sinner.

And of old, to Moses and to Aaron showed We favours:

And both of them, and their people, We rescued from the great distress:

And We succoured them, and they became the conquerors:

And We gave them (Moses and Aaron) each the lucid book:

And We guided them each into the right way:

And We left for them among posterity,

"Peace be on Moses and Aaron."

Lo, thus do We reward the well-doers;

Verily they were two of our believing servants.

And Elias truly was of our Sent Ones,

When he said to his people, "Fear ye not God?

Invoke ye Baal and forsake ye the most skilful Creator,

God your Lord, and Lord of your sires of old?"

But they treated him as a liar, and shall surely be consigned to punishment,

Except the servants of God who kept the true faith.

And We left for him among posterity,

"Peace be on Eliasin!"

Lo, thus do We reward the well-doers;

Verily he was one of our believing servants.

And Lot truly was of our Sent Ones,

When We rescued him and all his family,

Save an aged woman among those who tarried;

Afterward We destroyed the others.

And, lo! ye pass by their ruined dwellings in the morning

And at night: will ye not then understand?

And verily Jonas was one of the Apostles,

When he fled unto the laden ship,

And lots were cast, and he was doomed,

and the fish swallowed him, for he was blameworthy.

But had he not been of those who praise Us,

In its belly had he surely remained, till the day of resurrection.

And We cast him on the bare shore—and he was sick;

And We caused a gourd-plant to grow up over him,

And We sent him to a hundred thousand persons, or even more,

And because they believed, We continued their enjoyments for a season.

Inquire then of the Meccans whether thy Lord hath the daughters, and they, the sons?

Have We created angels females? and were they witnesses?

Is it not truly a falsehood of their own when they say,

"God hath begotten"? and they verily are the liars.

Hath He preferred daughters to sons?

What reason have ye for thus judging?

Will ye not then receive this warning?

Have ye a clear authority?

Bring forth your Book if ye speak truth.

And they make him to be of kin with the Djinn: but the Djinn know that these idolaters shall
be brought up before God:

High be the glory of God above what they impute to Him,

Except his servants, who are pure in their faith.

"Verily then, ye and what ye worship

Shall not stir up any against God,

Save him who shall burn in Hell.

And not one of us but hath his appointed place,

And verily we do range ourselves in order,

And verily we do celebrate His praises."

But the infidels say,

"Had we a warning from our forefathers,

We had surely been God's servants, pure in faith."

Yet they believe not the Koran—But they shall know its truth at last.

And our word came of old to our servants the Sent Ones,

That they should surely be the succoured,

And that verily our armies should gain victory for them.

Turn aside therefore from the unbelievers for a time,

And behold them, for they too shall in the end behold their doom.

Would they then hasten our vengeance?

But when it shall come down into their courts, an evil morning shall it be to those who have
had their warning:

Turn aside from them therefore for a time,

And behold them; for they too shall in the end behold their doom.

Far be the glory of thy Lord, Lord of greatness, above what they impute to Him!

And peace be on His Sent Ones!

And praise be to God, Lord of the worlds!

Source: *El-Koran; or, The Koran.* 2nd ed. Translated by J. M. Rodwell. London: Bernard Quaritch, 1876,
pp. 67–73 (verses 1–182).

7. Sir John Oldcastle: The Inquisition of a Protestant Layman

In its origins, the word inquisition *means simply "inquiry." In its technical sense, the Inquisition refers to the various legal procedures by which perceived heretics were investigated
and interrogated. Although the Spanish Inquisition, established in 1478, is well known for
the torture used on some suspects, most inquisitions in other places and time periods were
decidedly less violent in their interrogations, if not in their punishments. In the following
extract, which records the investigation of Sir John Oldcastle in England in 1413, the investigators simply ask the accused heretic to clarify his opinions on certain contentious theological issues. In fact, when Oldcastle fails to satisfy the inquisitors with his initial replies, they
give him a delay in which he can review the precise theological opinions with which they
wish him to agree. Only when he refuses to agree with these opinions is he confirmed as a
heretic. But although the trial was decidedly nonviolent, the punishment was not. Oldcastle*

was eventually burned in 1417. Although he could have avoided this fate by simply agreeing with the theological opinions presented to him, he preferred death to false agreement.

Lollardy was the heresy of which Sir John Oldcastle was accused, and the investigators, as the extract highlights, focused on the topics most associated with Lollard heresy: the Eucharist, Church authority, penance, and the cult of the saints. Whereas Lollardy held that the bread and wine in the Eucharist were symbolically Christ, orthodox Christianity held that the bread and wine in the Eucharist were materially Christ. "Material" here was a technical term meaning "in essence" or "in actuality." To use a trivial example, a chair in the shape of a toadstool might look like a toadstool, but it would be "materially" a chair. According to orthodox Catholics, therefore, the Eucharist might look like bread and wine, but it was materially Christ's body and blood.

Oldcastle, like other Lollards, held that Church officials held no authority; according to Lollards, God, who spoke primarily through the Bible, was the sole religious authority. Orthodox Catholicism, while recognizing that God was the ultimate head of religion, believed that the pope, bishops, and priests had been appointed by God to serve as administrators and judges of theological opinions. Partly as a result, Lollards contended that people did not have to confess their sins to a priest—God forgave sins directly. Orthodox Catholicism held that confession to a priest was necessary for forgiveness under normal circumstances.

Finally, Lollards, including Sir John Oldcastle, believed that orthodox Catholicism paid too much attention to the saints (deceased holy men and women) and that this attention to saints distracted from the worship of God. As a result, they rejected the honoring of statues or crosses and felt that pilgrimages to the graves of the saints were essentially wastes of time and money. All these beliefs conflicted with standard Catholic teaching. In the end, although Lollards viewed themselves as Catholics, the Church hierarchy viewed them as heretics.

Sir John Oldcastle was one of the most prominent Lollards ever convicted. The nobleman was a friend of both Henry IV and Henry V, and that special relationship underlies William Shakespeare's depiction of Sir John Falstaff in the I Henry IV plays. Nevertheless, Henry V brought Oldcastle reluctantly to trial when his heretical leanings became obvious. Although Oldcastle was convicted in 1413, he escaped from the Tower of London and led a Lollard uprising in January 1414, which failed disastrously. Oldcastle escaped the field of battle, however, and remained at large, fomenting dissent when possible, until 1417, when he was captured and executed. Sir John Oldcastle would later become a hero to sixteenth-century Protestants, who formed the core audience of Foxe's Acts and Monuments, from which the following extract is taken.

THE CATHOLIC FAITH AND CONFESSION OF THE LORD COBHAM

I John Oldcastle knight, Lord of Cobham, desire to make manifest unto all Christians, and God to be taken to witness, that I never thought otherwise or would think otherwise (by God's help) than with a steadfast & undoubted faith to embrace all those his Sacramentes which he hath instituted for the use of his Church.

Furthermore that I may the more plainly declare my mind in these 4 points of my faith:

First of all I believe the Sacrament of the altar to be the body of Christ under the form of bread, the very same body which was borne of his mother Mary, crucified for us, dead and buried, rose again the third day, sitteth on the right hand of his immortal father, now being a triumphant partaker with him of his eternal glory.

Then as touching the Sacrament of penance, this is my belief: that I do think the correction of a sinfull life to be most necessary for all such as desire to be saved and that they ought to take upon them such repentance of their former life by true confession, unfeigned contrition, and lawful satisfaction, as the word of God doth prescribe unto us. Otherwise there will be no hope of salvation.

Thirdly, as touching images, this is my opinion, that I do judge them no point of faith, but brought into the world after the faith of Christ by the sufferance of the Church, and so grown in use that they might serve for a calendar for the lay people and ignorant. By the beholding whereof they might the better call to remembrance the godly examples and martyrdom of Christ and other holy men: but if any man do otherwise abuse this representation, and give the reverence unto those Images, which is due unto the holy men whom they represent, or rather unto him whom the holy men themselves owe all their honor, setting all their trust and hope in them which ought to be referred unto God; or if they be so affected toward the dumb Images, that they do in any behalf addict unto them, either be more addicted unto one Saint than another, in my mind they do little differ from Idolatry, grievously offending against God the author of all honor.

Last of all I am thus persuaded that there be no inhabitants here in earth, but that we shall pass straight either to life or punishment; for whosoever doth so order his life that he stumble at the commandments of God, which either he knoweth not, or he will not be taught them, it is but in vain for him to look for salvation, although he ran over all the corners of the world. Contrarywise, he which observeth his commandments cannot perish, although in all his life time he walked no pilgrimage, neither to Rome, Canterbury, nor Compostella, or to any other place, whither as the common people are accustomed to walk.

This Schedule with the articles therein contained being read (as is aforesaid) by the said sir John, we with our fellow brethren aforesaid, and many other doctors and learned men had conference upon the same. And at the last by the counsel and consent of them, we spoke these words following unto the said sir John there present. Behold sir John, there are many good and catholic things contained in this schedule. But you have this time to answer unto other matters which savor of errors & heresies. Whereunto, by the contents of this schedule, it is not fully answered, and therefore you must answer thereunto & more plainly express and declare your faith and opinions as touching those points in the same bill. That is to say, whether you hold, believe and affirm, that in the sacrament of the altar, after the consecration rightly done, there remaineth material bread or not. Item, whether you hold, believe, and affirm, that it is necessary in the sacrament of penance for a man to confess his sins unto a priest appointed by the church.

The which articles in this manner delivered unto him, amongst many other things he answered plainly, that he would make no other declaration or answer thereunto than was conteined in the said Schedule. Whereupon we favoring the said sir John, with benign & gentle means, we spoke unto him in this manner. "Sir John, take heed, for if you do not plainly answer to these things, which are objected against you within a lawful time now granted you by the Judges, we may declare you to be an heretic," but the said sir John persevered as before, and would make no other answer. Consequently notwithstanding, we together with our said fellow brethren and others of our counsel took advice, and by their counsel declared unto the said sir John Oldcastle, that the said holy Church of Rome in this matter, following the saying of blessed S. Augustine, Jerome, Ambrose, and other holy men, hath determined, the which determinations every catholic ought to observe.

Whereupon the said sir John answered, that he would believe and observe whatsoever the holy Church determined, and whatsoever god would he should observe and believe. But that he would in no case affirm that our Lord the Pope, the cardinals, Archbishops, and Bishops or other prelates of the church have any power to determine any such matters. Whereunto, we yet favoring him, under hope of better advisement promised the said sir John; that we would give him in writing certain determinations upon the matter aforesaid. Whereunto he should more plainly answer, written in Latin, and for his better understanding, translated into English: whereupon, we commanded and heartily desired him that against Monday next following, he should give a plain and full answer, the which determinations we caused to be translated the same day and to be delivered unto him the Sunday next following. The tenor of which determinations here follow in this manner.

The faith and determination of that holy Church upon the holy Sacrament of the altar is this: that after the consecration done in the mass by the priest, the material bread shall be changed into the material body of Christ, and the material wine into the material blood of Christ. Therefore after the consecration there remaineth no more any substance of bread and wine, which was there before. What do you answer to this article?

Also the holy church hath determined that every christian dwelling upon earth ought to confess his sins unto a priest ordained by the Church, if he may come unto him. How think you by this article?

Christ ordained St. Peter his Vicar in earth, whose seat is in the Church of Rome, giving and granting the same authority which he gave unto Peter also to his successors which are now called Popes of Rome, in whose power it is to ordain and institute prelates in particular churches, as Archbishops, bishops, curates, and other ecclesiastical orders, unto whom the Christian people owe obedience according to the tradition of the church of Rome. This is the determination of the holy church. What think you by this article?

Besides this, the holy Church hath determined, that it is necessary for every christian to go on pilgrimage to holy places, & there specially to worship the holy relics of the Apostles, Martyrs, confessors, & all saints, whosoever the church of Rome hath allowed. What think you of this article?

Upon which Monday being the 25th day of the said month of September, before us and our fellow brethren aforesaid, having also taken unto us our reverend brother, Benedict, by the grace of God Bishop of Bangor, and by our commandment our counsellers and ministers: Master Henry official of our court of Cant., Philip Morgan D. of both laws, Dowell Kissin Doctor of the decretals, John Kempe and William Carlton Doctors of law, John Witnan, Thomas Palmer, Rob Wombewell, John Withe and Robert Chamberlayne, Richard Dotington & Thomas Walden professors of divinity, also James Cole, & I. Stevens our notaries appointed on this behalf. They all and every one being sworn upon that holy gospel of god, laying their hands upon the book that they should give their faithfull counsel in, and upon the manner aforesaid, and in every such cause and to the whole world. By and by, appeared sir Robert Morley Knight, Lieutenant of the Tower of London, and brought with him the foresaid Sir John Oldcastle, setting him before us. Unto whom we gently and familiarly rehearsed the acts of the day before passed. And as before we told him that he both is and was excommunicate, requiring and entreating him that he would desire and receive in due form the absolution of the Church. Unto whom the said Sir John then and there plainly answered, that in this behalf he would require no absolution at our hands, but only of God. Then afterward by gentle and soft means, we desired and required him to make plain answer unto the articles which were laid against him.

And first of all, as touching the Sacrament of the altar, to the which article, besides other things he answered and said thus: that as Christ being here in earth had in him both Godhead & manhood, notwithstanding the Godhead was covered and invisible under the humanity, the which was manifest and visible in him: so likewise in the sacrament of the altar there is the very body and very bread, bread which we do see, the body of Christ hidden under the same which we do not see. And plainly denied, that the faith as touching the said Sacrament determined by the Romish church and holy doctors and sent unto him by us in the said Schedule, to be the determination of the holy Church. But if it be the determination of the Church, he said that it was done contrary unto the scriptures, after the church was endowed, and that poison was poured into the Church and not afore.

Also as touching the Sacrament of penance and confession, he plainly said and affirmed then and there that if any man were in any grievous sin, out of the which he knew not how to rise, it were expedient and good for him to go unto some holy and discreet priest to take counsel of him. But that he should confess his sin to any proper Priest, or to any other although he might have the use of him, it is not necessary to salvation, for so much as by only contrition such sin can be wiped away, and the sinner himself purged.

As concerning the worshipping of the cross, he said and affirmed that only the body of Christ which did hang upon the cross is to be worshipped. And being demanded what honor he would do unto the Image of the cross. He answered by express words that he would only do it that honor that he would make it clean and lay it up safe.

As touching the power and authority of the keys, the Archbishops, Bishop, and other prelates, he said that the Pope is very Antichrist, that is the head: the Archbishops, Bishops and other prelates to be his members, and the Friars to be

Burning Heretics on Isle of Garnsey. This image from John Foxe's *Book of Martyrs* uses propaganda to depict the Church hierarchy as cruel and sadistic. In this scene, a baby bursts from a mother's womb as she is executed, naked, for heresy. © 2008 Jupiterimages Corporation.

his tail. The which Pope, Archbishops and bishops a man ought not to obey, but so far forth as they be followers of Christ and of Peter, in their life, manners and conversation, and that he is the successor of Peter, which is best and purest in life & manners. Furthermore, the said sir John spreading his hands with a loud voice, said thus to those which stood about him. "These men which judge and would condemn me, will seduce you all and themselves, and will lead you unto hell, therefore take heed of them."

When he had spoken those words, we again as oftentimes before with lamentable countenance, spoke unto the said sir John, exhorting him with as gentle words as we might that he would return to that unity of the church, to believe and hold that which the church of Rome doth believe and hold. Who expressly answered that he would not believe or hold otherwise than he had before declared. Wherefore, we perceiving as it appeared by him that we could not prevail: at the last with bitterness of heart, we proceeded to the pronouncing of a definitive sentence in this manner.

Source: Foxe, John. *Actes and Monuments of Matters Most Speciall and Memorable.* London: John Daye, 1583, p. 567. Spelling slightly modified by Lawrence Morris.

Priests and Rituals

Like any other sphere of life, religion has its own specialists and procedures. These specialists are generally called priests, monks, or ministers, and the procedures are called rituals. These two—priests and rituals—go together; priests perform rituals.

Within Christianity, the Eucharist (Document 12) is the central ritual. The Eucharist re-creates or memorializes Christ's last supper, in which Jesus gave his disciples bread and wine, calling it his body and blood. Although the Eucharist is specific to Christianity (other religions do have similar, though not identical, rituals), most religions do have some form of prayer. Thomas Roe was so struck by Muslim prayer (Document 13), for example, that he upbraided English Christians for not being as assiduous. Medieval Christianity, as seen in the *Rule of St. Benedict* (Document 8), also prized the ideal of frequent and constant prayer.

In addition to stressing constant prayer, the *Rule of St. Benedict* also strives to create an ideal community. According to the *Rule*, the monks have no personal possessions—everything is owned by the community and distributed as need arises. This ideal of personal poverty contrasts starkly with the forged *Donation of Constantine* (Document 9), which claimed that Emperor Constantine, who had converted to Christianity in the fourth century, essentially placed western Europe under the political, as well as spiritual, control of the pope. Far from being poor, as a result, the pope would be one of the largest landowners in Europe.

The tension between secular and religious hierarchies seen in *The Donation of Constantine* played out in small ways across Europe. In many Protestant countries, such as England, the king came to control the Church. As Document 10 shows, royal authority could control who became a preacher and what those preachers were allowed to preach about. The state controlled the Church, or at least attempted to control the Church. Religious officials, like other people, were not easy to control. Indeed, scandals involving churchmen were commonplace throughout the history of religion. Document 11 offers some advice to the minister who finds himself at the heart of a scandal: say nothing and look busy. Religious life easily moved from the heights of heaven to the mud of earth.

8. *Monastic Life According to the* **Rule of St. Benedict**

St. Benedict of Nursia (c. 480–c. 547) is often called the father of Western monasticism. Although Benedict was by no means the originator of monasticism—men and women, Christians and non-Christians, had long been forming separatist religious communities dedicated to religious rigor—Benedict did create a "rule," or set of monastic guidelines, that spread rapidly and became the veritable standard for Christian monastic life in western Europe throughout the Middle Ages.

The following extracts from the Rule of St. Benedict *highlight the essential principles of Benedictine monasticism: community, prayer, work. Community is central to monastic life; what separates a hermit from a monk is precisely the monk's intimate fellowship with other monks, whereas the hermit explicitly seeks isolation from all others. Clauses 3 and 33 show the ideal of community put into practice. Clause 3 stipulates that the abbot should consult all the monks about any important decisions instead of making the decision himself, although at the same time no individual monk is to believe that his own opinion is necessarily the best. Decisions, therefore, are made jointly; the individual's opinions yield to the community's decision. Clause 33, moreover, expands the concept of community to the arena of material property: no monk is allowed to own anything. Instead, all possessions are held by the monastic community as a whole. In the ideal Benedictine monastery, therefore, there is no "mine" or "yours," merely "ours." The singular of possessiveness yields to the plural of community. Although a monk could not own anything himself, this restriction did not necessarily make him poor; frequently, monastic communities, thanks to gifts from kings and others, could become quite rich, but the wealth remained in the hands of the community as a whole instead of in the hands of one individual.*

Ora et labora, Latin for "pray and work," served as a motto for monastic communities, and clause 48 demonstrates how this ideal worked in practice. As the clause indicates, most of the daylight hours were spent in manual labor, such as farming or similar tasks. The hottest part of the day, roughly 10 A.M. until 3 P.M., was given over in equal parts to study and slumber. The provisions for disciplining monks who were not reading suggest that many monks would take advantage of the study time to chitchat and simply to "hang out." The clause, however, does not mention the large amount of time spent in formal prayer both during the workday and during the night.

CLAUSE 3. ABOUT CALLING IN THE BROTHERS TO TAKE COUNSEL

Whenever anything of importance is to be done in the monastery, the abbot shall call together the whole congregation, and shall himself explain the matter in question, and, having heard the advice of the brothers, he shall do what he considers most advantageous. And for this reason, moreover, we have said that all ought to be called to take counsel, because often it is to a younger person that God reveals what is best. The brethren, moreover, with all subjection of humility, ought so to give their advice that they do not presume boldly to defend what seems good to them; but it should rather depend on the judgment of the abbot, so that, whatever he decides to be best, they should all agree to it. But even as it behooves the disciples to obey the master, so it is fitting that he should arrange all matters with care and justice. In all things, indeed, let every one follow the Rule as his guide; and let no one rashly deviate from it. Let no one in the monastery follow the inclination of his own heart. And let no one boldly presume to dispute with his abbot, within or without the monastery. But, if he should so presume, let him be subject to the discipline of the Rule.

CLAUSE 8. CONCERNING THE DIVINE OFFICES AT NIGHT

In the winter time, that is from the Calends of November until Easter, according to what is reasonable, they must rise at the eighth hour of the night, so that they rest a little more than half the night, and rise when they have already digested. But let the time that

Monk seated, writing with a stylus and eraser. Bible, Vulgate version. Northern France, ca. 1250–1300. Courtesy of the Library of Congress.

remains after vigils be kept for meditation by those brothers who are in any way behind hand with the psalter or lessons. From Easter, moreover, until the aforesaid Calends of November, let the hour of keeping vigils be so arranged that, a short interval being observed in which the brethren may go out for the necessities of nature, the matins, which are always to take place with the dawning light, may straightway follow.

CLAUSE 16. HOW DIVINE SERVICE SHALL BE HELD THROUGH THE DAY

As the prophet says: "Seven times in the day do I praise Thee." Which sacred number of seven will thus be fulfilled by us if, at matins, at the first, third, sixth, ninth hours, at vesper time and at "completorium" we perform the duties of our service; for it is of these hours of the day that he said: "Seven times in the day do I praise Thee." For concerning nocturnal vigils, the same prophet says: "At midnight I arose to confess unto thee." Therefore, at these times, let us give thanks to our Creator concerning the judgments of his righteousness; that is, at matins, etc.

CLAUSE 33. WHETHER THE MONKS SHOULD HAVE ANYTHING OF THEIR OWN

More than anything else is this special vice to be cut off root and branch from the monastery, that one should presume to give or receive anything without the order of the abbot, or should have anything of his own. He should have absolutely not anything, neither a book, nor tablets, nor a pen—nothing at all. For indeed it is not allowed to the monks to have their own bodies or wills in their own power. But all things necessary they must expect from the Father of the monastery; nor is it allowable to have anything which the abbot has not given or permitted. All things shall be held in common; as it is written, "Let not any man presume to call anything his own." But if any one shall have been discovered delighting in this most evil vice, being warned once and again, if he do not amend, let him be subjected to punishment.

CLAUSE 48. CONCERNING THE DAILY MANUAL LABOR

Idleness is the enemy of the soul. And therefore, at fixed times, the brothers ought to be occupied in manual labor; and again, at fixed times, in sacred reading. Therefore we believe that both seasons ought to be arranged after this manner, so that, from Easter until the October 1, going out early, from 6 a.m. until 10 a.m. they shall do what labor may be necessary. From 10 a.m. until about noon, they shall be free for reading. After the meal at noon, rising from the table, they shall rest in their beds with all silence, or, perchance, he that wishes to read may read to himself in such a way as not to disturb another. And the second meal shall be moderate and eaten about 2:30pm; and again they shall work at what is to be done until evening prayer. But, if the emergency or poverty of the place demands that they be occupied in picking fruits, they shall not be grieved; for they are truly monks if they live by the labors of their hands, as did also our fathers and the apostles. Let all things be done with moderation, however, on account of the faint-hearted.

In days of Lent they shall receive separate books from the library, which they shall read entirely through in order. These books are to be given out on the first day of Lent. Above all there shall be appointed without fail one or two elders, who shall go round the monastery at the hours in which the brothers are engaged in reading, and see to it that no troublesome brother be found who is given to idleness and trifling, and is not intent on his reading, being not only of no use to himself, but also stirring up others. If such a one (may it not happen!) be found, he shall be reproved once and a second time. If he does not amend, he shall be subject under the Rule to such punishment that the others may have fear. Nor shall brother join brother at unsuitable hours. Moreover, on Sunday all shall engage in reading, excepting those who are assigned to various duties. But if anyone be so negligent and lazy that he will not or can not read, some task shall be imposed upon him which he can do, so that he be not idle. On feeble or delicate brothers such a task or art is to be imposed, that they shall neither be idle nor so oppressed by the violence of labor as to be driven to take flight. Their weakness is to be taken into consideration by the abbot.

Sources: Ogg, Frederic Austin. *A Source Book of Mediaeval History*. New York: American, 1908, pp. 85–89. With slight modifications. Henderson, Ernest F. *Select Historical Documents of the Middle Ages*. London: Bell, 1921, pp. 281–83.

9. *Papal Power:* The Donation of Constantine

The document known as The Donation of Constantine, *which is reproduced here, played an important role in the development of ecclesiastical power in the Middle Ages. Modern scholars consider the document to be a forgery, but several medieval popes used the*

document, which first came to light in the ninth century, to justify the extension of their po-
litical influence. Urban II (d. 1099), for example, used The Donation *to claim Corsica,*
and Adrian IV (d. 1159), the only English pope, granted Ireland to England using The
Donation *as evidence for his own personal ownership of Ireland. Although these popes*
used The Donation *to strengthen papal power, other medieval thinkers such as Otto III*
(d. 1002) and Arnold of Brescia (fl. 1140) considered the document an outright lie. Just
like the popes, however, these individuals had their own personal motivations: Otto was
the Holy Roman Emperor, and an increase in papal power meant a decrease in his own
authority, and Arnold of Brescia was a radical reformer who severely condemned clerical
wealth in general.

The document itself depicts the Roman emperor Constantine (d. A.D. 337) granting
political control of the western Roman Empire to Pope Sylvester I (d. A.D. 335). Although
the story of this gift is fictional, Constantine was in fact the first emperor to profess Chris-
tianity, and he explicitly allowed the open practice of Christianity with the Edict of Milan
(A.D. 313). With this edict, Christianity was transformed from a secret, sometimes severely
persecuted religion, to a cult favored by the emperor himself. Within years, many high-
ranking Romans were Christians, and they granted the Church both wealth and power.
Although The Donation of Constantine *is not a true grant, it does recognize the pivotal*
role that Emperor Constantine played in transforming the Christian Church from a popular
but outlawed group of believers into a major political force.

According to The Donation, *Constantine was motivated to favor the Church through*
being healed miraculously from a leprosy-like disease. This miraculous cure, effected by
a regimen of penance imposed by Pope Sylvester, resulted in substantial rewards for the
Church. The pope is allowed to wear the same symbolic garments as the emperor—thereby
equating their status—and the pope is granted explicit control over the Western Empire
while the emperor changes his capital to Byzantium in the East. Constantine did in fact
move his capital from Rome to Byzantium, although the major motivation was the greater
wealth of the eastern empire. Although this arrangement does recognize a division between
church and state, in practice, the Church becomes state in western Europe in the rhetoric of
the document. The highest power is held not by the emperor, but by the pope.

Hereupon that same most blessed Sylvester our father, bishop of the city of Rome, imposed upon us a time of penance—within our Lateran palace, in the chapel, in a hair garment, so that I might obtain pardon from our Lord God Jesus Christ our Saviour by vigils, fasts, and tears and prayers, for all things that had been impiously done and unjustly ordered by me. Then through the imposition of the hands of the clergy, I came to the bishop himself; and there, renouncing the pomps of Satan and his works, and all idols made by hands, of my own will before all the people I confessed: that I believed in God the Father almighty, maker of Heaven and earth, and of all things visible and invisible; and in Jesus Christ, His only Son our Lord, who was born of the Holy Spirit and of the virgin Mary. And the font having been blessed, the wave of salvation purified me therewith at triple immersion. For there I, being placed at the bottom of the font, saw with my own eyes a hand from Heaven touching me; whence rising, clean, know that I was cleansed from all squalor of leprosy. And, I being raised from the venerable font—putting on white raiment, he administered to me the sign of the seven-fold holy Spirit, the unction of the holy oil; and he traced the sign of the holy cross on my brow, saying: God seals thee with the seal of His faith in the name of the Father and the Son and the Holy Spirit, to signalize thy faith. All the clergy replied: "Amen." The bishop added, "peace be with thee."

And so, on the first day after receiving the mystery of the holy baptism, and after the cure of my body from the squalor of leprosy, I recognized that there was no other God save the Father and the Son and the Holy Spirit; whom the most blessed Sylvester the pope doth preach; a trinity in one, a unity in three. For all the gods of the nations, whom I have worshipped up to this time, are proved to be demons; works made by the hand of men; inasmuch as that same venerable father told to us most clearly how much power in Heaven and on earth He, our Saviour, conferred on his apostle St. Peter, when finding him faithful after questioning him He said: "Thou are Peter, and upon this rock (petram) shall I build My Church, and the gates of hell shall not prevail against it." Give heed ye powerful, and incline the ear of your hearts to that which the good Lord and master added to His disciple, saying: "and I will give thee the keys of the kingdom of Heaven; and whatever thou shalt bind on earth shall be bound also in Heaven, and whatever thou shalt loose on earth shall be loosed also in Heaven." This is very wonderful and glorious, to bind and loose on earth and to have it bound and loosed in Heaven.

And when, the blessed Sylvester preaching them, I perceived these things, and learned that by the kindness of St. Peter himself I have been entirely restored to health: I—together with all our satraps and the whole senate and the nobles and all the Roman people, who are subject to the glory of our rule—considered it advisable that, as on earth he (Peter) is seen to have been constituted vicar of the Son of God, so the pontiffs, who are the representatives of that same chief of the apostles, should obtain from us and our empire the power of a supremacy greater than the earthly clemency of our imperial serenity is seen to have had conceded to it, we choosing that same prince of the apostles, or his vicars, to be our constant intercessors with God. And, to the extant of our earthly imperial power, we decree that his holy Roman church shall be honoured with veneration; and that, more than our empire and earthly throne, the most sacred seat of St. Peter shall be gloriously exalted; we giving to it the imperial power, and dignity of glory, and vigour and honour.

And we ordain and decree that he shall have the supremacy as well over the four chief seats Antioch, Alexandria, Constantinople and Jerusalem, as also over all the churches of God in the whole world. And he who for the time being shall be pontiff of that holy Roman church shall be more exalted than, and chief over, all the priests of the whole world; and, according to his judgment, every thing which is to be provided for the service of God or the stability of the faith of the Christians is to be administered. It is indeed just, that there the holy law should have the seat of its rule where the founder of holy laws, our Saviour, told St. Peter to take the chair of the apostleship; where also, sustaining the cross, he blissfully took the cup of death and appeared as imitator of his Lord and Master; and that there the people should bend their necks at the confession of Christ's name, where their teacher, St. Paul the apostle, extending his neck for Christ, was crowned with martyrdom. There, until the end, let them seek a teacher, where the holy body of the teacher lies; and there, prone and humiliated, let them perform the service of the heavenly king, God our Saviour Jesus Christ, where the proud were accustomed to serve under the rule of an earthly king.

Meanwhile we wish all the people, of all the races and nations throughout the whole world, to know: that we have constructed within our Lateran palace, to the same Saviour our Lord God Jesus Christ, a church with a baptistery from the foundations. And know that we have carried on our own shoulders, from its foundations, twelve baskets weighted with earth, according to the number of the holy apostles. Which holy Church we command to be spoken of, cherished, venerated and preached of, as the head and summit of all the churches in the whole world—as we have commanded through our other imperial decrees. We have also constructed the churches of St. Peter and St. Paul, chiefs of apostles, which we have enriched with gold and silver; where also, placing their most sacred bodies with great honour, we have constructed their caskets of electrum, against which no force of the elements prevails. And we have placed a cross of purest gold on each of their caskets, and fastened them with golden keys. And on these churches, for the providing of the lights, we have conferred estates, and have enriched them with different objects; and through our sacred imperial decrees, we have granted them our gift of land in the east as well as in the west; and even on the northern and southern coast; namely in Judea, Greece, Asia, Thrace, Africa, and Italy and the various islands: under this condition indeed, that all shall be administered by the hand of our most blessed father the pontiff Sylvester and his successors.

For let all the people and the nations of the races in the whole world rejoice with us; we exhorting all of you to give unbounded thanks, together with us, to our Lord and Saviour Jesus Christ. For He is God in Heaven above and on earth below, who, visiting us through His holy apostles, made us worthy to receive the holy sacrament of baptism and health of body. In return for which, to those same holy apostles, my masters, St. Peter and St. Paul; and, through them, also to St. Sylvester, our father, the chief pontiff and universal pope of the city of Rome, and to all the pontiffs his successors, who until the end of the world shall be about to sit in this seat of St. Peter: we concede and, by this present, do confer, our imperial Lateran palace, which is preferred to, and ranks above, all the palaces in the whole world; then a diadem, that is, the crown of our head, and at the same time the tiara; and, also, the shoulder band, that is, the collar that usually surrounds our imperial neck; and also the purple mantle, and crimson tunic, and all the imperial raiment; and the same rank as those presiding over the imperial cavalry; conferring also the imperial scepters, and, at the same time, the spears and standards; also the banners and different imperial ornaments, and all the advantage of our high imperial position, and the glory of our power.

And we decree, as to those most reverend men, the clergy who serve, in different orders, that same holy Roman church, that they shall have the same advantage, distinction, power and excellence by the glory of which our most illustrious senate is adorned; that is, that they shall be made patricians and consuls, we commanding that they shall also be decorated with the other imperial dignities. And even as the imperial soldiery, so, we decree, shall the clergy of the holy Roman church be adorned. And even as the imperial power is adorned by different offices—by the distinction, that is, of chamberlains, and door keepers, and all the guards, so we wish the holy Roman church to be adorned. And in order that the pontifical glory may shine forth more fully, we decree this also: that the clergy of this same holy Roman church may use saddle cloths of linen of the whitest colour; namely that their horses may be adorned and so be ridden, and that, as our senate uses shoes with goats' hair, so they may be distinguished by gleaming linen; in order that, as the celestial beings, so the terrestrial may be adorned to the glory of God. Above all things, moreover, we give permission to that same most holy one our father Sylvester, bishop of the city of Rome and pope, and to all the most blessed pontiffs who shall come after him and succeed him in all future times—for the honour and glory of Jesus Christ our Lord, to receive into that great catholic and apostolic church of God, even into the number of the monastic clergy, any one from the whole assembly of our nobles, who, in free choice, of his own accord, may wish to become a clerk; no one at all presuming thereby to act in a haughty manner.

We also decreed this, that this same venerable one our father Sylvester, the supreme pontiff; and all the pontiffs his successors, might use and bear upon their heads—to the praise of God and for the honor of St. Peter—the diadem; that is, the crown which we have granted him from our own head, of purest gold and precious gems. But he, the most holy pope, did not at all allow that crown of gold to be used over the clerical crown which he wears to the glory of St. Peter; but we placed upon his most holy head, with our own hands, a tiara of gleaming splendour representing the glorious resurrection of our Lord. And, holding the bridle of his horse, out of reverence for St. Peter we performed for him the duty of groom; decreeing that all the pontiffs his successors, and they alone, may use that tiara in processions.

In imitations of our own power, in order that for that cause the supreme pontificate may not deteriorate, but may rather be adorned with power and glory even more than is the dignity of an earthly rule: behold we—giving over to the oft-mentioned most blessed pontiff, our father Sylvester the universal pope, as well our palace, as has been said, as also the city of Rome and all the provinces, districts and cities of Italy or of the western regions; and relinquishing them, lay our inviolable gift, to the power and sway of himself or the pontiffs, his successors—do decree, by this our godlike charter and imperial constitution, that it shall be so arranged; and do concede that they (the palaces, provinces, etc.) shall lawfully remain with the holy Roman church.

Wherefore we have perceived it to be fitting that our empire and the power of our kingdom should be transferred and changed to the regions of the East; and that, in the province of Byzantium, in a most fitting place, a city should be built in our name; and that our empire should there be established. For, where the supremacy of priests and the head of the Christian religion has been established by a heavenly Ruler, it is not just that there an earthly ruler should have jurisdiction.

And we decree, moreover, that all these things which, through this our imperial charter and through other godlike commands, we have established and confirmed, shall remain uninjured and unshaken until the end of the world. Wherefore, before the living God, who commanded us to reign, and in the face of his terrible judgment, we conjure through this our imperial decree, all the emperors our successors, and all our nobles, the satraps also and the most glorious senate, and all the people in the whole world now and in all times previously subject to our rule: that no one of them, in any way, allow himself to oppose or disregard, or in any way seize, these things which, by our imperial sanction, have been conceded to the holy Roman church and to all its pontiffs. If anyone, moreover, which we do not believe, prove a scorner or despiser in this matter, he shall be subject and bound over to eternal damnation; and shall feel that the holy chiefs of the apostles of God, Peter and Paul, will be opposed to him in the present and in the future life. And, being burned in the nethermost hell, he shall perish with the devil and all the impious.

The page, moreover, of this our imperial decree, we, confirming it with our own hands, did place above the venerable body of St. Peter chief of the apostles; and there, promising to that same apostle of God that we would preserve inviolably all its provisions, and would leave in our commands to all the emperors our successors to preserve them, we did hand it over, to be enduringly and happily possessed, to our most blessed father Sylvester the supreme pontiff and universal pope, and, through him, to all the pontiffs his successors—God our Lord and our Saviour Jesus Christ consenting.

And the imperial subscription: May the Divinity preserve you for many years, oh most holy and blessed fathers.

Source: Henderson, Ernest F., ed. and trans. *Select Historical Documents of the Middle Ages.* London: Bell, 1921, pp. 323–29.

10. Licensed to Preach in England

Although the Protestant Reformation of the sixteenth century prized the individual's access to the Christian scriptures, these same Churches, once they had come to power, sought to control biblical interpretation. For example, the seventeenth-century document reproduced here, issued during the reign of the English King James I (r. 1603–1625), carefully outlines what a preacher can and cannot talk about. In essence, a priest lower than the rank of bishop can read homilies only from the approved two-volume collection. In particular, the lower-ranking priests are forbidden from discussing controversial issues such as predestination and from engaging in strenuous arguments about Catholicism or Puritanism. In fact, all higher-level theology is left in the hands of the bishops and theologians, so that the discussions will have the least impact on the common believer.

Behind much of this legislation lies the desire for political protection. As king, James I was head of the Anglican Church, and both the Catholic Church and the Puritan movement were potential threats to the Anglican Church and therefore to the king's preeminence. The king's orders, therefore, seek to create a stable theological environment that avoids contentious arguments, therefore promoting harmony. Such harmony built on extreme censorship proved impossible, and religious discontent continued to dominate the English political scene throughout the seventeenth century: two kings—Charles I and his son James II—were deposed in part because of their religious sympathies. Just as the Catholic hierarchy's attempts to contain heterodox theology through licensing preachers failed, the monarchy's attempts likewise proved ineffective.

THE KING'S MAJESTY'S LETTER TO THE LORDS . . ., TOUCHING PREACHING, AND PREACHERS

Most Reverend Father in God, Right trusty and right entirely beloved Counselor, We greet you well.

Forasmuch as the abuse and extravagancies of Preachers in the Pulpit, have been at all times repressed in this Land, by some Act of Council or State, with the advise and resolution of Grave and Reverend Preachers, insomuch as the very licensing of Preachers, had beginning by order in the Star-Chamber, the eighth of July, in the nineteenth year of King Henry the Eight, Our Noble Predecessor: And whereas at this present, diverse young Students, by reading of late Writers and ungrounded Divines, do preach many times unprofitable, unseasonable, seditious and dangerous doctrine, to the scandal of the Church, and disquieting of the State and present Government: We, upon humble presentation unto Us of these ill inconveniencies by your Self, and sundry other Grave and Reverend Prelates of this Church; as of our Princely care and desire, for the extirpation of Schism and Dissention growing from these seeds; and for the settling of a Religious and Peaceable Government both of Church and State: Do by these Our special Letters straightly charge and command you, to use all possible care and diligence, that these limitations and cautions herewith sent you concerning Preachers, be duely and strictly from henceforth observed, and put in practice by the several Bishops in their several Dioceses within your Jurisdiction. And to this end Our Pleasure is, that you send them forth several Copies of these Directions, to be by them speedily sent and communicated to every Parson, Vicar and Curate, Lecturer and Minister, in every Cathedral and Parish Church within their several Dioceses; and that ye earnestly require them, to employ their utmost endeavours for the performance of this so important a business: Letting them know, We have an especial eye to their proceedings, and expect a strict account thereof both from you and every of them, and this Our Letter shall be your sufficient warrant and discharge in this behalf.

Given under Our Signet at Our Castle of Windsor, the fourth day of August, in the twentieth year of Our Reign of England, France, and Ireland, and of Scotland. . . .

James I, King of England, bearing symbols of office and victory: a sceptre and laurel wreath. © 2008 Jupiterimages Corporation.

DIRECTIONS CONCERNING PREACHERS

1. That no Preacher, under the degree and calling of a Bishop, or Dean of a Cathedral or Collegiate Church, and they upon the King's days, and set Festivals, do take occasion by the expounding of any text of Scripture whatsoever, to fall into any set discourse or Commonplace (otherwise then by opening the coherence and division of his Text) which shall not be comprehended and warranted, in essence, substance and effect, or natural inference, within some one of the Articles of Religion set forth 1562, or in some of the Homilies set forth by authority in the Church of England, not only for a help for the Non-preaching, but withal for a pattern and a boundary (as it were) for the preaching Ministers, and for their further instructions: for the performance hereof, that they forthwith peruse over, and read diligently the said Articles, or the two books of Homilies.

2. That no Parson, Vicar, Curate, or Lecturer, shall preach any Sermon or Collation upon Sunday and Holy Days in the afternoon in any Cathedral or Parish Church throughout the Kingdom, but upon some part of the Catechism, or some text taken out of the Creed, ten Commandments, or Lords Prayer, (funeral Sermons only excepted) and that those Preachers be most encouraged and approved of, who spend these afternoon Exercises in examining the children in their Catechism, and in expounding of the several points and heads of the Catechism, which is the most ancient and laudable custom of teaching in the Church of England.

3. That no Preacher of what title soever, under the degree of a Bishop or Dean at the least, do from henceforth presume to preach in any populous auditory, the deep points of Predestination, Election, Reprobation; of the Universality, Efficacy, Resistability, or Irresistability of Gods grace, but leave those Themes to be handled by the learned men, and that moderately, and modestly, by way of use and application, rather then by way of positive doctrine, as being fitter for the Schools and University's, then for simple auditories.

4. That no Preacher of what title or denomination soever, shall presume from hence forth in any auditory in this Kingdom, to declare, limit, or bound out by positive doctrine, in any Lecture or Sermon, the Power, Prerogative, Jurisdiction, Authority, or Duty of Sovereign Princes; or otherwise meddle with these matters of State, and the references between Princes and the People, then as they are instructed and presidented in the Homily of obedience, and in the rest of the Homilies and Articles of Religion, set forth as is before mentioned by public authority; but rather confine themselves for those two heads, Faith and good Life, which are the subject of ancient Sermons and Homilies.

5. That no Preacher of what title or denomination soever, shall causelessly, and without invitation from the Text, fall into bitter invectives, and indecent railing speeches, against the persons of either Papist or Puritan, but modestly, and gravely when they are invited or occasioned thereunto by their text of Scripture, free both the Doctrine and Discipline of the Church of England, from the aspersion of either Adversary, especially where the auditory is suspected to be tainted with the one or the other infection.

6. Lastly, the Archbishops and Bishops of this kingdom (whom his Majesty hath good cause to blame for their former remissness) be more wary and choice in licensing Preachers, and revoke all grants made to any Chancellor, Official, or Commissary to license in this kind. And that all the Lecturers throughout the kingdom (a new body severed from the ancient Clergy of England, as being neither Parson, Vicar, nor Curate) be licensed henceforth in the Court of faculties, only upon recommendation of the party from the Bishop of the Diocese, under his hand and seal with a Fiat from the Lord Archbishop of Canterbury, and a confirmation of the great seal of England and that such as transgress any of these directions, be suspended by the Lord Bishop of the Diocese; in his default by the Lord Archbishop of the province, *ab Officio et Beneficio*, for a year and a day, until his Majesty by advice of the next Convocation shall prescribe some further punishment.

Source: Abbott, George. *The Coppie of a Letter Sent from My Lords Grace of Canterburie Shewing the Reasons Which Induced the Kings Majestie to Prescribe Directions for Preachers*. 1622. Spelling adapted by Lawrence Morris.

11. How a Minister Should Behave to Avoid Scandal

Scandals in the Church are hardly a new phenomenon. Geoffrey Chaucer in the fourteenth century was part of a long tradition of anti-clerical writing that portrayed monks and friars as sinful, but fun-loving villains and rapscallions. Throughout the Middle Ages, being Christian did not mean thinking that the local clergyman was a saint! In the following extract, an anonymous seventeenth-century author gives advice to any clergyman who may find himself at the center of a scandal.

According to this advice, the best course of action open to the clergyman is to avoid responding openly to the attack—denying the charges will just draw more attention to him. Instead, the pamphlet recommends that the clergyman throw himself even more into his work and avoid excessive socializing. In effect, the author is recommending a seventeenth-century method of image management—the clergyman must appear to be a serious, conscientious clergyman. The text, however, is not cynical; in those circumstances in which the scandal sticks to the clergyman, the pamphlet recommends that the minister be patient and think about the ways in which Christ himself was unjustly persecuted. The scandal, therefore, draws the minister closer to Christ. The language of the document is so close to modern English that the spelling of only a few words has been adjusted.

Dirt while it is green will not be struck off clear, but the very wiping of it fastens some stain, and spreads it further: Industrious Apologies, in such cases, beget suspicions, and raise more scandal: And 'tis a scandalous thing to have so much appearance of guilt, as to seem greatly concerned to clear ones Innocence; such lewd Reproaches will dye of themselves when they are let alone, and despised; but they are revived, and kept alive by much ado of answering, and refuting: The best way for any man to confute a slander, is to do it by the greater strictness of his Life: And if I was to counsel any Clergy man that was fallen under such circumstances of misfortune, I'll tell you how I would Advise.

1. I would perswade him to examine strictly, what occasion he may have given by any appearance of the vices with which he is reproach'd. 'Tis not sufficient for the Clergy to avoid evil, but they must stand off out of the shadow of it. Many things are lawful and harmless, that yet are not expedient, especially for men of sacred Character: And therefore if such a one find, that though his Conscience be clear, yet his prudence hath been defective; and that he hath not been enough cautious, and watchful in the midst of so many enemies; He ought to blame his own unwariness, and to resolve for the future upon more strictness in observing the Rules of expedience, as well as those of Duty: And not to content himself to fly from vice, but to get at what distance he can from any thing that looks like it.

2. If he be clear of the things imputed to him, He ought then to consider narrowly of what other sins he is guilty, that may be the reason of Gods leaving him to the fury of malicious Revilers. David did so when Shimei curst; He considered the permission of such an abuse as a judgement from Him, without discharging his rage on his railing enemy: And certainly when a man is exposed to causeless infamy, there is something more than malice, and misfortune in the case; God is to be remembered in it, and the provocations he hath received from our unquestionable sins. These he ought to call over in his thoughts, and to humble himself before the Divine Majesty under the

sense and apprehension of them. He should consider these as the main Adversaries that have hurt him, and execute his revenge here, in destroying, without mercy, these enemies of his soul, as well as of his credit: He should resolve to be more careful that his wayes please the Lord, and then his enemies will be at peace with him.

3. I would have him tye himself to a greater, and more severe Industry in the Duties of his place: And though he were constant, and laborious in those offices before; yet should he study to double his diligence, and be more assiduous (if possible) after such usage. He should joyn constant Catechising to constant Preaching, and frequent Sacraments to both; And study how otherwise to promote the spiritual advantage of his people; and endeavour to do it with all Conscience both towards God, and them. He should punctually perform all that his Rule requires, without deviations, or omissions; and not content with doing but just what is required of him, He should imploy himself in all those particular Industries (that the Law allows) that he judgeth tending to the Glory of God, the Honour of Religion, and the Edification of his charge: And take example for his practice from the strictest and most laborious Divines, yea and strive even to exceed them, in all painful and faithful diligence.

4. It is further adviseable, in my Opinion, That such an injured Minister, betake himself to great Privacy and Retiredness of living; That he be not frequent in unnecessary visits; that he mingle not ordinarily with common, and promiscuous companies; That he be not seen much abroad, but when he is about urgent affairs, and those especially that relate to his Office; That he go not without great cause to publick Houses, or places of resort: But that he stick close to his studies, and the preparations that are requisite for the due discharge of his great, and important business.

However severe these Rules may be thought, I judge they are exceedingly expedient, if not necessary, for a person in the Circumstances we suppose. And really there is so much wickedness, folly, and trifling in the ordinary conversations of the world, That methinks no serious, intelligent man should endure to be much in it. And as to the Clergy, There is so much captiousness, and malicious watching upon their words and actions; so much of what will give them just offence, and which they ought not to hear without reproof; And so much offence ready to be taken at them, and so many affronts ready to follow that, if they do reprove; That I see not how they can honestly and safely converse, except with a few known friends, though the malice of false reports hath not yet touch'd them. And in my judgement 'tis most adviseable for all the Clergy, in this evil Generation, to draw up (as far as is possible) into privacy, and retirement; For the Sea is too rough for them to be abroad upon it: But especially those on whom Envy, and ill-will have fastened any slanderous imputations, are of all Ministers, and all men, the most concern'd to live in as much silence, and reservedness, as their publick Office will permit.

These things, I know, (and by some experience) will contribute very much to the quiet and vindication of such an injured person, and more than all the verbal Apologies in the world: Or if they succeed not to clear his name, and restore him to the good opinion of men; There is yet no doubt but they will give him peace and approbation with God, and Conscience, which is infinitely better.

And if after all this, malice and Infamy should persecute him still; If it should continue upon him the old slanders, and out of nothing, and no appearance raise new ones to disquiet him, He need not, He ought not be concern'd, but may despise those impudent falshoods, and scorn to trouble himself to disprove them. He should not yield his enemies the satisfaction of having vext, and discomposed him: But rest himself contented with his Innocence, and the Testimony of his Conscience; blessing God that he is not such a person as they would render him to the world, and praying Him to give them a due sense of this their sin, and to pardon them upon their Repentance. In order to which excellent temper, He should frequently consider Him who with much long-suffering endured the contradictions of all sorts of sinners, and was reproach'd and vilified in his name, as well as injuriously treated in his person: And since they call'd Him, our Lord, Beelzebub, and publisht him for a Wine-Bibber, a Glutton, and a Friend of Publicans and Sinners, why should we care what they call us; or be at all moved at the Reproaches, which we have not deserv'd? Mens Tongues are their own, and they will speak; and let them say what they will, they cannot hurt us, while we are innocent, if our own niceness, and vitious tenderness of our names, do not assist their malice. This all good and wise men should endeavour to overcome, and outgrow; But chiefly the Clergy, and those of them especially of whom we are now speaking, ought to be well fortified against this weakness; That they may avoid the temptations to discouragement, impatience, and many other sins, and follies, that an over great concernment for Reputation doth expose men to: That they may go on with courage, and an equal mind, through good Report, and ill Report, in doing of their duty: That they may gain the noble height of wisdom, and Religion to count it a small thing to be approved and applauded by the judgement, and voices of men; and may attain the generosity of despising popular Fame, otherwise than as it may facilitate their doing good; considering, that This is most commonly given to the foolishest and worst of men, and things; while infamy and reproach is usually bestowed upon the worthiest and the best.

By such Exercises, and such Considerations as these; the scandall'd person shall either wipe off the slanders that are upon him: Or strengthen himself so as not to be hurt by them.

Thus I have let my pen run on as the humour of writing bad me: If to no other purpose; Yet the imployment hath given a little present diversion to my self: And I know you can be content that I should sometimes write for the little end of venting my own thoughts, in declaring my opinion, which I have now given you freely, in this matter . . .

Source: Anonymous. *An Apology and Advice for Some of the Clergy, Who Suffer under False and Scandalous Reports Written on the Occasion of the Second Part of the Rehearsal Transpros'd, in a Letter to a Friend, and by Him Publish'd.* London: A.E., 1674, pp. 8–12.

12. Preparing for Eucharistic Communion

The central ritual of most forms of Christianity is the Eucharist, the memorial of the Last Supper in which Jesus called bread and wine his body and blood and gave them to his disciples. Different denominations interpret this scene, and the corresponding ritual, in different ways. In traditional Catholicism, the bread and wine are viewed as substantially the body and blood of Christ. In other words, the substance—but not the appearance—of the bread and wine becomes the body and blood of Christ. This doctrine is called "transubstantiation." The word substance, however, is used in a philosophical sense—it does not mean atoms or raw materials; rather, it refers to the essence of a thing, regardless of what it looks like or what it is made out of. To use a comparison mentioned earlier, a chair in the shape of a mushroom and made out of plastic still has the essence or substance of a chair, although it looks like a mushroom and although it is made out of plastic; just so, the transubstantiated bread and wine have the essence of Christ's body and blood, although they continue to look like bread and wine.

Most Reformation theologians, such as John Calvin (see Document 3), did not interpret Christ's words so literally. According to these reformers, the Eucharist is a complex and effective symbol. The bread and wine do not literally become the body and blood of Christ, but they may have significant spiritual effects. The following document, written by two seventeenth-century Protestant Anglicans (members of the Church of England) with Puritan leanings, reflects this Reformation theology.

Throughout the document, the authors, William Bradshaw and Arthur Hildersam, stress that the Eucharist is a deep "mystery" that has considerable spiritual effects. Because the ritual is so closely bound up with Christ's death and the spiritual effects of that sacrifice, Christians must be certain to prepare themselves to receive the ritual bread and wine. They must think carefully about the meaning of the ritual and call to mind Christ's suffering and death, rather than thoughtlessly and distractedly receiving the Eucharist.

The very circumstance of time wherein our Saviour did administer it, showeth us, that this bread and wine, this eating and drinking, hath in this place a more than ordinarie use or end. Wee eat bread commonly to satisfie hunger, and to feed and nourish our bodies; and wee drinke wine to quench our thirst, and to revive and refresh our heavy spirits: but this is not the proper end of the eating of this bread, or of the drinking of this wine. For then Christ would never have administred it immediately after supper, and that a festivall supper, when they that were to receive it, were full of bread and wine before. And therefore in the receiving of this Sacrament, wee must not so much looke (as wee doe in other eatings and drinkings) to satisfie our hunger, to fill our bellies, and to quench our thirsts; but in this eating and drinking, wee must looke to satisfie and fill our souls with some heavenly and spirituall matters, shadowed in these outward signs, and conveyed unto our soules in the due receiving of them.

The mysteries then contained under these signs, and expressed by them, are the greatest that can be imagined, even the great and high mysterie of our redemption and salvation by Jesus Christ; our faith and belief whereof, we doe professe in the use of them, and the fruit whereof is sealed and confirmed unto us in the due receiving of them.

The breaking of the bread signifieth, in a mysterie, the breaking of Christ's body, that is, all the unspeakable torments that hee suffered in his own person for our sins, which were greater than if his living body had been rent and torn into a thousand pieces, and all his bones broken and beaten to dust and powder, Heb. 5.7. Esai 53.16.11. Matth. 27.46.

The eating of the bread thus broken, and the drinking of this wine, signifieth the speciall fruit that commeth unto all beleeuers, by the passion and sufferings of Jesus Christ. For Christ saith; This Bread is my Body which was broken for you: And this

Cuppe is the New Testament in my Blood. Or as hee speakes more plainly, Matt. 26.28. This is my Blood in the New Testament that was shed for many for the remission of their sins. And therefore hee bids them take and eat the one, and drinke the other; as though hee should more plainly say unto them: This bread, so broken as you see, shall bee a sign unto you, and unto all them that beleeue in my name, of that which I have suffered in my flesh for you. The wine in this Cuppe shall bee a sign even of the blood that in my Sacrifice upon the crosse was shed for you, to procure the pardon and remission of your sins, and of all their sins that shall beeleeve in me, which is not the blood of Oxen and sheepe, such as were offered in the Old Testament, but is in very deed the blood of God and man, whereby the new Testament is sealed and ratified, which offreth salvation unto al which shall beleeue in mee, and in the merits of this my blood: Therefore take ye and eat yee this mysticall bread, and drink this holy wine; and therein let it be a pledge unto you and to all the faithfull that shall in like manner receive the same, that the fruit of that which is shadowed thereby, belongs unto you; so that as verily as you eat this bread, and drinke this wine with your bodilie mouths, so verily shall your soules taste of, and, as it were, eat and drinke of the fruits of my death and passion, even the remission of sins, and life everlasting.

Is not this Sacrament then a mysterie to bee trembled at and adored? Is it not a great indignitie, that men should brutishly, without all preparation, come unto the same, as an horse to the manger, or a swine to the trough? If it were but a bare and simple eating of bread and drinking of wine for bodily necessity or pleasure, we ought not like beasts, without any show of reverence, seize upon them; but ought in the receiving of them, in some degree, lift up our hearts to God for them: Much more when there is such an heavenly use of these creatures, over and besides that naturall and common use, which cannot bee separated from them. It were a great indignitie offered to the worke of our redemption, but occasionally to speake or thinke of it without due reverence: but to deny reverence and honour unto it then when under such a speciall mysterie it is presented unto us, and when we are thereby called to a speciall consideration of it; yea wherein it is of purpose represented to our senses, that we might the better behold it, and be stirred up to praise and magnifie God for it: and which is more, when in a reverend use of this mysterie wee may spiritually partake even of all heavenly things that are shadowed by it, what a sin must this needs be, unreverently to rush upon these holy Rites? And what a forcible argument must it bee, to stirre us up to a worthy receiving of this Sacrament?

The fifth point of doctrine is concerning the consecration of this Sacrament, set down in these words: And when he had giuen thankes, hee brake it. This consecration was a speciall dedication of the elements in this Sacrament unto this mysticall and holy use, by prayer, and invocation upon the name of God, and specially by thanksgiving: wherein this thanksgiving specially consisted, is not revealed; most probable it is, that it was principally for our sake, to wit, for the great fruit of this Sacrament, that should redound unto all the worthie receivers thereof.

This showeth, that speciall thanks are due unto GOD from us for this Sacrament: For if Christ found cause to thank God for it, much more cause have wee, who reap all the fruit and benefit of it. And if the worthinesse of this Sacrament did draw thanks from Christ, it may challenge a worthy and reverend acceptance of us; yea it much more concerns us to administer and receive the same with prayer and thanksgiving. And it is great prophanenesse for us to presse unreuerently upon that which Christ himselfe would not enter upon, without speciall prayer; whereby hee sufficiently declareth, that this Sacrament is a speciall holy Ordinance, and therefore to bee used holily, and not in a prophane and unreverent manner. If Christ had but simply ordained it without any such speciall thanksgiving or prayer, it had beene our dutie notwithstanding, to receive it with all due reverence: But when he shall in this manner, by speciall prayer, institute and administer it, it must needs be great impietie for us to despise and contemne it, and not to make an high account and reckoning of it.

The Evangelist Matthew sayeth, Hee blessed the bread: By prayer and thanksgiving obtained a speciall blessing from God upon it. For that which Balac said of Balaam may bee more truely said of Christ, That which he blesseth, is blessed; and that which hee curseth, is cursed: So that this is a blessed Sacrament, which Christ Jesus, with his owne mouth, hath after such a speciall manner blessed: And the more hee hath blessed it, the more it will bee a means of blessing to the worthy receiver of it; and the more blessed it is of itself, the greater curse will it bring upon the prophane and unreverent abuser thereof. The sixth and last point of doctrine is concerning the main and most generall ends of this Sacrament, which are two; the first, respecting our selves: the second, others. That respecting our selves, is in these words; This doe ye in remembrance of mee: So that wee are to receive this Sacrament to this end and purpose, that in and by it we might be stirred up in a speciall manner to remember, and in remembring to meditate of Christ, and of his infinite love and mercy towards us, in the great work of our Redemption, which is shadowed and set forth by this Sacrament: When our speciall friends, upon their departure from us, bestow upon us a token of remembrance, they do it to this end, that so often as we looke upon the same, or use it, wee should call to minde the many loves they have showed unto us: And this is written in our nature, that when an occasion onely is offered unto us of remembring a friend departed from us, we use to show a speciall affection. Hence it is, that ignorant and superstitious persons will so heartily, upon every occasion of remembrance, pray the Lord to have mercy of their soules that are departed this life, whom they love and have been beholding unto. But when they behold a speciall memoriall of them in some token of their love, which brings to their minde some extraordinarie favours, then they use to be extraordinarily affected with the remembrance thereof; yea, and they use to show part of that love, affection, and honour, to the token and memoriall itselfe, which they beare to the person. They will carefully lay it up in their deskes and cabinets: They will (it may be) sometimes kisse it, and doe a kinde of honour unto it: So much do we use to be affected with any thing that brings into our minde the loves and favors of a deceased friend. And therefore seeing this Sacrament that was not only left unto us by the greatest friend that ever we had, but left of purpose to be a remembrance & a pledge unto us, of the greatest love that ever was showed to mortall creatures, and which hath the very effects and fruits of the love written upon it, nay ingraven in it, yea in some sort contained in it; is it a thing credible, that any that love and beleeve in Christ Jesus, should prophane and lightly regard this Sacrament?

But heere by the way we may observe how strangely forgetfull even those that are faithful, be of the great & unspeakable love of Christ, that they stand in need of such a remembrance: for unto them is this Sacrament given, as a helpe to bring to their mindes the consideration of this love. Is it possible that a man should forget the love of such a Lord and Master, that hath with a great price of money redeemed him from being a perpetuall Galley-slave, yea who for to redeem him, hath made himself a slave, yea hath purchased his servants libertie with his own death, and hath bestowed upon him all the honours and dignities that himselfe had, and even all that himselfe possessed? Were it not wonderfull that he should need a speciall remembrance when hee can no wayes cast his eyes, but hee shall behold the effects of his Lords love? Would not one thinke that hee should rather need some means to make him forget this love, and to put it out of his head, rather than to bring it unto his remembrance? This is the state and condition of all Christians; though Christ Jesus hath done a thousand times more for us than is possible for one man to doe for an other, though whatsoever wee have, we have it by his mercie and love, our soules, our bodies, our senses, our wit, our beautie, our wealth, our life; so that wee are compassed about with memorials of his kindnesse: and we cannot see, feele, heare, taste, or smell any thing, but it may put us in minde of his love, yea of his death and passion, by which the free use of these things have been purchased unto vs: yet for all this, wee stand in need, you see, of speciall remembrances; yea and yet (O sinfull wretches that we are!) wee are ready to prophane these speciall remembrances; yea, and which exceedeth all wonder, are prone, even in the midst of them, most all to forget the love of Christ, and to dishonour him.

Source: Bradshaw, William, and Arthur Hildersam. *A Direction for the Weaker Sort of Christians Shewing in What Manner They Ought to Fit and Prepare Themselues to the Worthy Receiuing of the Sacrament of the Body and Blood of Christ: With a Short Forme of Triall or Examination Annexed.* London: Hall, 1609, pp. 28–44.

13. A European Visitor Is Struck by the Zeal of Muslim Prayer

By the seventeenth century, when the following document was written, the Islamic world and the Christian world had been living side by side for centuries. Up until the late fifteenth century, for example, Muslims ruled much of the Spanish peninsula. In eastern Europe, moreover, Muslim governments had taken over the remains of the Byzantine Empire. Trade and crusading, meanwhile, had brought Muslims and Christians into frequent peaceful and violent contact. Nonetheless, the literature of the Middle Ages demonstrates that the average western European knew very little about authentic Muslim practices.

With the global expansion of west European empires (e.g., England, Spain, Portugal), however, increased contact with the Islamic world led to more informed discussions of Muslim practices. In this extract, the British ambassador Thomas Roe (c. 1581–1644), who had spent much of his life in Muslim lands, describes contemporary Muslim practices with an accuracy uncommon before this time period. Roe points out some of the major features of Muslim practice, which are still features of the faith today: praying five times per day, removing shoes before entering a mosque, using Arabic in prayer, and so on.

These ethnographic descriptions were not given, however, just to satisfy interest in for-
eign peoples. Writers like Roe interrogated their own cultures by comparing their home
culture with the foreign culture. In this case, although Roe accuses the Muslims (whom he
calls Mahometans) of practicing a false faith, he notes that their zeal in prayer puts to shame
many so-called Christians who barely pray five times in a year. According to Roe, such
Christians should not expect any more divine favor than the Muslims. Christian England,
then, has something to learn from the Muslim East.

The Mahometans have a set form of prayer in the Arabian Tongue, not understood by many of the common people, yet repeated by them as well as by the Moolaas: they likewise rehearse the Names of God and of their Mahomet certain times every day upon Beads, like the miss-led Papists, who seem to regard more the Number, then the weight of prayers.

But for the carriage of that people in their devotions, before they go into their Churches they wash their feet, and entring into them put off their shooes. As they begin their devotions they stop their ears, and fix their eyes, that nothing may divert their thoughts; then in a soft and still voice they utter their prayers, wherein are many words most significantly expressing the Omnipotency, and Greatness, and Eternity, and other Attributes of God. Many words likewise that seem to express much humiliation, they confessing in divers submissive gestures, their own unworthiness, when they pray casting themselves low upon their Face sundry times, and then acknowledge that they are burdens to the Earth, and poison to the Air, and the like, being so confounded and ashamed as that they seem not to dare so much as to lift up their eyes towards Heaven; but after all this, comfort themselves in the mercies of God, through the mediation of Mahomet.

If this people could as well conclude, as they can begin and continue their prayers, in respect of their expressions, and carriages in them, they might find comfort; but the conclusion of their devotions mars all. Yet this, for their commendation (who doubtless, if they knew better would pray better) that what diversions, and impediments soever they have arising either from pleasure or profit, the Mahometans pray five times a day. The Mogul doth so, who sits on the Throne; the Shepherd doth so that waits on his flock in the field (where, by the way, they do not follow their flocks; but their flocks, them) all sorts of Mahometans do thus whether fixed in a place or moving in a journey, when their times, or hours of prayer come, which in the morning are at Six, Nine, and Twelve of the clock; and at three and six in the afternoon.

When they pray, it is their manner to set their Faces that they may look towards Medina near Mecca in Arabia where their great Seducer Mahomet was buried, who promised them after one thousand years, to fetch them all to Heaven; which term, when it was out, and the promise not fulfilled, the Mahometans concluded that their Fore-fathers mis-took the time of the promise of his coming; and therefore resolve to wait for the accomplishment of it one thousand years more. In the mean time they do so reverence that place where the body of Mahomet was laid up, that whosoever hath been there (as there are divers which flock yearly thither in Pilgrimage) are for ever after called, and esteemed Hoggees, which signifies Holy men.

Mulsim pilgrims attempting to touch the Kaba stone in Mecca. © 2008 Jupiterimages Corporation.

And here the thing being rightly and seriously considered; it is a very great shame that a Mahometan should pray five times every day, that Pagans and Heathens should be very frequent in their devotions, and Christians (who only can hope for good answers in prayer) so negligent in that great prevailing duty. For a Mahometan to pray five times every day, what diversions soever he hath to hinder him, and for a Christian to let any thing interrupt his devotion; for a Mahometan to pray five times a day, and for one that is called a Christian not to pray (some believing themselves above this and other Ordinances) five times in a week, a month, a year!

But this will admit less cause of wonder if we consider how that many bearing the Names of Christians cannot pray at all, those I mean which are prophane and filthy, and who live as if there were no God to hear, or no judge, and no Hell to punish. Such as these can but babble, they cannot pray, for they blaspheme the Name of God, while they may think they adore it.

Source: Pietro della Valle. *The Travels of Sig. Pietro della Valle, a Noble Roman, into East India and Arabia Deserta in Which, the Several Countries, Together with the Customs, Manners, Traffique, and Rites Both Religious and Civil, of Those Oriental Princes and Nations, Are Faithfully Described: In Familiar Letters to His Friend Signior Mario Schipano: Whereunto Is Added a Relation of Sir Thomas Roe's Voyage into the East-Indies.* Translated by George Havers. London: J. Macock, 1665, pp. 423–24.

Death and the Afterlife

Stories of life after death are among the most prevalent worldwide. The human species seems to have almost unanimously rejected the idea that death is the end of independent conscious existence. That continued existence, however, may not always be happy. Xibalba (the *Maya* underworld), for example, contains houses of torment, such as the house of knives in which thrashing blades torture the inhabitants, but no houses of reward (Document 19). The *Anglo-Saxons*, likewise, envisioned souls of the dead leaping back and forth between a valley of intense cold and a land of fire, as the souls awaited Judgment Day (Document 18). One account from China depicts the souls of the dead being collected by a giant, who keeps them stuffed up his sleeve in unbearably cramped conditions; only devoted followers of Buddha could escape (Document 14).

Frequently, negative outcomes in the afterlife are the result of evildoing in this life. Dante's Italian lovers, punished by an eternal whirlwind in hell, have merited their lot in the afterlife because they allowed themselves to give in to carnal temptations in this life (Document 17). A Chinese gentleman, who witnessed his life flashing before his eyes on his deathbed, felt his blood boil painfully. Likewise, positive outcomes result from lives of goodness. The Chinese gentleman, for example, felt a sense of peace and calm when he recalled any virtuous act, and the souls of the righteous Anglo-Saxon dead await Judgment Day in a beautiful walled garden that is filled with a delicious and satisfying aroma. Good Muslims will be rewarded with beautiful maidens and feasting, according to the *Koran*, and the unrighteous will eat the bitter fruit of the Zakkoum tree (Document 16). Occasionally, however, the link between this life and the afterlife is less clear. The Japanese *Kojiki* does not present any clearly positive aspects about the *Shinto* underworld (Document 15), and there are no redeeming features to Xibalba.

Life and death are nevertheless still connected even in such grim underworlds as those of the Maya and the *Kojiki*. In the *Kojiki* account, His Augustness the Male Who Invites drops fruit to delay the pursuit of the servants of Her Augustness the Female Who Invites, who controls the underworld. The gendered difference of the gods—male and female—emphasizes the role of the underworld in fertility, which role is explicitly highlighted by the fruit in the story. Just as the dead crops of the previous autumn enrich the soil and provide the seeds for the next year's harvest, the land of death—the underworld—is a necessary component of life in general. Hun-Hunahpú in the Maya *Popul Vuh* may die, but his head becomes the fruit of the calabash tree. Death brings forth new life.

14. A Chinese Story of Resurrection

P'u Sung-ling, the seventeenth-century author of the following extract, spent much of his life working as a tutor, during which time he also collected the tales of fantasy that make up his Strange Tales from a Chinese Studio, published in 1679. P'u Sung-ling is famous for his literary style and has been called the "Last of the immortals."

In the following account, P'u Sung-ling sketches the afterlife experiences of one T'ang T'ing. Although we can assume that P'u Sung-ling elaborated what may have been a real experience, the details included indicate what a seventeenth-century Chinese audience expected the afterlife to be like. According to this description, the dead undergo a review of their good and evil actions in life and are punished with a boiling of their blood for evil actions and rewarded with a sense of peace for good actions. Once the soul passes out of the body, however, it is the subject of capricious beings. T'ang T'ing's soul, for example, is captured by a giant, who stores the soul in a coat sleeve, until T'ang T'ing is released by calling on the Buddha. After several more adventures, including a conversation with Confucius, the soul is returned to T'ang T'ing's body by a Bodhisatva (a monk who has reached nirvana) who throws clay over the soul. This recreation results in T'ang T'ing waking up in his coffin, returned once more to life. Ultimately, T'ang T'ing's perseverance, more than any other factor, results in his resurrection from the dead.

RAISING THE DEAD

Mr. T'ang T'ing, who took the highest degree in the year 1661, was suffering from a protracted illness, when suddenly he felt, as it were, a warm glow rising from his extremities upwards. By the time it had reached his knees, his feet were perfectly numb and without sensation; and before long his knees and the lower part of his body were similarly affected. Gradually this glow worked its way up until it attacked his heart, and then some painful moments ensued. Every single incident of Mr. T'ang's life from his boyhood upwards, no matter how trivial, seemed to surge through his mind, borne along on the tide of his heart's blood. At the revival of any virtuous act of his, he experienced a delicious feeling of peace and calm; but when any wicked deed passed before his mind, a painful disturbance took place within him, like oil boiling and fretting in a cauldron.

He was quite unable to describe the pain he suffered; however, he mentioned that he could recollect having stolen, being only seven or eight years old, some young birds from their nest, and having killed them; and for this alone, he said, boiling blood rushed through his heart during the space of an ordinary meal-time. Then when all the acts of his life had passed one after another in panorama before him, the warm glow proceeded up his throat, and entering the brain, issued out at the top of his head like smoke from a chimney. By-and-by Mr. T'ang's soul escaped from his body by the same aperture, and wandered far away, forgetting all about the tenement it had left behind. Just at that moment a huge giant came along, and seizing the soul, thrust it into his sleeve, where it remained cramped and confined, huddled up with a crowd of others, until existence was almost unbearable. Suddenly Mr. T'ang reflected that Buddha alone could save him from this horrible state, and forthwith he began to call on his holy name. At the third or fourth invocation he fell out of the giant's sleeve, whereupon the giant picked him up and put him back; but this happened several times, and at length the giant, wearied of picking him up, let him lie where he was. The soul lay there for some time, not knowing in which direction to proceed; however, it soon recollected that the land of Buddha was in the west, and westwards accordingly it began to shape its course. In a little while the soul came upon a Buddhist priest sitting by the roadside, and hastening forwards, respectfully inquired of him which was the right way. "The Book of Life and Death for scholars," replied the priest, "is in the hands of the God of Literature and Confucius; any application must receive the consent of both." The priest then directed Mr. T'ang on his way, and the latter journeyed along until he reached a Confucian temple, in which the Sage was sitting with his face to the south. On hearing his business, Confucius referred him to the God of Literature; and proceeding onwards in the direction indicated, Mr. T'ang by-and-by arrived at what seemed to be the palace of a king, within which sat the God of Literature precisely as we depict him on earth. "You are an upright man," replied the God, in reply to Mr. T'ang's prayer, "and are certainly entitled to a longer span of life; but by this time your mortal body has become decomposed, and unless you can secure the assistance of a Bodhisatva, I can give you no aid." So Mr. T'ang set off once more, and hurried along until he came to a magnificent shrine standing in a thick grove of tall bamboos; and entering in, he stood in the presence of the Bodhisatva, on whose head was the ushnisha, whose golden face was round like the full moon, and at whose side was a green willow-branch bending gracefully over the lip of a vase. Humbly Mr. T'ang prostrated himself on the ground, and repeated what Wen Ch'ang had said to him; but the Bodhisatva seemed to think that it would be impossible to grant his request, until one of the Lohans who stood by cried out. "O Bodhisatva, perform this miracle. Take earth and make his flesh; take a sprig of willow and make his bones." Thereupon the Bodhisatva broke off a piece from the willow-branch in the vase beside him; and pouring a little water on the ground, he made clay, and casting the whole over Mr. T'ang's soul, he bade an attendant lead the body back to the place where his coffin was. At that instant Mr. T'ang's family heard a groan come from within his coffin; and on rushing to it and helping out the lately deceased man, they found that he had quite recovered. He had then been dead seven days.

Source: Giles, Herbert A. *Gems of Chinese Literature: Prose.* 2nd ed. London: Bernard Quaritch, 1923, pp. 236–39.

15. The Japanese Land of the Dead

The Kojiki, from which the following extract is taken, contains an early-medieval Japanese story of creation and is a central text of the traditional Shinto religion. In this extract, the primal male deity goes in search of his younger sister, who has been transformed by death into the Great Deity of Hades. The word Hades (the name of the Greek underworld) is, of course, the translator's choice—the original Japanese account does not refer to the Greek underworld. When His Augustness the Male Who Invites sees his sister full of maggots and of Thunder Deities as a result of death, he flees. Her Augustness the Female Who Invites sends warriors in pursuit of the brother, who escapes ultimately by throwing down objects that turn into fruit.

The connections between gender, food, and the underworld are seen in many cultures. Whereas a brother visits a sister in Kojiki, "Good looks the playboy" goes in search of the fertility goddess Ishtar in Mesopotamian legend, and Hades snatches Persephone in Greek legend. Persephone cannot return permanently to the land of the living because she has eaten food in the underworld; food similarly detains the denizens of the underworld in the Kojiki, and in Irish folklore, people who have eaten food with the fairies cannot leave the fairy realm. These legends, ultimately concerned with fertility, reflect a widespread cultural understanding that death is a part of life and that life ultimately comes from death. The realm of the dead and the realm of the living are intricately connected. The emphasis on food in the underworld may also reflect rituals in which food was offered to the souls of the departed.

Thereupon [His Augustness the Male Who-Invites], wishing to meet and see his younger sister Her Augustness the Female-Who-Invites, followed after her to the Land of Hades. So when from the palace she raised the door and came out to meet him, His Augustness the Male-Who-Invites spoke, saying: "Thine Augustness my lovely younger sister! The lands that I and thou made are not yet finished making; so come back!" Then Her Augustness the Female-Who-Invites answered, saying: "Lamentable indeed that thou camest not sooner! I have eaten of the furnace of Hades. Nevertheless, as I reverence the entry here of Thine Augustness my lovely elder brother, I wish to return. Moreover, I will discuss it particularly with the Deities of Hades. Look not at me!" Having thus spoken, she went back inside the palace; and as she tarried there very long, he could not wait. So having taken and broken off one of the end-teeth of the multitudinous and close-toothed comb stuck in the august left bunch [of his hair], he lit one light and went in and looked. Maggots were swarming, and [she was] rotting, and in her head dwelt the Great-Thunder, in her breast dwelt the Fire-Thunder, in her left hand dwelt the Young-Thunder, in her right hand dwelt the Earth-Thunder, in her left foot dwelt the Rumbling-Thunder, in her right foot dwelt the Couchant-Thunder; altogether eight Thunder-Deities had been born and dwelt there. Hereupon His Augustness the Male-Who-Invites, overawed at the sight, fled back, whereupon his younger sister Her Augustness the Female-Who-Invites said: "Thou hast put me to shame," and at once sent the Ugly-Female-of-Hades to pursue him. So His Augustness the Male-Who-Invites took his black august head-dress and cast it down, and it instantly turned into grapes. While she picked them up and ate them, he fled on; but as she still pursued him, he took and broke the multitudinous and close-toothed comb in the right bunch [of his hair] and cast it down, and it instantly turned into bamboo-sprouts. While she pulled them up and ate them, he fled on. Again later [his Younger sister] sent the eight Thunder-Deities with a thousand and five hundred warriors of Hades to pursue him. So he, drawing the ten-grasp sabre that was augustly girded on him, fled forward brandishing it in his back hand; and as they still pursued, he took, on reaching the base of the Even Pass of Hades, three peaches that were growing at its base, and waited and smote [his pursuers therewith], so that they all fled back. Then His Augustness the Male-Who-Invites announced to the peaches: "Like as ye have helped me, so must ye help all living people in the Central Land of Reed-Plains when they shall fall into troublous circumstances and be harassed!" And he gave [to the peaches] the designation of Their Augustnesses Great-Divine-Fruit. Last of all, his younger sister Her Augustness the Princess-Who-Invites came out herself in pursuit. So he drew a thousand-draught rock, and [with it] blocked up the Even Pass of Hades, and placed the rock in the middle; and they stood opposite to one another and exchanged leave-takings; and Her Augustness the Female-Who-Invites said: "My lovely elder brother, thine Augustness! If thou do like this, I will in one day strangle to death a thousand of the folks of thy land." Then His Augustness the Male-Who-Invites replied: "My lovely younger sister, Thine Augustness! If *thou* do this, *I* will in one day set up a thousand and five hundred parturition-houses. In this manner each day a thousand people would surely be born." So Her Augustness the Female-Who-Invites is called the Great-Deity-of-Hades. Again it is said that, owing to her having pursued and reached [her elder brother], she is called the Road-Reaching-Great-Deity. Again the rock with which he blocked up the Pass of Hades is called the Great-Deity-of-the-Road-Turning-back, and again it is called the Blocking-Great-Deity-of-the-Door-of-Hades. So what was called the Even-Pass-of-Hades is now called the Ifuya-Pass in the Land of Idzumo.

Source: Chamberlain, Basil Hall. *Translation of "Ko-ji-ki": or "Records of Ancient Matters."* Kobe: Asiatic Society of Japan, 1919, pp. 38–41.

16. *Heaven and Hell in the Koran*

Like many other major religions, including Christianity and Buddhism, Islam teaches that the dead will be rewarded or punished in accordance with their deeds. Like Christianity, two major outcomes are possible: reward in paradise or torment in a kind of hell. In this manner, the day of judgment can be called by the Koran, as in the following extract, "Day that shall abase! Day that shall exalt!"

The rewards of the righteous are depicted with worldly imagery in the Koran. The righteous will feast on fruits and meat, and they will have houris (beautiful maidens) as companions; even their refreshing drink will not cause hangovers ("Their brows ache not from it, nor fails the sense"). Evildoers, however, will be punished with hot winds, boiling waters, and the bitter fruit of the Zakkoum tree.

Ultimately, the nature of creation serves as a rebuke to evil people. In this extract, God (using the plural "We") points out to the wicked that they are not the center and purpose of the universe. Indeed, human beings cannot force things to grow, cannot control the weather, and did not create the stars. The Koran suggests that human beings' own frailty points out their need of the Creator, and their resulting need to obey that Creator in choosing good over evil.

Sura LVI—The Inevitable

In the name of God, the Compassionate, the Merciful.
When the day that must come shall have come suddenly,
None shall treat its sudden coming as a lie:
Day that shall abase! Day that shall exalt!
When the earth shall be shaken with a shock,
And the mountains shall be crumbled with a crumbling,
And become scattered dust,
And into three bands shall ye be divided;
Then the people of the right hand—how happy the people of the right hand!
And the people of the left hand—how wretched the people of the left hand!
And they who were foremost on earth—the foremost still.
These are they who shall be brought close to God,
In gardens of delight;
A crowd from the ancients,
And a few from later generations;
On inwrought couches
Reclining on them face to face:
Immortal youths go round about to them
With goblets and ewers and a cup from a fountain;
Their brows ache not from it, nor fails the sense:
And with such fruits as they shall make choice of,
And with flesh of such birds as they shall long for:
And theirs shall be the Houris with large dark eyes like close-kept pearls,
A recompense for their labours past.
No vain discourse shall they hear therein, nor charge of sin,
But only the cry, "Peace! Peace!"
And the people of the right hand—how happy the people of the right hand!
Amid thornless lote-trees
And bananas clad with flowers,
And extended shade,
And flowing waters,
And abundant fruits,
Unfailing, and unforbidden,
And lofty couches.
Verily of a rare creation have We created the Houris,
And We have made them ever virgins,
Dear to their spouses, of equal age with them,
For the people of the right hand,
A crowd from the ancients,
And a crowd from later generations.
But the people of the left hand—how wretched shall be the people of the left hand!
Amid pestilential winds and in scalding water,
And the shadow of a black smoke,
Not cooling, not pleasant.
They truly, ere this, were blessed with worldly goods,
But persisted in heinous wickedness,
And were wont to say,
"When we have died, and become dust and bones, shall we indeed be raised?
And our fathers the men of yore?"
Say: Aye, the former and the latter.
Gathered shall they surely be before the time of a known day.

Then verily you, O you the erring, the imputers of falsehood,
Shall surely eat of the tree of Zakkoum,
And fill your bellies with it,
And thereupon shall ye drink of the boiling water,
And ye shall drink as the thirsty camel drinketh.
This shall be their repast in the day of reckoning!
We created you; will you not then credit Us?
What think you? The germs of life—
Is it you who create them? or are We their creator?
It is We who have decreed that death should be among you;
Yet are We not thereby hindered from replacing you with others, your likes, or from producing
    you again in a form which you know not!
And already you have known the first creation: will you not then reflect?
What think you? That which you sow—
Do ye cause its upgrowth, or are We the givers of it?
If We pleased We surely could so make it so dry and brittle that you would ever marvel
    and say,
"We have been indeed at cost, yet are we forbidden harvest."
What think you also of the water you drink?
Is it you who send it down from the clouds, or send We it down?
Brackish could We make it, if We pleased: will you not then be thankful?
What think ye too of the fire which ye obtain by friction—
Is it ye who rear its tree, or do We rear it?
It is We who have made it for a memorial and a benefit to the dwellers in the desert;
Praise therefore the name of thy Lord, the Great.
And I swear by the places where the stars do set,
And that is surely a great oath, if ye (only) knew it;
Verily it is the honorable Koran,
Written in the preserved Book:
Let none touch it but the purified,
It is a revelation from the Lord of the worlds.
Such tidings then as these will ye disdain?
And will ye make it your daily bread to gainsay them?
Why then when the soul of a dying man has reached the throat,
And ye then are looking on,
And We are nearer to him than ye, although ye see Us not:
Why could ye not, if ye are to escape all retribution,
Cause that soul to return? Tell me, if ye speak the truth.
But if he be one of those permitted to draw near to God,
His shall be repose and pleasure and a garden of delights;
And if he be of the people of the right hand—
From the people of the right hand shall be the greeting, "Peace be to thee:"
And if he be of those who treat the prophets as deceivers,
And of the erring,
His entertainment shall be of scalding water,
And the broiling of the hell-fire.
Verily this is a certain truth;
Praise therefore the name of thy Lord, the Great.

Source: *El-Kor'an, or, The Koran.* 2nd ed. Translated by J. M. Rodwell. London: Bernard Quaritch, 1876,
    pp. 51–55. With slight changes.

17. Dante: The Punishment of Literary Lust

The well-known Christian hell received its most famous and creative envisioning in the work of the Italian poet Dante Alighieri (1265–1321). Dante became famous in his own day, and his description of an imagined journey through hell, purgatory, and heaven has influenced countless generations of writers.

Throughout Dante's Divine Comedy, *the author carefully attempts to match the punishment or reward closely to the individual vice or virtue. In the following extract, depicting the punishment of the lustful, Dante depicts the damned as being blown almost continuously by a strong wind. As a result, the condemned sinners have no control over where they go or when they depart but are instead at the complete mercy of the capricious wind. This punishment presents Dante's understanding of the sin of lust itself. Like the wind, lust is difficult, even perhaps impossible, to control, especially if the victim does not take precautions against it. Moreover, the wind blows where it will just as love is blind, in the modern metaphor. Because lust, as Dante envisions it, is the result of lack of control and firm resolve instead of deliberate evil, Dante places the lustful in the outermost ring of hell, furthest from Satan. Although lust is a sin serious enough to cause damnation, it is the least evil of those serious sins; thus, these sinners are the furthest from the devil. This medieval understanding of lust as relatively minor challenges many modern perceptions of Christianity that view lust as a central and particularly pernicious sin.*

In Dante's catalog of sinners, the predominance of women is striking. Out of the eight named (or clearly identified) sinners, the majority are female. Indeed, the first four people named are all women, and the main spirit with whom Dante speaks is a woman. By highlighting women in this realm of hell, Dante suggests that women are more given to lust than men—another medieval conception that challenges modern stereotypes in which more men than women are driven by sex.

Finally, note the role of literature in promoting lust. Francesca and her lover first fall in love and kiss (which kiss we are led to believe leads to still further physical expressions of love) while reading a book about Lancelot, the Arthurian knight who adulterously loved Guinevere. By reading about adultery, the young couple themselves fall into fornication. Literature repeats itself in real life. This argument about fiction and reality has entered the modern world in the debate about violence in TV, movies, and video games. This question, in fact, has plagued humanity since at least Plato's Republic, *written in the fourth century* B.C.

Now again the rueful wailings are heard.
Now am I come where many a plaining voice
Smites on mine ear. Into a place I came
Where light was silent all. Bellowing there groaned
A noise as of a sea in tempest torn
By warring winds. The stormy blast of hell
With restless fury drives the spirits on,
Whirled round and dashed amain with sore annoy.
When they arrive before the ruinous sweep,
There shrieks are heard, there lamentations, moans,
And blasphemies against the good Power in heaven.
I understood that to this torment sad
The carnal sinners are condemned, in whom
Reason by lust is swayed. As in large troops

And multitudinous, when winter reigns,
The starlings on their wings are borne abroad;
So bears the tyrannous gust those evil souls.
On this side and on that, above, below,
It drives them: hope of rest to solace them
Is none, nor even of milder pang. As cranes,
Chanting their dolorous notes, traverse the sky,
Stretched out in long array: so I beheld
Spirits, who came loud wailing, hurried on
By their dire doom. Then I: "Instructor! Who
Are these, by the black air so scourged?"—"The first
Among those, of whom thou questionest," he replied,
"Over many tongues was empress. She in vice
Of luxury was so shameless, that she made
Liking be lawful by promulg'd decree,
To clear the blame she had herself incurred.
This is Semiramis, of whom 'tis writ,
That she succeeded Ninus her espoused;
And held the land, which now the Sultan rules.
The next in amorous fury slew herself,
And to Sicheus' ashes broke her faith:
Then follows Cleopatra, lustful queen."
There marked I Helen, for whose sake so long
The time was fraught with evil; there the great
Achilles, who with love fought to the end.
Paris I saw, and Tristan; and beside
A thousand more he showed me, and by name
Pointed them out, whom love bereaved of life.
When I had heard my sage instructor name
Those dames and knights of antique days, overpowered
By pity, well-nigh in amaze my mind
Was lost; and I began: "Bard! willingly
I would address those two together coming,
Which seem so light before the wind." He thus:
"Note thou, when nearer they to us approach.
"Then by that love which carries them along,
Entreat; and they will come." Soon as the wind
Swayed them toward us, I thus framed my speech:
"O wearied spirits! come, and hold discourse
With us, if by none else restrained." As doves
By fond desire invited, on wide wings
And firm, to their sweet nest returning home,
Cleave the air, wafted by their will along;
Thus issued from that troop, where Dido ranks,
They through the ill air speeding; with such force
My cry prevailed by strong affection urged.
"O gracious creature and benign! who goest
Visiting, through this element obscure,
Us, who the world with bloody stain imbrued;
If for a friend the King of all we owned,
Our prayer to him should for thy peace arise,

Since thou hast pity on our evil plight.
If whatsoever to hear or to discourse
It pleases thee, that will we hear, of that
Freely with thee discourse, while ever the wind,
As now, is mute. The land, that gave me birth,
Is situate on the coast, where Po descends
To rest in ocean with his sequent streams.
"Love, that in gentle heart is quickly learnt,
Entangled him by that fair form, from me
Taken in such cruel sort, as grieves me still:
Love, that denial takes from none beloved,
Caught me with pleasing him so passing well,
That, as thou seest, he yet deserts me not.
Love brought us to one death: Caina waits
The soul, who spilt our life." Such were their words;
At hearing which downward I bent my looks,
And held them there so long, that the bard cried:
"What art thou pondering?" I in answer thus:
"Alas! By what sweet thoughts, what fond desire,
Must they at length to that ill pass have reached!"
Then turning, I to them my speech addressed.
And thus began: "Francesca! Your sad fate
Even to tears my grief and pity moves.
But tell me; in the time of your sweet sighs,
By what, and how love granted, that ye knew
Your yet uncertain wishes?" She replied:
"No greater grief than to remember days
Of joy, when misery is at hand! That kens
Thy learned instructor. Yet so eagerly
If thou art bent to know the primal root,
From whence our love gat being, I will do,
As one, who weeps and tells his tale. One day
For our delight we read of Lancelot,
How him love thralled. Alone we were, and no
Suspicion near us. Ofttimes by that reading
Our eyes were drawn together, and the hue
Fled from our altered cheek. But at one point
Alone we fell. When of that smile we read,
The wished smile, rapturously kissed
By one so deep in love, then he, who never
From me shall separate, at once my lips
All trembling kissed. The book and writer both
Were love's purveyors. In its leaves that day
We read no more." While thus one spirit spake,
The other wailed so sorely, that heartstruck
I through compassion fainting, seemed not far
From death, and like a corpse fell to the ground.

Source: Dante Alighieri. *L'inferno,* canto 5, lines 27–138. In *The Vision of Hell,* trans. Henry Francis Cary. London: Cassel, 1892, pp. 62–65. Spelling has been regularized at the expense of meter.

Woodcut of Dante Alighieri, 1521. The background and Dante's serious expression represent both the author's exile from Florence and the author's major work: *The Divine Comedy.* © 2008 Jupiterimages Corporation.

18. Bede: An Out-of-Body Experience

In the following fascinating account of an out-of-body experience, the Anglo-Saxon monk Bede (c. 672–735) chronicles the journey of one Drihthelm Cunningham to purgatory, heaven, and hell. Cunningham fell apparently dead in the night and was waked by well-wishers, who fled when Cunningham stirred to life in the morning! Only his wife remained. As a result of his unearthly experiences, Drihthelm entered the monastery of Melrose and spent much of his remaining life in strict ascetic practices.

In accordance with early medieval associations of the north with evil, Drihthelm follows an angelic guide northward to visit hell. Hell itself is located in an intense blackness from which globes of flame, containing the souls of the damned, rise and fall and into which the laughs of demons merge with the laments of the condemned souls being dragged into the abyss. By contrast, heaven is an enclosed garden paradise filled with an odor of unsurpassed beauty and delight.

Purgatory, the waiting chamber of heaven reserved for souls that will not enter paradise until the day of judgment, contains a two-fold division that patterns the difference between heaven and hell. Those souls who repented late in life, thus receiving God's mercy despite their lack of positive good works, are forced to flit back and forth between a flaming valley and a valley of intense cold. Their punishment is severe enough that Drihthelm suspects this is hell, although the angelic guide informs him that, in fact, these souls will enter heaven on judgment day. Those souls, however, who lived more virtuous lives, though not lives worthy of entering heaven immediately, await the day of judgment in an enclosed garden that is explicitly paralleled to heaven, although the perfume and delights are less than those experienced in heaven.

Drihthelm's dramatic actions suggest that he really did experience a life-changing event. Drihthelm left his wife and family, having secured their financial future, and entered a monastery, where he became well known for his frequent practice of praying while submerged in the frozen waters of wintertime. Drihthelm's ascetic regimen matches the torments he saw in the next life, especially the valley of cold. By willingly undergoing painful correction in this life in an attempt to control the appetites of the body, Drihthelm prepared himself for a reception in the heavenly garden upon his death.

OF ONE AMONG THE NORTHUMBRIANS, WHO ROSE FROM THE DEAD, AND RELATED THE THINGS WHICH HE HAD SEEN, SOME EXCITING TERROR AND OTHERS DELIGHT. [A.D. 696.]

At this time a memorable miracle, and like to those of former days, was wrought in Britain; for, to the end that the living might be saved from the death of the soul, a certain person, who had been some time dead, rose again to life, and related many remarkable things he had seen; some of which I have thought fit here briefly to take notice of. There was a master of a family in that district of the Northumbrians which is called Cunningham, who led a religious life, as did also all that belonged to him. This man fell sick, and his distemper daily increasing, being brought to extremity, he died in the beginning of the night; but in the morning early, he suddenly came to life again, and sat up, upon which all those that sat about the body weeping, fled away in a great fright, only his wife, who loved him best, though in a great consternation and trembling, remained with him. He, comforting her, said, "Fear not, for I am now truly risen from death, and permitted again to live among men; however, I am not to live hereafter as I was wont, but from henceforward after a very different manner." Then rising immediately, he repaired to the oratory of the little town, and continuing in prayer till day, immediately divided all his substance into three parts; one whereof he gave to his wife, another to his children, and the third, belonging to himself, he instantly distributed among the poor. Not long after, he repaired to the monastery of Melrose, which is almost enclosed by the winding of the river Tweed, and having been shaven, went into a private dwelling, which the abbot had provided, where he continued till the day of his death, in such extraordinary contrition of mind and body, that though his tongue had been silent, his life declared that he had seen many things either to be dreaded or coveted, which others knew nothing of.

Thus he related what he had seen. "He that led me had a shining countenance and a bright garment, and we went on silently, as I thought, towards the north-east. Walking on, we came to a vale of great breadth and depth, but of infinite length; on the left it appeared full of dreadful flames, the other side was no less horrid for violent hail and cold snow flying in all directions; both places were full of men's souls, which seemed by turns to be tossed from one side to the other, as it were by a violent storm; for when the wretches could no longer endure the excess of heat, they leaped into the middle of the cutting cold; and finding no rest there, they leaped back again into the middle of the unquenchable flames. Now whereas an innumerable multitude of deformed spirits were thus alternately tormented far and near, as far as could be seen, without any intermission, I began to think that this perhaps might be hell, of whose intolerable flames I had often heard talk. My guide, who went before me, answered to my thought, saying, 'Do not believe so, for this is not the hell you imagine.'

"When he had conducted me, much frightened with that horrid spectacle, by degrees, to the farther end, on a sudden I saw the place begin to grow dusk and filled with darkness. When I came into it, the darkness, by degrees, grew so thick, that I could see nothing besides it and the shape and garment of him that led me. As we went on through the shades of night, on a sudden there appeared before us frequent globes of black flames, rising as it were out of a great pit, and falling back again into the same. When I had been conducted thither, my leader suddenly vanished, and left me alone in the midst of darkness and this horrid vision, whilst those same globes of fire, without intermission, at one time flew up and at another fell back into the bottom of the abyss; and I observed that all the flames, as they ascended, were full of human souls, which, like sparks flying up with smoke, were sometimes thrown on high, and again, when the vapor of the fire ceased, dropped down into the depth below. Moreover, an insufferable stench came forth with the vapors, and filled all those dark places.

Having stood there a long time in much dread, not knowing what to do, which way to turn, or what end I might expect, on a sudden I heard behind me the noise of a most hideous and wretched lamentation, and at the same time a loud laughing, as of a rude multitude insulting captured enemies. When that noise, growing plainer, came up to me, I observed a gang of evil spirits dragging the howling and lamenting souls of men into the midst of the darkness, whilst they themselves laughed and rejoiced. Among those men, as I could discern, there was one shorn like a clergyman, a layman, and a woman. The evil spirits that dragged them went down into the midst of the burning pit; and as they went down deeper, I could no longer distinguish between the lamentation of the men and the laughing of the devils, yet I still had a confused sound in my ears. In the meantime, some of the dark spirits ascended from that flaming abyss, and running forward, beset me on all sides, and much perplexed me with their glaring eyes and the stinking fire which proceeded from their mouths and nostrils; and threatened to lay hold on me with burning tongs, which they had in their hands, yet they durst not touch me, though they frightened me. Being thus on all sides enclosed with enemies and darkness, and looking about on every side for assistance, there appeared behind me, on the way that I came, as it were, the brightness of a star shining amidst the darkness; which increased by degrees, and came rapidly towards me: when it drew near, all those evil spirits, that sought to carry me away with their tongs, dispersed and fled.

"He, whose approach put them to flight, was the same that led me before; who, then turning towards the right began to lead me, as it were, towards the south-east, and having soon brought me out of the darkness, conducted me into an atmosphere of clear light. While he thus led me in open light, I saw a vast wall before us, the length and height of which, in every direction, seemed to be altogether boundless. I began to wonder why we went to the wall, seeing no door, window, or path through it. When we came to the wall, we were presently, I know not by what means, on the top of it, and within it was a vast and delightful field, so full of fragrant flowers that the odor of its delightful sweetness immediately dispelled the stink of the dark furnace, which had pierced me through and through. So great was the light in this place, that it seemed to exceed the brightness of the day, or the sun in its meridian height. In this field were innumerable assemblies of men in white, and many companies seated together rejoicing. As he led me through the midst of those happy inhabitants, I began to think that this might, perhaps, be the kingdom of heaven, of which I had often heard so much. He answered to my thought, saying, 'This is not the kingdom of heaven, as you imagine.'

"When we had passed those mansions of blessed souls and gone farther on, I discovered before me a much more beautiful light, and therein heard sweet voices of persons singing, and so wonderful a fragrance proceeded from the place, that the other which I had before thought most delicious, then seemed to me but very indifferent; even as that extraordinary brightness of the flowery field, compared with this, appeared mean and inconsiderable. When I began to hope we should enter that delightful place, my guide on a sudden stood still; and then turning back, led me back by the way we came.

"When we returned to those joyful mansions of the souls in white, he said to me, 'Do you know what all these things are which you have seen?' I answered. I did not; and then he replied, 'That vale you saw so dreadful for consuming flames and cutting cold, is the place in which the souls of those are tried and punished, who, delaying to confess and amend their crimes, at length have recourse to repentance at the point of death, and so depart this life; but nevertheless because they, even at their death, confessed and repented, they shall all be received into the kingdom of heaven at the day of judgment; but many are relieved before the day of judgment, by the prayers, alms, and fasting, of the living, and more especially by masses. That fiery and stinking pit, which you saw, is the mouth of hell, into which whosoever falls shall never be delivered to all eternity. This flowery place, in which you see these most beautiful young people, so bright and merry, is that into which the souls of those are received who depart the body in good works, but who are not so perfect as to deserve to be immediately admitted into the kingdom of heaven; yet they shall all, at the day of judgment, see Christ, and partake of the joys of his kingdom; For whoever are perfect in thought, word and deed, as soon is they depart the body, immediately enter into the kingdom of heaven; in the neighborhood, whereof that place is, where you heard the sound of sweet singing, with the fragrant odor and bright light. As for you, who are now to return to your body, and live among men again, if you will endeavor nicely to examine your actions, and direct your speech and behavior in righteousness and simplicity, you shall, after death, have a place or residence among these joyful troops of blessed souls; for when I left you for a while, it was to know how you were to be disposed of.' When he had said this to me, I much abhorred returning to my body, being delighted with the sweetness and beauty of the place I beheld, and with the company of those I saw in it. However, I durst not ask him any questions; but in the meantime, on a sudden, I found myself alive among men."

Now these and other things which this man of God saw, he would not relate to slothful persons and such as lived negligently; but only to those who, being terrified with the dread of torments, or delighted with the hopes of heavenly joys, would make use of his words to advance in piety. In the neighborhood of his cell lived one Hemgils, a monk, eminent in the priesthood, which he honored by his good works: he is still living, and leading a solitary life in Ireland, supporting his declining age with coarse bread and cold water. He often went to that man, and asking several questions, heard of him all the particulars of what he had seen when separated from his body; by whose relation we also came to the knowledge of those few particulars which we have briefly set down. He also related his visions to King Alfrid, a man most learned in all respects, and was by him so willingly and attentively heard, that at his request he was admitted into the monastery above mentioned, and received the monastic tonsure; and the said king, when he happened to be in those parts, very often went to hear him. At that time the religious and humble abbot and priest, Ethelwald, presided over the monastery, and now with worthy conduct possesses the episcopal see of the church of Lindisfarne.

He had a more private place of residence assigned him in that monastery, where he might apply himself to the service of his Creator in continual prayer. And as that place lay on the bank of the river, he was wont often to go into the same to do penance in his body, and many times to dip quite under the water, and to continue saying psalms or prayers in the same as long as he could endure it, standing still sometimes up to the middle, and sometimes to the neck in water; and when he went out from thence ashore, he never took off his cold and frozen garments till they grew warm and dry on his body. And when in the winter the half-broken pieces of ice were swimming about him, which he had himself broken, to make room to stand or dip himself in the river, those who beheld it would say, "It is wonderful, brother Drihthelm (for so he was called), that you are able to endure such violent cold; he simply answered, for he was a man of much simplicity and indifferent wit, "I have seen greater cold." And when they said, "It is strange that you will endure such

A monastic scribe. Throughout the early Middle Ages, scribes working for the Church, especially in monasteries, preserved and spread learning and ideas by copying and recopying books by hand. The Art Archive/British Library.

austerity;" he replied, "I have seen more austerity." Thus he continued, through an indefatigable desire of heavenly bliss, to subdue his aged body with daily fasting, till the day of his being called away; and thus he forwarded the salvation of many by his words and example.

Source: Bede. *The Ecclesiastical History of the English Nation.* Translated by John Stevens and Lionel C. Jane. New York: Dutton, 1910, book 5, ch. 12, pp. 241–46.

19. Xibalba: The Mayan Underworld

The Quiché Maya, in the Guatemalan highlands, were one of the most prosperous peoples of the region before the coming of the Spanish explorers. Shortly after the Spanish conquest of the 1520s, the Quiché wrote down some of their important legends in the book known as the Popul Vuh (Popol Wuj in the modern Quiché language), which means "Council Book." The Popul Vuh records the Maya creation legend and the exploits of the Hero Twins, Huhnapuh and Xbalanque, who eventually defeat the Lords of Xibalba (pronounced like "she-ball-buh"), which is the Maya underworld—a land of death and destruction.

In the following extract from the Popul Vuh, Hun-Hunahpú and Vuvub-Hunahpu, predecessors of the future Hero Twins, are called to Xibalba by the Lords of the Underworld; the Lords apparently want the playing gear of the siblings and plan to sacrifice the brothers to acquire their gear. This legend probably reflects a Maya custom of sacrificing captured warriors who were ritually defeated in the local ball game, which resembled somewhat a soccer game played with a hard ball.

According to the extract, Xibalba contains five separate halls of punishment: the house of gloom, the house of cold, the house of jaguars, the house of bats, and the house of knives. These different punishments resemble medieval Norse tradition, which contains a house of serpents, although general underworld accounts, such as Dante's, also delineate different areas of torment and suffering.

This extract also provides an etiological story of the calabash tree, that is, an explanation of how the calabash tree came to have its distinctively round, head-sized fruit. According to this account, when the head of the slain Hun-Hunahpú was placed upon a tree, the tree spontaneously brought forth fruit, and the head of Hun-Hunahpú was itself transformed into this fruit.

Although Xibalba does not contain any houses of heaven-like reward, the Popul Vuh does hint at the possibility of a positive reward after death. Once the Hero Twins descend to Xibalba and defeat its Lords, they ascend to heaven, becoming the sun and the moon, thereby governing time and the seasons. The very fact that the Lords of Xibalba can be defeated offers hope.

THE MESSENGERS OF HUN-CAMÉ AND VUCUB-CAMÉ ARRIVED IMMEDIATELY

"Go, Ahpop Achih!" they were told. "Go and call Hun-Hunahpú and Vucub-Hunahpú. Say to them, 'Come with us. The lords say that you must come.' They must come here to play ball with us so that they shall make us happy, for really they amaze us. So, then, they must come," said the lords. "And have them bring their playing gear, their rings, their gloves, and have them bring their rubber balls, too," said the lords. "Tell them to come quickly," they told the messengers.

And these messengers were owls: Chabi-Tucur, Huracán-Tucur, Caquix-Tucur and Holom-Tucur. These were the names of the messengers of Xibalba. Chabi-Tucur was swift as an arrow; Huracán-Tucur had only one leg; Caquix-Tucur had a red back, and Holom-Tucur had only a head, no legs, but he had wings. The four messengers had the rank of Ahpop-Achih. Leaving Xibalba, they arrived quickly, bringing their message to the court where Hun-Hunahpú and Vucub-Hunahpú were playing ball, at the ball-court which was called *Nim-Xob-Carchah*. The owl messengers went directly to the ball-court and delivered their message exactly as it was given to them by Hun-Camé, Vucub-Camé, Ahalpuh, Ahalganá, Chamiabac, Chamiaholom, Xiquiripat, Cuchumaquic, Ahalmez, Ahaltocob, Xic, and Patán, as the lords were called who sent the message by the owls.

"Did the Lords Hun-Camé and Vucub-Camé really say that we must go with you?" "They certainly said so, and 'Let them bring all their playing gear,' the lords said." "Very well," said the youths. "Wait for us, we are only going to say good-bye to our mother." And having gone straight home, they said to their mother, for their father was dead: "We are going, our mother, but our going is only for a while. The messengers of the lord have come to take us. 'They must come,' they said, according to the messengers. "We shall leave our ball here in pledge," they added. They went immediately to hang it in the space under the rooftree. "We will return to play," they said. And going to Hunbatz and Hunchouén they said to them: "Keep on playing the flute and singing, painting, and carving; warm our house and warm the heart of your grandmother." When they took leave of their mother, Xmucané was moved and burst into tears. "Do not worry, we are going, but we have not died yet," said Hun-Hunahpú and Vucub-Hunahpú as they left. Hun-Hunahpú and Vucub-Hunahpú went immediately and the messengers took them on the road.

Thus they were descending the road to Xibalba, by some very steep stairs. They went down until they came to the bank of a river which flowed rapidly between the ravines called *Nuziván cul* and *Cuziván*, and crossed it. Then they crossed the river which flows among thorny calabash trees. There were very many calabash trees, but they passed through them without hurting themselves. Then they came to the bank of a river of blood and crossed it without drinking its waters; they only went to the river bank and so they were not overcome.

They went on until they came to where four roads joined, and there at the crossroads they were overcome. One of the four roads was red, another black, another white, and another yellow. And the black road said to them: "I am the one you must take because I am the way of the Lord." So said the road. And from here on they were already overcome. They were taken over the road to Xibalba and when they arrived at the council room of the Lords of Xibalba, they had already lost the match. Well, the first ones who were seated there were only figures of wood, arranged by the men of Xibalba. These they greeted first: "How are you, Hun-Camé?" they said to the wooden man. "How are you, Vucub-Camé?" they said to the other wooden man. But they did not answer. Instantly the Lords of Xibalba burst into laughter and all the other lords began to laugh loudly, because they already took for granted the downfall and defeat of Hun-Hunahpú and Vucub-Hunahpú. And they continued to laugh.

Then Hun-Camé and Vucub-Camé spoke: "Very well," they said. "You have come. Tomorrow you shall prepare the mask, your rings, and your gloves," they said. "Come and sit down on our bench," they said. But the bench which they offered them was of hot stone, and when they sat down they were burned. They began to squirm around on the bench, and if they had not stood up they would have burned their seats. The Lords of Xibalba burst out laughing again; they were dying of laughter; they writhed from pain in their stomach, in their blood, and in their bones, caused by their laughter, all the Lords of Xibalba laughed.

"Go now to that house," they said. "There you will get your sticks of fat pine and your cigar and there you shall sleep." Immediately they arrived at the House of Gloom. There was only darkness within the house. Meanwhile the Lords of Xibalba discussed what they should do. "Let us sacrifice them tomorrow, let them die quickly, quickly, so that we can have their playing gear to use in play," said the Lords of Xibalba to each other. Well, their fat-pine sticks were round and were called *zaquitoc*, which is the pine of Xibalba. Their fat-pine sticks were pointed and filed and were as bright as bone; the pine of Xibalba was very hard. Hun-Hunahpú and Vucub-Hunahpú entered the House of Gloom. There they were given their fat-pine sticks, a single lighted stick which Hun-Camé and Vucub-Camé sent them, together with a lighted cigar for each of them which the lords had sent. They went to give them to Hun-Hunahpú and Vucub-Hunahpú.

Blood sacrifice. Mayan bas-relief of Lady Xoc pulling a rope through her tongue, kneeling before Shield Jaguar, Yaxchilan. Woodcut. North Wind Picture Archives.

They found them crouching in the darkness when the porters arrived with the fat-pine sticks and the cigars. As they entered, the pine sticks lighted the place brightly. "Each of you light your pine sticks and your cigars; come and bring them back at dawn, you must not burn them up, but you must return them whole; this is what the lords told us to say." So they said. And so they were defeated. They burned up the pine sticks, and they also finished the cigars which had been given to them.

There were many punishments in Xibalba; the punishments were of many kinds. The first was the House of Gloom, Quequma-ha, in which there was only darkness. The second was Xuxulim-ha, the house where everybody shivered, in which it was very cold. A cold, unbearable wind blew within. The third was the House of Jaguars, Balami-ha, it was called, in which there were nothing but jaguars which stalked about, jumped around, roared, and made fun. The jaguars were shut up in the house. Zotzi-há, the House of Bats, the fourth place of punishment was called. Within this house there were nothing but bats which squeaked and cried and flew around and around. The bats were shut in and could not get out. The fifth was called Chayim-há, the House of Knives, in which there were only sharp, pointed knives, silent or grating against each other in the house.

There were many places of torture in Xibalba, but Hun-Hunahpú and Vucub-Hunahpú did not enter them. We only mention the names of these houses of punishment. When Hun-Hunahpú and Vucub-Hunahpú came before Hun-Camé and Vucub-Camé, they said: "Where are my cigars? Where are my sticks of fat pine which I gave you last night?" "They are all gone, Sir." "Well. Today shall be the end of your days. Now you shall die. You shall be destroyed, we will break you into pieces and here your faces will stay hidden. You shall be sacrificed," said Hun-Camé and Vucub-Camé. They sacrificed them immediately and buried them in the Pucbal-Chah, as it was called. Before burying them, they cut off the head of Hun-Hunahpú and buried the older brother together with the younger brother. "Take the head and put it in that tree which is Planted on the road," said Hun-Camé and Vucub-Camé. And having put the head in the tree, instantly the tree, which had never borne fruit before the head of Hun-Hunahpú was placed among its branches, was covered with fruit. And this calabash tree, it is said, is the one which we now call the head of Hun-Hunahpú. Hun-Camé and Vucub-Camé looked in amazement at the fruit on the tree. The round fruit was everywhere; but they did not recognize the head of Hun-Hunahpú; it was exactly like the other fruit of the calabash tree. So it seemed to all of the people of Xibalba when they came to look at it. According to their judgment, the tree was miraculous, because of what had instantly occurred when they put Hun-Hunahpú's head among its branches.

And the Lords of Xibalba said: "Let no one come to pick this fruit. Let no one come and sit under this tree!" they said, and so the Lords of Xibalba resolved to keep everybody away. The head of Hun-Hunahpú did not appear again because it had become one and the same as the fruit of the gourd tree. Nevertheless, a girl heard the wonderful story. Now we shall tell about her arrival.

Source: *The Book of the People: Popul Vuh.* Translated by Delia Goetz and Sylvanus Griswold Morley, from Adrián Recino's translation. Los Angeles: Plantin Press, 1954, ii, ch. 2, pp. 75–79.

GLOSSARY OF INDIVIDUALS AND TERMS

See the appendix for biographical information on the authors of documents included in this volume.

Achilles. According to Greek mythology, Achilles was the strongest of the Greek warriors who fought against Troy. Despite his heroism, Homer writes in the *Odyssey* that Achilles, once he entered the underworld, would rather be a slave among the living than a king among the dead.

Alfred the Great (849–899). Alfred the Great was king of Wessex, an Anglo-Saxon kingdom in southwestern England, A.D. 871–899. During his reign, he successfully preserved Anglo-Saxon political autonomy from the Danes (Viking invaders) and oversaw a cultural renaissance.

Anglo-Saxons. The Anglo-Saxons are people descended from the commingled Germanic tribes that took England from the native British Celts starting in the mid-fifth century A.D. The Angles and Saxons originally came from the northwestern coasts of Denmark, Belgium, and the Netherlands.

Anti-Semitism. Anti-Semitism is prejudice against members of the Jewish race and against the Jewish religion.

Aztecs. The Aztecs are a Native American tribe whose empire was centered on Tenochtitlan (modern-day Mexico City); they dominated Mesoamerica in the fifteenth and sixteenth centuries. The Aztecs are also known as the Mexica (pronounced "meh-SHEE-ka").

Black Death. The Black Death refers to the outbreak of bubonic plague that swept Europe between A.D. 1347 and 1351, killing roughly one-third of the population.

Boudicca (d. A.D. 60). Also known as Boadicea ("boe-uh-di-SAY-uh"), Boudicca was a queen of the Celtic Iceni tribe in eastern Britain. She led a revolt against Roman rule in A.D. 60 that met with initial success before being quashed by the provincial governor Suetonius Paulinus.

Byzantine Empire. Byzantine Empire was the name given to the eastern part of the Roman Empire, which lasted until the fall of its capital, Byzantium, to the Ottoman

Turks in 1453. Byzantium (also known as Constantinople; modern-day Istanbul) controlled, for much of its history, the Balkan states, Greece, and Turkey.

Charlemagne (742–814). Charlemagne ruled the Frankish kingdom (roughly corresponding to modern-day France) from A.D. 768 to 814. From A.D. 800 until his death, he also held the title of Emperor of the Romans. His rule witnessed a cultural and educational flowering in western Europe. Charlemagne literally translates to "Charles the Great."

Charles I of England (1600–1649). Charles I, king of England and Ireland (ruled 1625–1649), fought a Civil War against Parliament in defense of the king's right to rule the country without Parliament's approval. Defeated, he was tried by Parliament and was publicly executed by decapitation; the English monarchy was then abolished.

Charles II of England (1630–1685). The son of Charles I, who had been executed in 1649, Charles II, king of England and Ireland (ruled 1660–1685), was invited to return to the English throne from French exile in 1660, when the English Commonwealth government faltered after the death of Oliver Cromwell. Charles II was an able politician, although his reign, known as the "Restoration," has become infamous for debauchery.

Chaucer, Geoffrey (c. 1342–1400). The English writer Geoffrey Chaucer authored *The Canterbury Tales*, a collection of varied stories that were esteemed in his own day and still remain a central classic of English literature. *The Canterbury Tales* was Chaucer's last work; earlier works, which had already earned him fame, include *The Book of the Duchess*, *The House of Fame*, and *Troilus and Criseyde*.

Christine de Pisan (1364–c. 1430). The daughter of an Italian astrologer who was resident at the court of the French king Charles V, Christine de Pisan was one of the leading female intellectuals of her time. Her most famous work, *The Book of the City of Ladies*, defended the innate talents and capabilities of women. Her other works included an autobiography, *La Vision de Christine*, and a biography of Charles V.

Confucianism. Confucianism encourages the adherence to the philosophical and religious principles of the Chinese thinker, Confucius (551–479 B.C.), who urged continual education in the pursuit of self-knowledge and self-cultivation.

Copernicus, Nicolaus (1473–1543). A Polish astronomer, Mikolaj Kopernik, best known by his Latin name Nicolaus Copernicus, proposed and supported a heliocentric theory of the solar system—that is, the idea that the sun is the center of the solar system and that the earth and other planets revolve around the sun.

Cortés, Hernán (1485–1547). The Spanish explorer Hernán Cortés extended Spanish control of Mesoamerica by leading an expedition from Cuba that eventually seized Tenochtitlan (modern-day Mexico City) in 1521 and conquered the native Aztec empire.

Edward the Confessor (c. 1003–1066). Edward the Confessor, king from 1042 to 1066, was the last Anglo-Saxon ruler of England. Upon his death, William, Duke of

Normandy, laid claim to the throne and defeated the Anglo-Saxon claimant, Harold. Later generations viewed Edward as a pious, religious, miracle-working king.

Edward I of England (1239–1307). Edward I, king of England from 1272 to 1307, strengthened the English monarchy, conquered Wales, and attempted unsuccessfully to impose his rule on Scotland.

Elizabeth I (1533–1603). Elizabeth I, the daughter of Henry VIII and queen of England from 1558 to 1603, led England during a period of great intellectual and political ferment. During Elizabeth's reign, England defeated the Spanish Armada, turned to Protestantism, and witnessed the creation of great literary works by William Shakespeare and other writers and poets.

Falstaff, Sir John. Sir John Falstaff is a comical character in four of William Shakespeare's plays: *Henry IV, Part 1*; *Henry IV, Part 2*; *Henry V*; and *The Merry Wives of Windsor*. Falstaff appears to have been modeled on Sir John Oldcastle, a former royal favorite of Henry V who was executed in 1417 for participating in the Lollard rebellion.

Giotto (1267–1337). Giotto, an Italian painter who dominated the artistic scene in fourteenth-century Italy, experimented with forms of linear perspective and helped to craft the realistic style of the following century.

Griffin. The griffin is a mythical animal, popular since at least the first millennium B.C., that had the body of a lion and the head of an eagle.

Henry V of England (1387–1422). Henry V, king of England from 1413 to 1422, triumphed over France during the early fifteenth-century phase of the Hundred Years' War, thereby making England one of the great military powers of western Europe. Henry won a great victory at Agincourt in 1415 and succeeded in having himself recognized as heir to the French throne, although he died before actually succeeding to the French crown.

Henry VIII (1491–1547). Henry VIII, king of England from 1509 to 1547, overthrew papal authority in England through the 1534 Act of Supremacy, which declared the king, and not the pope, head of the Church in England. Henry VIII famously married six times; two of the wives—Anne Boleyn and Katherine Howard—were executed by decapitation. By Anne Boleyn, Henry was the father of Elizabeth I.

Homer. Homer is the presumed author of the Greek epics *The Iliad* and *The Odyssey*. No historically reliable information about Homer remains, although—if he existed—he probably lived around 800 B.C.

Innocent III (c. 1161–1216). Pope Innocent III (reigned A.D. 1198–1216) consistently defended papal power against secular authorities and convoked the reforming fourth Lateran Council in 1215. In a dispute with King John, he placed all England under a papal ban.

James I of Great Britain (1566–1625). Known as James I in England, where he ruled from 1603 to 1625, and James VI in Scotland, where he was king from 1567, James sought to consolidate power in the hands of the monarch, instead of in Parliament.

James II of Great Britain (1633–1701). James II was king of England and, as James VII, king of Scotland, from 1685 to 1688. An ardent Roman Catholic, James angered Parliament and the Protestant majority among the people by attempting to increase the political power of the Roman Catholic Church. He was deposed by parliamentary forces in the so-called Glorious Revolution, which resulted in 1689 in the issuance of an invitation to his Protestant daughter and son-in-law to assume the English throne jointly as William III and Mary II.

John of England (1167–1216). John, king of England from 1199 to 1216, lost English control of Normandy and other English possessions in France to the king of France and was forced by rebellious barons in England to sign the Magna Carta (1215), which theoretically limited the powers of the monarch.

Justinian I (483–565). Justinian I, Byzantine emperor from 527 to 565, solidified the remnants of the Roman Empire in the wake of the Germanic migrations of the fifth century and produced the *Codex Justinianus*, a codification of Roman law that remained influential through the early modern era.

Kaaba. The Kaaba is a shrine in the Great Mosque in Mecca. Many Muslims consider the Kaaba to be the holiest spot on earth, a shrine originally erected by Adam and subsequently re-erected by Abraham. Pilgrims on the *hajj* walk around the Kaaba, and all Muslims say their prayers while facing in the direction of the Kaaba.

Kempe, Margery (c. 1373–c. 1440). Margery Kempe lived as a lay mystic and left behind one of the earliest autobiographies in the English language. Her sometimes outrageously self-centered preaching occasionally made her an object of ridicule.

Koran. The Koran, also spelled Qu'ran, is the main sacred text of Islam. Muslims believe that the angel Gabriel started to reveal the Koran to the prophet Muhammad in A.D. 610.

Liang Dynasty. A dynasty that ruled in southern China from A.D. 502 to 557. Some scholars see the rule of the dynasty as a "golden age" and its fall as a serious setback for Chinese political development, but this view is controversial.

Louis the Pious (778–840). Louis I "the Pious" was emperor of the Romans from 814 to 840; he inherited the throne upon the death of his father, Charlemagne, and attempted to weld the Frankish empire into a more cohesive unity.

Malthus, Thomas (1766–1834). Thomas Malthus, an English economist, predicted that the human population would always tend to outrun the food supply. This theory, known as Malthusianism, has not proved to be the case in the modern Western world.

Manco Capac. Manco Capac is the legendary first emperor of the Incas of Peru. Legend places his arrival at Cuzco (the future Inca capital) around A.D. 1200.

Maya. The Maya are an indigenous people of Mesoamerica. Maya territory stretches from southern Mexico, through Guatemala, to northern Belize. During the Classic period (A.D. 250–900), the Maya developed a complex cultural and political system. After the year 900, many Maya cities were abandoned, and the Maya returned, with notable exceptions, to a less organized and more agrarian society.

Mennonites. Mennonites are members of a Christian denomination that takes a literalist view of the Bible and forbids all warfare. Menno Simons, a Dutch priest, laid the foundation for the denomination with his preaching during the sixteenth century.

Moctezuma (1466–1520). Moctezuma, also known as Montezuma II, ruled the Aztec empire from 1502 to 1520 and was thus emperor when the Spanish conquistador Hernán Cortés came to Mexico in 1519. He was seized by Cortés and held hostage; when a revolt erupted in Tenochtitlan, he was injured while addressing the rebels and died of his wounds shortly thereafter.

Mughal Dynasty. The Muslim Mughal dynasty, also spelled Mogol, ruled northern India from the sixteenth to the eighteenth century.

Muhammad (570–632). Muhammad founded and spread the Islamic religion throughout Arabia. According to Muslim tradition, he started to receive visions from the angel Gabriel in A.D. 610.

Peasants' Revolt of 1381. The Peasants' Revolt refers to a popular uprising in southern England in June 1381. The immediate cause was an unpopular poll tax, but economic discontent had been troubling England ever since the Black Death of 1347–1350, which had prompted the passage by Parliament of legislation that attempted to restrain the rapid rise in laborers' wages resulting from a plague-caused decrease in the supply of skilled laborers.

Philip IV (1268–1314). Philip IV, king of France from 1285 to 1314, increased the power of the French monarchy at the expense of the papacy and at the expense of the nobility. During his reign, a series of French-dominated popes moved the Curia from Rome to Avignon. He also ruthlessly suppressed the Order of Knights Templar in France.

Puritans. The Puritans were sixteenth- and seventeenth-century English followers of the thought of sixteenth-century French Protestant reformer John Calvin. The Puritans sought, under Elizabeth I (r. 1558–1603), James I (r. 1603–1625), and Charles I (r. 1625–1649), to purge the English Church of its remaining Catholic elements and to adhere more closely to Calvinist doctrine and practice. Their ideology was embraced especially by the wealthier middle classes, and they came to dominate Parliament by the mid-seventeenth century. In the 1640s, the Puritan-controlled Parliament fought and won the English Civil War, which resulted in the execution of Charles I.

Quakers. Quakers are members of the Society of Friends, which was founded by the Englishman George Fox in the seventeenth century. Quakers seek to be guided by the Christian Holy Spirit and eschew traditional Christian ritual; they are generally pacifist and were occasionally persecuted for their refusal to conform to the dominant forms of Christianity.

Ramadan. Ramadan is the ninth month of the Muslim calendar and is the month of fasting. During Ramadan, Muslims fast from food and drink throughout the daylight hours.

Renaissance. The term Renaissance refers to the self-conscious attempt, made by Europeans from roughly the fourteenth century to the seventeenth, to reconnect with the learning of ancient Greece and Rome. The word literally means "rebirth" and refers to the rebirth of ancient Roman and Greek ideas. The Renaissance featured a cultural and intellectual flourishing in the arts and in scholarship.

Shinto. Shinto is the indigenous religion of Japan. Shinto has no fixed authorities, sacred texts, or religious teachings, but most Shinto worship involves physical shrines and a focus on mystical truths revealed by a *kami*, a spiritual entity beyond human understanding.

Tang Dynasty. The Tang dynasty ruled China from 618 to 907; the period of Tang rule witnessed a cultural flowering during which some of China's most valued poetry and art was produced.

Trent, Council of. A council of the Roman Catholic Church that met intermittently at Trent between 1545 and 1563, the Council of Trent clarified the official teaching of many Catholic doctrines, such as divine justification and the real presence in the Eucharist, and promoted self-reform within the Church. The council was called in large part as a response to the Protestant Reformation.

William the Conqueror (c. 1028–1087). William I "the Conqueror" was duke of Normandy from 1035 and king of England from 1066 to 1087. He won the Crown by defeating Harold, the last Anglo-Saxon king of England, at the Battle of Hastings in 1066. William united western France and England under one throne and is responsible, in large part, for the many French loanwords (such as *city*) that exist in the English language.

APPENDIX: BIOGRAPHIES OF DOCUMENT AUTHORS

Listed are the authors cited in the document introductions, with brief biographical information provided for each.

Ælfric (c. 995–1025): Ælfric of Eynsham helped to lead a cultural revival with his writings in Old English. His most important works are the *Catholic Homilies* and *The Lives of the Saints:* both works made important religious material, usually written in Latin, available to less learned clergy. His currently most famous work, however, is the *Colloquy,* a kind of phrase book for young Anglo-Saxons trying to learn Latin.

Al-Baladhuri (d. c. 892): Al-Baladhuri wrote an influential history of the early Muslim kingdoms. His work, *Futuh al-buldan,* became a standard reference for later historians.

Alberti, Leon Battista (1404–1472): Leon Battista Alberti offers a good example of the Renaissance polymath (an individual skilled in many different areas). Alberti dedicated his time to philosophy, art, and architecture. His *Della famiglia* (On Family) laid down a practical moral philosophy, and *Della pittura* (On Painting) outlined the contemporary principles of good painting and explained for the first time the science of linear perspective. His *De re aedificatoria* (On Building) made contributions to both the engineering and the aesthetics of architecture.

Ascham, Roger (c. 1515–1568): Roger Ascham was a leading scholar of Greek. A fellow of St. John's College, Cambridge, he tutored Princess, and later Queen, Elizabeth in Greek and assisted with other governmental matters. His most well-known book, *The Scholemaster,* discusses the best ways, in the author's opinion, to bestow a classical education.

Bede (c. 673–735): The Venerable Bede became the leading intellectual of western Europe during his lifetime. His commentaries on the Bible and his works on the Church calendar reached a large audience in his own day, but his *Historia ecclesiastica gentis Anglorum* (The Ecclesiastical History of the English Nation) offers the most interest for a modern audience. The *Historia ecclesiastica* traces the history of England and the role of God's providence in that history.

St. Benedict of Nursia (c. 480–c. 547): Benedict of Nursia founded the monastery of Monte Cassino and created a series of principles (called the "Benedictine Rule") to guide monastic life. As a result, Benedict is sometimes considered the father of Western monasticism.

Boetius, Hector (c. 1465–c. 1536): Hector Boece, or Boetius/Boethius in Latin, helped to found the University of Aberdeen and wrote an influential, though inaccurate, history of Scotland: *Scotorum historiae a prima gentis origine* (The Histories of the Scots from the First Beginnings of the People).

Boniface VIII (c. 1235–1303): Pope Boniface VIII (reigned 1294–1303) defended papal authority against the encroachments of King Philip IV of France. Boniface also helped to further codify canon (Church) law.

Bradshaw, William (1571–1618): William Bradshaw was a prolific Puritan author who objected strenuously to the Anglican Book of Common Prayer and to other high-church forms of worship.

Brahmagupta (598–c. 665): Brahmagupta, a Hindu Indian scientist, wrote an influential treatise on astronomy and mathematics—including arithmetic and algebra. The Arabic translation of his *Brahma-sphuta-siddhanta*, as his most famous work is generally called, transmitted Brahmagupta's findings across the Muslim world and into parts of Europe.

Brathwaite, Richard (1588–1673): Richard Brathwaite pursued a career as a London lawyer but found more success as a poet of light comedic verse before retiring to a country estate and writing *The English Gentleman* (1630) and *The English Gentlewoman* (1630), guides to proper conduct for the socially aspirant.

Calvin, John (1509–1564): John Calvin led the Protestant Reformation in France and influenced the development of Protestantism in many other countries. His *Institutes of the Christian Religion* (1536, 1559) remains a classic statement of low-church Protantism. Although many found Calvin's teaching persuasive, he resorted to physical force in establishing Protestantism in Geneva, Switzerland, his base for many of his later years.

Cavendish, Margaret (1623–1673): Margaret Cavendish, Duchess of Newcastle, followed Queen Elizabeth's example by earnestly pursuing intellectual endeavors, including poetry, philosophy, and autobiography. Her best-known work today, *A Description of a New World, Called The Blazing World* (1666), is an imaginative work bordering on science fiction. Her royalist sympathies and marriage to the exiled royalist officer William Cavendish (Duke of Newcastle) meant that she lived much of her life on the Continent.

Chen Tzu-ang (661–702): Chen Tzu-ang helped forge a new style of poetry in the early Tang dynasty.

Cranmer, Thomas (1489–1556): Thomas Cranmer promoted Protestantism under the reign of King Henry VIII of England and served as the Archbishop of Canterbury.

During the reign of the Catholic Queen Mary, Cranmer was found guilty of heresy and was executed by burning.

Dante Alighieri (1265–1321): Dante Alighieri wrote the most influential book in medieval Italian literature: *La Divina Commedia* (*The Divine Comedy*), in which the narrator journeys through hell, purgatory, and heaven. Dante was avidly involved also in philosophy and politics and was forced to live in exile from his native Florence from 1301 onward because of his imperial political opinions.

Díaz del Castillo, Bernal (1495–1584): Bernal Díaz del Castillo accompanied Hernán Cortés in the conquest of the Aztec empire. He wrote an eye-witness account of the expedition, titled *Historia verdadera de la conquista de la Nueva España* (The True History of the Conquest of Mexico).

Elyot, Thomas (c. 1490–1546): Sir Thomas Elyot served as a clerk of the Privy Council but achieved fame for his *Boke Named the Governour*, which set forth an influential educational plan for children of the aristocracy.

Firdawsi (c. 935–c. 1020): Firdawsi, also known as Abu Ol-qasem Mansur, wrote the Persian national epic: *Shah-nameh* (The Book of Kings).

Foxe, John (1516–1587): John Foxe, an English Puritan preacher, wrote *The Book of Martyrs*, which chronicled the sufferings endured by English Protestants under Catholic rule. Despite being fiercely anti-Catholic and producing a one-sided historical account of the English Reformation, Foxe objected to the execution of Anabaptists and Roman Catholics during Protestant rule.

Galileo Galilei (1564–1642): Galileo Galilei was an active mathematician and astronomer, whose most controversial theory—heliocentrism (the idea that the earth moves around the sun)—eventually resulted in his house-imprisonment from 1633 to the end of his life.

Garcilaso de la Vega (1539–1616): Garcilaso de la Vega, called El Inca, wrote an influential history of the Inca empire and the Spanish conquest. Garcilaso had unique insights into both cultures, in part because his father was a conquistador, and his mother was an Inca princess.

Gregory of Tours (c. 589–c. 594): The bishop St. Gregory of Tours wrote *Ten Books of Histories*, a major source of information about the early Merovingian kingdoms in France, as well as books about saints' lives and other religious works.

Han Wen-Kung (768–824): Han Wen-Kung, also known as Han Yu, was a leading Chinese poet, prose author, and proponent of Neo-Confucianism. Han Yu criticized in particular Taoism and Buddhism, which he viewed as imported foreign religions.

Harvey, William (1578–1657): William Harvey, a prominent physician and scientist, discovered how blood circulated in the human body. He published his findings in 1628.

Hildersam, Arthur (1563–1632): Arthur Hildersam was an avid Puritan preacher and a prolific author of religious tracts.

Jacques de Vitry (c. 1160–1240): Jacques de Vitry, Bishop of Acre, actively promoted crusades in the Middle East and in Europe. His *Historia Hierosomylitana* offers a first-hand account of thirteenth-century Palestine.

Julian of Norwich (1342–c. 1416): Julian of Norwich lived as an anchorite after being healed from a serious illness. As an anchorite, she lived in one room, which she never left, although many people visited her. Her *Revelations of Divine Love* records her mystical visions and her reflections upon those visions.

Li Po (701–762): Li Po, also called Li Bai, remains one of China's most esteemed poets. Although Li Po attempted to secure a court position, he spent most of his life wandering from patron to patron. Some of his most famous poems celebrate drinking, and legend reports that he died while admiring the moon, drunk, in a boat.

Li Shi-chen (1518–1593): Li Shi-chen, also known as Li Shizhen, codified the system of Chinese traditional medicine in his treatise *Bencao Gangmu*, which is sometimes also called by the Latin *Materia medica*.

Louis de Gaya (fl. seventeenth century): Louis de Gaya was a popular seventeenth-century author who wrote popular books concerning war and marriage customs.

Love, Nicholas (d. 1424): Nicholas Love was prior of the Carthusian abbey of Mount Grace in Yorkshire, England, during the early fifteenth century. His *Mirror of the Blessed Life of Jesus Christ* guided lay readers through a serious meditation on the life and passion of Christ.

Murasaki Shikibu (c. 978–c. 1014): Murasaki Shikibu, a female author in the Japanese court, wrote *The Tale of Genji* (*Genji monogatari*), a novel about court life. The *Genji monogatari* remains renowned as a classic of Japanese literature.

Petrarch (1304–1374): Petrarch, or Francesco Petrarca as he is known in Italian, helped to create the Renaissance by advocating a return to the classical ideals and styles of Cicero and the ancient Romans. In addition to scholarship, Petrarch also wrote a cycle of influential sonnets.

Po Chu-i (772–846): Po Chu-i, also known as Bai Juyi, used poetry to campaign actively against corruption and war in Tang dynasty China. He remains one of China's most important poets.

Polo, Marco (1254–1324): Marco Polo, a Venetian merchant and adventurer, traveled to Asia and stayed in China for 17 years. On his return, he published *Il Millione*, a famous description of the cultures he visited.

P'u Sung-ling (1640–1715): P'u Sung-ling, also known as Pu Songling, worked as a provincial schoolteacher, but his collection of ghost stories, *Strange Stories from a Chinese Studio*, became extremely popular when they were published, 51 years after his death.

Raymond d'Aguiliers (fl. eleventh century): Raymond d'Aguiliers published an eyewitness account of the eleventh-century First Crusade, which he accompanied as a chaplain.

Roe, Sir Thomas (c. 1581–1644): Sir Thomas Roe served as ambassador to the Mughal dynasty and to the Ottoman Empire. Sir Thomas's memoirs offer a solid description of the Muslim countries in which he traveled.

Shakespeare, William (1564–1616): William Shakespeare, the son of a relatively well-to-do Stratford family, became England's most famous poet and playwright. His important works include *King Lear*, *Romeo and Juliet*, *Hamlet*, and *Macbeth*, among many others.

Stanihurst, Richard (1547–1618): Richard Stanihurst, born in Ireland and educated at Oxford, wrote several learned treatises, including an influential history of Ireland.

Tsung Ch'en (1525–1560): Tsung Ch'en imitated the poetic styles prevalent during the high Tang dynasty.

Urban II (1088–1099): Pope Urban II (reigned 1035–1099) strengthened the political power of the papacy, continued the ecclesiastical reforms started by his predecessor, and launched the First Crusade in an effort to regain the Holy Lands.

Usamah ibn Munqidh (1095–1188): Usamah ibn Munqidh fought in the army of Saladin against the crusaders, though he later came to befriend several crusaders during the Europeans' presence in Palestine. His memoir records these cross-cultural interchanges, both violent and peaceful.

Walter of Henley (fl. thirteenth century): The thirteenth-century author Walter of Henley wrote a treatise on agricultural husbandry that remained the main reference work in England throughout the Middle Ages.

Yoshida Kenko (c. 1283–c. 1352): Yoshida Kenko was a Buddhist priest whose collection of essays (*Tsurezuregusa*, meaning "essays in idleness") discussing short-lived beauty and other aesthetic and philosophical ideas have become a classic of Japanese literature.

BIBLIOGRAPHY

SOURCE VOLUMES

A. T. *A Rich Storehouse or Treasury for the Diseased*. London: Thomas Purfoot and Ralph Blower, 1596.

Abbott, George. *The Coppie of a Letter Sent from my Lords Grace of Canterburie Shewing the Reasons Which Induced the Kings Majestie to Prescribe Directions for Preachers*. 1622.

al-Baladhuri, Abbas Ahmad ibn-Jabir. *The Origins of the Islamic State*. Translated by Philip Hitti. New York: Columbia University Press, 1916.

Alberti, Leon Battista. *On Painting*. Translated by John R. Spencer. New Haven, CT: Yale University Press, 1956.

Alexis, Guillaume. *Here Begynneth an Interlocucyon, with an Argument, betwixt Man and Woman and Which of Them Could Prove to Be Most Excellent*. London: Wynkyn de Worde, 1525.

Algebra, with Arithmetic and Mensuration, from the Sanscrit of Brahmegupta and Bhascara. Translated by Henry Thomas Colebrooke. London: John Murray, 1817.

Anonymous. *An Apology and Advice for Some of the Clergy, Who Suffer under False and Scandalous Reports Written on the Occasion of the Second Part of the Rehearsal Transpros'd, in a Letter to a Friend, and by Him Publish'd*. London: A.E., 1674.

Ascham, Roger. *The Scholemaster or Plaine and Perfite Way of Teaching Children to Understand, Write, and Speake the Latin Tong but Specially Purposed for the Private Bringing Up of Youth in Ientlemen and Noble Mens Houses, and Commodious Also for All Such as Have Forgot the Latin Tonge*. Aldersgate: John Day, 1573.

Attenborough, F. L., ed. and trans. *The Laws of the Earliest English Kings*. Cambridge: Cambridge University Press, 1922.

Bede. *The Ecclesiastical History of the English Nation*. Translated by L. C. Jane. New York: Dutton, 1910.

Boetius, Hector. *The Description of Scotland*. In *Chronicles of England, Scotland, and Ireland*, trans. Raphaell Holinshed. Vol. 5. London: Johnson, 1808 (originally published 1580).

Bongars. *Gesta Dei per Francos*. In *A Source Book for Medieval History*, ed. and trans. Oliver J. Thatcher and Edgar Holmes McNeal. New York: Scribners, 1905.

The Book of the People: Popul Vuh. Translated by Delia Goetz and Sylvanus Griswold Morley, from Adrián Recino's translation. Los Angeles: Plantin Press, 1954.

Bradshaw, William Bradshaw, and Arthur Hildersam. *A Direction for the Weaker Sort of Christians Shewing in What Manner They Ought to Fit and Prepare Themselues to the Worthy Receiuing of the Sacrament of the Body and Blood of Christ: With a Short Forme of Triall or Examination Annexed.* London: Hall, 1609.

Brathwaite, Richard. *The English Gentlewoman, Drawn Out to the Full Body: Expressing What Habilliments Doe Best Attire Her, What Ornaments Doe Best Adorne Her, What Complements Doe Best Accomplish Her.* London: B. Alsop and T. Fawcet, 1631.

Calvin, John. *Institutes of Christian Religion.* Translated by Henry Beveridge. Grand Rapids, MI: Eerdmans, 1989.

Cave, Roy, and Herbert Coulson. *A Source Book for Medieval Economic History.* New York: Biblo and Tannen, 1965.

Cavedish, Margaret, Duchess of Newcastle. *A True Relation of the Birth, Breeding, and Life of Margaret Cavendish, Duchess of Newcastle.* Edited by Sir Egerton Brydges. Kent: Johnson and Warwick, 1814.

Chamberlain, Basil Hall, trans. *Translation of "Ko-ji-ki": or "Records of Ancient Matters."* Kobe: Asiatic Society of Japan, 1919.

Chinese Materia Medica: Turtle and Shellfish Drugs. Translated by Bernard E. Read. Beijing: Peking Natural History Bulletin, 1937.

The Civil Law. Translated by S. P. Scott. Cincinnati: Central Trust Company, 1932.

The Council of Trent: The Twenty-Fifth Session; The Canons and Decrees of the Sacred and Oecumenical Council of Trent. Edited and translated by J. Waterworth. London: Dolman, 1848.

Cranmer, Thomas. *Certayne Sermons, or Homelies Appoynted by the Kynges Maiestie, to be Declared and Redde, by All Persones, Vicars, or Curates, Euery Sondaye in Their Churches, Where They Have Cure.* 1547.

Cunningham, W. *The Growth of English Industry and Commerce during the Early and Middle Ages.* Cambridge: Cambridge University Press, 1890.

Dante Alighieri. *The Convivio of Dante Alighieri.* Translated by Philip Wicksteed. London: Dent, [1903] 1924.

———. *L'inferno.* In *The Vision of Hell,* trans. Henry Francis Clay. London: Cassel, 1892.

Díaz del Castillo, Bernal. *The True History of the Conquest of Mexico.* London: Harrap, 1927.

El Inca Garcilaso de la Vega. *First Part of the Royal Commentaries of the Yncas.* Vol. 1. Translated by Clements R. Markham. London: Hakluyt Society, 1869.

El-Koran, or, The Koran. 2nd ed. Translated by J. M. Rodwell. London: Bernard Quaritch, 1876.

Elyot, Sir Thomas. *The Boke Named the Governour.* London: Thomas Berthelet, 1537.

Firdawsi. *Sháh Námeh.* In *Persian Literature, Comprising the Sháh Námeh, the Rubáiyát, the Divan and the Gulistan,* trans. James Atkinson. Rev. ed., vol. 1. World's Great Classics series. New York: Colonial, 1900.

The Fooles Complaint to Gotham College. London: Ridibundus, 1643.

Foxe, John. *Actes and Monuments of Matters Most Speciall and Memorable.* London: John Daye, 1583.

Furnivall, F. J., ed. *The Digby Plays.* London: Early English Text Society, 1896.

Galbert de Bruges. *De multro, traditione, et occisione gloriosi Karoli comitis Flandirarum.* In *University of Pennsylvania Translations and Reprints,* trans. Edward P. Cheyney, vol. 4, no. 3, p. 18. In Frederic Austin Ogg, *A Source Book of Mediaeval History.* New York: American, 1908.

Galilei, Galileo. *Dialogue on the Great World Systems in the Salusbury Translation.* Revised, annotated, and introduced by Giorgio de Santillana. Chicago: University of Chicago Press, 1953.

Gengler, H. G. *Germanische Rechtsdenkmäler.* Erlangen: F. Enke, 1875.

Giles, Herbert A. *Gems of Chinese Literature: Prose.* 2nd ed. London: Bernard Quaritch, 1923.

————. *A History of Chinese Literature*. New York: Appleton, 1901.

Harvey, William. *On the Motion of the Heart and Blood in Animals*. In *Great Books of the Western World*, trans. by Robert Willis. Vol. 26. Chicago: Encyclopaedia Britannica, 1990.

Henderson, Ernest F., ed. and trans. *Select Historical Documents of the Middle Ages*. London: n.p., 1896.

————, ed. and trans. *Select Historical Documents of the Middle Ages*. London: Bell, 1921.

Holinshed, Raphael. *Chronicles of England, Scotland, and Ireland*. London: Johnson, 1808.

Jacobs, Joseph. *Jewish Contributions to Civilization*. Philadelphia: Jewish Publication Society, 1919.

Krey, August. C. *The First Crusade: The Accounts of Eyewitnesses and Participants*. Princeton, NJ: Princeton University Press, 1921.

Leach, A. F., ed. *Beverley Town Documents*. London: Selden Society, 1900.

Louis de Gaya. *Matrimonial Customs, or, The Various Ceremonies and Divers Ways of Celebrating Weddings Practiced amongst All the Nations in the Whole World Done Out of French*. London: A.S., 1687.

Murasaki Shikibu. *Genji Monogatari*. In *Japanese Literature*, trans. Suyematz Kenchio. Rev. ed. World's Great Classics series. New York: Colonial, 1900.

Ogg, Frederic Austin. *A Source Book of Mediaeval History*. New York: American, 1908.

Petrarch. *Petrarch: The First Modern Scholar and Man of Letters*. Edited and translated by James Harvey Robinson. New York: G.P. Putnam, 1898.

Pietro della Valle. *The Travels of Sig. Pietro Della Valle, a Noble Roman, into East India and Arabia Deserta in Which, the Several Countries, Together with the Customs, Manners, Traffique, and Rites Both Religious and Civil, of Those Oriental Princes and Nations, Are Faithfully Described: In Familiar Letters to His Friend Signior Mario Schipano: Whereunto Is Added a Relation of Sir Thomas Roe's Voyage into the East-Indies*. Translated by George Havers. London: J. Macock, 1665.

Polo, Marco, and Rustichello of Pisa. *The Book of Ser Marco Polo the Venetian Concerning the Kingdoms and Marvels of the East*. Vol. 1. Edited by Henry Yule. London: John Murray, 1903.

————. *The Travels of Marco Polo: The Complete Yule-Cordier Edition*. Edited by Henry Yule and Henri Cordier. New York: Dover Publications, 1993.

Procopius. *Procopii Caesariensis Historiarum Temporis Sui Tetras Altera, De Bello Gótico*. Translated by Claudius Maltretus. Venice: n.p., 1729.

Revon, Michel. *Anthologie de la literature japonaise des origins au xxe siècle*. Paris: Delagrave, 1919.

Roe, Thomas. *A Voyage to East India*. In Pietro della Valle, *The Travels of Sig. Pietro Della Valle, a Noble Roman, into East-India and Arabia Deserta in Which, the Several Countries, Together with the Customs, Manners, Traffique, and Rites Both Religious and Civil, of Those Oriental Princes and Nations, Are Faithfully Described*. London: J. Macock, 1665.

Shakespeare, William. *The Merchant of Venice*. Edited by Robert Sharp. Richmond, VA: Johnson, 1903.

Sir Gawain and the Green Knight. 2nd ed. Edited by J.R.R. Tolkien and E. V. Gordon. Oxford: Clarendon Press, 1967.

Stanihurst, Richard. *A Treatise Conteining a Plaine and Perfect Description of Ireland, in Raphael Holinshed, Chronicles of England, Scotland, and Ireland*. Vol. 6. London: Johnson, 1808.

Stubbs, William, ed. *Select Charters and Other Illustrations of English Constitutional History from the Earliest Times to the Reign of Edward the First*. 9th ed. Revised by H.W.C. Davis. Oxford: Clarendon Press, 1913.

Symonds, John Addington. *Wine, Women, and Song: Mediaeval Latin Student's Songs*. London: n.p., 1884.

Thatcher, Oliver J., and Edgar Holmes McNeal, eds. *A Source Book for Medieval History*. New York: Scribner's, 1905.

Thorpe, Benjamin. *Ancient Laws and Institutes of England*. London: Eyre, 1840.

Tuberville, George. *Noble Arte of Venerie or Hunting* (1576). In *Tuberville's Book of Hunting*. Oxford: Clarendon Press, 1908.

Usamah ibn-Munqidh. *An Arab-Syrian Gentleman and Warrior in the Period of the Crusades: Memoirs of Usamah ibn-Munqidh*. Translated by Philip Hitti. New York: Columbia University Press, 1929.

W. C. *A Schoole of Nurture for Children, or The Duty of Children in Honouring Their Parents, Unfolded, Proved, and Applied*. London: Simon Miller, 1656.

Waley, Arthur, trans. *A Hundred and Seventy Chinese Poems*. London: Constable, 1918.

———, trans. *More Translations from the Chinese*. London: George Allen, 1919.

———, trans. *Tale of Genji*. Boston: Houghton, 1926.

Walter of Henley. *Husbandry*. Translated by Elizabeth Lamond. London: Longmans, 1890.

White, Albert Beebe, and Wallace Notestein, eds. *Source Problems in English History*. New York: Harper, 1915.

Wright, Thomas, trans. *Anglo-Saxon and Old English Vocabularies*. Vol. 1. London: Trubner, 1884.

SECONDARY INFORMATION RESOURCES

Anderson, James M. *Daily Life during the Spanish Inquisition*. Westport, CT: Greenwood Press, 2002.

Benn, Charles. *Daily Life in Traditional China: The Tang Dynasty*. Westport, CT: Greenwood Press, 2001.

Butt, John J. *Daily Life in the Age of Charlemagne*. Westport, CT: Greenwood Press, 2002.

Byrne, Joseph P. *Daily Life during the Black Death*. Westport, CT: Greenwood Press, 2006.

Carrasco, David, and Scott Sessions. *Daily Life of the Aztecs: People of the Sun and Earth*. Westport, CT: Greenwood Press, 1998.

Cohen, Elizabeth S., and Thomas V. Cohen. *Daily Life in Renaissance Italy*. Westport, CT: Greenwood Press, 2001.

Confer, Clarissa W. *Daily Life in Pre-Columbian Native America*. Westport, CT: Greenwood Press, 2007.

Crawford, Sally. *Daily Life in Anglo-Saxon England*. Westport, CT: Greenwood Press, 2008.

Forgeng, Jeffrey. *Daily Life in Stuart England*. Westport, CT: Greenwood Press, 2007.

Lane, George. *Daily Life in the Mongol Empire*. Westport, CT: Greenwood Press, 2006.

Lindsay, James E. *Daily Life in the Medieval Islamic World*. Westport, CT: Greenwood Press, 2005.

Malpass, Michael A. *Daily Life in the Inca Empire*. Westport, CT: Greenwood Press, 1996.

Rautman, Marcus. *Daily Life in the Byzantine Empire*. Westport, CT: Greenwood Press, 2006.

Roth, Norman. *Daily Life of the Jews in the Middle Ages*. Westport, CT. Greenwood Press, 2005.

Salisbury, Joyce E., ed. *The Greenwood Encyclopedia of Daily Life: A Tour through History from Ancient Times to the Present. Volume 2: The Medieval World*. Westport, CT: Greenwood Press, 2004.

———, ed. *The Greenwood Encyclopedia of Daily Life: A Tour through History from Ancient Times to the Present. Volume 3: 15th and 16th Centuries*. Lawrence Morris, vol. ed. Westport, CT: Greenwood Press, 2004.

Sharer, Robert J. *Daily Life in Maya Civilization*. Westport, CT: Greenwood Press, 1996.

Singman, Jeffrey L. *Daily Life in Elizabethan England*. Westport, CT: Greenwood Press, 1995.

———. *Daily Life in Medieval Europe*. Westport, CT: Greenwood Press, 1999.

Singman, Jeffrey L., and Will McLean. *Daily Life in Chaucer's England*. Westport, CT: Greenwood Press, 1995.

Wolf, Kirsten. *Daily Life of the Vikings*. Westport, CT: Greenwood Press, 2004.

INDEX

ABOUT THE EDITOR

LAWRENCE MORRIS is Assistant Professor of English at Albright College. He received his Ph.D. from Harvard University and has taught English literature and history at a variety of institutions including Harvard, University of Wisconsin–Green Bay, and Fitzwilliam College (Cambridge University). Morris is currently writing about the relationship between truth and literary fiction in the religious writing of the medieval British Isles.